HIDDEN MARKOV MODELS, THEORY AND APPLICATIONS

Edited by **Przemyslaw Dymarski**

Hidden Markov Models, Theory and Applications
Edited by Przemyslaw Dymarski

Published by InTech
Janeza Trdine 9, 51000 Rijeka, Croatia

Publishing Process Manager Ivana Lorkovic

Technical Editor Teodora Smiljanic

Cover Designer InTech Design Team

Additional hard copies can be obtained from orders@intechopen.com

Hidden Markov Models, Theory and Applications, Edited by Przemyslaw Dymarski
p. cm.
ISBN 978-953-307-208-1

For EU product safety concerns:
IN TECH d.o.o., Prolaz Marije Krucifikse Kozulić 3, 51000 Rijeka, Croatia,
info@intechopen.com or visit our website at intechopen.com.

Meet the editor

Przemyslaw Dymarski received the M.Sc. and Ph.D. degrees from the Wroclaw University of Technology, Poland, in 1974 and 1983, respectively, both in electrical engineering. In 2004 he received the D.Sc. degree in Telecommunications from the Faculty of Electronics and Information Technology of the Warsaw University of Technology. Now he is employed as a professor in the Institute of Telecommunications, Warsaw University of Technology. His research includes various aspects of digital signal processing, particularly speech and audio compression for telecommunications and multimedia, text-to-speech synthesis, speech recognition and audio watermarking.

Contents

Preface

Hidden Markov Models (HMMs), although known for decades, have made a big career nowadays and are still in state of development. This book presents theoretical issues and a variety of HMMs applications. Each of the 14 chapters addresses theoretical problems and refers to some applications, but the more theoretical parts are presented in Part 1 and the application oriented chapters are grouped in Part 2 and 3.

Chapter 1 has an introductory character: the basic concepts (e.g. Maximum Likelihood, Maximum a Posteriori and Maximum Mutual Information approaches to the HMM training) are explained. Problems of discriminative training are also discussed in[1] (2) and (5) – in particular the Large Margin approach. Chapter (3) discusses the united approach to the HMM segmentation (decoding) problem based on statistical learning. The Viterbi training is compared with the Baum-Welch training in (2). The HMM evaluation problem is analyzed in (4), where the probability of classification error in presence of corrupted observations (e.g. caused by sensor failures) is estimated. Chapter (6) presents the Global Variance constrained trajectory training algorithm for the HMMs used for speech signal generation. The Hidden Semi-Markov Models and Hidden Markov Trees are described in (7), the Pair HMMs in (8) and the Non-homogeneous HMMs in (10). The association of HMMs with other techniques, e.g. wavelet transforms (7) has proved useful for some applications.

The HMMs applications concerning recognition, classification and alignment of signals described in time domain are presented in Part 2. In (5) the hierarchical recognition of spoken commands and in (6) the HMMs application in the Text-To-Speech synthesis is described. Chapter (7) presents the algorithms of the ECG signal analysis and segmentation. In (8) HMM applications in neurosciences are discussed, i.e. the brain activity modeling, the separation of signals generated by single neurons given a muti-neuron recording and the identification and alignment of birdsong. In (9) the classification of seismic signals is described and in (10) multi-pollutant exceedances data are analyzed.

The applications referring to images, spatial structures and other data are presented in Part 3. Moving pictures (in forms of depth silhouettes) are recognized in the Human Activity Recognition System described in (11). Some applications concern computational

[1] Numbers of chapters are referred in parentheses

biology, bioinformatics and medicine. Predictions of gene functions and genetic abnormalities are discussed in (12), a 3-dimensional protein structure analyzer is described in (13) and a diagnosis of the sleep apnea syndrome is presented in (2). There are also applications in engineering: design of the energy efficient systems (e.g. server platforms) is described in (14) and condition-based maintenance of machines – in (2).

I hope that the reader will find this book useful and helpful for their own research.

Przemyslaw Dymarski
Warsaw University of Technology,Department of
Electronics and Information Technology,
Institute of Telecommunications
Poland

Part 1

Tutorials and Theoretical Issues

1

History and Theoretical Basics of Hidden Markov Models

Guy Leonard Kouemou
EADS Deutschland GmbH,
Germany

1. Introduction

The following chapter can be understood as one sort of brief introduction to the history and basics of the Hidden Markov Models.

Hidden Markov Models (HMMs) are learnable finite stochastic automates. Nowadays, they are considered as a specific form of dynamic Bayesian networks. Dynamic Bayesian networks are based on the theory of Bayes (Bayes & Price, 1763).

A Hidden Markov Model consists of two stochastic processes. The first stochastic process is a Markov chain that is characterized by states and transition probabilities. The states of the chain are externally not visible, therefore "hidden". The second stochastic process produces emissions observable at each moment, depending on a state-dependent probability distribution. It is important to notice that the denomination "hidden" while defining a Hidden Markov Model is referred to the states of the Markov chain, not to the parameters of the model.

The history of the HMMs consists of two parts. On the one hand there is the history of Markov process and Markov chains, and on the other hand there is the history of algorithms needed to develop Hidden Markov Models in order to solve problems in the modern applied sciences by using for example a computer or similar electronic devices.

1.1. Brief history of Markov process and Markov chains

Andrey Andreyevich Markov (June 14, 1856 – July 20, 1922) was a Russian mathematician. He is best known for his work on the theory of stochastic Markov processes. His research area later became known as Markov process and Markov chains.

Andrey Andreyevich Markov introduced the Markov chains in 1906 when he produced the first theoretical results for stochastic processes by using the term "chain" for the first time. In 1913 he calculated letter sequences of the Russian language.

A generalization to countable infinite state spaces was given by Kolmogorov (1931). Markov chains are related to Brownian motion and the ergodic hypothesis, two topics in physics which were important in the early years of the twentieth century. But Markov appears to have pursued this out of a mathematical motivation, namely the extension of the law of large numbers to dependent events.

Out of this approach grew a general statistical instrument, the so-called stochastic Markov process.

In mathematics generally, probability theory and statistics particularly, a Markov process can be considered as a time-varying random phenomenon for which Markov properties are

achieved. In a common description, a stochastic process with the Markov property, or memorylessness, is one for which conditions on the present state of the system, its future and past are independent (Markov1908),(Wikipedia1,2,3).
Markov processes arise in probability and statistics in one of two ways. A stochastic process, defined via a separate argument, may be shown (mathematically) to have the Markov property and as a consequence to have the properties that can be deduced from this for all Markov processes. Of more practical importance is the use of the assumption that the Markov property holds for a certain random process in order to construct a stochastic model for that process. In modelling terms, assuming that the Markov property holds is one of a limited number of simple ways of introducing statistical dependence into a model for a stochastic process in such a way that allows the strength of dependence at different lags to decline as the lag increases.
Often, the term Markov chain is used to mean a Markov process which has a discrete (finite or countable) state-space. Usually a Markov chain would be defined for a discrete set of times (i.e. a discrete-time Markov Chain) although some authors use the same terminology where "time" can take continuous values.

1.2 Brief history of algorithms need to develop Hidden Markov Models

With the strong development of computer sciences in the 1940's, after research results of scientist like John von Neuman, Turing, Conrad Zuse, the scientists all over the world tried to find algorithms solutions in order to solve many problems in real live by using deterministic automate as well as stochastic automate. Near the classical filter theory dominated by the linear filter theory, the non-linear and stochastic filter theory became more and more important. At the end of the 1950's and the 1960's we can notice in this category the domination of the "Luenberger-Observer", the "Wiener-Filter", the „Kalman-Filter" or the "Extended Kalman-Filter" as well as its derivatives (Foellinger1992), (Kalman1960).
At the same period in the middle of the 20th century, Claude Shannon (1916 - 2001), an American mathematician and electronic engineer, introduced in his paper "A mathematical theory of communication", first published in two parts in the July and October 1948 editions of the Bell System Technical Journal, a very important historical step, that boosted the need of implementation and integration of the deterministic as well as stochastic automate in computer and electrical devices.
Further important elements in the History of Algorithm Development are also needed in order to create, apply or understand Hidden Markov Models:
The expectation-maximization (EM) algorithm: The recent history of the expectation-maximization algorithm is related with history of the Maximum-likelihood at the beginning of the 20th century (Kouemou 2010, Wikipedia). R. A. Fisher strongly used to recommend, analyze and make the Maximum-likelihood popular between 1912 and 1922, although it had been used earlier by Gauss, Laplace, Thiele, and F. Y. Edgeworth. Several years later the EM algorithm was explained and given its name in a paper 1977 by Arthur Dempster, Nan Laird, and Donald Rubin in the Journal of the Royal Statistical Society. They pointed out that the method had been "proposed many times in special circumstances" by other authors, but the 1977 paper generalized the method and developed the theory behind it. An expectation-maximization (EM) algorithm is used in statistics for finding maximum likelihood estimates of parameters in probabilistic models, where the model depends on unobserved latent variables. EM alternates between performing an expectation (E) step, which computes an expectation of the likelihood by including the latent variables as if they

were observed, and maximization (M) step, which computes the maximum likelihood estimates of the parameters by maximizing the expected likelihood found on the E step. The parameters found on the M step are then used to begin another E step, and the process is repeated. EM is frequently used for data clustering in machine learning and computer vision. In natural language processing, two prominent instances of the algorithm are the Baum-Welch algorithm (also known as "forward-backward") and the inside-outside algorithm for unsupervised induction of probabilistic context-free grammars. Mathematical and algorithmic basics of Expectation Maximization algorithm, specifically for HMM-Applications, will be introduced in the following parts of this chapter.

The Baum-Welch algorithm: The Baum–Welch algorithm is a particular case of a generalized expectation-maximization (GEM) algorithm (Kouemou 2010, Wikipedia). The Baum–Welch algorithm is used to find the unknown parameters of a hidden Markov model (HMM). It makes use of the forward-backward algorithm and is named for Leonard E. Baum and Lloyd R. Welch. One of the introducing papers for the Baum-Welch algorithm was presented 1970 "A maximization technique occurring in the statistical analysis of probabilistic functions of Markov chains", (Baum1970). Mathematical and algorithmic basics of the Baum-Welch algorithm specifically for HMM-Applications will be introduced in the following parts of this chapter.

The Viterbi Algorithm: The Viterbi algorithm was conceived by Andrew Viterbi in 1967 as a decoding algorithm for convolution codes over noisy digital communication links. It is a dynamic programming algorithm (Kouemou 2010, Wikipedia). For finding the most likely sequence of hidden states, called the Viterbi path that results in a sequence of observed events. During the last years, this algorithm has found universal application in decoding the convolution codes, used for example in CDMA and GSM digital cellular, dial-up modems, satellite, deep-space communications, and 802.11 wireless LANs. It is now also commonly used in speech recognition applications, keyword spotting, computational linguistics, and bioinformatics. For example, in certain speech-to-text recognition devices, the acoustic signal is treated as the observed sequence of events, and a string of text is considered to be the "hidden cause" of the acoustic signal. The Viterbi algorithm finds the most likely string of text given the acoustic signal (Wikipedia, David Forney's). Mathematical and algorithmic basics of the Viterbi-Algorithm for HMM-Applications will be introduced in the following parts of this chapter.

The chapter consists of the next following parts:

- Part 2: Mathematical basics of Hidden Markov Models
- Part 3: Basics of HMM in stochastic modelling
- Part4: Types of Hidden Markov Models
- Part5: Basics of HMM in signal processing applications
- Part6: Conclusion and References

2. Mathematical basics of Hidden Markov Models

Definition of Hidden Markov Models

A Hidden Markov Model (cf. Figure 1) is a finite learnable stochastic automate.

It can be summarized as a kind of double stochastic process with the two following aspects:

- The first stochastic process is a finite set of states, where each of them is generally associated with a multidimensional probability distribution. The transitions between the different states are statistically organized by a set of probabilities called transition probabilities.

- In the second stochastic process, in any state an event can be observed. Since we will just analyze what we observe without seeing at which states it occurred, the states are "hidden" to the observer, therefore the name "Hidden Markov Model".

Each Hidden Markov Model is defined by states, state probabilities, transition probabilities, emission probabilities and initial probabilities.

In order to define an HMM completely, the following five Elements have to be defined:

1. The N states of the Model, defined by

$$S = \{S_1, ..., S_N\} \tag{1}$$

2. The M observation symbols per state $V = \{v_1, ..., v_M\}$. If the observations are continuous then M is infinite.
3. The State transition probability distribution $A = \{a_{ij}\}$, where a_{ij} is the probability that the state at time $t+1$ is S_j, is given when the state at time t is S_i. The structure of this stochastic matrix defines the connection structure of the model. If a coefficient a_{ij} is zero, it will remain zero even through the training process, so there will never be a transition from state S_i to

$$S_j. \; a_{ij} = p\{q_{t+1} = j \mid q_t = i\}, \quad 1 \le i, j \le N \tag{2}$$

Where q_t denotes the current state. The transition probabilities should satisfy the normal stochastic constraints, $a_{ij} \ge 0, \quad 1 \le i, j \le N$ and $\sum_{j=1}^{N} a_{ij} = 1, \quad 1 \le i \le N$.

4. The Observation symbol probability distribution in each state, $B = \{b_j(k)\}$ where $b_j(k)$ is the probability that symbol v_k is emitted in state S_j.

$$b_j(k) = p\{o_t = v_k \mid q_t = j\}, \quad 1 \le j \le N, \quad 1 \le k \le M \tag{3}$$

where v_k denotes the kth observation symbol in the alphabet, and o_t the current parameter vector.

The following stochastic constraints must be satisfied:

$$b_j(k) \ge 0, \quad 1 \le j \le N, \quad 1 \le k \le M \text{ and } \sum_{k=1}^{M} b_j(k) = 1, \quad 1 \le j \le N$$

If the observations are continuous, then we will have to use a continuous probability density function, instead of a set of discrete probabilities. In this case we specify the parameters of the probability density function. Usually the probability density is approximated by a weighted sum of M Gaussian distributions N,

$$b_j(o_t) = \sum_{m=1}^{M} c_{jm} N(\mu_{jm}, \Sigma_{jm}, o_t) \tag{4}$$

where $c_{jm} = \textit{weighting coefficients}$, $\mu_{jm} = \textit{mean vectors}$, and

$\Sigma_{jm} = Covariance\ matrices$. c_{jm} should also satisfy the stochastic assumptions $c_{jm} \geq 0,\ \ 1 \leq j \leq N,\ \ 1 \leq m \leq M$ and

$$\sum_{m=1}^{M} c_{jm} = 1, \quad 1 \leq j \leq N$$

5. The HMM is the initial state distribution $\pi = \{\pi_i\}$, where π_i is the probability that the model is in state S_i at the time $t = 0$ with

$$\pi_i = p\{q_1 = i\}\ and\ 1 \leq i \leq N \tag{5}$$

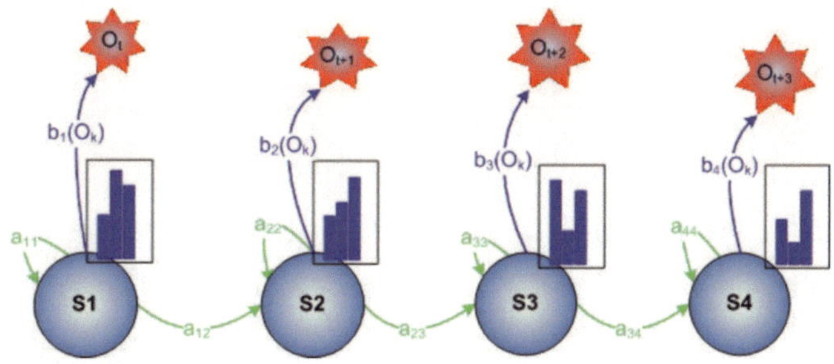

Fig. 1. Example of an HMM

By defining the HMM it is also very important to clarify if the model will be discrete, continuing or a mix form (Kouemou 2007).
The following notation is often used in the literature by several authors (Wikipedia):

$$\lambda = (A, B, \pi) \tag{6}$$

to denote a Discrete HMM, that means with discrete probability distributions, while

$$\lambda = \left(A, c_{jm}, \mu_{jm}, \Sigma_{jm}, \pi\right) \tag{7}$$

is often used to denote a Continuous HMM that means with exploitations statics are based here on continuous densities functions or distributions.
Application details to these different forms of HMM will be illustrated in the following parts of this chapter.

3. Basics of HMM in stochastic modelling

This part of the chapter is a sort of compendium from well known literature (Baum1970), (Huang1989), (Huang1990), (Kouemou2010), (Rabiner1986), (Rabiner1989), (Viterbi1967), (Warakagoda2010), (Wikipedia2010) in order to introduce the problematic of stochastic modelling using Hidden Markov Models.
In this part some important aspects of modelling Hidden Markov Models in order to solve real problems, for example using clearly defined statistical rules, will be presented. The stochastic modelling of an HMM automate consist of two steps:

- The first step is to define the model architecture
- The second to define the learning and operating algorithm

3.1 Definition of HMM architecture

The following diagram shows a generalized automate architecture of an operating HMM λ_i with the two integrated stochastic processes.

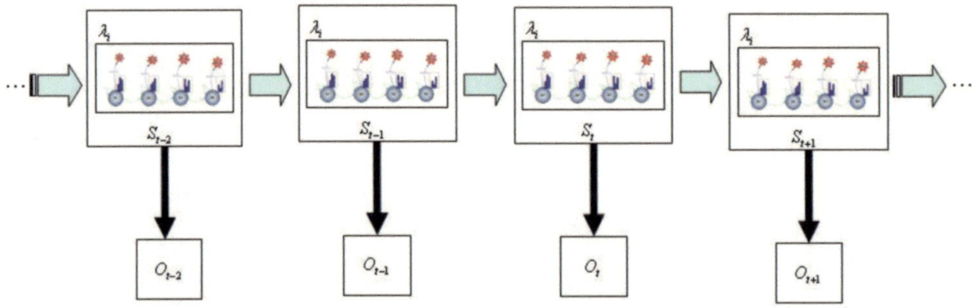

Fig. 2. Generalised Architecture of an operating Hidden Markov Model

Each shape represents a random variable that can adopt any of a number of values. The random variable *s*(*t*) is the hidden state at time *t*.

The random variable *o(t)* is the observation at the time *t*. The law of conditional probability of the Hidden Markov variable *s(t)* at the time *t*, knowing the values of the hidden variables at all times depends only on the value of the hidden variable *s(t-1)* at the time *t-1*. Every values before are not necessary anymore, so that the Markov property as defined before is satisfied.

By the second stochastic process, the value of the observed variable *o(t)* depends on the value of the hidden variable *s(t)* also at the time *t*.

3.2 Definition of the learning and operating algorithms – Three basic problems of HMMs

The task of the learning algorithm is to find the best set of state transitions and observation (sometimes also called emission) probabilities. Therefore, an output sequence or a set of these sequences is given.

In the following part we will first analyze the three well-known basic problems of Hidden Markov Models (Huang1990), (Kouemou2000), (Rabiner1989), (Warakagoda(2009):

1. The Evaluation Problem

What is the probability that the given observations $O = o_1, o_2, ..., o_T$ are generated by the model $p\{O \mid \lambda\}$ with a given HMM λ?

2. The Decoding Problem

What is the most likely state sequence in the given model λ that produced the given observations $O = o_1, o_2, ..., o_T$?

3. The Learning Problem

How should we adjust the model parameters $\{A, B, \pi\}$ in order to maximize $p\{O \mid \lambda\}$, whereat a model λ and a sequence of observations $O = o_1, o_2, ..., o_T$ are given?

The evaluation problem can be used for isolated (word) recognition. Decoding problem is related to the continuous recognition as well as to the segmentation. Learning problem must be solved, if we want to train an HMM for the subsequent use of recognition tasks.

3.2.1 The evaluation problem and the forward algorithm

Given a model $\lambda = (A, B, \pi)$ and a sequence of observations $O = o_1, o_2, ..., o_T$, $p\{O \mid \lambda\}$ needs to be found. Although this quantity can be calculated by the use of simple probabilistic arguments, it is not very practicable because the calculation involves number of operations in the order of N^T. But fortunately there is another calculation method with considerably low complexity that uses an auxiliary variable

$$\alpha_t(i) = p\{o_1, o_2, ..., o_t, q_t = i \mid \lambda\} \tag{8}$$

$\alpha_t(i)$ is called **forward variable**, and $o_1, o_2, ..., o_T$ is the partial observation sequence.
Out of this, the recursive relationship

$$\alpha_{t+1}(j) = b_j(o_{t+1}) \sum_{i=1}^{N} \alpha_t(i) o_{ij}, \quad 1 \le j \le N, \quad 1 \le t \le T-1 \tag{9}$$

with $\alpha_1(j) = \pi_j b_j(o_1), \quad 1 \le j \le N$ follows.

$\alpha_T(i), \quad 1 \le i \le N$ can be calculated using this recursion. So the required probability is given by

$$p\{O \mid \lambda\} = \sum_{i=1}^{N} \alpha_T(i) \tag{10}$$

This method is commonly known as the **forward algorithm**.
The backward variable $\beta_t(i)$ can be defined similar.

$$\beta_t(i) = p\{o_{t+1}, o_{t+2}, ..., o_t \mid q_t = i, \lambda\} \tag{11}$$

Given that the current state is *i*, $\beta_t(i)$ is the probability of the partial observation sequence $o_{t+1}, o_{t+2}, ..., o_T$.
$\beta_t(i)$ can also be calculated efficiently by using a recursive

$$\beta_t(i) = \sum_{j=1}^{N} \beta_{t+1}(j) a_{ij} b_j(o_{t+1}), \quad 1 \le i \le N, \quad 1 \le t \le T-1 \tag{12}$$

where $\beta_T(i) = 1, \quad 1 \le i \le N$
Further we can see that,

$$\alpha_t(i)\beta_t(i) = p\{O, q_t = i \mid \lambda\}, \quad 1 \le i \le N, \quad 1 \le t \le T \tag{13}$$

So there are two ways to calculate $p\{O \mid \lambda\}$, either using forward or backward variable:

$$p\{O \mid \lambda\} = \sum_{i=1}^{N} p\{O, q_t = i \mid \lambda\} = \sum_{i=1}^{N} \alpha_t(i)\beta_t(i) \tag{14}$$

This equation can be very useful, especially in deriving the formulas required for gradient based training.

3.2.2 The decoding problem and the Viterbi algorithm

Given a sequence of observations $O = o_1, o_2, ..., o_T$ and a model $\lambda = (A, B, \pi)$, we search for the most likely state sequence.

The definition of "likely state sequence" influences the solution of this problem. In one approach, we want to find the most likely state q_t and to concatenate all such 'q_t's. But because this approach sometimes does not result in a meaningful state sequence, we want to use another method, commonly known as Viterbi algorithm. Using the Viterbi algorithm, the whole state sequence with maximum likelihood is found.

An auxiliary variable is defined that gives the highest probability that partial observation sequence and state sequence up to *t=t* can have, given the current state is *i*.

$$\delta_t(i) = \max_{q_1, q_2 \cdots q_{t-1}} p\{q_1, q_2, ..., q_{t-1}, q_t = i, o_1, o_2, ..., o_{t-1} \mid \lambda\} \tag{15}$$

It follows that

$$\delta_{t+1}(j) = b_j(o_{t+1}) \left[\max_{1 \le i \le N} \delta_t(i) a_{ij} \right], \quad 1 \le i \le N, 1 \le t \le T-1 \tag{16}$$

with $\delta_1(j) = \pi_j b_j(o_1), \quad 1 \le j \le N$

So we start from the calculation of $\delta_T(j), \quad 1 \le j \le N$ to calculate the most likely state sequence. We always keep a pointer to the "winning state" in the maximum finding operation. It results in state j^*, where $j^* = \arg \max_{1 \le j \le N} \delta_T(j)$. We start from this state and back-track the sequence of states as the pointer in each state indicates. So we get the required set of states.

This whole algorithm can be interpreted as a search in a graph whose nodes are formed by the states of the HMM in each of the time instant $t, 1 \le t \le T$.

3.2.3 The Learning roblem

How can we adjust the HMM parameters in a way that a given set of observations (the *training set*) is represented by the model in the best way for the intended application? Depending on the application, the "quantity" that should be optimized during the learning process differs. So there are several optimization criteria for learning.

In literature, we can find two main optimization criteria: Maximum Likelihood (ML) and Maximum Mutual Information (MMI). The solutions for these criteria are described below.

3.2.3.1 Maximum Likelihood (ML) criterion

Given the HMM λ_w of the class *w*, we try to maximize the probability of a given sequence of observations O^w, belonging to a given class *w*, corresponding to the parameters of the model λ_w. Mathematically, this likelihood can be expressed as

$$L_{tot} = p\{O^w \mid \lambda_w\} \tag{17}$$

Dropping the subscript and superscript '*w*'s because we consider only one class *w* at a time, the ML can be given as

$$L_{tot} = p\{O \mid \lambda\} \tag{18}$$

The model $\lambda = (A, B, \pi)$ that maximizes the quantity L_{tot} cannot be solved analytically as there is known way for it. Using an iterative procedure, like Baum-Welch or a gradient based method, we can locally maximize it by choosing appropriate model parameters.

3.2.3.1.1 Baum-Welch Algorithm

The *Baum-Welch algorithm* is also known as *Forward-Backward algorithm* (Baum 1966), (Baum1970), (Rabiner1989).
This method can be derived as well known in the literature by using simple "occurrence counting" arguments or using calculus to maximize the auxiliary quantity

$$Q(\lambda, \overline{\lambda}) = \sum_{q} p\{q \mid O, \lambda\} \log\left[p\{O, q, \overline{\lambda}\}\right] \tag{19}$$

over $\overline{\lambda}$.
Additionally to the forward and backward variables we need to define two more auxiliary variables.
The first one of these variables is

$$\xi_t(i,j) = p\{q_t = i, q_{t+1} = j \mid O, \lambda\} \tag{20}$$

which can also be written as

$$\xi_t(i,j) = \frac{p\{q_t = i, q_{t+1} = j, O \mid \lambda\}}{p\{O \mid \lambda\}} \tag{21}$$

We can use forward and backward variables and these result in

$$\xi_t(i,j) = \frac{\alpha_t(i) a_{ij} \beta_{t+1}(j) b_j(o_{t+1})}{\sum_{i=1}^{N} \sum_{j=1}^{N} \alpha_t(i) a_{ij} \beta_{t+1}(j) b_j(o_{t+1})} \tag{22}$$

The second variable is the a posteriori probability,

$$\gamma_t(i) = p\{q_t = i \mid O, \lambda\} \tag{23}$$

In forward and backward variables this can be expressed by,

$$\gamma_t(i) = \left[\frac{\alpha_t(i)\beta_t(i)}{\sum_{i=1}^{N} \alpha_t(i)\beta_t(i)}\right] \tag{24}$$

So we can see that the relationship between $\gamma_t(i)$ and $\xi_t(i,j)$ is given by,

$$\gamma_t(i) = \sum_{j=1}^{N} \xi_t(i,j), \quad 1 \le i \le N, 1 \le t \le M \tag{25}$$

To maximize the quantity $p\{O \mid \lambda\}$, we can now describe the Baum-Welch learning process. We assume a starting model $\lambda = (A, B, \pi)$ and calculate the 'α's and 'β's. After this, we calculate the 'ξ 's and 'γ's. The next equations are known as *re-estimation formulas* and are used to update the HMM parameters:

$$\overline{\pi}_i = \gamma_1(i), \quad 1 \le i \le N \tag{26}$$

$$\overline{a}_{ij} = \frac{\sum_{t=1}^{T-1} \xi_t(i,j)}{\sum_{t=1}^{T-1} \gamma_t(i)}, \quad 1 \le i \le N, \quad 1 \le j \le N \tag{27}$$

$$\overline{b}_j(k) = \frac{\sum_{\substack{t=1 \\ o_t = v_k}}^{T} \gamma_t(j)}{\sum_{t=1}^{T} \gamma_t(j)}, \quad 1 \le j \le N, \quad 1 \le k \le M \tag{28}$$

These reestimation formulas can easily be modified to deal with the continuous density case too.

3.2.3.1.2 HMM Parameter Optimization

The optimization of the parameter κ of a given HMM λ is usually done by using Gradient related algorithms like shown in the following equation:

$$\kappa^t = \kappa^{t-1} - \varsigma \left[\frac{\partial \psi}{\partial \kappa} \right]_{\kappa^{t-1}} \tag{29}$$

By defining

$$\psi = -\log\left(p\{O|\lambda\}\right) \tag{30}$$

in order to find the maximum likelihood, the equation $\frac{\partial \psi}{\partial \kappa}$ for any parameter κ of the HMM λ has to be solved in order the minimized ψ.

The calculated ψ is therefore the expected Maximum Likelihood obtained by maximizing κ^t.

By associating ψ to the HMM model parameters introduced above (see equation 14), we then obtain

$$L_{tot} = \sum_{i=1}^{N} p\{O, q_t = i|\lambda\} = \sum_{i=1}^{N} \alpha_t(i)\beta_t(i) \tag{31}$$

The differentiation of the last equality in the equations (29) and (30) relative to the parameter κ of the HMM gives

$$\frac{\partial \psi}{\partial \kappa} = -\frac{1}{L_{tot}} \frac{\partial L_{tot}}{\partial \kappa} \tag{32}$$

The Equation (32) calculates $\frac{\partial \psi}{\partial \kappa}$ under the assumption, that $\frac{\partial L_{tot}}{\partial \kappa}$ is solvable. But this derivative depends on all the actual parameter of the HMM.

On the one side there are the transition probabilities α_{ij}, $1 \le i, N \ge j$ and on the other side the observation probabilities $b_j(k)$, $j \in \{1,...,N\}$, $k \in \{1,...,M\}$. For this reason we have to find the derivative for the both probabilities sets and therefore their gradient.

a) Maximum likelihood gradient depending on transition probabilities

In order to calculate the gradient depending on transition probabilities, the Markov rule is usually assumed like following:

$$\frac{\partial L_{tot}}{\partial \alpha_{ij}} = \sum_{t=1}^{T} \frac{\partial L_{tot}}{\partial \alpha_t(j)} \frac{\partial \alpha_t(j)}{\partial \alpha_{ij}} \tag{33}$$

The simple differentiation

$$\frac{\partial L_{tot}}{\partial \alpha_t(j)} = \beta_t(j) \tag{34}$$

as well as the time delay differentiation

$$\frac{\partial \alpha_t(j)}{\partial \alpha_{ij}} = b_j(\alpha_t)\alpha_{t-1}(i) \tag{35}$$

gives after parameter substitutions the well known result

$$\frac{\partial \psi}{\partial \alpha_{ij}} = -\frac{1}{L_{tot}} \sum_{t=1}^{T} \beta_t(j) b_j(\alpha_t)\alpha_{t-1}(i) \tag{36}$$

b) Maximum Likelihood gradient depending on observation probabilities

In a similar matter as introduced above, the gradient depending on observation probabilities using the Markov rule is calculated.
With

$$\frac{\partial L_{tot}}{\partial b_j(o_t)} = \frac{\partial L_{tot}}{\partial \alpha_t(j)} \frac{\partial \alpha_t(j)}{\partial b_j(o_t)} \tag{37}$$

and

$$\frac{\partial \alpha_t(j)}{\partial b_j(o_t)} = \frac{\alpha_t(j)}{b_j(o_t)} \tag{38}$$

the estimation probability is then calculated and results to

$$\frac{\partial\psi}{\partial b_j(o_t)} = -\frac{1}{L_{tot}}\frac{\alpha_t(j)\beta_t(j)}{b_j(o_t)} . \tag{39}$$

In the case of "Continuous Hidden-Markov-Models" or "Semi-Continuous Hidden-Markov-Models" the densities $\frac{\partial\psi}{\partial c_{jm}}, \frac{\partial\psi}{\partial\mu_{jm}}, \frac{\partial\psi}{\partial\sum_{jm}}$ are usually calculated similarly by just further propagating the derivative $\frac{\partial\psi}{\partial b_j(o_t)}$ assuming the Markov chain rules.

3.2.3.2 Maximum Mutual Information (MMI) criterion

Generally, in order to solve problems using Hidden Markov Models for example for engineering pattern recognition applications, there are two general types of stochastic optimization processes: on the one side, the Maximum Likelihood optimization process and on the other side the Maximum Mutual Information Process. The role of the Maximum Likelihood is to optimize the different parameters of a single given HMM class at a time independent of the HMM Parameters of the rest classes. This procedure will be repeated for every other HMM for each other class.

In addition to the Maximum Likelihood, differences of the Maximum Mutual Infomation Methods are usually used in practice in order to solve the discrimination problematic in pattern recognition applications between every class that has to be recognized in a given problem. At the end one can obtain a special robust trained HMM-based system, thanks to the well known "discriminative training methodics".

The basics of the Minimum Mutual Information calculations can be introduced by assuming a set of HMMs

$$\Lambda = \{\lambda_\nu , \nu \in \{1,...,V\}\} \tag{40}$$

of a given pattern recognition problem.

The purpose of the optimization criterion will consist here of minimizing the "conditional uncertainty" ν of one "complete unit by a given real world problem" given an observation sequence O^s of that class.

$$I\left(v\middle|O^s,\Lambda\right) = -\log p\left\{v\middle|O^s,\Lambda\right\} \tag{41}$$

This results in an art of minimization of the conditional entropy H, that can be also defined as the expectation of the conditional information I:

$$H\left(V\middle|O\right) = E\left[\left\{v\middle|O^s,\Lambda\right\}\right] \tag{42}$$

in which V is the set of all classes and O is the set of all observation sequences.

Therefore, the mutual information between the classes and observations

$$H\left(V\middle|O\right) = H(V) - H\left(V\middle|O^S\right) \tag{43}$$

is a maximized constant with $H(V)$, hence the name "Maximum Mutual Information" criterion (MMI).
In many literatures this technique is also well known as the "Maximum à Posteriori" method (MAP).

Generally Definition and Basics of the "Maximum à Posteriori" Estimation:

In Bayesian statistics, a maximum a posteriori probability (MAP) estimate is a mode of the posterior distribution. The MAP can be used to obtain a point estimate of an unobserved quantity on the basis of empirical data. It is closely related to Fisher's method of maximum likelihood (ML), but employs an augmented optimization objective which incorporates a prior distribution over the quantity one wants to estimate. MAP estimation can therefore be seen as a regularization of ML estimation.

Generally Description of the "Maximum à Posteriori" Estimation:

Assume that we want to estimate an unobserved Markov Model λ on the basis of observations o. By defining f as the sampling distribution of the observations o, so that $f(o|\lambda)$ is the probability of o when the underlying Markov Model is λ. The function $\lambda \mapsto f(o|\lambda)$ can be defined as the likelihood function, so the estimate

$$\hat{\lambda}_{ML}(o) = \arg\max_{\lambda} f(o|\lambda) \tag{44}$$

is the maximum likelihood estimate of the Markov Model λ.
Now when we assume that a prior distribution χ over the models λ exists, we can treat λ as a random variable as in the classical Bayesian statistics.
The posterior distribution of λ is therefore:

$$\lambda \mapsto f(\lambda|o) = \frac{f(o|\lambda)\chi(\lambda')}{\int_{\lambda' \in \Lambda} f(o|\lambda')\chi(\lambda')\partial\lambda'} \tag{45}$$

where χ is the density function of λ and Λ is the domain of χ as application of the Bayes' theorem.
The method of maximum a posteriori estimation then estimates the Markov Model λ as the mode of the posterior distribution of this random variable:

$$\hat{\lambda}_{ML}(o) = \arg\max_{\lambda} \frac{f(o|\lambda)\chi(\lambda)}{\int_{\lambda' \in \Lambda} f(o|\lambda')\chi(\lambda')\partial\lambda'} = \arg\max_{\lambda} f(o|\lambda)\chi(\lambda) \tag{46}$$

The denominator of the posterior distribution does not depend on λ and therefore plays no role in the optimization. The MAP estimate of the Markov Modells λ coincides with the ML estimate when the prior χ is uniform (that is, a constant function). The MAP estimate is a limit of Bayes estimators under a sequence of 0-1 loss functions.

Application of the "Maximum à Posteriori" for the HMM

According to these basics of the "Maximum à Posteriori" above, the posteriori probability $p\{v|O^c,\Lambda\}$ is maximised when the MMI criteria yields using the Bayes theorem to:

$$E_{MAP} = E_{MMI} = -\log p\{v|O^s, \Lambda\} = -\log \frac{p\{v, O^c|\Lambda\}}{p\{O^c|\Lambda\}} = -\log \frac{p\{v, O^c|\Lambda\}}{p\{\omega, O^c|\Lambda\}} \tag{47}$$

where ω is any possible class.
By using similar notation as in (17), the likelihoods can be written as following:

$$L_{tot}^{correct} = p\{v, O^c|\lambda\} \tag{48}$$

$$L_{tot}^{others} = \sum_{\omega} p\{\omega, O^c|\lambda\} \tag{49}$$

where indices "correct" and "others" distinguish between the correct class and all the other classes.
From the both equation above we then obtain expectations of the MMI or MAP as:

$$E_{MAP} = E_{MMI} = -\log \frac{L_{tot}^{correct}}{L_{tot}^{other}} \tag{50}$$

In analogy to the Maximum Likelihood, in order to minimize E_{MMI}, we can assume that $\psi = E_{MMI}$, and derive the gradients after $\frac{\partial \psi}{\partial \kappa}$ using the well known gradient related algorithms, where κ is an arbitrary parameter of the whole set of HMMs, Λ.
In analogy to the Maximum Likelihood estimation methods above, we then obtain

$$\frac{\partial \psi}{\partial \kappa} = \frac{1}{L_{tot}^{others}} \frac{\partial L_{tot}^{others}}{\partial \kappa} - \frac{1}{L_{tot}^{correct}} \frac{\partial L_{tot}^{correct}}{\partial \kappa} \tag{51}$$

with $L_{tot}^{correct} = \sum_{i \in class\ \upsilon} \alpha_t(i)\beta_t(i)$ and $L_{tot}^{others} = \sum_{\omega} \sum_{i \in class\ w} \alpha_t(i)\beta_t(i)$.

With the same procedure as for the Maximum Likelihood, the transition and observation probabilities must also be calculated as illustrated in the next steps by using the general law of the Markov chain.

a) Maximum Mutual Information gradient depending on transition probabilities

By using the well known Kronecker symbol $\delta_{k\upsilon}$, the calculation basics then yields to

$$\frac{\partial L_{tot}^{(correct\ or\ others)}}{\partial \alpha_{ij}} = \sum_{i=1}^{T} \frac{\partial L_{tot}^{(correct\ or\ others)}}{\partial \alpha_t(j)} \frac{\partial \alpha_t(j)}{\partial \alpha_{ij}} \tag{52}$$

with

$$\frac{\partial L_{tot}^{(correct)}}{\partial \alpha_{ij}} = \delta_{k\upsilon} \sum_{i=1}^{T} \beta_t(j) b_j(o_t) \partial \alpha_{t-1}(i) \tag{53}$$
$$i \in class\ k$$

and

$$\frac{\partial L_{tot}^{(others)}}{\partial \alpha_{ij}} = \sum_{i=1}^{T} \beta_t(j) b_j(o_t) \alpha_{t-1}(i) \tag{54}$$

After simplification one obtain

$$\underset{i \in class\ k}{\frac{\partial \psi}{\partial \alpha_{ij}}} = \left[\frac{1}{L_{tot}^{(others)}} - \frac{\delta_{kv}}{L_{tot}^{(correct)}} \right] \sum_{i=1}^{T} \beta_t(j) b_j(o_t) \alpha_{t-1}(i) \,. \tag{55}$$

b) Maximum Mutual Information gradient depending on observation probabilities

The calculation of the Maximum Mutual Information gradient depending on observation probabilities is similar to the description above according to the Markov chain rules as following:

$$\frac{\partial L_{tot}^{(correct\ or\ others)}}{\partial b_j(o_t)} = \frac{\partial L_{tot}^{(correct\ or\ others)}}{\partial \alpha_t(j)} \frac{\partial \alpha_t(j)}{\partial b_j(o_t)} \,. \tag{56}$$

After differentiation after $\alpha_t(j)$ and simplification using the Kronecker function δ_{kv}, the "correct" as well as the "others" variant are extracted usually as following:

$$\frac{\partial L_{tot}^{correct}}{\partial b_j(o_t)} = \delta_{kv} \frac{\alpha_t(j)\beta_t(j)}{b_j(o_t)} \quad j \in class\ k \tag{57}$$

and

$$\frac{\partial L_{tot}^{others}}{\partial b_j(o_t)} = \frac{\alpha_t(j)\beta_t(j)}{b_j(o_t)} \tag{58}$$

After further simplifications one obtain

$$\underset{j \in class\ k}{\frac{\partial \Psi}{\partial b_j(o_t)}} = \left[\frac{1}{L_{tot}^{others}} - \frac{\delta_{kv}}{L_{tot}^{correct}} \right] \frac{\alpha_t(j)\beta_t(j)}{b_j(o_t)} \tag{59}$$

With $\gamma_t(j)^{correct} = \delta_{kv} \frac{\alpha_t(j)\beta_t(j)}{L_{tot}^{correct}}$, $j \in class\ k$ and $\gamma_t(j)^{others} = \frac{\alpha_t(j)\beta_t(j)}{L_{tot}^{correct}}$

follows:

$$\frac{\partial \Psi}{\partial b_j(o_t)} = \frac{1}{b_j(o_t)} \left[\gamma_t(j)^{others} - \gamma_t(j)^{correct} \right]. \tag{60}$$

4. Types of Hidden Markov Models

Nowadays, depending on problem complexities, signal processing requirements and applications, it is indispensable to choose the appropriate type of HMM very early in the concept and design phase of modern HMM based systems. In this part different types of HMMs will be introduced and some generalized criteria will be shown for how to choose the right type in order to solve different kinds of problems (Huang1989), (Kouemou2008), (Rabiner1989).

4.1 Discrete HMM

Problematic: assuming that we have continuous valued feature vectors we will summarize in this section how to use Discrete Hidden Markov Models to solve this problem.

Generalized Methodology: the following three steps have to be processed:

1. A set of d-dimensional real valued vectors should be reduced to k d-dimensional vectors → vector quantization by codebook (k-means cluster algorithm)
2. Find the nearest codebook vector for the current feature vector
3. Use the index of this codebook vector for DHMM emission symbol / input

The following diagram illustrates the generalized steps needed.

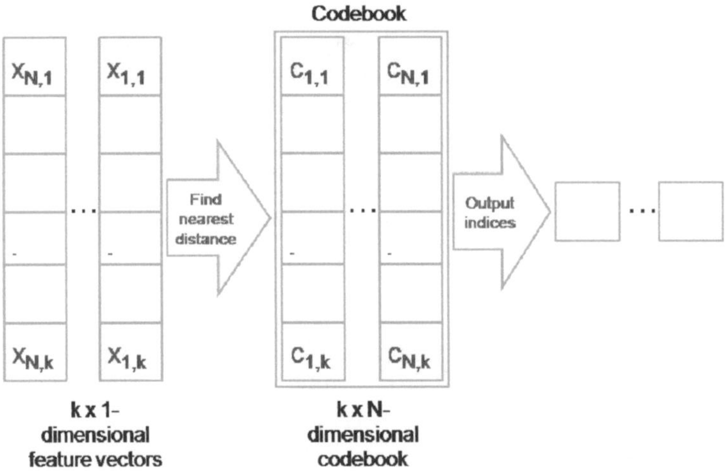

Fig. 3. Simplified Generation Procedure of a codebook by "Discrete Hidden Markov Model"

Details can be read in (Huang1989), (Kouemou2008), (Rabiner1989), (Warakagoda2010).

4.2 Continuous HMM

It is assumed that the output pdf can be written as

$$b_t(x) = \sum_{k=1}^{K} c_{jk} N(x \mid \theta_{jk}) \tag{61}$$

with $\sum_{k=1}^{K} c_{jk} = 1$, where c_{jk} is the mixture coefficient and $N(x \mid \theta_{jk})$ is the Gaussian density. For each state K multivariate Gaussian densities and K mixture coefficients have to be

estimated. This result in the following parameters for each state: covariance matrix, mean vector and mixture coefficients vector.
A continuous Hidden Markov Model is a three-layered stochastic process. The first part is, equal to DHMM, the selection of the next state. The second and the third part are similar to the selection of emission symbol with DHMM, whereas the second part of CHMM is the selection of the mixture density by mixture coefficient. The selection of the output symbol (vector) by the Gaussian density is the third and last part.
The classification and training algorithms have to be modified. There are only minor changes in the classification algorithm: the modified probability densities have to be substituted. The Baum-Welch/Viterbi trainings algorithms have to be modified by additional calculation.
The disadvantage is a high computational effort. The Gaussian distributions have to be evaluated and the high number of parameters probably may result in instabilities.

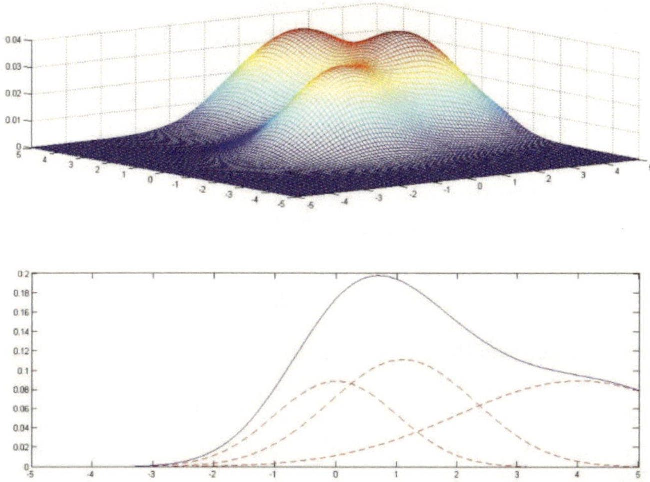

Fig. 4. Illustration of exemplary statistical distributions by continuous "Hidden Markov Models"

Details can be read in (Huang1989), (Kouemou2008), (Rabiner1989), (Warakagoda2010).

4.3 Semi-continuous HMM

The semi-continuous HMM can be seen as a compromise between DHMM and CHMM. It is assumed that the output pdf can be written as

$$b_t(x) = \sum_{k=1}^{K} c_{jk} P(x \mid \theta_k) \tag{62}$$

with $\sum_{k=1}^{K} c_{jk} = 1$, where c_{jk} is the mixture coefficient and $P(x \mid \theta_k)$ the Gaussian distribution.
Overall, K multivariate Gaussian distributions and K mixture coefficients have to be estimated. In contrast to the CHMM, we the same set of Gaussian mixture densities is used for all states.

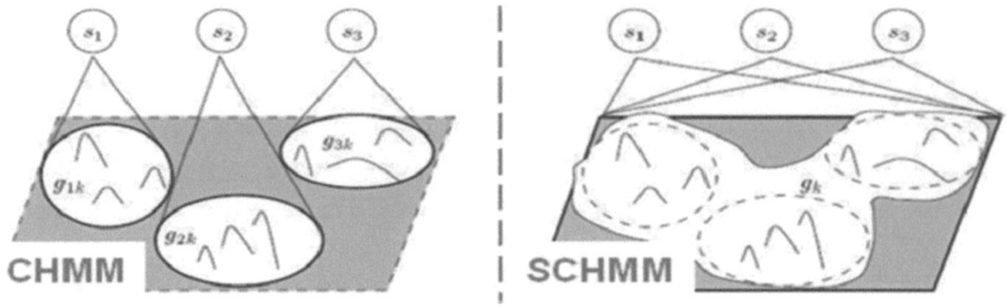

Fig. 5. Simple Illustration of the densities distribution CHMM vs. SCHMM.

Like the CHMM, the SCHMM is a three-layered stochastic process. After the next state has been selected, there will be the selection of the mixture density by the mixture coefficient. Third, the output symbol (vector) has to be selected by Gaussian density. The second and third step is similar to the selection of emission symbol with DHMM. There have to be some modifications of classification and training algorithms, too. For classification algorithm, the modified probability densities have to be modified and the Baum-Welch/Viterbi training algorithm are modified by additional calculations.
The disadvantage is a high computational effort. The Gaussian distributions have to be evaluated and the high number of parameters probably may result in instabilities.
Altogether, the modifications are similar to those in the CHMM, but the number of parameters is reduces significantly.
Details can be read in (Huang1989), (Kouemou2008), (Rabiner1989), (Warakagoda2010).

5. Basics of HMM in modern engineering processing applications

Nowadays, Hidden Markov Models are used in a lot of well-known systems all over the world. In this part of the chapter some general recommendations to be respected by creating an HMM for operational applications will first be introduced, followed by practical examples in the financial word, bioinformatics and speech recognition. This chapter part consists of the following under chapters:

- 5.1. General recommendations for creating HMMs in the practice
- 5.2. Application Examples in Financial Mathematics World, Bank and Assurances
- 5.3. Application Example in Bioinformatics and Genetics
- 5.4. Speech recognition and further Application Examples

5.1 General recommendations for creating HMMs in the practice

5.1.1 Creation of HMM architecture

The basis for creating an HMM for practical applications is a good understanding of the real world problem, e.g. the physical, chemical, biological or social behaviour of the process that should be modelled as well as its stochastic components. The first step is to check if the laws for Markov chains are fulfilled, that means if it is a Markov process as defined above.
If these laws are fulfilled, exemplary models can be structured with the help of the understanding of the relationships between the states of each Markov Model. Deterministic and stochastic characteristics in the process shall be clearly separated. After all of these steps are executed, the technical requirements of the system also have to be taken into consideration. It is very important to consider the specification of the signal processor in the running device.

5.1.2 Learning or adapting an HMM to a given real problem

First of all, different elements of the real problem to be analyzed have to be disaggregated in a form of Markov models. A set of Hidden Markov Models has to be defined that represents the whole real world problem. There are several points that have to be kept in mind, e.g. What should be recognized?, What is the input into the model, what is the output?

The whole learning process is done in two steps. In the first step learning data have to be organized, e.g. by performing measurements and data recording. If measurement is too complex or not possible, one can also recommend using simulated data. During the second step the learning session is started, that means the Markov parameters as explained in the chapters above are adapted.

5.2 Application examples in financial mathematics world, bank and assurances

Nowadays, many authors are known from literature for using HMMs and derivative in order to solve problems in the world of financial mathematics, banking and assurance (Ince2005), (Knab2000), (Knab2003), (Wichern2001). The following example was published by B. Knapp et.al. “Model-based clustering with Hidden Markov Model and its application to financial time-series data” and presents a method for clustering data which must be performed well for the task of generating statistic models for prediction of loan bank customer collectives. The generated clusters represent groups of customers with similar behaviour. The prediction quality exceeds the previously used k-mean based approach.

The following diagram gives an overview over the results of their experiment:

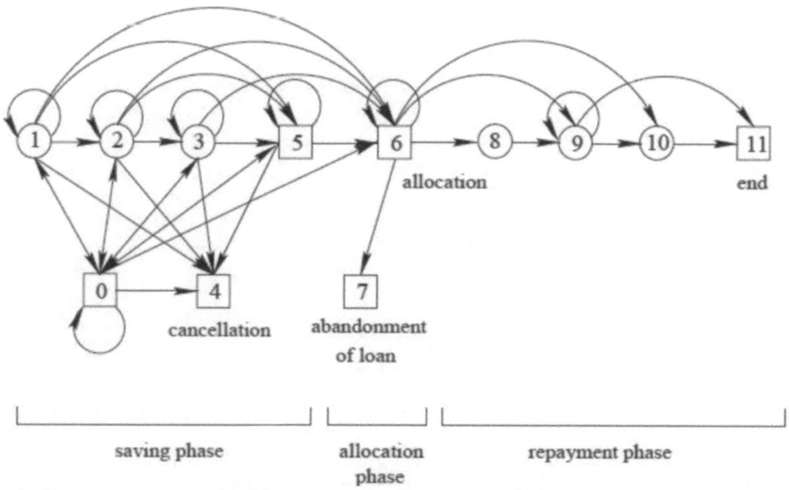

Fig. 6. Example of a Hidden Markov Model used by Knap et.al. in order to model the three phases of a loan banking contract

5.3 Application example in bioinformatics and genetics

Other areas where the use of HMMs and derivatives becomes more and more interesting are biosciences, bioinformatics and genetics (Asai1993), (Schliep2003), (Won2004), (Yada1994), (Yada1996), (Yada1998).

A. Schliep et al., presented 2003 for example, in the paper “Using hidden Markov models to analyze gene expression time course data”, a practical method which aim "to account for the

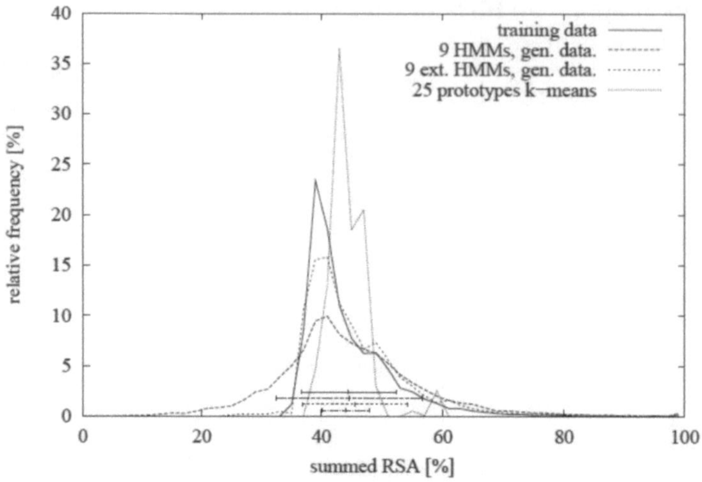

Fig. 7. Exemplary results of Knap et.al: examined "sum of relative saving amount per sequence" of the real data of bank customers and a prediction of three different models.

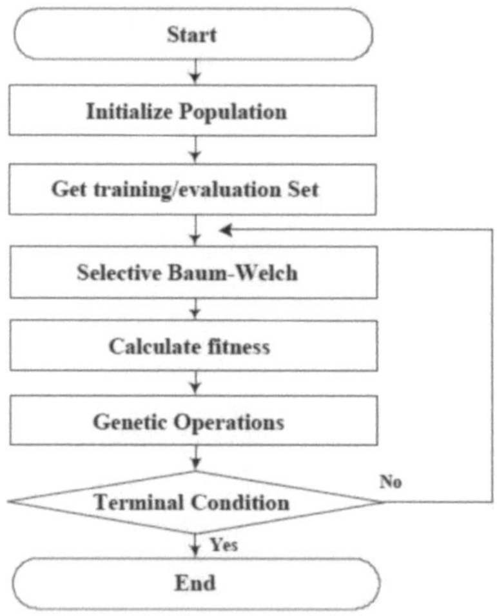

Fig. 8. Flow diagram of the Genetic Algorithm Hidden Markov Models (GA-HMM) algorithm according to K.J. Won et.al.

horizontal dependencies along the time axis in time course data" and "to cope with the prevalent errors and missing values" while observing, analysing and predicting the behaviour of gene data.

The experiments and evaluations were simulated using the "ghmm-software", a freely available tool of the "Max Planck Institute for Molecular Genetics", in Berlin Germany (GHMM2010).

K.J. Won et.al. presented, 2004, in the paper "Training HMM Structure with Genetic Algorithm for Biological Sequence Analysis" a training strategy using genetic algorithms for HMMs (GA-HMM). The purpose of that algorithm consists of using genetic algorithm and is tested on finding HMM structures for the promoter and coding region of the bacterium

C.jejuni. It also allows HMMs with different numbers of states to evolve. In order to prevent over-fitting, a separate data set is used for comparing the performance of the HMMs to that used for the Baum-Welch-Training. K.J. Won et.al. found out that the GA-HMM was capable of finding an HMM, comparable to a hand-coded HMM designed for the same task. The following figure shows the flow diagram of the published GA-HMM algorithm.

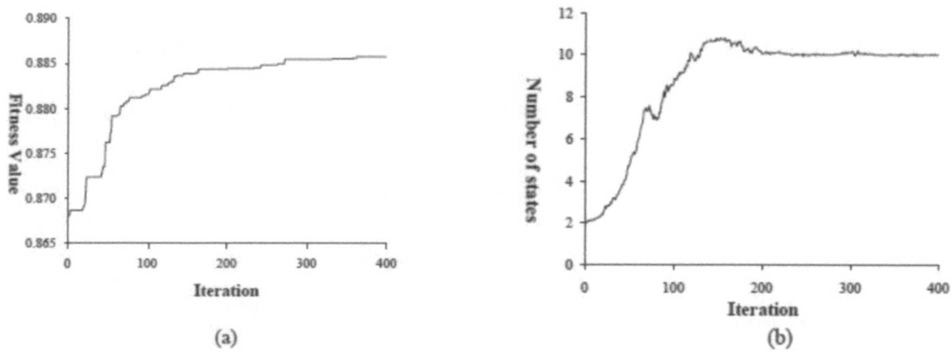

Fig. 9. Result during GA-HMM training after K.J. Won et.al.: (a) shows the fitness value of fittest individual on each iteration (b) shows average number of states for periodic signal. The GA started with a population consisting of 2 states. After 150 generations the HMM have a length of 10 states. Although the length does not significantly change thereafter the fitness continues to improve indicating that the finer structure is being fine tuned.

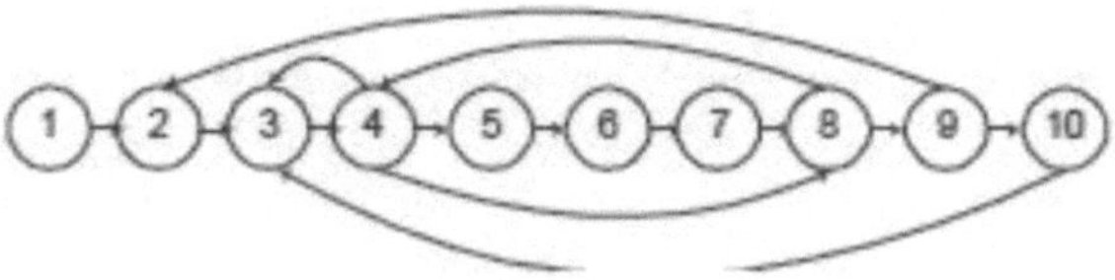

Fig. 10. Exemplary result of the GA-HMM structure model for a given periodic signal after training the C.jejuni sequences (K.J. Won).

5.4 Speech recognition and further application examples

Hidden Markov Models are also used in many other areas in modern sciences or engineering applications, e.g. in temporal pattern recognition such as speech, handwriting, gesture recognition, part-of-speech tagging, musical score following, partial discharges. Some authors even used HMM in order to explain or predict the behaviour of persons or group of persons in the area of social sciences or politics (Schrodt1998).

One of the leading application area were the HMMs are still predominant is the area of "speech recognition" (Baum1970), (Burke1958), (Charniak1993), (Huang1989), (Huang1990), (Lee1989,1), (Lee1989,2), (Lee1990), (Rabiner1989).

In all applications presented in this chapter, the "confusions matrices" is widely spread in order to evaluate the performance of HMM-based-Systems. Each row of the matrix represents the instances in a predicted class, while each column represents the instances in an actual class. One benefit of a confusion matrix is that it is easy to see if the system is confusing two classes (i.e. commonly mislabelling one as another). When a data set is

unbalanced, this usually happens when the number of samples in different classes varies greatly, the error rate of a classifier is not representative of the true performance of the classifier. This can easily be understood by an example: If there are 980 samples from class 1 and only 20 samples from class 2, the classifier can easily be biased towards class 1. If the classifier classifies all the samples as class 1, the accuracy will be 98%. This is not a good indication of the classifier's true performance. The classifier has a 100% recognition rate for class 1 but a 0% recognition rate for class 2.
The following diagram shows a simplified confusion-matrix of a specified character recognition device for the words "A","B","C","D","E" of the German language using a very simple "HMM-Model", trained data from 10 different persons and tested on 20 different persons, only for illustration purpose.

"Predicted" or "labeled as"	"A"	**99,5**	0	0	0	0	0,5
	"B"	0	**95**	1,4	1,6	0,5	1,5
	"C"	0	1,7	**95,1**	1,3	0,7	1,2
	"D"	0	1	1,6	**95,7**	0,4	1,3
	"E"	0	0,1	0,05	0,05	**99,6**	0,2
		"A"	"B"	"C"	"D"	"E"	rejected
		"Actual" or "Recognized as" or "Classified as"					

Table: Example of a Confusion Matrix for simple word recognition in the German language.

Depending on the values of the confusion matrix one call also derive typical performances of the HMM-based automate like: the general correct classification rate, the general false classification rate, the general confidences or sensitivities of the classifiers.

6. Conclusion

In this chapter the history and fundamentals of Hidden Markov Models were shown. The important basics and frameworks of mathematical modelling were introduced. Furthermore, some examples of HMMs and how they can be applied were introduced and discussed focussed on real engineering problems.
For more detailed analysis a considerable list of literature and state of the art is given.

7. References

Asai, K. & Hayamizu, S. & Handa, K. (1993). Prediction of protein secondary structure by the hidden Markov model. *Oxford Journals Bioinformatics*, Vol. 9, No. 2, 142-146

Baum, L.E. & Petrie, T. (1966). Statistical inference for probabilistic functions of finite Markov chains. *The Annals of Mathematical Statistics*, Vol. 37, No. 6, 1554-1563.

Baum, L.E. et al. (1970). A maximization technique occurring in the statistical analysis of probabilistic functions of Markov chains, *The Annals of Mathematical Statistics*, Vol. 41, No. 1, 164–171.

Bayes, T. & Price, R. (1763). An Essay towards solving a Problem in the Doctrine of Chances, In: *Philosophical Transactions of the Royal Society of London 53*, 370-418.

Burke, C. J. & Rosenblatt,M(1958). A Markovian Function of a Markov Chain. *The Annals of Mathematical Statistics*, Vol. 29, No. 4, 1112-1122.

Charniak, E.(1993). *Statistical Language Learning*, MIT Press, ISBN-10: 0-262-53141-0, Cambridge, Massachusetts.

Foellinger, O. (1992). Regelungstechnik, 7. Auflage, Hüthig Buch Verlag Heidelberg.GHMM, (2010). LGPL-ed C library implementing efficient data structures and algorithms for basic and extended HMMs. Internet connection: URL: http://www.ghmm.org. [14/08/2010]

Huang, X.D & Jack, M.A. (1989). Semi-continuous hidden Markov models for speech recognition, Ph.D. thesis, Department of Electrical Engineering, University of Edinburgh.

Huang,X. D. &Y. Ariki & M. A. Jack (1990). Hidden Markov Models for Speech Recognition. Edinburgh University Press.

Ince, H. T. & Weber, G.W. (2005). Analysis of Bauspar System and Model Based Clustering with Hidden Markov Models, Term Project in MSc Program "Financial Mathematics - Life Insurance", Institute of Applied Mathematics METU

Kalman, R.(1960): A New Approach to Linear Filtering and Prediction Problems. In: Transactions of the ASME-Journal of Basic Engineering

Kolmogorov, A. N. (1931). Über die analytischen Methoden in der Wahrscheinlichkeitsrechnung, In: *Mathematische Annalen 104*, 415.

Knab, B. (2000) Erweiterungen von Hidden-Markov-Modellen zur Analyse oekonomischer Zeitreihen. Dissertation, University of Cologne

Knab, B. & Schliep, A. & Steckemetz, B. & Wichern, B. (2003). Model-based clustering with Hidden Markov Models and its application to financial time-series data.

Kouemou, G. (2000). Atemgeräuscherkennung mit Markov-Modellen und Neuronalen Netzen beim Patientenmonitoring, Dissertation, University Karlsruhe.

Kouemou, G. et al. (2008). Radar Target Classification in Littoral Environment with HMMs Combined with a Track Based classifier, *Radar Conference*, Adelaide Australia.

Kouemou, G. (2010). *Radar Technology*, G. Kouemou (Ed.), INTECH, ISBN:978-953-307 029-2.

Lee, K.-F. (1989) "Large-vocabulary speaker-independent continuous speech recognition: The SPHINX system", Ph.D. thesis, Department of Computer Science, Carnegie-Mellon University.

Lee, K.-F. (1989) *Automatic Speech Recognition. The Development of the SPHINX System*, Kluwer Publishers, ISBN-10: 0898382963, Boston, MA.

Lee, K.-F.(1990) *Context-dependent phonetic hidden Markov models for speakerindependent continuous speech recognition*, Morgan Kaufmann Publishers, Inc., San Mateo, CA, 1990.

Markov, A. A. (1908). *Wahrscheinlichkeitsrechnung*, B. G. Teubner, Leipzig, Berlin

Petrie, T (1966). Probabilistic functions of finite state Markov chains. *The Annals of Mathematical Statistics*, Vol. 40, No. 1,:97-115.

Rabiner,L.R. & Wilpon, J.G. & Juang, B.H, (1986). A segmental k-means training procedure for connected word recognition, *AT&T Technical Journal*, Vol. 65, No. 3, pp.21-40

Rabiner, L. R. (1989). A tutorial on hidden Markov models and selected applications in speech recognition. *Proceedings of the IEEE*, Vol. 77, No. 2, 257-286.

Schliep, A.& Schönhuth, A. & Steinhoff, C. (2003). Using Hidden Markov Models to analyze gene expression time course data, *Bioinformatics,* Vol. 19, No. 1: i255–i263.

Schrodt, P. A. (1998). Pattern Recognition of International Crises using Hidden Markov Models, in D. Richards (ed.), Non-linear Models and Methods in Political Science, University of Michigan Press, Ann Arbor, MI.

Viterbi, A. (1967). Error bounds for convolutional codes and an asymptotically optimum decoding algorithm, In: *IEEE Transactions on Information Theory. 13, Nr. 2*,pp.260-269

Warakagoda, Narada (2009). Hidden Markov Models, internet connection, URL: http://jedlik.phy.bme.hu/~gerjanos/HMM/node2.html [14/08/2010]

Wichern, B (November 2001). Hidden-Markov-Modelle zur Analyse und Simulation von Finanzzeitreihen. PhD thesis. Cologne University

Wikipedia1, (2010). http://en.wikipedia.org/wiki/Andrey_Markov [20/08/2010]

Wikipedia2, (2010). http://en.wikipedia.org/wiki/Hidden_Markov_model [14/08/2010]

Wikipedia3, (2010). http://en.wikipedia.org/wiki/Markov_chain [14/08/2010]

Wikipedia4, (2010). http://en.wikipedia.org/wiki/Markov_process [14/08/2010]

Won, K..J. & Prügel-Bennett, A. & Krogh, A. (2004). Training HMM Structure with Genetic Algorithm for Biological Sequence Analysis, *Bioinformatics,* Vol. 20, No. 18, 3613-3619

Yada,T. & Ishikawa,M. & Tanaka,H. & Asai, K(1994). DNA Sequence Analysis using Hidden Markov Model and Genetic Algorithm. *Genome Informatics,* Vol.5, pp.178-179.

Yada, T. & Hirosawa, M. (1996). Gene recognition in cyanobacterium genomic sequence data using the hidden Markov model, Proceedings of the Fourth International Conference on Intelligent Systems for Molecular Biology, AAAI Press, Menlo Park, pp. 252–260.

Yada, T. (1998) Stochastic Models Representing DNA Sequence Data - Construction Algorithms and Their Applications to Prediction of Gene Structure and Function. Ph.D. thesis, University of Tokyo.

The author would like to thank his family {Dr. Ariane Hack (Germany), Jonathan Kouemou (Germany), Benedikt Kouemou (Germany)} for Supporting and Feedbacks.

Ulm, Germany, September 2010.

2

Hidden Markov Models in Dynamic System Modelling and Diagnosis

Tarik Al-ani
[1]*Laboratoire des Systèmes d'Ingénierie de Versailles, Université de Versailles Saint-Quentin, Centre Universitaire de Technologie, 10/12 Avenue de l'Europe - 78140 Vélizy, France*
[2] *Départment of Informatique, ESIEE-Paris, Cité Descartes-BP 99 93162 Noisy-Le-Grand France*

1. Introduction

Over the past few decades, Hidden Markov models *HMM*s have been widely applied as a *data-driven modeling* approach in automatic speech recognition (Rabiner, 1989). In this field, signals are encoded as temporal variation of a short time power spectrum. *HMM*s applications are now being extended to many fields such as pattern recognition (Fink, 2008); signal processing (Vaseghi, 2006); telecommunication (Hirsch, 2001); bioinformatics (Baldi et al., 2001), just to name a few applications.

Recently, *HMM*s represent in a natural way the individual component states of a dynamic system. This fact make them useful in biomedical signal analysis and in medical diagnosis (Al-ani et al., 2004; 2008; Al-ani & Trad, 2010a; Daidone et al., 2006; Helmy et al., 2008; Novák et al., 2004a;b;c;d). For the same reason, they are used in fault detection and mechanical system monitoring (Al-ani & Hamam, 2006; Bunks et al., 2000; Heck & McClellan, 1991; Miao et al., 2007; Smyth, 1994) as well in modelling, identification and control of dynamic systems (Elliot et al., 2004; Frankel, 2003; Fraser, 2010; Kwon1 et al., 2006; Myers et al., 1992; Tsontzos et al., 2007; Wren et al., 2000). An *HMM* may be used also to describe discrete stochastic changes in the system and then folds in the continuous dynamics, by associating a set of dynamic and algebraic equations with each HMM mode1. This leads to a model called *probabilistic hybrid automaton* (*PHA*) for short *hybrid complex Systems* (Hofbaur, 2005).

In these fields, it is essential to effectively learn all model parameters from a large amount of training data according to certain training criteria. It has been shown that success of *HMM*s highly depends on the goodness of estimated models and the underlying modeling technique plays an critical role in the final system performance.

The objective of this chapter is to sensitize the reader on two problems related to conventional *HMM*s which are important for dynamic system modelling and diagnosis: the training problem and the data-driven selection methods of the *structure* for the constructed *HMM* and then to introduce two application examples of *HMM*s in diagnosis of mechanical and medical dynamic systems.

2. Hidden Markov Models (*HMMs*)

This section introduces briefly the mathematical definition of Hidden Markov Models. We introduce only their conventional training aspects. The notations will be done to remain in the contexts cited by Rabiner (Rabiner, 1989).

The *HMMs* are double stochastic processes with one underlying process (state sequence) that is not observable but may be estimated through a set of processes that produce a sequence of observations. *HMMs* are a dominant technique for sequence analysis and they owe their success to the existence of many efficient and reliable algorithms.

Consider a discrete time Markov chain with a finite set of states $S = \{s_1, s_2, ..., s_N\}$. A *HMM* is defined by the following compact notation to indicate the complete parameter set of the model $\lambda = (\mathbf{\Pi}, \mathbf{A}, \mathbf{B})$ where $\mathbf{\Pi}$, $\mathbf{A}$ and $\mathbf{B}$ are the initial state distribution vector, matrix of state transition probabilities and the set of the observation probability distribution in each state, respectively (Rabiner, 1989).

$$\mathbf{\Pi} = [\pi_1, \pi_2, ..., \pi_N],\ \pi_i = P(q_1 = s_i), \mathbf{A} = [a_{ij}],\ a_{ij} = P(q_{t+1} = s_j | q_t = s_i),$$

$1 \le i, j \le N$, s_i, $s_j \in S$, $t \in \{1, 2, ..., T\}$. In the rest of this chapter, the states s_i and s_j will be written as i and j respectively for simplicity.

The observation at time t, $\mathbf{O}_t$, may be a discrete symbol (*Discrete HMMs* (*DHMMs*) case), $\mathbf{O}_t = v_k$, $v_k \in V = \{v_1, v_2, ..., v_M\}$, or continuous, $\mathbf{O}_t \in \mathbb{R}^K$. For a discrete observation, v_k will be written as z for simplicity.

The observation matrix $\mathbf{B}$ is defined by $\mathbf{B} = [b_i(\mathbf{O}_t)]$, where $b_i(\mathbf{O}_t)$ is the state conditional probability of the observation $\mathbf{O}_t$ defined by $b_i(\mathbf{O}_t) = P(\mathbf{O}_t = z | q_t = i)$, $1 \le i \le N$, $1 \le z \le M$. For a continuous observation (*Continuous HMMs* (*CHMMs*) case), $b_i(\mathbf{O}_t)$ is defined by a finite mixture of any log-concave or elliptically symmetric probability density function (pdf), e.g. Gaussian pdf, with state conditional observation mean vector μ_i and state conditional observation covariance matrix $\mathbf{\Sigma}_i$, so B may be defined as $\mathbf{B} = \{\mu_i,\ \mathbf{\Sigma}_i\}$, $i = 1, 2, ..., N$. The model parameters constraints for $1 \le i, j \le N$ are

$$\sum_{i=1}^{N} \pi_i = 1,\ \sum_{j=1}^{N} a_{ij} = 1,\ a_{ij} \ge 0,\ \sum_{k=1}^{M} b_i(\mathbf{O}_t = z) = 1 \ or\ \int_{-\infty}^{\infty} b_i(\mathbf{O}_t) d\mathbf{O}_t = 1.$$

In the case of *left-to-right HMMs* (Rabiner, 1989), multiple observation sequences must be used. Unlike the *ergodic HMM* case, the *left-to-right HMM* necessitates taking into account that the initial state probability is always equal to one. Thus, all the sequences are supposed to start with the same state. In this work, the specific structures are taken into account by weighting the values of the elements of the matrix $\mathbf{A}$. The weights are defined by zeros and ones elements corresponding to the structure of the matrix $\mathbf{A}$.

In general, at each instant of time t, the model is in one of the states i, $1 \le i \le N$. It outputs $\mathbf{O}_t$ according to a discrete probability (in the *DHMMs* case) or according to a a continuous density function (in the *CHMM* case) $b_j(\mathbf{O}_t)$ and then jumps to state j, $1 \le j \le N$ with probability a_{ij}. The state transition matrix defines the structure of the *HMM* (Rabiner, 1989).

The model λ may be obtained off-line using some training algorithm. In practice, given the observation sequence $O = \{\mathbf{O}_1\ \mathbf{O}_2\ ...\ \mathbf{O}_T\}$, and a model λ, the *HMMs* need three fundamental problems to be solved. Problem1 is how to calculate the likelihood $P(O|\lambda)$? The solution to this problem provides a score of how O belongs to the model λ. Problem 2 is how to determine the most likely state sequence that corresponds to O? The solution to this problem provides the sequence of the hidden states corresponding to the given observation sequence O. Problem

3 is how to adjust the model λ in order to maximize $P(O|\lambda)$? This is the problem of estimating the model parameters given a corpus of training observations sequences. Problems 1 and 2 are solved in the decoding stage using either the forward probability (Rabiner, 1989) or the *Viterbi decoding algorithm* (Viterbi, 1967), while problem 3 is solved during the training stage using either a conventional algorithm such as the *Baum-Welch* algorithm and the Viterbi-based algorithm, known as *segmental K-mean* in the case of *CHMMs* (Rabiner et al., 1986; Rabiner, 1989) or some other new training algorithm.

2.1 The decoding problem

In some applications, for a given *HMM*, the most probable state sequence $Q^* = \{q_1^* \, q_2^* \, ... \, q_T^*\}$ which generates a given observation sequence $O = \{\mathbf{O}_1 \, \mathbf{O}_2 \, ... \, \mathbf{O}_T\}$ could be desired. To estimate the optimum state sequence, the stochastic dynamic programming based *Viterbi algorithm* may be used. The Viterbi algorithm finds the state sequence Q^* such that

$$Q^* = arg \max_Q P(Q|O, \lambda) = arg \max_Q P(O, Q|\lambda)$$

We define the probability function $\delta_t(i)$ at the ith state, time t of the multi-stage by

$$\delta_t(i) = \max_{q_1 \, q_2 \, ... q_t} \ln p(q_1 \, q_2 \, ..., \, q_t = i, \mathbf{O}_1 \mathbf{O}_2 ... \mathbf{O}_t | \lambda, q_t),$$

$t \geq 1$, i.e. the maximum partial observation probability associated with state sequence of *HMM* at time t. In order to allow for path tracking, $\Psi_t(i)$ is also introduced to keep track of the most probable state sequence visited by an observation $\mathbf{O_t}$.

2.2 The training problem

The *HMMs* owe their success to the existence of many efficient and reliable *generative training* algorithms. The *generative training* has the advantage that one may impose all kinds of structure constraints, such as graphical models (Jordan, 2004). These constraints are related to inherent dependency or various relationship of data. More recently, a hybrid *generative/discriminative training* schemes were proposed for training. In a more general sense, the *discriminative training* of *generative models* may include any alternative estimation methods for traditional *generative models* based on a different training criterion rather than the *maximum likelihood estimation* (*MLE*). The *discriminative training* directly optimises a *mapping function* from the input data samples to the desired output labels by adjusting a decision boundary in the feature space. Several *mapping functions* can be estimated using some criteria that are directly relevant to the ultimate classification and regression purpose. The more used *mapping functions* in the literature are the *conditional maximum likelihood* (*CML*) (Jebara & Pentland, 1998), also known as *maximum mutual information* (*MMI*) estimation (Bahl et al., 1986; Woodland & Povey, 2002), empirical risk minimization (*ERM*) (Meir, 1995) and *large margin estimation* (*LME*) (Scholkopf & Smola, 2002; Smola et al., 2000).

2.2.1 *Conventional Baum-Welch training*

In many conventional *generative training* methods, a new set of parameters $\tilde{\lambda}$ is chosen such that $P(O|\tilde{\lambda})$ is maximized for a given observation sequence $O = \{\mathbf{O}_1 \, \mathbf{O}_2 \, ... \, \mathbf{O}_T\}$. In these methods, a new set of parameters $\tilde{\lambda}$ is chosen such that $P(O|\tilde{\lambda})$ is maximized for a given observation sequence $\mathbf{O}_{t+1} \, \mathbf{O}_{t+2} \, ... \, \mathbf{O}_T$. The re-estimation formulas of a given *HMM* (Rabiner,

1989) may be derived directly by maximizing (using standard constrained optimization techniques) the *Baum's auxiliary function* (Baum et al., 1970),

$$Q_{aux}(\lambda, \tilde{\lambda}) = \sum_{Q} P(O, Q|\lambda) \log P(O,\ Q|\tilde{\lambda}),$$

over $\tilde{\lambda}$. It has been proven by Bawm-Welch & Eagon (Baum & Eagon, 1967) that maximization of $Q_{aux}(\lambda, \tilde{\lambda})$ leads to increased likelihood, i.e.

$$\max_{\tilde{\lambda}}[Q_{aux}(\lambda, \tilde{\lambda})] \Rightarrow P(O|\tilde{\lambda}) \geq P(O|\lambda).$$

Eventually the likelihood function converges to a critical point.
In the literature, the solution space of *HMM*s is usually coded as a function of the model parameters $(\mathbf{\Pi}, \mathbf{A}, \mathbf{B})$. The *MLE* or the probability of the observation sequence associated to the *HMM* parameters may be applied. This may be obtained using the *Expectation-Maximization* algorithm (*EM*) (Dunmur & Titterington, 1998). This algorithm leads to *Baum-Welch reestimation formulas* which are based on the calculation of the forward and backward probabilities (Rabiner, 1989). The EM algorithm is slow, computationally expensive in practice and its estimation performance in the case of *CHMM*s depends on the given initial model.
The *Baum-Welsh* algorithm has become very popular due to its simplicity and efficiency. However, this algorithm may be easily trapped in a local optimum.

2.2.2 Conventional *K-mean* (Viterbi-based) training

Viterbi training (or *segmental K-means*) method is proposed as a *generative training* approach to speed up the learning process. The basic idea behind *Viterbi training* is to replace the computationally costly expectation E-step of the *EM* algorithm by an appropriate maximization step with fewer and simpler computations. Thus the MLE criterion can be approximated by maximizing the probability of the best *HMM* state sequence for each training sample, given the model. The most probable path for each training sequence is derived using *Viterbi decoding algorithm*. Based on this path, the state transition and observation emissions occurrences are estimated and used for the reestimation of the *HMM* parameters:

- Initialization: Choose model parameters randomly.
- Iteration:
  - Derive the most probable state sequence Q using the *Viterbi decoding algorithm*.
  - Calculate a_{ij} and $b_i(\mathbf{O}_t)$ for the given Q.
  - Estimate the new model parameters using the estimated occurrences of state transition and observation emissions.
- Termination: Stop, if convergence of the model parameters.

As mentioned by Rodríguez & Torres (Rodríguez & Torres, 2003) and by Koloydenko (Koloydenko, 2007), Viterbi training involves much less computational effort than Baum-Welch, still providing the same or slightly worse performance, so it is a common choice among designers of speech recognition systems.

2.2.3 New generative and discriminative training algorithms

There is no theoretical method to overcome the model initialisation and the local optimum problems. In practice, many *generative training* as well as *discriminative training* methods were proposed to overcome the limitations of the above conventional algorithms.

2.2.3.1 New generative training algorithms for the generative models

Some authors (Kanevsky, 2004; Povey & Kingsbury, 2007; Woodland & Povey, 2002) suggested an *Extended Baum-Welch* (*EBW*) algorithm which is an iterative algorithm that uses a specific set of update rules performed at each iteration. Huda et al. (Huda et al., 2006) proposed different initial guesses and the solution that corresponds to the local maximum with the largest probability is selected. The authors (Aupetit et al., 2007; Fengqin et al., 2008; Xue et al., 2006) used the *Particle Swarm Optimization* (*PSO*) algorithm (Kennedy et al., 2001). Wang et al. (Wang et al., 2008) proposed an*HMM* based on a *mixture of factor analysis* (*HMM-MFA*) to model the correlation between the feature vector elements in speech signals. Turner (Turner, 2008) proposed an effective implementation of a direct approach using an adaptation of the *Levenberg-Marquardt* algorithm. This approach is based on the possibility of maximizing the likelihood of *HMM*s by means of a direct *gradient-Hessian* approach, without resorting to the EM algorithm.

Meta-heuristics approaches such as *simulated annealing* or *Tabu search* algorithms (Aarts & Korst, 1990; Kinney et al., 2007; Kirkpartrick et al., 1983; Lee, 2008; Lyu et al., 1996; Mazumdar et al., 2007; McKendall & Shang, 2008) were used to minimize general energy or cost functions with the aim of finding global optimal solutions within the feasible parameter domain. Due to the non convexity of the *maximum likelihood criterion*, some meta-heuristics such as evolutionary programming and simulated annealing algorithms in their original implementation in the context of *HMM*s have been proposed (Andrieu et al., 2000; Eddy, 1995; Lee & Park, 2007; Paul, 1985; Pérez et al., 2007; Rao & Rose, 2001; Tang et al., 2006; Yang et al., 2008; Won et al., 2007; Zhao et al., 2007). In these works, the *simulated annealing* algorithm is applied to the *CHMM* parameters. It is well known in *simulated annealing* that the convergence and the size of the chain used at each temperature depend on the size of the solution space. A continuous coding of the solution space leads to an infinite size of this space which gives rise to convergence difficulties whereas the discrete coding of the solution space leads to a finite size of this space which gives rise to better convergence properties (Al-ani & Hamam, 2010b).

2.2.3.2 New *discriminative training* algorithms for the generative models

Based on the *mapping functions*, many *discriminative models* were developed (Jiang, 2010). Particularly, based on the *generalization bounds* in *statistical learning theory* (Vapnik, 1998), *large margin estimation* (*LME*) (Scholkopf & Smola, 2002; Smola et al., 2000) have been applied with success in several fields. However, as stated by Jiang (Jiang, 2010), there are still some limitations in the *discriminative training* scheme. For example, it is not straightforward to deal with *latent variables* and exploit the underlying structure of data in *discriminative models*. Moreover, computational complexity is considerably higher in discriminative training since it requires simultaneous consideration of data from all classes. Hence, no standalone discriminative model can yield comparable performance as *generative models*, i.e., *HMM*s, on any significant application task.

More recently, several hybrid algorithms have emerged combining *generative models* and *discriminative training* based on some *discriminative criteria* that are related to the application purposes (Altun et al., 2003; Jaakkola& Haussler, 1998; Jaakkola et al., 1999; Taskar et al., 2003).

This scheme makes possible to deal with latent variables and exploit the underlying structure of data. Discriminative training of *HMMs* have been applied in many fields:

- *Speech* and *handwritten* recognition (Altun et al., 2003; Arslan & Hansen, 1999; Bach & Jordan, 2005; Cheng et al., 2009; 2010; Do & Artières, 2009; Dong & Li, 2007; Ganapathiraju et al., 2000; Golowich & Sun, 2007; Gu et al., 2000; Jiang et al., 2006; Jiang & Li, 2006; Jiang, 2010; Krüger et al., 2005; 2006; Lee & Park, 2005; Li & Jiang, 2005; Li et al., 2005a;b; Li & Juang, 2006; Liu et al., 2007a;b; Markov et al., 2001; Sanguansat et al., 2004; Saon & Povey, 2008; Sha & Saul, 2009; Solin & Burshtein, 2008),
- *Computational biology* (Li & Noble, 2003),
- *Dialog act tagging* (Surendran & Levow, 2006),
- Analysis of *Facial expression temporal dynamics* (Valstar & Pantic, 2008)
- *Financial* applications (Rao & Hong, 2001),
- *Information extraction* (Altun et al., 2003),
- *Modeling chaotic nonlinear dynamical systems* (Myers et al., 1992),
- *Teleoperation tasks* (Castellani et al., 2004),
- *Temporal signals* and *EEG* analysis (Xu et al., 2005; 2006),

2.3 Selection of the number of states in *HMMs*

A practical implementation but fundamental issue to be addressed when using *HMMs* is the determination of their *structure*, namely the *topology* (or the transitions between the states) and the number of states. The *structure* of an *HMM* is determined by some constraints that may be introduced in the HMM *structure*, such as forcing the presence or absence of connections between certain states.

Several approaches were proposed for learning the *structure* of *HMMs*. Stolcke & Omohundro (Stolcke & Omohundro, 1993) proposed a data-driven technique where the induction process starts with the most specific model consistent with the training data and generalises by successively merging states. Both the choice of states to merge and the stopping criterion are guided by the Bayesian posterior probability. Takara et al. (Takara et al., 2007) proposed the application of a *genetic algorithm* (*GA*) to search out an optimal *structure*. Biem et al. (Biem et al., 2002; Biem, 2003) proposed a model selection criterion for classification problems. The criterion focuses on selecting models that are discriminant instead of models based on the Occam's razor principle of parsimony between accurate modeling and complexity. The criterion, dubbed *Discriminative Information Criterion* (*DIC*), was applied to the optimisation of *HMM topology* aimed at the recognition of cursively-handwritten digits. The results showed that *DIC* generated models achieve a good relative improvement in performance from a baseline system generated by the *Bayesian Information Criterion* (*BIC*). Bcego et al. (Bcego et al., 2003) proposed a technique which is able to deal with drawbacks of standard general purpose methods, like those based on the *Bayesian inference criterion* (*BIC*), i.e., computational requirements, and sensitivity to initialisation of the training procedures. The basic idea is to perform "decreasing" learning, starting each training how to learn model *structure* from data and how to make the best use of labeled and unlabeled data. They showed that a manually-constructed model that contains multiple states per extraction field outperforms a model with one state per field, and discussed strategies for learning the model *structure* automatically from data. They also demonstrated that the use of distantly-labeled data to set model parameters provides a significant improvement in extraction accuracy.

Siddiqi et al. (Siddiqi et al., 2007) proposed a new *state-splitting algorithm* that addresses two problems: choosing the *structure* (model selection) and estimating model parameters (learning).
Other approaches were also proposed for estimating the number of states. Celeux & Durand (Celeux & Durand, 2008) proposed a technique for selecting *HMM* state number with cross-validated Likelihood and they gave two approaches to compute cross-validated likelihood for a *HMM*. The first one consists of using a deterministic half-sampling procedure, and the second one consists of an adaptation of the *EM algorithm* for *HMMs*, to take into account randomly missing values induced by cross-validation. Gunter & Bunke (Gunter & Bunke, 2003) examined some optimization strategies for an *HMM* classifier that works with continuous feature values and uses the Baum-Welch training algorithm. The free parameters of the optimization procedure introduced in their paper are the number of states of a model, the number of training iterations, and the number of Gaussian mixtures for each state. The proposed optimization strategies are evaluated in the context of a handwritten word recognition task.

3. Some selected applications of *Hidden Markov models* in dynamic systems

In this section, we introduce two application examples on dynamic processes. The first application concerns the *condition-based maintenance* of machines using *HMMs* and the second one concerns the diagnosis in medicine. For more details, see (Al-ani et al., 2004; Bunks et al., 2000)

3.1 *Condition-based maintenance* of machines using *HMMs*

The term *condition-based maintenance* (*CBM*) is used to signify the monitoring of machines for the purpose of *diagnostics* and *prognostics*. *Diagnostics* are used to determine the current health status of a machine's internal components and *prognostics* are used to predict their remaining useful life. CBM has the potential to greatly reduce costs by helping to avoid catastrophic failures (an extremely important point, for example, for helicopter gearboxes) and by more efficiently determining the intervals required for maintenance schedules. The economic ramifications of CBM are many fold since they affect labour requirements, replacement part costs, and the logistics of scheduling routine maintenance. The reduction of maintenance to that which is strictly necessary can have the effect of prolonging machine life and that of diminishing the defects that can be introduced by the maintenance itself. Finally, the reduction of catastrophic failures which lead to the loss of life and equipment can have an important e!ect on insurance premiums.
One method for performing *CBM* is by using vibration measurements. The main objective is the detection of vibrational characteristics which correspond to physical changes in the machine which indicate abnormal operation. Examples of this could be chipping in a roller bearing or spalling on a pinion gear. The primary challenge is to achieve a high degree of precision in classifying a machine's health given that its vibrational characteristics will vary with many factors not all corresponding to defective components. For example, two identical, new machines will generally have different vibrational characteristics due to differences in the manufacturing process. Furthermore, a machine's underlying vibrational character is likely to change over time as a function of the operating conditions, the maintenance schedules it has undergone, and aging of the machine. Finally, the specific vibrational characteristics of the machine will change as torque loads vary. Clearly, it is important to be able to differentiate between vibrational changes which are due to machine component defects and

those due to changing operating conditions. Assuming that torque loads vary slowly with time, recorded vibration data should demonstrate practically stationary statistics over short intervals. Under these conditions the following approach suggests itself. First, all the different operating conditions which give rise to significantly different statistics in vibration data must be identified. Second, the statistics of vibration data for various defects must be determined either experimentally or by modelling. The combined sets of statistics would then serve as a universe of models with which hypothesis testing could be performed on segments of the data. Continuous processing of sequential segments of the data would result in classification of operating condition and defect type (if any) as a function of time. Prior knowledge of how a machine were to be operated or information about the relative frequency of the occurrence of different types of defects could also be used to improve the performance of the above classification algorithm. This would be accomplished by constructing a doubly stochastic process which describes probabilistically how the machine is likely to undergo transition from state to state and what the statistics are at each state. This type of process is well suited to the statistical modelling methodology defined by *HMMs*.

HMMs are well suited to modelling of quasi-stationary signals and thus, as will be discussed in what follows, can be used to perform detection and estimation for machine *diagnostics* and *prognostics*. Two features of HMMs are particularly useful in the monitoring of machine health. The first is that computationally efficient methods exist for computing likelihoods using *HMMs* (Van Trees, 1968). This feature is important since it promises that signal processing tools based on HMMs can be implemented cost effectively. Furthermore, there exist efficient techniques which can be used for system identification with *HMMs*. This means that HMMs can be used to build data-driven models of machines relieving somewhat the need to identify specific features in data to be used as health indicators.

Bunks et al. (Bunks et al., 2000) compared problems of speech processing, an area where *HMMs* have been applied extensively, to those of machine health monitoring. Their comparison was useful since it helped motivate the use of *HMMs* for *CBM* as well as indicated what some of the critical issues. Then, they used the Westland helicopter gearbox data to illustrate some of the characteristics of vibration data under different operating conditions and types of defects and to illustrate the application of *HMMs* to *CBM*.

3.1.1 The Westland helicopter gearbox data

The laboratory data set is made available by the Office of Naval Research for the evaluation of machine health monitoring algorithms. This data set consists of vibration measurements from a set of accelerometers placed on the casing of a Westland helicopter gearbox (Bunks et al., 2000). The gearbox was operated at various torque levels and with various seeded defects in a special test rig. This data set is used in examples of the application of *HMMs* to *CBM*.

The data set consists of 68 distinct operating conditions constituting nine different torque levels and eight different seeded defects (of which one is actually a no-defect case). For each operating condition time samples at a sampling rate of 100 kHz from eight accelerometers are available for analysis. Bunks et al. (Bunks et al., 2000) noted the following observations on the salient features of the Westland helicopter gearbox data set:

- The data are not stationary as a function of operating torque level.
- There are clear, although complex, differences in the spectra as a function of the types of defects.
- There are clear, although complex, differences in the spectra as a function of the severity of defect level.

These observations were important since they validated the comparisons made by Bunks et al. (Bunks et al., 2000), imply the feasibility of *prognostics*, and motivate the construction of *HMMs* models for *CBM*.

3.1.2 HMM modelling for the Westland helicopter gearbox data

The objective is to construct some HMM models which can be used on data from the Westland helicopter gearbox. *HMMs* are composed of two main components. There is the state transition matrix which probabilistically describes how the model moves from one stationary type of behaviour to another. There is also the probability distribution associated to each state which describes the statistics of the particular stationary model. In order to effectively model the Westland helicopter gearbox data presented briefly in the previous section it is necessary to construct a reasonable model for both of these components. This is achieved by first specifying the total number of states for the model and then by estimating the parameters of an appropriate probability density for each state. As for the state transition matrix this information can only be obtained by using a prior experimental knowledge of the frequency of occurrence of each defect and the average time spent operating at each of the torque levels. For the purposes of their work this information was not available; nevertheless, some effort was made Bunks et al. (Bunks et al., 2000) to construct a reasonable state transition model.

3.1.2.1 Modelling state probability densities

As noted in Section 3.1.1 the characteristics of the power spectra of the Westland data change significantly for different torque levels and for different defect types. For the Westland data set there are a total of 68 different torque-level defect-type pairs available. Thus, the *HMM* constructed contains the same number of states.

An essential part of applying *HMM* technology to any problem is to decide what the appropriate observations are. In general, the observations could be the raw data or some function or transformation of the data. A transformation of the data is preferable when the result allows for the diminution of the quantity of data which needs to be processed without losing the ability to effectively monitor the *HMM* process. This may be important for the Westland data since it is acquired at a rate of 100k samples per second for each of the eight sensors and thus represents a relatively heavy data volume.

Each state of the Markov chain associated to an HMM must have a state process model which implicitly or explicitly specifies a probability density function. In the *HMM* literature the Gaussian distribution is often used although multi-modal distributions are also used by taking mixtures of Gaussians (Liporace, 1982; Rabiner, 1989). Other common choices include mixtures of autoregressive and autoregressive moving-average models (Poritz, 1982). In this application a simple multi-dimensional Gaussian distribution was used. A different Gaussian is estimated for each of the 68 operating conditions. Each Gaussian is eight-dimensional (8D) (due to the eight sensors) and is estimated using the first 10k samples of each of the operating condition runs (i.e. the first 0.1 s of data). The mean vectors, μ_i, and covariance matrices, $\mathbf{\Sigma}_i$ for each of the $i = 1, 2, .., 68$ cases were obtained using the following formulas:

$$\mu_i = \frac{1}{T}\sum_{t=1}^{T} y_i(t) \tag{1}$$

$$\mathbf{\Sigma}_i = \frac{1}{T}\sum_{t=1}^{T} [y_i(t) - \mu_i][y_i(t) - \mu_i]^T \tag{2}$$

where T=10000 and $y_i(t)$ is the 8-vector of observations at time $t\Delta t$ for data from operating condition i.

We note that, in principle, the vibration data should be zero mean since having a DC level of vibration is meaningless. Nevertheless, it is important to take the sample mean into account to cancel the effects of bias coming from electronic amplification. We further note that modelling the time sample data as an independent and identically distributed 8D Gaussian process does not take advantage of the spectrally banded features of the data that were pointed out in Section 3.1.1. The choice does have, however, a physical interpretation. Since the mean does not contain any information the difference in data can only be contained in the second-order statistics, namely the covariance. Looking at the broadband covariance matrix associated to an operating condition yields information about the *rms* vibrational power on each sensor (the diagonal terms of the covariance matrix) as well as the *rms* cross-power between sensors. Since the various sensors are distributed equally around the gearbox it can be concluded that this model provides information on proximity (i.e. relative power) and multipath effects (i.e. events that lead to high correlation between sensors). As shown by Bunks et al. (Bunks et al., 2000), this model results in an extremely robust classification of the Westland helicopter gearbox data.

To measure the ability of the 68 Gaussian models to discriminate the data they were used in three classification experiments. The experiments were conducted by testing which of the 68 models maximized the likelihood of observed data. This was done with varying sample lengths for the observed data (10k, 1k, and 200 samples). The three tests were performed using the fourth second of data. Note that since the models were created using the first 0.1 s of data that these tests are performed by applying the models to data removed by 3.9 s. The results of the above three experiments are illustrated in Fig. 1.

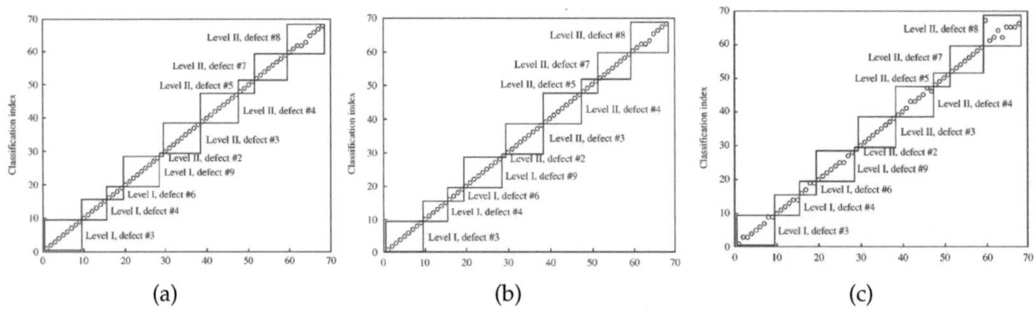

(a) (b) (c)

Fig. 1. Classification test using fourth second's first (a) 10k samples. (b) 1k samples. (c) 200 samples (Bunks et al., 2000).

Each sub-figure illustrates the classification index (1-68) vs the data set index (also 1-68). Thus, each circle in Fig. 1 (a) yields the result of deciding which is the best model (classification) given the data set specified on the independent axis. Perfect classification requires that all the circles lie on the diagonal as they almost do in Fig. 1 (a). The classification indices were chosen to group operating conditions together by defect type. The ensemble of rectangular boxes in Fig. 1 (a) indicates groups of indices whose defect type and level are the same. As shown in the figure each rectangle is labelled by the defect type and level it represents. Finally, inside each rectangle the torque level is increasing from the lower left to the upper right of the box.

As can be seen in Fig. 1 (a) the classification of the 68 cases only has minor errors consisting of two torque-level misclassifications. In particular, for the level 2 defect d8 the torque at

50% is misclassiëd to be 45% and that of 60% is taken to be 50%. Thus, it can be concluded that using eight-dimensional Gaussian distributions to model the data is sufficient to identify defect types and almost sufficient to identify all torque levels. This remains true when the observed data set is reduced to only 1000 samples as is seen in Fig. 1 (b). However, as shown in Fig. 1 (c), when the number of samples is reduced to only 200 the classification of the 68 cases starts to show a more significant number of errors. Nevertheless, these errors continue to consist of only torque-level classification errors and none are defect-type errors.

The next test shows how the above classification procedure might work on a data set from an operating helicopter gearbox. The tests are made using a composite data set which was created by splicing together data from 10 of the 68 different operating conditions. An example of this data set for the port quill shaft sensor is illustrated in Fig. 2.

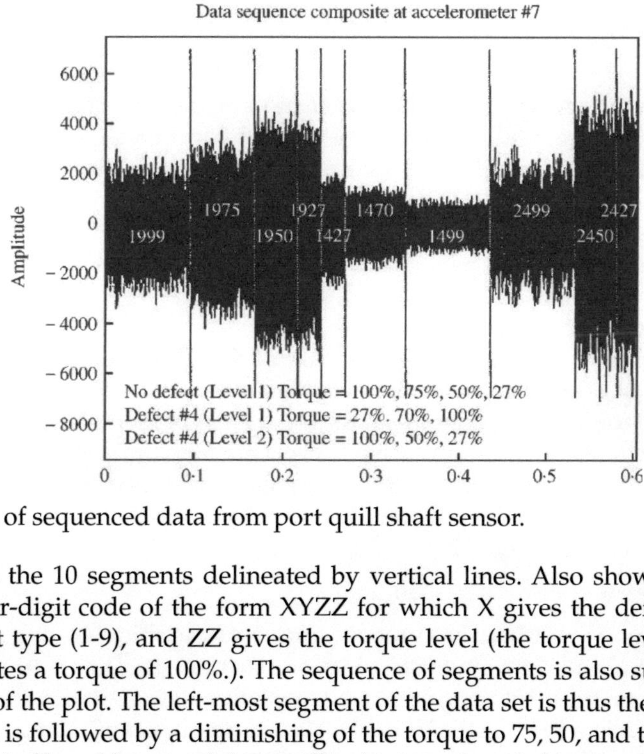

Fig. 2. Illustration of sequenced data from port quill shaft sensor.

The figure shows the 10 segments delineated by vertical lines. Also shown on each of the segments is a four-digit code of the form XYZZ for which X gives the defect level (1 or 2), Y gives the defect type (1-9), and ZZ gives the torque level (the torque level designated by 99 actually indicates a torque of 100%.). The sequence of segments is also summarized in the lower-left corner of the plot. The left-most segment of the data set is thus the no-defect case at 100% torque. This is followed by a diminishing of the torque to 75, 50, and then 27% at which point defect #4 (spiral bevel input opinion spalling) is introduced also at a torque level of 27%. The torque level is then increased to 70 and then 100% with this defect. The situation then becomes more serious evolving to a level-2 defect #4 at 100% torque. The torque level then decreases to 50 and then 27% for this defect level.

It is interesting to note that in the sequence presented in Fig. 2 the amplitude of vibration is higher for low torque levels than for high torque levels. This was already noted previously in the examination of power spectra (see Fig. 1 and the associated comments). The sequenced data set for all eight sensors (of which only one is illustrated in Fig. 2) were used to perform three classification experiments. Each experiment was conducted by applying a sliding window (with no overlap) of length 1k, 200, and 100 samples, respectively, over the data. The models used in the prior examples were used to classify the data output from the sliding window at each step. The results are shown in Fig. 3.

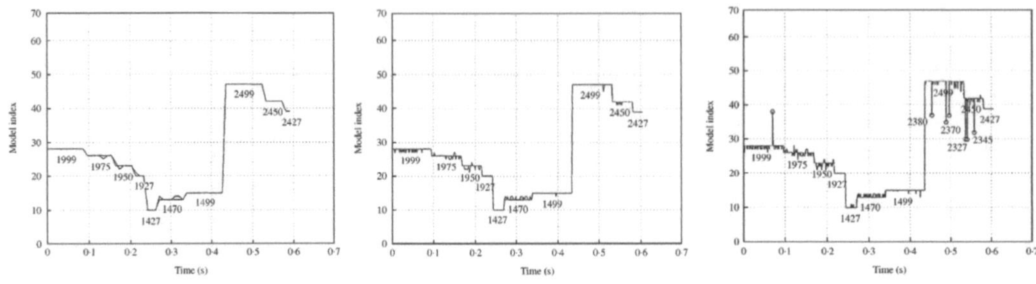

(a) (b) (c)

Fig. 3. Comparison of classification and true sequence with (a) a sliding window 1000 samples wide. (b) a sliding window 200 samples wide. (c) a sliding window 100 samples wide (Bunks et al., 2000).

In Fig. 3 (a) there are very few errors of classification for the case where a sliding window of 1k samples is used. Since model index is organized by torque as was illustrated in Fig. 1 it can be seen that the several small errors are torque-level classification errors only. For the case of the sliding window using 200 samples shown in Fig. 3 (b) there are more errors but they remain small and are still only slight torque-level discrepancies. Finally, in Fig. 3 (c) which illustrates the case of the sliding window with 100 sample points, there are several important errors which give rise to misclassifications in the type of defect. These errors are indicated by circles and are labelled by their type codes.

The tests presented in the preceding figures indicate that the 68 models are quite robust and are quite capable of performing accurate classification of defects and even classification of torque level. Furthermore, the examples show that the use of more samples is preferable since it improves the accuracy of classification and proportionally diminishes the amount of data to consider. It is important to note that the computational burden necessary to obtain the decision statistics is quite light depending only on a number of multiplies proportional to the number of samples as defined in Equation 2.

3.1.2.2 Modelling state transition probabilities

The construction of a state transition model improves classification performance over that obtained from simply using a finite set of unrelated models. That is to say the additional information obtained from knowing what are the relative state visitation frequencies provides a smoothing mechanism to the estimation of state (i.e. classification). Detection and estimation algorithms based on *HMM*s incorporate state transition information in a Bayesian way.

In the previous section, a description of how to model state probability densities for the Westland helicopter gearbox data was described and the resulting models were shown to be effective in discriminating between various types of seeded defects. The models were also shown to be robust and sufficiently discriminating to determine the operating torque levels of the gearbox. These results seem to be sufficiently good to forego the need for the construction of a state transition model. However, the Westland data set is a high-quality laboratory test set. Under true helicopter-operating conditions the recorded data would certainly be a lot noisier and would most likely contain features not apparent in the test data.

Another important point is that for general problems of machine health monitoring there will not always be laboratory test data from which state probability densities can be estimated as was done in the previous subsection. Under these circumstances it may be necessary to determine these densities from explicit modelling using only the knowledge of the physical characteristics of the various machine components (for a description of how to do this with gears see (Mark, 1992)). Consequently, additional statistical information obtained from the state transition model is very important for the performance of any classification computations.

This section discusses a state transition model for the gearbox data. This model should be based on prior information about the frequency of occurrence of each defect and the average time spent operating at each of the torque levels. Although, for the Westland helicopter gearbox data set, this information is not available it is still useful to discuss a potential model. The model describes how a simple state transition diagram might reasonably be constructed. The model is illustrated in Fig. 4 which shows three rows of states the top one for no-defect, the middle one for a level 1 defect, and the bottom one for a level 2 defect.

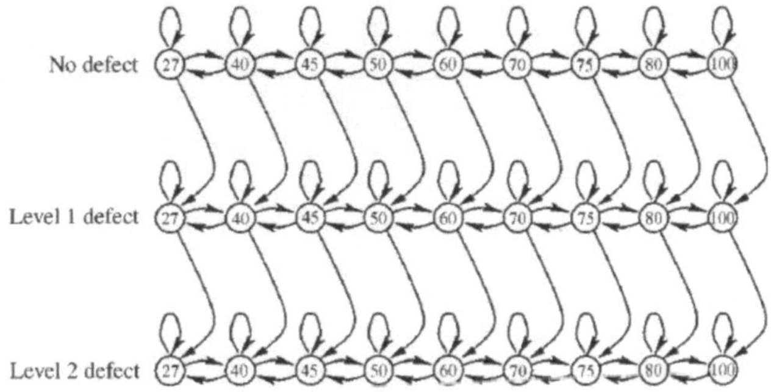

Fig. 4. Transition diagram for Westland helicopter gearbox.

Each row contains nine states representing the nine torque levels under which the Westland helicopter gearbox was operated. The arrows between torque levels are associated with probabilities for transitioning from one torque level to the next. As shown in the diagram they indicate that the torque can only increase or decrease by increments. The torque level can also stay the same. The arrows between defect levels are associated with probabilities for transitioning from no defect to a level-1 defect and subsequently to a level-2 defect. Notice that once a no-defect state is left there is no way to return. This is also true for the transition from a level-1 defect to a level-2 defect.

The state diagram in Fig. 4 illustrates a model for transitions from a no-defect to a single-defect case. Since the Westland data set consists of seven distinct defect types the full-state transition diagram would be based on Fig. 4 where the bottom two rows would be repeated six more times and each attached in parallel to the top row. The full-state diagram model would then permit a transition from the no-defect case to any one of the seven defect cases. The state transition model could then be made more complex by allowing multiple defects to be simultaneously present. Under these circumstances, additional branches representing the multiple defect cases would be added to the state transition diagram. The new branches would be appropriately attached to the single defect states. For example, simultaneous defects A and B could be accessed by transitioning from either the single defect A or the single defect B (not necessarily with the same probability).

3.1.2.3 *Prognostics*

An important problem in *CBM* is planning essential maintenance. Maintenance must be performed before the expiration of the remaining useful life of critical machine components.

Nevertheless, performing machine maintenance before it is needed gives rise to unnecessary costs and can lead to maintenance-caused defects (damage inflicted on the machine via the maintenance procedure). Thus, the estimation of mean useful life, known as *prognostics*, is an interesting and important problem. *HMMs* provide a natural framework within which problems of *prognostics* can be formulated. To illustrate this, Fig. 5 shows an HMM which can be used for estimating the mean remaining useful life. In the figure, each state represents the degree of incipient failure of a particular machine defect. The random process of each state is determined by a row of Fig. 4. That is, state 1 in Fig. 5 is associated to a random process generated by the top row of Fig. 4 (i.e. for no-defects). State 2 in Fig. 4 gets its random process from the middle row of Fig. 4 and so on. For each state n there is a probability of remaining in that state, a_{nn}, and a probability of leaving it, $a_{n,n+1}$. Since defects always become worse and never improve the chain only allows transitions in the direction of increasing defect.

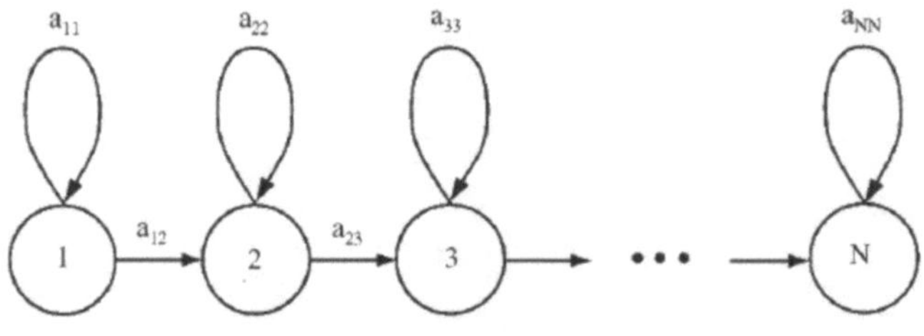

Fig. 5. Hidden Markov model for prognostics.

Thus, if state N represents the state of zero remaining useful life then the mean time, t^*, to this state given that the current state, n, is calculated as a function of the mean number of steps required to go from state n to state N. From the definition of expectation this is accomplished by calculating the probability, p_k, of going from state n to state N in exactly k steps and then forming the sum

$$t^* = \sum_{k=1}^{\infty} k p_k \tag{3}$$

This shows, at least in principle, how the problem of prognostics can be formulated if the appropriate transition probabilities can be determined. Transition probabilities are determined from experiential knowledge. As an example, it is well known that timing belts on cars fail at around 70 000 miles. This sort of information is known for many types of machine components and can be incorporated into the HMM in Fig. 5 as transition probabilities. Used in conjunction with observations of vibration data it helps to determine the current state in the HMM and the transition probabilities can then be used to compute a mean remaining useful life estimate. This also illustrates how *HMMs* can be used in a hierarchical way to build up complex models from simpler ones.

This application example does not answer all questions of how to apply *HMMs* to *CBM* and many issues remain to be resolved. In particular, it is important to explore the practical question of how to train *HMMs* for *CBM*. Since it is impractical to test each machine for each operating condition that might be encountered, Bunks et al. (Bunks et al., 2000) suggested a dynamic modelling approach for synthetically generating vibration data.

3.2 *Sleep apnea* diagnosis using *HMMs*

In this example, an automatic diagnosis approach based on *HMMs* is proposed for the diagnosis of *sleep apnea syndrome* (Al-ani et al., 2004; 2008).

Sleep apnea Syndrome (*SAS*) (American Academy of Sleep Medicine Task Force, 1999), is a very common *sleep disorder*. SAS is considered as clinically relevant when the breath stops during more than 10 seconds and occurs more than five times per sleep hour. These non breathing episodes may sometimes occur more than 300 times a night. Health studies affirm that more than 30 of these non breathing episodes per night should be considered abnormal. There exist two kinds of *apneic events* that may cause insufficient pulmonary ventilation during *sleep apnea* and *hypopnoea*. *Apnea* is defined as the total absence of airflow, followed by the reduction of oxygen levels in arterial blood. The term *hypopnoea* is used when the breath doesn't stop but decrease over 50% of its normal value , followed by the reduction of oxygen levels in arterial blood. The *SAS* is present mainly in adults and in 11% of children especially in the male population (Eliot et al., 2003). Different form of *apnea/hypopnoea* may be distinguished: *obstructive*, and *mixed*. *Obstructive sleep apnea* (*OSA*) is the most common type of *sleep apnea*. *OSA* occurs when the upper airway occludes (either partially or fully) but the effort to continue breathing is persistent. The primary causes of upper airway obstruction are lack of muscle tone during sleep, excess tissue in the upper airway, and anatomic abnormalities in the upper airway and jaw.

The treatment of *SAS* depends on the diagnosis quality of the *apnea/hypopnoea* event by the expert physician. Nowadays the *sleep apnea*s are classified manually by the expert physician thanks to the nocturnal *polysomnographic* monitoring that simultaneously records several vital signals during the entire sleeping process (*Nasal airflow* (*NAF*), *electrocardiogram* (*ECG*), *electroencephalogram* (*EEG*), *electromyogram* (*EMG*), *esophageal pressure* (*Pes*), *gastric pressure* (*Pgas*), *Oxygen Saturation* (*OS*), ...). A *sleep apnea diagnosis* is a very time consuming, expensive and tedious task consisting of expert visual evaluation all 10 minutes pieces of approximately 8 hour recording with a setting of many channels.

Al-ani et al. (Al-ani et al., 2004), demonstrated that *sleep apnea* classification may be done automatically using three simultaneous records of *NAF*, *Peso* and *Pgas* issued from the current techniques of investigating patients with suspected sleep disordered breathing. The inference method of this approach translates parameter values into interpretations of physiological and pathophysiological states. If the interpretation is extended to sequences of states in time, a state-space trajectory may be obtained. The identification of state-space trajectories is a useful concept in diagnosis because some disorders may only be distinguished from each other by time sequences of pathophysiological states. The probabilistic concept of *HMMs* captures the uncertainty inherent in state interpretation. A major interest of using *HMMs* is their capabilities for predictive inference. This inference makes our diagnosis system useful in the evaluation of treatment plans, in the optimization of treatment plans, in the predictive alarming.

The proposed diagnosis system, Fig. 6, is organized in such a manner that to be interactive with the expert. It is organized as three phases: training phase, state interpretation phase and detection phase.

3.2.1 Training phase

In the training phase, a real polysomnographic clinical records (observations) were used. These records were organised as a *multiple observation sequences* of observations vectors. Each vector contains three vital signals: *NAF*, *Peso* and *Pgas*. In Patient monitoring, we may represent the evolution of the processes, modelled by different *HMMs* (*normal respiration*, *snoring*, *hypopnea*, *apnea*, ...), by some intrinsic hidden states corresponding to some events of interest (e.g., two events *normal inspiration* and *normal expiration in the case of* normal

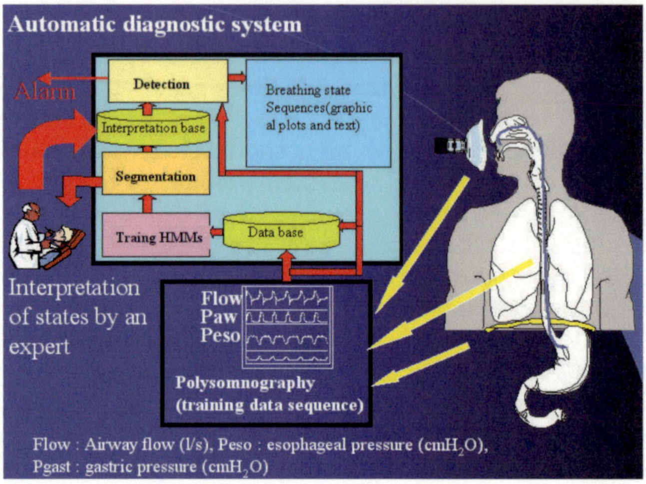

Fig. 6. Diagnosis system.

respiration. *Simulated annealing algorithm* (Al-ani & Hamam, 2010b) was used to construct these *HMM*s.

3.2.2 Segmentation of the training data sequence into different pathophysiological state sequence - state interpretation phase

Given the training observation sequences and their corresponding *HMM*s, this phase allows an expert to decode, off-line, their corresponding state labels using *Viterbi decoding algorithm*. The expert may then interpret these decoded state labels by some *pathophysiological* state interpretations (e.g. snoring, inspiration, expiration, obstructive apnea, etc.), Fig. 7. The interpretation of each state will be useful in on-line detection and interpretation of the on-line state sequence. The identification of state-space trajectories is useful concept in diagnosis since some disorders can only be distinguished from each other by the sequences of pathophysiological states that they follow in time.

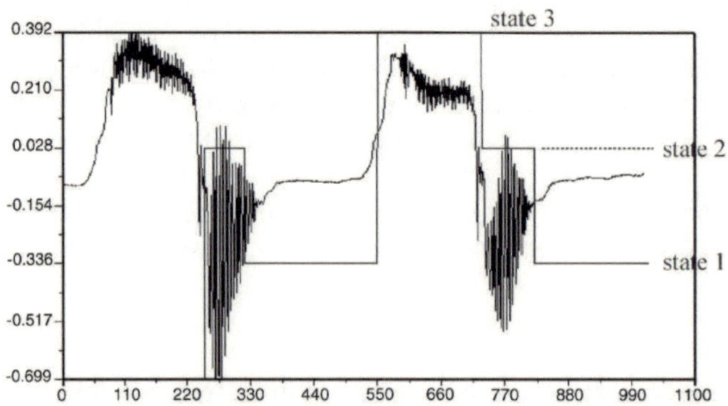

Fig. 7. An example of data segmentation of the air flow into different states and their interpretations. Event model contains three states: state 1: week airflow, state 2: snoring during expiration and state 3: snoring during inspiration.

3.2.3 Off-line or on-line detection phase

Once the *HMMs* are available, the detection of hidden *pathophysiological* states in a given observation sequence becomes possible. This may be done by two consecutive steps. At step1, select the model that gives the maximum likelihood and at step 2, detect the *Pathophysiological* state using *Viterbi algorithm*. Two modes of detection are possible: off-line detection using the complete length of the observation sequence or on-line detection using a sliding window on the observation sequence stream.

In the above work, it was demonstrated that *sleep apnea* classification may be done automatically using three simultaneous records of *NAF*, *Peso* and *Pgas* issued from the current techniques of investigating patients with suspected sleep disordered breathing. Correctly identifying obstructive hypopneas and episodes of upper airway resistance needs a sensitive measure of airflow and inspiratory effort. The measurement of swings in pleural pressure by esophageal manometry is the current gold standard techniques for detecting changes in respiratory effort. However, the placement of an esophageal catheter is often uncomfortable and unacceptable, it may modify the upper airway dynamics, and some believe that it contributes to the sleep disturbance during the sleep study. Furthermore, this technique is available in only a proportion of sleep laboratories and, if performed, adds significantly to the cost of the sleep study. For all these reasons, a new preliminary approach on detecting and classifying *sleep apneas* and other *breathing disorders* is realised using mainly the *ECG* (Al-ani et al., 2008). In this work, the observation sequences were obtained by feature extraction technique which is based on *Heart Rate Variability* (*HRV*) defined in term of *RR intervals* of *ECG* signals.

4. Conclusions

We tried throughout this chapter to sensitize the reader

1. on two problems related to conventional *HMMs*: the training problem and the selection of a convenient *structure* for the constructed *HMM*. We recommend the reader to explore some of the new training schemes introduced in section 2.2.3 that may significantly improve the modelling results. The hybrid *generative/discriminative* approach is more sensitive to change detection in dynamic systems than the purely *generative* or the purely discriminative methods.

   Concerning the choice of the *structure*, when it have a clear domain interpretation, as for example in fault monitoring, the *structure* may be naturally dictated by the domain. When the *structure* is not so conveniently available, however, we can employ some of the data-driven selection methods introduced in section 2.3 to discover an appropriate *structure*.

2. to the use of *HMMs* as a powerful tool for dynamic system modelling, fault detection and diagnosis applications.

5. References

Aarts, E. & Korst, J. (1990). Simulated Annealing and Boltzmann Machines - A Stochastic Approach to Combinatorial Optimization and Neural Computing. J. Wiley & Sons, New York.

Al-ani, T.; Hamam, Y.; Fodil, R.; Lofaso, F. & Isabey, D. (2004). Using hidden Markov models for sleep disordered breathing identification. Simulation Practice and Theory, Vol. 12, No. 2, pp. 117-128.

Al-ani T. & Hamam, Y.. (2006). A learning based stochastic approach for fault diagnosis in a continuous stirred tank reactor. MESM'06, Alexandria, August 28-30.

Al-ani, T.; Karmakar, C.K. ; Khandoker, A.H. ; Palaniswami, M. (2008). Automatic Recognition of Obstructive Sleep apnoea Syndrome Using Power Spectral Analysis of Electrocardiogram and Hidden Markov Models. International Conference on Intelligent Sensors, Sensor Networks and Information Processing (ISSNIP), Sydney, NSW, 15-18 Dec., pp. 285-290.

Al-ani, T. & Trad, D. (2010). Signal Processing and Classification Approaches for Brain-computer Interface", In : Intelligent and Biosensors, Edited by Vernon S. Somerset, pp. 25-66.

Al-ani, T. & Hamam, Y. (2010). A low Complexity Simulated Annealing Approach For Training Hidden Markov Models. International Journal of Operational Research, Vol. 8, No.4 pp. 483-510.

Altun, Y.; Tsochantaridis, I. & Hofmann, T. (2003). Hidden Markov support vector machines. In: Proceedings of the 20th International Conference on Machine Learning (ICML-2003), Washington, DC.

American Academy of Sleep Medicine Task Force. (1999). Sleep-related breathing disorders in adults: recommendations for syndrome definition and measurement techniques in clinical research. The report of an American Academy of Sleep Medicine Task Force. Sleep, Vol. 22, No. 5, pp. 662-689.

Andrieu, C. & Doucet, A. (2000). Simulated annealing for maximum a posteriori parameter estimation of hidden Markov models. IEEE Transactions on Information Theory, Vol. 46, No. 3, pp. 994-1004.

Arslan, L.M. & Hansen, J.H.L. (1999). Selective Training in Hidden Markov Model Recognition. IEEE Transactions on Speech & Audio Processing, Vol. 7, No. 1, pp. 46-54.

Aupetit, S.; Monmarche, N. & Slimane, M. (2007). Hidden Markov models training by a particle swarm optimization algorithm. Journal of Mathematical Modelling and Algorithms, Vol. 6, No. 2, pp. 175-193.

Bach, F.R. & Jordan, M.I. (2005). Discriminative Training of Hidden Markov models for Multiple Pitch Tracking. In ICASSP.

Bahl, L.R., Brown, P.F., De Souza, P.V. & Mercer, R.L. (1986). Maximum mutual information estimation of hidden Markov model parameters for speech recognition. In: Proceedings of IEEE International Conference on Acoustic, Speech, and Signal Processing (ICASSP'86), Tokyo, Japan, pp. 49-52.

Baldi, P. & Brunak, S. (2001). Bioinformatics. A Bradford Book, The MIT Press, Cambridge.

Baum, L.E. & Eagon, J.A. (1967). An inequality with application to statistical estimation for probabilistic functions of Markov processes and to a model for ecology. Accounting, Organizations and Society, Vol. 21, Issue 2, pp. 360-363.

Baum, L.E.; Petrie, T. ; Soules, G. & Weiss, N. (1970). A maximization technique occurring in the statistical analysis of probabilistic functions of Markov chains. The Annals of Mathematical Statistics, Vol. 41, No. 1, pp. 164-171.

Bunks, C.; McCarthy, D. & Al-ani, T. (2000). Condition-based maintenance of machines using hidden Markov models. Mechanical Systems and Signal Processing, Vol. 14, No. 4, pp. 597-612.

Bicego, M.; Murino, V. & Figueiredo, M.A.T. (2003). A sequential pruning strategy for the selection of the number of states in Hidden Markov Models. Pattern Recognition Letters , Vol. 24, pp. 1395-1407.

Biem, A.; Jin-Young, Ha & Subrahmonia, J. (2002). A Bayesian model selection criterion for HMM topology optimization. IEEE International Conference on Acoustics, Speech, and Signal Processing (ICASSP), Orlando, FL , USA. Proceedings, Vol. 1 pp. I-989 - I-992.

Biem, A. (2003). A Model Selection Criterion for Classification: Application to HMM Topology Optimization. Seventh International Conference on Document Analysis and Recognition. Proceedings, Vol. 1, pp. 104-108.

Castellani, A.; Botturi, D.; Bicego, M. & Fiorini P. (2004). Hybrid HMM/SVM :Model for the Analysis and Segmentation of Teleoperation Tasks. Proceedings of the 2004 IEEE International Conference on Robotics & Automation New Orleans. LA, April 2004.

Celeux, G. & Durand, J.-B. (2008). Selecting hidden Markov model state number with cross-validated likelihood. Computational Statistics, Vol. 23, No. 4, pp. 541-564.

Cheng, C.-C.; Sha, F. & Saul, L.K. (2009). A fast online algorithm for large margin training of continuous-density hidden Markov models. In Proceedings of the Tenth Annual Conference of the International Speech Communication Association (Interspeech-09), pp. 668-671. Brighton, UK.

Cheng, C.-C.; Sha, F. & Saul, L.K. (2010). Online Learning and Acoustic Feature Adaptation in Large Margin Hidden Markov Models. To appear in IEEE Journal of Selected Topics in Signal Processing.

Daidone, A.; Di Giandomenico, F.; Chiaradonna, S. & Bondavalli, A. Hidden Markov Models as a Support for Diagnosis: Formalization of the Problem and Synthesis of the Solution. 25th IEEE Symposium on Reliable Distributed Systems, SRDS '06.

Do, T-M-T & Artières, T. (2009). Large Margin Training for Hidden Markov Models with Partially Observed States. Proceedings of the 26th International Conference on Machine Learning, Montreal, Canada, 2009.

Dong, Y. & Li, D. (2007). Large-Margin Discriminative Training of Hidden Markov Models for Speech Recognition. Proceedings of the International Conference on Semantic Computing, pp. 429-438.

Dunmur, A.P. & Titterington, D.M. (1998). The influence of initial conditions on maximum likelihood estimation of the parameters of a binary hidden Markov model. Statistics & Probability Letters, Vol. 40, No. 1, pp. 67-73.

Eddy, S.R. (1995). Multiple alignment using hidden Markov models. Proc. Third International Conference on Intelligent Systems for Molecular Biology, C. Rawlings et al., eds. AAAI Press, Menlo Park, Vol. 3, pp. 114-120.

Eliot, S.K.; Janita L.; Cheryl B. & Carole L.M. (2003). Transit Time as a measure of arousal and respiratory effort in children with sleep-disorder breathing. In: Pediatric research, Vol. 53, No. 4, pp. 580-588.

Elliot, R. J.; Aggoun, L.; & Moore, J. B. (2004). Hidden Markov Models: Estimation and Control, Vol. 29 of Applications of Mathematics. New York: *Springer-Verlag*.

Fengqin, Y. & Changhai, Z. (2008). An effective hybrid optimization algorithm for HMM. Proc. of the 2008 Fourth International Conference on Natural Computation, Vol. 4, pp. 80-84.

Fink, G. A. (1989). Markov Models for Pattern Recognition. From Theory to Applications, *Springer*.

Frankel, J. Linear Dynamic Models for Automatic Speech Recognition. Ph.D. Thesis, The Centre for Speech Technology Research, University of Edinburgh, Edinburgh, UK.

Fraser, A.M. Hidden Markov Models and Dynamical Systems, Cambridge University Press.

Ganapathiraju, A.; Hamaker, J. E.& Picone, J. (2000).Hybrid SVM/HMM architectures for speech recognition. In Proc. ICSLP-2000, Vol. 4, pp. 504-507, Beijing, China.

Golowich, S.E. & Sun, D.X. (2007). A Support Vector/Hidden Markov Model Approach to Phoneme Recognition. Applied Soft Computing. Vol. 7, No. 3, pp. 828-839.

Gu, L.; Nayak, J. & Rose, K. (2000). Discriminative training of tied-mixture HMM by deterministic annealing. ICSLP 2000, Beijing, China, October.

Gunter, S. & Bunke, H. (2003). Optimizing the Number of States, Training Iterations and Gaussians in an HMM-based Handwritten Word Recognizer. Seventh International Conference on Document Analysis and Recognition, 3-6 Aug. Proceedings, Vol. 1, pp. 472-476.

Heck, L.P. & McClellan, J.H. (1991). Mechanical system monitoring using hidden Markov models. Proceedings International Conference on Acoustics, Speech and Signal Processing, Toronto, Ont., Canada., Vol. 3, pp. 1697-1700.

Helmy, S.; Al-ani, T.; Hamam, Y. & El-madbouly, E. (2008). P300 Based Brain-Computer Interface Using Hidden Markov Models. International Conference on Intelligent Sensors, Sensor Networks and Information Processing (ISSNIP), Sydney, NSW, 15-18 Dec., pp. 127-132.

Hirsch H-G (2001). HMM adaptation for applications in telecommunication. Speech Communication, Vol. 34, Issues 1-2, April 2001, pp. 127-139.

Hofbaur, M.W. Hybrid Estimation of Complex Systems. Lecture Notes in Control and Information Sciences, Vol. 319. Thoma, M.& Morari, M. (Editors).

Huda, Md.S.; Ghosh R. & Yearwood J. (2006). A Variable Initialization Approach to the EM Algorithm for Better Estimation of the Parameters of Hidden Markov Model Based Acoustic Modeling of Speech Signals. Lecture Notes in Artificial Intelligence. Advances in Data Mining: Applications in Medicine, Web Mining, Marketing, Image and Signal Mining, Vol. 4065, pp. 416-430, Springer-Verlag, Berlin.

Jaakkola, T. & Haussler, D. (1998). Exploiting generative models in discriminative classifiers. In: Proceedings of Advances in Neural Information Processing Systems, vol. 11.

Jaakkola, T.; Meila, M. & Jebara, T. (1999). Maximum entropy discrimination. In: Proceedings of Advances in Neural Information Processing Systems, vol. 12.

Jebara, T., Pentland, A. (1998). Maximum conditional likelihood via bound maximization and the CEM algorithm. In: Proceedings of Advances in Neural Information Processing Systems, Vol. 11.

Jiang, H.; Li, X. & Liu, C. (2006a). Large Margin Hidden Markov Models for Speech Recognition. IEEE Transactions On Audio, Speech, and Language Processing, Vol. 14, No. 5, pp. 1584-1595.

Jordan, M.I. (2004). Graphical models. Statistical Science 19 (Special Issue on Bayesian Statistics), pp. 140-155.

Jiang, H.; Li, X. & Liu, C. (2006b). Solving Large Margin Estimation of HMMS Via Semidefinite Programming. In: Proc. Interspeech, pp. 2414-2417.

Jiang, H. (2010). Discriminative training of HMMs for automatic speech recognition: A survey. Computer Speech and Language, Vol. 24, pp. 589-608.

Kinney, G.W.; Barnes, J.W. & Colletti, B.W. (2007). A Reactive Tabu Search Algorithm with Variable Clustering for the Unicost Set Covering Problem. International Journal of Operational Research, Vol. 2, No. 2, pp. 156-172.

Kirkpartrick, S.; Gelatt, C.D. & Vecchi, Jr. M.P. (1983). Optimization by simulated annealing, Science, Vol. 220, No. 4598, pp. 671-680.

Kanevsky, D. (2004). Extended Baum Transformations for General Functions. Proceeding ICASSP 2004, Vol. 1, pp. 821-4.

Kennedy, J.; Eberhart, R.C. & Shi, Y. (2001). Swarm intelligence. Morgan Kaufmann Publishers Inc., San Francisco, CA.

Koloydenko, A. (2007). On adjusted Viterbi training. Acta Applicandae Mathematicae, Vol. 9, No. 2, pp. 111-126.

Krüger S.E.; Schafföner M.; Katz M.; Andelic E. & Wendemuth A. (2005). Speech recognition with support vector machines in a hybrid system. In Proc. EuroSpeech, pp. 993-996.

Krüger S.E.; Schafföner M.; Katz M.; Andelic E. & Wendemuth A. (2006). Mixture of Support Vector Machines for HMM based Speech Recognition. In 18th International Conference on Pattern Recognition (ICPR).

Kwon1, K.-C; J.-H. Kim2 & Seong, P.-H. (2002). Hidden Markov model-based real-time transient identifications in nuclear power plants. Special Issue: Intelligent Systems for Process Monitoring and Diagnosis, Vol. 17, No. 8, pp. 791-811.

Lee, J.-S. & Park, C.H. (2007). Training hidden Markov models by hybrid simulated annealing for visual speech recognition. Conference Proceedings - IEEE International Conference on Systems, Man and Cybernetics, Vol. 1, pp. 198-20.

Lee, J-S & Park, C.H. (2005). Discriminative Training of Hidden Markov Models by Multiobjective Optimization for Visual Speech Recognition. Proceedings of International Joint Conference on Neural Networks, Montreal, Canada, July 31 - August 4, pp. 2053-2058.

Lee, Z.-H. (2008). On-line MTO lead-time scheduling: a probabilistic approach. The International Journal of Operational Research, Vol. 3, No. 1-2, pp. 183 - 200.

Li, L. & Noble, W.S. (2003). Combining Pairwise Sequence Similarity and Support Vector Machines for Detecting Remote Protein Evolutionary and Structural Relationships. Journal of computational biology, Vol. 10, No. 6.

Li, X.; Jiang, H. (2005). A Constrained Joint Optimization Method for Large Margin HMM Estimation. IEEE Automatic Speech Recognition and Understanding Workshop (ASRU), Cancun, Mexico, November 27 - December 1.

Li, X.; Jiang, H. & Liu C. (2005a). Large Margin HMMS for Speech Recognition. the 30th IEEE International Conference on Acoustics, Speech, and Signal Processing (ICASSP), Philadelphia , March 18-23.

Li, X.; Jiang, H. & Liu C. (2005b). Discriminative Training of CDHMMs for Maximum Relative Separation Margin, the 30th IEEE International Conference on Acoustics, Speech, and Signal Processing (ICASSP), Philadelphia, March 18-23.

Li, Q. & Juang, B-H. (2006). Study of a Fast Discriminative Training Algorithm for Pattern Recognition. IEEE Transactions on Neural Networks, Vol. 17, No. 5, pp. 1212-1221.

Liporace, L. A. (1982). Maximum likelihood estimation for multivariate observations of Markov sources. IEEE Transactions on Information Theory IT-28, pp. 729-734.

Liu, J.; Wang, Z. & Xiao, X. (2007a). A hybrid SVM/DDBHMM decision fusion modeling for robust continuous digital speech recognition. Pattern Recognition Letters, Vol. 28, pp. 912-920.

Liu, C.; Jiang, H. & Li, X. (2007b). Discriminative training of CDHMMS for maximum relative separation margin. IEEE Transactions on Audio, Speech, and Language Processing, Vol. 15, No. 8, pp. 2383-2392.

Lyu, J.J.; Gunasekaran, A. & Ding, J.H. (1996). Simulated Annealing Algorithms for Solving the Single Machine Early/Tardy Problem. International Journal of Systems Science, Vol. 27, No. 7, pp. 605-610.

Paul, D.B. (1985). Training of hmm recognizers by simulated annealing. Proceedings IEEE International Conference Acoustics, Speech and Signal Process, Vol. 10, pp. 13-16.

Pérez, O′.; Piccardi, M.; Garci′a, J.; Patricio, M.A. & Molina, J.M. (2007). Comparison between genetic algorithms and the Baum-Welch algorithm in learning HMMs for human activity classification. Lecture Notes in Computer Science, Vol. 4448, pp. 399-406, Springer Berlin.

Poritz, A.B. (1982). Linear predictive hidden Markov models and the speech signal. Proceedings of ICASSP, Paris, France, May, pp. 1291-1294.

Povey, D. & Kingsbury, B. (2007). Evaluation of Proposed Modifications to MPE for Large Scale Discriminative Training. ICASSP'07, Vol. 4, pp. 321-324.

Mark, W.D. (1992). In Noise and vibration Control Engineering: Principles and Applications, pp. 735-770. New York: John Wiley & Sons. Elements of gear noise prediction.

Markov, K.; Nakagawa, S. & Nakamura, S. (2001). Discriminative training of HMM using maximum normalized likelihood algorithm. In Proc. IEEE Int. Conf. Acoustics, Speech, Signal Processing, pp. 497-500.

Mazumdar, C.S., Mathirajan M., Gopinath, R. and Sivakumar A.I. (2007). Tabu Search methods for scheduling a burn-in oven with non-identical job sizes and secondary resource constraints. International Journal of Operational Research, Vol. 3, No. 1-2, pp. 119-139.

McKendall Jr, A. R. & Shang, J. (2008). Tabu Search Heuristics for the Crane Sequencing Problem. International Journal of Operational Research, Vol. 3, No.4, pp. 412-429.

Meir, R. (1995). Empirical risk minimization versus maximum likelihood estimation: a case study. Neural Computation Vol. 7, No. 1, pp. 144-157.

Miao, Q.; Huang, H.-Z. & Fan, X. (2007). A Comparison Study of Support Vector Machines and Hidden Markov Models in Machinery Condition Monitoring. Journal of Mechanical Science and Technology, Vol. 21, pp. 607-615.

Myers, C.; Singer, A.; Shin, F. & Church, E. (1992). Modeling chaotic systems with hidden Markov models. IEEE International Conference on Acoustics, Speech, and Signal Processing, Vol.4, 23-26 Mar, San Francisco, CA , USA, pp. 565-568.

Novák, D.; Cuesta-Frau, D.; Al ani, T.; Aboy, M.; Mico, R. & Lhotska, L. (2004). Speech Recognition Methods Applied to Biomedical Signals Processing. 26th Annual International Conference of the IEEE Engineering in Medicine and Biology Society (EMBEC), San Francisco, CA, 1-5 Sept, pp. 118-121 , Vol.1.

Novák, D.; Al-ani T.; Hamam, Y. & L. Lhotska, (2004). Ëlectroencephalogram processing using Hidden Markov Models", 5th EUROSIM Congress on Modelling and Simulation, September, 06-10, Paris.

Novák, D.; Al-ani T.; Hamam, Y.; Cuesta-Frau, D.; Aboy, M. & Lhotska, L. (2004). Morphology Analysis of Biological Signals Using Hidden Markov Models. 17th conference of the International Association for Pattern Recognition (ICPR), 23-26 August, Cambridge,UK.

Novák, D.; Al-ani T.; Hamam, Y.; Cuesta-Frau, D; Mico, P. &, Lhotska, L. (2004). Unsupervised Learning of Holter ECG signals using HMM optimized by simulated annealing. In Analysis of Biomedical Signals and Images. Brno: VUTIUM Press, pp. 60-62.

Vaseghi, S. V. (2006). Advanced Digital Signal Processing and Noise Reduction. 4th Edition, *Wiley*.

Rabiner, L.R.; Wilpon, J.G. & Juang B.H. (1986). A segmental K-mean training procedure for connected word recognition. AT&T Technical J., Vol. 65, pp. 21-31.

Rabiner, L. R. (1989). A tutorial on hidden Markov models and selected applications in speech recognition. Proc. IEEE, Vol. 77, pp. 257-286.

Rao, A.V. & Rose, K. (2001). Deterministically annealed design of hidden Markov model speech recognizers. IEEE Transactions on Speech and Audio Processing, Vol. 9, No. 2, pp. 111-126.

Rao, S. & Hong, J. (2010). Analysis of Hidden Markov Models and Support Vector Machines in Financial Applications. Technical Report No. UCB/EECS-2010-63.

Rodríguez, L.J. & Torres, I. (2003). Comparative Study of the Baum-Welch and Viterbi Training Algorithms Applied to Read and Spontaneous Speech Recognition. Lecture Notes in Computer Science, Pattern Recognition and Image Analysis, Vol. 2652, pp. 847-857, *Springer*.

Sanguansat, P.; Asdornwised, W. & Jitapunkul, S. (2004). Online Thai handwritten character recognition using hidden Markov models and support vector machines. IEEE International Symposium on Communications and Information Technology,ISCIT.

Saon, G. & Povey, D. (2008). Penalty function maximization for large margin HMM training. In Proc. Interspeech.

Scholkopf, B. & Smola, A.J. (2002). Learning with Kernels: Support vector Machine, Regularization, Optimization, and Beyond. The MIT Press, Cambridge.

Seymore, K.; Mccallum, A. & Rosenfeld, R. (1999). Learning Hidden Markov Model Structure for Information Extraction. In AAAI 99 Workshop on Machine Learning for Information Extraction, pp. 37-42.

Sha, F. & Saul, L. K. (2009). Large Margin Training of Continuous Density Hidden Markov Models, in Automatic Speech and Speaker Recognition - Large Margin and Kernel Methods, Editor: Joseph Keshet, Samy Bengio.

Siddiqi, S.M.; Gordon, G. & A. Moore. (2007). Fast State Discovery for HMM Model Selection and Learning,Proceedings of the Eleventh International Conference on Artificial Intelligence and Statistics. (AI-STATS), 2007.

Sloin, A. & Burshtein, D. (2008). Support Vector Machine Training for Improved Hidden Markov Modeling. IEEE Transactions On Signal Processing, Vol. 56, No. 1, pp. 172-188.

Smola, A.J.; Bartlett, P.; Scholkopf, B. & Schuurmans, D., (Ed.) (2000). Advances in Large Margin Classifiers, The MIT Press.

Smyth, P. (1994). Hidden Markov models for fault detection in dynamic systems. Pattern Recognition, Vol. 27, pp. 149-164.

Stolcke, A. & Omohundro, S. (1993). Hidden Markov model induction by Bayesian model merging. In S. J. Hanson, J. D. Cowan, and C. L. Giles, editors, Advances in Neural Information Processing Systems 5, San Francisco, CA. Morgan Kaufmann, pp. 11-18.

Surendran, D. & Levow, G. (2006). Dialog Act Tagging with Support Vector Machines and Hidden Markov Models. Proceedings of Interspeech 2006, pp. 1950-1953.

Takara, T.; Iha, Y. & Nagayama, I. (1998) SSelection of the Optimal Structure of the Continuous HMM Using the Genetic Algorithm. 5th Int. Conf. On Spoken Language Processing. 3, pp. 751-754.

Tang, J.; Zhu, J.-H. & Sun, Z.-Q. (2006). Evolutionary hidden Markov modeling for dynamic agent systems. Kongzhi yu Juece-Control and Decision, Vol. 21, No. 2, pp. 189-192.

Taskar, B.; Guestrin, C. & Koller, D. (2003). Max-margin Markov networks. In: Proceedings of Neural Information Processing Systems Conference (NIPS03), Vancouver, Canada.

Tsontzos, G.; Diakoloukas, V.; Koniaris, C. & Digalakis, V. (2007). Estimation of General Identifiable Linear Dynamic Models with an Application in Speech Recognition. IEEE International Conference on Acoustics, Speech and Signal Processing (ICASSP).

Turner, R. (2008). Direct maximization of the likelihood of a hidden Markov model. Computational Statistics and Data Analysis, Vol. 52, No. 9, pp. 4147-4160.

Valstar, M.F. & Pantic, M. (2008). Combined Support Vector Machines and Hidden Markov Models for Modeling Facial Action Temporal Dynamics. Proceedings of Belgium-Netherlands Conf. ArtificialIntelligence (BNAIC'08), pp. 367-368, Boekelo, the Netherlands, October.

Van Trees, H. L. (1968). Detection, Estimation, and Modulation theory: Part I. New York: John Wiley & Sons.

Viterbi, A.J. (1967). Error bounds for convolutional codes and asymptotically optimum decoding algorithm. IEEE Transactions On Information Theory, Vol. 13, No. 2, pp. 260-269.

Xue, L.; Yin, J.; Ji, Z. & Jiang, L. (2006). A particle swarm optimization for hidden Markov model training. 8th International Conference on Signal Processing, Vol. 1, pp. 16-20.

Yang, F.; Zhang, C. & Bai, G. (2008). A novel genetic algorithm based on tabu search for HMM optimization. 4th International Conference on Natural Computation, ICNC '08, 18-20 Oct., Vol. 4, pp. 57-61.

Vapnik, V.N. (1998). Statistical Learning Theory. Wiley.

Wang, X.-M.; Wang, Q. & Yao, T.-R. (2008). Training algorithm of hidden Markov model based on mixture of factor analysis. Journal of System Simulation, Vol. 20 , No. 15, pp. 3969-3972.

Wren, C.R.; Clarkson, B.P. & Pentland, A.P. (2000). Understanding purposeful human motion. Fourth IEEE International Conference on Automatic Face and Gesture Recognition, 2000. Proceedings. pp. 378-383

Woodland, P.C. & Povey, D. (2002). Large Scale Discriminative Training of hidden Markov models for Speech Recognition. Computer Speech and Language, Vol. 16, No. 1, pp. 25-47.

Won, K.-J.; Hamelryck, T.; Prügel-Bennett, A. & Krogh, A. (2007). An evolutionary method for learning HMM structure: Prediction of protein secondary structure. BMC Bioinformatics, Vol. 8, No. 357, doi:10.1186/1471-2105-8-357.

Xu, W.; Wu, J.; Huang, Z. & Guan, C., (2005). Kernel based hidden Markov model with applications to EEG signal classification. IASTED ICBE, pp. 401-404.

Xu, W.; Wu, J. & Huang, Z. (2006). A maximum margin discriminative learning algorithm for temporal signals. The 18th International Conference on Pattern Recognition (ICPR'06)

Zhao, Z-J; Zheng, S-L; Xu, C-Y & Kong, X-Z (2007). Discrete channel modelling based on genetic algorithm and simulated annealing for training hidden Markov model. Chinese Physics, Vol. 16, No. 6, pp. 1619-1623.

3

Theory of Segmentation

Jüri Lember[1], Kristi Kuljus[2] and Alexey Koloydenko[3]
[1]*University of Tartu*
[2]*Swedish University of Agricultural Sciences*
[3]*Royal Holloway, University of London*
[1]*Estonia*
[2]*Sweden*
[3]*UK*

1. Introduction

1.1 Preliminaries

In this chapter we focus on what Rabiner in his popular tutorial (Rabiner, 1989) calls "uncovering the hidden part of the model" or "Problem 2", that is, *hidden path inference*. We consider a hidden Markov model $(X, Y) = \{(X_t, Y_t)\}_{t\in\mathbb{Z}}$, where $Y = \{Y_t\}_{t\in\mathbb{Z}}$ is an unobservable, or *hidden*, homogeneous Markov chain with a finite state space $S = \{1, \ldots, K\}$, transition matrix $\mathbb{P} = (p_{i,j})_{i,j\in S}$ and, whenever relevant, the initial probabilities $\pi_s = \mathbf{P}(Y_1 = s)$, $s \in S$. A reader interested in extensions to the continuous case is referred to (Cappé et al., 2005; Chigansky & Ritov, 2010). The Markov chain will be further assumed to be of the first order, bearing in mind that a higher order chain can always be converted to a first order one by expanding the state space. To simplify the mathematics, we assume that the Markov chain Y is stationary and ergodic. This assumption is needed for the asymptotic results in Section 3, but not for the finite time-horizon in Section 2. In fact, Section 2 does not even require the assumption of homogeneity. The second component $X = \{X_t\}_{t\in\mathbb{Z}}$ is an observable process with X_t taking values in $\mathcal{X}$ that is typically a subspace of the Euclidean space, i.e. $\mathcal{X} \subset \mathbb{R}^d$. The process X can be thought of as a noisy version of Y. In order for (X, Y) to be a hidden Markov model, the following properties need to be satisfied:

1) given $\{Y_t\}$, the random variables $\{X_t\}$ are conditionally independent,
2) the distribution of X_t depends on $\{Y_t\}$ only through Y_t.

The process X is sometimes called a *hidden Markov process*. It is well known that the ergodicity of Y implies that of X (see, e.g. (Ephraim & Merhav, 2002; Genon-Catalot et al., 2000; Leroux, 1992)). The conditional distributions $P_s = \mathbf{P}(X_1 \in \cdot | Y_1 = s)$ are called *emission distributions*. Without loss of generality, we will assume that the emission distributions P_s all have densities f_s with respect to a common reference measure μ.

We often restrict the general process defined above to time interval I, where I is either $\{1, \ldots, n\}$ for some $n \geq 1$ (Section 2), or $I = \mathbb{N}$ (Section 3). Thus $\{(X_t, Y_t)\}_{t\geq 1}$ is a restriction of the doubly-infinite HMM to the positive integers and clearly, this process is ergodic as well. Since our study is mainly motivated by statistical and machine learning, our notation reverses the notation used in the mainstream HMM literature, e.g. (Cappé et al., 2005), where the hidden Markov chain is denoted by X and the observed process by Y.

Given a set $\mathcal{A}$, integers m and n, $m < n$, and a sequence $a_1, a_2, \ldots \in \mathcal{A}^\infty$, we write a_m^n for the subsequence $(a_m, \ldots, a_n)$; when $m = 1$, it will usually be suppressed, e.g. $a_1^n \in \mathcal{A}^n$ will be written as a^n. With a slight abuse of notation, we will denote the conditional probability $\mathbf{P}(Y_k^l = y_k^l | X^n = x^n)$ by $p(y_k^l | x^n)$. We will often use the so-called *smoothing probabilities* $p_t(s|x^n) := \mathbf{P}(Y_t = s | X^n = x^n)$, where $s \in S$ and $1 \le t \le n$. We will denote the probability of x^n by $p(x^n)$ and, for any $s^n \in S^n$, we will write $p(s^n) = \mathbf{P}(Y^n = s^n)$ for the probability of Y^n having the outcome s^n; the distinction should be clear from the context.

1.2 The segmentation problem in the framework of statistical learning

By *segmentation* we refer to estimation of the unobserved realization $y^n = (y_1, \ldots, y_n)$ of the underlying Markov chain Y, given the observations $x^n = (x_1, \ldots, x_n)$ of X^n. In communications literature segmentation is also known as *decoding* (Bahl et al., 1974; Viterbi, 1967) or *state sequence detection* (Hayes et al., 1982). Segmentation is often the primary interest of the HMM-based inference, but it can also be an intermediate step of a larger problem such as estimation of the model parameters (Lember & Koloydenko, 2008; Rabiner, 1989), which will be discussed in Subsection 4.2. Despite its importance in the HMM-based methodology, a systematic study of different segmentation methods and their properties has been overdue (Lember & Koloydenko, 2010b). Here we present a unified approach to the segmentation problem based on statistical learning, and describe the commonly used as well as recently proposed solutions.

Formally we seek a mapping $g : \mathcal{X}^n \to S^n$ called a *classifier*, that maps every sequence of observations to a state sequence or *path*, which is sometimes also referred to as an *alignment* (Lember & Koloydenko, 2008)[1]. In order to assess the overall quality of g, it is natural to first measure the quality of each individual path $s^n \in S^n$ via a function known as *risk*. Thus, for a given x^n, let us denote the risk of s^n by $R(s^n|x^n)$. A natural approach to solving the segmentation problem is then to compute a state sequence with the minimum risk. In the framework of statistical decision and pattern recognition theory (Bishop, 2006) the risk is usually specified via a more basic entity known as a *loss function* $L : S^n \times S^n \to [0, \infty]$, where $L(a^n, b^n)$ is the loss incurred by estimating the actual state sequence a^n to be b^n. Then for any state sequence $s^n \in S^n$ the risk $R(s^n|x^n)$ is the conditional expectation of the loss $L(Y^n, s^n)$ given that $X^n = x^n$, i.e. $R(s^n|x^n) := E[L(Y^n, s^n)|X^n = x^n]$.

One popular loss function is the *zero-one* loss defined as

$$L_\infty(a^n, b^n) = \begin{cases} 1, \text{ if } a^n \neq b^n; \\ 0, \text{ if } a^n = b^n. \end{cases}$$

The minimizer of the risk $R_\infty(s^n|x^n)$ based on L_∞ is a sequence with maximum posterior probability $p(s^n|x^n)$, hence it is called the *maximum a posteriori (MAP) path*. The MAP-path is also called the *Viterbi path* after the *Viterbi algorithm* (Forney, 1973; Rabiner, 1989; Viterbi, 1967) used for its efficient computation.

Another popular approach is based on pointwise loss functions of the form

$$L_1(a^n, b^n) = \frac{1}{n} \sum_{t=1}^{n} l(a_t, b_t), \tag{1}$$

[1] This usage of the term "alignment" is broader than that of the HMM-based "multiple sequence alignment" in the bioinformatics context .

where $l(a_t, b_t) \geq 0$ is the loss of classifying the tth symbol as b_t when the truth is a_t. Most commonly $l(s, s') = I_{\{s \neq s'\}}$, where I_A is the indicator function of a set A. Then the corresponding risk function $R_1(s^n|x^n)$ is simply the expected misclassification rate given the data x^n. Hence, the minimizer of this risk is a sequence with the lowest expected number of misclassifications. We refer to such sequences as *pointwise maximum a posteriori (PMAP)* alignments (Lember & Koloydenko, 2010b). The name refers to the fact that given x^n, the PMAP-alignment maximizes $\sum_{t=1}^n p_t(s_t|x^n)$ that obviously can be done pointwise. Note that the PMAP-alignment equivalently maximizes the product $\prod_{t=1}^n p_t(s_t|x^n)$, and therefore minimizes the *pointwise log* risk

$$\bar{R}_1(s^n|x^n) := -\frac{1}{n}\sum_{t=1}^{n} \log p_t(s_t|x^n). \tag{2}$$

Since the purpose is to maximize the expected number of correctly classified states, this is also known as the *optimal accuracy* alignment (Holmes & Durbin, 1998). In statistics, this type of estimation is known as *marginal posterior mode* (Winkler, 2003) or *maximum posterior marginals* (Rue, 1995) (MPM) estimation. In computational biology, this is also known as the *posterior decoding* (PD) (Brejová et al., 2008). In the wider context of biological applications of discrete high-dimensional probability models this has also been called "consensus estimation", and in the absence of constraints, "centroid estimation" (Carvalho & Lawrence, 2008). In communications applications of HMMs, largely influenced by (Bahl et al., 1974), the terms "optimal symbol-by-symbol detection" (Hayes et al., 1982), "symbol-by-symbol MAP estimation" (Robertson et al., 1995), and "MAP state estimation" (Brushe et al., 1998) have been used to refer to this method.

Note that the introduced risk-based formalism does not impose any special conditions on Y. In particular, in this and in the next Section the chain Y need not be homogeneous and the conditional distribution of X_t given Y_t can, in principle, vary with t.

2. Hybrid classifiers

2.1 The problem

The Viterbi classifier has several drawbacks. First, the obtained alignment is not optimal and it can actually be quite poor in terms of accuracy as measured by the number of correctly classified states. Related to this is the reluctance of this decoder to switch states as can be seen from the following simple example taken from (Koloydenko & Lember, 2010).

Example 1. A long sequence has been simulated from an HMM with the following parameters:

$$\mathbb{P} = \begin{pmatrix} 0.99 & 0.01 & 0 \\ 0.3 & 0.3 & 0.4 \\ 0 & 0.02 & 0.98 \end{pmatrix}, \qquad \pi = \begin{pmatrix} 0.5882 \\ 0.0196 \\ 0.3922 \end{pmatrix}, \qquad \pi^{\mathrm{t}} = \pi^{\mathrm{t}}\mathbb{P},$$

and the emission distributions

$$p_1 = (0.3, 0.2, 0.2, 0.3), \quad p_2 = (0.1, 0.3, 0.3, 0.3), \quad p_3 = (1/6, 1/6, 1/6, 1/2).$$

The sequence is then decoded with several classifiers including the Viterbi and PMAP ones. Figure 1 gives two fragments of the ground truth and decoded outputs; the complete output can be found in (Koloydenko & Lember, 2010). The example illustrates the typical tendency of the Viterbi classifier to get stuck in a state of sizable probability and therefore systematically

True:	1111111112333333333333333211111111111111111111 · · · 11111111111111111111111111111111111111
Viterbi:	1111111111111111111111111111111111111111111111 · · · 11111111111111111111111111111111111111
PMAP:	1111113333333333333333333333333333333331111111 · · · 11133333333333333333333333333333333311
PairMAP:	1111111113333333333333333333333333333331111111 · · · 11133333333333333333333333333333333311
PVD:	1111123333333333333333333333333333211111111111 · · · 11111233333333333333333333333333333321
CnstrPMAP:	1111112333333333333333333333333333333321111111 · · · 11123333333333333333333333333333333321
HybridK2:	1111123333333333333333333333333333333333333211 · · · 11111111111111111111111111111111111111

Fig. 1. Decoding performance of different classifiers.

misclassify less frequent states. In its extreme form, this behavior would predict a constant sequence of *Heads* even when the *Heads* side of the coin is only slightly heavier than the *Tails* one. In HMMs, the inaccuracy problem can be alleviated by exploiting the PMAP-classifier. However, as can be noted from the forbidden transitions between states 1 and 3 along the PMAP-path in Figure 1, the PMAP-decoding allows alignments of low or even zero probability. In computational biology, for example, such paths would violate biological constraints and hence be *inadmissible*. We will return to this example when considering alternative classifiers.

As it has been shown in (Käll et al., 2005), it is possible to explicitly constrain the PMAP-classifier to avoid inadmissible paths. The constrained PMAP-alignment is the solution of the following optimization problem

$$\min_{s^n:\, p(s^n|x^n)>0} R_1(s^n|x^n) \quad \Leftrightarrow \quad \max_{s^n:\, p(s^n|x^n)>0} \sum_{t=1}^{n} p_t(s_t|x^n). \tag{3}$$

In our example the solution of (3) is seen in Figure 1 under the name CnstrPMAP. The solution is indeed admissible, i.e. the forbidden zero-probability transitions are not any more present. Observe that in the presence of path constraints, minimizing the R_1-risk is not any more equivalent to minimizing the $\bar{R}_1$-risk, therefore (3) is not equivalent to the optimization problem

$$\min_{s^n:\, p(s^n|x^n)>0} \bar{R}_1(s^n|x^n) \quad \Leftrightarrow \quad \max_{s^n:\, p(s^n|x^n)>0} \sum_{t=1}^{n} \log p_t(s_t|x^n). \tag{4}$$

The solution of (4) was recently used in (Fariselli et al., 2005) under the name *posterior Viterbi decoding* (PVD). On their tasks of predicting membrane proteins, PVD has shown results superior to the Viterbi and PMAP-classifiers. In our example, the solution of (4) is seen in Figure 1 under the name PVD. Note that it differs from the constrained PMAP but it is still admissible.

To summarize: since the overall error rate is not the only measure of accuracy and since PMAP may fail 100% in detecting an infrequent state, such as state 2 in our example, constraining the PMAP-classifier is not an ultimate answer. Also, in some applications such as gene-finding, region-based measures of accuracy are no less important than the pointwise ones, but direct minimization of the corresponding risks generally does not lead to efficient decoding algorithms.

2.2 Further issues and alternative solutions

Another serious drawback of the Viterbi decoding is that "there might be many similar paths through the model with probabilities that add up to a higher probability than the single most probable path" (Käll et al., 2005). In fact, Viterbi paths need not be representative of the overall posterior probability distribution (Carvalho & Lawrence, 2008) and can be significantly atypical (Lember & Koloydenko, 2010a). Indeed, imagine having to estimate the transition probabilities from the Viterbi path in Figure 1. This second problem of the Viterbi segmentation has been addressed by moving from single path inference towards envelops (Holmes & Durbin, 1998) and centroids (Carvalho & Lawrence, 2008). The most common approach here is to aggregate individual states into a smaller number of semantic labels (e.g. codon, intron, intergenic). In effect, this would realize the notion of path similarity by mapping many "similar" state paths to a single label path or *annotation* (Brejová et al., 2008; Fariselli et al., 2005; Käll et al., 2005; Krogh, 1997). However, this leads to the problem of *multiple paths*, which in practically important HMMs renders the dynamic programming approach of the Viterbi algorithm NP-hard (Brejová et al., 2007; Brown & Truszkowski, 2010). Unlike the Viterbi classifier, PMAP handles annotations as easily as it does state paths, including the enforcement of the positivity constraint (Käll et al., 2005). A number of heuristic approaches are also known to alleviate these problems, but none appears to be fully satisfactory (Brejová et al., 2008). Note that mapping optimal state paths to the corresponding annotations need not lead to optimal annotations and can give poor results (Brejová et al., 2007).

Although the Viterbi and PMAP-classifiers have been by far the most popular segmentation methods in practice, their aforementioned drawbacks have invited debates on the trade-off between the path accuracy and probability, and alternative approaches have demonstrated significantly higher performance in, for example, predicting various biological features.

In Subsection 2.3 below, which is based on (Lember & Koloydenko, 2010b), we show how several relevant risks can be combined within a very general penalized risk minimization problem with a small number of penalty terms. Tuning one of the penalty parameters allows us to "interpolate" between the PMAP- and Viterbi classifiers in a natural way, whereas the other terms give further interesting extensions. The minimization problem can then be solved by a dynamic programming algorithm similar to the Viterbi algorithm. We would like to remark that the idea of interpolation between the Viterbi and PMAP-estimators was already hinted at in the seminal tutorial (Rabiner, 1989) and then considered in (Brushe et al., 1998). In spite of those, no general systematic study of hybridization of the Viterbi and PMAP-classifiers has been published before.

2.3 Generalized risk-based hybrid classifiers

Although the constrained PMAP-classifier and PVD guarantee admissible paths, as can also be noted from Figure 1, the (posterior) probability of such paths can still be very low. Hence, it seems natural to consider instead of (3) the following penalized optimization problem:

$$\max_{s^n}\Big[\sum_{t=1}^{n} p_t(s_t|x^n)+\log p(s^n)\Big] \quad\Leftrightarrow\quad \min_{s^n}\Big[R_1(s^n|x^n)+\bar{R}_\infty(s^n)\Big], \tag{5}$$

where

$$\bar{R}_\infty(s^n) := -\frac{1}{n}\log p(s^n)$$

is the prior log risk which does not depend on the data. The logic behind (5) is clear: we aim to look for the alignment that simultaneously minimizes the R_1-risk and maximizes the path probability. A more general problem can be written in the form

$$\min_{s^n}\Big[R_1(s^n|x^n)+Ch(s^n)\Big], \tag{6}$$

where $C \geq 0$ and h is some penalty function. Taking $Ch(s^n) = \infty \times (1 - \text{sign}\,(p(s^n))$ reduces problem (6) to problem (3).
Similarly, instead of (4), the following problem can be considered:

$$\max_{s^n} \left[\sum_{t=1}^{n} \log p_t(s_t|x^n) + \log p(s^n) \right] \quad \Leftrightarrow \quad \min_{s^n} \left[\bar{R}_1(s^n|x^n) + \bar{R}_\infty(s^n) \right].$$

Again, the problem above can be generalized as

$$\min_{s^n} \left[\bar{R}_1(s^n|x^n) + Ch(s^n) \right]. \tag{7}$$

Taking $Ch(s^n) = \infty \times (1 - \text{sign}\,(p(s^n))$, reduces problem (7) to problem (4).

2.3.1 A general family of classifiers

Motivated by the previous argument, we consider the following yet more general problem:

$$\min_{s^n} \left[C_1 \bar{R}_1(s^n|x^n) + C_2 \bar{R}_\infty(s^n|x^n) + C_3 \bar{R}_1(s^n) + C_4 \bar{R}_\infty(s^n) \right], \tag{8}$$

where $C_1, \ldots, C_4 \geq 0$, $C_1 + \cdots + C_4 > 0$, and

$$\bar{R}_1(s^n|x^n) = -\frac{1}{n} \sum_{t=1}^{n} \log p_t(s_t|x^n), \text{ as defined in equation (2) above,}$$

$$\bar{R}_\infty(s^n|x^n) := \bar{R}_\infty(s^n; x^n) + \frac{1}{n} \log p(x^n),$$

$$\bar{R}_\infty(s^n; x^n) := -\frac{1}{n} \left[\log \pi_{s_1} + \sum_{t=1}^{n-1} \log p_{s_t s_{t+1}} + \sum_{t=1}^{n} \log f_{s_t}(x_t) \right] = -\frac{1}{n} \left[\log p(s^n) + \sum_{t=1}^{n} \log f_{s_t}(x_t) \right],$$

$$\bar{R}_1(s^n) := -\frac{1}{n} \sum_{t=1}^{n} \log \mathbf{P}(Y_t = s_t),$$

$$\bar{R}_\infty(s^n) = -\frac{1}{n} \left[\log \pi_{s_1} + \sum_{t=1}^{n-1} \log p_{s_t s_{t+1}} \right] = -\frac{1}{n} \log p(s^n).$$

The newly introduced risk $\bar{R}_1(s^n)$ is the prior pointwise log risk. Evidently, the combination $C_1 = C_3 = C_4 = 0$ gives the Viterbi alignment, the combination $C_2 = C_3 = C_4 = 0$ yields the PMAP-alignment, whereas the combinations $C_1 = C_2 = C_3 = 0$ and $C_1 = C_2 = C_4 = 0$ give the *maximum prior probability* decoding and *marginal prior mode* decoding, respectively. The case $C_2 = C_3 = 0$ subsumes (7), and the case $C_1 = C_3 = 0$ is the problem

$$\min_{s^n} \left[\bar{R}_\infty(s^n|x^n) + C\bar{R}_\infty(s^n) \right]. \tag{9}$$

Thus, a solution to (9) is a generalization of the Viterbi decoding which allows for suppressed ($C > 0$) contribution of the data. It is important to note that with $C_2 > 0$ every solution of (8) is admissible.
Similarly to the generalized risk minimization problem in (8), a relevant generalization of (6) emerges as follows:

$$\min_{s^n} \left[C_1 R_1(s^n|x^n) + C_2 \bar{R}_\infty(s^n|x^n) + C_3 R_1(s^n) + C_4 \bar{R}_\infty(s^n) \right], \tag{10}$$

where

$$R_1(s^n) := \frac{1}{n}\sum_{t=1}^{n}\mathbf{P}(Y_t \neq s_t)$$

is the error rate when the data are ignored.

2.3.2 Solving (8) and (10)

The problems (8) and (10) would only be of theoretical interest if there were not an effective way to solve them. We now present a dynamical programming algorithm (similar to the Viterbi algorithm) for solving these problems. The algorithm requires the smoothing probabilities $p_t(j|x^n)$ for $t = 1,\ldots,n$ and $j \in S$, which can be computed by the usual forward-backward algorithm (Rabiner, 1989). For every $t = 1,\ldots,n$ and $s \in S$, let

$$g_t(s) := C_1 \log p_t(s|x^n) + C_2 \log f_s(x_t) + C_3 \log \mathbf{P}(Y_t = s).$$

Note that the function g_t depends on all the data x^n. For every $j \in S$ and for every $t = 1,2,\ldots,n-1$, define the scores

$$\delta_1(j) := C_1 \log p_1(j|x^n) + (C_2 + C_3 + C_4)\log \pi_j + C_2 \log f_j(x_1), \tag{11}$$

$$\delta_{t+1}(j) := \max_i \left(\delta_t(i) + (C_2 + C_4)\log p_{ij}\right) + g_{t+1}(j). \tag{12}$$

Using the scores $\delta_t(j)$, let for every $t = 1,\ldots,n$,

$$i_t(j) := \begin{cases} \arg\max_{i\in S}[\delta_t(i) + (C_2 + C_4)\log p_{ij}], & \text{when } t = 1,\ldots,n-1, \\ \arg\max_{i\in S}\delta_n(i), & \text{when } t = n; \end{cases} \tag{13}$$

$$\hat{s}^t(j) := \begin{cases} i_1(j), & \text{when } t = 1, \\ (\hat{s}^{t-1}(i_{t-1}(j)), j), & \text{when } t = 2,\ldots,n. \end{cases}$$

It is now not hard to see (see Th. 3.1 in (Lember & Koloydenko, 2010b)) that recursions (11)-(12) solve (8), meaning that any solution of (8) is in the form $\hat{s}^n(i_n)$, provided the ties in (13) are broken accordingly.

By a similar argument, problem (10) can be solved by the following recursions:

$$\delta_1(j) := C_1 p_1(j|x^n) + (C_2 + C_4)\log \pi_j + C_2 \log f_j(x_1) + C_3 \pi_j,$$

$$\delta_{t+1}(j) := \max_i \left(\delta_t(i) + (C_2 + C_4)\log p_{ij}\right) + g_{t+1}(j),$$

where now

$$g_t(s) = C_1 p_t(s|x^n) + C_2 \log f_s(x_t) + C_3 \mathbf{P}(Y_t = j).$$

2.4 k-block PMAP-alignment

As an idea for interpolating between the PMAP- and Viterbi classifiers, Rabiner mentions in his seminal tutorial (Rabiner, 1989) the possibility of maximizing the expected number of correctly estimated pairs or triples of (adjacent) states rather than the expected number of correct single states. With k being the length of the block ($k = 2,3,\ldots$) this entails minimizing the conditional risk

$$R_k(s^n|x^n) := 1 - \frac{1}{n-k+1}\sum_{t=1}^{n-k+1} p(s_t^{t+k-1}|x^n) \tag{14}$$

based on the following loss function:

$$L_k(y^n, s^n) := \frac{1}{n-k+1} \sum_{t=1}^{n-k+1} I_{\{s_t^{t+k-1} \neq y_t^{t+k-1}\}}.$$

Obviously, for $k = 1$ this gives the usual R_1-minimizer – the PMAP-alignment – which is known to allow inadmissible paths. It is natural to think that the minimizer of $R_k(s^n|x^n)$ evolves towards the Viterbi alignment "monotonically" as k increases to n. Indeed, when $k = n$, minimization of $R_k(s^n|x^n)$ in (14) is equivalent to minimization of $\bar{R}_\infty(s^n|x^n)$, which is achieved by the Viterbi alignment. In Figure 1 the minimizer of (14) for $k = 2$ appears under the name PairMAP, and, as the example shows, it still has zero probability. This is a major drawback of using the loss L_k.

We now show that this drawback can be overcome when the sum in (14) is replaced by the product. This is not an equivalent problem, but with the product the k-block idea works well – the longer the block, the bigger the probability and the solution is guaranteed to be admissible even for $k = 2$. Moreover, this gives another interpretation to the risk $\bar{R}_1(s^n|x^n) + C\bar{R}_\infty(s^n|x^n)$. Let $k \in \mathbb{N}$. We define

$$\bar{U}_k(s^n|x^n) := \prod_{j=1-k}^{n-1} p(s_{(j+1)\vee 1}^{(j+k)\wedge n}|x^n), \quad \bar{R}_k(s^n|x^n) := -\frac{1}{n} \log \bar{U}_k(s^n|x^n).$$

Thus $\bar{U}_k(s^n|x^n) = U_1^k \cdot U_2^k \cdot U_3^k$, where

$$U_1^k := p(s_1|x^n) \cdots p(s_1^{k-2}|x^n) p(s_1^{k-1}|x^n)$$
$$U_2^k := p(s_1^k|x^n) p(s_2^{k+1}|x^n) \cdots p(s_{n-k}^{n-1}|x^n) p(s_{n-k+1}^n|x^n)$$
$$U_3^k := p(s_{n-k+2}^n|x^n) p(s_{n-k+3}^n|x^n) \cdots p(s_n|x^n).$$

Clearly, for $k = 1$, $\bar{R}_k$ equals $\bar{R}_1(s^n|x^n)$ defined in (2), so it is a natural generalization of $\bar{R}_1$. The meaning of the risk $\bar{R}_k$ will be transparent from the following equality proved in (Lember & Koloydenko, 2010b): for every s^n,

$$\bar{R}_k(s^n|x^n) = (k-1)\bar{R}_\infty(s^n|x^n) + \bar{R}_1(s^n|x^n).$$

Thus, the minimizer of $\bar{R}_k(s^n|x^n)$ is a solution of (8) with $C_1 = 1$, $C_2 = k - 1$, $C_3 = C_4 = 0$. Note that the solution is admissible for every $k > 1$. It is easy to see that increasing the block length k increases the posterior probability as well as the $\bar{R}_1$-risk of the solution. Hence, this provides a natural interpolation between the Viterbi and the PMAP-alignments. In Figure 1 the minimizer of $\bar{R}_2(s^n|x^n)$ for $k = 2$ is shown under the name HybridK2. The difference between the HybridK2-alignment and the PairMAP-alignment (the minimizer of the R_2-risk) is clearly visible; in particular, the HybridK2-alignment is of positive probability. From the figure it is also evident that the HybridK2-alignment possesses the properties of both the Viterbi and PMAP-alignments.

3. Infinite segmentation

In the previous section, several alignments for segmenting the observations $x^n = (x_1, \ldots, x_n)$ were defined. The next question one can ask is the following: what are the long-run properties of these different classifiers? This question is not easy to answer, since in general there is no obvious notion of infinite (asymptotic) alignment. Indeed, if $(g_1,\ldots,g_n) = g(x_1,\ldots,x_n)$ is an alignment, then adding one more observation x_{n+1} can in principle change the whole alignment so that $g_t(x^n) \neq g_t(x^{n+1})$ for every t, where $g_t(x^n)$ stands for the tth element of $g(x^n)$. On the other hand, it is intuitively expected that such a situation is rather atypical and that a few, say k, first elements of g will be fixed *almost surely* as n goes to infinity. If this is the case, then an infinite classifier can be defined as follows.

Def. For every $n \in \mathbb{N}$, let $g^n : \mathcal{X}^n \to S^n$ be a classifier. We say that the sequence $\{g^n\}$ of classifiers can be *extended to infinity*, if there exists a function $g : \mathcal{X}^\infty \to S^\infty$ such that for almost every realization $x^\infty \in \mathcal{X}^\infty$ the following holds: for every $k \in \mathbb{N}$ there exists $m \geq k$ (depending on x^∞) such that for every $n \geq m$ the first k elements of $g^n(x^n)$ are the same as the first k elements of $g(x^\infty)$, i.e. $g^n(x^n)_i = g(x^\infty)_i$, $i = 1,\ldots,k$. The function g will be referred to as an *infinite classifier*. If an infinite classifier exists, then applying it to the observations x^∞ gives us an *infinite alignment* $g(x^\infty)$, and applying it to the process X^∞ gives us a random S-valued process $g(X^\infty)$ that is called the *alignment process*. ◇

Hence, to study the asymptotic properties of various classifiers, the existence of an infinite alignment is the first problem to be addressed. It is also desirable that various SLLN-type results hold for the alignment process. This is guaranteed if the alignment process is regenerative or ergodic. Despite the unified risk-based representation of the different classifiers presented here, proving the existence of the infinite alignment for them requires different mathematical tools.

3.1 Infinite Viterbi alignment and Viterbi process

Justified or not, the Viterbi classifier is the most popular one in practice. In (Lember & Koloydenko, 2008; 2010a), under rather general assumptions on the HMM, a constructive proof of the existence of the infinite Viterbi classifier was given. We shall now explain the basic ideas behind the construction.

3.1.1 The idea of piecewise alignments

The proof is based on the existence of the so-called *barriers*. We believe that the following oversimplified but insightful example will help the reader to understand this concept. Suppose there is a state, say 1, and a set of observations $A \subset \mathcal{X}$ such that $P_1(A) > 0$ while $P_l(A) = 0$ for $l = 2,\ldots,K$. Thus, at time u any observation $x_u \in A$ is almost surely generated under $Y_u = 1$, and we say that x_u *indicates its state*. Consider n to be the terminal time and note that any positive probability path, including the MAP/Viterbi ones, has to go through state 1 at time u. This allows us to split the Viterbi alignment $v(x^n)$ into v_1^u and v_{u+1}^n, an alignment from time 1 through time u, and a conditional alignment from time $u+1$ through time n, respectively. Moreover, it is clear that the first piece v_1^u maximizes $p(s^u|x_1^u)$ over all paths from time 1 through time u, $v_u = 1$, and the second piece v_{u+1}^n maximizes $\mathbf{P}(Y_{u+1}^n = s^{n-u}|X_{u+1}^n = x_{u+1}^n, Y_u = 1)$. Clearly, any additional observations x_{n+1}^m do not change the fact that x_u indicates its state. Hence, for any extension of x^n the first part of the alignment is always v_1^u. Thus, any observation that indicates its state also fixes the beginning of the alignment for every $n > u$. Suppose now that x_t, $u < t < n$, is another observation that indicates its state, say, also 1. By the same argument, the piece v_{u+1}^n can be split into pieces v_{u+1}^t and v_{t+1}^n, where v_{u+1}^t maximizes $\mathbf{P}(Y_{u+1}^t = s^{t-u}|X_{u+1}^t = x_{u+1}^t, Y_u = 1)$ and terminates in 1, i.e. $v_t = 1$. Again, increasing n does not change the fact that x_t indicates its state, so that v_u^t is independent of all the observations before u and after t. Therefore, the Viterbi alignment up to t can be constructed independently of the observations x_{t+1}^n by concatenating the pieces

v_1^u and v_{u+1}^t. Since our HMM is now a stationary process that has a positive probability to generate state-indicating observations, there will be infinitely many such observations *almost surely*. Since the Viterbi alignment between two such observations x_u and x_t can be be found as the maximizer of $p(\cdot|x_u^t)$, the infinite alignment can be constructed by concatenating the corresponding pieces. We say that the alignment can be constructed *piecewise*.

3.1.2 Nodes

The example above is rather exceptional and we next define nodes to generalize the idea of state-indicating observations. Recall that the Viterbi algorithm is a special case of the general dynamic programming algorithm introduced in Subsection 2.3 with $C_2 = 1$ and $C_1 = C_3 = C_4 = 0$. In particular, the basic recursion for obtaining the scores (11) and (12) for the Viterbi algorithm is as follows: for every $j \in S$ and $t = 1, \dots, n-1$,

$$\begin{aligned}\delta_1(j) &= \log \pi_j + \log f_j(x_1),\\ \delta_{t+1}(j) &= \max_i \left(\delta_t(i) + \log p_{ij}\right) + \log f_j(x_{t+1}).\end{aligned}$$

The Viterbi alignment $v(x^n)$ is given by $v^n(i_n)$, where for every $j \in S$, the paths $v^t(j)$, $t = 1, \dots, n$, are obtained recursively:

$$v^t(j) = \begin{cases} i_1(j), & \text{when } t = 1,\\ (v^{t-1}(i_{t-1}(j)), j), & \text{when } t = 2, \dots, n; \end{cases}$$

with $i_t(j)$ being (recall (13))

$$i_t(j) = \begin{cases} \arg\max_{i \in S}[\delta_t(i) + \log p_{ij}], & \text{when } t = 1, \dots, n-1,\\ \arg\max_{i \in S} \delta_n(i), & \text{when } t = n. \end{cases}$$

Def. Given the first u observations, the observation x_u is said to be an *l-node* (of order zero) if

$$\delta_u(l) + \log p_{lj} \geq \delta_u(i) + \log p_{ij}, \quad \forall i, j \in S. \tag{15}$$

We also say that x_u is a *node* if it is an l-node for some $l \in S$. We say that x_u is a strong node if the inequalities in (15) are strict for every $i, j \in S$, $i \neq l$. $\diamond$

In other words, x_u is an l-node if for appropriate tie-breaking $i_u(j) = l$ for every $j \in S$ (see also Figure 2). This obviously implies that (under the same tie-breaking) the first u elements of the Viterbi alignment are fixed independently of the observations x_{u+1}^n. If the node is strong, then all the Viterbi alignments must coalesce at u. Thus, the concept of strong nodes circumvents the inconveniences caused by non-uniqueness: no matter how the ties are broken, every alignment is forced into l at u, and any tie-breaking rule would suffice for the purpose of obtaining the fixed alignments. However tempting, strong nodes unlike the general ones are quite restrictive. Indeed, suppose that the observation x_u indicates its state, say 1. Then $f_1(x_u) > 0$ and $f_i(x_u) = 0$ for $i \neq 1$. Hence $\delta_u(1) > -\infty$ and $\delta_u(i) = -\infty$ for every $i \in S$, $i \neq 1$. Thus (15) holds and x_u is a 1-node. In other words, every observation that indicates its state is a node. If in addition $p_{1j} > 0$ for every $j \in S$, then for every $i, j \in S$, $i \neq 1$, the right-hand side of (15) is $-\infty$, whereas the left-hand side is finite, making x_u a strong node. If, however, there is j such that $p_{1j} = 0$, which can easily happen if $K > 2$, then for such j both sides are $-\infty$ and x_u is not strong anymore.

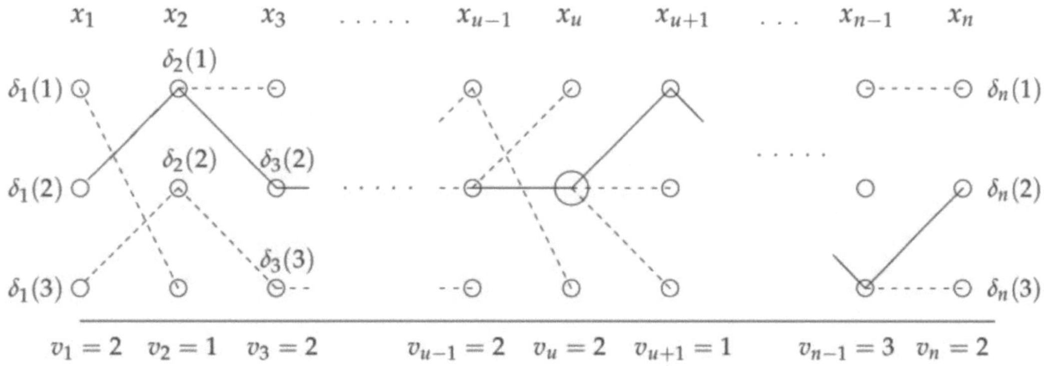

Fig. 2. An example of the Viterbi algorithm in action. The solid line corresponds to the final alignment $v(x^n)$. The dashed links are of the form $(t, i_t(j)) - (t+1, j)$ and are not part of the final alignment. E.g., $(1,3) - (2,2)$ is because $3 = i_1(2)$ and $2 = i_2(3)$. The observation x_u is a 2-node since we have $2 = i_u(j)$ for every $j \in S$.

3.1.3 Higher order nodes

We next extend the notion of nodes to account for the fact that a general ergodic $\mathbb{P}$ can have a zero in every row, in which case nodes of order zero need not exist. Indeed, suppose x^u is such that $\delta_u(i) > -\infty$ for every i. In this case, (15) implies $p_{lj} > 0$ for every $j \in S$, i.e. the lth row of $\mathbb{P}$ must be positive, and (15) is equivalent to

$$\delta_u(l) \geq \max_i [\max_j (\log p_{ij} - \log p_{lj}) + \delta_u(i)].$$

First, we introduce $p_{ij}^{(r)}(u)$, the maximum probability over the paths connecting states i and j at times u and $u+r+1$, respectively. For each $u \geq 1$ and $r \geq 1$, let

$$p_{ij}^{(r)}(u) := \max_{q^r \in S^r} p_{iq_1} f_{q_1}(x_{u+1}) p_{q_1 q_2} f_{q_2}(x_{u+2}) p_{q_2 q_3} \cdots p_{q_{r-1} q_r} f_{q_r}(x_{u+r}) p_{q_r j}.$$

Note that for $r \geq 1$, $p_{ij}^{(r)}(u)$ depends on the observations x_{u+1}^{u+r}. By defining

$$i_t^{(r)}(j) := \arg\max_{i \in S} [\delta_t(i) + \log p_{ij}^{(r)}],$$

we get that for every $t = 1, \ldots, n$ and $j \in S$ it holds that the $(t-r-1)^{\text{th}}$ element of $v^t(j)$ equals $i_{t-r-1}^{(r)}(j)$, i.e.

$$v_{t-r-1}^t(j) = i_{t-r-1}^{(r)}(j). \tag{16}$$

Def. Given the first $u+r$ observations, the observation x_u is said to be an *l-node of order r* if

$$\delta_u(l) + \log p_{lj}^{(r)}(u) \geq \delta_u(i) + \log p_{ij}^{(r)}(u), \quad \forall i, j \in S. \tag{17}$$

The observation x_u is said to be an rth order node if it is an rth-order l-node for some $l \in S$. The node is said to be *strong* if the inequalities in (17) are strict for every $i, j \in S, i \neq l$. ⋄
Note that any r^{th}-order node is also a node of order r' for any integer $r \leq r' < n$, and thus by the order of a node we will mean the minimal such r. Note also that for $K = 2$, a node of any order is a node of order zero. Hence, positive order nodes emerge for $K \geq 3$ only.

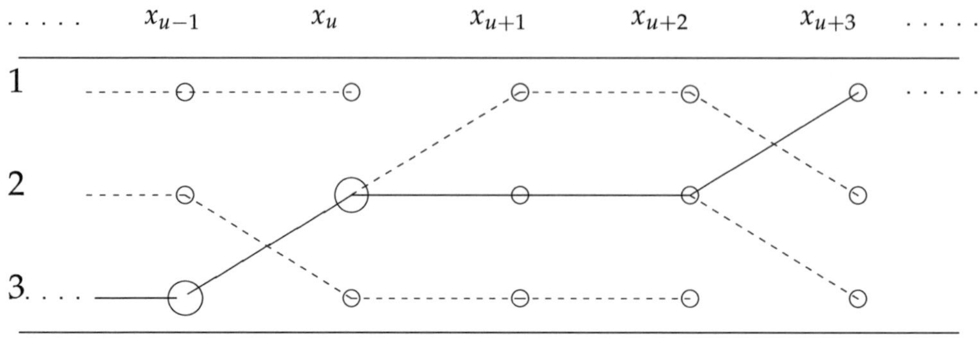

Fig. 3. Suppose $u < n$, and x_u is a 2nd order 2-node, and x_{u-1} is a 3rd order 3-node. Therefore, any alignment $v(x^n)$ has $v(x^n)_u = 2$.

This definition implies that x_u is an l-node of order r if and only if (under suitable tie breaking) $i_u^{(r)}(j) = l$ for every $j \in S$. By (16), this means that $v_u^{u+r+1}(j) = l$ for every $j \in S$, implying that the first u elements of the Viterbi alignment are fixed independently of the observations x_{u+r+1}^n (see Figure 3). This means that the role of higher order nodes is similar to the role of nodes. Suppose now that the realization x^∞ contains infinitely many r^{th} order l-nodes $u_1 < u_2 < \ldots$. Then, as explained in Subsection 3.1.1, the infinite Viterbi alignment $v(x^\infty)$ can be constructed piecewise, i.e. the observations x^{u_1+r} fix the piece v^{u_1}, then the observations $x_{u_1+1}^{u_2+r}$ fix the piece $v_{u_1+1}^{u_2}$, and so on. In the absence of ties, the resulting piecewise infinite alignment is unique. In the presence of ties we require that the ties be broken consistently, and always so that the alignment goes through l at times u_i. Then the resulting infinite Viterbi alignment is called *proper* (see (Lember & Koloydenko, 2008) for details).

3.1.4 Barriers

Recall that nodes of order r at time u are defined relative to the entire realization x^{u+r}. Thus, whether x_u is a node or not depends, in principle, on all observations up to x_{u+r}. On the other hand, the observation that indicates its state is a node independently of the observations before or after it. This property is generalized by the concept of *barrier*. Informally speaking, a barrier is a block of observations that is guaranteed to contain a (probably higher order) node independently of the observations before and after this block. The formal definition is as follows.

Def. Given $l \in S$, a block of observations $z^M \in \mathcal{X}^M$ is called a (strong) *l-barrier* of order $r \geq 0$ and length $M \geq 1$ if for any realization x^n, $M \leq n \leq \infty$, such that $x_{t-M+1}^t = z^M$ for some t, $M \leq t \leq n$, the observation x_{t-r} is a (strong) l-node of order r. $\diamond$

According to this definition, any observation that indicates its state is a barrier of length one. Usually a set $A \subset \mathcal{X}$ can be found such that any observation from A indicates its state. More typically, however, there is a set $B \subset \mathcal{X}^M$ such that any sequence from B is a barrier. Hence barriers can be detected by a sliding window of length M. More importantly, when such a subset B is constructed, then by ergodicity of X almost every realization x^∞ contains infinitely many barriers provided that the set B has a positive probability to occur. As already explained, having infinitely many barriers guarantees infinitely many (usually higher order) nodes, and based on these nodes, the infinite Viterbi alignment can be constructed piecewise.

Thus, everything boils down to the construction of the barrier set B. We are able to do this under some mild assumptions on the HMM. Next we state and discuss briefly these assumptions.
Recall that f_s, $s \in S$, are the densities of $P_s := \mathbf{P}(X_1 \in \cdot | Y_1 = s)$ with respect to some reference measure μ. For each $s \in S$, let $G_s := \{x \in \mathcal{X} : f_s(x) > 0\}$.
Def. We call a non-empty subset $C \subset S$ *a cluster* if the following conditions are satisfied:

$$\min_{j \in C} P_j(\cap_{s \in C} G_s) > 0 \quad \text{and} \quad \text{either } C = S \quad \text{or} \quad \max_{j \notin C} P_j(\cap_{s \in C} G_s) = 0. \qquad \diamond$$

Therefore, a cluster is a maximal subset of states such that $G_C = \cap_{s \in C} G_s$, the intersection of the supports of the corresponding emission distributions, is "detectable". There always exists at least one cluster; distinct clusters need not be disjoint, and a cluster can consist of a single state. In this latter case such a state is not hidden, since it is exposed by any observation it emits. If $K = 2$, then S is the only cluster possible, because otherwise the underlying Markov chain would cease to be hidden. Our first assumption is the following.
A1 (cluster-assumption): There exists a cluster $C \subset S$ such that the sub-stochastic matrix $R = (p_{ij})_{i,j \in C}$ is primitive, i.e. there is a positive integer r such that the rth power of R is strictly positive.
The cluster assumption **A1** is often met in practice. It is clearly satisfied if all elements of the matrix $\mathbb{P}$ are positive. Since any irreducible aperiodic matrix is primitive, the assumption **A1** is also satisfied in this case if the densities f_s satisfy the following condition: for every $x \in \mathcal{X}$, $\min_{s \in S} f_s(x) > 0$, i.e. for all $s \in S$, $G_s = \mathcal{X}$. Thus, **A1** is more general than the *strong mixing condition* (Assumption 4.2.21 in (Cappé et al., 2005)) and also weaker than Assumption 4.3.29 in (Cappé et al., 2005). Note that **A1** implies aperiodicity of Y, but not vice versa.
Our second assumption is the following.
A2: For each state $l \in S$,

$$P_l\Big(\{x \in \mathcal{X} : f_l(x) p_l^* > \max_{s, s \neq l} f_s(x) p_s^*\}\Big) > 0, \quad \text{where} \quad p_l^* = \max_j p_{jl}, \quad \forall l \in S. \tag{18}$$

The assumption **A2** is more technical in nature. In (Koloydenko & Lember, 2008) it was shown that for a two-state HMM, (18) always holds for one state, and this is sufficient for the infinite Viterbi alignment to exist. Hence, for the case $K = 2$, **A2** can be relaxed. Other possibilities for relaxing **A2** are discussed in (Lember & Koloydenko, 2008; 2010a). To summarize: we believe that the cluster assumption **A1** is essential for HMMs, while the assumption **A2**, although natural and satisfied for many models, can be relaxed. For more general discussion about these assumptions, see (Koloydenko & Lember, 2008; Lember, 2011; Lember & Koloydenko, 2008; 2010a). The following Lemma is the core of our proof of the existence of the infinite Viterbi alignment.

Lemma 3.1. *Assume* **A1** *and* **A2**. *Then for some integers M and r, $M > r \geq 0$, there exist a set $B = B_1 \times \cdots \times B_M \subset \mathcal{X}^M$, an M-tuple of states $y^M \in S^M$ and a state $l \in S$, such that every $z^M \in B$ is an l-barrier of order r, $y_{M-r} = l$ and $\mathbf{P}(X^M \in B, \quad Y^M = y^M) > 0$.*

Lemma 3.1 is proved in (Lember & Koloydenko, 2010a), and implies that $\mathbf{P}(X^M \in B) > 0$. Hence almost every realization of X contains infinitely many barriers, which makes the piecewise construction possible.

3.1.5 Viterbi process and its regenerativity.

If **A1** and **A2** hold, then by Lemma 3.1 and the piecewise construction there exists an infinite Viterbi classifier $v : \mathcal{X}^\infty \to S^\infty$. By applying v to HMM we obtain the alignment process $V = v(X)$. We shall call the process $V = \{V_t\}_{t=1}^\infty$ the *Viterbi process*. The existence of the Viterbi process follows from the existence of infinitely many barriers. Now recall that Lemma 3.1 states more than merely the existence of infinitely many barriers. Namely, the Lemma actually also states that *almost every* realization of a two-dimensional process (X,Y) contains infinitely many barriers from B synchronized with y^M. In other words, almost every realization of (X,Y) contains infinitely many pairs (z^M, y^M) such that $z^M \in B$. Let τ_i be the random time of the rth order l-node in the ith such pair. Thus $X_{\tau_1}, X_{\tau_2}, \ldots$ are r^{th} order l-nodes. By the assumptions on y^M we also know that for every i,

$$Y_{\tau_i+r-M+1}^{\tau_i+r} = y^M \quad \text{and} \quad Y_{\tau_i} = l.$$

Hence the two-dimensional process (X,Y) is clearly regenerative with respect to the random times $\{\tau_i\}_{i=1}^\infty$. Moreover, the proper piecewise construction ensures that the Viterbi process V is also regenerative with respect to $\{\tau_i\}$, see (Lember & Koloydenko, 2008). The random variables $\tau_1, \tau_2 - \tau_1, \tau_3 - \tau_2, \ldots$ are independent and $\tau_2 - \tau_1, \tau_3 - \tau_2, \ldots$ are i.i.d. Thus, defining $S_i := \tau_{i+1}$, $i = 0, 1, \ldots$, we obtain that the three-dimensional process $Z = (X, Y, V)$ is regenerative with respect to the delayed renewal process $\{S_t\}_{t=0}^\infty$. Let $\tilde{V}^n := v^n(X^n)$, where v^n is a finite Viterbi alignment. The discussion above can be summarized as the following theorem (see (Kuljus & Lember, 2010) for details).

Theorem 3.1. *Let $(X,Y) = \{(X_t, Y_t)\}_{t=1}^\infty$ be an ergodic HMM satisfying* **A1** *and* **A2**. *Then there exists an infinite Viterbi alignment $v : \mathcal{X}^\infty \to S^\infty$. Moreover, the finite Viterbi alignments $v^n : \mathcal{X}^n \to S^n$ can be chosen so that the following conditions are satisfied:*

R1 *the process $Z := (X, Y, V)$, where $V := \{V_t\}_{t=1}^\infty$ is the alignment process, is a positive recurrent aperiodic regenerative process with respect to some renewal process $\{S_t\}_{t=0}^\infty$;*

R2 *there exists a nonnegative integer $m < \infty$ such that for every $j \geq 0$, $\tilde{V}_t^n = V_t$ for all $n \geq S_j + m$ and $t \leq S_j$.*

We actually know that m relates to r, the order of the barriers in Lemma 3.1, as $m = r + 1$. Aperiodicity of Z follows from aperiodicity of Y, the latter being a consequence of **A1**. Obviously, the choice of v^n becomes an issue only if the finite Viterbi alignment is not unique. In what follows, we always assume that the finite Viterbi alignments $v^n : \mathcal{X}^n \to S^n$ are chosen according to Theorem 3.1. With such choices, the process $\tilde{Z}^n := \{(\tilde{V}_t^n, X_t, Y_t)\}_{t=1}^n$ satisfies by **R2** the following property: $\tilde{Z}_t^n = Z_t$ for every $t = 1, \ldots, S_{k(n)}$, where $k(n) = \max\{k \geq 0 : S_k + m \leq n\}$.

Regenerativity of Z makes it possible to obtain without any remarkable effort the SLLN for $\tilde{Z}^n$. To be more precise, let g_p be a measurable function for some $p \in \mathbb{N}$ and let $n \geq p$, and consider the following random variables

$$\tilde{U}_i^n := g_p(\tilde{Z}_{i-p+1}^n, \ldots, \tilde{Z}_i^n), \quad i = p, \ldots, n.$$

Note that if $i \leq S_{k(n)}$, then $\tilde{U}_i^n = U_i := g_p(Z_{i-p+1}, \ldots, Z_i)$. Let

$$M_k := \max_{S_k < i \leq S_{k+1}} |\tilde{U}_{S_k+1}^i + \cdots + \tilde{U}_i^i|.$$

The random variables $M_p, M_{p+1}, \ldots$ are identically distributed, but for $p > 1$ not necessarily independent. The following Theorem in a sense generalizes Th. VI.3.1 in (Asmussen, 2003), and is an important tool for the applications in Subsection 4.1. The process Z^* appearing in the theorem is a stationary version of Z. For the proof and details see (Kuljus & Lember, 2010).

Theorem 3.2. *Let g_p be such that $EM_p < \infty$ and $E|g_p(Z_1^*, \ldots, Z_p^*)| < \infty$. Then we have*

$$\frac{1}{n-p+1} \sum_{i=p}^{n} \tilde{U}_i^n \underset{n\to\infty}{\to} EU_p = Eg_p(Z_1^*, \ldots, Z_p^*) \quad \text{a.s. and in } L_1.$$

3.1.6 Doubly-infinite HMMs

Recall that $\{(X_t, Y_t)\}_{t\geq 1}$ is a restriction of the doubly-infinite HMM $\{X_t, Y_t\}_{t\in\mathbb{Z}}$ to the positive integers. A great advantage of the barrier-based approach is that it allows us to construct a piecewise infinite Viterbi alignment also for the doubly-infinite HMM. Thus, there exists a doubly-infinite Viterbi alignment $v : \mathcal{X}^{\mathbb{Z}} \to S^{\mathbb{Z}}$ that is an extension of finite Viterbi alignments. For the formal definition of a doubly-infinite alignment see (Kuljus & Lember, 2010). An important feature of the doubly-infinite Viterbi alignment is that the decoding process v is stationary, i.e. shifting the realization $x_{-\infty}^{\infty}$ by one time-unit (Bernoulli shift) entails the same shift of the decoded sequence $v(x_{-\infty}^{\infty})$. Hence, applying v to an ergodic doubly-infinite process X gives us an ergodic doubly-infinite Viterbi process $v(X)$. The following theorem (Th. 2.2 in (Kuljus & Lember, 2010)) is a doubly-infinite counterpart of Theorem 3.1.

Theorem 3.3. *Let $(X, Y) = \{(X_t, Y_t)\}_{t\in\mathbb{Z}}$ be a doubly-infinite ergodic HMM satisfying* **A1** *and* **A2**. *Then there exists an infinite Viterbi alignment $v : \mathcal{X}^{\mathbb{Z}} \to S^{\mathbb{Z}}$. Moreover, the finite Viterbi alignments $v_{z_1}^{z_2}$ can be chosen so that the following conditions are satisfied:*

RD1 *the process (X, Y, V), where $V := \{V_t\}_{t\in\mathbb{Z}}$ is the alignment process, is a positively recurrent aperiodic regenerative process with respect to some renewal process $\{S_t\}_{t\in\mathbb{Z}}$;*

RD2 *there exists a nonnegative integer $m < \infty$ such that for every $j \geq 0$, $\tilde{V}_t^n = V_t$ for all $n \geq S_j + m$ and $S_0 \leq t \leq S_j$;*

RD3 *the mapping v is stationary, i.e. $v(\theta(X)) = \theta v(X)$, where θ is the usual shift operator, i.e. $\theta(\ldots, x_{-1}, x_0, x_1, \ldots) = (\ldots, x_0, x_1, x_2, \ldots)$.*

Note the difference between **R2** and **RD2**. Also, as explained above, property **RD3** is important because it guarantees that the doubly-infinite alignment process $V = \{V_t\}_{t\in\mathbb{Z}}$ as well as $Z = \{(X_t, Y_t, V_t)\}_{t\in\mathbb{Z}}$ is ergodic. Hence, by Birkhoff's ergodic theorem it holds that for any integrable function f,

$$\frac{1}{n} \sum_{t=1}^{n} f(\ldots, Z_{t-1}, Z_t, Z_{t+1}, \ldots) \underset{n\to\infty}{\to} E[f(\ldots, Z_{-1}, Z_0, Z_1, \ldots)] \quad \text{a.s. and in } L_1. \tag{19}$$

The convergence (19) is an important tool in proving limit theorems. Let Z^* denote the restriction of $\{(X_t, Y_t, V_t)\}_{t=-\infty}^{\infty}$ to the positive integers, i.e. $Z^* = \{(X_t, Y_t, V_t)\}_{t=1}^{\infty}$. By **RD2**, Z^* is a stationary version of Z as in **R1**. Thus $(X_0, Y_0, V_0) \overset{D}{=} (X_1^*, Y_1^*, V_1^*) := Z_1^*$. Note that the singly-infinite Viterbi process V in **R1** is not defined at time zero so that the random variable V_0 always refers to the doubly-infinite, and hence stationary, case.

3.1.7 Two-state HMM

The two-state HMM is special in many ways. First, since the underlying Markov chain is aperiodic and irreducible, all entries of $\mathbb{P}^2$ are positive. This implies that the cluster-assumption **A1** is always satisfied. Clearly the models of interest have only one cluster consisting of both states. Positiveness of the transition probabilities also suggests that there is no real need to consider either higher order nodes (and therefore higher order barriers) or nodes that are not strong. That all makes the analysis for the case $K = 2$ significantly simpler. The two-state case was first considered in (Caliebe, 2006; Caliebe & Rösler, 2002), where the existence of infinite Viterbi alignments and regenerativity of the Viterbi process were proved under several additional assumptions. The proof is based on the central limit theorem and cannot be extended beyond the two-state case (see (Koloydenko & Lember, 2008; Lember & Koloydenko, 2008) for a detailed discussion). The barrier-based construction for two-state HMMs was considered in detail in (Koloydenko & Lember, 2008). The main result of this paper states that for $K = 2$ also the assumption **A2** can be removed. The only assumption that remains is the natural assumption that the emission measures P_1 and P_2 are different. The main theorem of (Koloydenko & Lember, 2008) states that under this assumption almost every realization of X has infinitely many strong barriers. This result significantly generalizes those in (Caliebe & Rösler, 2002).

3.2 Exponential forgetting and infinite PMAP-alignment

The existence of an infinite PMAP-classifier follows from the convergence of the so-called *smoothing probabilities* as detailed below: for every $s \in S$, $t, z \in \mathbb{Z}$ such that $t \geq z$, we have

$$\mathbf{P}(Y_t = s|X_z, \ldots, X_n) \underset{n\to\infty}{\to} \mathbf{P}(Y_t = s|X_z, X_{z+1} \ldots) =: \mathbf{P}(Y_t = s|X_z^\infty) \quad \text{a.s.} \tag{20}$$

The convergence (20) in its turn follows from Levy's martingale convergence Theorem. When the model is such that for every t there exists s' satisfying

$$\mathbf{P}(Y_t = s'|X^\infty) > \mathbf{P}(Y_t = s|X^\infty), \quad \forall s \neq s' \quad \text{a.s.,} \tag{21}$$

then the existence of infinite PMAP-alignment follows from (20) with $z = 1$, because then

$$\arg\max_s \mathbf{P}(Y_t = s|X^n) = \arg\max_s \mathbf{P}(Y_t = s|X^\infty) \quad \text{eventually,} \quad \text{a.s.}$$

Condition (21) guarantees that $\arg\max_s \mathbf{P}(Y_t = s|X^\infty)$ is almost surely unique. The drawback of the easy construction of the infinite PMAP-alignment (given (21) holds) is that the ergodic properties of the PMAP-process still need to be established. In particular, an analogue of Theorem 3.2 has not yet been established, although we conjecture that under some assumptions it holds.

At the same time, employing Levy's martingale convergence Theorem again, we have

$$\lim_{z\to-\infty} \mathbf{P}(Y_t = s|X_z^\infty) = \mathbf{P}(Y_t = s|\cdots, X_{-1}, X_0, X_1, \ldots) =: \mathbf{P}(Y_t = s|X_{-\infty}^\infty) \quad \text{a.s.}$$

In (Lember, 2011), the rates of the above convergences are studied. In particular, the following *exponential forgetting* Theorem (Th. 2.1 in (Lember, 2011)) is proved. In this Theorem, for every z_1, z_2 such that $-\infty \leq z_1 < z_2 \leq \infty$, $\mathbf{P}(Y_t \in \cdot|X_{z_1}^{z_2})$ denotes the K-dimensional vector of probabilities and $\|\cdot\|$ stands for the total variation distance.

Theorem 3.4. *Assume* **A1**. *Then there exists a finite random variable C and $\rho \in (0,1)$ such that for every z, t, n satisfying $z \leq t \leq n$,*

$$\|\mathbf{P}(Y_t \in \cdot|X_z^n) - \mathbf{P}(Y_t \in \cdot|X_{-\infty}^{\infty})\| \leq C(\rho^{t-z} + \rho^{n-t}) \quad \text{a.s.} \tag{22}$$

The proof of Theorem 3.4 is based on an approach developed in (Cappé et al., 2005). The approach is based on the fact that given x^n, the conditional distribution of the underlying chain Y is still Markov (albeit generally inhomogeneous). Using this, the difference between the smoothing probabilities can be bounded by the Dobrushin coefficient of the product of the (data-dependent) transition matrices. Condition **A1** allows us to bound the Dobrushin coefficient also in the case when the strong mixing condition fails. This is why Theorem 3.4 is more general than the previous similar results where the transition matrix was assumed to have only positive entries or the emission densities f_i were assumed to be all positive (Cappé et al., 2005; Gerencser & Molnar-Saska, 2002; Gland & Mevel, 2000). It is important to note that although the technique used in proving the exponential forgetting inequality differs completely from the one used in proving the infinite Viterbi alignment, the same assumption **A1** appears in both the situations. This gives us a reason to believe that **A1** is indeed essential for HMMs.

4. Applications of infinite segmentation

4.1 Asymptotic risks

Recall (Subsection 1.2) that the quantity $R(g, x^n) := R(g(x^n)|x^n)$ measures the quality of classifier g when it is applied to observations x^n. We are interested in the random variable $R(g, X^n)$. In particular, we ask whether there exists a constant R such that $R(g, X^n) \underset{n\to\infty}{\to} R$ *almost surely*. This constant, when it exists, will be called *asymptotic risk* and for a given risk function, its asymptotic risk depends only on the model and the classifier. Therefore, asymptotic risks can be used to characterize the long-run properties of different classifiers for a given HMM. They provide a tool for comparing how well different segmentation methods work for a particular model. In the following, we present some risk convergence results that were originally proved in (Kuljus & Lember, 2010; Lember, 2011). We also give the main ideas behind the proofs. It should be noted that although the risk-based approach allows us to consider several segmentation methods in a unified framework, we are not aware of any unified method for proving the convergence of the corresponding risks. Therefore, every specific risk as well as any particular classifier requires individual treatment. In the following, we will denote the Viterbi alignment by v and the PMAP-alignment by u.

4.1.1 The R_1-risk

The R_1-risk is based on the pointwise loss function L_1 that was defined in (1). When measuring the goodness of segmentation with the R_1-risk, the quantity of actual interest is the so-called *empirical or true* risk

$$R_1(g, Y^n, X^n) := \frac{1}{n} \sum_{t=1}^{n} l(Y_t, g_t(X^n)),$$

where $g_t(X^n)$ is the tth element of the n-dimensional vector $g(X^n)$. Since Y^n is hidden, the empirical risk $R_1(g, Y^n, X^n)$ cannot be found. If g is the Viterbi classifier, then

$$R_1(v, Y^n, X^n) = \frac{1}{n} \sum_{t=1}^{n} l(Y_t, \tilde{V}_t^n),$$

and from Theorem 3.2 it follows that

$$R_1(v, Y^n, X^n) \underset{n\to\infty}{\to} El(Y_0, V_0) =: R_1 \quad \text{a.s. and in } L_1. \tag{23}$$

The risk $R_1(v, X^n)$ is the conditional expectation of the empirical risk, i.e.

$$R_1(v, X^n) = E[R_1(v, Y^n, X^n)|X^n].$$

In (Kuljus & Lember, 2010) it is shown that (23) implies also convergence of the conditional expectations. Let us summarize this as the following Theorem (Th. 5 in (Kuljus & Lember, 2010)).

Theorem 4.1. *Let $\{(Y_t, X_t)\}_{t=1}^{\infty}$ be an ergodic HMM satisfying* **A1** *and* **A2**. *Then there exists a constant $R_1 \geq 0$ such that*

$$\lim_{n\to\infty} R_1(v, Y^n, X^n) = \lim_{n\to\infty} R_1(v, X^n) = R_1 \quad \text{a.s. and in } L_1.$$

From the convergence in L_1 (or by the bounded convergence Theorem) it obviously follows that the expected risk of the Viterbi alignment converges to R_1 as well: $ER_1(v, X^n) \to R_1$.
Assuming that the asymptotic risk R_1 has been found (by simulations, for example), one could now be interested in a large deviation type upper bound on $\mathbf{P}(R_1(v, Y^n, X^n) - R_1 > \epsilon)$. In (Ghosh et al., 2009) it has been shown that under the same assumptions as in the present paper, the following large deviation principle holds:

$$\lim_{n\to\infty} \frac{1}{n} \log \mathbf{P}(R_1(v, Y^n, X^n) > \epsilon + R_1) = -I(R_1 + \epsilon),$$

where I is a rate function and ϵ is small enough. The authors of (Ghosh et al., 2009) do not state the exact bound on the probability $\mathbf{P}(R_1(v, Y^n, X^n) - R_1 > \epsilon)$, but it could be derived from their proof of the above result. We would like to draw the reader's attention to how this theme is different from supervised learning. In supervised learning (pattern recognition) the model is often unknown, but the variables Y^n are observable, thus the empirical risk $R_1(g, Y^n, X^n)$ for any classifier could be calculated. The main object of interest then is the unknown asymptotic risk and the large deviation inequalities are used to estimate the unknown asymptotic risk by the known empirical risk. In our setting the data Y^n are hidden, but the model, and therefore the asymptotic risk, is known, thus it can be used to estimate the unknown empirical risk.
Consider now the R_1-risk for the PMAP-classifier u, that is the minimizer of this risk. Birkhoff's ergodic theorem together with the exponential smoothing inequality (22) immediately imply the existence of a constant R_1^* such that $R_1(u, X^n) \to R_1^*$ almost surely. Indeed, from (19) it follows that

$$\frac{1}{n}\sum_{t=1}^{n} \min_s \Big(\sum_{a\in S} l(a,s) P(Y_t = a|X_{-\infty}^{\infty}) \Big) \underset{n\to\infty}{\to} E \min_s \Big(\sum_{a\in S} l(a,s) P(Y_0 = a|X_{-\infty}^{\infty}) \Big) =: R_1^* \quad \text{a.s.}$$

The forgetting bound (22) yields

$$\Big| R_1(u, X^n) - \frac{1}{n}\sum_{t=1}^{n} \min_{s\in S} \Big(\sum_{a\in S} l(a,s) P(Y_t = a|X_{-\infty}^{\infty}) \Big) \Big| \leq \frac{C}{n}\sum_{t=1}^{n} (\rho^{t-1} + \rho^{n-t}) \quad \text{a.s.,} \tag{24}$$

see (Lember, 2011) for details. The right-hand side of (24) converges to zero almost surely as n grows. Thus, the following Theorem holds (Th. 3.1 in (Lember, 2011)).

Theorem 4.2. *Let* $\{(Y_t, X_t)\}_{t=1}^{\infty}$ *be an ergodic HMM satisfying* **A1**. *Then there exists a constant* R_1^* *such that* $R_1(u, X^n) \underset{n\to\infty}{\to} R_1^*$ *a.s. and in* L_1.

The asymptotic risk R_1^* measures in the long run the average loss incurred by classifying one symbol. Since the PMAP-classifier is optimal for the R_1-risk, then clearly $R_1^* \leq R_1$ and their difference indicates how well the Viterbi segmentation performs in the sense of R_1-risk in comparison to the best classifier in the sense of R_1-risk. For example, if the pointwise loss function l is symmetric, then the optimal classifier in the sense of misclassification error makes on average about $R_1^* n$ classification mistakes and no other classifier does better.

4.1.2 The $\bar{R}_1$-risk

Recall (2) which defines the $\bar{R}_1$-risk to be

$$\bar{R}_1(s^n|x^n) = -\frac{1}{n}\sum_{t=1}^{n} \log p_t(s_t|x^n).$$

To show the convergence of $\bar{R}_1(v, X^n)$, we use Theorem 3.3. According to **RD3**, the doubly-infinite alignment process v is stationary. Consider the function $f : \mathcal{X}^{\mathbb{Z}} \to (-\infty, 0]$, where

$$f(x_{-\infty}^{\infty}) := \log p_0(v_0(x_{-\infty}^{\infty})|x_{-\infty}^{\infty}) = \log \mathbf{P}(Y_0 = V_0|X_{-\infty}^{\infty} = x_{-\infty}^{\infty}).$$

It is not hard to see that $f(\theta^{(t)}(x_{-\infty}^{\infty})) = \log \mathbf{P}(Y_t = V_t|X_{-\infty}^{\infty} = x_{-\infty}^{\infty})$. Thus, by (19),

$$-\frac{1}{n}\sum_{t=1}^{n} \log \mathbf{P}(Y_t = V_t|X_{-\infty}^{\infty}) \underset{n\to\infty}{\to} -E\big(\log \mathbf{P}(Y_0 = V_0|X_{-\infty}^{\infty})\big) =: \bar{R}_1 \quad \text{a.s. and in } L_1,$$

provided the expectation is finite. This convergence suggests that by suitable approximation the following convergence also holds:

$$\lim_{n\to\infty} \bar{R}_1(v, X^n) = \lim_{n\to\infty} -\frac{1}{n}\sum_{t=1}^{n} \log \mathbf{P}(Y_t = \tilde{V}_t^n|X^n) = \bar{R}_1 \quad \text{a.s.} \tag{25}$$

The difficulties with proving the convergence of $\bar{R}_1(v, X^n)$ are caused mainly by the fact that the exponential forgetting inequality in (22) does not necessarily hold for the logarithms. This inequality would hold if the probability $\mathbf{P}(Y_0 = V_0|X_{-\infty}^{\infty})$ were bounded below, i.e. if

$$\mathbf{P}(Y_0 = V_0|X_{-\infty}^{\infty}) > \epsilon \quad \text{a.s.} \tag{26}$$

held for some $\epsilon > 0$. Then by (22) it would hold that almost surely $\mathbf{P}(Y_t = V_t|X^{\infty}) > \frac{\epsilon}{2}$ eventually, and the inequality $|\log a - \log b| \leq \frac{1}{\min\{a,b\}}|a - b|$ together with (22) would imply

$$-\frac{1}{n}\sum_{t=1}^{n} \log \mathbf{P}(Y_t = V_t|X^n) \underset{n\to\infty}{\to} \bar{R}_1 \quad \text{a.s.}$$

Then, by an argument similar to the one in the proof of Theorem 3.2, the convergence (25) would follow. Unfortunately, (26) need not necessarily hold. In (Kuljus & Lember, 2010) the condition (26) is replaced by the following weaker condition: there exists $\alpha > 0$ such that

$$E\Big(\frac{1}{\mathbf{P}(Y_0 = V_0|X_{-\infty}^{\infty})}\Big)^{\alpha} < \infty. \tag{27}$$

It can be shown (Prop. 4.1 and Lemma 3 in (Kuljus & Lember, 2010)) that under **A1** the inequality (27) holds. The condition in (27) turns out to be sufficient to prove the convergence of $\bar{R}_1(v, X^n)$. The discussion above can be summarized in the following theorem (Th. 4.1 in (Kuljus & Lember, 2010)).

Theorem 4.3. *Let* $\{(Y_t, X_t)\}_{t=1}^{\infty}$ *be an ergodic HMM satisfying* **A1** *and* **A2**. *Then*

$$\lim_{n\to\infty} \bar{R}_1(v, X^n) = \bar{R}_1 \quad \text{a.s. and in } L_1 .$$

From the preceding argument it is clear that the convergence of the $\bar{R}_1$-risk is rather easy to prove when instead of the Viterbi alignment the PMAP-alignment is used. Indeed, by (19),

$$-\frac{1}{n}\sum_{t=1}^{n} \max_{s\in S} \log \mathbf{P}(Y_t = s|X_{-\infty}^{\infty}) \underset{n\to\infty}{\to} E[\max_{s\in S} \log \mathbf{P}(Y_0 = s|X_{-\infty}^{\infty})] =: \bar{R}_1^* \quad \text{a.s. and in } L_1.$$

Since $\max_{s\in S} \mathbf{P}(Y_t = s|X^n) \geq K^{-1}$, for the PMAP-alignment the condition (26) is trivially satisfied. From the exponential forgetting inequality (22) it then follows (Cor. 4.2 in (Kuljus & Lember, 2010)) that

$$\bar{R}_1(u, X^n) = -\frac{1}{n}\sum_{t=1}^{n} \max_{s\in S} \log \mathbf{P}(Y_t = s|X^n) \underset{n\to\infty}{\to} \bar{R}_1^* \quad \text{a.s. and in } L_1 .$$

Again, since the $\bar{R}_1$-risk is minimized by the PMAP-classifier, it holds that $\bar{R}_1^* \leq \bar{R}_1$.

4.1.3 The $\bar{R}_\infty$-risk

Recall (Subsection 2.3.1) that the $\bar{R}_\infty$-risk is defined as the negative log-posterior probability given observations x^n, i.e. $\bar{R}_\infty(s^n|x^n) = -\frac{1}{n}\log p(s^n|x^n)$. Let $p(x^n)$ denote the likelihood of x^n. Then

$$p(\tilde{V}^n|X^n) = \mathbf{P}(Y^n = \tilde{V}^n|X^n) = \frac{p(X^n|\tilde{V}^n)\mathbf{P}(Y^n = \tilde{V}^n)}{p(X^n)},$$

therefore

$$\bar{R}_\infty(v, X^n) = -\frac{1}{n}\Big(\log p(X^n|\tilde{V}^n) + \log \mathbf{P}(Y^n = \tilde{V}^n) - \log p(X^n)\Big).$$

By Theorem 3.2, the following convergences hold (see (Kuljus & Lember, 2010) for details):

$$\frac{1}{n}\log p(X^n|\tilde{V}^n) \underset{n\to\infty}{\to} \sum_{s\in S} E\big(\log f_s(X_0) I_s(V_0)\big) \quad \text{a.s.,} \qquad \frac{1}{n}\log \mathbf{P}(Y^n = \tilde{V}^n) \underset{n\to\infty}{\to} E(\log p_{V_0 V_1}) \quad \text{a.s.}$$

The last convergence $-\frac{1}{n}\log p(X^n) \to H_X$, where H_X is the entropy rate of X, follows from the Shannon-McMillan-Breiman Theorem. The ideas above are formalized in the following Theorem (Th. 5.1 in (Kuljus & Lember, 2010)).

Theorem 4.4. *Let for every* $s \in S$ *the function* $\log f_s$ *be* P_s*-integrable. Then there exists a constant* $\bar{R}_\infty$ *such that*

$$\bar{R}_\infty(v, X^n) \underset{n\to\infty}{\to} \bar{R}_\infty \quad \text{a.s. and in } L_1.$$

By the same argument, there exists another constant $\bar{R}^Y_\infty$ such that

$$-\frac{1}{n}\log \mathbf{P}(Y^n|X^n) \underset{n\to\infty}{\to} \bar{R}^Y_\infty \quad \text{a.s. and in } L_1.$$

Since $E[\log \mathbf{P}(Y^n|X^n)] = -H(Y^n|X^n)$, where $H(Y^n|X^n)$ stands for the conditional entropy of Y^n given X^n, the limit $\bar{R}^Y_\infty$ could be interpreted as the conditional entropy rate of Y given X, it is not the entropy rate of Y. Clearly, $\bar{R}_\infty \leq \bar{R}^Y_\infty$, and the difference of these two numbers shows how much the Viterbi alignment inflates the posterior probability.

4.2 Adjusted Viterbi training

So far we have assumed that the model is known, i.e. both the transition matrix as well as the emission distributions P_s are given. Often the model is given up to parametrization and then parameter estimation becomes of interest. Hence, in this subsection we assume that all emission densities are of the form $f_s(x;\theta_s)$, where $\theta_s \in \Theta_s$ is the emission parameter to be estimated. In practice, e.g. in speech recognition, the transition matrix is often assumed to be known and the emission parameters are the only parameters to be estimated, sometimes however the transition matrix $\mathbb{P} = (p_{ij})$ is to be estimated as well. Thus, in general, the set of unknown parameters is $\psi = (\mathbb{P},\theta)$, where $\theta = (\theta_1,\theta_2,\ldots,\theta_K)$. (We ignore π, the initial distribution, since in the stationary regime π is determined by $\mathbb{P}$, whereas otherwise its estimation would require multiple samples x^n.)

The classical algorithm for finding the maximum likelihood estimators of HMM-parameters is the so-called *EM-training* (see, e.g. (Cappé et al., 2005; Ephraim & Merhav, 2002; Rabiner, 1989)). Although theoretically justified, the EM-training might be very slow and computationally expensive. Therefore, in practice, the EM-training is sometimes replaced by the much quicker *Viterbi training* (VT), where the expectation over all alignments (E-step) is replaced by the maximum a posteriori alignment. In other words, in the kth iteration the Viterbi alignment is performed using $\psi^{(k)}$, the current estimate of the parameters. According to this alignment, the observations x^n are divided into K subsamples, where the sth subsample consists of those observations that are aligned with the state s. In each subsample the maximum likelihood estimator $\hat{\mu}_s$ of θ_s is found. The estimate of the transition probability $\hat{p}_{ij}$ is the proportion of states i followed by the state j in the Viterbi alignment. The formal algorithm of VT estimation is as follows.

Viterbi training (VT)

1. Choose initial values for the parameters $\psi^{(k)} = (\mathbb{P}^{(k)},\theta^{(k)})$, $k = 0$.
2. Given the current parameters $\psi^{(k)}$, obtain the Viterbi alignment $v^{(k)} = v(x^n;\psi^{(k)})$.
3. Update the regime parameters $\mathbb{P}^{(k+1)} := (\hat{p}^n_{ij})$, $i,j \in S$, as given below:

$$\hat{p}^n_{ij} := \begin{cases} \dfrac{\sum_{m=1}^{n-1} I_{\{i\}}(v^{(k)}_m) I_{\{j\}}(v^{(k)}_{m+1})}{\sum_{m=1}^{n-1} I_{\{i\}}(v^{(k)}_m)}, & \text{if } \sum_{m=1}^{n-1} I_{\{i\}}(v^{(k)}_m) > 0, \\ \mathbb{P}^{(k)}_{ij}, & \text{otherwise.} \end{cases}$$

4. Assign x_m, $m = 1,2,\ldots,n$, to the class $v^{(k)}_m$. Equivalently, define empirical measures

$$\hat{P}^n_s(A;\psi^{(k)},x^n) := \frac{\sum_{m=1}^n I_{A\times\{s\}}(x_m, v^{(k)}_m)}{\sum_{m=1}^n I_{\{s\}}(v^{(k)}_m)}, \quad A \in \mathcal{B}, \quad s \in S.$$

5. For each class $s \in S$, obtain the ML estimator $\hat{\mu}_s^n(\psi^{(k)}, x^n)$ of θ_s, given by:

$$\hat{\mu}_s^n(\psi^{(k)}, x^n) := \arg\max_{\theta_s' \in \Theta_s} \int \log f_s(x; \theta_s') \hat{P}_s^n(dx; \psi^{(k)}, x^n),$$

$$\text{and for all } s \in S \text{ let } \theta_s^{(k+1)} := \begin{cases} \hat{\mu}_s^n(\psi^{(k)}, x^n), & \text{if } \sum_{m=1}^{n} I_{\{s\}}(v_m^{(k)}) > 0, \\ \theta_s^{(k)}, & \text{otherwise.} \end{cases}$$

For better interpretation of VT, suppose that at some step k, $\psi^{(k)} = \psi$, thus $v^{(k)}$ is obtained using the true parameters. Let y^n be the actual hidden realization of Y^n. The training pretends that the alignment $v^{(k)}$ is perfect, i.e. $v^{(k)} = y^n$. If the alignment were perfect, the empirical measures $\hat{P}_s^n$, $s \in S$, would be obtained from the i.i.d. samples generated from the true emission measures P_s and the ML estimators $\hat{\mu}_s^n$ would be natural estimators to use. Under these assumptions $\hat{P}_s^n \Rightarrow P_s$ *almost surely*, and provided that $\{f_s(\cdot;\theta_s) : \theta_s \in \Theta_s\}$ is a P_s-Glivenko-Cantelli class and Θ_s is equipped with a suitable metric, we would have $\lim_{n\to\infty} \hat{\mu}_s^n = \theta_s$ *almost surely*. Hence, if n is sufficiently large, then $\hat{P}_s^n \approx P_s$ and $\theta_s^{(k+1)} = \hat{\mu}_s^n \approx \theta_s = \theta_s^{(k)}$ for every $s \in S$. Similarly, if the alignment were perfect, then $\lim_{n\to\infty} \hat{p}_{ij}^n = \mathbf{P}(Y_2 = j | Y_1 = i) = p_{ij}$ *almost surely*. Thus, for the perfect alignment

$$\psi^{(k+1)} = (\mathbb{P}^{(k+1)}, \theta^{(k+1)}) \approx (\mathbb{P}^{(k)}, \theta^{(k)}) = \psi^{(k)} = \psi,$$

i.e. ψ would be approximately a fixed point of the training algorithm.
Certainly the Viterbi alignment in general is not perfect even when it is computed with the true parameters. The empirical measures $\hat{P}_s^n$ can be rather far from those based on the i.i.d. samples from the true emission measures P_s even when the Viterbi alignment is performed with the true parameters. Hence we have no reason to expect that $\lim_{n\to\infty} \hat{\mu}_s^n(\psi, X^n) = \theta_s$ and $\lim_{n\to\infty} \hat{p}_{ij}^n(\psi, X^n) = p_{ij}$ *almost surely*. Moreover, we do not even know whether the sequences of empirical measures $\hat{P}_s^n(\psi, X^n)$ or the ML estimators $\hat{\mu}_s^n(\psi, X^n)$ and $\hat{p}_{ij}^n(\psi, X^n)$ converge *almost surely* at all. Here again Theorem 3.2 answers the question. From Theorem 3.2 it follows that for any measurable set A, $\hat{P}_s^n(A) \to \mathbf{P}(X_0 \in A | V_0 = s) =: Q_s(A)$ a.s., where $\hat{P}_s^n = \hat{P}_s^n(\psi, X^n)$. This implies that the empirical measures $\hat{P}_s^n$ converge weakly to the measures Q_s *almost surely*, i.e. for every $s \in S$,

$$\hat{P}_s^n \Rightarrow Q_s \quad \text{a.s.} \tag{28}$$

Convergence (28) is the main statement of Theorem 4.1 in (Lember & Koloydenko, 2008). In (Koloydenko et al., 2007) it has been shown that if $f_s(x;\theta_s)$ satisfy some general conditions and if Θ_s are closed subsets of $\mathbb{R}^d$, then convergence (28) implies convergence of $\hat{\mu}_s^n(\psi, X^n)$, i.e.

$$\hat{\mu}_s^n(\psi, X^n) \underset{n\to\infty}{\to} \mu_s \text{ a.s.,} \quad \text{where } \mu_s(\psi) := \arg\max_{\theta_s' \in \Theta_s} \int \log f_s(x; \theta_s') Q_s(dx). \tag{29}$$

Since in general $Q_s \neq P_s(\theta_s)$, clearly μ_s need not equal $\theta_s = \arg\max_{\theta_s'} \int \log f_s(x;\theta_s') P_s(dx)$.

Similarly, Theorem 3.2 also implies that

$$\hat{p}_{ij}^n(\psi; X^n) \underset{n\to\infty}{\to} \mathbf{P}(V_1 = j | V_0 = i) =: q_{ij} \quad \text{a.s.} \tag{30}$$

Again, in general $p_{ij} \neq q_{ij}$. In order to reduce the biases $\theta_s - \mu_s$ and $p_{ij} - q_{ij}$, we have proposed the *adjusted Viterbi training*. We know that convergences (29) and (30) hold for any parameter ψ given that **A1** and **A2** hold. Since the limits μ_s and q_{ij} depend on the true parameters, we can consider the mappings

$$\psi \mapsto \mu_s(\psi), \quad \psi \mapsto q_{ij}(\psi), \quad s,i,j = 1,\ldots,K. \tag{31}$$

These mappings do not depend on the observations x^n, hence the following corrections are well-defined:

$$\Delta_s(\psi) := \theta_s - \mu_s(\psi), \quad R_{ij}(\psi) := p_{ij} - q_{ij}(\psi), \quad s,i,j = 1,\ldots,K. \tag{32}$$

Based on (32), the *adjusted Viterbi training* can be defined as follows.
Adjusted Viterbi training (VA)

1. Choose initial values for the parameters $\psi^{(k)} = (\mathbb{P}^{(k)}, \theta^{(k)}), k = 0$.
2. Given the current parameters $\psi^{(k)}$, obtain the Viterbi alignment $v^{(k)} = v(x^n; \psi^{(k)})$.
3. Update the regime parameters $\mathbb{P}^{(k+1)} := \left(p_{ij}^{(k+1)}\right)$ as follows:

$$p_{ij}^{(k+1)} := \hat{p}_{ij}^n + R_{ij}(\psi^{(k)}),$$

   where $\hat{p}_{ij}^n$ is defined as in VT.

4. Based on $v^{(k)}$, define empirical measures $\hat{P}_s^n$, $s \in S$, as in VT.
5. Update the emission parameters as follows:

$$\theta_s^{(k+1)} := \Delta_s(\psi^{(k)}) + \begin{cases} \hat{\mu}_s^n(\psi^{(k)}, x^n), & \text{if } \sum_{m=1}^n I_{\{s\}}(v_m^{(k)}) > 0, \\ \theta_s^{(k)}, & \text{otherwise.} \end{cases}$$

   Here $\hat{\mu}_s^n(\psi^{(k)}, x^n)$ is as in VT.

Provided n is sufficiently large, VA has approximately the true parameters ψ as its fixed point as desired. Indeed, suppose $\psi^{(k)} = \psi$. From (29) we obtain that for every $s \in S$,

$$\hat{\mu}_s^n(\psi^{(k)}, x^n) = \hat{\mu}_s^n(\psi, x^n) \approx \mu_s(\psi) = \mu_s(\psi^{(k)}).$$

Similarly, (30) gives that for all $i, j \in S$,

$$\hat{p}_{ij}^n(\psi^{(k)}, x^n) = \hat{p}_{ij}^n(\psi, x^n) \approx q_{ij}(\psi) = q_{ij}(\psi^{(k)}).$$

Thus, for every $s, i, j \in S$,

$$\theta_s^{(k+1)} = \hat{\mu}_s^n(\psi, x^n) + \Delta_s(\psi) \approx \mu_s(\psi) + \Delta_s(\psi) = \theta_s = \theta_s^{(k)},$$
$$p_{ij}^{(k+1)} = \hat{p}_{ij}^n(\psi, x^n) + R_{ij}(\psi) \approx q_{ij}(\psi) + R_{ij}(\psi) = p_{ij} = p_{ij}^{(k)}.$$

Hence, $\psi^{(k+1)} = (\mathbb{P}^{(k+1)}, \theta^{(k+1)}) \approx (\mathbb{P}^{(k)}, \theta^{(k)}) = \psi^{(k)}$. The simulations in (Koloydenko et al., 2007; Lember & Koloydenko, 2007), presented in part in Example 2 below, show that the asymptotic fixed point property does make a difference. Namely, unlike the VT estimates, the VA ones are nearly as accurate (and can even be more accurate than) as the ones obtained by the EM-training. At the same time, VA is comparable to VT in terms of the computational cost, and therefore may be preferred to EM.

4.2.1 Example 2

The following simulation study is adapted from (Koloydenko et al., 2007). We consider a two-state HMM with the transition matrix

$$\mathbb{P} = \begin{pmatrix} 1-\epsilon & \epsilon \\ \epsilon & 1-\epsilon \end{pmatrix}, \quad \epsilon \in (0, 0.5],$$

and with the emission distributions $P_1 = \mathcal{N}(\theta_1, 1)$ and $P_2 = \mathcal{N}(\theta_2, 1)$. Thus, there are two emission parameters θ_1 and θ_2 and one regime parameter ϵ in this model. Assume without loss of generality that $\theta_1 < \theta_2$ and let $a = 0.5(\theta_2 - \theta_1)$. With $\epsilon = 0.5$ this model reduces to the i.i.d. (mixture) model. The correction function $\Delta(a, \epsilon)$ was estimated off-line by simulations and achieves its maximum at $\epsilon = 0.5$, i.e. in the i.i.d. case. Using the obtained Δ-function, we apply the adjusted Viterbi training and compare it with the VT- and EM-algorithms. Tables 1-2 present simulation results obtained from samples of size 10^6 and focus on estimation of the emission parameters. The iterations were initialized by setting $\theta_1^{(0)}$ and $\theta_2^{(0)}$ to the first and third quartiles of $x_1, x_2, \ldots, x_n$, respectively, and stopped as soon as the L_∞-distance between successive estimates fell below 0.01. From Tables 1-2 it can be seen that the Viterbi training is quickest to converge, but its estimates are evidently biased. Accuracy of the adjusted Viterbi training is comparable to that of the EM-algorithm, while VA converges somewhat more rapidly than EM. Each step of EM requires significantly more intensive computations, so that one should expect the overall run-time of VA to be notably shorter than that of EM. Using the same stopping rule as before, we also test the three algorithms for the fixed point property. From Tables 3-4 it is evident that both EM and VA do approximately satisfy this property, whereas VT moves the true parameters to a notably different location.

	EM	VT	VA
Step 0	(-0.689,0.687)	(-0.689,0.687)	(-0.689,0.687)
Step 1	(-0.477,0.475)	(-0.537,0.536)	(-0.460,0.459)
Step 2	(-0.385,0.384)	(-0.474,0.474)	(-0.359,0.358)
Step 3	(-0.335,0.333)	(-0.445,0.445)	(-0.305,0.307)
Step 4	(-0.303,0.301)	(-0.429,0.430)	(-0.273,0.274)
Step 5	(-0.281,0.279)	(-0.420,0.422)	(-0.252,0.254)
Step 6	(-0.265,0.264)		(-0.239,0.241)
Step 7	(-0.253,0.252)		(-0.229,0.232)
Step 8	(-0.244,0.243)		
L_1 error	0.087	0.442	0.061
L_2 error	0.061	0.312	0.043
L_∞ error	0.044	0.222	0.032

Table 1. Estimating θ_1 and θ_2, when $\epsilon = 0.2$, $a = 0.2$, $\theta_1 = -0.2$ and $\theta_2 = 0.2$.

	EM	VT	VA
Step 0	(-1.050,1.053)	(-1.050,1.053)	(-1.050,1.053)
Step 1	(-1.013,1.015)	(-1.166,1.169)	(-1.014,1.016)
Step 2	(-1.003,1.005)	(-1.165,1.169)	(-1.004,1.006)
L_1 error	0.008	0.334	0.010
L_2 error	0.006	0.236	0.007
L_∞ error	0.005	0.169	0.006

Table 2. Estimating θ_1 and θ_2, when $\epsilon = 0.5$, $a = 1$, $\theta_1 = -1$ and $\theta_2 = 1$.

	EM	VT	VA
Step 0	(-0.200,0.200)	(-0.200,0.200)	(-0.200,0.200)
Step 1	(-0.198,0.202)	(-0.252,0.254)	(-0.198,0.200)
Step 2		(-0.298,0.302)	
Step 3		(-0.333,0.339)	
Step 4		(-0.357,0.367)	
Step 5		(-0.373,0.386)	
Step 6		(-0.383,0.399)	
Step 7		(-0.387,0.408)	
L_1 error	0.003	0.396	0.002
L_2 error	0.002	0.280	0.002
L_∞ error	0.002	0.208	0.002

Table 3. Comparison of algorithms for $\epsilon = 0.2$ and $a = 0.2$, and $\theta_1^{(0)} = \theta_1$ and $\theta_2^{(0)} = \theta_2$.

	EM	VT	VA
Step 0	(-1.000,1.000)	(-1.000,1.000)	(-1.000,1.000)
Step 1	(-0.998,1.000)	(-1.165,1.167)	(-0.998,1.000)
Step 2		(-1.165,1.167)	
L_1 error	0.002	0.332	0.002
L_2 error	0.002	0.235	0.002
L_∞ error	0.002	0.167	0.002

Table 4. Comparison of algorithms for $\epsilon = 0.5$ and $a = 1$, and $\theta_1^{(0)} = \theta_1$ and $\theta_2^{(0)} = \theta_2$.

4.3 Generalizations, other training ideas and implementation

4.3.1 Segmentation-based training

As we have seen above, the drawback of VT stems from the fact that the Viterbi process differs systematically from the underlying chain, so that the empirical measures obtained by the Viterbi segmentation can differ significantly from the true emission distributions P_s even when the parameters used to obtain the Viterbi alignment were correct and n were arbitrarily large. Hence, using the Viterbi alignment for segmentation in the training procedure is not theoretically justified.

Since the PMAP-alignment minimizes the error rate, using the PMAP-segmentation in the training procedure could be the lesser of the two evils. The empirical measures obtained by the PMAP-alignment would, of course, also differ from the emission measures even when the parameters are correct and n is arbitrarily large, and in particular the transition probability estimators can easily be biased. However, since the PMAP-alignment has more correctly estimated states in the long run, the emission estimators $\hat{\mu}_n$ obtained by the PMAP-alignment are expected to be closer to the ML estimators that would have been obtained if the underlying state sequence were known. A tandem training that would synergize the Viterbi and PMAP alignments may also be worth considering.

In general, one can speak about *segmentation-based training*, where the observations are divided into K subsamples (empirical measures) according to a segmentation procedure with current parameter estimates. Every subsample is considered to be an i.i.d. sample from P_s and the corresponding MLE is found. The transition probabilities are directly obtained from the segmentation. Once again, the PMAP-training should give more precise estimates of the emission parameters than the Viterbi training, but the PMAP-alignment might produce forbidden transitions (Section 1.2). Thus, even when a transition probability is set to zero initially, or turns zero at some iteration, it would not necessarily remain zero at later iterations

of the PMAP training. This is different from VT which cannot turn a zero transition probability positive. This more liberal behavior of the PMAP-training can easily be constrained "by hand", which would be appropriate when, for example, the forbidden transitions are known a priori. More generally, the k-block alignment defined in Subsection 2.4 could be considered in the training procedure which would automatically preserve zero transition probabilities. Preservation of zero transition probabilities is not necessarily a goal in itself as it can prevent the algorithm from detecting rare transitions. However, using the k-block alignment for segmentation based training is worth considering as further optimization may be achieved by varying k.
Recall that the adjusted Viterbi training is largely based on Theorem 3.2, since this is the main theoretical result behind the existence of the adjustments in (32). Although not yet proved, we believe that a counterpart of Theorem 3.2 holds for many alignments other than Viterbi. Now, if the training is based on an alignment for which the above result does hold, the adjusted version of the training can then be defined along the lines of the Viterbi training.

4.3.2 Independent training

The order of the observations $x^n = (x_1, \ldots, x_n)$ provides information about the transition probabilities. When we reorder the observations, we loose all information about the transitions, but the information about the emission distributions remains. Often the emission parameters are the primary interest of the training procedure, the transition matrix could for example be known or considered to be a nuisance parameter. Then it makes sense to estimate the emission parameters by treating the observations $x_1, \ldots, x_n$ as an i.i.d. sample from a mixture density $\sum_s \pi_s f_s(\cdot; \theta_s)$, assuming π to be the invariant distribution of $\mathbb{P}$. This approach is introduced in (Koloydenko et al., 2007; Lember & Koloydenko, 2008) under the name of *independent training*. Besides the EM-training the Viterbi training can also be used for data that is regarded as independent, and in this case it is equivalent to the PMAP-training. As shown in (Koloydenko et al., 2007) (see Subsection 4.2.1), the bias Δ_s is relatively large for the i.i.d. case, which makes the replacement of VT by VA particularly attractive in this case. The advantage of the VA-based independent training over VA is that training is usually significantly easier in the i.i.d. case. In particular, the adjustment terms Δ_s are more likely to be found theoretically. Also, the i.i.d. case is usually computationally much cheaper. Another appealing procedure that could be applied for independent training is VA2 that will be described next. For a more detailed discussion about independent training, see (Koloydenko et al., 2007; Lember & Koloydenko, 2008). For VA in the i.i.d. case, see (Lember & Koloydenko, 2007).

4.3.3 VA2

For the case of i.i.d. data from a mixture density $\sum_s \pi_s f_s(\cdot; \theta_s)$, a slightly modified version of VA was proposed in (Lember & Koloydenko, 2007). To explain the main idea, assume that the weights π_s are known so that the emission parameters $\theta = (\theta_1, \ldots, \theta_K)$ are the only parameters to be estimated. VA2 is based on the observation that for the i.i.d. case the segmentation of the data into subsamples is induced by a partition of the sample space. Indeed, given the current estimates $\theta^{(k)}$, the observation x_t belongs to the subsample corresponding to state 1 if and only if $x_t \in \mathcal{S}_1 := \{x : \pi_1 f_1(x; \theta_1^{(k)}) \geq \pi_s f_s(x; \theta_s^{(k)}),\ \forall s \in S\}$. The sets $\mathcal{S}_1, \ldots, \mathcal{S}_K$ form a partition of X (upto the ties) that depends only on $\theta^{(k)}$. It is intuitively clear, especially in the case of $K = 2$, that many different parameters θ could induce the same partition. In particular, $\theta^{(k)}$ could induce the partition corresponding to the true parameter θ^* even when $\theta^{(k)} \neq \theta^*$. In that case, the ML estimates $\hat{\mu}_s$ would be the same for both $\theta^{(k)}$ and θ^*. However, since the correction term $\Delta(\theta^{(k)})$ does depend on $\theta^{(k)}$, it follows that the adjusted estimate $\theta^{(k+1)}$ need not be close to θ^*. The adjustment in VA2 tries to overcome the mentioned deficiency. In particular, the parameters $\theta^{(k)}$ are taken into account via their induced partition only. Given the partition and the ML estimates $\hat{\mu}_s$, the new adjustment seeks θ that would asymptotically induce the given partition and the given estimates. Now, if the partition corresponded to θ^*, then $\theta^{(k+1)}$ obtained in such a way would be close to θ^*. For details, see (Lember & Koloydenko, 2007).

4.3.4 Implementation

The difficulties in implementing VA are caused by the fact that apart from the i.i.d. case, finding the adjustment functions $\Delta(\psi)$ theoretically is very hard. However, since the adjustments do not depend on the data, they can be found by simulations independently of the data. It is important to point out that even if such simulations require significant effort, they are done *off-line* and can be reused with the same model.

Another, computationally less demanding approach, is the so called *stochastically adjusted Viterbi training* (SVA). Instead of estimating the correction at every point as in the previous approach, SVA estimates the correction by simulations at every iteration and therefore only at the points visited by the algorithm. Clearly, if the number of iterations is relatively small, this method should require less overall computing. On the other hand, if a model is to be used repeatedly, estimating the correction function off-line as in the previous example might still be preferable.

Several implementation ideas for the i.i.d. case, i.e. for estimating mixture parameters, are discussed in (Lember & Koloydenko, 2007). The implementation of VA2 depends on the model. Instead of calculating the correction function Δ, for VA2 a certain inverse function should be found. This might be difficult to do even for simple models, but when it is done, it can be reused again and again.

4.4 Segmentation with partially revealed observations

Consider the situation where some hidden states can be revealed on request, albeit possibly at a very high cost. The purpose of uncovering a number of states is to improve the alignment by reducing the number of incorrectly estimated states. With the additional information a constrained alignment can be obtained, which in general will lower the empirical risk considerably. The decision on how many and which states to reveal is a trade-off between the cost of learning an unknown state and the reduction in the alignment risk.

One way to approach the problem of which states to reveal is to study the conditional misclassification probabilities at every time point $t = 1, \dots, n$, given the observations $X_1, \dots, X_n$. One can order the calculated conditional probability $\mathbf{P}(Y_t \neq g_t(X^n)|X^n = x^n)$, $t = 1, \dots, n$, and ask for the actual states of the points with the largest probability. This approach involves finding the alignment and computing the conditional probabilities for every single realization. In order to use this approach, one needs to know the conditional probability of incorrect segmentation given a certain observation, or a segment of observations, in advance. Let us denote the conditional misclassification probability given an observation x by $P(incorrect|x)$.

4.4.1 Definition of misclassification probability for Viterbi alignment

In this section $l(a_t, b_t)$ stands for the symmetric pointwise loss: $l(a_t, b_t) = 1$ if $a_t \neq b_t$ and 0 otherwise. Thus the R_1-risk measures the expected number of misclassified observations. Recall that (X_0, Y_0, V_0) belongs to the stationary version of (X_t, Y_t, V_t). Define for every measurable A,

$$P^{correct}(A) := \mathbf{P}(X_0 \in A | Y_0 = V_0),$$
$$P^{incorrect}(A) := \mathbf{P}(X_0 \in A | Y_0 \neq V_0).$$

The probability measure $P^{(in)correct}$ can be interpreted as the asymptotic distribution of an observation given the Viterbi alignment at that point is (in)correct. Because of stationarity of X the distribution of every observation is given by

$$\begin{aligned} P(A) &= \mathbf{P}(X_0 \in A) = \mathbf{P}(X_0 \in A | Y_0 = V_0)\mathbf{P}(Y_0 = V_0) + \mathbf{P}(X_0 \in A | Y_0 \neq V_0)\mathbf{P}(Y_0 \neq V_0) \\ &= P^{correct}(A)(1 - R_1) + P^{incorrect}(A)R_1, \end{aligned}$$

where R_1 is the asymptotic risk as defined in Subsection 4.1.1. Thus, the probability $P(incorrect|\cdot)$ can be defined as follows:

$$P(incorrect|A) := \mathbf{P}(Y_0 \neq V_0 | X_0 \in A) = \frac{P^{incorrect}(A)R_1}{P^{correct}(A)(1 - R_1) + P^{incorrect}(A)R_1}.$$

The probability distribution of any observation of X can be written as a weighted sum of emission distributions P_s: $P_X = \sum_{s \in S} \pi_s P_s$. Because the emission distributions P_s have densities f_s with respect to some measure μ, from the equality $P(A) = P^{correct}(A)(1 - R_1) + P^{incorrect}(A)R_1$ it follows that $P^{(in)correct}$ have densities with respect to μ, we denote them by $f^{(in)correct}$. The conditional probability that the Viterbi alignment makes a mistake given that the observation is x, can now be defined as

$$P(incorrect|x) := \mathbf{P}(Y_0 \neq V_0 | x) = \frac{f^{incorrect}(x)R_1}{f^{correct}(x)(1 - R_1) + f^{incorrect}(x)R_1}. \tag{33}$$

Observe that $P(incorrect|x)$ depends only on the model. This implies that once the alignment error probability for a given x is estimated, we can use this value whenever working with the same model. It is also important to emphasize that $P(incorrect|x)$ is a function of both $f^{correct}$ and $f^{incorrect}$, thus it takes into account both the proportions of correctly and incorrectly classified states that emit x. For example, if $f^{incorrect}(x_t)$ and $f^{incorrect}(x_u)$ are both large but $f^{correct}(x_t)$ is much smaller than $f^{correct}(x_u)$, then it makes more sense to seek more information on Y at time t.

One way to estimate $P(incorrect|x)$ is from simulations by using empirical measures. If we would know the true underlying states $Y_1, \ldots, Y_n$ for a given sequence of observations $X_1, \ldots, X_n$, we could after performing the Viterbi segmentation calculate the number of correctly and incorrectly classified states. We could also tally (in)correctly classified states with emissions in A. Thus, we can consider empirical measures $P_n^{correct}$ and $P_n^{incorrect}$ defined as follows:

$$P_n^{correct}(A) := \frac{\sum_{t=1}^n I_{A \times \{0\}}(X_t, l(Y_t, v_t(X^n)))}{\sum_{t=1}^n I_{\{0\}}(l(Y_t, v_t(X^n)))} = \frac{\sum_{t=1}^n I_A(X_t) I_{\{Y_t = \tilde{V}_t^n\}}}{\sum_{t=1}^n I_{\{Y_t = \tilde{V}_t^n\}}},$$

$$P_n^{incorrect}(A) := \frac{\sum_{t=1}^n I_{A \times \{1\}}(X_t, l(Y_t, v_t(X^n)))}{\sum_{t=1}^n I_{\{1\}}(l(Y_t, v_t(X^n)))} = \frac{\sum_{t=1}^n I_A(X_t) I_{\{Y_t \neq \tilde{V}_t^n\}}}{\sum_{t=1}^n I_{\{Y_t \neq \tilde{V}_t^n\}}}.$$

Similarly, we can define the empirical measure $P_n(incorrect|\cdot)$ that calculates the proportion of classification errors given the observation belongs to $A \in \mathcal{B}$:

$$P_n(incorrect|A) := \frac{\sum_{t=1}^{n} I_{A\times\{1\}}(X_t, l(Y_t, \tilde{V}_t^n))}{\sum_{t=1}^{n} I_A(X_t)} = \frac{\sum_{t=1}^{n} I_A(X_t) I_{\{Y_t \neq \tilde{V}_t^n\}}}{\sum_{t=1}^{n} I_A(X_t)}.$$

In practice, the empirical measures defined above are unknown. It follows directly from Theorem 3.2 that the empirical measures $P_n^{(in)correct}$ and $P_n(incorrect|\cdot)$ converge almost surely to $P^{(in)correct}$ and $P(incorrect|\cdot)$ respectively, i.e. for every $A \in \mathcal{B}$,

$$P_n^{(in)correct}(A) \to P^{(in)correct}(A), \qquad P_n(incorrect|A) \to P(incorrect|A) \quad a.s.$$

These convergences allow us to estimate the densities $f^{(in)correct}$, R_1, and hence also $P(incorrect|x)$, when it is difficult to find any of these quantities analytically.

Example 3. This example demonstrates estimation of $f^{correct}$, $f^{incorrect}$ and $P(incorrect|x)$ by simulations. A two-state HMM with emission distributions $\mathcal{N}(3, 2^2)$ and $\mathcal{N}(10, 3^2)$ and transition matrix

$$\mathbb{P} = \begin{pmatrix} 0.3 & 0.7 \\ 0.7 & 0.3 \end{pmatrix}$$

was considered. The estimates of the densities $f^{correct}$, $f^{incorrect}$ and $P(incorrect|x)$ for a sample of size $n = 100000$ are presented in Figure 4 graphs (a), (b) and (c), respectively. The R-package 'HiddenMarkov' (Harte, 2010) was used for these simulations.

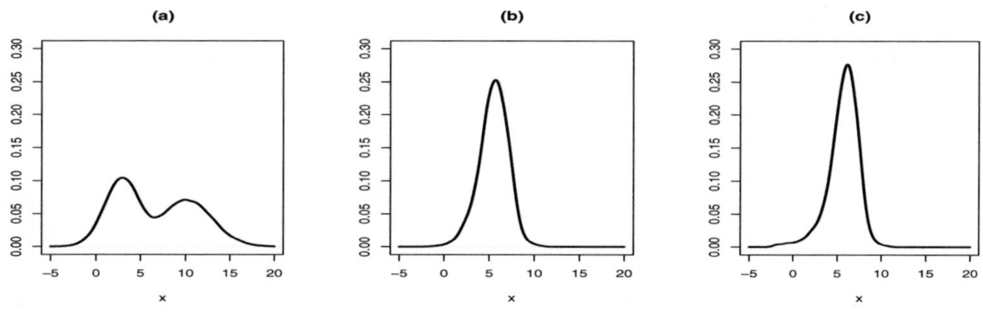

Fig. 4. Estimates of $f^{correct}$, $f^{incorrect}$ and $P(incorrect|x)$.

In (Raag, 2009), the decrease in the number of Viterbi alignment errors when a number of true states are uncovered, is compared for the following three cases: states are revealed randomly, the states with largest conditional point risk are uncovered, the states with the largest misclassification error are revealed. The simulation studies in (Raag, 2009) investigate for example, how the number of mistakes of the constrained alignments depends on the transition probabilities or dependence between the states, and how the decrease in the number of errors is affected by the number of states in the model.

4.4.2 Generalization

Thus far, we have defined the misclassification probability conditionally given a single observation on X. Stationarity makes this probability time invariant. Now we are going to generalize this definition and take into account also information from the neighbors of X. We

will consider a $(2k+1)$-tuple of observations $X_{t-k}, \ldots, X_t, \ldots, X_{t+k}$, $k > 0$. In the following, the tuples $X^k_{-k}, Y^k_{-k}, V^k_{-k}$ are from the doubly-infinite and hence stationary process Z.
Let $A_1 \times \ldots \times A_{2k+1} \in \mathcal{B}^{2k+1}$. By analogy with the single observation case, for $(2k+1)$-tuples of observations we can define the following measures:

$$\begin{aligned} P^{incorrect}(A_1 \times \ldots \times A_{2k+1}) &= \mathbf{P}(X_{-k} \in A_1, \ldots, X_k \in A_{2k+1} | Y_0 \neq V_0) \\ P^{correct}(A_1 \times \ldots \times A_{2k+1}) &= \mathbf{P}(X_{-k} \in A_1, \ldots, X_k \in A_{2k+1} | Y_0 = V_0) \\ P(incorrect | A_1 \times \ldots \times A_{2k+1}) &= \mathbf{P}(Y_0 \neq V_0 | X_{-k} \in A_1, \ldots, X_k \in A_{2k+1}) \end{aligned}$$

Clearly, the decomposition

$$\begin{aligned} \mathbf{P}(X_{-k} \in A_1, \ldots, X_k \in A_{2k+1}) = & \; P^{incorrect}(A_1 \times \ldots \times A_{2k+1}) R_1 \\ & + P^{correct}(A_1 \times \ldots \times A_{2k+1})(1 - R_1) \end{aligned} \tag{34}$$

holds. Since the random variables X_i have densities with respect to μ, it follows that the vector X^k_{-k} has the density with respect to the product measure μ^{2k+1}. From (34) it now follows that the measures $P^{(in)correct}$ have densities $f^{(in)correct}$ with respect to μ^{2k+1} as well so that (33) generalizes as follows:

$$P(incorrect | x^{2k+1}) := \mathbf{P}(Y_0 \neq V_0 | X^k_{-k} = x^{2k+1}) = \frac{f^{incorrect}(x^{2k+1}) R_1}{f^{correct}(x^{2k+1})(1 - R_1) + f^{incorrect}(x^{2k+1}) R_1}.$$

The probability $P(incorrect | x^{2k+1})$ is the asymptotic conditional misclassification probability given the neighbors. It is interesting to note that for some neighborhood this probability can be bigger than 0.5, see Figure 5. Obviously, as in the single observation case, the probability $P(incorrect | x^{2k+1})$ could be estimated by simulation. For this, one can define the empirical measures

$$P_n^{correct}(A_1 \times \ldots \times A_{2k+1}) = \frac{\sum_{t=k+1}^{n-k} I_{\{A_1 \times \ldots \times A_{2k+1}\} \times \{0\}}(X_{t-k}, \ldots, X_{t+k}, l(Y_t, \tilde{V}^n_t))}{\sum_{t=k+1}^{n-k} I_{\{0\}}(l(Y_t, \tilde{V}^n_t))},$$

$$P_n^{incorrect}(A_1 \times \ldots \times A_{2k+1}) = \frac{\sum_{t=k+1}^{n-k} I_{\{A_1 \times \ldots \times A_{2k+1}\} \times \{1\}}(X_{t-k}, \ldots, X_{t+k}, l(Y_t, \tilde{V}^n_t))}{\sum_{t=k+1}^{n-k} I_{\{1\}}(l(Y_t, \tilde{V}^n_t))},$$

$$P_n(incorrect | A_1 \times \ldots \times A_{2k+1}) = \frac{\sum_{t=k+1}^{n-k} I_{\{A_1 \times \ldots \times A_{2k+1}\} \times \{1\}}(X_{t-k}, \ldots, X_{t+k}, l(Y_t, \tilde{V}^n_t))}{\sum_{t=k+1}^{n-k} I_{\{A_1 \times \ldots \times A_{2k+1}\}}(X_{t-k}, \ldots, X_{t+k})}.$$

From Theorem 3.2 it follows again that the empirical measures converge to the corresponding theoretical ones at every Borel set almost surely (hence the measures converge weakly almost surely). Therefore, the densities $f^{(in)correct}$ as well as the probabilities $P(incorrect | x^{2k+1})$ could be estimated.

Example 4. This example illustrates how the misclassification error $P(incorrect | x^{2k+1})$, $k = 1$, depends on the transition probabilities. We consider a two-state HMM, where the process X can take on the values $1, 2, 3, 4$. The transition probability matrix and the emission distributions are as follows:

$$\mathbb{P} = \begin{pmatrix} 1-\epsilon & \epsilon \\ \epsilon & 1-\epsilon \end{pmatrix}, \quad P_1 = (1/2, 1/8, 1/8, 1/4), \quad P_2 = (1/5, 1/5, 1/10, 1/2).$$

For each value of ϵ a chain of $n = 10000$ observations was simulated and the misclassification probabilities $P(incorrect|111)$ and $P(incorrect|141)$ were estimated. To estimate the standard deviations of the estimators, the simulations were replicated 100 times. In Figure 5, the estimated probabilities are plotted together with their $+/-$ one standard deviation bands.

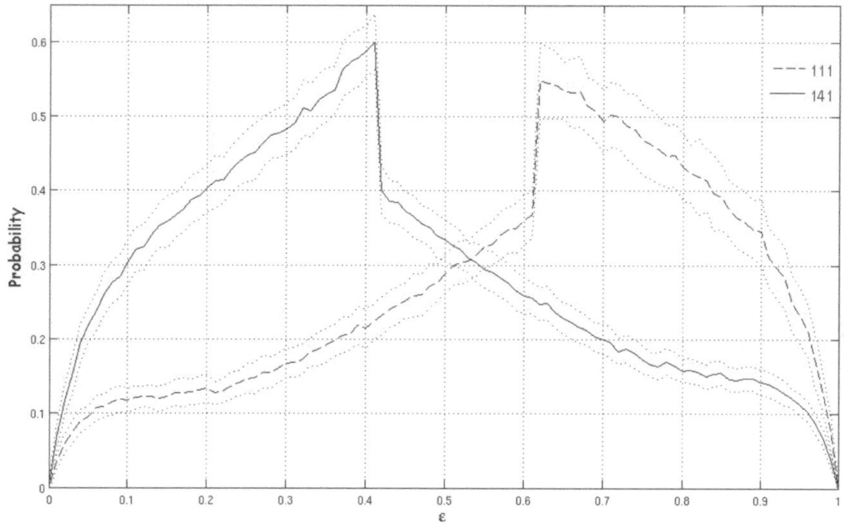

Fig. 5. Estimates of $P(incorrect|111)$ and $P(incorrect|141)$.

Example 5. In the previous example, $P(incorrect|141) \approx 0.6$ for $\epsilon = 0.41$, see Figure 5. Now we consider the HMM of Example 4 for $\epsilon = 0.41$ and study how $P(incorrect|141)$ is affected when we intervene in the Viterbi segmentation process with an increasing intensity. Let m denote the number of occurrences of the word 141 in the simulated process. Then, for example, the intensity 0.2 means that we would intervene in classification the process at $0.2m$ sites. The following four types of interventions were studied:

1) at uniformly distributed random times t, $\tilde{V}_t^n$ was replaced by the opposite state;
2) at uniformly distributed random times t, $\tilde{V}_t^n$ was replaced by the true state Y_t;
3) at the times of occurrence of 141, $\tilde{V}_t^n$ was replaced by the opposite state;
4) at the times of occurrence of 141, $\tilde{V}_t^n$ was replaced by the true state Y_t.

For each thereby constrained Viterbi segmentation, the error rate – the proportion of misclassified states of the constrained alignment – was computed. The results are plotted in Figure 6. The most interesting is of course to see, how the number of Viterbi alignment errors decreases depending on how many true states are revealed.

5. Acknowledgment

J. Lember is supported by Estonian Science Foundation grant 7553.

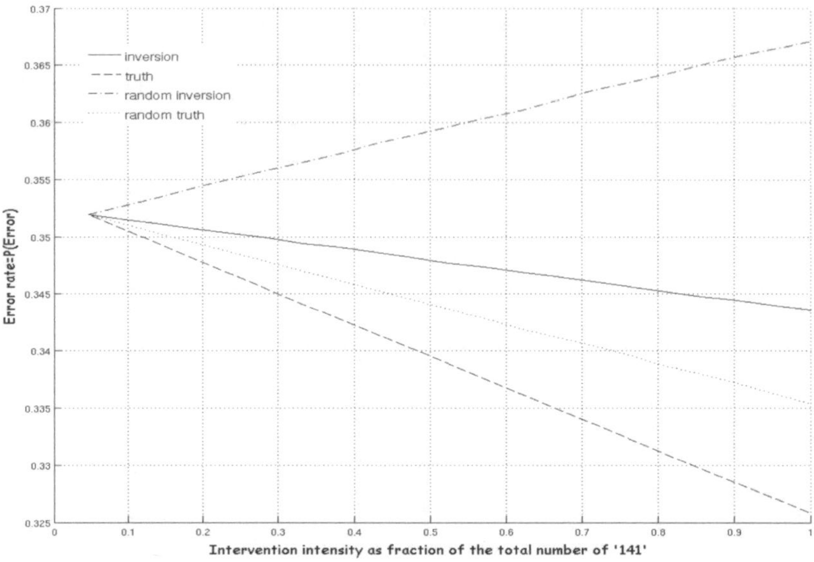

Fig. 6. Misclassification probability as a function of intervention rate.

6. References

Asmussen, S. (2003). *Applied Probability and Queues*, Springer.

Bahl, L., Cocke, J., Jelinek, F. & Raviv, J. (1974). Optimal decoding of linear codes for minimizing symbol error rate (Corresp.), *IEEE Trans. Inform. Theory* 20(2): 284–287.

Bishop, C. (2006). *Pattern Recognition and Machine Learning*, Springer, New York.

Brejová, B., Brown, D. & Vinař, T. (2007). The most probable annotation problem in HMMs and its application to bioinformatics, *J. Comput. Syst. Sci.* 73(7): 1060 – 1077.

Brejová, B., Brown, D. & Vinař, T. (2008). Advances in hidden Markov models for sequence annotation, *in* I. Măndoiu & A. Zelikovsky (eds), *Bioinformatics Algorithms: Techniques and Applications*, Wiley, chapter 4, pp. 55–92.

Brown, D. & Truszkowski, J. (2010). New decoding algorithms for Hidden Markov Models using distance measures on labellings, *BMC Bioinformatics* 11(Suppl 1): S40.

Brushe, G., Mahony, R. & Moore, J. (1998). A soft output hybrid algorithm for ML/MAP sequence estimation, *IEEE Trans. Inform. Theory* 44(7): 3129–3134.

Caliebe, A. (2006). Properties of the maximum a posteriori path estimator in hidden Markov models, *IEEE Trans. Inform. Theory* 52(1): 41–51.

Caliebe, A. & Rösler, U. (2002). Convergence of the maximum a posteriori path estimator in hidden Markov models, *IEEE Trans. Inform. Theory* 48(7): 1750–1758.

Cappé, O., Moulines, E. & Rydén, T. (2005). *Inference in Hidden Markov Models*, Springer Series in Statistics, Springer, New York.

Carvalho, L. & Lawrence, C. (2008). Centroid estimation in discrete high-dimensional spaces with applications in biology, *PNAS* 105(9): 3209–3214. URL: *http://www.pnas.org/content/105/9/3209.abstract*

Chigansky, P. & Ritov, Y. (2010). On the Viterbi process with continuous state space, *Bernoulli*. To appear. URL: *http://arxiv.org/abs/0909.2139v1*

Ephraim, Y. & Merhav, N. (2002). Hidden Markov processes, *IEEE Trans. Inform. Theory* 48(6): 1518–1569. Special issue on Shannon theory: perspective, trends, and applications.

Fariselli, P., Martelli, P. & Casadio, R. (2005). A new decoding algorithm for hidden Markov models improves the prediction of the topology of all-beta membrane proteins, *BMC Bioinformatics* 6(Suppl 4): S12.

Forney, G. (1973). The Viterbi algorithm, *Proc. IEEE* 61(3): 268–278.

Genon-Catalot, V., Jeantheau, T. & Larédo, C. (2000). Stochastic volatility models as hidden Markov models and statistical applications, *Bernoulli* 6(6): 1051–1079.

Gerencser, L. & Molnar-Saska, G. (2002). A new method for the analysis of Hidden Markov model estimates, *Proceedings of the 15th IFAC World Congress*, Vol. 15.

Ghosh, A., Kleiman, E. & Roitershtein, A. (2009). Large deviation bounds for functionals of Viterbi paths. Accepted with revision in IEEE Trans. Inform. Theory.
URL: *http://www.public.iastate.edu*

Gland, F. L. & Mevel, L. (2000). Exponential forgetting and geometric ergodicity in hidden Markov models, *Math. Control Signals Systems* 13: 63 – 93.

Harte, D. (2010). *Package 'Hidden Markov'*, Statistics Research Associates, Wellington, New Zealand.
URL: *http://cran.at.r-project.org/web/packages/HiddenMarkov*

Hayes, J., Cover, T. & Riera, J. (1982). Optimal sequence detection and optimal symbol-by-symbol detection: similar algorithms, *IEEE Transactions on Communications* 30(1): 152–157.

Holmes, I. & Durbin, R. (1998). Dynamic programming alignment accuracy, *J. Comput. Biol.* 5(3): 493–504.

Käll, L., Krogh, A. & Sonnhammer, E. (2005). An HMM posterior decoder for sequence feature prediction that includes homology information, *Bioinformatics* 21(Suppl. 1): i251–i257.

Koloydenko, A., Käärik, M. & Lember, J. (2007). On adjusted Viterbi training, *Acta Appl. Math.* 96(1-3): 309–326.

Koloydenko, A. & Lember, J. (2008). Infinite Viterbi alignments in the two state hidden Markov models, *Acta Comment. Univ. Tartu. Math.* (12): 109–124. Proc. 8th Tartu Conf. Multivariate Statist. June 2007.

Koloydenko, A. & Lember, J. (2010). Hidden path inference, *Technical report*, Mathematics Department, Royal Holloway, University of London. http://personal.rhul.ac.uk/utah/113/pfinds/index.html.

Krogh, A. (1997). Two methods for improving performance of an HMM and their application for gene finding, *ISMB-97 Proceedings*, AAAI, pp. 179–186.

Kuljus, K. & Lember, J. (2010). Asymptotic risks of Viterbi segmentation, http://arxiv.org/abs/1002.3509. submitted.

Lember, J. (2011). On approximation of smoothing probabilities for hidden Markov models, *Statistics and Probability Letters* . To appear.

Lember, J. & Koloydenko, A. (2007). Adjusted Viterbi training: A proof of concept, *Probab. Eng. Inf. Sci.* 21(3): 451–475.

Lember, J. & Koloydenko, A. (2008). The Adjusted Viterbi training for hidden Markov models, *Bernoulli* 14(1): 180–206.

Lember, J. & Koloydenko, A. (2010a). A constructive proof of the existence of Viterbi processes, *IEEE Trans. Inform. Theory* 56(4): 2017–2033.

Lember, J. & Koloydenko, A. (2010b). A generalized risk-based approach to segmentation based on hidden Markov models, http://arxiv.org/abs/1007.3622v1. submitted. URL: *http://arxiv.org/abs/1007.3622v1*

Leroux, B. (1992). Maximum-likelihood estimation for hidden Markov models, *Stochastic Process. Appl.* 40(1): 127–143.

Raag, M. (2009). Risk and errors of Viterbi alignment, Master Thesis. in Estonian.

Rabiner, L. (1989). A tutorial on hidden Markov models and selected applications in speech recognition, *Proc. IEEE* 77(2): 257–286.

Robertson, P., Villebrun, E. & Hoeher, P. (1995). A comparison of optimal and sub-optimal MAP decoding algorithms operating in the log domain, *ICC '95 Seattle, 'Gateway to Globalization', 1995 IEEE International Conference on Communications*, Vol. 2, pp. 1009–1013.

Rue, H. (1995). New loss functions in Bayesian imaging, *J. Am. Stat. Assoc.* 90(431): 900–908. URL: *http://www.jstor.org/stable/2291324*

Viterbi, A. (1967). Error bounds for convolutional codes and an asymptotically optimum decoding algorithm, *IEEE Trans. Inform. Theory* 13(2): 260–269.

Winkler, G. (2003). *Image Analysis, Random Fields and Markov Chain Monte Carlo Methods. A Mathematical Introduction*, Vol. 27 of *Applications of Mathematics (New York)*, Springer-Verlag, Berlin.

4

Classification of Hidden Markov Models: Obtaining Bounds on the Probability of Error and Dealing with Possibly Corrupted Observations

Eleftheria Athanasopoulou[1] and Christoforos N. Hadjicostis[2,1]
[1]*University of Illinois, Urbana-Champaign*
[2]*University of Cyprus, Nicosia*
[1,2]*USA*
[2]*Cyprus*

1. Introduction

In this chapter we consider classification of systems that can be modeled as hidden Markov models (HMMs). Given two[1] known HMMs, we discuss how to build an optimal classifier to determine, with minimal probability of error, which competing model has most likely produced a given sequence of observations. The main issue when dealing with HMMs is that the state cannot be directly observed but, instead, only the (possibly non-unique) output associated with the state and/or the transition of the model can be observed. Apart from describing how to optimally perform the classification task (in a way that minimizes the probability of error), we analyze the classification scheme by characterizing the effectiveness of the classifier in terms of a bound on the associated probability of error. We also analyze a more challenging scenario where the observations are possibly erroneous.

The likelihood that a given observed sequence has been generated from a particular HMM can be calculated as the sum of the probabilities of all possible state sequences that are consistent with the sequence of observations. This can be done using an iterative algorithm similar to the forward algorithm (Rabiner, 1989), which solves the evaluation problem in HMMs and is used frequently in speech recognition applications (Jelinek, 1998), (Rabiner, 1989), (Poritz, 1988). More specifically, given a model and an observed sequence, the evaluation problem consists of computing the probability that the observed sequence was produced by the model. When there are many competing models, these probabilities can be used to choose the model which best matches the observations, in a way that minimizes the probability of error. The forward algorithm is also used in pattern recognition applications (Fu, 1982), (Vidal et al., 2005) to solve the syntax analysis or parsing problem, i.e., to recognize a pattern by classifying it to the appropriate generating grammar, and in bioinformatics (Durbin et al., 1998), (Koski, 2001) to evaluate whether a DNA sequence or a protein sequence belongs to a particular family of sequences.

This chapter begins with an overview of optimal classification schemes for HMMs where the goal is to minimize the probability of error of the classifier. Given a particular sequence of

[1] We can easily generalize the discussion in this chapter to deal with classification of more than two models, but choose to focus on the case of two models for clarity/brevity purposes.

observations, these techniques can be used to choose the HMM that most likely generated the sequence of observations and, in the process, also characterize the associated probability of error (for the given sequence of observations). However, in order to measure the classification capability of the classifier *before* making any observations, one needs to compute the *a priori* probability that the classifier makes an incorrect decision for *any* of the possible sequences of observations. Enumerating all possible sequences of a given length (in order to evaluate their contribution to the probability of error) is prohibitively expensive for long sequences; thus, we describe ways to avoid this computational complexity and obtain an upper bound on the probability that the classifier makes an error without having to enumerate all possible output sequences. Specifically, we present a constructive approach that bounds the probability of error as a function of the observation step. We also discuss necessary and sufficient conditions for this bound on the probability of error to go to zero as the number of observations increases.
After obtaining bounds on the probability of erroneous classification, we consider the additional challenge that the observed sequence is corrupted, due to noise coming from sensor malfunctions, communication limitations, or other adversarial conditions. For example, depending on the underlying application, the information that the sensors provide may be corrupted due to inaccurate measurements, limited resolution, or degraded sensor performance (due to aging or hardware failures). We consider unreliable sensors that may cause outputs to be deleted, inserted, substituted or transposed with certain known probabilities. Under such sensor malfunctions, the length of the observed sequence will generally not equal the length of the output sequence and, in fact, several output sequences may correspond to a given observed sequence. Thus, one would need to first identify all possible state sequences and the probabilities with which they agree with *both* the underlying model and the observations (after allowing, of course, for sensor failures). In particular, if symbols in the output sequence can be *deleted*, there may be an infinite number of output sequences that agree with a given observed sequence, which makes the standard forward algorithm inapplicable for classification. This inability of the standard forward algorithm can be overcome via an iterative algorithm that allows us to efficiently compute the probability that a certain model matches the observed sequence: each time a new observation is made, the algorithm simply updates the information it keeps track of and outputs on demand the probability that a given model has produced the sequence observed so far. The iterative algorithm we describe relates to (and generalizes) iterative algorithms for the evaluation problem in HMMs (Rabiner, 1989), the parsing problem in probabilistic automata (PA) (Fu, 1982), (Vidal et al., 2005), and the trellis-based decoding of variable length codes (VLC) (Bauer and Hagenauer, 2000), (Guyader et al., 2001), all of which can be modified to deal with some types of sensor failures but are not quite as general (or effective) as the iterative algorithm we describe.
We motivate the study of the above problems (bounding the probability of classification error and dealing with corrupted observations) using examples from the areas of failure diagnosis and computational biology. For instance, the problem of failure diagnosis in systems that can be modeled as finite state machines (FSMs) with known input statistics can be converted to the problem of classification of HMMs (Athanasopoulou, 2007). FSMs form a particular class of discrete event systems (DESs) that have discrete state spaces and whose evolution is event-driven, i.e., only the occurrence of discrete events forces the systems to take state transitions. Any large scale dynamic system, such as a computer system, a telecommunication network, a sensor network, a manufacturing system, a chemical process or a semiconductor manufacturing process, can be modeled as an FSM at some level of abstraction. In addition,

network protocols that describe the rules and conditions for exchanging information in distributed environments can also be modeled by FSMs. Given two known FSMs (one corresponding to the fault-free version of the underlying system and the other corresponding to a faulty version of the system) and an associated input distribution, a classifier (called diagnoser in this case) can be used to determine which of the two competing models has most likely produced a given sequence of observations. Work in this area by the authors has appeared in (Athanasopoulou et al., 2010), (Athanasopoulou and Hadjicostis, 2008). HMMs are also used in the area of computational biology to capture the behavior of DNA sequences; as we will see via examples in this chapter, these models can then be used to perform classification in order to characterize various properties of interest in DNA sequences.

2. Preliminaries and notation: FSMs, Markov chains, and hidden Markov models

A finite state machine (FSM) is a four-tuple (Q, X, δ, q_0), where $Q = \{0, 1, 2, ..., |Q| - 1\}$ is the finite set of states; X is the finite set of inputs; δ is the state transition function; and q_0 is the initial state. The FSMs we consider here are event-driven and we use n to denote the time epoch between the occurrence of the nth and $(n+1)^{st}$ input. The state $Q[n+1]$ of the FSM at time epoch $n+1$ is specified by its state $Q[n]$ at time epoch n and its input $X[n+1]$ via the state transition function δ as $Q[n+1] = \delta(Q[n], X[n+1])$. A finite state machine (FSM) with outputs is described by a six-tuple $(Q, X, Y, \delta, \lambda, q_0)$, where (Q, X, δ, q_0) is an FSM; Y is the finite set of outputs; and λ is the output function. The output $Y[n+1]$ is determined by the state $Q[n]$ and the input $X[n+1]$ via the output function, i.e., $Y[n+1] = \lambda(Q[n], X[n+1])$, which maps a state and input pair to an output from the finite set of outputs Y.

We denote a time homogeneous Markov chain by $(Q, \Delta, \pi[0])$, where $Q = \{0, 1, 2, ..., |Q| - 1\}$ is the finite set of states; $\pi[0]$ is the initial state probability distribution vector; and Δ captures the state transition probabilities, i.e., $\Delta(q, q') = P(Q[n+1] = q' \mid Q[n] = q)$, for $q, q' \in Q$. If we denote the state transition probabilities by $a_{jk} = P\{(Q[n+1] = j) \mid (Q[n] = k)\}$, the state transition matrix of the Markov chain associated with the given system is $\mathcal{A} = (a_{jk})_{j,k=0,1,...,|Q|-1}$. (To keep the notation clean, the rows and columns of all matrices are indexed starting from 0 and not 1.) The state transition matrix $\mathcal{A}$ captures how state probabilities evolve in time via the evolution equation $\pi[n+1] = \mathcal{A}\pi[n]$, for $n = 0, 1, 2, \ldots$. Here, $\pi[n]$ is a $|Q|$-dimensional vector, whose j^{th} entry denotes the probability that the Markov chain is in state j at time epoch n. In our development later on, we will find it useful to define the notion of a time homogeneous Markov chain with inputs, which we denote by $(Q, X, \Delta, \pi[0])$; here, $Q = \{0, 1, 2, ..., |Q| - 1\}$ is the finite set of states; X is the finite set of inputs; $\pi[0]$ is the initial state probability distribution vector; and Δ captures the state and input transition probabilities, i.e., $\Delta(q, x_i, q') = P(Q[n+1] = q' \mid Q[n] = q, X[n+1] = x_i)$, for $q, q' \in Q$, $x_i \in X$.

An HMM is described by a five-tuple $(Q, Y, \Delta, \Lambda, \boldsymbol{\rho}[0])$, where $Q = \{0, 1, 2, ..., |Q| - 1\}$ is the finite set of states; Y is the finite set of outputs; Δ captures the state transition probabilities; Λ captures the output probabilities associated with transitions; and $\boldsymbol{\rho}[0]$ is the initial state probability distribution vector. More specifically, for $q, q' \in Q$ and $\sigma \in Y$, the state transition probabilities are given by $\Delta(q, q') = P(Q[n+1] = q' \mid Q[n] = q)$ and the output probabilities associated with transitions are given by $\Lambda(q, \sigma, q') = P(Q[n+1] = q', Y[n+1] = \sigma \mid Q[n] = q)$, where Λ denotes the output function that assigns a probability to the output σ associated with the transition from state $Q[n]$ to state $Q[n+1]$. We define the $|Q| \times |Q|$ matrix $\mathcal{A}_\sigma$, associated with output $\sigma \in Y$ of the HMM, as follows: the entry at the $(j,k)^{th}$ position of $\mathcal{A}_\sigma$ captures the probability of a transition from state k to state j that produces output σ. Note that

$\sum_{\sigma \in Y} \mathcal{A}_\sigma = \mathcal{A}$, i.e., the transition matrix whose $(j,k)^{th}$ entry denotes the probability of taking a transition from state k to state j. The joint probability of the state at step n and the observation sequence $y[1], \ldots, y[n]$ is captured by the vector $\boldsymbol{\rho}[n]$ where the entry $\boldsymbol{\rho}[n](j)$ denotes the probability that the HMM is in state j at step n and the sequence $y_1^n = y[1], \ldots, y[n]$ has been observed. More formally, $\boldsymbol{\rho}[n](j) = P(Q[n] = j, Y_1^n = y_1^n)$ (note that $\boldsymbol{\rho}$ is not necessarily a probability vector).

3. Posterior probability calculation with uncorrupted observations

In this section, we examine the simplest case where no sensor failures are present. It will become apparent later that this case does not involve any complications, such as loops in the trellis diagram, and the calculations can be easily performed iteratively by a forward-like algorithm.

Given the observation sequence $Y_1^L = y_1^L =< y[1], y[2], ..., y[L] >$ and two candidate HMMs S_1 and S_2 (together with their initial state probability distributions and their *prior* probabilities P_1 and $P_2 = 1 - P_1$), the classifier that minimizes the probability of error needs to implement the maximum *a posteriori* probability (MAP) rule by comparing $P(S_1 \mid y_1^L) \underset{<}{>} P(S_2 \mid y_1^L) \Rightarrow \frac{P(y_1^L \mid S_1)}{P(y_1^L \mid S_2)} \underset{<}{>} \frac{P_2}{P_1}$, and deciding in favor of S_1 (S_2) if the left (right) quantity is larger.

To calculate the probability $P(y_1^L \mid S)$ of the observed sequence given a particular model S, we first capture the evolution of S as a function of time for a given observed sequence by constructing the trellis diagram of S. The state sequences that agree with the observed sequence (consistent sequences) are those that start from any valid initial state and end at any final state while ensuring that the output at each step n matches the observed output $y[n]$. Due to the Markovian property, the probability of a specific consistent state sequence can be easily calculated as the product of the initial state probability and the state transition probabilities at each time step. Thus, to calculate the probability $P(y_1^L \mid S)$ we need to first identify all consistent sequences and their probabilities and then sum up the total probability.

The computation of $P(y_1^L \mid S)$ is not iterative in respect to the number of observation steps, hence it is not amenable for online monitoring. To make the computation iterative we can use a forward-like algorithm. For candidate HMM S, we can update $\boldsymbol{\rho}_S$ iteratively as

$$\boldsymbol{\rho}_S[n+1] = \mathcal{A}_{S,y[n+1]} \boldsymbol{\rho}_S[n], \quad n = 0, 1, ..., L-1,$$

where $\boldsymbol{\rho}_S[0]$ is taken to be the probability distribution of the initial states for model S and $\mathcal{A}_{S,y[n+1]}$ is the matrix that describes the state transition probabilities under the output observed at time epoch $n+1$. If L is the last step, the probability that the observation sequence was produced by FSM S is equal to the sum of the entries of $\boldsymbol{\rho}_S[L]$, i.e., $P(y_1^L \mid S) = \sum_{j=0}^{|Q|-1} \boldsymbol{\rho}_S[L](j)$. This iterative algorithm is the standard forward algorithm that is used to solve the evaluation problem in HMMs.

Example 1.a: In this example we consider the finite state machine (FSM) S with known input distribution shown on the left of Figure 1: S has four states $Q = \{0, 1, 2, 3\}$, three inputs $X = \{x_1, x_2, x_3\}$, and three outputs $Y = \{a, b, c\}$. Each transition is labeled as $x_i \mid \sigma$, where $x_i \in X$ denotes the input that drives the FSM and $\sigma \in Y$ denotes the associated output produced by the FSM. If we assign equal prior probabilities to the inputs, i.e., if each input has probability $1/3$ of occurring, the resulting HMM is shown on the right of Figure 1: each transition in the HMM is labeled as $p \mid \sigma$, where p denotes the probability of the transition and $\sigma \in Y$ denotes the output produced.

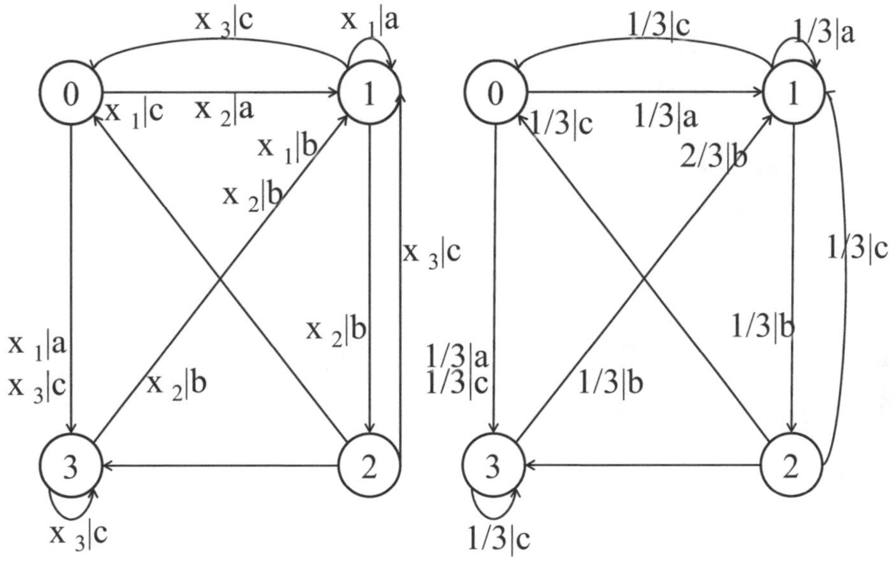

Fig. 1. State transition diagram of FSM S of Example 1 (left) and its corresponding HMM (right).

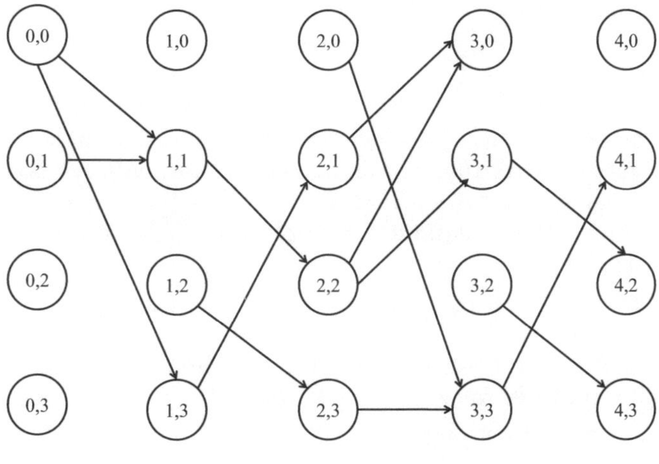

Fig. 2. Trellis diagram corresponding to S of Example 1 for observation sequence $y_1^4 =< abcb >$ (transition probabilities are not included for clarity).

Suppose that we monitor S for $L = 4$ steps and we observe the sequence $y_1^4 =< abcb >$. The corresponding trellis diagram is shown in Figure 2 (pairs of states that are associated with zero transition probabilities are not connected in the diagram and transition probabilities are

n	$\rho_S^T[n]$				$P(y_1^n \mid S)$
0	[0.2500	0.2500	0.2500	0.2500]	1
1	[0	0.1667	0	0.0833]	0.2500
2	[0	0.0556	0.0556	0]	0.1112
3	[0.0370	0.0185	0	0]	0.0555
4	[0	0	0.0062	0]	0.0062

Table 1. Iterative calculations for vector $\boldsymbol{\rho}_S$ for the sequence of observations $y_1^4 =< abcb >$.

not included for clarity of presentation). Each state of the trellis diagram is identified by a pair (m, j), where $m = 0, 1, 2, 3, 4$ denotes the observation step and $j \in \{0, 1, 2, 3\}$ denotes the state of S. For example, the probability of a transition from state $(0, 0)$ to state $(1, 3)$ producing output a is $1/3$. Assuming uniform initial distribution, the probability that the observations were produced by S can be calculated iteratively and is given by $P(y_1^4 \mid S) = 0.0062$. Note that this probability is expected to go down as the number of observations increases. Table 1 shows the sequence of iterations in order to obtain the vector $\boldsymbol{\rho}_S[n]$ as observations are coming in. □

Example 1.b:

As another example, we consider a problem from computational biology. Specifically, we concentrate on identifying CpG islands in a DNA sequence, where the alphabet consists of the four nucleotides A, C, G, T (Durbin et al., 1998). Regions that are characterized by higher than usual concentration of CpG dinucleotides (more generally, higher concentration of C and G nucleotides) are called CpG islands.[2] It is important to be able to identify these regions because they typically appear around the promoters or start regions of many genes (Fatemi et al., 2005). Consider the following task: given a short stretch of genomic sequence, can we decide whether it comes from a CpG island or not? For illustration purposes, we assume that we are only capable of observing two output symbols, α and β, as follows: we observe the symbol α when the true output is A or C and we observe the symbol β when the true output is G or T (this could be used, for instance, to model situations where instruments are unable to distinguish between specific pairs of nucleotides). We assume that we are given two HMMs, CpG^+ and CpG^-, with known structure, which model respectively regions with and without CpG islands. As shown in Figure 3, CpG^+ and CpG^- have four states $Q = \{A, C, G, T\}$, and two outputs $Y = \{\alpha, \beta\}$. We also assume (for simplicity) that the *priors* of the two models are $p_{CpG^+} = p_{CpG^-} = 0.5$.

Suppose that we observe the sequence $y_1^4 =< \alpha\beta\alpha\beta >$ and our goal is to determine which of the two HMMs (CpG^+ or CpG^-) has most likely generated the observed sequence. According to the previously described iterative algorithm, we need to first define the transition probability matrices for each symbol for each one of the two HMMs ($\mathcal{A}_{CpG^+,\alpha}$, $\mathcal{A}_{CpG^+,\beta}$, $\mathcal{A}_{CpG^-,\alpha}$, $\mathcal{A}_{CpG^-,\beta}$); for example, for HMM CpG^+, we have

$$\mathcal{A}_{CpG^+,\alpha} = \begin{bmatrix} & A & C & G & T \\ A & 0.18 & 0.17 & 0.16 & 0.08 \\ C & 0.27 & 0.37 & 0.34 & 0.36 \\ G & 0 & 0 & 0 & 0 \\ T & 0 & 0 & 0 & 0 \end{bmatrix}$$

[2] The formal definition of a CpG island is a region with at least 200 base pairs that has a GC percentage that is greater than 50% and an observed/expected CpG ratio that is greater than 60 (Gardiner-Garden and Frommer, 1987).

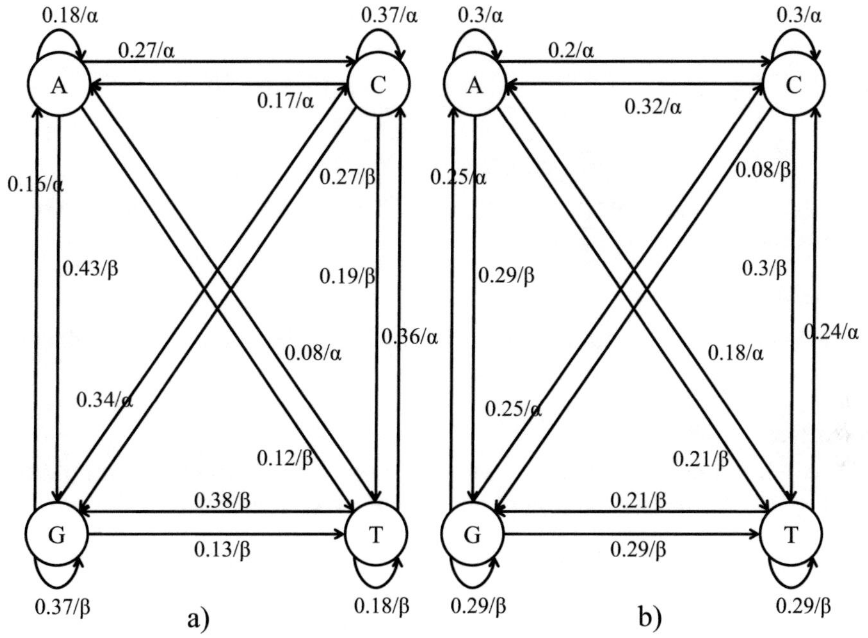

Fig. 3. State transition diagram of the two HMMs used to identify regions with or without CpG islands in Example 1.b: (a) CpG^+ (left), and (b) CpG^- (right).

n	$\rho_+^T[n]$				$P(y_1^n \mid CpG^+)$
0	[0.2500	0.2500	0.2500	0.2500]	1
1	[0.1475	0.3350	0	0]	0.4825
2	[0	0	0.1539	0.0814]	0.2353
3	[0.0311	0.0816	0	0]	0.1127
4	[0	0	0.0354	0.0192]	0.0546

Table 2. Iterative calculations for posterior probabilities for the sequence of observations $y_1^4 =< \alpha\beta\alpha\beta >$ for the model CpG^+.

Given our previous discussion, we can calculate

$$\begin{aligned} \text{æ}_+[4] &= \mathcal{A}_{CpG^+,\beta} \cdot \mathcal{A}_{CpG^+,\alpha} \cdot \mathcal{A}_{CpG^+,\beta} \cdot \mathcal{A}_{CpG^+,\alpha} \cdot \boldsymbol{\rho}_{CpG^+}[0] \\ \text{æ}_-[4] &= \mathcal{A}_{CpG^-,\beta} \cdot \mathcal{A}_{CpG^-,\alpha} \cdot \mathcal{A}_{CpG^-,\beta} \cdot \mathcal{A}_{CpG^-,\alpha} \cdot \boldsymbol{\rho}_{CpG^-}[0] \end{aligned}$$

and obtain $P(y_1^4 \mid CpG^+) = 0.0546$ and $P(y_1^4 \mid CpG^-) = 0.0445$. We can now apply the MAP rule $\frac{P(y_1^4 \mid CpG^+)}{P(y_1^4 \mid CpG^-)} \gtrless \frac{p_{CpG^+}}{p_{CpG^-}}$ which reduces to $\frac{0.0546}{0.0445} \gtrless 1$, and decide in favor of CpG^+ since the left quantity is larger. Tables 2 and 3 show the various values obtained for the vectors $\boldsymbol{\rho}_+$ and $\boldsymbol{\rho}_-$ (corresponding to CpG^+ and CpG^- respectively) during the iteration.

n	$\rho_-^T[n]$				$P(y_1^n \mid CpG^-)$
0	[0.2500	0.2500	0.2500	0.2500]	1
1	[0.2625	0.2475	0	0]	0.51
2	[0	0	0.0959	0.1294]	0.2253
3	[0.0473	0.0550	0	0]	0.1023
4	[0	0	0.0181	0.0264]	0.0445

Table 3. Iterative calculations for posterior probabilities for the sequence of observations $y_1^4 =< \alpha\beta\alpha\beta >$ for the model CpG^-.

4. Probability of error

In this section we focus on bounding the probability of classification error, i.e., the probability that the classifier makes the incorrect decision.

4.1 Preliminaries

We start by conditioning on a given observation sequence y_1^L and we compute online the conditional probability that the classifier makes an incorrect decision as follows:

$$\begin{aligned} P(\text{error at } L \mid y_1^L) &= P(\text{decide } S_2 \text{ at } L,\ S_1 \mid y_1^L) + P(\text{decide } S_1 \text{ at } L,\ S_2 \mid y_1^L) \\ &= P(\text{decide } S_2 \text{ at } L \mid S_1,\ y_1^L) \cdot P(S_1 \mid y_1^L) + \\ &\quad P(\text{decide } S_1 \text{ at } L \mid S_2,\ y_1^L) \cdot P(S_2 \mid y_1^L) \\ &= \min\{P(S_2 \mid y_1^L),\ P(S_1 \mid y_1^L)\}. \end{aligned}$$

Since both *posteriors* are already computed (for use in the MAP rule comparison), the probability of error given the observation sequence y_1^n as a function of n can be easily computed online along with the maximum likelihood decision. At each step, the classifier chooses the model with the larger *posterior* and makes an error with probability equal to the *posterior* of the other model (of course, the *posteriors* need to be normalized so that they sum up to one).

Our goal is to find a measure of the classification capability of the classifier *a priori*, i.e., before any observation is made. The probability of error at step L is given by

$$P(\text{error at } L) = \sum_{y_1^L} \left(P(y_1^L) \cdot \min\{P(S_2 \mid y_1^L),\ P(S_1 \mid y_1^L)\} \right).$$

To perform such computation, we need to find each possible observation sequence y_1^L, along with its probability of occurring, and use it to compute the *posterior* of each model conditioned on this observation sequence. To avoid the possibly prohibitively high computational complexity (especially for large L) we will focus on obtaining an easily computable upper bound and then show that, under certain conditions on the underlying HMMs, this bound on the probability of error decays exponentially to zero with the number of observation steps L.

A classifier that uses the MAP rule necessarily chooses model S_1 (S_2) if the observation sequence cannot be produced by S_2 (S_1), with no risk of making an incorrect decision. However, if the observation sequence can be produced by both models, the classifier chooses the model with the highest *posterior*, thereby risking to make an incorrect decision. The bound we obtain considers the worst case scenario where, when both models are consistent with the observation sequence y_1^L (i.e., when $P(S_i \mid y_1^L) > 0$ for $i = 1$ and 2), the classifier is assumed to always make the incorrect decision; specifically, one has

$$\begin{aligned}
P(\text{error at } L) &= \sum_{y_1^L} \min\{P(S_1 \mid y_1^L), P(S_2 \mid y_1^L)\} \cdot P(y_1^L) \\
&= 1 - \sum_{y_1^L} \max\{P(S_1 \mid y_1^L), P(S_2 \mid y_1^L)\} \cdot P(y_1^L) \\
&= 1 - \sum_{\substack{y_1^L : P(S_i \mid y_1^L)=0 \\ \text{for } i=1 \text{ or } 2}} P(y_1^L) - \sum_{\substack{y_1^L : P(S_i \mid y_1^L)>0 \\ \text{for } i=1 \text{ and } 2}} \max\{P(S_1 \mid y_1^L), P(S_2 \mid y_1^L)\} \cdot P(y_1^L) \\
&\leq 1 - \sum_{\substack{y_1^L : P(S_i \mid y_1^L)=0 \\ \text{for } i=1 \text{ or } 2}} P(y_1^L) - \frac{1}{2} \sum_{\substack{y_1^L : P(S_i \mid y_1^L)>0 \\ \text{for } i=1 \text{ and } 2}} P(y_1^L) \\
&= 1 - \sum_{\substack{y_1^L : P(S_i \mid y_1^L)=0 \\ \text{for } i=1 \text{ or } 2}} P(y_1^L) - \frac{1}{2}\Big(1 - \sum_{\substack{y_1^L : P(S_i \mid y_1^L)=0 \\ \text{for } i=1 \text{ or } 2}} P(y_1^L)\Big) \\
&= \tfrac{1}{2}\Big(1 - \sum_{\substack{y_1^L : P(S_i \mid y_1^L)=0 \\ \text{for } i=1 \text{ or } 2}} P(y_1^L)\Big) \\
&= \tfrac{1}{2}\Big(1 - P_1 \sum_{\substack{y_1^L : S_2 \\ \text{incons.}}} P(y_1^L \mid S_1) - P_2 \sum_{\substack{y_1^L : S_1 \\ \text{incons.}}} P(y_1^L \mid S_2)\Big).
\end{aligned}$$

In the previous formulas we used the fact that, when both S_1 and S_2 are consistent with the observations, then the maximum of their *posteriors* is greater than or equal to half.

4.2 Calculation of bound on probability of error

Initially, our objective is to capture the set of observation sequences that are consistent with S_1 but not with S_2 (or sequences that are consistent with S_2 but not with S_1), i.e., to capture the set of output sequences that can be produced by S_1 but not by S_2 (or the other way around). Once we have identified this set of output sequences, we need to find its probability of occurring. First, we construct the Markov chain $S_{12|1}$ (respectively MC $S_{12|2}$) to help us compute the bound on the probability that S_2 (respectively S_1) becomes inconsistent with the observations, given that the actual model is S_1 (respectively S_2). In particular, we explain how to construct MC $S_{12|1}$ starting from HMMs S_1 and S_2 in the following five steps (a similar procedure can be followed to construct MC $S_{12|2}$).

Step 1. Construct FSMs S_{1ND} and S_{2ND} from HMMs S_1 and S_2 respectively.

The set of input sequences that S_{iND} accepts is the set of output sequences that S_i is capable of producing (where $i = 1, 2$). Recall that HMM S_i is denoted by $(Q_i, Y, \Delta_i, \Lambda_i, \boldsymbol{\rho}_i[0])$ (without loss of generality[3] we assume that $Y_1 = Y_2 = Y$). Ignoring the transition probabilities of HMM S_i, we build the possibly nondeterministic FSM S_{iND} which has the same set of states as S_i and its set of inputs is equal to the set of outputs of S_i. The state transition functionality of S_{iND} is determined by the output functionality of S_i which is captured by Λ_i (although the probabilities are not important at this point). More formally, FSM S_{iND} is denoted by $S_{iND} = (Q_{iND}, X_{iND}, \delta_{iND}, q_{iND0})$, where $Q_{iND} = Q_i$; $X_{iND} = Y$; $q_{iND0} = \{j \mid \boldsymbol{\rho}_i[0](j) > 0\}$ (i.e., q_{iND0} includes all states of S_i with nonzero initial probability); and $\delta_{iND}(q_{iND}, \sigma) = \{q'_{iND} \in Q_{iND} \mid \Lambda_i(q_{iND}, \sigma, q'_{iND}) > 0\}$.

Step 2. Construct FSMs S_{1D} and S_{2D} from FSMs S_{1ND} and S_{2ND} respectively.

We can think of FSM S_{iD} as an observer for S_i because each state of S_{iD} contains the set of

[3] We can always redefine $Y = Y_1 \cup Y_2$ to be the output of both machines if Y_1 and Y_2 are different.

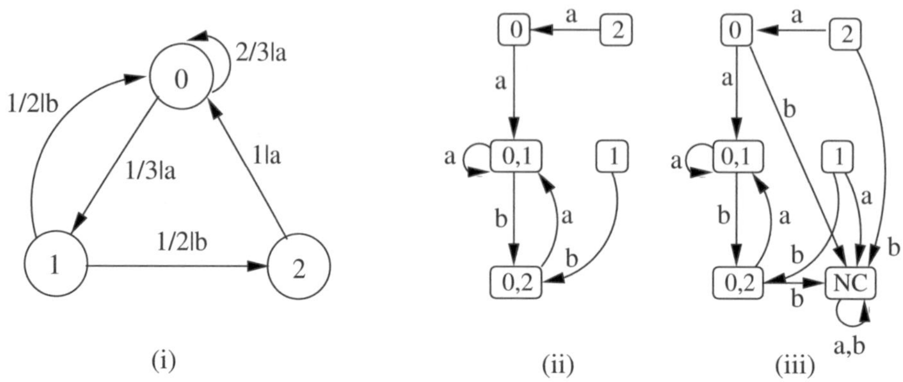

Fig. 4. State transition diagrams of (i) HMM S_1, (ii) FSM S_{1D}, and (iii) FSM S_{1DNC} of Example 2.

states that S_i may be in given the observation sequence. The number of states of S_{iD}, i.e., the deterministic version of S_{iND} could be as high as $2^{|Q_{iND}|}$. Although this may raise complexity issues, it is very common in practical scenarios for S_{iD} to have roughly the same number of states as S_{iND} (Hopcroft et al., 2001). Following the procedure of subset construction (Hopcroft et al., 2001) we use S_{iND} to build the deterministic, equivalent machine $S_{iD} = (Q_{iD}, X_{iD}, \delta_{iD}, q_{iD0})$, where Q_{iD} contains subsets of states in the set Q_i (recall that $Q_{iND} = Q_i$); the set of inputs are the same as the set of inputs of S_{iND}, i.e., $X_{iD} = Y$ (recall that $X_i = Y$); $q_{iD0} = q_{i0}$; and δ_{iD} is determined from S_{iND} by the procedure of subset construction, i.e., for $Q_S \subset Q_i$ and $\sigma \in Y$, $\delta_{iD}(Q_S, \sigma) = \{k \mid \exists j \in Q_S, k \in \delta_{iND}(j, \sigma)\}$.

Step 3. Construct FSM S_{2DNC} from FSM S_{2ND}.

Next, we append the inconsistent state NC to S_{2D} to obtain FSM S_{2DNC}. As mentioned earlier, FSM S_{2D} accepts all sequences that can be produced by S_2. FSM S_{2DNC} accepts not only the sequences that can be produced by S_2, but also all other sequences (that cannot be produced by S_2). In fact, all sequences that cannot be produced by S_2 will lead S_{2DNC} to its inconsistent state NC. More specifically, $S_{2DNC} = (Q_{2DNC}, X_{2DNC}, \delta_{2DNC}, q_{2DNC0})$, where $Q_{2DNC} = Q_{2D} \cup \{NC\}$; $X_{2DNC} = Y$; $q_{2DNC0} = q_{2D0}$ and δ_{2DNC} is given by $\delta_{2DNC}(q_{2DNC}, \sigma) =$

$$\begin{cases} \delta_{2D}(q_{2DNC}, \sigma), & \text{if } q_{2DNC} \neq NC, \delta_{2D}(q_{2DNC}, \sigma) \neq \emptyset, \\ NC, & \text{otherwise.} \end{cases}$$

Step 4. Construct FSM S_{1D2DNC} from FSMs S_{1D} and S_{2DNC}.

To capture the set of observations that can be produced by S_1 but not by S_2, we need to build the product FSM S_{1D2DNC}. FSM S_{1D2DNC} accepts all sequences that can be produced by S_1; from all of these sequences, the ones that cannot be produced by S_2 lead S_{1D2DNC} to a state of the form $\{q_{1D}, NC\}$. More specifically, $S_{1D2DNC} = S_{1D} \times S_{2DNC}$, i.e., $S_{1D2DNC} = (Q_{1D2DNC}, X_{1D2DNC}, \delta_{1D2DNC}, q_{0,1D2DNC})$, where $Q_{1D2DNC} = Q_{1D} \times Q_{2DNC}$; $X_{1D2DNC} = Y$ (recall that $X_{1D} = X_{2DNC} = Y$); $q_{0,1D2DNC} = q_{0,1D} \times q_{0,2DNC}$; and δ_{1D2DNC} is given by $\delta_{1D2DNC}(\{q_{1D}, q_{2DNC}\}, \sigma) = \{\delta_{1D}(q_{1D}, \sigma), \delta_{2DNC}(q_{2DNC}, \sigma)\}$, $\sigma \in Y$. Note that $\delta_{1D2DNC}(\{q_{1D}, q_{2DNC}\}, \sigma)$ is undefined if $\delta_{1D}(q_{1D}, \sigma)$ is undefined.

Step 5. Construct MC $S_{12|1}$ from FSM S_{1D2DNC} or from S_1, S_{1D}, and S_{2D}.

To compute the probabilities of the sequences captured by S_{1D2DNC} we construct the Markov chain with inputs $S_{12|1} = (Q_{12|1}\ X_{12|1}, \Delta_{12|1}, \rho_{12|1}[0])$, where $Q_{12|1} = Q_1 \times Q_{1D2DNC}$; $X_{12|1} =$

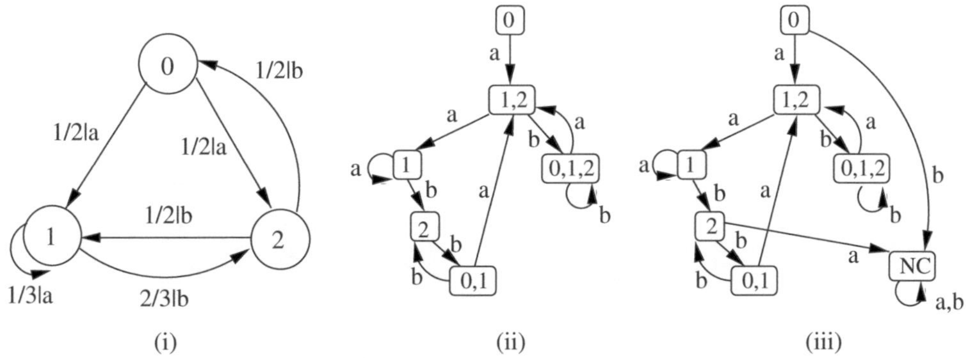

Fig. 5. State transition diagrams of (i) HMM S_2, (ii) FSM S_{2D}, and (iii) FSM S_{2DNC} of Example 2.

Y; $\rho_{12|1}[0](\{q_1, q_{0,1D2DNC}\}) = \rho_1[0](q_1)$, for every $q_1 \in Q_1$ and zero otherwise;[4] and $\Delta_{12|1}$ is given by $\Delta_{12|1}$ $(\{q_1, q_{1D}, q_{2DNC}\}, \sigma, \{q_1', \delta_{1D}(q_{1D}, \sigma), \delta_{2DNC}(q_{2DNC}, \sigma)\}) = \Lambda_1(q_1, \sigma, q_1')$ for all $\sigma \in Y$ such that $\delta_{1D}(q_{1D}, \sigma) \neq \emptyset$. We group all states of the form $\{q_1, q_{1D}, NC\}$ in one new state and call it NC; we also add a self-loop at state NC with probability one.

Alternatively we can build MC $S_{12|1}$ from S_1, S_{1D}, and S_{2D} as follows: $S_{12|1} = (Q_{12|1}, X_{12|1}, \Delta_{12|1}, \rho_{12|1}[0])$, where $Q_{12|1} = Q_1 \times Q_{1D} \times Q_{2D}$; $X_{12|1} = Y$; $\rho_{12|1}[0](\{q_1, q_{1D}, q_{2D}\}) = \rho_1[0](q_1)$, for every $q_1 \in Q_1$, $q_{1D} \in Q_{1D}$, and $q_{2D} \in Q_{2D}$; and $\Delta_{12|1}$ is given by $\Delta_{12|1}(\{q_1, q_{1D}, q_{2DNC}\}, \sigma, \{q_1', \delta_{1D}(q_{1D}, \sigma), \delta_{2DNC}(q_{2DNC}, \sigma)\}) = \Lambda_1(q_1, \sigma, q_1')$, for all $\sigma \in Y$ such that $\delta_{1D}(q_{1D}, \sigma) \neq \emptyset$ and $\delta_{2D}(q_{2D}, \sigma) \neq \emptyset$ or $\Delta_{12|1}$ $(\{q_1, q_{1D}, q_{2DNC}\}, \sigma, \{q_1', \delta_{1D}(q_{1D}, \sigma), NC\}) = \Lambda_1(q_1, \sigma, q_1')$, for all $\sigma \in Y$ such that $\delta_{1D}(q_{1D}, \sigma) \neq \emptyset$ and $\delta_{2D}(q_{2D}, \sigma) = \emptyset$. (Note that for all q_{2D} and all σ we have $\delta_{1D}(q_{1D}, \sigma) \neq \emptyset$.) As mentioned before, we group all states of the form $\{q_1, q_{1D}, NC\}$ in one new state and call it NC; then we add a self-loop at state NC with probability one.

Notice that any path in $S_{12|1}$ that ends up in state NC represents a sequence that can be produced by S_1 but not by S_2; the probability of such path is easily computed using the Markovian property. Recall that our objective is to calculate the probability that HMM S_2 is inconsistent with the observations given that the observations are produced by S_1 (i.e., we would like to calculate $\sum_{y_1^L : S_2 \text{ incons.}} P(y_1^L \mid S_1)$). Therefore, we are interested in the probability of $S_{12|1}$ being in the inconsistent state NC as a function of the observation step given by $P(S_{12|1}$ in state NC at $L) = \pi_{12|1}[L](NC)$, where $\pi_{12|1}[L](NC)$ denotes the entry of $\pi_{12|1}[L]$ that captures the probability that $S_{12|1}$ is in the inconsistent state NC at L. Note that $\pi_{12|1}[L] = \mathcal{A}_{12|1}^L \pi_{12|1}[0]$, where $\mathcal{A}_{12|1}$ is the matrix that captures the transition probabilities for MC $S_{12|1}$ and $\pi_{12|1}[0] = \rho_{12|1}[0]$ (note that at this point the particular inputs associated with a transition are not needed and are ignored — only the probabilities of these transitions matter).

[4] Abusing notation, we use $\rho_{12|1}[0](\{q_1, q_{1D2DNC}\})$ to denote the entry of $\rho_{12|1}[0]$ that corresponds to state $\{q_1, q_{1D2DNC}\}$; of course, $\rho_1[0](q_1)$ denotes the entry of $\rho_1[0]$ that corresponds to state q_1.

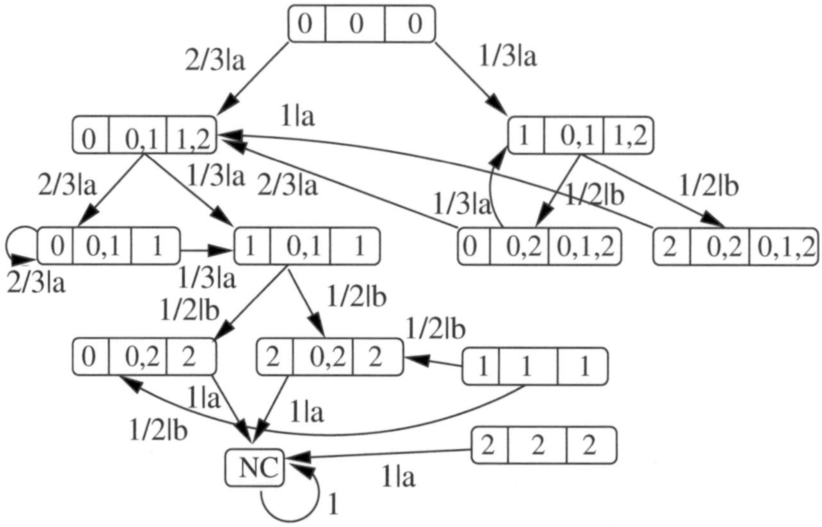

Fig. 6. State transition diagram of MC $S_{12|1}$ of Example 2.

Proposition 1: The probability of error as a function of the observation step is given by

$$\begin{aligned} P(\text{error at } L) &\leq \frac{1}{2}\Big(1 - P_1 \cdot \sum_{\substack{y_1^L : S_2 \\ \text{incons.}}} P(y_1^L \mid S_1) - P_2 \cdot \sum_{\substack{y_1^L : S_1 \\ \text{incons.}}} P(y_1^L \mid S_2)\Big) \\ &= \frac{1}{2} - \frac{1}{2}P_1 \cdot \pi_{12|1}[L](NC) - \frac{1}{2}P_2 \cdot \pi_{12|2}[L](NC), \end{aligned}$$

where $\pi_{12|1}[L](NC)$ captures the probability of $S_{12|1}$ being in state NC at step L, $\pi_{12|2}[L](NC)$ captures the probability of $S_{12|2}$ being in state NC at step L, and P_1 and P_2 denote the *priors* of S_1 and S_2. □

Example 2: We consider two candidate HMMs S_1 and S_2 with $Q_1 = Q_2 = \{0,1,2\}$, $Y_1 = Y_2 = \{a,b\}$, initial state $\{0\}$, and transition functionality, as shown in Figures 4.(i) and 5.(i), where each transition is labeled by $p_i \mid \sigma$, i.e., the probability of the transition and the output it produces. Following the procedure of subset construction we construct the deterministic FSMs S_{1D} and S_{2D} as shown in Figures 4.(ii) and 5.(ii), respectively (notice that we include states $\{1\}$ and $\{2\}$ in the state transition diagram of S_{1D} for completeness although they are not reachable from the initial state $\{0\}$). Adding the inconsistent state for each machine we get FSMs S_{1DNC} and S_{2DNC} as shown in Figures 4.(iii) and 5.(iii), respectively. Then, we construct MCs $S_{12|1}$ and $S_{12|2}$ with state transition diagrams as shown in Figures 6 and 7, respectively. For example, the sequence $< a\ a\ b\ a >$ can be produced by S_1 but not by S_2 (hence, given that this is the observation sequence, the probability that the classifier makes an incorrect decision is zero). In fact, all sequences in $S_{12|1}$ that end up in state NC can be produced by S_1 but not by S_2. □

4.3 Properties of bound on probability of error

The inconsistent state NC in MC $S_{12|1}$ is an absorbing state by construction. Therefore, the probability that $S_{12|1}$ is in state NC does not decrease as a function of the observation step; the same property holds for $S_{12|2}$. From Proposition 1 it is clear that the bound on the probability of error is a nonincreasing function of the observation step.

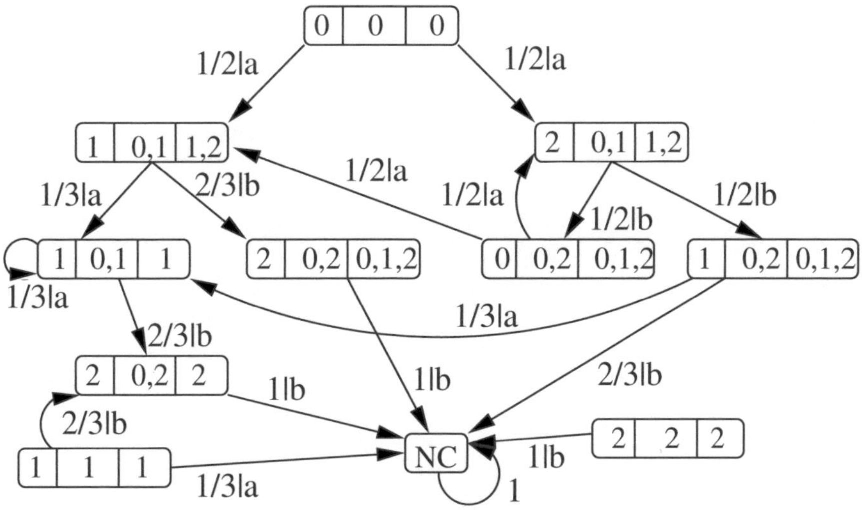

Fig. 7. State transition diagram of MC $S_{12|2}$ of Example 2.

Proposition 2: The bound on the probability of error given by Proposition 1 is a nonincreasing function of the number of observation steps. □

In fact, if MCs $S_{12|1}$ and $S_{12|2}$ have a single absorbing state each, i.e., state NC is the only absorbing state in each model, then the bound goes to zero as the number of observation steps increases. The expected number of steps to absorption, given that the initial state is the 0th state of $S_{12|1}$, can be calculated using the fundamental matrix of the absorbing Markov chain $S_{12|1}$ (Kemeny et al., 1976). If $\mathcal{A}_{T12|1}$ is the substochastic transition matrix of $S_{12|1}$ that captures the transitions among all transient states (all but NC) then the fundamental matrix is given by $\sum_{i=0}^{\infty} {\mathcal{A}_{T12|1}}^{i} = (I - \mathcal{A}_{T12|1})^{-1}$ and its $(j,k)^{th}$ entry captures the expected number of transitions from state k to state j before absorption. The expected number of steps to absorption, given that the initial state is state $\{0\}$, is equal to the sum of the elements of the 0th column of the fundamental matrix. In fact, the rate of convergence to absorption depends on the largest eigenvalue of the substochastic matrix $\mathcal{A}_{T12|1}$ (because the rate of convergence of matrix $\mathcal{A}^{m}_{T12|1}$ is captured by the rate of convergence of $\lambda^{m}_{12|1}$, where $\lambda_{12|1}$ is the largest eigenvalue of $\mathcal{A}_{T12|1}$ and m denotes the number of steps (Kemeny et al., 1976)).

Let us now consider the scenario where neither $S_{12|1}$ nor $S_{12|2}$ includes the inconsistent state NC in their set of states. Then the bound on the probability of error will not go to zero; in fact, it will always be equal to half, thereby providing us with no useful information. This scenario corresponds to the case where all output sequences that can be produced by S_1 can also be produced by S_2 and vice versa. For this to be true, S_1 and S_2 need to be equivalent, i.e., generate the same regular language (i.e., the same set of output sequences). Of course, although the set of output sequences is the same for both models, the probabilities associated with an output sequence could be different for each model. However, the *posteriors* of the candidate models in this case would be strictly greater than zero for any observation sequence; hence, the error in the MAP decision will always be nonzero. We can check whether S_1 and S_2 are equivalent using standard approaches with complexity $O((|Q_{1D}| + |Q_{2D}|)^2)$ (Hopcroft et al., 2001). We can also easily check equivalence by using S_{1D2DNC} and S_{1DNC2D} which we have already constructed: if the inconsistent state in either S_{1D2DNC} or S_{1DNC2D} (and

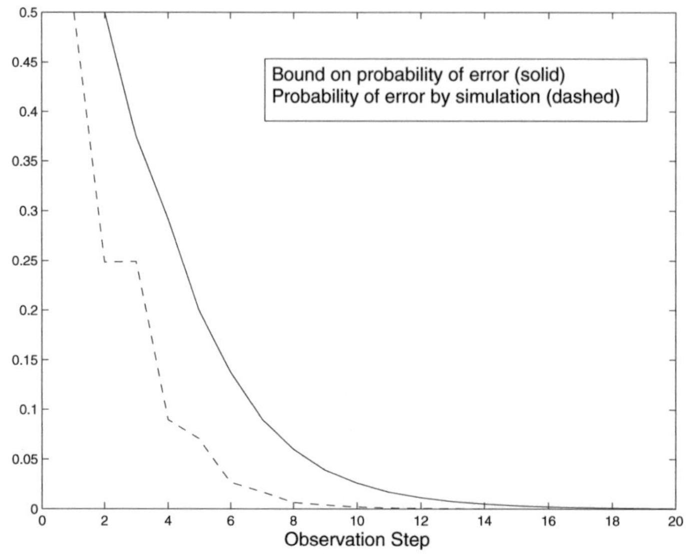

Fig. 8. Plot of the bound on the probability of error (solid) and the empirical probability of error obtained by simulation (dashed) in Example 2, both shown as functions of the observation step.

consequently $S_{12|1}$ or $S_{12|2}$) can be reached starting from the initial state, then the two models are not equivalent.

If MC $S_{12|1}$ has no absorbing state and MC $S_{12|2}$ has only the state NC as an absorbing state, then the bound on the probability of error goes to the value $\frac{P_1}{2}$. This case corresponds to the language generated by S_1 being a subset of the language generated by S_2, i.e., the set of output sequences that can be produced by S_1 can also be produced by S_2. To check for this scenario, we can check whether the inconsistent state in S_{1D2DNC} is reachable from the initial state. We formalize the above discussion in the following proposition.

Proposition 3: For two HMMs S_1 and S_2, the upper bound on the probability of error for the classification decision

- tends to zero exponentially with the number of observation steps, if (and only if) each of FSMs S_{1D2DNC} and S_{1DNC2D} has a unique absorbing state, namely the inconsistent state;
- tends to the value $P_1/2$ exponentially with the number of observation steps, if FSM S_{1D2DNC} has no inconsistent state and FSM S_{1DNC2D} has a unique absorbing state, i.e., the inconsistent state;
- tends to the value $P_2/2$ exponentially with the number of observation steps, if FSM S_{1D2DNC} has no inconsistent state and FSM S_{1DNC2D} has a unique absorbing state, i.e., the inconsistent state;
- is equal to $1/2$, if (and only if) FSMs S_{1D2DNC} and S_{1DNC2D} have no inconsistent states. □

Example 2 (continued): As shown in Figures 6 and 7, each of $S_{12|1}$ and $S_{12|2}$ have NC as the unique absorbing state. Thus, the bound on the probability of error goes to zero exponentially with the observation time; this is evident in Figure 8 where we assume equal *priors* (i.e., $P_1 =$

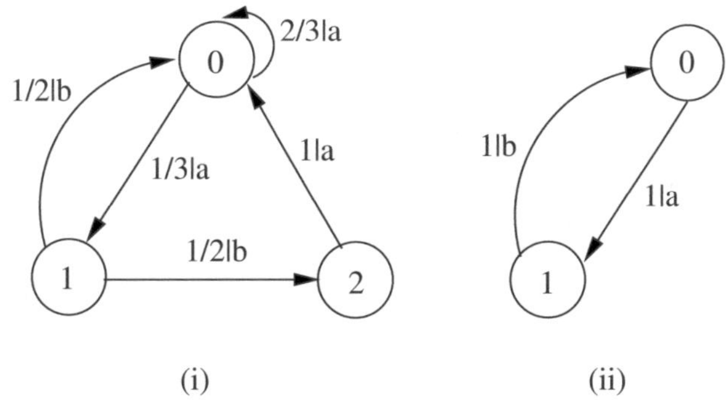

Fig. 9. State transition diagram of (i) HMM S_1 and (ii) HMM S_3 of Example 3.

$P_2 = 0.5$). After running simulations, half with the actual model being S_1 and the other half with the actual model being S_2, we obtain the empirical probability of error given S_1 (and given S_2) by recording the fraction of simulations for which the classifier incorrectly decided S_2 (and S_1, respectively). The empirical probability of error as a function of the observation step is shown in Figure 8. The expected time to absorption for $S_{12|1}$ is calculated to be 6.8 steps and the expected time to absorption for $S_{12|2}$ is 6.3 steps; hence, for equal *priors*, the expected number of steps for the bound on the probability of error to become zero is 6.55 steps. □

Example 3: Consider HMM S_1 and HMM S_3 shown in Figure 9, and assume equal *priors*. Notice that any output sequence that can be produced by S_3 can also be produced by S_1; thus, there is no inconsistent state in $S_{13|3}$ and the probability $\sum_{y_1^L:P(S_1|y_1^L)=0} P(y_1^L \mid S_3)$ is always equal to zero. On the other hand, $S_{13|3}$ has a unique absorbing inconsistent state. According to the proposition, we expect the bound on the probability of error to go to $P_1/2 = 0.25$. From Figure 10 we see that, although the bound on the probability of error indeed goes to 0.25 (as expected), the simulations show that the empirical probability of error goes to zero as the number of steps increases; for this set of candidate models, the bound is not tight, even as the number of observation steps goes to infinity. □

5. Posterior probability calculation with corrupted observations

So far, we have assumed that the output sequence of the HMM is correctly observed by the classifier. Next, we consider the scenario where sensor failures may convert the output sequence to a corrupted observed sequence.

5.1 Sensor failure model

The output sequence $y_1^L =< y[1], y[2], ..., y[L] >$ produced by the system under classification may become corrupted due to noise or sensor unreliability. When sensor failures are possible, what is actually observed by the system, denoted by $z_1^{L_z} =< z[1], z[2], ..., z[L_z] >$, may be different from the output sequence. In fact, if sensor failures are allowed to insert and/or delete outputs, the length of the observed sequence $z_1^{L_z}$ may be different from the length of the output sequence (i.e., it could be that $L_z \neq L$). We consider sensor failures that may result in the deletion, insertion, or substitution of output symbols, or the transposition of adjacent output symbols. We assume that sensor failures are transient and occur independently at each observation step with certain (known) probabilities that could *depend* on the observation step, e.g., the probability of such transient errors could vary as a function of time. We also make

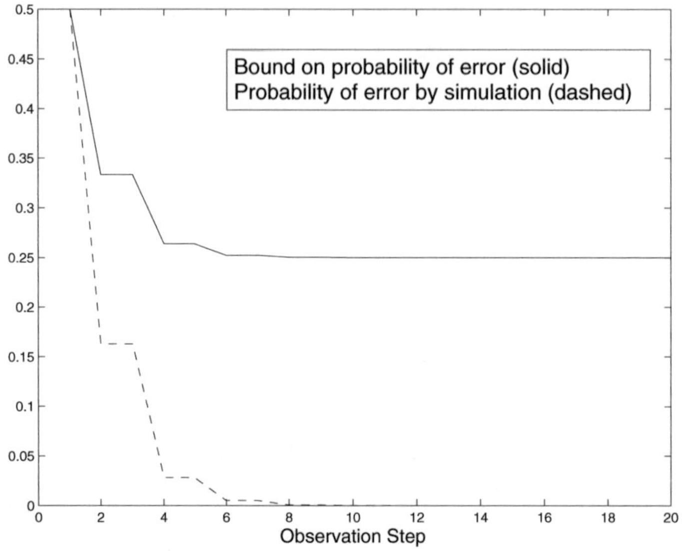

Fig. 10. Plot of the bound on the probability of error (solid) and the empirical probability of error obtained by simulation (dashed) in Example 3, both shown as functions of the observation step.

the reasonable assumption that sensor failures are conditionally independent from the HMM given the observation sequence.

If an output $\sigma \in Y$ is deleted by the sensor, then we do not observe the output, i.e., the deletion causes $\sigma \rightarrow \varepsilon$, where ε denotes the empty label. Similarly, if an output $\sigma \in Y$ is inserted by the sensor, then we observe σ instead of ε, i.e., the insertion causes $\varepsilon \rightarrow \sigma$. Also, if an output $\sigma_j \in Y$ is substituted by $\sigma_k \in Y$, then we observe σ_k, i.e., the substitution causes $\sigma_j \rightarrow \sigma_k$. Lastly, the corruption of subsequence $< \sigma_j \sigma_k >$ to $< \sigma_k \sigma_j >$ is referred to as a transposition error.

To perform the posterior probability calculation, we construct the trellis diagram of S as before but modify it to capture the sensor failures. Note that we call each column of the trellis diagram a *stage* to reflect the notion of an observation step. Deletions appear in the trellis diagram as vertical transitions within the same stage and insertions appear as one-step forward transitions. A substitution appearing at a particular observation step results in a change of the transition functionality of the HMM for that step. The transposition of two adjacent outputs appears in the trellis diagram as an erroneous transition that spans two columns.

Given the sensor failure model, we can assign probabilities to all types of errors on the observed sequence. Since the probabilities of sensor failures are known and are (conditionally) independent from the transition probabilities of the HMM, we can easily determine the probabilities associated with transitions in the modified trellis diagram that accounts for sensor failures. Due to space limitations, we focus on deletions which is the most challenging case of sensor failures because they may produce vertical cycles in the trellis diagram; the interested reader can find more details in (Athanasopoulou, 2007).

We assume that a deletion $d_{\sigma'}$ of output σ' occurs with known probability $p_{d_{\sigma'}}[m+1]$ at observation step $m+1$ when S is in a state from which a transition that outputs σ' is possible. Let $D = \{d_{\sigma_1}, d_{\sigma_2}, ..., d_{\sigma_{|D|}} \mid \sigma_1, \sigma_2, ..., \sigma_{|D|} \in Y\}$ be the set of deletions and define a function out to allow us to recover the corresponding output in the set Y given a deletion, i.e., $out(d_{\sigma'}) = \sigma'$. When constructing the trellis diagram, we assign probabilities to the transitions as follows:

1. each forward (normal) transition from state (m, j) to state $(m+1, k)$ associated with output σ is assigned probability
$$(1 - \sum_{\substack{\forall d_{\sigma'} \in D \text{ s.t.} \\ \delta(j, out(d_{\sigma'})) \neq \emptyset}} p_{d_{\sigma'}}[m]) \cdot \mathcal{A}_\sigma(k, j),$$
where $(1 - \sum_{\substack{\forall d_{\sigma'} \in D \text{ s.t.} \\ \delta(j, out(d_{\sigma'})) \neq \emptyset}} p_{d_{\sigma'}}[m])$ is the probability that no deletion (possible from state j) occurs and where $\mathcal{A}_\sigma(k, j)$ is the probability of going from state j to state k while producing output σ;
2. each vertical transition (corresponding to deletions) from state (m, j) to state (m, k) is assigned probability
$$\sum_{\substack{\forall d_{\sigma'} \in D \text{ s. t.} \\ \delta(j, out(d_{\sigma'})) = k}} (p_{d_{\sigma'}}[m] \cdot \mathcal{A}_{\sigma'}(k, j)).$$

Note that other ways of defining these probabilities (or obtaining them from a particular sensor failure model) are possible, e.g., under different models of sensor failures. What is important (and a challenge) here are not the specific values of these probabilities but the structure of the trellis diagram (in particular the loops that are present).

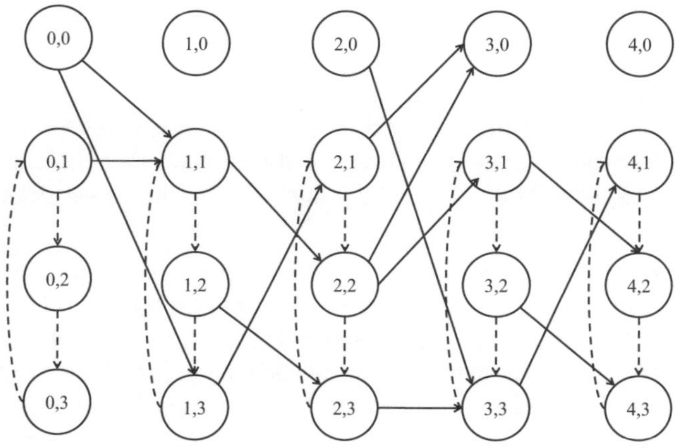

Fig. 11. Trellis diagram corresponding to S of Example 1 with deletions due to sensor failures (transition probabilities are not included for clarity).

Example 1 (continued): In S of Example 1 suppose that deletion of b may occur and that the observed sequence is $z_1^4 =< abcb >$. The output sequence y_1^L could be of any length; examples of possible output sequences are $< abbbcb >$, $< babcb >$, and $< babbcbbb >$. The resulting trellis diagram is shown in Figure 11, where dashed arcs represent transitions due to the deletion of b. In this example, we assume that the deletion probability p_{d_b} is fixed for all observation steps. The probabilities of transitions are not included in the figure for clarity, but they can be computed as explained before the example. For instance, the (normal) transition from state $(0,0)$ to state $(1,3)$ when symbol a is observed has probability $\mathcal{A}_a(3,0)$, which is equal to the probability that S took a transition from state 0 to state 3 and produced output a. Similarly, the (erroneous) transition from state $(0,1)$ to state $(0,2)$ has probability $p_{d_b} \cdot \mathcal{A}_b(2,1)$, which is the probability that b was produced by S and then it was deleted by the sensors. □

5.2 Posterior probability calculation

The iterative algorithm described in Section 3 cannot be applied in the case of sensor unreliability (see Figure 11) because the vertical arcs within a stage can possibly form loops (as in our example) and be traversed any number of times (more loop traversals occur, of course, with lower probability). Next, we establish some notation which will help us perform the iteration.

We can view the trellis diagram for a given observed sequence $z_1^{L_z}$ as a probabilistic FSM H with $|Q_H| = (L_z+1) \cdot |Q|$ states and probabilities on transitions determined by the trellis diagram. The transition probabilities do not generally satisfy the Markovian property and the matrix $\mathcal{A}_H$ that describes the transition probabilities of FSM H is not stochastic. We can easily build H' by modifying H, so that the assigned transition probabilities produce a Markov chain and, in particular, an absorbing Markov chain. More specifically, we append $|Q|+1$ states as described in the following two steps:

1. We add an extra stage at the end of the trellis diagram, i.e., we add $|Q|$ states of the form (L_z+1, j) so that from each state of the form (L_z, j) there exists a transition with probability one to state $(L_z+1, j), j \in \{0, 1, 2, ..., |Q|-1\}$; we also add a self-loop with probability one at each state of the form (L_z+1, j). We call each state of the form (L_z+1, j) a *consistent* state because H' being in that state implies that S is consistent with the observed sequence $z_1^{L_z}$.
2. We add state q_{in} to represent the *inconsistent* state, i.e., H is in state q_{in} when the observed sequence is not consistent with S. To achieve this, we add transitions from each state of FSM H to the inconsistent state q_{in} with probability such that the sum of the transition probabilities leaving each state is equal to one; we also add a self-loop at state q_{in} with probability one.

The resulting Markov chain H' has $|Q_{H'}| = (L_z+2) \cdot |Q| + 1$ states. The only self-loops in H' with probability one are those in the consistent states (of the form (L_z+1, j)) and in the inconsistent state (q_{in}). In fact, due to the particular structure of H' (and given that there is a nonzero probability to leave the vertical loop at each stage), the consistent and inconsistent states are the only absorbing states, while the rest of the states are transient. Therefore, when H' reaches its stationary distribution, only the absorbing states will have nonzero probabilities (summing up to one). We are interested in the stationary distribution of H' so that we can account for output sequences y_1^L of any length that correspond to the observed sequence $z_1^{L_z}$, i.e., for $L = L_z, L_z+1, \ldots, \infty$. (Recall that without sensor failures we have $L = L_z$.)

More formally, we arrange the states of H' in the order $(0,0)$, $(0,1), \ldots, (0, |Q|-1), (1,0), (1,1), \ldots, (1, |Q|-1), \ldots, (L_z+1, 0), (L_z+1, 1), \ldots, (L_z+1, |Q|-1), q_{in}$. Let $\pi_{H'}[0]$ be a vector with $|Q_{H'}|$ entries, each of which represents the initial probability of a corresponding state of H'. We are interested in the stationary probability distribution of H' denoted by

$$\pi_{H'} = \lim_{n\to\infty} \pi_{H'}[n] = \lim_{n\to\infty} \mathcal{A}_{H'}^{n} \cdot \pi_{H'}[0],$$

where the state transition matrix $\mathcal{A}_{H'}$ of H' is in its canonical form given by

$$\mathcal{A}_{H'} = \begin{bmatrix} \mathcal{A}_H & 0 \\ R & I \end{bmatrix}. \quad (1)$$

Here $\mathcal{A}_H$ captures the behavior of the transient states of H', the $(|Q|+1) \times |Q_H|$ matrix R captures the transitions from the transient states to the absorbing states, 0 is a matrix of appropriate dimensions with all zero entries, and I is the identity matrix of appropriate dimensions. Note that since H' is an absorbing Markov chain, the limit $\lim_{n\to\infty} \mathcal{A}_{H'}^{n}$ exists and it is given by

$$\lim_{n\to\infty} \mathcal{A}_{H'}^{n} = \begin{bmatrix} 0 & 0 \\ (I-\mathcal{A}_H)^{-1}R & I \end{bmatrix}, \quad (2)$$

where $(I-\mathcal{A}_H)^{-1}$ is called the fundamental matrix (Kemeny et al., 1976).
The only nonzero entries of $\pi_{H'}$ are those that correspond to the consistent and inconsistent states. In fact, the probability that H' ends up in a consistent state is equal to the complement of the probability that H' ends up in the inconsistent state and it is equal to the probability of the observed sequence $z_1^{L_z}$ given the FSM model S, i.e.,

$$P(z_1^{L_z} \mid S) = \sum_{j=L_z\cdot|Q|}^{|Q_H|-1} \pi_{H'}(j) = 1 - \pi_{H'}(|Q_{H'}|).$$

Note that the above approach for the posterior probability calculation is consistent with the one obtained in (Athanasopoulou et al., 2010) using the notion of the observation FSM and its composition with S.

5.3 Iterative posterior probability calculation with corrupted observations

In this section we exploit the structure of matrix $\mathcal{A}_{H'}$ which captures the transition probabilities of H' to perform the posterior probability calculations in an efficient manner. We first define the following submatrices which will be used to express $\mathcal{A}_{H'}$.

- Matrices $B_{m,m+1}$, $m = 0,1,...,L_z$, capture the transitions from any state of H' at stage m to any state of H' at stage $m+1$. They can be obtained from $\mathcal{A}_{H'}$ as $B_{m,m+1}(k,j) = \mathcal{A}_{H'}((m+1)\cdot|Q|+k, m\cdot|Q|+j)$, where $k,j = 0,1,...,|Q|-1$.
- Matrices B_m, $m = 0,1,...,L_z$, capture the vertical transitions and account for deletions. They can be obtained from $\mathcal{A}_{H'}$ as $B_m(k,j) = \mathcal{A}_{H'}(m\cdot|Q|+k, m\cdot|Q|+j)$, where $k,j = 0,1,...,|Q|-1$. (Note that if deletions occur at each observation step with the same probability, then $B_m = B$, $m = 0,1,...,L_z$.)
- C^T is a row vector with entries $C^T(j) = 1 - \sum_{k=1}^{|Q_H|} \mathcal{A}_H(k,j)$, for $j = 1,2,...,|Q_H|$, i.e., C^T ensures that the sum of each column of $\mathcal{A}_{H'}$ is equal to 1.

We should note here that an alternative way to compute the block matrices $B_{m,m+1}$ and B_m directly, without the help of the modified trellis diagram, is by using the following equations:

$$B_m(k,j) = \sum_{\substack{\forall d_{\sigma'} \in D \text{ s.t.} \\ \delta(j, out(d_{\sigma'}))=k}} (p_{d_{\sigma'}}[m] \cdot \mathcal{A}_{\sigma'}(k,j)),$$

$$B_{m,m+1}(k,j) = (1 - \sum_{\substack{\forall d_{\sigma'} \in D \text{ s.t.} \\ \delta(j, out(d_{\sigma'}))\neq\emptyset}} p_{d_{\sigma'}}[m]) \cdot \mathcal{A}_{z[m+1]}(k,j),$$

where $k, j = 0, 1, ..., |Q| - 1$ and $p_{d_{\sigma'}}[m]$, $\mathcal{A}_\sigma$ were defined earlier.
Using the above notation, we can decompose the matrix $\mathcal{A}_{H'}$ in blocks and express it as

$$\mathcal{A}_{H'} = \left[\begin{array}{ccccccc|cc} B_0 & 0 & 0 & \dots & 0 & 0 & 0 & 0 \\ B_{0,1} & B_1 & 0 & \dots & 0 & 0 & 0 & 0 \\ 0 & B_{1,2} & B_2 & \dots & 0 & 0 & 0 & 0 \\ \vdots & \vdots & \vdots & \dots & \vdots & \vdots & \vdots & \vdots \\ 0 & 0 & 0 & \dots & B_{L_z-1} & 0 & 0 & 0 \\ 0 & 0 & 0 & \dots & B_{L_z-1,L_z} & B_{L_z} & 0 & 0 \\ \hline 0 & 0 & 0 & \dots & 0 & I - B_{L_z} & I & 0 \\ & & & C^T & & & 0 & 1 \end{array}\right].$$

Recall that the matrix $\mathcal{A}_{H'}$ is in its canonical form (see (1)), where the submatrices $\mathcal{A}_H$ and R are given by

$$\begin{array}{rcl} \mathcal{A}_H & = & \left[\begin{array}{cccccc} B_0 & 0 & 0 & \dots & 0 & 0 \\ B_{0,1} & B_1 & 0 & \dots & 0 & 0 \\ 0 & B_{1,2} & B_2 & \dots & 0 & 0 \\ \vdots & \vdots & \vdots & \dots & \vdots & \vdots \\ 0 & 0 & 0 & \dots & B_{L_z-1} & 0 \\ 0 & 0 & 0 & \dots & B_{L_z-1,L_z} & B_{L_z} \end{array}\right], \\ R & = & \left[\begin{array}{cccc} 0 & \dots & 0 & I - B_{L_z} \\ & & C^T & \end{array}\right]. \end{array}$$

In the initial probability distribution vector $\pi_{H'}[0]$ the only nonzero entries are its first $|Q|$ entries, i.e., $\pi_H[0] = (\rho[0]\ 0\ ...\ 0)^T$, where $\rho[0]$ denotes the initial probability distribution of S (i.e., it is a $|Q|$-dimensional vector, whose j^{th} entry denotes the probability that S is initially in state j). Recall that $\pi_{H'}$ denotes the stationary probability distribution vector of H' and has nonzero entries only in the absorbing states, i.e., its last $|Q|+1$ states. Hence, given the observed sequence $z_1^{L_z}$, we can express $\pi_{H'}$ as $\pi_{H'} = (0\ ...\ 0\ \rho[L_z+1]\ p_{in}[L_z+1])^T$, where $\rho[L_z+1]$ captures the probabilities of the consistent states and $p_{in}[L_z+1]$ denotes the probability of the inconsistent state. The following equations hold:

$$\begin{array}{rcl} \pi_{H'} & = & \lim_{n\to\infty} \mathcal{A}_{H'}^n \cdot \pi_{H'}[0] \\ (0\ ...\ 0\ \rho[L_z+1]\ p_{in}[L_z+1])^T & = & \lim_{n\to\infty} \mathcal{A}_{H'}^n \cdot (\rho[0]\ ...\ 0)^T \\ \rho[L_z+1] & = & \lim_{n\to\infty} \mathcal{A}_{H'}^n(L_z+2,1) \cdot \rho[0]. \end{array}$$

Therefore, in order to calculate the probability of the consistent states we only need the initial distribution of S and the $(L_z+2,1)^{st}$ block of the matrix $\lim_{n\to\infty} \mathcal{A}_{H'}^n$.

Next, we argue that we can compute the $\lim_{n\to\infty} \mathcal{A}_H^n(L_z+2,1)$ with much less complexity than the standard computation in (2). For simplicity, we illustrate this for the case where the observed sequence is of length 2, i.e., $L_z = 2$. The state transition matrix $\mathcal{A}_{H'}$ is given by

$$\mathcal{A}_{H'} = \left[\begin{array}{ccc|cc} B_0 & 0 & 0 & 0 & 0 \\ B_{0,1} & B_1 & 0 & 0 & 0 \\ 0 & B_{1,2} & B_2 & 0 & 0 \\ \hline 0 & 0 & I-B_2 & I & 0 \\ & C^T & & 0 & 1 \end{array}\right].$$

We can compute by induction the matrix $\mathcal{A}_{H'}$ raised to the power n and consequently find the limit of $\mathcal{A}_{H'}^n(4,1)$ as n tends to infinity as follows:

$$\begin{aligned} \lim_{n\to\infty} \mathcal{A}_H^n(4,1) &= \lim_{n\to\infty} \sum_{j_1+j_2+j_3+j_4=n-3} I^{j_4}\, I\, B_2^{j_3} B_{1,2} B_1^{j_2} B_{0,1} B_0^{j_1} \\ &= (I+B_2+B_2^2+\ldots)B_{1,2}(I+B_1+B_1^2+\ldots)B_{0,1}(I+B_0+B_0^2+\ldots) \\ &= \left(\sum_{j=0}^{\infty} B_2^j\right) B_{1,2} \left(\sum_{j=0}^{\infty} B_1^j\right) B_{0,1} \left(\sum_{j=0}^{\infty} B_0^j\right) \\ &= (I-B_2)^{-1}B_{1,2}(I-B_1)^{-1}B_{0,1}(I-B_0)^{-1}\,. \end{aligned}$$

(The detailed proof is omitted due to space limitations; it can be found in (Athanasopoulou, 2007).)

As explained earlier, we are interested in the state probabilities of the *consistent* states, which will be given by the entries of the vector $\boldsymbol{\rho}[3] = \lim_{n\to\infty} \mathcal{A}_H^n(4,1)\ \boldsymbol{\rho}[0]$. From the above equation, we get

$$\boldsymbol{\rho}[3] = ((I-B_2)^{-1}B_{1,2}(I-B_1)^{-1}B_{0,1}(I-B_0)^{-1})\boldsymbol{\rho}[0].$$

To simplify notation let us define $B'_{m,m+1} = (I-B_{m+1})^{-1}B_{m,m+1}$, $m = 0,1,2$. Hence, $\boldsymbol{\rho}[3] = B'_{1,2}B'_{0,1}(I-B_0)^{-1}\boldsymbol{\rho}[0]$.

Generalizing the above computation for any number of observations L_z, the vector that describes the probabilities of the consistent states given the observed sequence $z_1^{L_z}$ satisfies

$$\boldsymbol{\rho}[L_z+1] = \left(\prod_{i=0}^{L_z-1} B'_{m,m+1}\right)(I-B_0)^{-1}\,\boldsymbol{\rho}[0], \tag{3}$$

where $B'_{m,m+1} = (I-B_{m+1})^{-1}B_{m,m+1}$, $m = 0,1,\ldots,L_z$.

By inspection of (3) we notice that the computation of $\boldsymbol{\rho}[L_z+1]$ can be performed iteratively as follows:

$$\begin{aligned} \boldsymbol{\rho}[1] &= B'_{0,1}(I-B_0)^{-1}\,\boldsymbol{\rho}[0], \\ \boldsymbol{\rho}[m+1] &= B'_{m,m+1}\,\boldsymbol{\rho}[m],\ m = 1,2,\ldots,L_z, \end{aligned} \tag{4}$$

where $\boldsymbol{\rho}[m+1]$ represents the probability of consistent states given the observed sequence z_1^m. The probability that the observed sequence $z_1^{L_z}$ was produced by the particular FSM S is equal to the sum of the elements of the state probability distribution vector $\boldsymbol{\rho}[L_z+1]$, i.e., $P(z_1^{L_z} \mid S) = \sum_{j=0}^{|Q|-1} \boldsymbol{\rho}[L_z+1](j)$.

The above algorithm is described in pseudocode below.

Algorithm

Input: Matrices $\{B_m\}$, $\{B_{m,m+1}\}$, where $m = 0, 1, \ldots, L_z$; an observed (possibly corrupted) output sequence $z_1^{L_z} = \{z[1], z[2], ..., z[L_z]\}$ and the initial probability distribution $\boldsymbol{\rho}[0]$.

1. Initialization. Let $m = 0$, $z[m] = \emptyset$,

compute $B'_{0,1} = (I - B_1)^{-1} B_{0,1}$,

compute $\boldsymbol{\rho}[1] = B'_{0,1}(I - B_0)^{-1}\ \boldsymbol{\rho}[0]$.

2. Let $m = 1$.
3. Consider the output $z[m]$, do

compute $B'_{m,m+1} = (I - B_{m+1})^{-1} B_{m,m+1}$,

compute $\boldsymbol{\rho}[m+1] = B'_{m,m+1}\boldsymbol{\rho}[m]$.

4. $m = m + 1$.
5. If $m = L_z + 1$, Goto 6; else Goto 3.
6. Compute $P(z_1^{L_z} \mid S) = \sum_{j=0}^{|Q|-1} \boldsymbol{\rho}[L_z + 1](j)$. □

To gain some intuition regarding the iteration, let us consider for now the case of reliable sensors. This case corresponds to matrices B_m in $\mathcal{A}_{H'}$ being equal to zero, which means that there are no vertical transitions (transitions within the same stage) in the trellis diagram. In this case, iteration (4) becomes

$$\boldsymbol{\rho}[m+1] = B_{m,m+1}\ \boldsymbol{\rho}[m], \quad m = 0, 1, \ldots, L_z.$$

This latter equation is the same as the iterative equation that appeared in Section 3 for the case of reliable sensors (where we denoted $B_{m,m+1}$ by $\mathcal{A}_{y[m+1]}$). Intuitively, every time we get a new observation we update the current probability vector by multiplying it with the state transition matrix of S that corresponds to the new observation. With the above intuition at hand, we now return to the case of sensor failures. Here, we also need to take into consideration the fact that any number of vertical transitions may occur. Therefore, every time we get a new observation $z[m+1]$, we multiply the current probability vector with the state transition matrix of S that corresponds to the new observation (as before) and also with $(I - B_{m+1})^{-1} = \sum_{j=0}^{\infty} B_{m+1}^j$ thereby taking into account the vertical transitions at stage $m + 1$.

The matrices $B_{m,m+1}$ have dimension $|Q| \times |Q|$, while the matrix $\mathcal{A}_H$ has dimension $|Q_H| \times |Q_H|$, where $|Q_H| = (L_z + 2) \cdot |Q|$. If we calculate π_H without taking advantage of the structure of $\mathcal{A}_H$, the computational complexity is proportional to $O(((L_z + 2) \cdot |Q|)^3) = O(L_z^3 \cdot |Q|^3)$. If we use the iterative approach instead, the computational complexity reduces significantly to $O((L_z + 2) \cdot (|Q|^2 + |Q|^3)) = O(L_z \cdot |Q|^3)$ (each stage requires the inversion of a new $|Q| \times |Q|$ matrix which has complexity $O(|Q|^3)$ and dominates the computational complexity associated with that particular stage). If sensor failure probabilities remain invariant at each stage, then matrix B_m at stage m only needs to be inverted once and the complexity of the iterative approach is $O((L_z + 2) \cdot |Q|^2 + |Q|^3) = O(L_z \cdot |Q|^2 + |Q|^3)$. In addition to complexity gains, the iterative nature of the calculations allows us to monitor the system under classification online and calculate the probability of the observed sequence at each observation step by first updating the state probability vector and then summing up its entries.

5.4 Discussion

We discuss here how the presented iterative algorithm relates to other known algorithms. As mentioned earlier, the techniques that we use relate to the evaluation problem in HMMs or the parsing problem in probabilistic automata with vertical loops in the resulting trellis diagram. The forward algorithm is used to evaluate the probability that a given sequence of observations is produced by a certain HMM. To do that, the standard forward algorithm uses the HMM to build a trellis diagram based on the given sequence of observations and performs the likelihood calculation online. However, the standard forward algorithm cannot handle the existence of vertical cycles in the trellis diagram. Ways around vertical cycles in the trellis diagram have been suggested in speech recognition applications, where HMMs are used to model speech patterns (Rabiner, 1989), (Ephraim and Merhav, 2002), (Jelinek, 1998), (Poritz, 1988) and may include null transitions (i.e., the HMM may move from the current state to the next state without producing any output (Jelinek, 1998), (Bahl and Jelinek, 1975)), as well as in the area of pattern recognition, where one may have to deal with null transitions when solving the parsing problem for a given probabilistic finite state automaton (Vidal et al., 2005).

While in most HMM formulations one deals with state observations, several authors have also studied the evaluation problem in HMMs with transition observations, including null transitions (i.e., transitions with no outputs). For instance, the authors of (Bahl and Jelinek, 1975), (Bahl et al., 1983), (Jelinek, 1998), develop HMMs that capture the generation of codewords in speech recognition applications via observations that are associated with transitions rather than states. These HMMs also include null transitions, i.e., transitions that change the state without producing outputs. To avoid loops in the resulting trellis diagram, the authors of (Bahl and Jelinek, 1975) eliminate them via an appropriate modification of the underlying HMM *before* constructing the trellis diagram. In (Vidal et al., 2005), an algorithm is presented to solve the parsing problem in pattern recognition applications for the case where null transitions exist in a probabilistic finite-state automaton (PFSA) model (as pointed out in (Dupont et al., 2005), HMMs are equivalent to PFSAs with no final probabilities). The authors evaluate recursively the probability that a sequence is produced by a λ-PFSA (i.e., a PFSA that includes null transitions) and their approach can be shown, after some manipulation, to be a special case of the algorithm we described here.

Also related to the described likelihood computation algorithm is the well-known Viterbi algorithm (Forney, 1973), (Viterbi, 1967), which solves the related problem of maximum-likelihood decoding of convolutional codes by choosing the most likely state sequence based on a given sequence of observations. In fact, the Viterbi algorithm is a dynamic programming algorithm amenable to online use with applications in various fields; for example, in HMMs it finds the most likely (hidden) state sequence corresponding to the observed output sequence (Rabiner, 1989). Note that, in contrast to the Viterbi algorithm, the maximum likelihood approach in this work considers the total probability of *all* paths (rather than the cost of the *most likely* path) which can be generated from the initial state(s) to the final state(s). As a consequence of this requirement, the Viterbi algorithm (or variations of it) do not obtain a solution for the problem considered here. However, it is worth pointing out that the Viterbi algorithm has been frequently suggested as a suboptimal alternative for likelihood evaluation in some applications (Rabiner, 1989). Also note that a modified Viterbi algorithm was proposed in (Bouloutas et al., 1991) to identify the correct strings of data given an FSM representation of a possibly erroneous output sequence; in (Hart and Bouloutas, 1993) the same authors proposed a channel inversion algorithm for correcting symbol sequences that have been corrupted by errors (associated with costs) which can be described in terms of finite state automata. The work in (Amengual and Vital, 1998) proposes an efficient implementation of the Viterbi algorithm to perform error-correcting parsing using an FSM and an error model. The Viterbi algorithm can handle the case where vertical cycles exist by unwrapping cycles so that each state on the cycle is visited at most once (to avoid adding cost or decreasing the probability of the path — recall that the Viterbi algorithm only searches for the most likely path).

Before closing this discussion, it is worth pointing out that the techniques used to solve our problem also relate to maximum a posteriori (MAP) decoding of variable length codes (VLC). In MAP decoding of VLC, symbols that are generated by a source may give rise to a different number of output bits and, given an observed bit sequence, one has to recover the symbols that are transmitted according to the source codewords. The authors in (Bauer and Hagenauer, 2000), (Guyader et al., 2001) constructed a two-dimensional (symbol and bit) trellis diagram representation of the variable length coded data and then applied the BCJR algorithm (Bahl et al., 1974) to do either symbol or bit decoding. This setup resembles the setup described here when only a *finite* number of sensor failures exist in the observed sequence (in such case, one can appropriately enlarge the underlying model since no vertical cycles are present). In our formulation, however, deletions may cause vertical loops in the associated trellis diagram resulting in an infinite number of possible output sequences matching a given sequence of observations. As a consequence, the standard BCJR algorithm is insufficient for solving our problem and the techniques that we describe are crucial in obtaining the probabilities needed for our trellis-based analysis.

To summarize, the approach presented here is more general than the aforementioned approaches because it can handle different kinds of loops at different stages of the trellis diagram (loops in our setup are not introduced by null transitions in the underlying model but rather by errors in the observed sequence which can occur with time-varying probabilities). Thus, the associated probabilities in the trellis diagram can be changing with time (which cannot be handled as effectively using the techniques in (Vidal et al., 2005) or in (Bahl and Jelinek, 1975)). The problem is that the modification of the underlying model so as to match the requirements of these earlier approaches results in a quite complex HMM (in which the evaluation problem can still benefit from the techniques we describe here). Therefore, the attractive feature of the described iterative algorithm for likelihood calculation is that it can handle time-varying and infinite number of sensor failures (or, equivalently, vertical cycles in the trellis diagram) with reduced complexity.

6. Conclusions

In this chapter we considered the problem of optimal classification of HMMs in order to minimize the probability of error. Given two candidate HMMs along with their *prior* probabilities, a classifier that aims to minimize the probability of error (misclassification) needs to determine which candidate model has most likely produced the observation sequence of the system under classification. In order to find the *a priori* probability that the classifier makes an incorrect decision as a function of the observation step, one could in principle calculate all possible observation sequences (of that length), find their probabilities, and determine their contribution to the probability of misclassification. Since the complexity for calculating the exact probability of error can be prohibitively high, we described ways to obtain an upper bound on this probability, as well as necessary and sufficient conditions for the bound to go exponentially to zero as the number of observation steps increases.

Additionally, we presented an iterative methodology to calculate the probability of a given HMM under possibly erroneous observations. Our goal was to determine which of two candidate HMMs has most likely produced the observed sequence under sensor failures which can corrupt the observed sequence. Using the trellis diagram which includes all possible sequences consistent with both the observations and the given HMMs, we described an iterative algorithm that efficiently computes the total probability with which each HMM, together with a combination of sensor failures, can generate the observed sequence. The described algorithm can deal with vertical loops in the trellis diagrams which can be caused by output deletions.
As examples we considered the classification of CpG islands in DNA sequences and a failure diagnosis scenario where a system is classified as faulty or non-faulty depending on the observation sequence. The described techniques can be easily extended to classification of several hidden Markov models with applications in various fields such as document or image classification, pattern recognition, and bioinformatics.

7. Acknowledgement

The authors would like to thank Christoforos Keroglou for help with Example 1.b and for proof reading several parts of this chapter.

8. References

J. C. Amengual and E. Vidal. (1998). Efficient error-correcting Viterbi parsing, *IEEE Trans. on Pattern Analysis and Machine Intelligence*, vol. 20, no. 10, pp. 1109–1116.

E. Athanasopoulou, L. Li, and C. N. Hadjicostis. (2010). Maximum likelihood failure diagnosis in finite state machines under unreliable observations, *IEEE Trans. Automatic Control*, vol. 55, no. 3, pp. 579–593.

E. Athanasopoulou and C. N. Hadjicostis. (2008). Probability of error bounds for failure diagnosis and classification in hidden Markov models, *IEEE Proc. of the 47th IEEE Conf. on Decision and Control*, pp. 1477-1482.

E. Athanasopoulou. (2007). *Diagnosis of finite state models under partial or unreliable observations.* Ph.D. Thesis, Department of Electrical and Computer Engineering, University of Illinois, IL.

L. R. Bahl, F. Jelinek and R. L. Mercer. (1983). A maximum likelihood approach to continuous speech recognition, *IEEE Trans. Pattern Analysis and Machine Intelligence*, vol. PAMI-5, no. 2, pp. 179–190.

L. R. Bahl and F. Jelinek. (1975). Decoding for channels with insertions, deletions and substitutions with applications to speech recognition," *IEEE Trans. Information Theory*, vol. IT-21, no. 4, pp. 404–411.

L. R. Bahl, J. Cocke, F. Jelinek, and J. Raviv. (1974). Optimal decoding of linear codes for minimizing label error rate, *IEEE Trans. Information Theory*, vol. IT-20, pp. 284–287.

R. Bauer and J. Hagenauer. (2000). Symbol-by-symbol MAP decoding of variable length codes, in *Proc. 3rd ITG Conf. on Source and Channel Coding*, pp. 111–116.

A. Bouloutas, G. W. Hart, and M. Schwartz. (1991). Two extensions of the Viterbi algorithm, *IEEE Trans. Information Theory*, vol. 37, no. 2, pp. 430–436.

P. Dupont, F. Denis, and Y. Esposito. (2005). Links between probabilistic automata and hidden Markov models: probability distributions, learning models and induction algorithms, *Pattern Recognition*, vol. 38, no. 9, pp. 1349–1371.

R. Durbin, S. R. Eddy, A. Krogh, and G. Mitchison. (1998). *Biological Sequence Analysis: Probabilistic Models of Proteins and Nucleic Acids.* Cambridge University Press, Cambridge, UK.

Y. Ephraim and N. Merhav. (2002). Hidden Markov processes, *IEEE Trans. Information Theory,* vol. 48, no. 6, pp. 1518–1569.

M. Fatemi, M. M. Pao, S. Jeong, E. N. Gal-Yam, G. Egger, D. J. Weisenberger, and P. A. Jones. (2005). Footprinting of mammalian promoters: use of a *CpG* DNA methyltransferase revealing nucleosome positions at a single molecule level, *Nucleic Acids Research,* vol. 33, no. 20, pp. e176.

G. D. Forney, Jr.. (1973). The Viterbi algorithm, *Proc. IEEE,* vol. 61, pp. 268–278.

K. S. Fu. (1982). *Syntactic Pattern Recognition and Applications.* Prentice-Hall, New York, NY.

M. Gardiner-Garden and M. Frommer (1987). *CpG* Islands in vertebrate genomes, *Journal of Molecular Biology,* vol. 196, no. 2, pp. 261-282.

A. Guyader, E. Fabre, C. Guillemot, and M. Robert. (2001). Joint source-channel turbo decoding of entropy-coded sources," *IEEE Journal on Selected Areas in Communications,* vol. 19, no. 9, pp. 1680–1696.

G. W. Hart and A. T. Bouloutas. (1993). Correcting dependent errors in sequences generated by finite-state processes, *IEEE Trans. Information Theory,* vol. 39, no. 4, pp. 1249–1260.

J. E. Hopcroft, R. Motwani, and J. D. Ullman. (2001). *Introduction to Automata Theory, Languages, and Computation,* Addison Wesley, Reading, MA.

F. Jelinek. (1998). *Statistical Methods for Speech Recognition,* The MIT Press, Cambridge, MA.

J. G. Kemeny, J. L. Snell, and A. W. Knapp. (1976). *Denumerable Markov Chains.* 2nd ed., Springer-Verlag, New York, NY.

T. Koski. (2001). *Hidden Markov Models of Bioinformatics.* Kluwer Academic Publishers, Boston, MA.

A. M. Poritz. (1998). Hidden Markov models: A guided tour, *Proc. 1988 IEEE Conf. Acoustics, Speech, and Signal Processing,* vol. 1, pp. 7–13.

L. R. Rabiner. (1989). A tutorial on hidden Markov models and selected applications in speech recognition, *Proc. IEEE,* vol. 77, no. 2, pp. 257–286.

E. Vidal, F. Thollard, C. de la Higuera, F. Casacuberta, and R. C. Carrasco. (2005). Probabilistic finite-state machines–part I, *IEEE Trans. Pattern Analysis and Machine Intelligence,* vol. 27, no. 7, pp. 1013–1025.

A. D. Viterbi. (1967). Error bounds for convolutional codes and an asymptotically optimum decoding algorithm, *IEEE Trans. Inform. Theory,* vol. IT-13, pp. 260–269.

Part 2

Hidden Markov Models in Speech and Time-domain Signals Processing

5

Hierarchical Command Recognition Based on Large Margin Hidden Markov Models

Przemyslaw Dymarski
Warsaw University of Technology,Department of Electronics and Information Technology, Institute of Telecommunications
Poland

1. Introduction

The dominant role of Hidden Markov Models (HMMs) in automatic speech recognition (ASR) is not to be denied. At first, the HMMs were trained using the Maximum Likelihood (ML) approach, using the Baum- Welch or Expectation Maximization algorithms (Rabiner, 1989). Then, discriminative training methods emerged, i.e. the Minimum Classification Error (Sha & Saul, 2007; Siohan et al., 1998), the Conditional Maximum Likelihood, the Maximum Mutual Information (Bahl et al., 1986), the Maximum Entropy (Kuo & Gao, 2006; Macherey & Ney, 2003) and the Large Margin (LM) approach (Jiang et al., 2006; Sha & Saul, 2007). These methods enabled an improvement of class separation (e.g. phonemes or words), but generally suffered from computational complexity, slow convergence or ill conditioning of computational algorithms.

In this work the Large Margin HMMs are used, but the training algorithm is based on the iterative use of the well conditioned Baum - Welch algorithm, so there are no problems with its convergence. Such a corrective HMM training yields an improvement of class separation, which is tested on the speaker independent commands recognition and the spoken digits recognition tasks.

This text is partially based on the publication (Dymarski & Wydra, 2008), but it contains new concepts and not yet published results, e.g. the corrective training approach is extended to simultaneous design of a whole set of HMMs (not only two), the selective optimization concept is presented and the hierarchical command recognition system is designed and tested.

2. Discriminative training of the HMM

The Hidden Markov Model (HMM) consists of N states, described with observation models. The n-dimensional observation vector contains a set of speech parameters e.g. the mel-cepstrum coefficients. In the case of DHMM (Discrete HMM) the observation vector exhibits M distinct values with probabilities delivered by the observation model. In the case of CHMM (Continuous HMM) the observation model has a form of a probability density function of speech parameters (e.g. gaussian or gaussian mixture pdf). The CHMMs outperform the DHMMs in speech recognition tasks, because the DHMMs require clustering of the observation vectors (e.g. using the k-means algorithm), which introduces quantization error. Therefore in this chapter we shall concentrate on the CHMM. In fact any HMM (also the CHMM) is discrete in time domain, because only N distinct states are available - this is an inherent disadvantage of this kind of models.

The commonly used maximum likelihood (ML) approach to a word recognition task may be described as follows: Having a set of observations $\mathbf{X}$ (i.e. a set of n-dimensional vectors), characterizing an unknown word, and having a set of HMMs $\{\lambda_i\}$, the HMM maximizing the probability (in case of DHMM) or the pdf (in case of CHMM) is chosen:

$$\arg\max_i \; p(\mathbf{X}|\lambda_i) \tag{1}$$

Design of a HMM λ_i for the i-th word consists in calculating transition probabilities between states, observation models for each state and initial probabilities for each state (if the initial state is not set a priori). Usually the Baum-Welch (or *Expectation Maximization* - EM) method is used (Rabiner, 1989), maximizing the likelihood

$$\prod_k p(\mathbf{X}_i^k|\lambda_i) \tag{2}$$

where $\mathbf{X}_i^k$ is the k-th element (instance) of the i-th observation set (describing e.g. the k-th utterance of the i-th word, stored in a speech database). In practice, due to the extremely small likelihood values, the logarithm of the probability (or the pdf), i.e. the log-likelihood is maximized:

$$Loglik(\mathbf{X}_i|\lambda_i) = \sum_k \log\left[p(\mathbf{X}_i^k|\lambda_i)\right] = \sum_k loglik(\mathbf{X}_i^k|\lambda_i) \tag{3}$$

where $loglik(\mathbf{X}_i^k|\lambda_i) = \log\left[p(\mathbf{X}_i^k|\lambda_i)\right]$.

The above criterion yields the best HMM (in a maximum likelihood sense) for a given database $\mathbf{X}_i = \{\mathbf{X}_i^k\}$, but it does not take into consideration the discriminative properties of this model. If for some other model λ_j, and for an observation set $\mathbf{X}_i^k$ (characterizing the k-th instance of a i-th word) $loglik(\mathbf{X}_i^k|\lambda_j) > loglik(\mathbf{X}_i^k|\lambda_i)$, then the recognition error appears. Therefore, a difference

$$d_{i,j}(\mathbf{X}_i^k) \;=\; loglik(\mathbf{X}_i^k|\lambda_i) \;-\; loglik(\mathbf{X}_i^k|\lambda_j) \tag{4}$$

contributes to a measure of separation of the classes i and j and should be considered in training of the HMM λ_i (Jiang et al., 2006).

In most applications class i must be well separated not only from a single class j, but from any class $j = 1, 2, ..., L_w$, $j \neq i$, where L_w is a number od commands being recognized, e.g. 10 for the recognition of spoken digits. Thus the separation of the k-th instance of an i-th word from the other classes may be measured using the smallest difference $d_{i,j}$, $j = 1, ..., L_w$, $j \neq i$:

$$\begin{aligned} d_i(\mathbf{X}_i^k) \;&=\; \min_{j\neq i}\; d_{i,j}(\mathbf{X}_i^k) \\ d_i(\mathbf{X}_i^k) \;&=\; loglik(\mathbf{X}_i^k|\lambda_i) \;-\; \max_{j\neq i}\; loglik(\mathbf{X}_i^k|\lambda_j) \end{aligned} \tag{5}$$

In Fig.1 some instances of the same word i are analyzed: the log-likelihood for the proper HMM λ_i and for the other HMMs λ_j, $j \neq i$, the differences $d_{i,j}$ and the minimum differences d_i are shown.

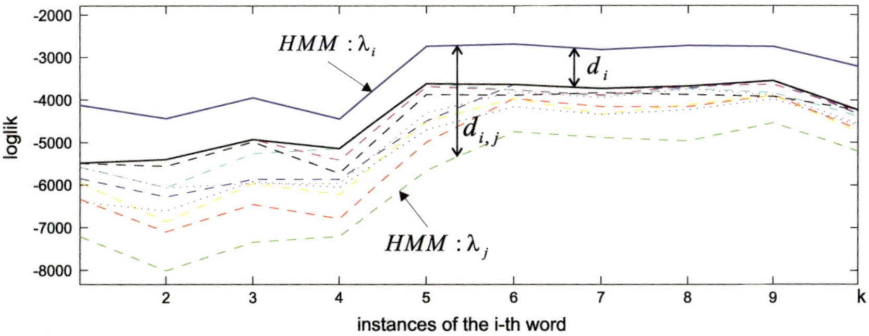

Fig. 1. Log-likelihoods $loglik(\mathbf{X}_i^k|\lambda_i)$, $loglik(\mathbf{X}_i^k|\lambda_j), j = 1, ..., 10, j \neq i$, differences $d_{i,j}(\mathbf{X}_i^k)$ and $d_i(\mathbf{X}_i^k)$ for 10 utterances (instances) of the same, i-th word

The discriminative properties of the set of HMMs may be improved, by choosing the proper parameters being the components of the observation vector. The mel-cepstrum parameters with their first and second derivatives are usually chosen, but in (Dymarski & Wydra, 2008; Wydra, 2007) some improvement in isolated words recognition task is reported due to replacement of the 3 last mel-cepstrum coefficients with 3 parameters characterizing voicing of spoken phonemes. In (Hosseinzadeh & Krishnan, 2008) many spectral features were tested with success in the speaker recognition task.

The structure of the HMM may be adapted to the particular words or the other acoustic units, in order to improve its discriminative properties. E.g. the number of states may be chosen according to the number of phonemes in a word being modeled (see (Wydra, 2007), some new results are also reported in this chapter). However care must be taken, because mixing different HMM structures in one system may give poor results (e.g. ergodic HMMs yield generally greater log-likelihood values despite of their rather poor discriminative properties). The application of discriminative methods of the HMM design (Bahl et al., 1986; Chang & Glass, 2009; Jiang et al., 2006; Kuo & Gao, 2006; Macherey & Ney, 2003; Schlueter et al., 1997; Sha & Saul, 2007) is a straightforward approach to improve the class separation (described e.g. with the d_i values). The following methods of discriminative training became popular:

- Minimum Classification Error approach (Sha & Saul, 2007; Siohan et al., 1998). The criterion is a number of errors, i.e. number of instances generating negative values of $d_i(\mathbf{X}_i^k)$. This criterion is not a continuous function which causes problems with its minimization. If it attains zero, then the design procedure is stopped, therefore it is often replaced by a continuous sigmoidal function and gradient methods are used for its minimization.
- Conditional Maximum Likelihood and Maximum Mutual Information approach (Bahl et al., 1986). Unlike the ML approach, these methods consider the whole set of HMMs, when updating the i-th HMM. In the Maximum Mutual Information approach the probability of occurrence of words is also taken into consideration. Gradient optimization methods are used, or the Extended Baum - Welch algorithm (Schlueter et al., 1997).
- Maximum Entropy (ME) (Kuo & Gao, 2006; Macherey & Ney, 2003). As described in (Macherey & Ney, 2003), ME training looks for a model "consistent with constraints derived from the training data while making as little assumptions as possible". Finally

it leads to the log-linear models, somewhat different from the HMMs (observations are associated with state transitions, not with states). The *Generalized Iterative Scaling* algorithm, used for model design, is rather complex and slowly convergent.

- Large Margin (LM) classification methods (Jiang et al., 2006; Sha & Saul, 2007), maximizing the class separation, i.e. a margin, being a function of the distances d_i (5). Gradient optimization methods may be used, but there are problems with their convergence (Jiang et al., 2006; Sha & Saul, 2007). Unconstrained optimization may lead to the infinite value of a margin while the log-likelihood $Loglik(\mathbf{X}_i|\lambda_i)$ tends to $-\infty$. Therefore, constraints are needed, which make the design process complex. If the margin is described with a few critical observation sets (for which d_i attain the minimum values), the Support Vector Machine may be used as a Large Margin Classifier. It is possible to construct such a classifier as a HMM (Altun et al., 2003).

The Large Margin (LM) approach is the most promising one, however it suffers from a high computational complexity of the HMM design algorithms. In this chapter it is shown, that the margin may be increased by the iterative use of the Baum-Welch (or EM) algorithm - a basic tool for the Maximum Likelihood HMM design. Using the *Iterative Localized Optimization* strategy (in each iteration only one HMM is modified) (Jiang et al., 2006) and *corrective training approach* (only the margin forming sets of observations influence the HMM design) (Schlueter et al., 1997) new algorithms are described in this work (see sect. 3 - some of them were proposed before by the author and S.Wydra in (Dymarski & Wydra, 2008)). These algorithms include:

- Optimization of all HMMs (obtained at first with the classical ML algorithm) using the Large Margin (LM) training
- Selective LM training, i.e. modification of only these HMMs, which generate recognition errors
- LM training of pairs: the HMM for the i-th word and the HMM for all but the i-th word (the reference model, the world model)
- LM training of pairs: the HMM for the word "i" versus the HMM for the word "j".
- Hierarchical system:
  - at the first stage the classical ML HMMs (or the HMMs after the selective training) are used,
  - at the second stage the words disambiguation is performed using the LM trained pairs: the HMM for the word "i" versus the HMM for the word "j".

The best compromise between recognition quality and algorithm complexity is reached in the hierarchical system. Hierarchical recognition structures were studied in the literature (Chang & Glass, 2009; Fine et al., 2002; Gosztolya & Kocsor, 2005; Yang et al., 2002), but the structure proposed in this chapter is somewhat different: it avoids merging of words, the first stage is a complete recognition system and the disambiguation stage may be even removed from the system. The first stage is optimized with respect to the HMM structure (the chain structure with any path achieving the final state has better discriminative properties than Bakis and ergodic structures), the number of states etc.
The pairwise training using a word model and a reference (world) model has been applied in the problem of recognition of speakers having similar voice characteristics in the text

dependent speaker verification system (Dymarski & Wydra, 2008). Similar corrective training algorithm was used, yielding greater distance (margin) between the authorized person and the impostors.
For a small number of words (e.g. the spoken digits recognition) a recognition system may be based on pairs of LM HMMs, trained for recognition of only two words. The pairwise training yields a good separation of classes and the final decision is made by voting (sect. 5)

3. Design of the Large Margin HMMs

A set of observations $\mathbf{X}_i^k$ (describing the k-th instance of the i-th word) and the HMM λ_i yield the log-likelihood $loglik(\mathbf{X}_i^k|\lambda_i) = \log\left[p(\mathbf{X}_i^k|\lambda_i)\right]$. The classical approach to HMM design consists in maximizing the log-likelihood for the whole database representing a given class i, i.e. maximizing of $Loglik(\mathbf{X}_i|\lambda_i) = \sum_k loglik(\mathbf{X}_i^k|\lambda_i)$ (3). In Fig.1 this yields a maximum value of the integral of the upper curve without considering the lower ones (values of $loglik(\mathbf{X}_i^k|\lambda_j)$ are not considered in the design process).
The measure of separation of the class i from the other classes $j = 1, 2, ..., L_w, \ j \neq i$ may be defined as a function of $d_i(\mathbf{X}_i^k)$. E.g. the sum

$$D_i(\mathbf{X}_i) = \sum_k d_i(\mathbf{X}_i^k) \tag{6}$$

may be used as a class separation measure. In Fig.1 it represents the area between the upper curve ($loglik(\mathbf{X}_i^k|\lambda_i)$) and a solid line representing $\max_{j\neq i} loglik(\mathbf{X}_i^k|\lambda_j)$. Such a measure may be used as a criterion for HMM design, but it must be considered, that increasing of the $d_i(\mathbf{X}_i^k)$ having already large values has no sense, because these instances do not contribute to recognition errors. In order to get rid of recognition errors negative values of $d_i(\mathbf{X}_i^k)$ should be eliminated. This suggests that a proper class separation measure should depend only on these negative values. However, for small databases it is quite easy to eliminate errors, but it is no guarantee that errors will not appear for instances not included in a database.
Therefore, in order to obtain a proper separation measure, not only negative values of $d_i(\mathbf{X}_i^k)$ should be considered, but also small positive values. These values correspond to a critical set (or a support vector set (Jiang et al., 2006; Vapnik, 1998)) and define a margin between the class i and the other classes. By maximizing the margin for a given database, the number of errors outside of the database is reduced (Jiang et al., 2006). As it is shown in (Vapnik, 1998), the greater the margin, the smaller the VC-dimension of the classifier, and the better its performance outside of a training set. The margin may be defined as a mean distance for the instances belonging to the critical set:

$$M_i(\mathbf{X}_i) = \frac{1}{s_i} \sum_{k \in S_i} d_i(\mathbf{X}_i^k) \tag{7}$$

where S_i- critical set, s_i- number of elements in the critical set. Here a critical set is defined as 10% of instances, yielding the smallest values of $d_i(\mathbf{X}_i^k)$.
In this work a Large Margin HMM training algorithm is proposed, based on an iterative application of the Baum-Welch procedure. It is partially based on suggestions appearing in (Jiang et al., 2006) and (Schlueter et al., 1997). As in (Jiang et al., 2006), only one HMM is optimized in a single iteration and the remaining ones are left unchanged (the *Iterative*

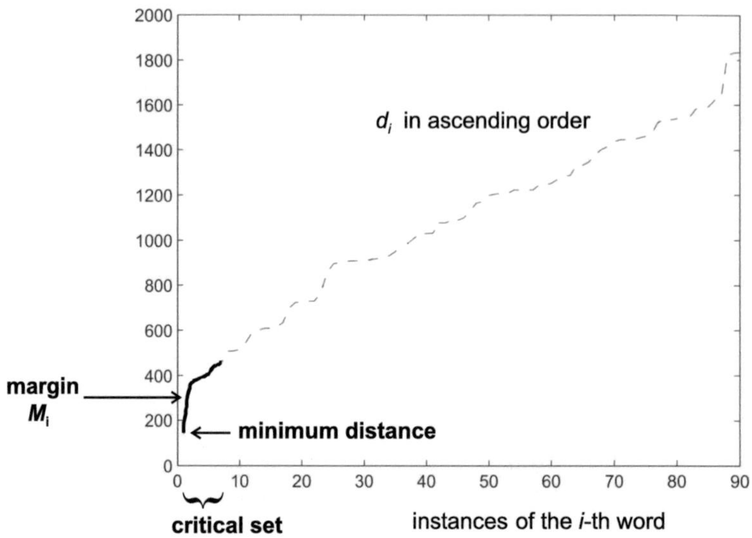

Fig. 2. The critical set of instances of the i-th word, the margin M_i and the minimum distance $d_{i,min}$

Localized Optimization approach). As in (Schlueter et al., 1997), the *corrective training* is used: the erroneously recognized elements are used to re-design of the HMM at each stage. The corrective training approach has been modified in this work: the whole database is used for HMM design, but the critical set has greater influence on the design process. To attain this, the critical set, re-defined in each iteration, is appended to the database. Thus the speech database is growing during the HMM design process, because the critical instances are duplicated and added to it.

The generic form of a proposed LM training algorithm may be described as follows:

1. Using the classical ML approach (Baum-Welch algorithm) calculate the initial HMMs for all L_w words, i.e. for the database $\mathbf{X}_i = \{\mathbf{X}_i^k\}$ calculate parameters of the HMM λ_i.
2. For each word $i = 1, \ldots, L_w$:
   - For each element of the database $\{\mathbf{X}_i^k\}$ (i.e. the k-th instance of the i-th word) calculate its distances to the other words $d_{i,j}(\mathbf{X}_i^k)$, $j = 1, \ldots, L_w$, $j \neq i$ and the measure of separation $d_i(\mathbf{X}_i^k)$
   - Define a critical set S_i and append the critical set to the database $\mathbf{X}_i = \{\mathbf{X}_i^k\}$
   - Recalculate the HMM λ_i using the Baum-Welch algorithm and the augmented database $\mathbf{X}_i = \{\mathbf{X}_i^k\}$
3. Check the stopping condition (e.g. the number of iterations). If it is not fulfilled, go to the step 2

Using the above algorithm, L_w models are modified consecutively. Several variants may be considered, which have been mentioned in the previous section:

- In the selective training, only selected HMMs are updated (e.g. only one HMM, generating most of the recognition errors).

- In the pairwise training, two HMMs are designed in the same time. Each iteration consists of two stages: firstly λ_i is modified and λ_j left unchanged, then λ_j is modified and λ_i left unchanged. The algorithm uses two databases $\{\mathbf{X}_i^k\}$ and $\{\mathbf{X}_j^k\}$. Note that in this case $d_i = d_{i,j}$. In the word disambiguation stage of the hierarchical recognition system, both HMMs (λ_i and λ_j) describe the phonetically similar words.

- In the pairwise training using the reference (world) model the first database $\{\mathbf{X}_i^k\}$ represents the i-th word and the second database $\{\mathbf{X}_j^k\}$ - all but the i-th word. In this notation j means "not i" so it will be replaced with $\bar{i}$. During the recognition phase, the differences

$$d_{i,\bar{i}}(\mathbf{X}_i^k) = loglik(\mathbf{X}_i^k|\lambda_i) - loglik(\mathbf{X}_i^k|\lambda_{\bar{i}}) \quad (8)$$

are used as a criterion. The model $\lambda_{\bar{i}}$ is used as a reference model for the i-th word. This approach has been used in the speaker recognition/verification task (Dymarski & Wydra, 2008).

4. Large Margin HMMs in command recognition

4.1 The ASR system based on the ML HMMs

The speaker independent ASR system, described in (Dymarski & Wydra, 2008),(Wydra, 2007), recognizes 20 robot controlling commands. The database (developed at the Military University of Technology, Warsaw) consisted of 143 instances of each command, uttered by 16 speakers: 90 instances were used for HMM design and 53 for testing. The content has been reviewed and the instances which have been damaged by the Voice Activity Detector were removed (e.g. *tar* which is a trimmed version od the word *start*). Therefore the results obtained using the classical (ML) HMM design are better than those reported in (Dymarski & Wydra, 2008; Wydra, 2007). As a simulation tool, the Murphy's Toolbox (Murphy, 2005) was used with modified procedures forcing the end of any path in a predefined state.
The Large Margin HMM design algorithms, proposed in previous section, start from the classical models obtained using the Maximum Likelihood (ML) approach. Therefore these classical models have been optimized, taking into consideration their structure, number of states, observation model, etc. If the ergodic or Bakis structure is used (the Bakis structure enables any transition "from the left to the right"), then e.g. the word *pje~ts'* (in phonetic SAMPA transcription (Sampa, n.d.)) is very often taken for *dz'evje~ts'*. In the chain structure (transitions "from the left to the right" without "jumps") this error appears very seldom. This conclusion is confirmed in Table 1: the mean margin increases for the chain structure. For the proper recognition of e.g. the words *os'* - *os'em* it is important that each state is visited (transitions "from the left to the right" without "jumps" and the final state being the right hand state) - Fig.3.
The number of states N should depend on the number of phonemes L_f in a word (Wydra, 2007), the choice $N = L_f + 2$ seems to be reasonable (Table 1).
The observation vector consisted of the energy, 10 mel-cepstrum coefficients and 3 coefficients characterizing voicing of speech (see (Wydra, 2007) for details). With the first and second derivatives there are 42 parameters, modeled with the gaussian pdf. The Gaussian Mixture Models were tested, but the results for the test instances were not better (about 3% of errors). The observed decrease of generalization ability may be due to the increase of HMM complexity, which influences its VC-dimension (Vapnik, 1998).

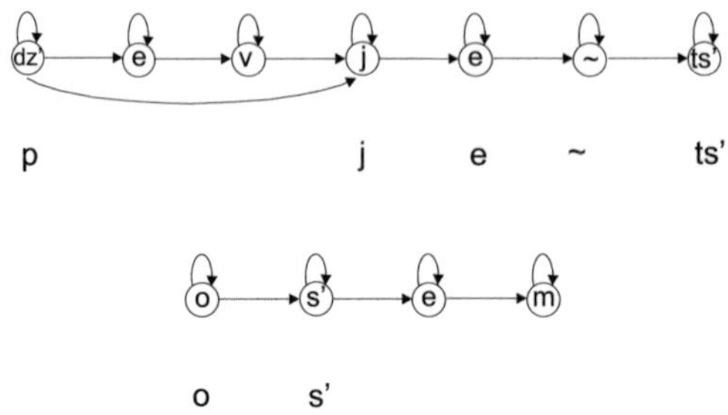

Fig. 3. Problems in recognizing pairs $dz'evje \sim ts'$ - $pje \sim ts'$ and $os'em$ - os' - (Dymarski & Wydra, 2008)

Thus, a good recognition system may be obtained using a chain HMM with the number of states $N = L_f + 2$ and gaussian observation models. Any path through the HMM must start in the left hand state and achieve the right hand state.

structure	nr of states	err % base	Margin base	err % test	Margin test
ergodic	$L_f + 2$	0.05	266	2.55*	141
Bakis	$L_f + 2$	0	259	2.74	138
Bakis-end	$L_f + 2$	0	250	3.20	122
chain	$L_f + 2$	0.05	298	0.94	180
chain-end	$L_f + 2$	**0.05**	**301**	**0.66**	**192**
chain-end	$L_f + 1$	0.05	259	1.32	166
chain-end	$L_f + 3$	0.05	311	0.75	200
chain-end	$L_f + 4$	0.05	372	1.04	216

* confidence interval ± 0.3 at 70% confidence for results $\approx 1\%$

Table 1. ML training: comparison of HMM structures (L_f - number of phonemes in a word, chain-end - chain structure with any state visited, Margin - the mean margin for 20 words, base - instances used for HMM design, test - instances used for testing)

4.2 Large Margin HMMs obtained by corrective and selective training

Further improvement of the class separation is obtained by using the Large Margin HMM design algorithms described in sect. 3. At first, the corrective training of all the 20 HMMs was tested. In consecutive iterations a constant increase of the margin is observed for the base instances (Fig.4). One recognition error (0.05% in Tab.1 for a chain-end structure) disappeared in the first iteration. However, the margin for the test instances increases very slowly and the error rate oscillates between 0.66% and 1.04%. This may be explained as follows: All the models are jointly optimized and maximization of the margin of the i-th word influences a large set of distances $d_{l,i}(\mathbf{X}_l^k)$. Some of them decrease, which may introduce new errors.
Better results may be obtained if only some of the HMMs are optimized - the selected ones, which exhibit errors or are characterized by a small margin. E.g. in the recognition system based on the "chain-end" HMM models (Tab.1, in bold) all the errors (7 for the test instances) were caused by the HMMs of the words $start$ and $stop$. Note the negative margins in Tab.2 for these words: -19 and -95. After 8 iterations of the corrective training algorithm, involving only the HMM describing the word $start$ there were only 5 errors, and after 1 iteration involving the HMM describing the word $stop$ the number of errors dropped to 4 (0.38%). The corresponding

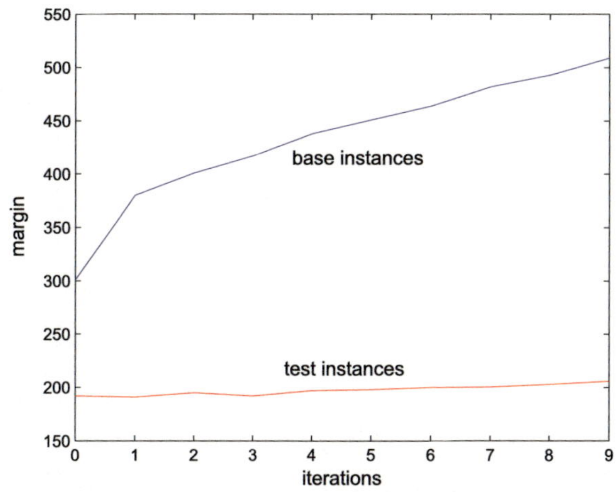

Fig. 4. Corrective training: mean margin for 20 words for the database instances and the test instances versus number of iterations

margins increased, but remained negative (-18 and -28). Thus the selective LM training has better generalization ability than the corrective LM training of all the HMMs. It is to be noted that the selective training improves the margins for the chosen HMMs (in this case two HMMs of the words *start* and *stop*), but does not change much the margins of the remaining HMMs (Tab.2).

4.3 Hierarchical ASR system based on the Large Margin HMMs

Further improvement is possible, if the phonetically similar words are passed to the second stage of the recognition system, i.e. a disambiguation stage. In this case pairs of models are trained, using the LM corrective training algorithm described in section 3.

This version of the corrective training algorithm has a "complementary" character, two HMMs (representing e.g. phonetically similar words i and j) are designed in the same time. Each iteration consists of two stages: first $\lambda_{i,j}$ (HMM of the word i yielding the maximum distance to the word j) is modified and $\lambda_{j,i}$ left unchanged, then $\lambda_{j,i}$ is modified and $\lambda_{i,j}$ left unchanged. The algorithm uses two databases $\{\mathbf{X}_i^k\}$ and $\{\mathbf{X}_j^k\}$. The following steps are performed N^{iter} times:

- For the database $\{\mathbf{X}_i^k\}$ calculate parameters of the HMM $\lambda_{i,j}$ using the Baum-Welch algorithm.
- For each element of the database $\{\mathbf{X}_i^k\}$ calculate a distance $d_{i,j}(\mathbf{X}_i^k)$, then define a critical set S_i (instances of the word i exhibiting small distances $d_{i,j}$) and append the critical set to the database.
- For the database $\{\mathbf{X}_j^k\}$ calculate parameters of the HMM $\lambda_{j,i}$ using the Baum-Welch algorithm.
- For each element of the database $\{\mathbf{X}_j^k\}$ calculate a distance $d_{j,i}(\mathbf{X}_j^k)$, then define a critical set S_j and append the critical set to the database.

word (SAMPA)	ML base	LMs base	LMh base	ML test	LMs test	LMh test
zero	360	360	360	150	150	150
jeden	356	356	356	206	206	206
dva	161	159	169	23	23	47
tSI	241	241	241	144	144	144
tSterI	271	271	271	93	93	93
$pje \sim ts'$	169	169	169	67	67	67
$Ses'ts'$	568	568	568	632	632	632
$s'edem$	311	311	311	165	165	165
$os'em$	804	805	805	752	752	752
$dz'evje \sim ts'$	361	361	361	287	287	287
xvItak	468	451	451	347	347	347
duw	307	305	305	228	224	224
gura	241	247	247	161	161	161
levo	248	248	248	179	179	179
os'	83	118	118	91	89	89
pravo	289	289	289	227	218	218
$pus'ts'$	203	205	205	123	125	125
start	**102**	**211**	**215**	**-19**	**-18**	**16**
stop	**142**	**184**	**198**	**-95**	**-28**	**33**
zwap	320	316	364	76	76	123
mean value	301	309	313	192	195	203

Table 2. Margins for 20 commands: ML- training using the Baum-Welch algorithm, LMs- selective training of the LM HMMs, LMh- hierarchical system, base - instances used for HMM design, test - instances used for testing)

This approach has several advantages:
- For each pair different HMM structure and different parameters (number of states, observation model) may be used,
- The *loglik* values may be modified using offset values, chosen for each pair. If the positive offset $o_{i,j}$ is added to any *loglik* obtained with the HMM $\lambda_{i,j}$, then the distance $d_{i,j}$ increases and $d_{j,i}$ decreases (4). A proper choice of $o_{i,j}$ may force any distance to be positive, which indicates lack of recognition errors.

In Figures 5 and 6 a problem of disambiguation of the pair *start* and *stop* is presented. Before the corrective training both ML HMMs yield some negative distances, i.e. errors are inevitable (Fig.5). After the optimization of HMM parameters (chain-end structure, 6 states for the $\lambda_{start,stop}$ and 4 states for the $\lambda_{stop,start}$, observation modeling using the gaussian pdf with a diagonal covariance matrix), application of LM discriminative training and the offset $o_{stop,start} = 85$ the distances became positive and errors disappeared (Fig.6).

The problem remains, which words should be selected for the second (disambiguation) stage of the recognition algorithm. The phonetic similarity may be used as a criterion (e.g. a pair *start* and *stop*) or the distances $d_{i,j}$ for the base instances used to HMM design may be considered (negative and small positive distances suggest passing to the disambiguation stage). Finally, the most frequent recognition errors may be noted (e.g. users of the spoken digits recognition system may complain that a digit 5 ($pje \sim ts'$) is frequently recognized as 9 ($dz'evje \sim ts'$)). For the 20 commands recognition system the following structure is adopted:

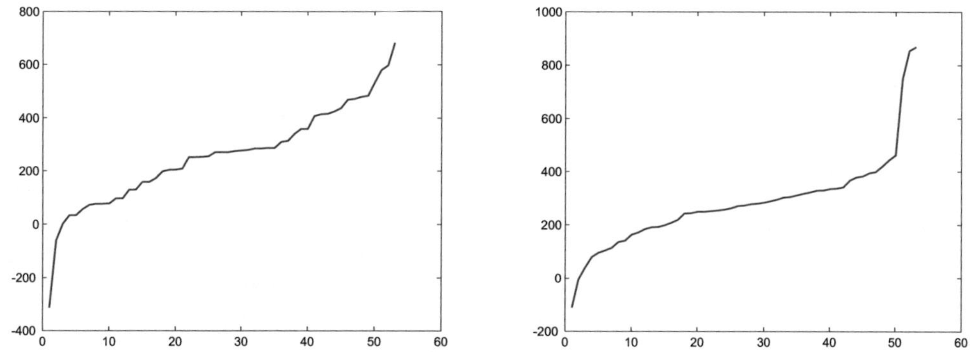

Fig. 5. Left side: distances $d_{stop,start}$ (in ascending order) for the test instances of the word *stop*, Right side: distances $d_{start,stop}$ for the test instances of the word *start*, ML HMM

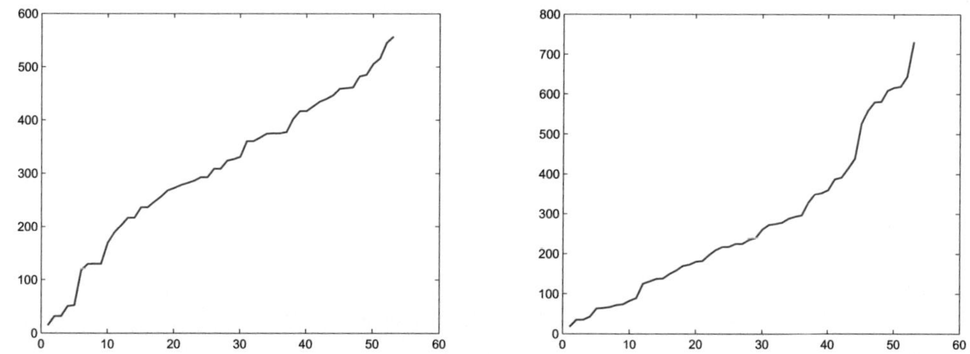

Fig. 6. Left side: distances $d_{stop,start}$ (in ascending order) for the test instances of the word *stop*, Right side: distances $d_{start,stop}$ for the test instances of the word *start*, LM HMM

1. **First stage:** For a given observation set **X**, representing an unknown spoken command, make a preliminary decision *prelim* yielding maximum log-likelihood:

$$prelim = \arg\max_i \; loglik(\mathbf{X}|\lambda_i)$$

   where $\{\lambda_i\}$ - HMMs used at the first stage of the recognition system.

2. **Second stage:** Set the final decision $final$ equal to the preliminary decision, except of the following cases:
   - If $prelim = start$ calculate the distance

$$d_{stop,start}(\mathbf{X}) = loglik(\mathbf{X}|\lambda_{stop,start}) + o_{stop,start} - \left[loglik(\mathbf{X}|\lambda_{start,stop}) + o_{start,stop}\right]$$

     If $d_{stop,start}(\mathbf{X}) > 0$ set $final = stop$.
   - If $prelim = stop$ calculate $d_{start,stop}(\mathbf{X})$. If $d_{start,stop}(\mathbf{X}) > 0$ set $final = start$.
   - If $prelim = zero$ calculate $d_{start,zero}(\mathbf{X})$. If $d_{start,zero}(\mathbf{X}) > 0$ set $final = start$.
   - If $prelim = zwap$ calculate $d_{dva,zwap}(\mathbf{X})$. If $d_{dva,zwap}(\mathbf{X}) > 0$ set $final = dva$.

- If $prelim = dva$ calculate $d_{zwap,dva}(\mathbf{X})$. If $d_{zwap,dva}(\mathbf{X}) > 0$ set $final = zwap$.
- If $prelim = tSterI$ calculate $d_{stop,tSterI}(\mathbf{X})$. If $d_{stop,tSterI}(\mathbf{X}) > 0$ set $final = stop$.
- If $prelim = pravo$ calculate $d_{start,pravo}(\mathbf{X})$. If $d_{start,pravo}(\mathbf{X}) > 0$ set $final = start$.

At the first stage of the proposed hierarchical system the HMMs obtained with selective training algorithm are used (see subsection 4.2). At this stage there are only 4 errors: (*stop* is taken for *start* and vice versa, *start* is taken for *zero*), but there are many small positive distances (e.g. concerning the words *dva* and *zwap*). At the disambiguation stage all errors disappeared and margins of the critical words increased (Tab.2). Note the positive margins for the test instances of the words *start* and *stop*, 16 and 33 correspondingly.

The probability of error is reduced at the disambiguation stage, because of better discriminative properties of complementary pairs of HMMs. At the first stage the distances (4)

$$d_{i,j}(\mathbf{X}_i^k) \ = \ loglik(\mathbf{X}_i^k|\lambda_i) \ - \ loglik(\mathbf{X}_i^k|\lambda_j)$$

are generally smaller than the distances used at the disambiguation stage:

$$d_{i,j}(\mathbf{X}_i^k) = loglik(\mathbf{X}_i^k|\lambda_{i,j}) + o_{i,j} - \left[loglik(\mathbf{X}_i^k|\lambda_{j,i}) + o_{j,i}\right] \tag{9}$$

Thus the corresponding margins increase and the probability of error drops.

5. Recognition of spoken digits using pairs of Large Margin HMMs

It has been observed (subsection 4.3) that pairs of LM HMMs $\lambda_{i,j}$ and $\lambda_{j,i}$ exhibit better discriminative properties than the whole system, consisting of the LM HMMs $\lambda_i, \ i = 1, \ldots, L_w$. Obviously, it is easier to solve the discrimination problem for two classes than for $L_w > 2$ classes. Discriminative training exploits differences of corresponding classes, therefore better results may be expected in solving the problem "is the observed word an instance of the spoken digit 5 or 9?" than solving the problem "is it 5 or any other spoken digit?". Thus, having L_w classes, it would be interesting to decompose the discrimination task to a series of binary discriminations. The number of these elementary tasks equals $\frac{L_w\ (L_w-1)}{2}$ and for each task a pair of HMMs is needed. Generally this approach is computationally too expensive, but for small number of classes it is feasible.

A good example is a system for spoken digits recognition, which may be decomposed to 45 binary discrimination tasks. The same database was used (143 instances of each command, uttered by 16 speakers: 90 instances for HMM design and 53 for testing). The observation vector consisted of the energy and 13 mel-cepstrum coefficients. With the first and second derivatives there are 42 parameters, modeled with the gaussian pdf. As before, the chain HMMs with the number of states $N = L_f + 2$ were used, with any path starting in the left hand state and achieving the right hand state.

At first, the classic ML HMMs $\lambda_i, \ i = 0, \ldots, 9$ were designed, using the Baum-Welch algorithm (the HMM λ_i represents the spoken digit i). Results (margins for the spoken digits) are given in Tab.3. Note the small values (48) for the test instances of the digits 4 (*tSterI*) and 5 (*pje* $\sim$ *ts'*). Indeed, there was an error (4 was taken for 0) and a series of small positive distances for digit 5 (usually "menaced" by the digit 9). This may be also observed in Fig.7 (note the negative distance for one of the test instances of the digit 4 and the ML HMM) and in Fig.9 (note a series of small positive distances for instances of the digit 5). In Fig.8

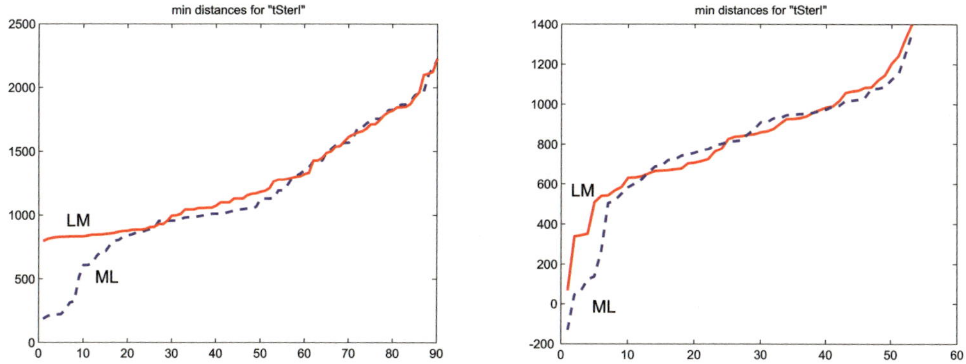

Fig. 7. Left side: distances $d_4 = min_{j \neq 4}(d_{4,j})$ for the database instances of the spoken digit 4 ($tSterI$), right side: the same for the test instances, ML- maximum likelihood HMMs, LM - large margin HMMs

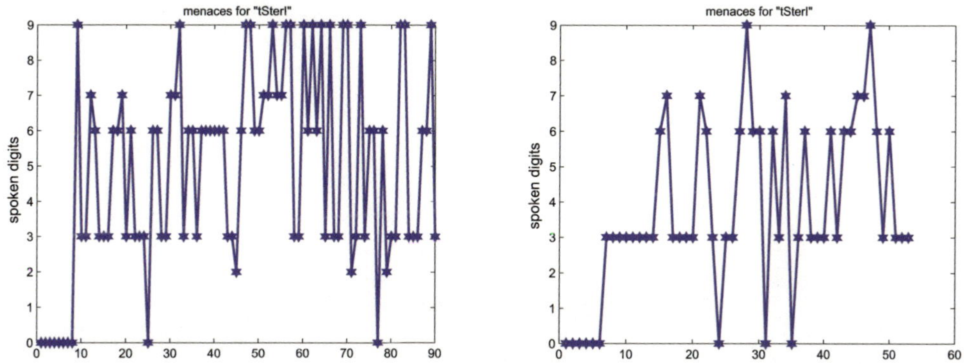

Fig. 8. Left side: competing words generating the minimum distances $d_4 = min_{j \neq 4}(d_{4,j})$ for the database instances of the spoken digit 4 ($tSterI$), right side: the same for the test instances, only for the maximum likelihood HMMs

the "menacing" digits are displayed for instances of the digit 4 - one can see that the small distances are due to the HMM of the word *zero* (instances on the x-axis are reordered as in the Fig.7). The second example concerns the digits 5 and 9 (Fig.11)- due to the phonetic similarity the digit 5 is usually menaced by 9 and vice versa.

In order to solve a problem of small and negative distances, pairs of the Large Margin HMMs $\lambda_{i,j}$ and $\lambda_{j,i}$ were designed, using the corrective training described in subsection 4.3. The problem remains, how to combine the results of 45 binary discriminations to make a final decision. For an observation set $\mathbf{X}$ representing an unknown digit, the binary discriminations are performed, yielding 45 distances (see equation 9):

$$d_{i,j}(\mathbf{X}) = loglik(\mathbf{X}|\lambda_{i,j}) + o_{i,j} - \left[loglik(\mathbf{X}|\lambda_{j,i}) + o_{j,i}\right] \tag{10}$$

These distances are stored in a 10×10 array $\mathbf{D}$ with an empty diagonal and $d_{j,i}(\mathbf{X}) = -d_{i,j}(\mathbf{X})$. Values stored in the i-th row correspond to the hypothesis that the observation set $\mathbf{X}$ represents

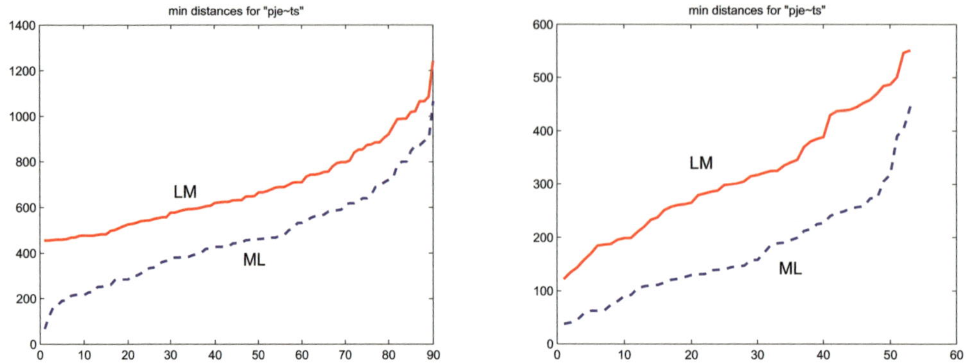

Fig. 9. Left side: distances $d_5 = min_{j \neq 5}(d_{5,j})$ for the database instances of the spoken digit 5 ($pje \sim ts'$), right side: the same for the test instances, ML- maximum likelihood HMMs, LM - large margin HMMs

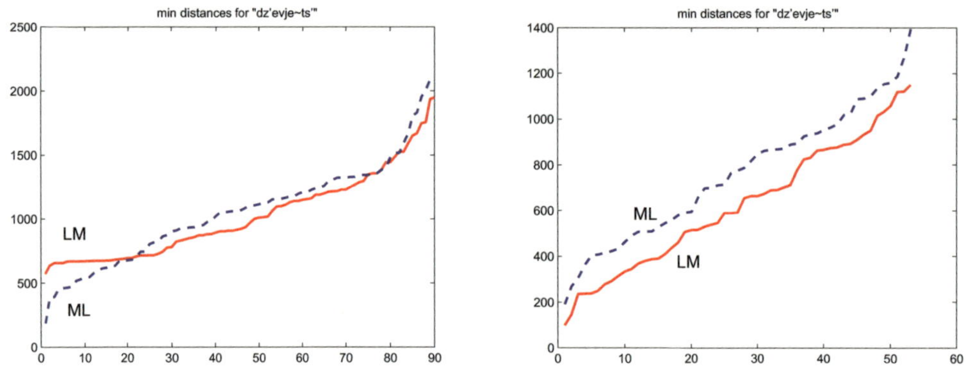

Fig. 10. Left side: distances $d_9 = min_{j \neq 9}(d_{9,j})$ for the database instances of the spoken digit 9 ($dz'evje \sim ts'$), right side: the same for the test instances, ML- maximum likelihood HMMs, LM - large margin HMMs

the digit i. The number of positive distances in this row may be regarded as a number of votes for the digit i. This number varies from 0 to 9. An example is shown in Fig.12: the numbers of positive votes in the upper row ($i = 0$) are displayed for instances of the spoken digit 4 ($\mathbf{X} = \mathbf{X}_4^k$) and the numbers of positive votes in the row $i = 4$ are displayed for instances of the spoken digit 0 ($\mathbf{X} = \mathbf{X}_0^k$). Note that the number of positive votes is variable and never attains the maximum value equal to 9. Different results are obtained for a pair of phonetically similar words 5 ($pje \sim ts'$) and 9 ($dz'evje \sim ts'$). Here (Fig.13) the number of positive votes equals 8 in most cases, but never attains 9. The maximum number of 9 votes is obtained only in the row $i = 5$ for instances of the word 5 ($\mathbf{X} = \mathbf{X}_5^k$) and in the row $i = 9$ for instances of the word 9 ($\mathbf{X} = \mathbf{X}_9^k$). The number of votes suggests the final decision. Problem may occur, if the maximum number of positive votes (e.g. 8) is obtained in two or more rows. In this case a "tie-break" algorithm may be used, e.g. taking into consideration the sum of entries in these rows. This algorithm, however, was not necessary: in any case the proper decision was made using the maximum number of positive votes. Note also a substantial increase of the margin

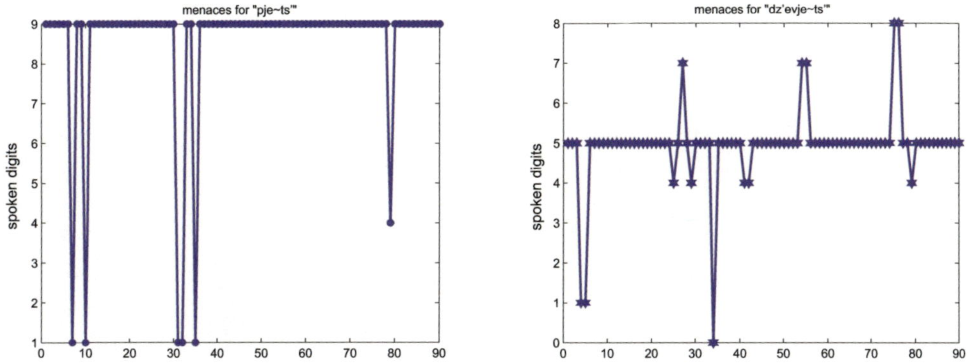

Fig. 11. Left side: competing words generating the minimum distances $d_5 = min_{j \neq 5}(d_{5,j})$ for the database instances of the spoken digit 5 ($pje \sim ts'$), right side: the same for the spoken digit 9 ($dz'evje \sim ts'$), only for the maximum likelihood HMMs

calculated for the database instances and an increase of the previously smallest margins for digits 4 and 5 (Tab.3). The same observation stems from Fig.7: note a substantial increase of the distances for the database instances and lack of errors (positive distances) for the digit 4. The proper choice of the offset value yields similar margins for the digits 5 and 9 (compare the results for LM HMMs in Fig.9 and Fig.10). In general, recognition system based on pairs of the LM HMMs yields greater distances and margins than the classical system based on ML HMMs.

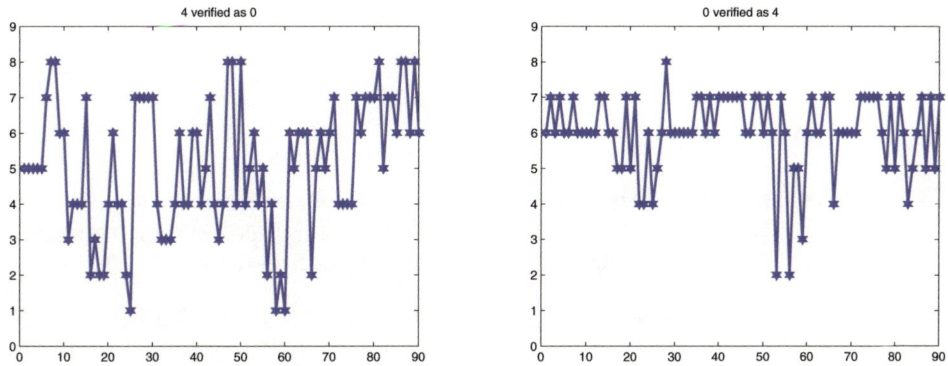

Fig. 12. Left side: verification of the hypothesis "Is it 0?" for instances of the spoken digit 4; right side: the hypothesis "Is it 4?" is verified for instances of the spoken digit 0 (x axis: database instances of the spoken digit, y axis: number of positive votes)

6. Conclusion

The class separation properties of different HMM structures and design methods are compared. The margin was selected as a measure of class separation. It is shown that margin may be increased by the iterative application of the classical Baum-Welch (or EM) algorithm and duplication of the critical instances. A series of algorithms of Large Margin HMM design

digit	word (SAMPA)	ML base	LMp base	ML test	LMp test
0	*zero*	556	672	372	344
1	*jeden*	452	785	259	266
2	*dva*	332	613	197	314
3	*tSI*	312	747	213	358
4	*tSterI*	275	823	48	321
5	$pje \sim ts'$	171	462	48	145
6	$Ses'ts'$	665	798	601	484
7	$s'edem$	497	732	387	327
8	$os'em$	888	1129	763	602
9	$dz'evje \sim ts'$	429	650	306	190
	mean value	458	741	319	335

Table 3. Margins for 10 spoken digits: ML- Maximum Likelihood training using the Baum-Welch algorithm, LMp- pairwise training of the LM HMMs, base - instances used for HMM design, test - instances used for testing)

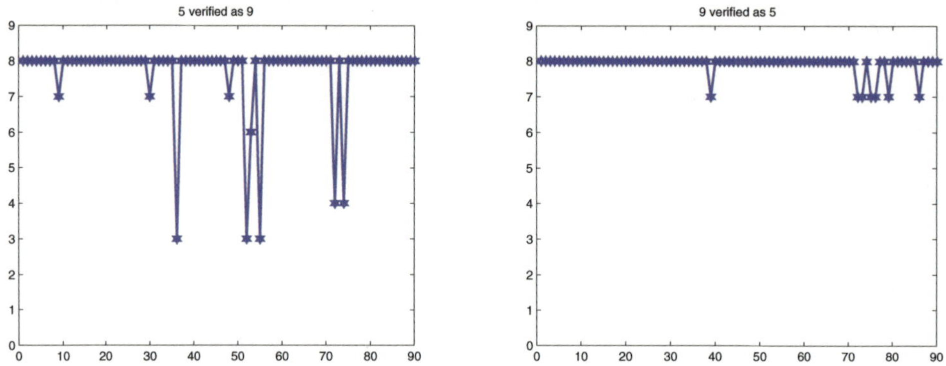

Fig. 13. Left side: verification of the hypothesis "Is it 9?" for instances of the spoken digit 5; right side: the hypothesis "Is it 5?" is verified for instances of the spoken digit 9 (x axis: database instances of the spoken digit, y axis: number of positive votes)

was proposed, based on corrective training and Iterative Localized Optimization. These algorithms exhibit good convergence properties and relatively low complexity. Particularly good results were obtained for pairs of HMMs optimized for two classes. It should be noted that the proposed Large Margin HMM training algorithms may be easily implemented using existing software (Baum-Welch or EM procedures). The Large Margin effect is obtained by the manipulation of the database.

The proposed algorithms were tested in a speaker independent system of robot controlling commands recognition. The best results were obtained for a two-stage hierarchical recognition. In the first stage either the classical HMMs or the Large Margin HMMs obtained with the selective optimization algorithm were applied. In the second stage a disambiguation of phonetically similar words was carried out, using pairs of Large Margin HMMs adapted to the words being processed.

For small number of classes (e.g. the spoken digits) the whole recognition system may be based on pairs of Large Margin HMMs. Tests confirm the improvement of performance (greater inter-class margin) in comparison to the classical recognition system based on the Maximum Likelihood approach.

7. References

Altun, Y., Tsochantaridis, I. & Hofmann, T. (2003). Hidden Markov Support Vector Machines, *Proceedings of the Twentieth International Conference on Machine Learning - ICML-2003*, Washington DC.

Bahl, L., Brown, P., deSouza, P. & L.R., M. (1986). Maximum mutual information estimation of Hidden Markov Model parameters for speech recognition, *Proc. ICASSP 1986*, Tokyo, Japan, pp. 49–52.

Chang, H. & Glass, J. (2009). Discriminative training of hierarchical acoustic models for large vocabulary continuous speech recognition, *Proc. ICASSP 2009*, pp. 4481–4484.

Dymarski, P. & Wydra, S. (2008). Large Margin Hidden Markov Models in command recognition and speaker verification problems, *Proc. of IWSSIP - International Conference on Systems, Signals and Image Processing*, Bratislava, Slovakia, pp. 221–224.

Fine, S., Saon, G. & Gopinath, R. (2002). Digit recognition in noisy environment via a sequential GMM/SVM system, *Proc. ICASSP 2002, vol.1*, pp. 49–52.

Gosztolya, G. & Kocsor, A. (2005). A hierarchical evaluation methodology in speech recognition, *Acta Cybernetica* Vol. 17: 213–224.

Hosseinzadeh, D. & Krishnan, S. (2008). On the use of complementary spectral features for speaker recognition, *EURASIP J. on Advances in Signal Proc.* vol. 2008, art.ID 258184.

Jiang, H., Li, X. & Liu, C. (2006). Large Margin Hidden Markov Models for speech recognition, *IEEE Trans. on Audio, Speech and Language Processing* Vol. 14(No. 5).

Kuo, H. & Gao, Y. (2006). Maximum entropy direct models for speech recognition, *IEEE Trans. on Audio, Speech and Language Processing* Vol. 14(No. 3).

Macherey, W. & Ney, H. (2003). A comparative study on maximum entropy and discriminative training for acoustic modeling in automatic speech recognition, *Proc. Eurospeech 2003*, Geneva, Switzerland, pp. 493–496.

Murphy, K. (2005). Hidden Markov Model (HMM) toolbox for Matlab. URL: *www.cs.ubc.ca/ murphyk/Software/HMM/hmm.html*

Rabiner, L. (1989). A tutorial on Hidden Markov Models and selected applications in speech recognition, *Proc. of the IEEE* Vol. 77(No. 2).

Sampa (n.d.). Sampa - computer readable phonetic alphabet. URL: *http://www.phon.ucl.ac.uk/home/sampa/polish.htm*

Schlueter, R., Macherey, W., Kanthak, S., Ney, H. & Welling, L. (1997). Comparison of optimization methods for discriminative training criteria, *Proc. Eurospeech 1997*, pp. 15–18.

Sha, F. & Saul, L. (2007). Comparison of large margin training to other discriminative methods for phonetic recognition by Hidden Markov Models, *Proc. ICASSP 2007*, Honolulu, Hawaii.

Siohan, O., Rosenberg, A. & Parthasarathy, S. (1998). Speaker identification using minimum classification error training, *Proc. ICASSP 1998*, pp. 109–112.

Vapnik, V. (1998). *Statistical Learning Theory*, John Wiley and Sons.

Wydra, S. (2007). Recognition quality improvement in automatic speech recognition system for Polish, *Proc. IEEE EUROCON 2007*, Warsaw, Poland.

Yang, D., Xu, M. & Wu, W. (2002). Study on the strategy for hierarchical speech recognition, *Proc. ISCSLP 2002, paper 111*.

6

Modeling of Speech Parameter Sequence Considering Global Variance for HMM-Based Speech Synthesis

Tomoki Toda
Nara Institute of Science and Technology
Japan

1. Introduction

Speech technologies such as speech recognition and speech synthesis have many potential applications since speech is the main way in which most people communicate. Various linguistic sounds are produced by controlling the configuration of oral cavities to convey a message in speech communication. The produced speech sounds temporally vary and are significantly affected by coarticulation effects. Thus, it is not straightforward to segment speech signals into corresponding linguistic symbols. Moreover, the acoustics of speech vary even if the same words are uttered by the same speaker due to differences in the manner of speaking and articulatory organs. Therefore, it is essential to stochastically model them in speech processing.

The hidden Markov model (HMM) is an effective framework for modeling the acoustics of speech. Its introduction has enabled significant progress in speech and language technologies. In particular, there have been numerous efforts to develop HMM-based acoustic modeling techniques in speech recognition, and continuous density HMMs have been widely used in modern continuous speech recognition systems (Gales & Young (2008)). Moreover, several approaches have been proposed for applying the HMM-based acoustic modeling techniques to speech synthesis technologies (Donovan & Woodland (1995); Huang et al. (1996)) such as Text-to-Speech (TTS), which is ... from a given text. Recently, HMM-based speech synthesis has been proposed (Yoshimura et al. (1999)) and has generated interest owing to its various attractive features such as completely data-driven voice building, flexible voice quality control, speaker adaptation, small footprint, and so forth (Zen et al. (2009)).

A basic framework of HMM-based speech synthesis consists of training and synthesis processes. In the training process, speech parameters such as spectral envelope and fundamental frequency (F_0) are extracted from speech waveforms and then their time sequences are modeled by context-dependent phoneme HMMs. To model the dynamic characteristics of speech acoustics with HMMs, which assume piecewise constant statistics within an HMM state and conditional independence, a joint vector of static and dynamic features is usually used as an observation vector. In the synthesis process, a smoothly varying speech parameter trajectory is generated by maximizing the likelihood of a composite sentence HMM subject to a constraint between static and dynamic features with respect to not the observation vector sequence including both static and dynamic features but the static feature vector sequence (Tokuda et al. (2000)). Finally, a vocoding technique is employed to generate a speech waveform from the generated speech parameters. This framework for directly generating speech parameters from the HMMs has the potential to be used for developing very flexible TTS systems. On the other hand, the quality of the synthetic speech is noticeably degraded compared with the original spoken audio. It is known that the static feature vectors generated from the HMMs are often oversmoothed, which is one of the main factors causing the muffled effect in synthetic speech.

There have been some attempts to model new features of speech acoustics to ensure that the generated parameters exhibit similar properties to those of natural speech, thus reducing the oversmoothing effect. As one of the most effective features for capturing properties not well modeled by traditional HMMs, Toda and Tokuda (Toda & Tokuda (2007)) proposed the global variance (GV), which is the variance of the static feature vectors calculated over a time sequence (*e.g.*, over an utterance). It has been found that the GV is inversely correlated with the oversmoothing effect. Therefore, a metric on the GV of the generated parameters effectively acts as a penalty term in the parameter generation process. Several papers (Toda & Tokuda (2007); Zen et al. (2007a; 2008)) have reported that the naturalness of synthetic speech is significantly improved by considering the GV in HMM-based speech synthesis. Moreover, it has been reported that the use of the GV is also effective for improving other statistical parametric speech synthesis techniques such as voice conversion (Toda et al. (2007)). It is not an exaggeration to say that GV modeling has significantly contributed to the recent improvements in those techniques.

This chapter presents an overview of the techniques for modeling a speech parameter sequence considering the GV for HMM-based speech synthesis. First, the traditional framework for HMM-based speech synthesis and its weaknesses are described. Then, the parameter generation algorithm considering the GV (Toda & Tokuda (2007)) is presented as an effective approach to addressing the oversmoothing problem caused by the traditional modeling process. This algorithm is capable of generating the parameter trajectory, yielding a significant improvement in synthetic speech quality while maintaining its GV close to its natural value. Furthermore, a training method considering the GV (Toda & Young (2009)) is presented, which is derived by introducing the GV-based parameter generation into the HMM training process. It is shown that this method yields some additional advantages such as the use of a consistent optimization criterion between the training and synthesis processes and the use of a closed-form solution for parameter generation, whereas only an iterative solution is available if the GV is considered in only the parameter generation process. Finally, several experimental results are presented to demonstrate that these methods yield a significant improvement in the naturalness of synthetic speech.

2. Basic framework of HMM-based speech synthesis

Figure 1 shows a schematic image of the basic training and synthesis processes of HMM-based speech synthesis. In the training process, the time sequence of the static feature vectors $\boldsymbol{c}$ is linearly transformed into a higher-dimensional space using the linear transformation function $f_o(\boldsymbol{c})$. Then, the transformed feature vector sequence consisting of static and dynamic feature vectors $\boldsymbol{o}$ is modeled with HMMs. In the synthesis process, the static feature vector sequence is determined by maximizing the likelihood of the HMMs for the static and dynamic feature vectors with respect to only the static feature vectors under the constraint given by the linear transformation function. The following subsections give more details of these training and synthesis processes.

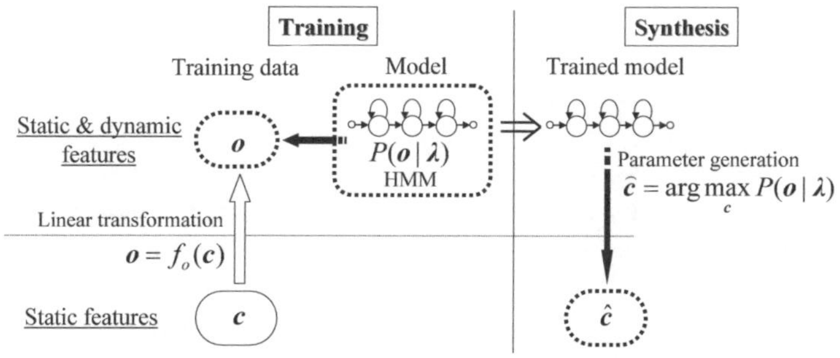

Fig. 1. Schematic image of basic training and synthesis processes of HMM-based speech synthesis.

2.1 Speech parameter sequence modeling

Let us assume a D-dimensional static feature vector of a speech parameter $\boldsymbol{c}_t = [c_t(1), c_t(2), \cdots, c_t(d), \cdots, c_t(D)]^\top$ at frame t. To suitably model the dynamic properties of the speech parameter with HMMs, the first dynamic feature vector $\Delta^{(1)}\boldsymbol{c}_t$ and the second dynamic feature vector $\Delta^{(2)}\boldsymbol{c}_t$ are calculated frame by frame as follows:

$$\Delta^{(n)}\boldsymbol{c}_t = \sum_{\tau=-L_-^{(n)}}^{L_+^{(n)}} w^{(n)}(\tau)\boldsymbol{c}_{t+\tau}, \quad n = 1,2, \tag{1}$$

where $w^{(n)}(t)$ is a regression coefficient used to calculate the dynamic features from the current frame, $L_-^{(n)}$ previous frames, and $L_+^{(n)}$ succeeding frames,[1] and then a joint static and dynamic feature vector $\boldsymbol{o}_t = \left[\boldsymbol{c}_t^\top, \Delta^{(1)}\boldsymbol{c}_t^\top, \Delta^{(2)}\boldsymbol{c}_t^\top\right]^\top$ is used as the observation vector. The time sequence vectors of the joint static and dynamic feature vector $\boldsymbol{o}_t$ and the static feature vector $\boldsymbol{c}_t$ are written as $\boldsymbol{o} = \left[\boldsymbol{o}_1^\top, \boldsymbol{o}_2^\top, \cdots, \boldsymbol{o}_t^\top, \cdots, \boldsymbol{o}_T^\top\right]^\top$ and $\boldsymbol{c} = \left[\boldsymbol{c}_1^\top, \boldsymbol{c}_2^\top, \cdots, \boldsymbol{c}_t^\top, \cdots, \boldsymbol{c}_T^\top\right]^\top$, respectively. The relationship between these two time sequence vectors is represented as a linear transformation as follows:

$$\boldsymbol{o} = \boldsymbol{W}\boldsymbol{c}, \tag{2}$$

where $\boldsymbol{W}$ is the $3DT$-by-DT matrix written as

$$\boldsymbol{W} = [\boldsymbol{W}_1, \boldsymbol{W}_2, \cdots, \boldsymbol{W}_t, \cdots, \boldsymbol{W}_T]^\top \otimes \boldsymbol{I}_{D\times D}, \tag{3}$$

$$\boldsymbol{W}_t = \left[\boldsymbol{w}_t^{(0)}, \boldsymbol{w}_t^{(1)}, \boldsymbol{w}_t^{(2)}\right], \tag{4}$$

$$\boldsymbol{w}_t^{(n)} = \Big[\underbrace{0}_{\text{1st}}, \cdots, 0, \underbrace{w^{(n)}(-L_-^{(n)})}_{\left(t-L_-^{(n)}\right)\text{-th}}, \cdots, \underbrace{w^{(n)}(0)}_{(t)\text{-th}}, \cdots, \underbrace{w^{(n)}(L_+^{(n)})}_{\left(t+L_+^{(n)}\right)\text{-th}}, 0, \cdots, \underbrace{0}_{T\text{-th}}\Big]^\top, \tag{5}$$

[1] For example, when the number of frames to be used for calculating dynamic features is set to $L_-^{(1)} = L_+^{(1)} = 1$ and $L_-^{(2)} = L_+^{(2)} = 1$, the regression coefficients can be set to $w^{(1)}(t-1) = -0.5$, $w^{(1)}(t) = 0$, $w^{(1)}(t+1) = 0.5$, $w^{(2)}(t-1) = 1$, $w^{(2)}(t) = -2$, and $w^{(2)}(t+1) = 1$.

where $L_{-}^{(0)} = L_{+}^{(0)} = 0$, and $w^{(0)}(0) = 1$. The operator $\otimes$ denotes the Kronecker product. The matrix $\boldsymbol{I}_{D \times D}$ denotes the D-by-D identity matrix. It is important to note that the joint static and dynamic feature vector sequence $\boldsymbol{o}$ is generated from the static feature vector sequence $\boldsymbol{c}$ using the linear transformation function given by Eq. (2).

The observation sequence vector $\boldsymbol{o}$ is modeled by context-dependent phoneme HMMs, whose the parameter set is denoted by $\boldsymbol{\lambda}$. The state output probability density function (p.d.f.) of $\boldsymbol{o}_t$ at an HMM state q is usually modeled by a single multivariate Gaussian distribution as follows:

$$\mathcal{N}\left(\boldsymbol{o}_t; \boldsymbol{\mu}_q, \boldsymbol{U}_q\right) = \frac{1}{\sqrt{(2\pi)^{3D}|\boldsymbol{U}_q|}} \exp\left(-\frac{1}{2}\left(\boldsymbol{o}_t - \boldsymbol{\mu}_q\right)^{\top} \boldsymbol{U}_q^{-1}\left(\boldsymbol{o}_t - \boldsymbol{\mu}_q\right)\right), \tag{6}$$

where $\boldsymbol{\mu}_q$ and $\boldsymbol{U}_q$ are the mean vector and the covariance matrix, respectively. The p.d.f. of the observation sequence vector $\boldsymbol{o}$ given an HMM state sequence $\boldsymbol{q} = \{q_1, q_2, \cdots, q_t, \cdots, q_T\}$ is written as

$$\begin{aligned} P(\boldsymbol{o}|\boldsymbol{q}, \boldsymbol{\lambda}) &= \prod_{t=1}^{T} \mathcal{N}\left(\boldsymbol{o}_t; \boldsymbol{\mu}_{q_t}, \boldsymbol{U}_{q_t}\right) \\ &= \mathcal{N}\left(\boldsymbol{o}; \boldsymbol{\mu}_{\boldsymbol{q}}, \boldsymbol{U}_{\boldsymbol{q}}\right), \end{aligned} \tag{7}$$

where $\boldsymbol{\mu}_{\boldsymbol{q}}$ and $\boldsymbol{U}_{\boldsymbol{q}}$ are the $3D$-by-1 mean vector and the $3D$-by-$3D$ covariance matrix, respectively, which are given by

$$\boldsymbol{\mu}_{\boldsymbol{q}} = \left[\boldsymbol{\mu}_{q_1}^{\top}, \boldsymbol{\mu}_{q_2}^{\top}, \cdots, \boldsymbol{\mu}_{q_t}^{\top}, \cdots, \boldsymbol{\mu}_{q_T}^{\top}\right]^{\top}, \tag{8}$$

$$\begin{aligned} \boldsymbol{U}_{\boldsymbol{q}} &= \mathrm{diag}\left[\boldsymbol{U}_{q_1}, \boldsymbol{U}_{q_2}, \cdots, \boldsymbol{U}_{q_t}, \cdots, \boldsymbol{U}_{q_T}\right] \\ &= \begin{bmatrix} \boldsymbol{U}_{q_1} & & & \\ & \boldsymbol{U}_{q_2} & & \\ & & \ddots & \\ & & & \boldsymbol{U}_{q_T} \end{bmatrix}. \end{aligned} \tag{9}$$

The operator diag$[\cdot]$ denotes the transformation from a rectangular matrix (or a vector) to a block diagonal matrix (or a diagonal matrix). The likelihood function given the HMM set for the observation sequence vector $\boldsymbol{o}$ is given by

$$\begin{aligned} P(\boldsymbol{o}|\boldsymbol{\lambda}) &= \sum_{\text{all } \boldsymbol{q}} P(\boldsymbol{o}, \boldsymbol{q}|\boldsymbol{\lambda}) \\ &= \sum_{\text{all } \boldsymbol{q}} P(\boldsymbol{o}|\boldsymbol{q}, \boldsymbol{\lambda}) P(\boldsymbol{q}|\boldsymbol{\lambda}), \end{aligned} \tag{10}$$

where $P(\boldsymbol{q}|\boldsymbol{\lambda})$ is usually modeled by state transition probabilities in speech recognition. However, in speech synthesis explicit duration models are often incorporated into the HMMs to model the temporal structure of a speech parameter sequence appropriately (Yoshimura et al. (1999); Zen et al. (2007b)). In training, the HMM parameter set $\boldsymbol{\lambda}$ is optimized for the given observation sequence vectors $\boldsymbol{o}^{(1)}, \boldsymbol{o}^{(2)}, \cdots, \boldsymbol{o}^{(k)}, \cdots, \boldsymbol{o}^{(K)}$ in the sense of maximum likelihood

(ML) as follows:

$$\hat{\boldsymbol{\lambda}} = \arg\max_{\boldsymbol{\lambda}} \prod_{k=1}^{K} P\left(\boldsymbol{o}^{(k)}|\boldsymbol{\lambda}\right), \tag{11}$$

where K is the total number of observation sequence vectors.

2.2 Parameter generation based on maximum likelihood criterion

In synthesis, a time sequence of static feature vectors is determined by maximizing the HMM likelihood under the condition given by Eq. (2) as follows:

$$\hat{\boldsymbol{c}} = \operatorname*{argmax}_{\boldsymbol{c}} P(\boldsymbol{o}|\boldsymbol{\lambda}) \qquad \text{subject to} \quad \boldsymbol{o} = \boldsymbol{W}\boldsymbol{c}. \tag{12}$$

To reduce the computational cost, the HMM likelihood is usually approximated with a single HMM state sequence as follows:

$$P(\boldsymbol{o}|\boldsymbol{\lambda}) \simeq P(\boldsymbol{o}|\boldsymbol{q},\boldsymbol{\lambda})P(\boldsymbol{q}|\boldsymbol{\lambda}), \tag{13}$$

and then the HMM state sequence and the static feature vector sequence are sequentially determined. First a suboptimum HMM state sequence is determined by

$$\hat{\boldsymbol{q}} = \operatorname{argmax} P(\boldsymbol{q}|\boldsymbol{\lambda}). \tag{14}$$

Then, the static feature vector sequence is determined by maximizing the HMM likelihood given the HMM state sequence $\boldsymbol{q}$ as follows:

$$\hat{\boldsymbol{c}} = \operatorname{argmax} P(\boldsymbol{o}|\boldsymbol{q},\boldsymbol{\lambda}) \qquad \text{subject to} \quad \boldsymbol{o} = \boldsymbol{W}\boldsymbol{c}. \tag{15}$$

The objective function $\mathcal{L}_q$ to be maximized with respect to the static feature vector sequence is given by

$$\begin{aligned}
\mathcal{L}_q &= \log P(\boldsymbol{o}|\boldsymbol{q},\boldsymbol{\lambda}) && (16)\\
&\propto -\frac{1}{2}\boldsymbol{o}^\top \boldsymbol{U}_q^{-1}\boldsymbol{o} + \boldsymbol{o}^\top \boldsymbol{U}_q^{-1}\boldsymbol{\mu}_q \\
&= -\frac{1}{2}\boldsymbol{c}^\top \boldsymbol{W}^\top \boldsymbol{U}_q^{-1}\boldsymbol{W}\boldsymbol{c} + \boldsymbol{c}^\top \boldsymbol{W}^\top \boldsymbol{U}_q^{-1}\boldsymbol{\mu}_q \\
&= -\frac{1}{2}\boldsymbol{c}^\top \boldsymbol{R}_q\boldsymbol{c} + \boldsymbol{c}^\top \boldsymbol{r}_q, && (17)
\end{aligned}$$

where

$$\boldsymbol{R}_q = \boldsymbol{W}^\top \boldsymbol{U}_q^{-1}\boldsymbol{W}, \tag{18}$$

$$\boldsymbol{r}_q = \boldsymbol{W}^\top \boldsymbol{U}_q^{-1}\boldsymbol{\mu}_q. \tag{19}$$

The ML estimate of the static feature vector sequence $\overline{\boldsymbol{c}}_q$ is given by

$$\overline{\boldsymbol{c}}_q = \boldsymbol{P}_q\boldsymbol{r}_q, \tag{20}$$

$$\boldsymbol{P}_q = \boldsymbol{R}_q^{-1}. \tag{21}$$

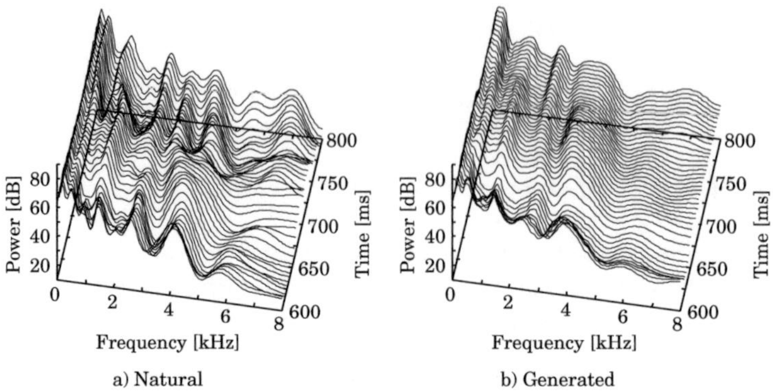

Fig. 2. An example of natural and generated spectral segments.

Since the matrix $\boldsymbol{P}_q$ is generally full owing to the inverse of the band matrix $\boldsymbol{R}_q$, the state output p.d.f. at each HMM state affects the ML estimates of the static feature vectors at all frames over a time sequence. This parameter generation algorithm is capable of generating speech parameter trajectories that vary frame by frame from the p.d.f. sequence corresponding to discrete state sequences so that the generated trajectories exhibit suitable static and dynamic properties.

The calculation of the ML estimate is efficiently performed by the Cholesky decomposition of $\boldsymbol{R}_q$ and the forward/backward substitution operation. It is also possible to implement a recursive estimation process so as to generate the static feature vectors frame by frame (Tokuda et al. (1995)). Furthermore, although only the case of using a single multivariate Gaussian distribution as the state output p.d.f. is described in this section, Gaussian mixture models can also be employed in this framework by using the Expectation-Maximization (EM) algorithm (Tokuda et al. (2000)).

2.3 Oversmoothing effect

In HMM-based speech synthesis, speech samples synthesized with the generated speech parameters often sound muffled. One of the factors causing the muffled sound is the oversmoothing of the generated speech parameters. **Figure 2** shows an example of natural and generated spectral segments. It can be observed from this figure that the generated spectra are often excessively smoothed compared with the natural spectra. The statistical modeling process with HMMs tends to remove the details of spectral structures. Although this smoothing results in reduced error in the generation of spectra, it also causes the degradation of naturalness of synthetic speech because the removed structures are still necessary for synthesizing high-quality speech.

3. Parameter generation considering global variance

To reduce oversmoothing, a parameter generation algorithm considering the GV has been proposed (Toda & Tokuda (2007)). A schematic image of the training and synthesis processes is shown in **Figure 3**. In the training process, the linearly transformed feature vector sequence consisting of static and dynamic feature vectors $\boldsymbol{o}$ is modeled with HMMs in the same manner as discussed in **Section 2**. Also, the time sequence of the static feature vectors $\boldsymbol{c}$ is nonlinearly transformed into the GV $\boldsymbol{v}$ using the nonlinear transformation function $f_v(\boldsymbol{c})$, and then its p.d.f. is modeled with a continuous density distribution. In the synthesis process, the static feature vector sequence is determined by maximizing the product of the HMM likelihood and

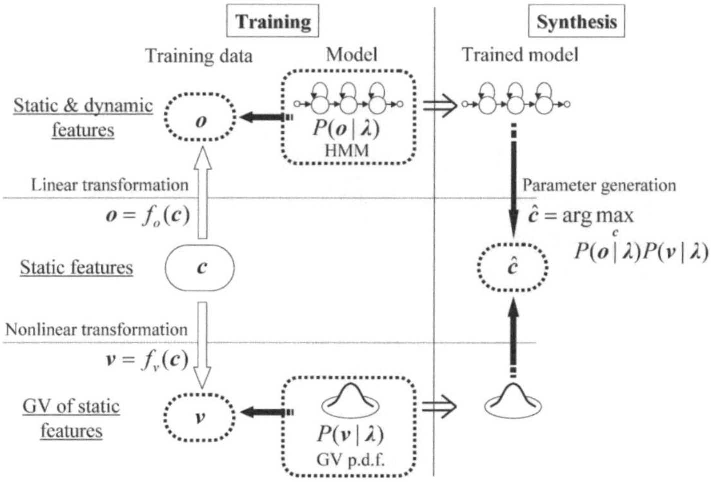

Fig. 3. Schematic image of training and synthesis processes of HMM-based speech synthesis with GV-based parameter generation algorithm.

the GV likelihood. The following subsections give more details of these training and synthesis processes.

3.1 Global Variance (GV)

The GV vector $\boldsymbol{v}(\boldsymbol{c}) = [v(1), \cdots, v(d), \cdots, v(D)]^\top$ of a static feature vector sequence $\boldsymbol{c}$ is calculated by

$$v(d) = \frac{1}{T} \sum_{t=1}^{T} \left(c_t(d) - \langle c(d) \rangle\right)^2, \tag{22}$$

where

$$\langle c(d) \rangle = \frac{1}{T} \sum_{\tau=1}^{T} c_\tau(d). \tag{23}$$

The GV is often calculated utterance by utterance.

Figure 4 shows a time sequence of the 2nd mel-cepstral coefficients extracted from natural speech and that generated from the HMM, where mel-cepstrum is one of the most effective spectral parameters (Tokuda et al. (1994)). It can be observed that the GV of the generated mel-cepstra (given by Eq. (20)) is smaller than that of the natural ones. The ML criterion usually makes the generated trajectory close to the mean vector sequence of the HMM. Consequently, the reduction of GV is often observed.

3.2 Parameter generation algorithm considering GV

To consider the GV in the parameter generation process, the p.d.f. of the GV is modeled by a single multivariate Gaussian distribution, which is given by

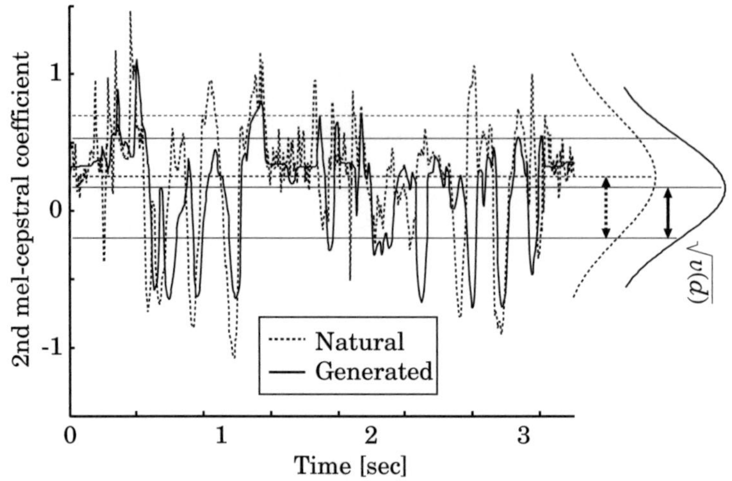

Fig. 4. Natural and generated mel-cepstrum sequences. The square root of the GV of each sequence is shown as a bidirectional arrow.

$$P(\boldsymbol{v}(\boldsymbol{c})|\boldsymbol{\lambda}_v) = \mathcal{N}(\boldsymbol{v}(\boldsymbol{c}); \boldsymbol{\mu}_v, \boldsymbol{U}_v)$$
$$= \frac{1}{\sqrt{(2\pi)^D |\boldsymbol{U}_v|}} \exp\left(-\frac{1}{2}(\boldsymbol{v}(\boldsymbol{c}) - \boldsymbol{\mu}_v)^\top \boldsymbol{U}_v^{-1} (\boldsymbol{v}(\boldsymbol{c}) - \boldsymbol{\mu}_v)\right), \quad (24)$$

where $\boldsymbol{\lambda}_v$ denotes the GV parameter set consisting of the mean vector $\boldsymbol{\mu}_v$ and the covariance matrix $\boldsymbol{U}_v$. The GV parameter set $\boldsymbol{\lambda}_v$ and the HMM parameter set $\boldsymbol{\lambda}$ are independently trained from speech samples in the training data.

In the synthesis process, given a suboptimum HMM state sequence $\boldsymbol{q}$, the static feature vector sequence is determined by maximizing a new likelihood function given by a product of the HMM likelihood for the static and dynamic feature vectors and the GV likelihood as follows:

$$\hat{\boldsymbol{c}} = \operatorname{argmax} P(\boldsymbol{o}|\boldsymbol{q}, \boldsymbol{\lambda}) P(\boldsymbol{v}(\boldsymbol{c})|\boldsymbol{\lambda}_v)^{\omega T} \qquad \text{subject to} \quad \boldsymbol{o} = \boldsymbol{W}\boldsymbol{c}, \quad (25)$$

where the constant ω denotes the GV weight, used for controlling the balance between the two likelihoods, which is usually set to the ratio between the number of dimensions of vectors $\boldsymbol{v}(\boldsymbol{c})$ and $\boldsymbol{o}$ (*i.e.*, $\omega = 3$). Note that this likelihood function with an additional constraint on the GV of the generated trajectory is still a function of the static feature vector sequence $\boldsymbol{c}$. The GV likelihood $P(\boldsymbol{v}(\boldsymbol{c})|\boldsymbol{\lambda}_v)$ can be viewed as a penalty term for a reduction of the GV. The objective function $\mathcal{L}_{\boldsymbol{q}}^{(GV)}$ to be maximized with respect to the static feature vector sequence is written as

$$\mathcal{L}_{\boldsymbol{q}}^{(GV)} = \log P(\boldsymbol{o}|\boldsymbol{q}, \boldsymbol{\lambda}) + \omega T \log P(\boldsymbol{v}(\boldsymbol{c})|\boldsymbol{\lambda}_v) \quad (26)$$
$$\propto -\frac{1}{2}\boldsymbol{c}^\top \boldsymbol{R}_{\boldsymbol{q}} \boldsymbol{c} + \boldsymbol{c}^\top \boldsymbol{r}_{\boldsymbol{q}} + \omega T \left(-\frac{1}{2}\boldsymbol{v}(\boldsymbol{c})^\top \boldsymbol{U}_v^{-1} \boldsymbol{v}(\boldsymbol{c}) + \boldsymbol{v}(\boldsymbol{c})^\top \boldsymbol{U}_v^{-1} \boldsymbol{\mu}_v\right). \quad (27)$$

This objective function is equivalent to the traditional function given by Eq. (16) when the GV weight ω is set to 0. To determine the static feature vector sequence maximizing the objective function, an iterative process for updating $\hat{\boldsymbol{c}}$ employing the gradient method is necessary as follows:

$$\hat{\boldsymbol{c}}^{(i+1)\text{-th}} = \hat{\boldsymbol{c}}^{(i)\text{-th}} + \alpha \cdot \delta\hat{\boldsymbol{c}}^{(i)\text{-th}}, \tag{28}$$

where α is the step size parameter. The following two gradient methods are basically employed to calculate the vector $\delta\hat{\boldsymbol{c}}^{(i)\text{-th}}$.

Steepest descent algorithm: Using the steepest descent algorithm, $\delta\hat{\boldsymbol{c}}^{(i)\text{-th}}$ is written as

$$\delta\hat{\boldsymbol{c}}^{(i)\text{-th}} = \left.\frac{\partial \mathcal{L}_{\boldsymbol{q}}^{(GV)}}{\partial \boldsymbol{c}}\right|_{\boldsymbol{c}=\hat{\boldsymbol{c}}^{(i)\text{-th}}}. \tag{29}$$

The first derivative is calculated by

$$\frac{\partial \mathcal{L}_{\boldsymbol{q}}^{(GV)}}{\partial \boldsymbol{c}} = -\boldsymbol{R}_{\boldsymbol{q}}\boldsymbol{c} + \boldsymbol{r}_{\boldsymbol{q}} + \omega \boldsymbol{x}, \tag{30}$$

$$\boldsymbol{x} = \left[\boldsymbol{x}_1^\top, \boldsymbol{x}_2^\top, \cdots, \boldsymbol{x}_t^\top, \cdots, \boldsymbol{x}_T^\top\right]^\top, \tag{31}$$

$$\boldsymbol{x}_t = \left[x_t(1), x_t(2), \cdots, x_t(d), \cdots, x_t(D)\right]^\top, \tag{32}$$

$$x_t(d) = -2\left(c_t(d) - \langle c(d)\rangle\right)\left(\boldsymbol{v}(\boldsymbol{c}) - \boldsymbol{\mu}_v\right)^\top \boldsymbol{p}_v^{(d)}, \tag{33}$$

where $\boldsymbol{p}_v^{(d)}$ is the d-th column vector of the precision matrix $\boldsymbol{P}_v (= \boldsymbol{U}_v^{-1})$.

Newton-Raphson method: If the initial value of the static feature vector sequence $\hat{\boldsymbol{c}}^{(0)\text{-th}}$ is close to the optimum value, the Newton-Raphson method using not only the first derivative but also the second derivative, *i.e.*, the Hessian matrix, may also be used. The vector $\delta\hat{\boldsymbol{c}}^{(i)\text{-th}}$ is written as

$$\delta\hat{\boldsymbol{c}}^{(i)\text{-th}} = -\left.\left(\frac{\partial^2 \mathcal{L}_{\boldsymbol{q}}^{(GV)}}{\partial \boldsymbol{c}\partial \boldsymbol{c}^\top}\right)^{-1} \frac{\partial \mathcal{L}_{\boldsymbol{q}}^{(GV)}}{\partial \boldsymbol{c}}\right|_{\boldsymbol{c}=\hat{\boldsymbol{c}}^{(i)\text{-th}}}. \tag{34}$$

Because a Hessian matrix is not always a positive-definite matrix, the following second derivative, approximated using only diagonal elements, is used:

$$\frac{\partial^2 \mathcal{L}_{\boldsymbol{q}}^{(GV)}}{\partial \boldsymbol{c}\partial \boldsymbol{c}^\top} \simeq \mathrm{diag}\left[-\mathrm{diag}^{-1}\left[\boldsymbol{R}_{\boldsymbol{q}}\right] + \omega \boldsymbol{y}\right], \tag{35}$$

$$\boldsymbol{y} = \left[\boldsymbol{y}_1^\top, \boldsymbol{y}_2^\top, \cdots, \boldsymbol{y}_t^\top, \cdots, \boldsymbol{y}_T^\top\right]^\top, \tag{36}$$

$$\boldsymbol{y}_t = \left[\frac{\delta x_t(1)}{\delta c_t(1)}, \frac{\delta x_t(2)}{\delta c_t(2)}, \cdots, \frac{\delta x_t(d)}{\delta c_t(d)}, \cdots, \frac{\delta x_t(D)}{\delta c_t(D)}\right]^\top, \tag{37}$$

$$\frac{\delta x_t(d)}{\delta c_t(d)} = -\frac{2}{T}\left\{(T-1)\left(\boldsymbol{v}(\boldsymbol{c}) - \boldsymbol{\mu}_v\right)^\top \boldsymbol{p}_v^{(d)} + 2\left(c_t(d) - \langle c(d)\rangle\right)^2 p_v^{(d)}(d)\right\}, \tag{38}$$

where the operator $\mathrm{diag}^{-1}[\cdot]$ denotes the inverse operation of $\mathrm{diag}[\cdot]$; *i.e.*, the extraction of only the diagonal elements (or block diagonal matrices) from a square matrix.

There are two main methods for setting the initial value of the static feature vector sequence $\hat{c}^{(0)\text{-th}}$. One is to use the ML estimate $\bar{c}_q$ given by Eq. (20) in the traditional parameter generation process. The other is to use the static feature vector sequence c' linearly converted from the ML estimate so that its GV is equivalent to the mean vector of the GV p.d.f., μ_v, as follows:

$$c'_t(d) = \sqrt{\frac{\mu_v(d)}{v(d)}} \left(c_t(d) - \langle c(d) \rangle\right) + \langle c(d) \rangle, \tag{39}$$

where $\mu_v(d)$ is the d-th element of the mean vector μ_v. The former sequence maximizes the HMM likelihood $P(o|q,\lambda)$, while the latter sequence maximizes the GV likelihood $P(v(c)|\lambda_v)$. It is reasonable to start the iterative update from the static feature vector sequence yielding a higher value of the objective function given by Eq. (26).

3.3 Effectiveness of considering GV

It is well known that postfiltering to increase the sharpness of spectral peaks is effective for improving synthetic speech quality (Koishida et al. (1995)), in which it is necessary to empirically adjust a parameter to control the degree of emphasis. Moreover, this parameter is usually kept constant over different frames. On the other hand, when considering the GV, at a certain dimension the trajectory movements are greatly emphasized, but at another dimension they remain almost the same. The degree of emphasis varies between individual dimensions and frames, and it is automatically determined from the objective function given by Eq. (26). This process may be regarded as statistical postfiltering.

Using more mixture components to model the probability density also reduces oversmoothing. However, it also causes another problem of overtraining due to an increase in the number of model parameters, which often causes performance degradation for data samples not included in the training data. One of the advantages of considering the GV is that the number of parameters is kept almost equal to that when not considering the GV. In addition, since the proposed framework is based on a statistical process, it retains many advantages of statistical parametric speech synthesis, such as allowing model adaptation (Yamagishi et al. (2009)) in a manner supported mathematically.

3.4 Weakness

The main weakness of considering the GV is the inconsistency between the training and synthesis criteria. In the training, the likelihood for the joint static and dynamic feature vectors is used to optimize the HMM parameters and the likelihood for the GV is used to optimize the GV p.d.f. parameters. These two models are independently optimized. On the other hand, in the synthesis, the product of these two likelihoods is used to optimize only the static feature vectors. Consequently, the trained model parameters are not optimum for this parameter generation process.

The GV p.d.f. given by Eq. (24) is context-independent. Hence, it does not capture variations of the GV caused by different contextual factors. A context-dependent model may be used as the GV p.d.f. to capture them. However, if the GV is calculated utterance by utterance, the number of GV samples used to train the context-dependent model is relatively small; *i.e.*, only the number of utterances in the training data. Therefore, the number of context-dependent GV p.d.f.s is often limited to avoid the overtraining problem.

The parameter generation process with the GV requires the gradient method. Thus, it has a greater computational cost than the traditional parameter generation process, for which the closed-form solution can be used.

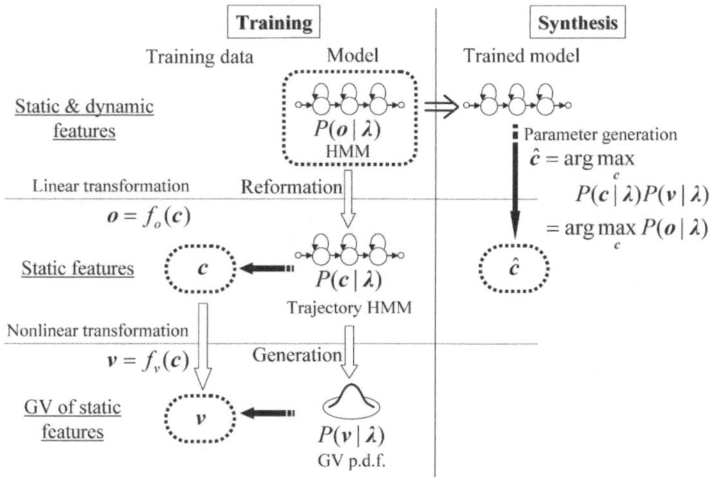

Fig. 5. Schematic image of training and synthesis processes of HMM-based speech synthesis with GV-constrained trajectory training algorithm.

4. HMM training considering global variance

The traditional framework described in **Section 2** also suffers from the inconsistency between the training and synthesis criteria. To address this issue, Zen *et al.* (Zen et al. (2007c)) proposed the trajectory HMM, which is derived by imposing an explicit relationship between static and dynamic features on the traditional HMM. This method allows the utilization of a unified criterion, *i.e.*, the trajectory likelihood, in both training and synthesis processes. In a similar spirit, Wu and Wang (Wu & Wang (2006)) proposed minimum generation error (MGE) training. This method optimizes the HMM parameters so that the error between the generated and natural parameters is minimized.

Inspired by these approaches, the idea of considering the GV has been introduced to the model training process to make it possible to use the same objective function consisting of the GV metric in both the training process and the synthesis process (Toda & Young (2009)). A schematic image of the training and synthesis processes is shown in **Figure 5**. The basic HMMs that model the p.d.f. of the joint static and dynamic feature vector sequence are reformulated as the trajectory HMM, which models the p.d.f. of the static feature vector sequence by imposing the constraint given by the linear transformation function $f_o(\boldsymbol{c})$. Furthermore, the GV p.d.f. is generated from the trajectory HMM based on the constraint given by the nonlinear transformation function $f_v(\boldsymbol{c})$. Then, the basic HMM parameters are optimized so that the objective function defined as the product of the likelihood of the trajectory HMM and the likelihood of the generated GV p.d.f. is maximized. In the synthesis process, the static feature vector sequence is determined by maximizing the same objective function. The following subsections give more details of these training and synthesis processes.

4.1 Trajectory HMM

The traditional HMM is reformulated as a trajectory HMM by imposing an explicit relationship between static and dynamic features, which is given by Eq. (2) (Zen et al. (2007c)).

The p.d.f. of $\boldsymbol{c}$ in the trajectory HMM is given by

$$P(\boldsymbol{c}|\boldsymbol{\lambda}) = \sum_{\text{all } \boldsymbol{q}} P(\boldsymbol{c}|\boldsymbol{q},\boldsymbol{\lambda}) P(\boldsymbol{q}|\boldsymbol{\lambda}), \quad (40)$$

$$\begin{aligned} P(\boldsymbol{c}|\boldsymbol{q},\boldsymbol{\lambda}) &= \frac{1}{Z_{\boldsymbol{q}}} P(\boldsymbol{o}|\boldsymbol{q},\boldsymbol{\lambda}) \\ &= \mathcal{N}(\boldsymbol{c};\bar{\boldsymbol{c}}_{\boldsymbol{q}},\boldsymbol{P}_{\boldsymbol{q}}), \end{aligned} \quad (41)$$

where the normalization term $Z_{\boldsymbol{q}}$ is given by

$$\begin{aligned} Z_{\boldsymbol{q}} &= \int P(\boldsymbol{o}|\boldsymbol{q},\boldsymbol{\lambda}) d\boldsymbol{c} \\ &= \frac{\sqrt{(2\pi)^{DT}|\boldsymbol{P}_{\boldsymbol{q}}|}}{\sqrt{(2\pi)^{3DT}|\boldsymbol{U}_{\boldsymbol{q}}|}} \exp\left(-\frac{1}{2}(\boldsymbol{\mu}_{\boldsymbol{q}}^{\top}\boldsymbol{U}_{\boldsymbol{q}}^{-1}\boldsymbol{\mu}_{\boldsymbol{q}} - \boldsymbol{r}_{\boldsymbol{q}}^{\top}\boldsymbol{P}_{\boldsymbol{q}}\boldsymbol{r}_{\boldsymbol{q}})\right). \end{aligned} \quad (42)$$

In Eq. (41), the mean vector $\bar{\boldsymbol{c}}_{\boldsymbol{q}}$ (given by Eq. (20)) varies within the states, and the interframe correlation is modeled by the temporal covariance matrix $\boldsymbol{P}_{\boldsymbol{q}}$ (given by Eq. (21)) even when using the same number of model parameters as in the traditional HMM. Note that the mean vector of the trajectory HMM is equivalent to the ML estimate of the generated static feature sequence in the traditional parameter generation process. Namely, the traditional parameter generation process is equivalent to the maximization process of the likelihood function of the trajectory HMM with respect to the static feature vector sequence. The utilization of the trajectory likelihood as a unified criterion in both training and synthesis processes makes it possible to optimize the HMM parameters for parameter generation.

4.2 GV-constrained trajectory training

The parameter generation process considering the GV given by Eq. (25) has been modified and integrated into a training framework as follows:

$$\hat{\boldsymbol{\lambda}} = \arg\max_{\boldsymbol{\lambda}} P(\boldsymbol{c}|\boldsymbol{q},\boldsymbol{\lambda}) P(\boldsymbol{v}(\boldsymbol{c})|\boldsymbol{q},\boldsymbol{\lambda})^{\omega T}, \quad (43)$$

where $P(\boldsymbol{c}|\boldsymbol{q},\boldsymbol{\lambda})$ is given by Eq. (41) and $P(\boldsymbol{v}(\boldsymbol{c})|\boldsymbol{q},\boldsymbol{\lambda})$ is the modified GV p.d.f., which is given by

$$P(\boldsymbol{v}(\boldsymbol{c})|\boldsymbol{q},\boldsymbol{\lambda}) = \mathcal{N}\left(\boldsymbol{v}(\boldsymbol{c});\boldsymbol{v}(\bar{\boldsymbol{c}}_{\boldsymbol{q}}),\boldsymbol{U}_{v}\right). \quad (44)$$

Note that the mean vector of the GV p.d.f. is defined as the GV of the mean vector of the trajectory HMM, which is equivalent to the GV of the generated parameters from the HMMs given by Eq. (20). Hence, the GV likelihood $P(\boldsymbol{v}(\boldsymbol{c})|\boldsymbol{q},\boldsymbol{\lambda})$ acts as a penalty term to make the GV of the generated parameters close to that of the natural ones. The balance between the two likelihoods $P(\boldsymbol{c}|\boldsymbol{q},\boldsymbol{\lambda})$ and $P(\boldsymbol{v}(\boldsymbol{c})|\boldsymbol{q},\boldsymbol{\lambda})$ is controlled by the GV weight ω. The objective function $\mathcal{L}_{\boldsymbol{q}}^{(GV)'}$ used in both training and synthesis processes is given by

$$\mathcal{L}_{\boldsymbol{q}}^{(GV)'} = \log P(\boldsymbol{c}|\boldsymbol{q},\boldsymbol{\lambda}) + \omega T \log P(\boldsymbol{v}(\boldsymbol{c})|\boldsymbol{q},\boldsymbol{\lambda}). \quad (45)$$

Given the HMM state sequence $\boldsymbol{q}$,[2] the GV weight ω, and the GV covariance matrix $\boldsymbol{U}_v$, the HMM parameter set is optimized by maximizing the proposed objective function $\mathcal{L}_{\boldsymbol{q}}^{(GV)'}$. The mean vectors and diagonal precision matrices at all HMM states (from 1 to N), which are given by

$$\boldsymbol{m} = \left[\boldsymbol{\mu}_1^\top, \boldsymbol{\mu}_2^\top, \cdots, \boldsymbol{\mu}_N^\top\right]^\top, \tag{46}$$

$$\boldsymbol{\Sigma}^{-1} = \left[\boldsymbol{U}_1^{-1}, \boldsymbol{U}_2^{-1}, \cdots, \boldsymbol{U}_N^{-1}\right]^\top, \tag{47}$$

are simultaneously updated since they depend on each other. The mean vectors $\boldsymbol{m}$ are iteratively updated using the following gradient:

$$\frac{\partial \mathcal{L}_{\boldsymbol{q}}^{(GV)'}}{\partial \boldsymbol{m}} = \boldsymbol{A}_{\boldsymbol{q}}^\top \boldsymbol{U}_{\boldsymbol{q}}^{-1} \boldsymbol{W} \left(\boldsymbol{c} - \overline{\boldsymbol{c}}_{\boldsymbol{q}} + \omega \boldsymbol{P}_{\boldsymbol{q}} \overline{\boldsymbol{x}}_{\boldsymbol{q}}\right), \tag{48}$$

where

$$\overline{\boldsymbol{x}}_{\boldsymbol{q}} = \left[\overline{\boldsymbol{x}}_{\boldsymbol{q},1}^\top, \overline{\boldsymbol{x}}_{\boldsymbol{q},2}^\top, \cdots, \overline{\boldsymbol{x}}_{\boldsymbol{q},t}^\top, \cdots, \overline{\boldsymbol{x}}_{\boldsymbol{q},T}^\top\right]^\top, \tag{49}$$

$$\overline{\boldsymbol{x}}_{\boldsymbol{q},t} = \left[\overline{x}_{\boldsymbol{q},t}(1), \overline{x}_{\boldsymbol{q},t}(2), \cdots, \overline{x}_{\boldsymbol{q},t}(d), \cdots, \overline{x}_{\boldsymbol{q},t}(D)\right]^\top, \tag{50}$$

$$\overline{x}_{\boldsymbol{q},t}(d) = -2\left(\overline{c}_{\boldsymbol{q},t}(d) - \langle \overline{c}_{\boldsymbol{q}}(d)\rangle\right)\left(\boldsymbol{v}(\overline{\boldsymbol{c}}_{\boldsymbol{q}}) - \boldsymbol{v}(\boldsymbol{c})\right)^\top \boldsymbol{p}_v^{(d)}, \tag{51}$$

and $\boldsymbol{A}_{\boldsymbol{q}}$ is a $3DT$-by-$3DN$ matrix whose elements are 0 or 1 depending on the state sequence $\boldsymbol{q}$. The precision matrices $\boldsymbol{\Sigma}^{-1}$ are iteratively updated using the following gradient:

$$\begin{aligned}\frac{\partial \mathcal{L}_{\boldsymbol{q}}^{(GV)'}}{\partial \boldsymbol{\Sigma}^{-1}} = \frac{1}{2}\boldsymbol{A}_{\boldsymbol{q}}^\top \mathrm{diag}^{-1}\Big[&\boldsymbol{W}(\boldsymbol{P}_{\boldsymbol{q}} + \overline{\boldsymbol{c}}_{\boldsymbol{q}}\overline{\boldsymbol{c}}_{\boldsymbol{q}}^\top - \boldsymbol{c}\boldsymbol{c}^\top)\boldsymbol{W}^\top - 2\boldsymbol{\mu}_{\boldsymbol{q}}(\overline{\boldsymbol{c}}_{\boldsymbol{q}} - \boldsymbol{c}_{\boldsymbol{q}})^\top \boldsymbol{W}^\top \\ &+ 2\omega \boldsymbol{W}\boldsymbol{P}_{\boldsymbol{q}}\overline{\boldsymbol{x}}_{\boldsymbol{q}}(\boldsymbol{\mu}_{\boldsymbol{q}} - \boldsymbol{W}\overline{\boldsymbol{c}}_{\boldsymbol{q}})^\top\Big].\end{aligned} \tag{52}$$

This update is performed on a logarithmic domain to ensure that the updated covariance matrices are positive definite. Although only the case of using a single observation sequence for training data is described here, it is straightforward to extend this training algorithm to multiple observation sequences. This training algorithm enables the HMM parameters to be optimized so that both the generated parameter trajectory and its GV are close to the natural ones.

The proposed objective function $\mathcal{L}_{\boldsymbol{q}}'$ is also used in parameter generation. The static feature vector sequence is determined by

$$\begin{aligned}\hat{\boldsymbol{c}} &= \arg\max_{\boldsymbol{c}} \mathcal{L}_{\boldsymbol{q}}^{(GV)'} \\ &= \arg\max_{\boldsymbol{c}} \mathcal{N}(\boldsymbol{c}; \overline{\boldsymbol{c}}_{\boldsymbol{q}}, \boldsymbol{P}_{\boldsymbol{q}})\mathcal{N}(\boldsymbol{v}(\boldsymbol{c}); \boldsymbol{v}(\overline{\boldsymbol{c}}_{\boldsymbol{q}}), \boldsymbol{U}_v) \\ &= \overline{\boldsymbol{c}}_{\boldsymbol{q}}.\end{aligned} \tag{53}$$

[2] A suboptimum HMM state sequence may be determined by the Viterbi algorithm with the traditional likelihood, *i.e.*, $P(\boldsymbol{q}|\boldsymbol{\lambda})P(\boldsymbol{o}|\boldsymbol{q}, \boldsymbol{\lambda})$.

Note that this estimate is equivalent to the ML estimate (given by Eq. (20)) in the traditional parameter generation algorithm because the GV likelihood is always maximized by setting the generated parameters to the mean vector of the trajectory HMM. Therefore, it is no longer necessary to practically consider the GV term in parameter generation, and the traditional parameter generation algorithm can be directly employed. Note that the traditional algorithm is computationally much more efficient than the parameter generation algorithm considering the GV, which requires an iterative process as mentioned in **Section 3.2**.

4.3 Discussion

GV-constrained trajectory training addresses some of the issues of parameter generation considering the GV described in **Section 3.4**. It provides a unified framework using the same objective function in both training and synthesis processes. It also allows the closed-form solution to be used in parameter generation. This makes it possible to implement the recursive estimation process, which generates the static feature vectors frame by frame (Tokuda et al. (1995)), which is very effective for achieving a low-delay synthesis process. Moreover, context-dependent GV modeling can be easily implemented without increasing the number of model parameters. It has been found that the variations of the GV tend to be larger with decreasing number of frames (*i.e.,* the total duration of an utterance). Therefore, the parameter generation algorithm considering the GV sometimes causes highly artificial sounds in synthetic speech when synthesizing very short utterances such as one word. This problem is effectively addressed by GV-constrained trajectory training.

In an attempt to apply the idea of considering the GV in the HMM training process, Wu *et al.* (Wu et al. (2008)) proposed MGE training that considers the error in the GV between natural and generated parameters as well as the generation error mentioned above. The HMM parameters are optimized so that both the generated parameters and their GV are similar to the natural ones. This method is similar to GV-constrained trajectory training. One of the differences between these two methods is that not only frame-by-frame (weighted) generation errors but also the correlation between the errors over a time sequence is considered in GV-constrained trajectory training because of the use of the temporal covariance matrix of the trajectory HMM, $\boldsymbol{P_q}$.

5. Experimental evaluation

The effectiveness of parameter generation considering the GV and that of GV-constrained trajectory training were evaluated separately.

5.1 Experimental conditions

The 0th through 24th mel-cepstral coefficients were used as spectral parameters and log-scaled F_0 was used as the excitation parameter. A high-quality speech analysis-synthesis method called Speech Transformation and Representation using Adaptive Interpolation of weiGHTed spectrum (STRAIGHT) (Kawahara et al. (1999)) was employed for the analysis-synthesis method. Each speech parameter vector included the static features and their delta and delta-deltas. The frame shift was set to 5 ms.

Context-dependent phoneme HMMs were trained for each of the spectral and F_0 components using a decision-tree-based context-clustering technique based on the minimum description length (MDL) criterion (Shinoda & Watanabe (2000)). The spectral component was modeled by the continuous density HMM, of which each state output p.d.f. was modeled by a single Gaussian with a diagonal covariance matrix. The F_0 component was modeled by the multispace probability distribution HMM (MSD-HMM) (Tokuda et al. (2002)) to model a time

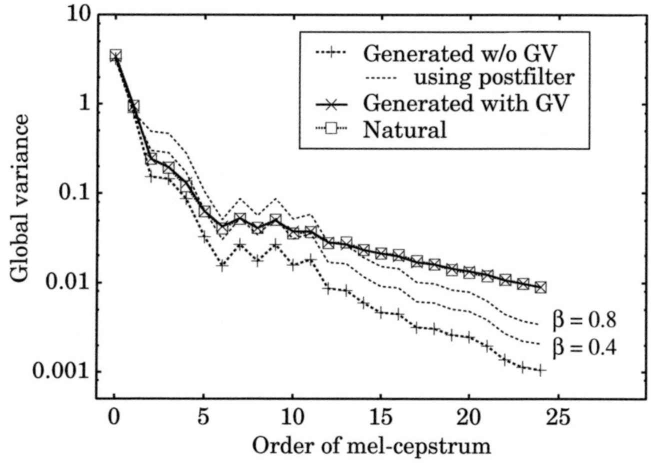

Fig. 6. GVs of several mel-cepstrum sequences. The values shown are GV mean values over all test sentences and speakers.

sequence consisting of continuous values, *i.e.*, log-scaled values of F_0, and discrete symbols that represent unvoiced frames. Static, delta, and delta-delta values of F_0 were modeled in different streams (Yoshimura et al. (1999)). Context-dependent duration models for modeling the state duration probabilities were also trained.

In the synthesis, a sentence HMM for given input contexts was constructed by concatenating the context-dependent phoneme HMMs, and then a suboptimum state sequence was determined from the state duration model. Mel-cepstrum and F_0 sequences were directly generated from p.d.f. sequences corresponding to the determined suboptimum state sequence. A speech waveform was synthesized by filtering the excitation signal, which was designed using the generated excitation parameters, based on the generated mel-cepstra with the Mel Log Spectrum Approximation (MLSA) filter (Imai (1983)).

5.2 Evaluations of parameter generation considering GV

To evaluate the parameter generation algorithm considering the GV, voices were built for four Japanese speakers (two males, MHT and MYI, and two females, FTK and FYM) in the ATR Japanese speech database B-set (Sagisaka et al. (1990)), which consists of 503 phonetically balanced sentences. For each speaker, 450 sentences were used as training data and the other 53 sentences were used for evaluation. Context-dependent labels were prepared from phoneme and linguistic labels included in the ATR database. A Gaussian distribution of the GV p.d.f. for each of the spectral and F_0 components was trained using the GVs calculated from individual utterances in the training data. The GV weight ω was set to 1.0.

Figure 6 shows the GVs of mel-cepstra generated with the traditional generation algorithm and those with the generation algorithm considering the GV. For the traditional algorithm, the GVs of the generated mel-cepstra when using the postfilter to emphasize the mel-cepstra (Koishida et al. (1995)) are also shown. The filtering coefficient β was set to 0.4 or 0.8. The GV of the natural mel-cepstra is also shown in the figure as a reference. It can be seen that the GV of the mel-cepstra generated with the traditional algorithm is small. Although postfiltering increases the GV, the GV characteristics of the emphasized mel-cepstra are obviously different from those of the natural ones. On the other hand, mel-cepstra whose GV is almost equal to that of the natural ones are generated when considering the GV.

Generation method	MOS ± 95% confidence interval
Generated w/o GV	2.53 ± 0.12
Generated with GV	3.46 ± 0.15
Natural (analysis-synthesized)	4.35 ± 0.12

Table 1. Mean opinion score (MOS) on naturalness given in opinion test to evaluate parameter generation with GV.

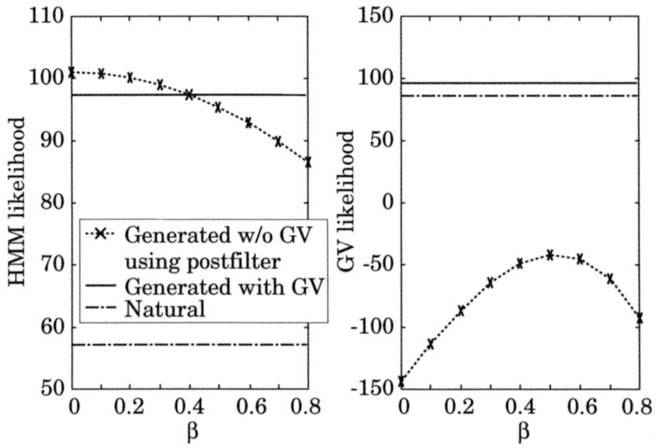

Fig. 7. Log-scaled HMM and GV likelihoods on mel-cepstrum sequences as a function of postfilter coefficient β. The HMM likelihoods are normalized by the number of frames.

Figure 7 shows the logarithmic HMM and GV likelihoods on mel-cepstrum sequences, which are normalized by the number of frames. It is reasonable that the largest HMM likelihood is yielded by the traditional algorithm ($\beta = 0.0$) and that it decreases when the postfilter is applied or the GV is considered. An interesting point is that the HMM likelihood for the natural sequence is smaller than those for the generated sequences. This implies that we do not necessarily generate the speech parameter sequence that maximizes only the HMM likelihood, although it seems reasonable to keep the likelihood larger than that for the natural sequence. The GV likelihoods are very small when using the traditional algorithm because of the GV reduction shown in **Figure 6**. Although it is observed that they are recovered by postfiltering, the resulting likelihoods are still much smaller than that for the natural sequence. On the other hand, the algorithm considering the GV generates a sequence for which the GV likelihood is sufficiently large. Consequently, it makes both HMM and GV likelihoods exceed those for the natural sequence. These results demonstrate that the algorithm considering the GV is capable of generating more similar speech parameter sequences to those of natural speech from the viewpoint of satisfying a greater variety of characteristics than the traditional algorithm.

Table 1 shows the result of a subjective evaluation based on an opinion test on the naturalness of the synthetic speech. The opinion score was set to a 5-point scale (5: excellent, 4: good, 3: fair, 2: poor, 1: bad) and ten Japanese listeners participated in the test. It is observed that the generation algorithm considering the GV yields significant quality improvements compared with the traditional generation algorithm. It effectively reduces muffled sounds of synthetic

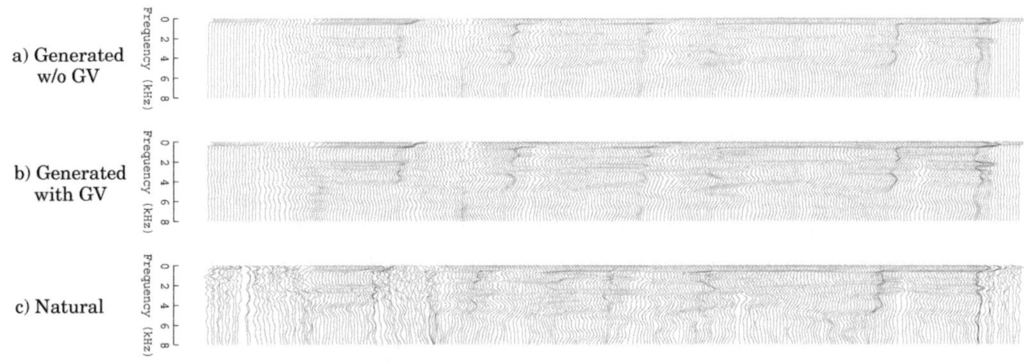

Fig. 8. Examples of spectrum sequences of generated speech using traditional algorithm, generated speech using generation algorithm considering GV, and natural speech. Note that the phoneme duration of the natural sequence is different from those of the generated sequences.

voices caused by the oversmoothing effect.[3] An example of spectrum sequences is shown in **Figure 8**. The algorithm considering the GV generates much sharper spectral peaks than those generated by the conventional algorithm. Note that increasing the GV usually causes an increase in mel-cepstral distortion between the generated sequence and the natural sequence, which is strongly correlated with the decrease in the HMM likelihood shown in **Figure 7**. It is possible that simply increasing the GV will cause the quality degradation of synthetic speech because it does not always make the generated sequence close to the natural one. The GV-based generation algorithm increases the GV by considering the GV likelihood while also considering the HMM likelihood to reduce the quality degradation due to the excessive increase in the GV.

5.3 Evaluation of GV-constrained trajectory training

To evaluate the GV-constrained trajectory training method, voices were built for four English speakers (2 males: bdl and rms, and 2 females: clb and slt) in the CMU ARCTIC database (Kominek & Black (2003)). For each speaker, we used subset A, which consists of about 600 sentences as training data and the remaining subset B, which consists of about 500 sentences for evaluation. Context-dependent labels were automatically generated from texts using a text analyzer. After initializing the HMM parameters in the traditional training process, trajectory training was performed for the spectral and F_0 components. Finally, GV-constrained trajectory training was performed for both components. The covariance matrix of the GV p.d.f. for each component was previously trained using the GVs calculated from individual utterances in the training data. The GV weight ω was empirically set to 0.125.

Table 2 shows the log-scaled trajectory likelihood, GV likelihood, and total likelihood for the training data and evaluation data, where the total likelihood is calculated as the product of the trajectory and GV likelihoods. All values are normalized by the number of frames. The trajectory training causes significant improvements in the trajectory likelihoods because the HMM parameters are optimized so as to directly maximize the trajectory likelihoods. It is interesting to note that the trajectory training also causes improvements in the GV likelihood, although the improvements are not large. These results suggest that the trajectory training

[3] Several samples are available from http://isw3.naist.jp/~tomoki/INTECH/ModelGV/index.html

Training method	Training data			Evaluation data		
	Trajectory	GV	Total	Trajectory	GV	Total
Traditional	19.06	-67.63	-48.57	16.26	-67.86	-51.60
Trajectory	30.78	-32.35	-1.57	29.30	-33.33	-4.03
GV-constrained	30.36	94.98	125.34	28.89	82.51	111.40

Table 2. Log-scaled trajectory likelihood given by Eq. (41), GV likelihood given by Eq. (44), and total likelihood given by Eq. (43) ($\omega = 1.0$) for each training method.

Training method	MOS $\pm$ 95% confidence interval
Traditional	2.35 ± 0.14
Trajectory	2.79 ± 0.12
GV-constrained	3.46 ± 0.15
Natural (analysis-synthesized)	4.38 ± 0.13

Table 3. Mean opinion score (MOS) on naturalness given in opinion test to evaluate GV-constrained trajectory training.

generates better parameter trajectories than the traditional training. The GV likelihoods are dramatically improved by GV-constrained trajectory training. Note that this training method does not cause significant reductions to the trajectory likelihoods. This can be observed in both the training and evaluation data. Overall, these results suggest that the GV-constrained trajectory training method leads to parameter trajectories that more closely resemble the various characteristic features of real speech.

Table 3 shows the result of a subjective evaluation based on an opinion test on the naturalness of the synthetic speech. The opinion score was set to the same 5-point scale as before and ten listeners participated in the test. GV-constrained trajectory training yields significant quality improvements compared with the traditional training. This tendency is similar to that observed when considering the GV in the parameter generation process, as shown in **Table 1**. The trajectory training also yields significant quality improvements, but these improvements are much smaller than those yielded by GV-constrained trajectory training. [4]

6. Summary

This chapter has described the two main techniques for modeling a speech parameter sequence considering the global variance (GV) for HMM-based speech synthesis: the parameter generation algorithm considering the GV and GV-constrained trajectory training. The traditional framework of HMM-based speech synthesis suffers from the oversmoothing effect in speech parameters generated from the HMM, which makes the synthetic speech sound muffled. Since the GV is inversely correlated with the oversmoothing effect, a metric on the GV of the generated parameters is effectively used to reduce muffled sounds. The parameter generation algorithm considering the GV uses not only an HMM likelihood but also a GV likelihood to determine the generated parameters. GV-constrained trajectory training has been proposed by integrating this idea into a training framework. Consequently, it provides a unified framework for training and synthesizing speech using a common criterion, context-dependent GV modeling, and a more efficient parameter generation process with the GV based on a closed-form solution. Experimental results have demonstrated that both

[4] Several samples are available from http://isw3.naist.jp/~tomoki/INTECH/ModelGV/index.html

methods yield very significant improvements in the naturalness of synthetic speech and that GV modeling is very effective in HMM-based speech synthesis.

Acknowledgements: This research was supported in part by MEXT Grant-in-Aid for Young Scientists (A).

7. References

Donovan, R. & Woodland, P. Improvements in an HMM-based speech synthesiser. *Proceedings of Euro. Conf. on Speech Commun. & Tech. (EUROSPEECH)* pp. 573–576, Madrid, Spain, Sept. 1995.

Gales, M. & Young, S. The application of hidden Markov models in speech recognition. *Foundations & Trends in Signal Processing* Vol. 1, No. 3, pp. 195–304, 2008.

Huang, X.; Acero, A.; Adcock, J.; Hon, H.-W.; Goldsmith, J.; Liu, J. & Plumpe, M. Whistler: a trainable text-to-speech system. *Proceedings of Int. Conf. on Spoken Lang. Process. (ICSLP)*, pp. 2387–2390, Philadelphia, USA, Oct. 1996.

Imai, S. Cepstral analysis synthesis on the mel frequency scale. *Proceedings of IEEE Int. Conf. on Acoust., Speech, & Signal Process. (ICASSP)*, pp. 93–96, Boston, USA, Apr. 1983.

Kawahara, H.; Masuda-Katsuse, I. & de Cheveigné, A. Restructuring speech representations using a pitch-adaptive time-frequency smoothing and an instantaneous-frequency-based F_0 extraction: possible role of a repetitive structure in sounds. *Speech Commun.*, Vol. 27, No. 3–4, pp. 187–207, 1999.

Koishida, K.; Tokuda, K.; Kobayashi, T. & Imai, S. CELP coding based on mel-cepstral analysis. *Proceedings of IEEE Int. Conf. on Acoust., Speech, & Signal Process. (ICASSP)*, pp. 33–36, Detroit, USA, May 1995.

Kominek, J. & Black, A.W. CMU ARCTIC databases for speech synthesis. *Technical Report*, CMU-LTI-03-177, Language Technologies Institute, Carnegie Mellon University, 2003.

Sagisaka, Y.; Takeda, K.; Abe, M.; Katagiri, S.; Umeda, T. & Kuwabara, H. A large-scale Japanese speech database. *Proceedings of Int. Conf. on Spoken Lang. Process. (ICSLP)*, pp. 1089–1092, Kobe, Japan, Nov. 1990.

Shinoda, K. & Watanabe, T. MDL-based context-dependent subword modeling for speech recognition. *J. Acoust. Soc. Jpn. (E)*, Vol. 21, No. 2, pp. 79–86, 2000.

Toda, T. & Tokuda, K. A speech parameter generation algorithm considering global variance for HMM-based speech synthesis. *IEICE Trans. Inf. & Syst.*, Vol. E90-D, No. 5, pp. 816–824, 2007.

Toda, T.; Black, A.W. & Tokuda, K. Voice conversion based on maximum likelihood estimation of spectral parameter trajectory. *IEEE Trans. Audio, Speech & Lang. Process.*, Vol. 15, No. 8, pp. 2222–2235, 2007.

Toda, T. & Young, S. Trajectory training considering global variance for HMM-based speech synthesis. *Proceedings of IEEE Int. Conf. on Acoust., Speech, & Signal Process. (ICASSP)*, pp. 4025–4028, Taipei, Taiwan, Apr. 2009.

Tokuda, K.; Kobayashi, T.; Masuko, T. & Imai, S. Mel-generalized cepstral analysis – a unified approach to speech spectral estimation. *Proceedings of Int. Conf. on Spoken Lang. Process. (ICSLP)*, pp. 1043–1045, Yokohama, Japan, Sept. 1994.

Tokuda, K.; Kobayashi, T. & Imai, S. Speech parameter generation from HMM using dynamic features. *Proceedings of IEEE Int. Conf. on Acoust., Speech, & Signal Process. (ICASSP)*, pp. 660–663, Detroit, USA, May 1995.

Tokuda, K.; Yoshimura, T.; Masuko, T.; Kobayashi, T. & Kitamura, T. Speech parameter generation algorithms for HMM-based speech synthesis. *Proceedings of IEEE Int. Conf.*

on Acoust., Speech, & Signal Process. (ICASSP), pp. 1315–1318, Istanbul, Turkey, June 2000.

Tokuda, K.; Masuko, T.; Miyazaki, N. & Kobayashi, T. Multi-space probability distribution HMM. *IEICE Trans. Inf. & Syst.*, Vol. E85-D, No. 3, pp. 455–464, 2002.

Wu, Y.-J. & Wang, R.H. Minimum generation error training for HMM-based speech synthesis. *Proceedings of IEEE Int. Conf. on Acoust., Speech, & Signal Process. (ICASSP)*, pp. 89–92, Toulouse, France, May 2006.

Wu, Y.-J.; Zen, H.; Nankaku, Y. & Tokuda, K. Minimum generation error criterion considering global/local variance for HMM-based speech synthesis. *Proceedings of IEEE Int. Conf. on Acoust., Speech, & Signal Process. (ICASSP)*, pp. 4621–4624, Las Vegas, USA, Mar. 2008.

Yamagishi, J.; Nose, T.; Zen, H.; Ling, Z.-H.; Toda, T.; Tokuda, K.; King, S. & Renals, S. Robust speaker-adaptive HMM-based text-to-speech synthesis. *IEEE Trans. Audio, Speech & Lang. Process.*, Vol. 17, No. 6, pp. 1208–1230, 2009.

Yoshimura, T.; Tokuda, K.; Masuko, T.; Kobayashi, T. & Kitamura, T. Simultaneous modeling of spectrum, pitch and duration in HMM-based speech synthesis. *Proceedings of Euro. Conf. on Speech Commun. & Tech. (EUROSPEECH)* pp. 2347–2350, Budapest, Hungary, Sept. 1999.

Zen, H.; Toda, T.; Nakamura, M. & Tokuda, K. Details of the Nitech HMM-based speech synthesis system for the Blizzard Challenge 2005. *IEICE Trans. Inf. & Syst.*, Vol. E90-D, No. 1, pp. 325–333, 2007a.

Zen, H.; Tokuda, K.; Masuko, T.; Kobayashi, T. & Kitamura, T. A hidden semi-Markov model-based speech synthesis system. *IEICE Trans. Inf. & Syst.*, Vol. E90-D, No. 5, pp. 825–834, 2007b.

Zen, H.; Tokuda, K. & Kitamura, T. Reformulating the HMM as a trajectory model by imposing explicit relationships between static and dynamic feature vector sequences. *Computer Speech & Lang.*, Vol. 21, No. 1, pp. 153–173, 2007c.

Zen, H.; Toda, T. & Tokuda, K. The Nitech-NAIST HMM-based speech synthesis system for the Blizzard Challenge 2006. *IEICE Trans. Inf. & Syst.*, Vol. E91-D, No. 6, pp. 1764–1773, 2008.

Zen, H.; Tokuda, K. & Black, A.W. Statistical parametric speech synthesis. *Speech Commun.*, Vol. 51, No. 11, pp. 1039–1064, 2009.

7

Using Hidden Markov Models for ECG Characterisation

Krimi Samar, Ouni Kaïs and Ellouze Noureddine
Engineering National School of Tunis/Signal,
Image and Pattern Recognition research unit
University Tunis El Manar Tunis
Tunisia

1. Introduction

Recent research on biomedical signal processing especially ECG analysis mostly focused on the use of Hidden Markov Models (HMM). The general aim of any signal segmentation method is to partition a given signal into consecutive regions of interest. In the context of the ECG then, the role of segmentation is to determine as accurately as possible the onset and offset boundaries, as well as the peak locations, of the various waveform features, such that the ECG interval measurements may be computed automatically and the study of waveform patterns will be facilitated (Sayadi & Shamsollahi, 2009). Ad hoc algorithms have been developed in order to help cardiologists to segment large amounts of ECGs. But these algorithms do not provide a precise segmentation, and repetitive corrections have to be made. Wavelet parametrisation is known to highlight discontinuities in the signal, and has proven to give good results for ECG segmentation (Kawaja et al., 2006; Thomas et al., 2006).
A statistical model helps to regularize the detection, resulting in a more robust delineation. One of the advantages of probabilistic models over traditional methods is that a confidence measure for each segmented signal is given by the log likelihood of the observed signal given the model (Thomas et al., 2006).
The main focus of this chapter is to introduce some new and robust HMM associated with wavelet transform based methods for ECG analysis. The chapter begins with a review of the literature on the use of HMM to analyse ECG signals. We then consider in detail the suitability of HMM to provide a faithful statistical description of the ECG. In particular, we examine the validity of the various assumptions inherent in the HMM framework in the context of the ECG. Following this, we consider a number of specific issues in developing an HMM for ECG segmentation, including the choice of model architecture, type of observation models. Then a combination of HMM approach with wavelet properties will be explained.

1.1 Previous works

The use of hidden semi-Markov models (HSMM) for ECG segmentation has been considered previously in (Thoraval et al. 1994), the segmentation process is effected by an HSMM, where each state in the model corresponds to a particular aspect of a given ECG waveform feature. Specifically, the model architecture makes use of separate onset, middle and offset states for each waveform feature. This enhanced state space is motivated by the need to match the stationarity assumption for each HSMM state, with the transitory nature of the observations over the time course of a particular ECG waveform. The observation and duration densities for the HSMM are modelled by Gaussians (with diagonal covariance matrices in the specific case of the observations). The performance of the model is demonstrated qualitatively on a sample ECG waveform (Hughes, 2006).

Wavelets and statistical methods can be used complementarily for ECG delineation, as reported previously in (Clavier et al., 1998, 2002), to associate a local and a global segmentation. Hidden Markov models (HMM), are applied to the coefficients of an ECG wavelet transform. This transform also showed the signal singularities, but it was too sensitive to noise. The association of the two methods made it possible to solve cases where they would fail if they were used alone. The ECG was segmented in three steps: first, a redundant multiresolution analysis was applied to the ECG signal; secondly, the R-wave was detected by a threshold on the wavelet coefficients; thirdly, a segmentation algorithm based on an HMM representing a beat was applied to isolate the P wave. The observations were the wavelet coefficients, whose probability densities were estimated by a non-parametric model.

Lepage et al., 2000, have presented a HMM associated with wavelets to improve an automatic segmentation of the ECG signal. While HMM describes the dynamical mean evolution of cardiac cycle, the use of wavelet analysis in association with the HMM leads to take into account local singularities. The parameters of this HMM model (means, variances and transition probabilities) are estimated using EM algorithm by modifying the parameter estimation by using the stochastic expectation maximisation algorithm (SEM) instead of the EM which avoids staying in local minima. Some good results were obtained at several scales, showing the good localization properties of wavelet, but the results were not as reliable as those obtained with the 10 state HMM method. It is sometimes really difficult to choose the coefficient that represents the beginning, the middle or the end of a wave, when the changes of state are too close or too numerous.

Graja &Boucher, 2005, have proposed a new ECG delineation method which uses a hidden Markov tree (HMT) model. Using wavelet coefficients to characterize the different ECG waves and, then linking these coefficients by a tree structure enabling wave change to be detected. The idea is to develop probability models for the wavelet transform of a signal and to analyze the dependency of wavelet coefficients through scales. In fact, it is well-known that wavelet coefficients have a non-Gaussian distribution. Making the assumption that it can be described by a mixture of Gaussian distributions. To pick up the relationships between states, they use a HMM on a wavelet tree with a hypothesis of clustering and persistence (Crouse et al., 1998).

Thomas et al., 2006, have used machine learning approach to ECG segmentation consists in building a model λ of the signal, and in using the most likely state sequence for a given observation sequence in order to find the wave transitions. To be able to segment unspecified ECGs with high accuracy, they implemented a multi-HMM approach. This method consists in performing a Bayesian clustering of the training base (Li, & Biswas, 2000). The training base is divided in K classes of ECGs which have similarities and K HMM are trained and exploited to provide great generalization capabilities and high accuracy at the same time. This HMM clustering algorithm is simply a variation of the K-Means algorithm, where the clusters are defined by HMM rather than by centers in the data space (Thomas et al., 2007).

Online HMM adaptation for ECG analysis has been successfully carried out by Müler et al., 2006, they have introduced the online HMM adaptation for the patient ECG signal adaptation problem. Two adaptive methods were implemented, namely the incremental version of the expectation maximization (EM) and segmental k-means algorithms. The system is adapted to the ECG of the individual in an unsupervised way. For that, the segmentation output is used to reestimate the HMM parameters of each waveform.
Andreão et al., 2007, have presented an original HMM approach for online beat segmentation. The HMM framework is highly suitable for the ECG problem. This approach addresses a large panel of topics like : waveforms modelling, multichannel beat segmentation and classification, and unsupervised adaptation to the patient's ECG. The segmentation task is carried out by generic HMM of each beat waveform. One important feature of this approach is the generic model adaptation strategy to each individual, which is non supervised (there is no need of manual labels). The HMM are used to carry out beat detection and segmentation. The main contributions are based on the following (Andreão et al. 2003, 2004, 2006). Firstly, waveform modelling (and not beat modelling) using generic HMM (trained through examples from several individuals). In this way, HMM are trained taking into account the morphology diversity of each waveform. Secondly, better waveform segmentation precision by adapting a generic model to each individual. The model adaptation is done in an unsupervised way, eliminating waveform manual labelling (Laguna et al., 1997).

1.2 Contributions and chapter organization

In our works, we have developed three original hybrid segmentation algorithms based on :
Firstly, Modulus Maxima Wavelet Transform (MMWT) that has been successfully combined with Hidden Markov Models (HMM) providing reliable beat segmentation results (Krimi et al. 2008). In the MMWT, the wavelet transform local extrema is used to characterize singularities in the signal. One very successful method described in (Cuiwei et al., 1995), uses the ECG wavelet transform modulus maxima properties to characterize the different ECG complexes. A rule based system is used to detect QRS waves and differentiate them from T waves and noise artifacts. This method has also been extended for T and P wave's detection (Jouck, 2004).
Secondly, Pitch Synchronous Wavelet Transform (PSWT) and Hidden Semi-Markov Models (HSMM) (Krimi et al., 2007). The combination of these two methods has shown to be very efficient tool for ECG delineation. As noted in other studies on the HMM, the self transitions of the HMM cause an incorrect modelling of segment durations. An extension of the HMM, the Hidden Semi Markov model HSMM, largely solves this problem. PSWT, has been effectively used in speech, music signals (Evangelista, 1993) and waveform interpolation coding scheme (Chong et al., 2000). The (PSWT) is based on a modelling concept, which is able to capture period to period signal fluctuation by basis elements means that are comb-like in the frequency domain. This technique relies primarily on the high peaks positions corresponding to the ECG R wave. The principle consists in estimating the periodicity (pitch period) with the autocorrelation function and dividing the original signal into pseudo-periodic segments using the time points obtained from the considered pitch detector algorithm; this segmentation leads to the pitch synchronous representation. By applying the wavelet transform to this representation and synthesis only the approximation component we can obtain the dominating pitched signal's behaviour, so the ECG estimation.

Thirdly (in progress), Multiscale Product Wavelet Transform (MPWT) in association with Hidden Markov Tree (HMT). The idea of this study is to detect singularity not via local maxima of the wavelet coefficients signals but via the product of the wavelet coefficients. Rosenfeld and co-workers (Rosenfeld, 1970) suggested forming multiscale point-wise products. This is intended to enhance multiscale peaks due to edges, while suppressing noise, by exploiting the multiscale correlation due to the presence of the desired signal (Besrour & al., 2009). MPWT is based on Mallat's and Hwang's approach (Mallat & Hwang, 1992) for singularity detection via local maxima of the wavelet coefficients signals. It acted as the parameter extraction stage necessary to build the observation sequence of our original HMT based segmentation approach.

2. Background information

This section provides a brief review of Hidden Markov Models (HMM), Hidden Markov Tree (HMT) and Hidden Semi-Markov Models (HSMM).

2.1 Hidden Markov Models (HMM)

To model a sequence $W = w^1, w^2, ..., w^T$; with $w^t \in \mathbb{R}^N$, a continuous HMM is defined with the structure $\vartheta = \langle Q, A, \pi, B \rangle$ where (Milone et al., 2010) :

i. $Q = \{Q\}$ is the set of states, where Q is a discrete random state variable taking values $q \in \{1, 2, ..., N_Q\}$

ii. $A = \left[a_{ij} \right]$ is the matrix of transition probabilities with $a_{ij} = \Pr\left(Q^t = j \mid Q^{t-1} = i \right) \forall i, j \in Q$, where $Q^t \in Q$ is the model state at time $t \in \{1, 2, ..., T\}$, $a_{ij} \geq 0 \forall i, j$ and $\sum_j a_{ij} = 1 \forall i$

iii. $\pi = \left[\pi_j = \Pr\left(Q^1 = j \right) \right]$ is the initial state probability vector. In the case of left to right HMM this vector is $\pi = \delta_1$

iv. $B = \left\{ b_k\left(w^t \right) \right\}$ is the set of observation (or emission) probability distributions $b_k\left(w^t \right) = \Pr\left(W^t = w^t \mid Q^t = k \right) \forall k \in Q$

Assuming a first order Markov process and the statistical independence of the observations, the HMM likelihood can be defined using the probability of the observed data given the model:

$$L_\vartheta(W) = \sum_{\forall q} L_\vartheta(W, q) \triangleq \sum_{\forall q} \prod_t a_{q^{t-1} q^t} b_{q^t}\left(w^t \right) \tag{1}$$

where $\forall q$ stands for over all possible state sequences $q = q^1, q^2, ..., q^T \in Q$ and $a_{01} = \pi_1 = 1$.
To simplify the notation, we will indicate $\Pr\left(w^t \mid q^t \right)$ as equivalent to $\Pr\left(W^t = w^t \mid Q^t = q^t \right)$ or in a similar way $\Pr\left(q^t \mid q^{t-1} \right) \equiv \Pr\left(Q^t = q^t \mid Q^{t-1} = q^{t-1} \right)$
The EM algorithm is the most widely used way to maximize this likelihood (Duda et al., 2001). The forward–backward algorithm provides an efficient method for the expectation step (Baum et al., 1970) . The expected values for the state probabilities in ϑ can be calculated with the recursions

$$\alpha^t(j) \triangleq \Pr\left(w^1,...,w^t,q^t = j \mid \vartheta\right) = b_j\left(w^t\right)\sum_i \alpha^{t-1}(i)a_{ij} \tag{2}$$

$$\beta^t(j) \triangleq \Pr\left(w^{t+1},...,w^T,q^t = j \mid \vartheta\right) = \sum_k a_{jk}b_k\left(w^{t+1}\right)\beta^{t+1}(k) \tag{3}$$

Initialized with $\alpha^1(i) = \pi_i b_i\left(w^1\right)\forall i$ and $\beta^T(k) = 1\forall k$. Then, the probability of being in state i at time t is

$$\gamma^t(i) \triangleq \Pr\left(q^t = j \mid W,\vartheta\right) = \frac{\alpha^t(i)\beta^t(i)}{\sum_i \alpha^t(i)\beta^t(i)} \tag{4}$$

And the probability of being in state i at time t-1, and in state j at time t is

$$\xi^t(i,j) \triangleq \Pr\left(q^{t-1} = i, q^t = j \mid W,\vartheta\right) = \frac{\alpha^{t-1}(i)a_{ij}b_j\left(w^t\right)\beta^t(j)}{\sum_i \alpha^t(i)\beta^t(i)} \tag{5}$$

The learning rules can be obtained by maximizing the likelihood of the data as a function of the model parameters (Huang et al., 1990). Thus, the transition probabilities can be estimated with

$$a_{ij} = \frac{\sum_t \xi^t(i,j)}{\sum_t \gamma^t(i)} \tag{6}$$

These equations can be easily extended for training from multiple observation sequences (Liporace, 1982).
The corresponding learning rules for the parameters of the observation distributions are dependent on the chosen model for $b_k\left(w^t\right)$.

2.2 Hidden Markov Tree (HMT)

Let $W = \left[w_1, w_2, ..., w_N\right]$ be the concatenation of the wavelet coefficients obtained after performing a DWT with J scales, without including w_0, the approximation coefficient at the coarsest scale. Therefore, $N = 2^J - 1$. The HMT can be defined with the structure $\theta = \langle U, \Re, \pi, \varepsilon, F\rangle$, where (Milone et al., 2010) :

i. $U = \{u\}$ with $u \in \{1,2,...,N\}$, is the set of nodes in the tree.

ii. $\Re = \bigcup_u \Re_u$ is the set of states in all the nodes of the tree, denoting with $\Re_u = \{R_u\}$ the set of discrete random state variables in the node u, and R_u taking values $r_u \in \{1,2,...,M\}$

iii. $\varepsilon = \left[\varepsilon_{u,mn}\right]$ with $\varepsilon_{u,mn} = \Pr\left(R_u = m, \mid R_{\rho(u)} = n\right)\forall m \in \Re_u, \forall n \in \Re_{\rho(u)}$ is the array whose elements hold the conditional probability of node u, being in state m, given that the state in its parent node $\rho(u)$ is n and satisfy $\sum_m \varepsilon_{u,mn} = 1$

iv. $\pi = \left[\pi_p\right]$ with $\pi_p = \Pr(R_1 = p) \forall p \in \Re_1$ the probabilities fort he root node being on state p.

v. $F = \{f_{u,m}(w_u)\}$ are the observation probability distributions, with $f_{u,m}(w_u) = \Pr(W_u = w_u \mid R_u = m)$ the probability of observing the wavelet coefficient w_u with the state m (in the node u).

Additionally, the following notation will be used :

- $C(u) = \{c_1(u), \ldots, c_{N_u}(u)\}$ is the set of children of the node u.
- T_u is the subtree observed from the node u (including all its descendants).
- $T_{u \setminus v}$ is the subtree from node u but excluding node v and all its descendants.

As in the sequence q for HMM, we will use the notation $r = [r_1, r_2, \ldots, r_N]$ to refer a particular combination of hidden states in the HMT nodes.

Assuming that the following three basic properties in the HMT are true :

1. $\Pr(r_u = m \mid \{r_v / v \neq u\}) = \Pr\left(r_u = m \mid \left\{r_{\rho(u)}, r_{c_1(u)}, r_{c_2(u)}, \ldots, r_{c_{N_u}(u)}\right\}\right)$

the Markovian dependencies for trees

2. $\Pr(W \mid r) = \prod_u \Pr(w_u \mid r)$ the statistical independence of the observed data given the hidden states
3. $\Pr(w_u \mid r) = \prod_u \Pr(w_u \mid r_u)$ the statistical independence of the observed coefficient in node u to the states in the other nodes of the tree and using the standard definition $L_\theta(w, r) \triangleq \Pr(w, r \mid \theta)$ the HMT likelihood is

$$L_\theta(w) = \sum_{\forall r} L_\theta(w, r) \triangleq \sum_{\forall r} \prod_u \varepsilon_{u}, {}_{r_u r_{\rho(u)}} f_{u}, {}_{r_u}(w_u) \tag{7}$$

where $\forall r$ means that we include all the possible combinations of hidden states in the tree nodes and $\varepsilon_1, {}_{r_1 r_{\rho(1)}} = \pi_{r_1}$

For the computation of the expected values in the EM algorithm, the upward-downward recursions are used, in a similar way than the forward-backward ones in HMM. For this algorithm the following quantities are defined (Ronen et al., 1995) :

$$\alpha_u(n) \triangleq \Pr\left(T_{1\setminus u}, r_u = n \mid \theta\right) \tag{8}$$

$$\beta_u(n) \triangleq \Pr(T_u \mid r_u = n, \theta) \tag{9}$$

$$\beta_{\rho(u),u}(n) \triangleq \Pr\left(T_u \mid r_{\rho(u)} = n, \theta\right) \tag{10}$$

In the upward step the β quantities are computed as

$$\beta_u(n) = f_{u,n}(w_u) \prod_{v \in C(u)} \beta_u(m) \varepsilon_{u,mn} \tag{11}$$

Initialized with $\beta_u(n) = f_{u,n}(w_u) \forall u$ in the finest scale. Then, $\beta_{\rho(u),u}(n)$ is computed and the iterative process follows in the previous level, in an upward inductive tree traversal.

When the upward step reaches the root node, the downward step computes

$$\alpha_u(n) = \sum_m \frac{\varepsilon_{u,nm}\beta_{\rho(u)}(m)\alpha_{\rho(u)}(m)}{\beta_{\rho(u),u}(m)} \tag{12}$$

Starting from $\alpha_1(m) = \Pr(r_1 = m \mid \theta) = \pi_m$. The other two useful quantities are the probability of being in state m of node u

$$\gamma_u(m) \triangleq \Pr(r_u = m \mid w, \theta) = \frac{\alpha_u(m)\beta_u(m)}{\sum_n \alpha_u(n)\beta_u(n)} \tag{13}$$

And the probability of being in state m at node u, and the state n at its parent node $\rho(u)$

$$\xi_u(m,n) \triangleq \Pr\left(r_u = m, r_{\rho(u)} = n \mid w, \theta\right) = \frac{\beta_u(m)\varepsilon_{u,mn}\alpha_{\rho(u)}(n)\beta_{\rho(u)}(n) / \beta_{\rho(u),u}(n)}{\sum_n \alpha_u(n)\beta_u(n)} \tag{14}$$

If we consider the maximization for multiple observations $W = \{w^1, w^2, \dots, w^L\}$, with $w \in \mathbb{R}^N$, the conditional probabilities $\varepsilon_{u,mn}$ can be estimated from $\varepsilon_{u,mn} = \frac{\sum_l \xi_u^l(m,n)}{\sum_l \gamma_{\rho(u)}^l(n)}$ and using a normal distribution for the observation probability distributions

$$f_{u,r_u}(w_u) = \frac{1}{\sqrt{2\pi\sigma}} \exp\left(-\frac{1}{2}\frac{\left(w_u - \mu_{u,r_u}\right)^2}{\sigma_{u,r_u}^2}\right) \tag{15}$$

We have (Crouse, et al., 1998)

$$\mu_{u,m}(w_u) = \frac{\sum_l w_u^l \gamma_u^l(m)}{\sum_l \gamma_u^l(m)} \tag{16}$$

$$\sigma_{u,m}^2 = \frac{\sum_l \left(w_u^l - \mu_{u,m}\right)^2 \gamma_u^l(m)}{\sum_l \gamma_u^l(m)} \tag{17}$$

2.3 Hidden Semi-Markov Models (HSMM)

A HSMM consists of a pair of discrete-time stochastic processes $\{S_t\}$ and $\{X_t\}$. Similar to HMM, the observed process $\{X_t\}$ is related to the unobserved semi-Markovian state process $\{S_t\}$ by the so-called conditional distributions (Bulla et al., 2010).

Let $X_T^1 := (X_1, \dots, X_T)$ denote the observed sequence of length T. The same convention is used for the state sequence S_t, and θ denotes the set of model parameters. The state process is a finite-state semi-Markov chain, which is constructed as follows. A homogeneous Markov chain with J states, labelled 1,…,J models the transitions between different states.

The stochastic process $\{S_t\}$ is specified by the initial probabilities $\pi_j := P(S_1 = j)$ with :

$\sum_j \pi_j = 1$ and the transition probabilities p_{ij}. For states $i, j \in \{1,...,J\}$ with $j \neq i$, these are given by

$$p_{ij} := P(S_{t+1} = j \mid S_{t+1} \neq i, S_t = i) \tag{18}$$

Satisfying $\sum_j p_{ij} = 1$ and $p_{ii} = 0$. The diagonal elements of the transition probability matrix (TPM) of a HSMM are required to be zero, since we separately model the run length distribution and do not consider the case of absorbing states. This distribution, also referred to as sojourn time distribution, is associated with each state. It models the duration the process $\{S_t\}$ remains in the state j and is defined by

$$d_j(u) := P(S_{t+u+1} \neq j \mid S_{t+u} = j,...,S_{t+2} = j \mid S_{t+1} = j, S_t \neq j) \tag{19}$$

The combination of a Markov chain, modelling state changes, and runlength distributions, determining the sojourn times in the states, define $\{S_t\}$ and illustrate the main difference between the HMM and the HSMM. The semi-Markovian state process $\{S_t\}$ of a HSMM does not have the Markov property at each time t, but is Markovian at the times of state changes only.
The observed process $\{X_t\}$ at time t is related to the state process $\{S_t\}$ by the conditional distributions $b_j(x_t)$, which are either probability functions in the case of discrete conditional distributions or probability densities in the case of continuous conditional distributions :

$$b_j(x_t) = \begin{cases} P(X_t = x_t \mid S_t = j) & \text{for discrete } X_t \\ f(X_t = x_t \mid S_t = j) & \text{for continuous } X_t \end{cases} \tag{20}$$

For the observation component, the so-called conditional independence property is fulfilled:

$$P\left(X_t = x_t \mid X_T^1 = x_T^1,...,S_1^{t-1} = s_1^{t-1}, S_t = j, S_{t+1}^T = s_{t+1}^T\right) = P(X_t = x_t \mid S_t = j) \tag{21}$$

That is, the output process at time t depends only on the value of S_t .

3. Proposed ECG segmentation techniques

3.1 Modulus maxima wavelet transforms and hidden Markov models based method

This technique is based on the combination of two mathematical techniques namely the Wavelet Transform (WT) and Hidden Markov Models (HMM). In this method, we first localize edges in the ECG by wavelet coefficients, then, features extracted from the edges serve as input for the HMM. This new approach was tested and evaluated on the manually annotated database QT database (Laguna & al., 1997), which is regarded as a very important benchmark for ECG analysis. We obtained a sensitivity Se= 99,40% for QRS detection and a sensitivity Se= 94,65% for T wave detection.

3.1.1 Modulus maxima wavelet transforms

The modulus maximum describe any point u_0, s_0 such that the $|W_{s_0} f(u)|$ is locally maximum at $u = u_0$. This implies that (Chen, 2006)

$$\frac{\partial W_{S_0} f(u)}{\partial u}\bigg|_{u=u_0} = 0 \qquad (22)$$

When the WT is at fine scale, singularities are detected by finding the abscissa where the wavelet modulus maxima converge (Mallat & Hwang, 1992). The zero-crossings of the WT, which is also at fine scale, correspond to the maxima or minima of the smoothed uniphase signal (Mallat, 1991).

$$W_s f(u) = \int_{-\infty}^{+\infty} f(t) \frac{1}{\sqrt{s}} \Psi^*(\frac{t-u}{s}) dt \qquad (23)$$

The singularities in the arrhythmia waveform can be conveniently detected by employing wavelet transform (WT). WT of a function f is a convolution product of the time series with the scaled and translated kernel Ψ , and is given by (Strang & Nguyen, 1996) :

$$W_{s,u_0}(f) = \int_{-\infty}^{+\infty} \frac{1}{s} \Psi(\frac{u-u_0}{s}) f(x) dx \qquad (24)$$

$$W_{s,u_0}(f) \alpha |s|^{h(u_0)} \quad s \to 0^+ \qquad (25)$$

Where s is the scale parameter and u_0 is the translation parameter. The ability of WT to reveal even the weaker singularities within the time series by adjusting s makes it an indispensable tool for singularity analysis.
The continuous WT described in Equation (24) is an extremely redundant and a computationally expensive representation. The wavelet transform modulus maxima (WTMM) method (Hwang, 1994) changes the continuous sum over space into a discrete sum by taking the local maxima of $|W_{s,u_0}(f)|$ considered as a function of u . An important feature of these maxima lines is that, each time the analyzed signal has a local Hölder exponent $h(u_0)$ less than the analyzing wavelet, there is at least one maxima line pointing toward u_0 along which Equation (25) holds (Arneodo, 1995, Joshi, 2006).

3.1.2 Selecting edge localization

First, In the WTMM (Mallat, 1999), the WT local extrema is used to characterize singularities in the signal. One very successful method described in (Cuiwei et al., 1995), uses the ECG wavelet transform modulus maxima properties to characterize the different ECG complexes. A rule based system is used to detect QRS waves and differentiate them from T waves and noise artifacts. This method has also been extended for T and P wave's detection (Jouck, 2004). In the ECG substantial information is carried in the peaks, so if we want to use a segment model, it would be preferable to model a segment around the ECG peaks. The rising and falling edges in a signal can be easily identified by the WT coefficients.
A positive modulus maximum corresponds to a rising edge and a modulus maxima corresponds to a falling edge. The modulus maximum alone do not provide sufficient information to determine the edge onset and offset. When the analyzing wavelet is the derivative of a smoothing function $\theta(u)$, the wavelet transform can be interpreted as the derivative of the original signal $f(u)$ smoothed by $\theta(u)$.

As the zero crossings of $Wf(u,s)$ correspond to zero crossings of $df(u)/du$ - the derivative of $f(u)$ - a rising or falling edge onset and offset can be derived from the zero crossings in $Wf(u,s)$. So, by determining the modulus maxima locations and the zero crossing near the modulus maxima, the onset and offset as well as the point of inflection of an edge can be determined. The area between the ECG onset and offset is characterized by constant sign wavelet coefficients - either all positive or all negative. The scale selection u, determines the resolution details of $f(u)$ that are visible in the $Wf(u,s)$, and thus also the edges resolutions that can be detected. When only coarse scales are selected, only coarse details of $f(u)$ are detectable. When only fine scales are selected, the fast varying details of $f(u)$ are visible. As fine scales give a better time-resolution, it would be preferable to use fine scales to more precisely determine the edge onset and offset.

However, ECG signals are often subject to high frequency noise, and at small scales this noise distorts the wavelet transform. So, we want to select scales such that the ECG peaks oscillations are visible in the wavelet transform, but not so small that the noise in the signal becomes too dominant in the wavelet transform. From empirical tests, it became apparent that selecting only one scale to detect edges did not suffice. The edges resolutions make up the ECG peaks are too broad to be captured by one scale WT. Therefore it is necessary to use multiple scales to detect edges. Unfortunately, it is not guaranteed, that if the wavelet coefficients at one scale have constant sign in one area, that the wavelet coefficients in that area on another scale also have constant sign. In order to deal with this, the area in which an edge of $f(u)$ is localized is determined as follows :

We selected two scales that respond well to the edges time-frequency resolution that make up the ECG peaks. The finest of the two scales has the best time resolution to determine the edges onset and offset, but the high frequency noise in the ECG is also visible at this scale. In the wavelet coefficients on the more coarse scale, noise is less dominant, but some time resolution is lost. Therefore the wavelet transform at both scales is combined to detect edges. An edge is only detected, when in a certain signal $f(u_t,...,u_{t+d})$ area, wavelet coefficients on both scales $Wf(u_t,...,u_{t+d},s)$ have the same sign.

3.1.3 ECG edges localisation as HMM front end

The edges in the ECG are localized and features extracted from the edges serve as input for the HMM. The Viterbi algorithm for the HMM (Koski, 1996) can be interpreted as a search in the model state-time space. In the optimal solution search, states are assigned to observations to maximize the likelihood function. In other words, segments are modelled around observations that have a high probability to belong to a certain state when a Gaussian mixture model is used to model the observation probabilities (the wavelet coefficients). It is known that important information about the signal is carried in the wavelet transform modulus maxima. This information can improve discrimination between the ECG characteristics. The problem is that in the Viterbi algorithm the whole signal is searched, and that in some search areas no modulus maxima are present. For this reason it is hard to model the modulus maxima information into the probability calculations for the HMM observations.

This problem can be solved if only parts of the signal where modulus maxima are present are processed. In the edge wavelet transform at least one modulus maxima must be present. The segment is modelled from one zero crossing in the one scale wavelet coefficients the next zero crossing. Somewhere between the zero crossings we must have an inflection point, where the wavelet coefficients change direction (from rising to falling or vice versa), otherwise all wavelet coefficients in the segment would have to be zero. So, when a segment has been localized, further information from the wavelet coefficients in the segment can be extracted. This information is then used as an observation for the HMM. In contrast to the previous Markov models implementation, the observations no longer correspond to an ECG time sample, but an ECG segment time.

3.1.4 Experiments and results

In order to evaluate our performance method for ECG delineation, we use a standard *QT* database (Laguna & al., 1997). This is a manually annotated database, consisting of 105 records, two leads each. The records contain both automatic and manual annotations. The automatic annotations are available for the whole signal; the manual annotations are made for 30 to 100 beats for each record. In the tests performed, only the manual annotations are used as a reference. Not all records are used in the evaluation, some records have no T peak annotation or normal beat annotations, these records have been excluded. To asses the detection performance of the different waves we calculated the sensitivity Se and the positive predictivity P_+ of several events. In the QT database, when a QRS_{peak} is annotated, the rest of the beat is also annotated (at least the QRS_{on} and QRS_{off} and the T_{peak} and T_{end}). Therefore, the P_+ can only be calculated for other events then the QRS_{peak}. In an annotated beat, each absent manual annotation in the automatic detection neighbourhood can be considered as a false positive. Therefore, the wave detection rates are calculated as follows : a true positive is calculated for the QRS complex and the T wave, when at the annotated QRS_{peak} or T_{peak} the HMM of our method is in the QRS or T state respectively. When this is not the case, a false negative is recorded. For our method there are several states that relate to the QRS complex and T wave. The states related to the QRS complex are the states $\{Q,R,S,RST\}$,those related to the T wave are the states $\{T_1,T_2,RST\}$. The $\{RST\}$ state models a weak transition from the QRS complex to the T wave, therefore both the QRS complex and the T wave are associated with this state. As argued above, the P_+ can not be computed for QRS detection, but this can be computed for the QRS complex onset QRS_{on}, and the T wave offset T_{off}. For these events the Se and P_+ are calculated, as well as the mean (m) and the standard deviation (s) of the time differences between the cardiologist and automatic annotations. Furthermore, for the beats annotated by the cardiologist in the QT database, the QT time mean and standard deviation of these beats is measured *manQTt*. The mean and standard deviation of the time difference between the manual and automatic QT times is measures as εQTt. These differ from the errors of QRS_{on} and T_{off}, as they are calculated over all manual annotations and all automatic annotations. The proposed method is only trained on the whole concatenated test set and not on individual records. The results are shown in Table 1.

In this method only parts of the ECG signal that are detected by the edge localization method can be classified. As a consequence, when an edge is not detected when it should be, this part of the signal is always misclassified. Furthermore, the edge detection algorithm determines the edges onset and offset. The results of the T_{off} error mean show a positive bias (45ms). This means that most edges related to the T-wave are truncated too late in comparison to the cardiologist's annotations. Edges are truncated, when at the finest scale, the wavelet coefficients change sign. This is a very simple and straight forward approach,

Parameter	QRS	QRS_{on}	T	T_{off}	manQTt	εQTt
Se (%)	99,40	95,34	94,65	86,16	-	-
P+ (%)	-	90,75	-	83,56	-	-
m(ms)	-	-5,80	-	45	422,10	38
s (ms)	-	31,10	-	77,30	72,20	74,3
# annotations	3473	3473	3512	3512	-	-

Table 1. WTMM and HMM based method detection results

but unfortunately, often this does not concur with the cardiologists annotations. A possible solution to this is to truncate an edge sooner. For instance by using an even finer wavelet scale, or by truncating an edge when the wavelet coefficients cross at a certain threshold value, instead of zero. It should be noted, that these measures might increase T_{off} delineation precision (*m* and *s*) and the T_{off} sensitivity *Se*, but they would have little impact on detection rates (T sensitivity). Our HMM topology is able to model a great variety of ECG morphologies. Still, there are many different topologies possible, which may improve performance. This is an elementary problem in hidden Markov modelling; the topology and some of the model parameters are determined by experimentation and thus most likely to be suboptimal. The HMM model used has more states than annotated events present in the database. This is because some ECG waveforms are segmented more precise then in the manual annotations. As a result, it is hard to calculate the right parameters for the states related to the segments that are not annotated explicitly in the database. The obvious solution is to annotate the database more precisely, but this is a time consuming and expensive job. The resulting parameters can still not be proved to be optimal, and another HMM topology might be required, which would issue another database annotation. For this reason some of the states share parameters, these are the parameters that can be easily extracted from the database. The segment features that have been chosen as observations for the proposed HMM have shown to be discriminative between states.

3.2 Pitch synchronous wavelet transform and hidden semi-Markov models based method

In this technique we develop a new approach to ECG analysis, combining Pitch Synchronous Wavelet Transform (PSWT) and Hidden Semi-Markov Model (HSMM) for tracking the typical ECG cycle. The combination of these two techniques was examined in a way that the PSWT of an ECG signal was an input for the HSMM. This approach was tested and evaluated on the manually annotated QT database. Experimental results show the accuracy of the proposed technique for all corrupted ECG tested reaching a sensitivity Se=99,95% for QRS detection and Se=97,79% for T detection.

3.2.1 Pitch synchronous wavelet transform

The Pitch Synchronous Wavelet Transform (PSWT) is developed as an extension of the wavelet transform that is suitable for pseudo periodic signals like speech signals; electroencephalogram (EEG) signals; seismic signals and so more. Electrocardiogram (ECG) signals, i.e. heartbeat signals, exhibit pseudo-periodic behaviour. Nearby pulses are very similar in shape, but of course various evolutionary changes in the behaviour are medically significant (Goodwin, 1997).

PSWT is a periodic and pseudo periodic signals decomposition approach. It is based on a pitch synchronous technique which leads to convert the signal into a whole of vectors having variable length and to apply thereafter to the sequence obtained a traditional wavelet transform. This shows its capacity on one hand to analyze according to a periodic approach and on several scales the signals with periodic behaviour and on the other hand to take account of signal variabilities period per period (Evangelista, 1995)

A pseudo-periodic signal $x[n]$ is first converted into a sequence $v[k]=\{v_q[k]\}$ of variable length vector $v_q[k]$, each containing the sample of one period signal. The indexes $q=0,...,p[k]-1$ and k are respectively the inter-period and the period count index and $p[k]$ is a sequence of integer local pitch periods extracted from $x[n]$. Based on this representation the sequences of components are, then, analysed by means of an array of wavelet transform. Given a set of decomposition levels $l=1,2,...,L$, the pitch synchronous wavelet expansion of the signal $x[n]$ is defined by the following sum :

$$x[n]=\sum_{l=1}^{L} w_l[n]+r_L[n] \tag{26}$$

Where the scaling residue (estimation) $r_L[n]$ represents the average behaviour of $x[n]$ while the partial (details) $w_L[n]$ represents the fluctuations at scale 2^L local periods. In the transform domain the scaling residue and the partial are represented by the expressions :

$$x[n]=\sum_{l=1}^{L} w_l[n]+r_L[n] \tag{27}$$

$$w_l[n]=\sum_{m,q} S_{l,m,q}\xi_{l,m,q}[n] \tag{28}$$

Where $\xi_{l,m,q}[n]$, $\vartheta_{L,m,q}[n]$ (m,q integers adapted to the periodicity of the signal $x[n]$), $\sigma_{L,m,q}$ and $S_{l,m,q}$ represent a finite scale pitch synchronous wavelet, L level scaling sequences and the expansion coefficients, respectively (Elloumi et al., 2004).

3.2.2 Pitch synchronous wavelet transform as HSMM front end

The PSWT coefficients can be employed as a front end to a Markov Model as individual samples (the normal HMM) or as a segment of samples (the HSMM or Segmental Markov Model). In the sample based model, a state transition is made at each time step, and the occurrence probability of a given state is calculated from one observation O_t - that represents the wavelet coefficients from one time-sample $W_u(t,s)$ - In the segment based model, a state transition is made only after a certain number of time steps, *d*, and the probability for a state is calculated from multiple observations $O_t...O_{t+d}$ - that represent multiple pitch synchronous wavelet coefficients, $W_u(t...t+d,a)$ - In the HSMM, the probability of the segment observations $P(O_t,...,O_{t+d})$, is calculated as the product of the individual observations that make up the segment, as if they where independent identically distributed observations.

3.2.3 Experiments and results

The results of our method trained on individual records of the test database are considerably high. There are only a small number of records who fail good detection.

Record *sel36*, has the worst detection rate. This record has a rhythm of one or two normal beats followed by PVC (Premature Ventricular Contraction). As a result, the durations of the QRS complexes that are recorded are divided into two clusters : One for the normal QRS complexes that have a relatively short duration, and one for the PVC's that have a long duration. From the sensibility Se and the positive predictivity P_+ values, we can gather that there are slightly more false positives than false negatives. This may be a disadvantage for applications in which we need to be sure that only QRS complexes are detected. It may be possible to change this relation by changing parameters in our future work analysis. This extensive model which models the ECG waveforms more accurate might improve detection rates. The results shown in Table 2 are considerably high. There are only a small number of records who fail good detection, Se=99,95% and P_+=97,39% for QRS_{on} and Se=95,68% and P_+=96,57% for T_{off}.

Parameter	QRS	QRSon	T	Toff	manQTt	εQTt
Se (%)	99,95	99,95	97,79	95,68	-	-
P+ (%)	-	97,39	-	96,57	-	-
m(ms)	-	9,95	-	0,76	408,8	-9,7
s (ms)	-	7,2	-	22,7	52,1	14,1
# annotations	2093	2093	2131	2131	-	-

Table 2. PSWT and HSMM based method detection results

3.3 Multiscale product wavelet transform and hidden Markov tree based method

3.3.1 Multiscale product wavelet transform

The WT is a multi-scale analysis which has been shown to be very well suited for speech processing as Glottal Closure Instant (GCI) detection, pitch estimation, speech enhancement and recognition and so on. Moreover, a speech signal can be analysed at specific scales corresponding to the range of human speech (Berman & Baras 1993, Kadambe, 1992). (Witkin, 1981) provided the foundation for scale space theory by generalizing Rosenfeld's work (Rosenfeld, 1970), in which smoothing filters at dyadic scales were used. Based essentially on forming multiscale products of smoothed gradient estimates, this approach attempts to enhance the peaks of the gradients caused by true edges, while suppressing false peaks due to noise. The wavelet transform acts as an edge detector, and the detail coefficients should be equivalent to the estimated gradients. This method was first used in image processing (Xu et al., 1994) rely on the variations in the WT decomposition level. They use multiplication of WT of the image at adjacent scales to distinguish important edges from noise. Continuous WT produces modulus maxima at signal singularities allowing their localisation. However, one-scale analysis is not accurate. So, decision algorithm using multiple scales is proposed by different works to circumvent this problem (Bouzid & Ellouze, 2007, 2009).

So if the wavelet is chosen to have one vanishing moment, modulus maxima appear at discontinuities of the signal and represent the maxima of the first derivative of the smoothed signal. The MP (Sadler & Swami, 1999) consists of making the product of wavelet transform coefficients of the function f(n) at some successive dyadic scales as follows

$$p(n) = \prod_{j} w_{2^j} f(n) \tag{29}$$

Where $w_{2^j} f(n)$ is the wavelet transform of the function $f(n)$ at scale 2^j.
This expression is distinctly a non linear function. The product p(n) reveals peaks at signal edges, and has relatively small values elsewhere. Singularities produce cross-scale peaks in wavelet transform coefficients, these peaks are reinforced by the product p(n). Although particular smoothing levels may not be optimal, the non linear combination tends to reinforce the peaks while suppressing spurious peaks. The signal peaks will align across scales for the first few scales, but not for all scales because increasing the amount of smoothing will spread the response and cause singularities separated in time to interact. Thus, choosing too large scales will result in misaligned peaks in p(n). An odd number of terms in p(n) preserves the sign of the edge (Bouzid et al., 2006).
Motivated by the efficiency of the multiscale product in improving the edge detection, this method is applied on ECG signal and then can outperform the wavelet transform precision in weak singularity detection (Besrour et al., 2009).

4. Conclusion and future work

In this chapter, we have proposed some new techniques for ECG characterisation based on modulus maxima wavelet transform, pitch synchronous wavelet transform and in the future work multiscale product wavelet transform as respectively front ends of hidden Markov models, hidden semi-Markov models and hidden Markov tree. These innovative methods were then applied to the conventional QT database, according to the first method we have a Se= 99,40% for QRS detection and a Se= 94,65% for T wave detection. The second method have reached a Se=99,95% for QRS detection and a Se=97,79% for T detection.
The combination of these techniques has shown to be very efficient tool for ECG delineation; the good time-frequency resolution of the wavelet transform can successfully overcome some of the inherent problems of the ECG signal, such as noise and baseline drift. The HMM Markov chain can successfully capture the structural ECG properties, such as the cyclic ECG characteristics occurrences. These methods have a more intuitive approach to ECG delineation : focusing on relevant ECG parts, that are easily distinguishable, instead of ECG individual samples. It can be concluded, that the results of our methods can compete with other published work, and is a good candidate for further development.

5. References

Sayadi, O. & Shamsollahi, M.B. (2009). A Model-based Bayesian Framework for ECG Beat Segmentation. *International Journal of Physiolgical Measurement,* Vol.30, No.3, (March 2009), pp. 335-352

Kawaja, A.; Sanyal, S. & Dössel, O. (2005). A Wavelet-based Multi-channel ECG Delineator. *Proceedings of the 3rd European Medical and Biological Engineering Conference,* Singapore, 2005

Thomas, J.; Rose C. & Charpillet F. (2006). A Multi-HMM Approach to ECG Segmentation. *proceedings of the 18th IEEE International Conference on Tools with Artificial Intelligence,* pp. 609-616, ISBN 1082-3409, Washington D.C., United States, 2006

Thomas, J.; Rose C. & Charpillet F. (2007). A Support System for ECG Segmentation Based on Hidden Markov Models. *proceedings of the 29th Annual International Conference of the IEEE Engineering in Medicine and Biology Society,* pp. 3228-3231, SBN 978-1-4244-0787-3, Lyon, France, August 22-26, 2007

Li, C. & Biswas, G. (2000). A Bayesian Approach to Temporal Data Clustering Using Hidden Markov Models. *Proceedings of the 7th International Conference on Machine Learning*, pp. 543-550, ISBN 1-55860-707-2, Stanford, California, 2000

Thoraval, L.; Carrault, G. & Bellanger, J.J. (1994). Heart Signal Recognition by Hidden Markov Models : the ECG Case, *International Journal of Methods of Information in Medicine*, Vol. 33, No.1, (1994), pp. 10-14, ISSN 0026-1270

Hughes, N.P (2006). Probabilistic Models for Automated ECG Interval Analysis. Department of Engineering Science, University of Oxford, Ph.D. Thesis 2006

Clavier, L.; Boucher, J.-M. & Pollard, E. (1998). Hidden Markov Models Compared to the Wavelet Transform for P-wave Segmentation in ECG Signals. *Proceedings of the 9th European Signal Processing Conference*, pp. 2453–2456, ISBN 960-7620-05-4, Rhodes, Greece, September 8-11, 1998

Clavier, L.; Boucher, J.-M.; Lepage, R.; Blanc, J.-J. & Cornily, J.-C. (2002). Automatic P-wave Analysis of Patients Prone to Atrial Fibrillation. *International Journal of Medical and Biological Engineering and Computing*, Vol.40, No.1, (January 2002), pp. 63-71, ISSN 0140-0118

Lepage, R.; Provost, K.; Boucher, J.-M.; Cornily, J.-C; Blanc J.-J. (2000). Wavelet and HMM Association for ECG Segmentation. *Proceedings of the 10th European Signal Processing Conference*, pp. 525-528, ISBN 952-15-0443-9, Tampere, Finland, September 4-8, 2000

Graja, S. & Boucher J.-M. (2005). Hidden Markov Tree Model Applied to ECG Delineation. *IEEE Transactions on Instrumentation and Measurement*, Vol.54, No.6, (December 2005), pp. 2163 - 2168, ISSN 1729-8806

Crouse, M.S.; Novak, R.D. & Baraniuk, R.G. (1998). Wavelet-Based Statistical Signal Processing Using Hidden Markov Models. *IEEE Transactions on Signal Processing*, Vol.46, No.4, (April 1998), pp. 886-902

Muller, S.M.T. Andreao, R.V. Boudy, J. Garcia-Salicetti, S. Filho, T.F.B. Filho, M.S. (2006). Online HMM Adaptation Applied to ECG Signal Analysis. *IEEE International Symposium on Industrial Electronics*, pp. 511-514, ISBN 1-4244-0496-7, Montreal, Canada, July 9-13, 2006

Andreão, R.V.; Dorizzi, B.; Boudy J. & Mota, J.C.M. (2003). Transformée en Ondelettes et Modèles de Markov Cachés pour la Segmentation Automatique du Signal ECG. *Proceedings du 19ème colloque GRETSI*, Paris, France, 2003

Andreão, R.V.; Dorizzi, B.; Boudy J. & Mota, J.C.M. (2004). Online Beat Segmentation and Classification through Hidden Markov Models, *Proceedings of the International Federation for Medical and Biological Engineering*, João Pessoa, Brazil, 2004

Andreão, R.V.; Dorizzi, B.; Boudy J. (2006). ECG Signal Analysis through Hidden Markov. *IEEE Transactions on Biomedical Engineering*, Vol.53, No.8, (August 2006), pp. 1541-1549, ISSN 0018-9294

Laguna, P.; Mark, R.G., Goldberger, A. & Moody, G.B. (1997). A Database for Evaluation of Algorithms for Measurement of QT and Other Waveform Intervals in the ECG. *Proceedings of the 24th Annual Meeting on Computers in Cardiology*, pp. 673-676, ISBN 0-7803-4445-6, Lund, Sweden, September 7-10, 1997

Available from http://www.physionet.org/physiobank/database/qtdb

Evangelista, G. (1993). Pitch Synchronous Wavelet Representation of Speech and Music Signals. *IEEE transactions on signal processing*, Vol.41, No.12, (1993), pp. 3313-3330, ISSN 1053-587X

Chong, N.R.; Burnett I.S. & Chicharo, J.F. (2000). A New Waveform Interpolation Coding Scheme Based on Pitch Synchronous Wavelet Transform Decomposition, *IEEE*

Transactions on Speech and Audio Processing,Vol.8,No.3, (2000), pp. 345-348, ISSN 1063-6676

Krimi, S.; Ouni, K. & Ellouze, N. (2007). Pitch Synchronous Wavelet and Hidden Semi-Markov Models Based Method for ECG Analysis. *Proceedings of the 15th European Signal Processing Conference*, pp. 1407-1411, Poznan-Poland, September 3-7, 2007

Cuiwei, L.; Zheng, C. & Tai, C. (1995). Detection of ECG Characteristic Points Using Wavelet Transforms, *IEEE Transactions on Biomedical Engineering*, Vol.42, No.1, (1995), pp. 21-28, ISSN 0018-9294

Jouck, P. (2004). Application of the Wavelet Transform Modulus Maxima Method to T-Wave Detection in Cardiac Signals. Master's Thesis, Maastricht University, 2004

Krimi, S.; Ouni, K. & Ellouze, N. (2008). An Approach Combining Wavelet Transform and Hidden Markov Models for ECG Segmentation. *Proceedings of the 3rd International Conference on Information and Communication Technologies: From Theory to Applications*, pp. 1-6, ISBN 978-1-4244-1751-3, Damascus, Syria, April 7-11, 2008

Mallat, S. & Hwang, W.L. (1992). Singularity Detection and Processing with Wavelets. *IEEE Transactions on Information Theory*, Vol.38, No.2, (March 1992), pp. 617-643,

Sadler, B.M. & Swami, A. (1999). Analysis of Multiscale Products for Step Detection and Estimation. *IEEE Transactions on Information Theory*, Vol.45, No. 3, (1999), pp. 1043-1051, ISSN 0018-9448

Besrour, R; Lachiri, Z. & Ellouze, N. (2009). Using Multiscale Product for ECG Characterization. *Research Letters in Signal Processing*, ISSN 1687-6911

Milone, D.H.; Di Persia, L.E., & Torres, M.E. (2010). Denoising and Recognition Using Hidden Markov Models with Observation Distributions Modelled by Hidden Markov Trees. *Journal of Pattern Recognition*, Vol.43, No.4, (2010), pp. 1577-1589, ISSN 0031-3203

Duda, R.O.; Hart, P.E. & Stork, D.G. (2001). *Pattern Classification*, second ed., Wiley, ISBN 978-0-471-05669-0, New York

Baum, L.; Petric, T., Soules, G., Weiss, N.A. (1970). Maximization Technique Occurring in the Statistical Analysis of Probabilistic Functions of Markov Chains. *Annals Mathematical Statistics*, Vol. 41, No.1, (1970), pp. 164-171

Huang, X.D.; Ariki, Y., Jack, M.A. (1990). Hidden Markov Models for Speech Recognition. *Edinburgh University Press*, Edinburgh, ISBN 0748601627

Liporace, L. (1982). Maximum Likelihood Estimation form Multivariate Stochastic Observations of Markov Chains. *IEEE Transactions on Information Theory*, Vol.28, No.5, (1982), pp. 724-734, ISSN 0018-9448

Ronen, O.; Rohlicek, J.R. & Ostendorf, M. (1995). Parameter Estimation of Dependence Tree Models Using the EM Algorithm. *IEEE Signal Processing Letters*, Vol. 2, No.8, (1995), pp. 157-159, ISSN 1070-9908

Bulla, J.; Bulla, I.; Nenadic, O. (2010). Hsmm—An R Package for Analyzing Hidden Semi-Markov Models. *Journal of Computational Statistics & Data Analysis*, Vol.54, No.3, (2010), pp. 611-619, ISSN 0167-9473

Chen, P.C.; Lee, S. & Kuo, C.D. (2006). Delineation of T-Wave in ECG by Wavelet Transform Using Multiscale Differential Operator. *IEEE Transactions on Biomedical Engineering*, Vol.53, No.7, (July 2006), pp. 1429-1433, ISSN 0018-9294

Mallat, S. (1991). Zero-Crossings of a Wavelet Transform. *IEEE transactions on information theory*, Vol.37, No.4, pp. 1019-1033, (July 1991), ISSN 0018-9448

Strang, G. & Nguyen, T. (1996). Wavelets and Filter Banks. *Wellesley-Cambridge Press*, ISBN 09614088 71 978 09614088 79

Hwang, W.L. & Mallat, S. (1994) .Characterization of Self-Similar Multifractals with Wavelet Maxima. *International Journal of Applied and Computational Harmonic Analysis*, Vol.1, No.4, (1994), pp.316-328, 1994

Arneodo, A.; Bacry, E. & Muzy, J.F. (1995). The Thermodynamics of Fractals Revisited with Wavelets. *Physica A*, 213, pp. 232–275

Joshi, A.J. (2006). Data Mining of Biomedical Signals. *Progress Report of PhD*, Department of Computer Science and Engineering Indian Institute of Technology, Bombay, Mumbai, 2006

Mallat, S. (1999). A Wavelet Tour of Signal Processing. *Academic Press*, second edition

Koski, A. (1996). Modelling ECG Signal with Hidden Markov Models. *Journal of Artificial Intelligence in Medicine*, Vol. 8, No. 5, (1996), pp. 453-471

Evangelista, G. (1994). Comb and Multiplexed Wavelet Transforms and their Applications to Signal Processing. *IEEE transactions on Signal Processing*, Vol.42, No.2, (1994), pp. 292-303, ISSN 1053-587X

Goodwin, M. (1997). Adaptive Signal Models : Theory Algorithms and Audio Applications. *PhD Thesis*, Department of Electrical Engineering, University of California, Berkeley, 1997

Elloumi, A.; Lachiri Z. & Ellouze, N. (2004). Pitch Synchronous Wavelet Based Foetal ECG Extraction. *Symposium on the 1st International Control, Communications and Signal Processing*, pp. 239-242, ISBN 0-7803-8379-6, 2004

Berman, Z. & Baras, J.S. (1993). Properties of the Multiscale Maxima and Zero-Crossings Representations. *IEEE Transactions on Signal Processing*, Vol.41, No.12, (1993), pp. 3216–3231, ISSN 1053-587X

Kadambe, S. & Boudreaux-Bartels, G.F. (1992). Application of the Wavelet Transform for Pitch Detection of Speech Signals. *IEEE Transactions of Information Theory*. Vol.38, No.2,(1992), pp.917–924, ISSN 0018-9448

Xu, Y.; Weaver, J.B, Healy, D.M. & Lu, J. (1994). Wavelet Transform Domain Filters : a Spatially Selective Noise Filtration Technique. *IEEE Transactions on Image Processing*, Vol.3, No.6, (1994), pp.747-758

Bouzid, A. & Ellouze, N. (2009). Voice Source Parameter Measurement Based on Multi-scale Analysis of Electroglottographic Signal. *Journal of Speech Communication*, Elseiver, Vol.51, No.9, (2009), pp.782-792, ISSN 0167-6393

Bouzid, A. & Ellouze, N. (2007). Open Quotient Measurements Based on Multiscale Product of Speech Signal Wavelet Transform. *Research Letters in Signal Processing*, pp. 1-6. Hindawi Publishing

Bouzid, A. & Ellouze, N. (2006). Singularity Detection of Electroglottogram Signal by Multiscale Product Method. *The 14th European Signal Processing Conference*, Florence, Italie, September 4-8, 2006

Sadler, B.M.; Pham, T. & Sadler, L.C. (1998). Optimal and Wavelet-based Shock wave Detection and Estimation. *Journal of Acoustical Society of America*, Vol.104, No.2, (1998), pp. 955-963

Witkin, A.P. (1983). Scale-Space Filtering. *Proceedings of the 8th International Joint Conference in Artificial. Intelligence*, pp. 1019-1022, 1983

Rosenfeld, A. (1970). A Non Linear Edge Detection, *Proc. IEEE*, Vol.58, (May 1970), pp. 814-816

Mallat, S. & Zhong, S. (1992). Characterization of Signals from Multiscale Edges. *IEEE Transactions on Pattern Analysis and Machine Intelligence*, Vol.14, No.7, (1992) pp. 710-732, ISSN 0162-8828

8

Hidden Markov Models in the Neurosciences

Blaettler Florian, Kollmorgen Sepp,
Herbst Joshua and Hahnloser Richard
Institute of Neuroinformatics,
University of Zurich / ETH Zurich
Switzerland

1. Introduction

HMMs are useful tools for model-based analyses of complex behavioral and neurophysiological data. They make inference of unobserved parameters possible whilst taking into account the probabilistic nature of behavior and brain activity. The trend in neuroscience is to observe and manipulate brain activity in freely moving animals during natural behaviors and to record from several dozens of neurons at the same time. The richness of the data generated in such experiments constitutes a major challenge in data analysis, a challenge that can be addressed partly using HMMs. For example, an experimenter could be interested in recovering from noisy measurements of brain activity the underlying electrical activity of single brain cells using the constraint that activity has to agree with cellular biophysics (such as in the spike sorting problem). Or, the experimenter may want to describe the variance in some behavior and relate it to causes encoded in the neural recordings. We here review recent HMM applications to illustrate how HMMs enhance the experimental read out and provide insights into neural population coding. We discuss HMMs for identifying repetitive motifs in natural behaviors, in particular birdsong and for extracting and comparing patterns of single-neuron activity in multi-neuron recordings. Finally, we introduce a pair HMM for sequence alignment that is free of distance measures and aligns sequences by matching their self-similarities. We demonstrate the workings of the new pair HMM by aligning the song of a pupil bird to that of its tutor.

2. General overview

HMMs are widely applied in neuroscience research, ranging from studies of behavior, to neuron assemblies, and to individual ion channels. The observed variable (the output of the HMM) can be a test subject's decision, or an animal's motor output. In other cases, the observed variable is neural activity measured using electrophysiology, electroencephalography (EEG), magnetoencephalography (MEG), or imaging. What many studies have in common is the quest to identify underlying brain states that correlate with the measured signals. Also, many studies create the need of segmenting behavioral or neural sequences into recurring elements and transitions between them.

2.1 Decoding of neural data with HMMs

Spike data recorded from single or multiple nerve cells (neurons) is amenable to modeling with HMMs. Neurons emit action potentials. These are brief and stereotyped electrical events that can be recorded with extracellular electrodes in behaving animals. A popular application of HMMs is decoding information from recorded spike data. For instance, Pawelzik et al. (Pawelzik, Bauer et al. 1992) used an HMM to model neuronal responses in the cat's visual cortex. Their model distinguishes periods of oscillatory versus stochastic firing. Gat and Tishby (Gat and Tishby 1993) modeled monkey cortical activity as a multivariate time-dependent Poisson process. The Poisson means are hidden parameters. The recorded spike trains were divided into small time bins in which the spike counts were assumed to obey a Poisson distribution with time-dependent mean rate. Gat and Tishby's model yielded a temporal segmentation of spike data into a sequence of 'cognitive' states, each with its distinguished vector of Poisson means. Along the same lines, Radons et al. (Radons, Becker et al. 1994) employed HMMs for decoding the identity of visual stimuli from recorded neural responses. They simultaneously recorded neuronal spiking activity from several neurons in the visual cortex of monkeys during presentation of different visual stimuli. For each stimulus, they trained an HMM on a subset of the respective trials. HMM outputs were formed from the neural activity of the simultaneously recorded cells, assuming Poisson spike statistics. After learning, the hidden states of the HMMs corresponded to various regimes of multi-unit activity. Radons et al. then used the trained HMMs to decode stimulus identity from neural responses by selecting the stimulus for which the HMM gives the largest likelihood for generating the neural responses. Using this procedure they were able to identify the presented visual stimulus with high accuracy.

Related to these studies, several authors have investigated the idea of cell assemblies and their associated sequential or attractor dynamics. A state of a cell assembly is given by a particular pattern of activity in that assembly. States and transitions of assemblies are thought to bear functional relevance and can be efficiently modeled using HMMs (Gat, Tishby et al. 1997; Nicolelis, Fanselow et al. 1997; Rainer and Miller 2000). Thereby, insights can be gained into the mechanisms of neuron firing under different pharmacological conditions (Camproux, Saunier et al. 1996). Also, rich patterns of neural activity have been observed during sleep; these patterns often resemble motor-related activity during the day and are thought to constitute a form of replay activity. Such replay activity has, for example, been observed in songbirds (Dave and Margoliash 2000; Hahnloser, Kozhevnikov et al. 2002; Weber and Hahnloser 2007). HMMs have helped to gain insights into such activity patterns by segmenting them into discrete global states. One successful method for doing this is to assume that for each global (hidden) state of the neuron population, neurons have renewal firing statistics determined by the probability density of their interspike intervals (Camproux, Saunier et al. 1996; Danoczy and Hahnloser 2006). By training an HMM on the simultaneously recorded spike trains, each model neuron learns to fire spike patterns with renewal statistics that can be different for each of the hidden states. Using this procedure, it was found that sleep-related activity in songbirds is characterized by frequent switching between two awake-like firing states, one in which the bird is singing, and one in which it is not singing (Danoczy and Hahnloser 2006; Weber and Hahnloser 2007).

Several authors have explored HMM based decoding of neural or nerve activity for control purposes, for example, to control a robot arm. Chan and Englehart (Chan and Englehart 2005) recorded myoelectric signals from the forearm during six different kind of movements, represented by six hidden states in their HMM. Their goal was to infer the

correct arm movement (the correct hidden state) from the recorded myoelectric signal. Knowing the regular dynamics of limb movements, and to avoid overfitting, the authors constrained the transition matrix of the HMM down to a single parameter alpha, the probability of remaining in the same hidden state in two consecutive time steps (32 ms). All transitions to other states were equally probable. Emission distributions were modeled as Gaussians; their parameters were directly estimated from the training data. Using this model, Chan and Englehart reach a classification rate of 94.6% correct, which exceeds the performance of other algorithms. One of the advantages of using a probabilistic model is that it allows, through continuous training, to continuously adapt to long term system changes, such as changes in the electrode-skin interface. Other neuroprosthetics work relies solely on neural recordings to control the robotic arm. Recordings are usually made in brain areas that are responsible for motor planning or motor commands. The activity of recorded cells is decoded and related to a certain motion of the robot arm. Abeles and others (Abeles, Bergman et al. 1995; Seidemann, Meilijson et al. 1996; Gat, Tishby et al. 1997) analyzed neural population data from the frontal cortex of monkeys performing a delayed localization task. The monkeys were trained to perform a delayed instructed arm movement. This task made it possible to record from neurons during the planning phase in which the monkey knew what to do, but was not moving yet, and during the movement phase itself. In such experiments it is possible to use an HMM to estimate the upcoming motor output from the recorded neural signal during the planning phase and control the prosthetic robot arm using decoded planning-related activity. Poisson firing statistics are usually assumed whereby the mean firing rate depends on the current state of the neuron population that is hidden from the observer. Movements or movement intentions can be decoded in such scenarios for example by thresholding the posterior probabilities of hidden states (Kemere, Santhanam et al. 2008).
HMMs have also been used to model neural activity on a much smaller scale. Action potentials are formed by different ion channels that can either be closed or open, i.e. permeable for a special type of ion or not. The state of single ion channels can be recorded using cell-attached recording modes. The state (open or closed) of a single ion channel is probabilistic and depends on its own history and the history of membrane voltage amongst other factors. HMMs can model the dynamics of single ion channels and be used to estimate their state trajectory from noisy recordings (Chung, Moore et al. 1990; Becker, Honerkamp et al. 1994).

2.2 HMMs as tools in data analysis

In contrast to the abovementioned cases in which HMMs are used to directly model a hidden parameter of interest, HMMs are also commonly used as intermediate steps in data analysis, e.g. artifact correction. Dombeck et al. (Dombeck, Khabbaz et al. 2007) describe an experimental apparatus for two-photon fluorescence imaging in behaving mice; the mice are head-restrained while their limbs rest on a Styrofoam ball. The mice maneuver on the spherical treadmill while their head remains motionless. In such experiments it is common to observe running-associated motion artifacts in the focal plane of the microscope. The displacement of the brain relative to the microscope throughout the scanning process can be described by a (hidden) random walk on a finite two-dimensional grid. Key to artifact correction is the fit of the scanned image at a given time point and displacement compared to the reference image. The parameters of the displacement can be learned by maximizing over the joint probability of displacements and image similarities with the expectation maximization algorithm. After correcting the motion artifacts in the image sequence, the cleaned data can be further analyzed to study the neural code or other questions of interest.

2.3 Analysis of psychophysical data with HMMs

HMMs have been used to infer when learning occurs in behaving subjects and shown to provide better estimation of learning curves than other methods. Smith et al. (Smith, Frank et al. 2004) studied learning in a binary choice task – subjects had to make a choice out of two possibilities (correct versus incorrect). In this case the observed data are a time series of Boolean values. The authors assumed that the subject's answers followed a Bernoulli distribution that depends on a hidden state, reflecting the subject's performance. Using this latent variable model they quantified the probability that subjects performed better than chance, as follows. The first estimated the hidden learning dynamics, which allowed them to estimate the subject's performance on a fine timescale, essentially on a trial by trial basis. Using a confidence bound on the inferred learning curve they estimated the exact trial when learning has occurred. This trial happened usually much earlier than when determined using less elaborate methods, revealing the superiority of the hidden-state approach.

2.4 Analysis of natural behavior with HMMs

Natural behaviors are increasingly the target of neuroscience research but they are much more difficult to characterize than controlled behaviors because of their many inherent degrees of freedom. In typical experiments, natural behaviors are captured by means of movies or sound recordings, or by placing sensors or emitters on critical body parts. It is often difficult to classify natural behaviors. For example, to classify the swimming behaviors of fish, or the mating behaviors of flies, human experimenters usually must painstakingly analyze the various image frames and inspect them for repetitive movement patterns. Obviously, it would be much more convenient to automate such processes and let machines do the pattern extraction. Today, efforts are underway to develop such techniques and HMMs are a key methodology with great potential.

In the following, we introduce HMMs for analyses of complex vocal output, namely the songs of songbirds. The birdsong analysis problem bears resemblance with the speech recognition problem. However, the nature of birdsong learning creates different challenges for birdsong analysis. Therefore, different HMM approaches may be required as we will see next.

3. Alignment of birdsong with HMMs

Songbirds learn their songs from a tutor early during life, much like children learn their mother tongue from their parents. Songs in many species are composed of repetitions of a song motif that is composed of several syllables. The song motifs and syllables in closed-end learners such as the zebra finch are very stereotyped and do not change much during adulthood (Immelmann 1969). Song development, on the other hand, is more complex, and at any time juvenile birds can alter the spectral or temporal features of their songs: young birds can morph a syllable into another, drop an existing syllable, or introduce new syllables (Tchernichovski, Nottebohm et al. 2000; Tchernichovski, Mitra et al. 2001; Gardner, Naef et al. 2005). During development, song syllables may change independently of each other. Furthermore, songs can vary in speed from rendition to rendition (Gardner, Naef et al. 2005; Glaze and Troyer 2006).

A standard problem in birdsong analysis is that of segmenting the songs into motifs and into syllables. HMMs are useful for automated segmentation of birdsongs (Kogan and Margoliash 1998) because they can adequately deal with variable song tempo and spectral variability of song syllables.

However, in many circumstances song analysis goes beyond segmentation. A typical situation for a birdsong researcher is that he or she wants to compare the song of a juvenile bird to that of his tutor, to find out how much the pupil has already learned. To track song development through time, corresponding song elements have to be reliably identified across developmental phases. Below, we illustrate the use of HMMs for song comparison. The goal is twofold: first, it is to measure the similarity between two songs in terms of a single scalar quantity; and, second, to identify matching elements in the two songs. Assessment of song similarity has proven to be a very useful tool for developmental studies in which enabling or disabling influences on song learning are studied (Tchernichovski, Nottebohm et al. 2000; Tchernichovski, Mitra et al. 2001; Gardner, Naef et al. 2005; London and Clayton 2008) . The identification of matching song elements between different birds is of relevance in multi tutor studies in which we would like to trace back song elements to the tutor they have been learned from (Rodriguez-Noriega, Gonzalez-Diaz et al. 2010).

To compare two different songs with each other bears resemblance with comparing the genomes of two different species, in which insertions or deletions of long strands of DNA sequences are frequently encountered. The problem of finding correspondences between sequences is often referred to as the alignment problem (Brown, Cocke et al. 1990; Durbin 1998). Clearly birdsong alignment is different from genome alignment, because in the former both spectral and temporal features change during development, whereas there is no analogy of spectral changes in genomes (the four letter alphabet of nucleotides has been preserved by evolution).

3.1 Pair HMMs for birdsong alignment

Computational approaches to the alignment problem, like minimal edit distance algorithms (Wagner and Fischer 1974), have been around for quite some time and recently pair hidden Markov models (pair HHMs) have become very common. They offer a unified probabilistic framework that entails these more basic techniques but is much more general (Durbin 1998). One advantage of pair HMMs in alignment over more standard dynamic programming techniques is that pair HMMs do not require ad-hoc parameter setting: the trade-off between insertions, deletions, and matches can be learned from the data and does not have to be set by hand. Before we introduce a new pair HMM architecture and apply it to birdsong alignment, we first illustrate the general problem of alignment using a toy example.

Consider the following two sequences: *ABAC* and *AADC*. The second sequence results from the first by deleting *B* and inserting *D* at a different location. A possible way to describe the relationship between the two sequences is thus through the alignment *(Match, Deletion, Match, Insertion, Match)*. This alignment is not unique, however. For example, it would also be possible to align the sequences using matches only *(Match, Match, Match, Match)*, with the disadvantage that unequal symbols are matched onto each other (*B* onto *A* and *A* onto *D*), but the advantage that fewer alignment steps are required in the process. To decide which alignments are better, we define costs for the various matches, insertions, and deletions. Given these costs, the problem of finding the best sequence alignment can be solved by dynamic programming using minimum edit distance algorithms.

If we adopt a probabilistic view on the alignment problem (instead of the simpler cost perspective), we can represent the different types of mini-alignments (e.g. *Match, Insertion, Deletion*) by states of an HMM. Because such an HMM operates on pairs of sequences, we denote it with pair HMM (Durbin 1998). A simple pair HMM and an example alignment is depicted in Figure 1.

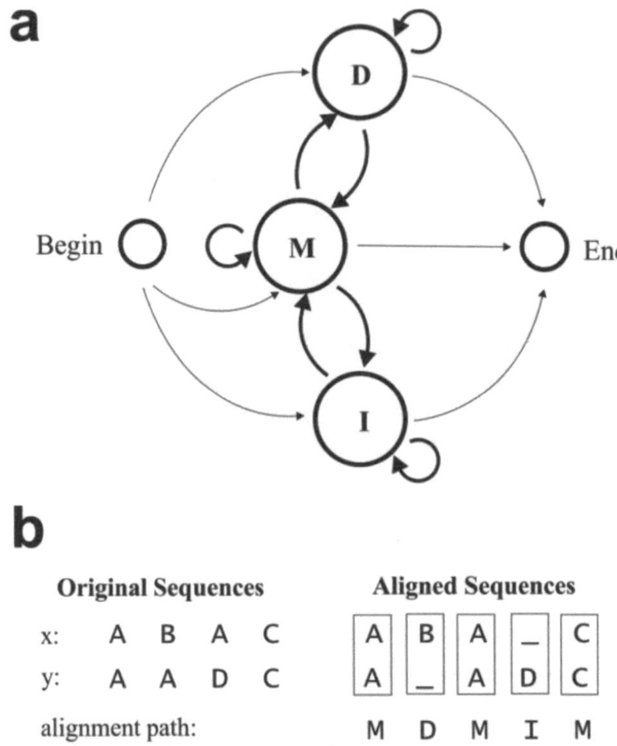

Fig. 1. A simple pair HMM for alignment (after Durbin, 1998) and alignments produced by it. (**a**) A pair HMM with one match state (M), one insertion state (I) and one deletion state (D) as well as a begin and an end state. (**b**) Two sequences x and y (left) and their alignment (right) by virtue of the state sequence: M, D, M, I, M (Match, Deletion, Match, Insertion, Match).

Using pair HMMs, the best sequence alignment is given by the most probable state path, which can be computed using an analogue to the Viterbi algorithm (Durbin 1998). We can also efficiently compute the probability that two sequences are related by *any* alignment using the forward algorithm. Independence of the scalar similarity of two sequences from any particular alignment is an advantage over the simpler dynamic programming approach outlined above, which allows only sequence comparisons by virtue of specific alignments. For example, the second and third best alignments might all be very good, which would so contribute to the similarity estimate of the pair HMM, whereas in the simple dynamic programming approach it does not. Hence, pair HMMs can provide a more robust similarity estimate than estimates based on the best alignment only.

Another advantage is that using pair HMMs we are not dependent on pre-specified costs for insertions, deletions and matches, but these parameters are embedded in emission and transition probabilities than can be learned from data using a variant of the Baum-Welch algorithm (Rabiner 1989). Note that the Viterbi, forward, backward, and Baum-Welch algorithms for pair HMMs are derived in a straight forward manner from their standard HMM counterparts (Durbin 1998).

In the following we introduce a new pair HMM architecture that deviates from Durbin's original proposal in some significant ways. The pair HMMs contain three different types of hidden states (match, insertion, and deletion) and a continuous emission alphabet (compare Figure 1a). Durbin's model operated only on discrete observations, which is adequate for problems such as genome alignment. However, when dealing with continuous data such as birdsong, models with continuous emission probability distributions are more convenient, because they can reflect the acoustic features of song on a continuous scale.

We denote the two sequences by $x_1, x_2, \ldots, x_T$ and $y_1, y_2, \ldots, y_U$. The pair HMM contains m deletion, m insertion, and n match states. In our notation these hidden states are distinguished by the index j: $j \in Deletion = \{1, \ldots, m\}$ correspond to deletions states, $j \in Insertion = \{m+1, \ldots, 2m\}$ correspond to insertion states, $j \in Match = \{2m+1, \ldots, 2m+n\}$ correspond to match states. Furthermore, we denote

a_{ij} : transition probability from hidden state i onto hidden state j

$b_j(x_t)$: emission probability of symbol x_t given hidden state $j \in Deletion$

$b_j(y_u)$: emission probability of symbol y_u given hidden state $j \in Insertion$

$b_j(x_t, y_u)$: emission probability of symbols x_t and y_u given hidden state $j \in Match$

For our pair HMM, the recursive equations of the Viterbi algorithm are given by:

$$\forall j \in Match: \quad V_j(t,u) = b_j(x_t, y_u) \cdot \max_i \left(a_{ij} V_i(t-1, u-1) \right) \tag{1}$$

$$\forall j \in Deletion: \quad V_j(t,u) = b_j(x_t) \cdot \max_i \left(a_{ij} V_i(t-1, u) \right) \tag{2}$$

$$\forall j \in Insertion: \quad V_j(t,u) = b_j(y_u) \cdot \max_i \left(a_{ij} V_i(t, u-1) \right) \tag{3}$$

Where V is the best score (highest probability) along a single path, at times t in the first sequence and u in the second sequence, which accounts for the first t and u observations and ends in state j. In the following, we consider two realizations this pair HMM architecture.

3.1.1 Pair HMM with three states and distance metric

First we consider a very simple realization of the aforementioned architecture: a three-state pair HMM with one match, one deletion, and one insertion state. Its parameters are predetermined and not learned. Its transition matrix a is parameterized by three free parameters:

$$a = \begin{bmatrix} 1-2\delta-\tau & \delta & \delta \\ 1-\varepsilon-\tau & \varepsilon & 0 \\ 1-\varepsilon-\tau & o & \varepsilon \end{bmatrix} \tag{4}$$

The parameter ε is the probability of remaining in the insertion or deletion state, whereas δ is to probability of entering a deletion or insertion state from the match state and τ is the probability to transit to the end state. Transitions from deletions to insertions and vice versa are not allowed in this model (compare Figure 1a).

For the emission probability densities, we assume $b_j(x_t)=1$ for $j \in Deletion$ and $b_j(y_u)=1$ for $j \in Insertion$. The emission probability density $b_j(x_t, y_u)$ of the match state depends on the Euclidean distance between observations x_t and y_u as follows:

$$b_j(x_t, y_u) = k e^{-\frac{|x_t - y_u|^2}{2\sigma^2}} \tag{5}$$

where k is the trade-off factor between matches and insertions/deletions and σ is the standard deviation of the Gaussian distance metric. A good choice of k is such that the expectation of the right hand side of equation 5 over all observation pairs x_t and y_u equals 1. This reflects the assumption that random pairs x_t and y_u are about as likely to match as to form inserts or deletions. With the exception of our choice of emission probabilities $b_j(x_t, y_u)$ in the match state, this model architecture corresponds to the one presented in (Durbin 1998).

To obtain discrete-time observations x_t and y_u from birdsong, we binned the continuous-time acoustic signal. A standard practice, that we also adopted here, is to use a time-frequency representation of the signal (columns of log-power spectrograms, in our case with time-steps 5.8 ms between columns and frequency resolution 86 Hz, from 0 to 11025 Hz). The observations x_t and y_u are given by normalized columns of the spectrogram. Figure 2b depicts an alignment of two birdsongs (a tutor song and a pupil song) that was computed using the 3 state HMM.

3.1.2 Pair HMM with many states and no distance metric

Next we introduce a more powerful pair HMM with many more states and more general alignment capabilities. Songs consist of sequences of distinct syllables in which the tempo of some syllable may vary more than others. Also, when songs of two different birds have to be aligned to each other (such as tutor song and pupil song), the spectral features of their songs might be quite different so it may be difficult to find an adequate distance measure. The expansion of the simple pair HMM from the previous section solves both these problems, i.e. temporal variability can be modeled locally and songs can be aligned even if the spectral mismatch is high.

HMMs can serve as generative models of song (Kogan and Margoliash 1998). However, the pair HMM in our previous section is not a generative model of song. To adopt this capability and model single song elements by discrete states, we choose an expansion of the pair HMM as follows: we define a set of individual states for each operation (deletion, insertion, match) instead of single state each. Further, we are dealing with a full transition matrix a. Note: In the case of working solely with insertion and deletion states, such a model would be equivalent to an HMM for each song separately. We choose as model for emissions a sum of Gaussians. Such models can be trained using the Baum-Welch-algorithm.

Formally, the emission probabilities in the model are joint probability distributions over pairs of columns (for the match state) and distributions over single columns (insertion and

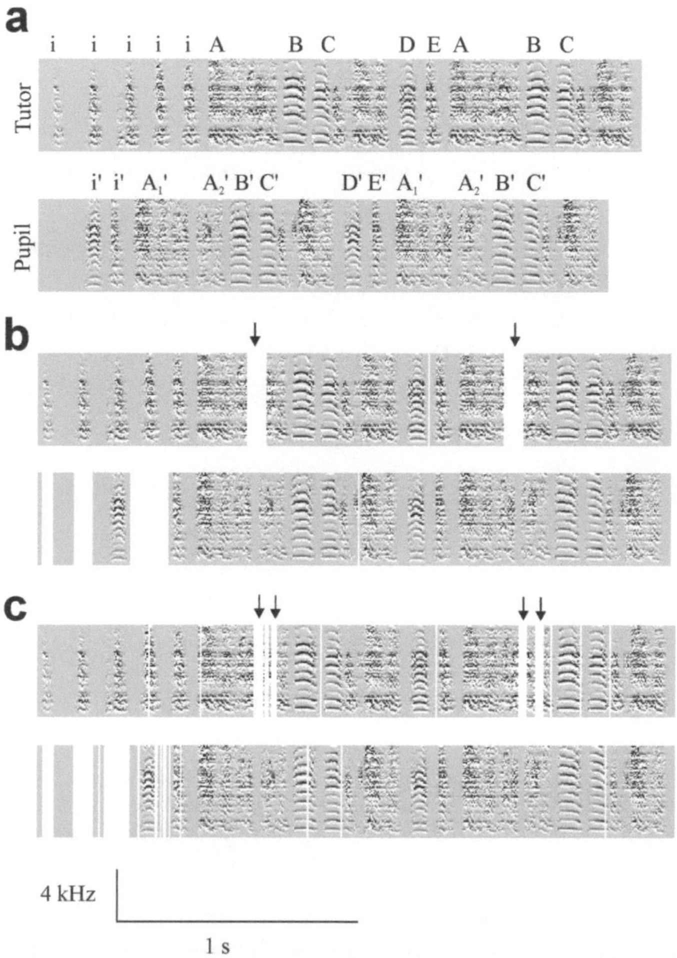

Fig. 2. Alignment of tutor song and pupil song. (**a**) Derivative spectrogram of tutor song and the pupil song. Visibly, the pupil copied the song of his tutor remarkably well. The main difference is Syllable A: In the tutor's song Syllable A consists of 4 parts, whereas the pupil divided that syllable into two syllables: Syllable A_1 (consisting of 3 parts) and Syllable A_2 (consisting of 1 part). (**b**) Alignment of the two songs by the Viterbi path using the 3 state model. Syllable A in the tutor song is split into 2 and correctly aligned to Syllables A_1 and A_2 of the pupil's song (arrows). All other syllables are correctly aligned as well. (**c**) Alignment of the same two songs by the Viterbi-path of a 40-state pair HMM. The model consists of $n = 20$ match states, $m = 10$ deletion states, and $m = 10$ insertion states. Emission probabilities of deletion and insertion states are modeled as the sum of two 128-dimensional Gaussians defined on the spectrum of the corresponding song. The emission probability of the match state is defined as the sum of two 256-dimensional Gaussians (defined on the spectrum of both songs). The alignment in this 40-state model is similar to the alignment in the 3-state model. However, Syllable A of the tutor song is split in 3 or 4 parts (instead of two parts), marked by the arrows. The first split accounts for the break between Syllables A_1 and A_2 in the pupil's song, whereas the other splits account for Syllable A_2 that is sung slower than the fourth part of the tutor Syllable A.

deletion), all of which can be learned from the data. In the example presented in Figure 2c, we have modeled the emissions probability densities for each state as a sum of two Gaussians with diagonal covariance matrix

$$b_j(x_t) = \sum_{k=1}^{2} c_{jk} \cdot \left|2\pi\Sigma_{jk}\right|^{-1/2} \exp\left(-\frac{1}{2}\left(x_t - \mu_{jk}\right)^T \Sigma_{jk}^{-1}\left(x_t - \mu_{jk}\right)\right) \tag{6}$$

for deletion states and similarly for the other states. The transition probabilities a_{ij} as well as the means μ_{jk}, the weights c_{jk}, and the covariance matrix Σ_{jk} of each Gaussian were trained using the Baum-Welch algorithm on seven pairings of tutor and pupil song. The forward probabilities in our pair HMM (the probabilities $\alpha_j(t,u)$ of observing partial output sequences until times t and u and of being in hidden state j at these times obey the recursive equations

$$\forall j \in Match: \qquad \alpha_j(t,u) = b_j(x_t, y_u)\sum a_{ij}\alpha_i(t-1,u-1) \tag{7}$$

$$\forall j \in Deletion: \qquad \alpha_j(t,u) = b_j(x_t)\sum a_{ij}\alpha_i(t-1,u) \tag{8}$$

$$\forall j \in Insertion: \qquad \alpha_j(t,u) = b_j(y_u)\sum a_{ij}\alpha_i(t,u-1). \tag{9}$$

The backward probabilities $\beta_i(t,u)$ are calculated analogously:

$$\begin{aligned}\beta_i(t,u) = \sum_{j\in Match} a_{ij}b_j(x_{t+1}, y_{u+1})\beta_j(t+1,u+1) + \sum_{j\in Deletion} a_{ij}b_j(x_{t+1})\beta_j(t+1,u) + \\ + \sum_{j\in Insertions} a_{ij}b_j(y_{u+1})\beta_j(t,u+1).\end{aligned} \tag{10}$$

The only parameters we have to define beforehand are the number m of deletion and insertion states, the number n of match states, and the number of Gaussians in the emission model. But there is no need to define a (spectral) distance measure; hence the spectrograms in the songs to be aligned are never directly compared to each other. The emission probabilities $b_j(x_t, y_u)$ of match states represent spectral features which are acquired during training by matching similar spectral-temporal dynamics in both songs.

3.2 Advantages and limitations of pair HMMs for birdsong alignment

As outlined above, the main use for pair HMMs is the identification of corresponding syllables in songs from either a single bird or from two different birds. However, corresponding elements can in principle also be identified by different approaches. One could for example segment the audio signal into syllables by thresholding sound amplitude, then extract suitable features and cluster all syllables based on these features. Note that in this case, we fix a priori what constitutes similarity by virtue of our choice of the features and clustering algorithm. This is not at all a problem if we are dealing with simple similarity relationships, for instance, if the songs to be aligned are highly similar and their difference can be ascribed to a source of additive noise for example. It is also not a problem if we have sufficient knowledge of the invariances of the problem, i.e. the dimensions that do not play a role in establishing similarity, because, in that case, we can select our features accordingly.

If, however, the similarity relationship is more complex and we have no a priori knowledge of it, we may prefer to learn the similarity relationship from the data using as few assumptions as possible. That is what pair HMMs can give us. If two songs can be aligned using matches, insertions, and deletions as provided by pair HMMs, we can learn the similarity relationship between them using for example the Baum Welch algorithm. In this manner our pair HMMs can deal with the case of a pupil that correctly learns the tutor song except that the pupil's song has higher pitch (or song pitch varies randomly from trial to trial). Given sufficient data, the pair HMMs would be able to detect that pitch is an invariant feature with respect to the similarity relation, it would detect that pitch essentially does not matter. Furthermore, from our pair HMM we can conveniently read out the similarity relationship from the parameters of learned emissions in match states and, in principle, also from the transitions probabilities.

Such learning does of course require computational resources. The multi-state pair HMM, outlined in 3.1.2 requires more computational resources than the simple three-state model from section 3.1.1 and many pairs of songs are needed in order to learn faithful model parameters. The computation time and memory requirements scale quadratic with the lengths of observation sequences to be aligned (compared to a linear increase in the case of normal HMMs). If we use a 100-state pair HMM and align sequences of 10^4 observation each, than we have to calculate and store $10^{10}=10^4\cdot10^4\cdot100$ forward and backward probabilities α and β in the course of processing one sequence pair with the Baum Welch algorithm. This underlines the importance of faster approximations of the Baum Welch algorithm (e.g. Viterbi training) in the context of sequence alignment.

A more conceptual problem that we face when trying to align birdsongs, are swaps of single syllables. When learning the tutor song the pupil might change the order of syllables, e.g. the tutor sings ABCD and the pupil A'C'B'D'. Clearly, we would somehow like to have a model that can align the sequence by swapping B and C instead of using insertions and deletions. However, the Viterbi algorithm provides only one global path which in the best case either includes B and B' or C and C'. We can overcome this problem by using the idea of the Smith-Waterman algorithm (Smith and Waterman 1981) to extend the Viterbi algorithm, in order to search for local instead of global alignments. In this extension the best score of match states in Equation (1) is thresholded by a power of the free parameter θ:

$$\forall j \in Match: \qquad V_j(t,u)=b_j(x_t,y_u)\cdot\max\begin{cases}\max\limits_i\left(a_{ij}V_i(t-1,u-1)\right)\\ \theta^{t+u}\end{cases}. \qquad (11)$$

The formula for the deletion and insertion states are similarly changed to include θ. The results are regions in which the probability $V_j(t,u)$ surpasses the threshold θ^{t+u}. In these regions we backtrack the scores in order to find the local alignments. There is the risk that the Baum-Welch algorithm will entrain the alignment of B with C′ and C with B′. Such misalignment could probably be avoided by also adapting the Baum-Welch algorithm to consider possible local alignments instead of all possible global alignments.

4. Alignment of spike trains with HMMs

A common problem in neuroscience is to quantify how similar the spiking activities of two neurons are. One approach is to align the spike trains and take some alignment score as similarity measure. To that end, Victor and Purpura (Victor and Purpura 1998) introduced a spike-train similarity measure based on the physiological hypotheses that the presence of a spike is probabilistic and that there is some jitter in spike timing. Victor and Purpura introduce two similarity measures: $D^{spike}[q]$ based on spike times and $D^{interval}[q]$ based on inter-spike intervals, where q is a free parameter. They also propose an efficient algorithm to calculate these similarity measures. In this section, we outline how Victor and Purpura's method can be implemented using pair HMMs. We discuss the advantages of a pair HMM implementation and possible generalizations. First, we briefly introduce their measures:

a) $D^{interval}[q]$

Imagine two spike trains S_1 and S_2 both represented by vectors of inter-spike intervals. Their method transforms one spike train into the other by (i) adding spike intervals, (ii) removing spike intervals and (iii) changing the duration of a spike interval by Δt . There is a unit cost for (i) and (ii), and a cost of $q * \Delta t$ for (iii). The 'distance' or dissimilarity between two spike trains is defined as the minimal cost to transform S_1 into S_2 using (i-iii). This measure can be calculated efficiently using dynamic programming.

b) $D^{spike}[q]$

This is very similar to (a). Instead of considering spike intervals, we deal with exact spike times, where the parameter q now determines the cost of shifting a spike in time. Again, spikes can also be added or removed.

(a) and (b) are computed using the same underlying efficient algorithm. Victor and Purpura use their measures to analyze spike trains elicited by a set of different stimuli. By using stimulus-dependent clustering based on their measures, they determine how well the different classes of spike trains can be separated. They find that the degree to which these classes are separable depends on the chosen value of the parameter q . They explore a range of different values for q, but find that there is no single optimal value for all cases: the choice of q needs to be made based on trial and error.

The two measures (a) and (b) can also be realized using a pair HMM. In such a pair HMM there are two states corresponding to unmatched inter-spike intervals in the two sequences, which are dealt with by adding or removing spike inter-spike intervals, respectively. Also, there is one match state in which the two inter-spike intervals are matched with associated emission probability $b_M(\Delta t) = \exp(-q\Delta t)$, where q is a free parameter and Δt the interval difference. The total costs of adding, removing, and matching intervals are encoded in the emission and transition probabilities of the pair HMM. This pair HMM can be trained on a group of spike trains that belong to a given stimulus class. Thereby, the parameter q is learned from the data. Such a simple procedure of identifying the optimal q is advantageous compared to exploring a range of possible values or even choosing a value for q a priori.

In addition to its flexibility, another advantage of the pair HMM approach is that we can now define a novel similarity measure for spike trains, based not on a particular alignment, but based on all possible alignments. Instead of defining the similarity of two spike trains as the probability of the most likely transformation, we define it as the overall probability of observing the spike trains given the model parameters. This measure corresponds to the forward probability of the pair HMM and takes into consideration all possible transformations between the two spike trains, weighed by their probability. To make the similarity measure independent of the lengths of the spike trains, it can be defined as the average forward probability per step:

$$S(x,y) = P(x,y|\lambda)^{\frac{1}{\max(T,U)}} \tag{12}$$

where T and U are the respective lengths of the spike trains. A spike train measure based on a probabilistic approach has also been introduced by Douwels (Dauwels, Vialatte et al. 2007). Their approach of stochastic event synchrony assumes that spike trains are equal apart from global shifts, the introduction or removal of spikes, and temporal jitter of single spikes. Such transformations can be described by a triplet of parameters describing the shift offset, the standard deviation of the timing jitter, and the percentage of spurious spikes. These parameters can be derived via cyclic maximization or expectation maximization.

5. Spike sorting with HMMs

To study the underlying neural code of complex behaviors, electrophysiology is the method of choice. For example, by implanting recording electrodes into a songbird's brain, mounted on motorized microdrives, it is possible to record from neurons while the bird engages in its normal singing behavior. The neurons spike trains are often recorded in the extracellular space using low impedance electrodes that typically pick up the activity of several neurons simultaneously (so called multi-unit activity). Correspondingly, telling the activity from the different cells apart (finding out which unit fired which spike) is an important problem, when dealing with multi unit recordings.

The identification and classification of spikes from the raw data is called spike sorting. Most spike sorting methods consist of two steps. In a first step, spike events are extracted from the raw data. In a second step these events are classified. Difficulties arise when spikes overlap on the recorded trace (arising when neurons are densely packed and fire at high rate), compare Fig. 3. These 'overlaps' are notoriously difficult to sort. The shape of such an overlap can be complex, because the number of different spikes contributing to the shape is unknown, as is the exact time delay between them.

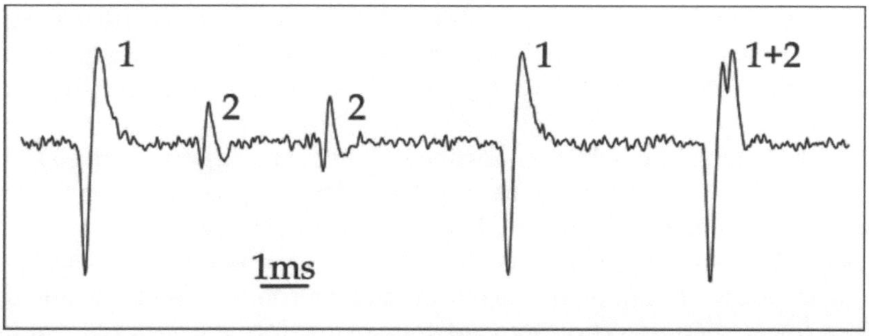

Fig. 3. Example of a multi-unit recording: Spike waveforms of two different neurons (1 and 2) are recorded on the same electrode. The rightmost waveform (1+2) represents a spike overlap.

HMMs provide a framework for addressing the spike sorting problem (Herbst, Gammeter et al. 2008). Spikes can be described by independent random variables (the hidden variables), whereas the recorded voltage is the probabilistic outcome conditional on the state of the hidden variables.

The transient nature of spikes allows us to describe neural activity by a discrete-time Markov chain with a ring structure, Fig. 4a. The first state in the ring is the resting state of the neuron, and the remaining states represent a spike. The resting state decays with fixed probability p per unit time (a free parameter), after which states along the ring are visited with unit probability (spikes are never incomplete). The recorded voltage level on the electrode is modeled as a Gaussian probability density with state-dependent mean (free model parameter) and state-independent variance (free model parameter), Fig. 4b.

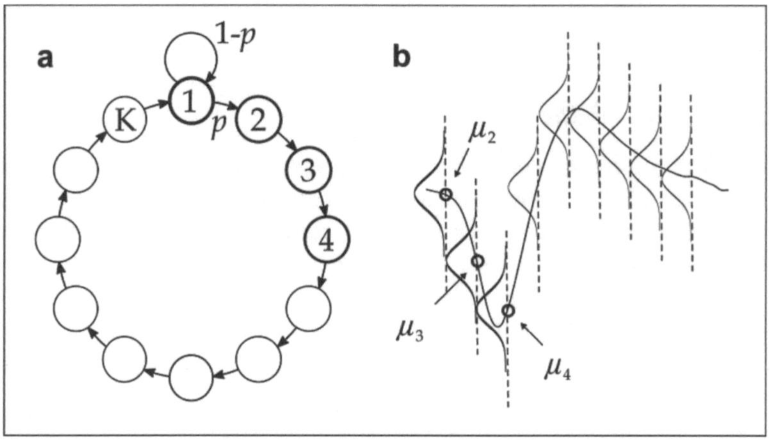

Fig. 4. (**a**) The state space of the hidden variable: There is a resting state that is left with probability p. Once the resting state is left, state 2 to K are visited with unit probability. (**b**) For each state k there is a free parameter μ_k, the mean of the Gaussian output probability. The means of the Gaussians represent the mean spike waveform.

A single ring is used to sort extracellular spikes from a single neuron, as follows: The model parameters (means, variance, spike probability) are learned by using algorithms such as the Baum-Welch algorithm. Thereafter, these parameters are used to calculate the most probable hidden state sequence with the Viterbi algorithm. The spike times are given by the time points at which the hidden variable visits state 2 (visited states start revolving around the ring).

This HMM can be extended to allow for sorting of multi-unit activity. In this extension, each neuron is modeled as an independent ring-like Markov process as in Figure 4a. The extracellular voltage signal is again modeled as a Gaussian random variable with fixed variance (free model parameter). The mean of the Gaussian is formed by summing up the state-dependent means of each neuron. Hence, each neuron contributes to the mean of the Gaussian in a linear manner. The extended framework forms a factorial hidden Markov model (fHMM) (Ghahramani and Jordan 1997).

The learning of model parameters can be performed using the expectation maximization algorithm (Baum-Welch) or using structured variational inference (Saul, Jaakkola et al. 1996). After model parameters are learned, spike sorting is performed using the Viterbi algorithm. Using an HMM approach, spike sorting can be done in a single framework, we do not have to separate the sorting problem into separate frameworks for spike extraction and spike classification as is common using other sorting methods. The HMM operates on the recorded data from the first to the last step of the spike sorting. There is no need for pre-processing, such as spike identification, feature extraction or even manual inspection, all of which are error prone.

HMM-based spike sorting is permissive to spike overlaps. Most overlap-permissive algorithms first classify isolated spikes and then split overlapping cases to the according classes. The advantage of the HMM algorithm is that it is overlap robust both during parameter learning and during spike-sorting itself; for the model there is no difference whether spikes appear as single or overlapping events. The parameters for a neuron can even be learned in the case where the spikes are always overlapping and never appear as single events.

The HMM can easily be extended to sort spikes recorded with tetrodes. Tetrodes are electrode bundles with contacts lying within a few micrometers of each other. Depending on the distance between spiking neurons and the electrodes, the signal is picked up by several electrodes at the same time, with varying amplitude on each electrode. The signal on these electrodes is thus strongly correlated and this additional information can be incorporated into the HMM. The observed voltage level is now modeled by a multivariate Gaussian probability density with a state-dependent mean vector (free model parameters) and fixed covariance matrix (free model parameters).

Apart from spike overlaps, there are other difficulties that are often encountered in electrophysiological recordings: signal outliers (or artifacts) and nonstationarities of the data, due to bursts or electrode drift. Electrode drifts lead to a sustained change of recorded spike shape. Drifts happen slowly, they can be dealt with by updating model parameters (few iterations of the Baum-Welch algorithm) from time to time. That way the parameters are able follow the drift. Spikes produced in a very short time period, so called bursts, usually change their shape due to biophysical constraints. Spikes in bursts usually have similar spike shape as single spikes but smaller amplitudes, because not all ion channels are ready to open again. Bursting neurons can be modeled using several state rings per neuron, one ring for the first spike in a burst and the other rings for successive spikes. The introduction of new parameters can be kept to a minimum by introducing one new parameter for every ring, namely the scaling factor by which the spike template (common to all rings) is multiplied. Signal outliers should be classified as such. The HMM allows us to identify outliers both during learning and sorting as follows: the probability of an observation sequence up to time t can be calculated and can be plotted against t. From this probability trajectory one can identify the times at which the model fits the data poorly and exclude that data from learning and sorting.

The main downside of the HMM approach for spike sorting is the computational cost involved. Assume a model with K states per ring, B rings per neuron (to model bursts) and N neurons. The number of hidden states, $(KB)^N$, grows exponentially with the number of neurons. The problem can be made tractable by imposing restrictions on the activity patterns modelled. For instance, by restricting the number of neurons that can be co-active at the same time to M, the number of hidden states can be reduced to $\binom{N}{M}(KB)^M$.

6. References

Abeles, M., H. Bergman, et al. (1995). "Cortical activity flips among quasi-stationary states." Proc Natl Acad Sci U S A 92(19): 8616-8620.

Becker, J. D., J. Honerkamp, et al. (1994). "Analysing ion channels with hidden Markov models." Pflugers Arch 426(3-4): 328-332.

Brown, P., J. Cocke, et al. (1990). "A statistical approach to machine translation." Computational linguistics 16(2): 85.

Camproux, A. C., F. Saunier, et al. (1996). "A hidden Markov model approach to neuron firing patterns." Biophys J 71(5): 2404-2412.

Chan, A. D. and K. B. Englehart (2005). "Continuous myoelectric control for powered prostheses using hidden Markov models." IEEE Trans Biomed Eng 52(1): 121-124.

Chung, S. H., J. B. Moore, et al. (1990). "Characterization of single channel currents using digital signal processing techniques based on Hidden Markov Models." Philos Trans R Soc Lond B Biol Sci 329(1254): 265-285.

Danoczy, M. and R. Hahnloser (2006). "Efficient estimation of hidden state dynamics from spike trains." Advances in Neural Information Processing Systems, MIT Press 18: 227--234.

Dauwels, J., F. Vialatte, et al. (2007). A Novel Measure for Synchrony and its Application to Neural Signals. Acoustics, Speech and Signal Processing, 2007. ICASSP 2007. IEEE International Conference on.

Dave, A. S. and D. Margoliash (2000). "Song replay during sleep and computational rules for sensorimotor vocal learning." Science 290(5492): 812-816.

Dombeck, D. A., A. N. Khabbaz, et al. (2007). "Imaging large-scale neural activity with cellular resolution in awake, mobile mice." Neuron 56(1): 43-57.

Durbin, R. (1998). Biological sequence analysis: Probabilistic models of proteins and nucleic acids, Cambridge Univ Pr.

Gardner, T., F. Naef, et al. (2005). "Freedom and rules: the acquisition and reprogramming of a bird's learned song." Science 308(5724): 1046.

Gat, I. and N. Tishby (1993). Statistical Modeling of Cell Assemblies Activities in Associative Cortex of Behaving Monkeys. Advances in Neural Information Processing Systems 5, [NIPS Conference], Morgan Kaufmann Publishers Inc.

Gat, I., N. Tishby, et al. (1997). "Hidden Markov modelling of simultaneously recorded cells in the associative cortex of behaving monkeys." Network: Computation in neural systems 8(3): 297-322.

Gat, I., N. Tishby, et al. (1997). "Hidden Markov modelling of simultaneously recorded cells in the associative cortex of behaving monkeys." Network: Computation in Neural Systems 8: 297-322.

Ghahramani, Z. and M. I. Jordan (1997). "Factorial Hidden Markov Models." Machine Learning 29(2): 245-273.

Glaze, C. and T. Troyer (2006). "Temporal structure in zebra finch song: implications for motor coding." Journal of Neuroscience 26(3): 991.

Hahnloser, R. H., A. A. Kozhevnikov, et al. (2002). "An ultra-sparse code underlies the generation of neural sequences in a songbird." Nature 419(6902): 65-70.

Herbst, J. A., S. Gammeter, et al. (2008). "Spike sorting with hidden Markov models." J Neurosci Methods.

Immelmann, K. (1969). "Song development in the zebra finch and other estrildid finches." Bird Vocalizations: 61–74.

Kemere, C., G. Santhanam, et al. (2008). "Detecting neural-state transitions using hidden Markov models for motor cortical prostheses." J Neurophysiol 100(4): 2441-2452.

Kogan, J. A. and D. Margoliash (1998). "Automated recognition of bird song elements from continuous recordings using dynamic time warping and hidden Markov models: a comparative study." J Acoust Soc Am 103(4): 2185-2196.

London, S. E. and D. F. Clayton (2008). "Functional identification of sensory mechanisms required for developmental song learning." Nat Neurosci 11(5): 579-586.

Nicolelis, M., E. Fanselow, et al. (1997). "Hebb's dream: the resurgence of cell assemblies." Neuron 19(2): 219.

Pawelzik, K., H. Bauer, et al. (1992). How oscillatory neuronal responses reflect bistability and switching of the hidden assembly dynamics, Morgan Kaufmann Publishers Inc.

Rabiner, L. (1989). "A tutorial on hidden Markov models and selected applications inspeech recognition." Proceedings of the IEEE 77(2): 257-286.

Radons, G., J. D. Becker, et al. (1994). "Analysis, classification, and coding of multielectrode spike trains with hidden Markov models." Biol Cybern 71(4): 359-373.

Rainer, G. and E. Miller (2000). "Neural ensemble states in prefrontal cortex identi" ed using a hidden Markov model with a modi" ed EM algorithm."

Rodriguez-Noriega, E., E. Gonzalez-Diaz, et al. (2010). "Hospital triage system for adult patients using an influenza-like illness scoring system during the 2009 pandemic--Mexico." PLoS One 5(5): e10658.

Saul, L. K., T. Jaakkola, et al. (1996). "Mean Field Theory for Sigmoid Belief Networks." arxiv.org cs.AI/9603102.

Seidemann, E., I. Meilijson, et al. (1996). "Simultaneously recorded single units in the frontal cortex go through sequences of discrete and stable states in monkeys performing a delayed localization task." J Neurosci 16(2): 752-768.

Smith, A. C., L. M. Frank, et al. (2004). "Dynamic analysis of learning in behavioral experiments." J Neurosci 24(2): 447-461.

Smith, T. F. and M. S. Waterman (1981). "Identification of common molecular subsequences." J Mol Biol 147(1): 195-197.

Tchernichovski, O., P. Mitra, et al. (2001). "Dynamics of the vocal imitation process: how a zebra finch learns its song." Science 291(5513): 2564.

Tchernichovski, O., F. Nottebohm, et al. (2000). "A procedure for an automated measurement of song similarity." Animal Behaviour 59(6): 1167-1176.

Victor, J. and K. Purpura (1998). Metric-space analysis of spike trains: theory, algorithms, and application.

Wagner, R. and M. Fischer (1974). "The string-to-string correction problem." Journal of the ACM (JACM) 21(1): 168-173.

Weber, A. P. and R. H. Hahnloser (2007). "Spike correlations in a songbird agree with a simple markov population model." PLoS Comput Biol 3(12): e249.

9

Volcano-Seismic Signal Detection and Classification Processing Using Hidden Markov Models - Application to San Cristóbal and Telica Volcanoes, Nicaragua

Gutiérrez, Ligdamis[1], Ramírez, Javier[1],
Ibañez, Jesús[2] and Benítez, Carmen[1]
[1]*Dep. Signal Theory Networking and Communications University of Granada, Granada*
[2]*Instituto Andaluz de Geofísica. Campus de Cartuja s/n. University of Granada, Granada*
Spain

1. Introduction

The identification and classification of seismic signals is one of primary work that a volcano observatory must do, and this work should be done in a period of time as close as possible to the real time". Each seismic event is related to a different source process, and its time and spatial distribution could be used as elements of an early warning system of volcanic eruption (see for example Chouet el el 1996 [1, 2], or Chouet 2003 [3]).
Moreover, the recognition system is based on the HMM theory, published in the late 60s by Baum et al. (1966) [4] and Baum et al. (1970) [5]. Nowadays, the Hidden Markov Models technique is the more effective one to implement voice recognition systems. Over the past years, Hidden Markov Models have been widely applied in several models like pattern [6, 7], pathologies [8] or speech recognition [9, 10], and DNA sequence analysis [11, 12]. On the other hand, previous works [13, 14, 15, 16, 16a, 16b] have probed the parallelism among speech and volcano-seismic events in terms of signal complexity and real time requirements. At the present many observatories perform this work observing on the screen or in paper the seismograms, and a technician decides the type of event under their appearance in the time domain and their experience. This work is in many cases difficulty if the rate of occurrence of seismic events per hour is high, or if weather or local conditions increase the level of seismic noise. A more detailed analysis, including for example spectral characteristics, would be too time-consuming to be carried out in real time. Furthermore, in a crisis situation, there is a need to make fast decisions that can affect the public safety. This is the reason because many researchers are focussing their efforts in the development of a robust automatic discrimination algorithm of seismic events, enabling technicians to focus their efforts in the interpretation of the situation or to analyze only a reduced number of signals. Recently Del Pezzo et al.[17] and Scarpeta et al.[18] have presented the application of neuronal networks for discrimination and classification of volcanic and artificial signals at Vesuvius Volcano and Phlegraean Fields (Italy). These methods have been successfully applied to discriminate signals for local and volcanic seismicity. However, a limitation of

these systems is that they require a manual pre-processing of the data to select a subset of recordings, each one containing just one seismic event to be classified. On the other hand, Ornhberger [19] has studied discrete hidden Markov modelling (HMM) tools for continuous seismic event classification. Just as neural networks, these methods have been successfully applied to discriminate signals for local and volcanic seismicity without the limitations of the first. Gutiérrez et al. [16], Ibañez et al [16a], Cortes et al.[16b] and Benítez et al. [13] improved the continuous HMMbased seismic event classification and monitoring system and applied the algorithm to the detection and classification of four kind of volcanic events recorded at Etna, Stromboli (Italy), Popocatepetl, Colima (México) and Deception Island (Antarctica). This system is based on the state of the art of HMM-based pattern recognition techniques, successfully applied to other disciplines such as robust automatic speech recognition (ASR) systems.

In this sense, we recordings of different seismic event types are studied at two active volcanoes; San Cristóbal and Telica in Nicaragua. The objective of the present work is to observe the validity of the method using data from active volcanoes, and to check if it is possible to exchange different databases to recognize signals belonging to different volcanoes. We use data from one single field survey carried out in February to March 2006. In this work we initially proceeded to identify the signals and to segment them to obtain a model for each class of events. Then we applied separately the model for each volcano data set and finally we mixed both data set to have a joint test of capability and accuracy of the system.

2. Regional setting

2.1 Nicaragua volcanic chain

In Nicaragua exists more than 200 volcanic structures. Some experts refer at more than 600. Counting their multiple small crater lakes (gaps) of volcanic origin, domes, maar, etc. The Nicaragua volcanic chain has produced all the mechanisms and volcanic products known in the world. The volcanic activity combined with tectonic processes taking place above the subduction zone along the Pacific Coast of Central America, formed the Volcanic Chain of Nicaragua. This chain is a part of the Central American Volcanic Front, which includes 18 volcanic centres in Nicaragua, of which eight are active. The chain is underlain by Middle Miocene – Late Pliocene volcanics and volcanogenic sediments (the widest spread Coyol and/or Tamarindo Formations).

Young volcanoes are clustered in several morphologically well defined complexes, in some cases, separated one from another by NE trending, siniestral strike-slip faults (van Wyk de Vries, 1993 [20]), Carr and Stoiber, 1977 [21]). In Nicaragua exist ten main individual volcanic complexes, as listed below

a. Cosigüina shield volcano
b. San Cristóbal - Casita complex
c. Telica complex
d. El Hoyo - Cerro Negro complex
e. Momotombo - Malpaisillo - La Paz Centro complex
f. Apoyeque silicic shield volcano
g. Miraflores - Nejapa volcano - tectonic zone
h. Masaya volcanic complex
i. Apoyo / Mombacho / Zapatera volcanic complex

j. Nandaime - Granada volcano - tectonic Aligneament
k. Ometepe island volcanoes

The respective volcanic complexes are situated in the Nicaraguan Depression, which is interpreted as an asymmetric graben. The two volcanoes of this work, San Cristóbal and Telica are the major active volcanoes in the complexes of the same name (Fig 2.1).

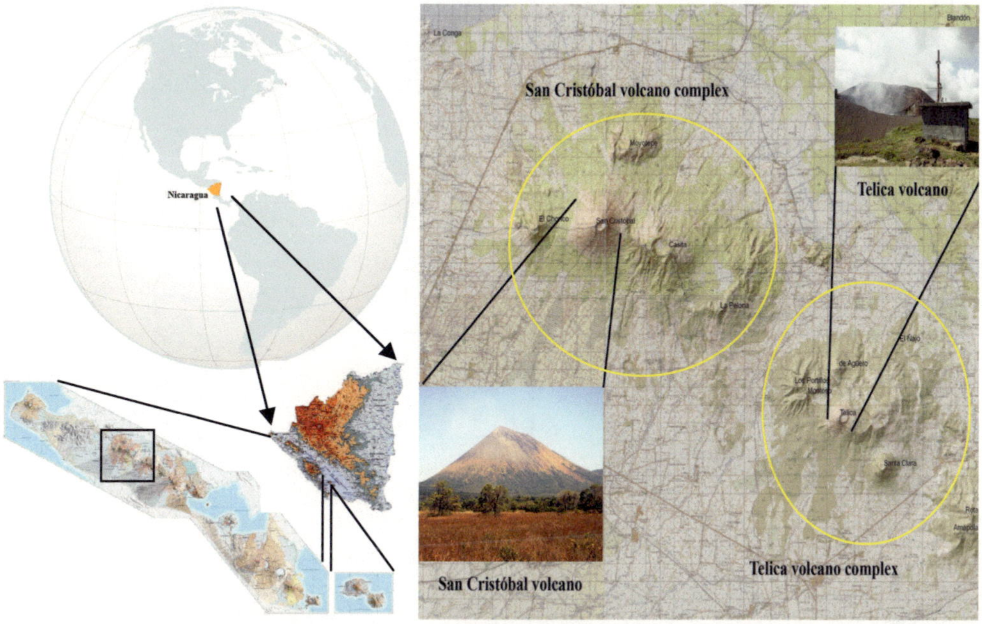

Fig. 2.1 San Cristóbal and Telica volcano complex in Nicaragua volcanic chain

The San Cristóbal volcanic complex, 100 kilometers northwest of Managua, consists of five principal volcanic edifices. The symmetrical youngest cone, San Cristóbal (also known as El Viejo) is the highest peak of the Maribios Range, and is capped by a 500 x 600 meter wide crater. The San Cristóbal is a Quaternary stratovolcano. Historical eruptions from San Cristóbal, consisting of small-to-moderate explosive activity, have been reported since the 16th century.

Telica is a Quaternary stratovolcano located in the western part of Nicaragua. It has six cones, the tallest of which is 1061 meters high. The Telica volcano, *(1,061 meters)* one of Nicaragua's most active volcanoes. Telica has erupted frequently since the Spanish Era. The Telica volcano group consists of several interlocking cones and vents with a general northwest alignment. Sixteenth-century eruptions have been reported at symmetrical Santa Clara volcano, at the southwest end of the Telica group.

3. Data instruments and sities

More than 600 hours of data in each volcano were analyzed and 431 seismic events in San Cristóbal and 1224 in Telica were registered at short period stations. The first step in the data analysis, after the revision of the files, is the visual inspection and segmentation of the signals. Each file is 300-s-long and could have different types of volcanic signals. Fig 3.1 and 3.2 shows the Histogram of the duration (in seconds) for each one of the seismic events. The

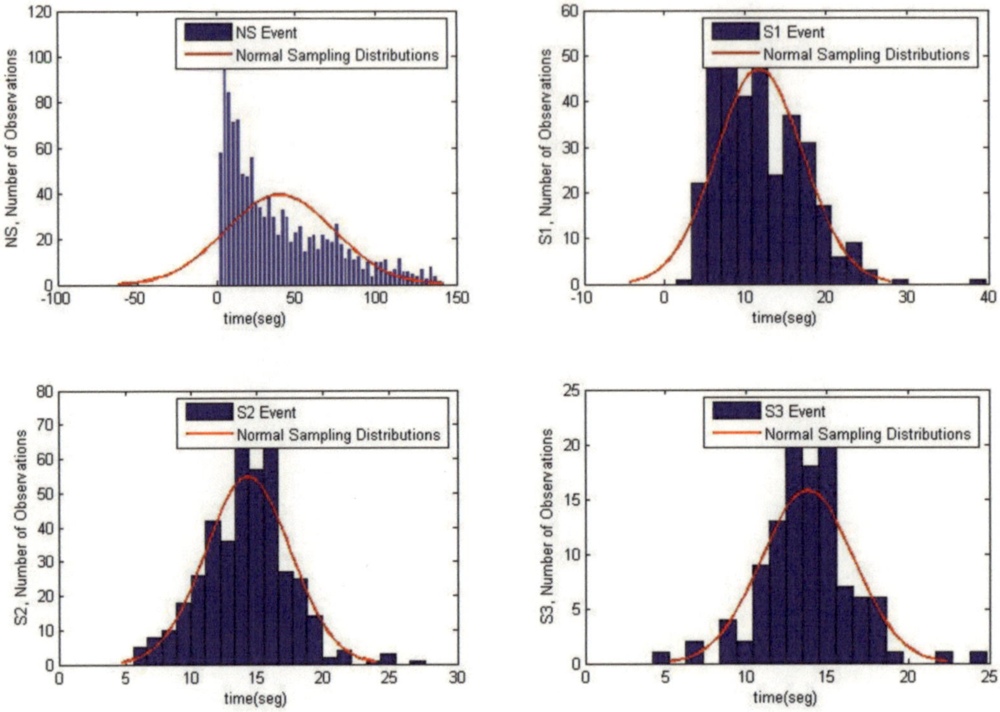

Fig. 3.1 Histogram of the duration (in seconds) for each one of the seismic events in San Cristóbal volcano.

durations of the event range between 10 and 40 seconds and tremor background noise 20-120 seconds.

For our study we proceeded to distinguish three types of signals events in the San Cristóbal volcano; San Cristóbal Long Period signal, Strombolian and San Cristóbal explosions, volcanic tremor and background seismic noise. We have defined these types as S1, S2 and S3. Additionally, we have defined the tremor background seismic noise as NS. Fig 3.3 shows and example of San Cristóbal explosion signal (S2) and Fig 3.4 shows and example of background seismic noise (NS) in which is presented a harmonic tremor.

For Telica volcano we define four types of seismic signals; Strombolian explosions, Telica explosions, Telica Long Period signal, volcanic tremor and background seismic noise. We have defined these types as T1, T2, T3 and T4. Additionally, we have defined the tremor background seismic noise as NT. Fig 3.5 shows and example of Telica signal (T1) and Fig 3.6 shows and example of Telica signal (T4).

The characteristics of the San Cristóbal explosion quakes have peaks from 3 to 8 Hz in the S1 event, 5 Hz in the S2 event to 6 Hz in the S3 event. The first 3 seconds of the signal are dominated by frequencies between 0.5 and 2 Hz, while the successive phases show a broader frequency content (see "zoom frequency spectrogram (d)" in fig. 3.3). Fig 3.4 shows and example of harmonic tremor in San Cristóbal, the signal are dominated by frequencies between 2.5 and 3.5 Hz. In the figure three bands of energy can be observed, the highest peak is about 2.8 Hz. For Telica volcano the durations of the event range between 10 and 60 seconds, and for the background noise between 20 and 140 s. The rest of the volcanic signals were not considered. In fact, In order to have an adequate model of every class of volcanic

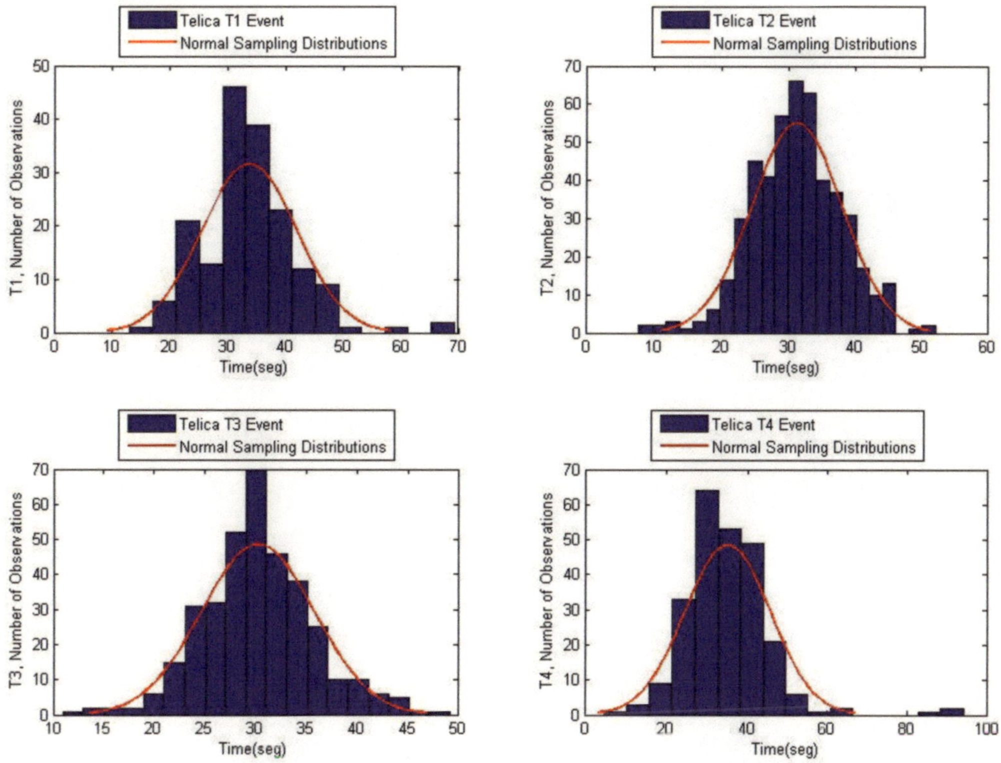

Fig. 3.2 Histogram of the duration (in seconds) for each one of the seismic events in Telica volcano

signals we need a number of events as large as possible, and only the above cited three classes in San Cristóbal and four classes in Telica could provide a number of events large enough to build a well-defined model.

The segmentation process consists in setting marks on the seismograms to define the data segments that contain a particular seismic event. Then, a label is added to declare the type of event that occurred at each segment. This procedure was done manually by a single expert, who set the beginnings and endings of the seismic events by waveform inspection and decided which class they belong to. In this way we ensure the use of the same criteria in the selection process.

For San Cristóbal volcano we segmented 224 samples of S1, 330 samples of S2, 544 samples of S3 and 1,746 samples of background noise (NS) events. For Telica volcano we segmented 360 samples of T1, 502 samples of T2, 429 samples of T3, 298 samples of T4 and 2,855 samples of background noise (NT) events.

4. Method

4.1 Introduction

We initially proceeded to identify the signals visually, and to segment the data to obtain a model for each event class. Once the recordings were manually segmented and labelled, the recognition system was carefully trained using the available Baum-Welch reestimation

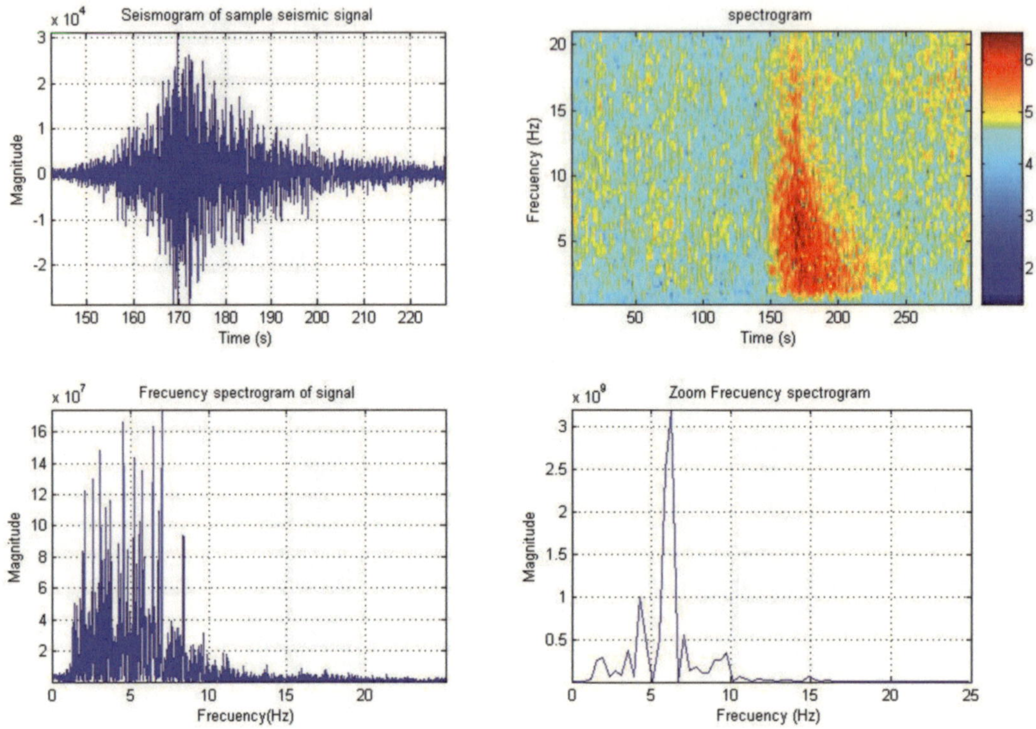

Fig. 3.3 **S2** seismic signal analysis at San Cristóbal volcano.

algorithms [22] using the Hidden Markov Model Toolkit (HTK) software [23]. Fig 4.1 shows a four-state left-to-right HMM non-emitting entry and exit states. The models were defined as left-to-right HMMs where only transitions from state *i* to state *i*+1 are allowed. The optimal length of the HMMs is mainly determined by the mean duration of the explosions and tremor events being modelled. Several experiments were carried out in order to determine the best choice. On the other, the HMM emission probabilities at each state were previously defined as Gaussian mixture densities and, during the training process, HMM models with increasing number of Gaussians were built in order to determine the best trade-off between recognition accuracy and performance. For our work we defined the models with 13-state HMMs with 16 Gaussians. Fig 4.2 shows the architecture of a general purpose HMM-based pattern recognition system. The training database and transcriptions are used to build the models. We applied these models separately for the volcano data set and finally mixed both data sets as a test of the portability of the system. The method analyzes the seismograms comparing the characteristics of the data to a number of event classes defined beforehand. If a signal is present, the method detects its occurrence and produces a classification. The recognition and classification system based on HMM is a powerful, effective, and successful tool [24]. From the application performed over our data set, we have demonstrated that in order to have a reliable result, a careful and adequate segmentation process is crucial. Also, each type of signals requires its own characterization. That is, each signal type must be represented by its own specific model, which would include the effects of source, path and sites.

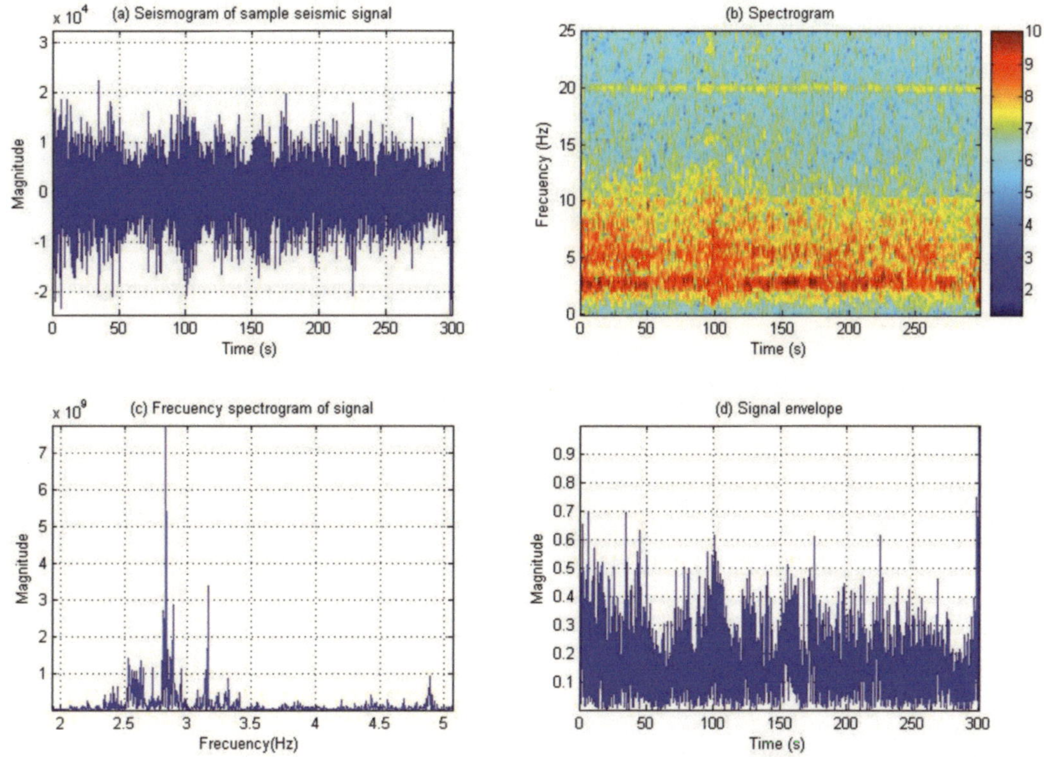

Fig. 3.4 Harmonic tremor in a **NS** background seismic noise in San Cristóbal volcano.

4.2 Description of the recognition system

An HMM-based seismic event recognition system [13,16,16a,16b] assumes that the signal is a realization of a sequence of one or more symbols. In order to perform the recognition process the recognizer decomposes the incoming signal as a sequence of feature vectors. This sequence is assumed to be a precise representation of the seismic signal while the length of the analysis window is such that the seismic waveform can be considered as stationary. The goal of a seismic event recognition system is to perform a mapping between a sequence of feature vectors and the corresponding sequence of seismic events.

4.3 Seismic event recognition

Let a sequence of seismic events $\mathbf{w} = \{w_1, w_2, \ldots, w_l\}$ be represented as a sequence of feature vectors $\mathbf{o}_t$ or observations $\mathbf{O}$, defined as

$$\mathbf{O} = \mathbf{o}_1, \mathbf{o}_2, \ldots, \mathbf{o}_t, \ldots, \mathbf{o}_T \quad (1)$$

where $\mathbf{o}_t$ is the feature vector observed at time t. The solution to the problem of continuous event recognition is to select the sequence of events $\mathbf{w}$ with the maximum probability $P(\mathbf{w} \mid \mathbf{O})$, that is:

$$\underset{\mathbf{w}}{\arg\max} \quad P(\mathbf{w} \mid \mathbf{O}) \quad (2)$$

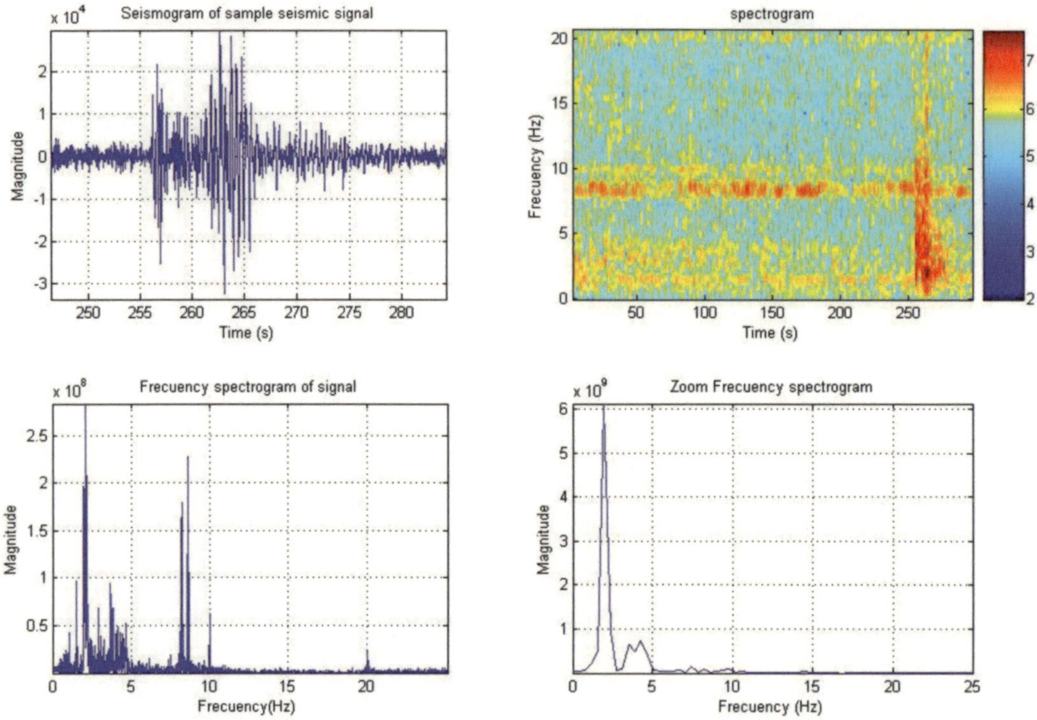

Fig. 3.5 **T1** seismic signal analysis at Telica volcano

4.4 HMM-based seismic event classification

HMM-based pattern recognition systems normally assume that the sequence of observed feature vectors corresponding to each event is generated by a Markov model. A Markov model is essentially a finite state machine with several states. Figure 4.1 shows a four-state left-to-right HMM with non-emitting entry and exit states. A change of state takes place every time unit and a feature vector $\mathbf{o}_t$ is generated from a probability density $b_j(\mathbf{o}_t)$ determined during the training process. Moreover, transition from state i to state j is governed by the transition probabilities a_{ij} which are used to model the delay in each of the states and the transitions through the entire model.

Figure 4.2 shows the architecture of a general purpose HMM-based pattern recognition system. The training database and transcriptions are used to build the models. Once the models are initiated, the recognition system performs feature extraction and decoding based on the Viterbi algorithm (Fig. 4.3). The output is the sequence of recognized events, confidence measures and global accuracy scores.

4.5 Signal processing and feature extraction

The first step of the recognition process is the signal processing feature extraction which converts the volcano seismic waveform in a parametric representation, with less redundant information, for further analysis and processing. As the short-time spectral envelop representation of the signal has been widely used, with good results, in speech recognition systems (Rabiner and Juang,1993) [25], a similar representation for our volcano seismic recognition system is used in this work. The feature extraction process is described as

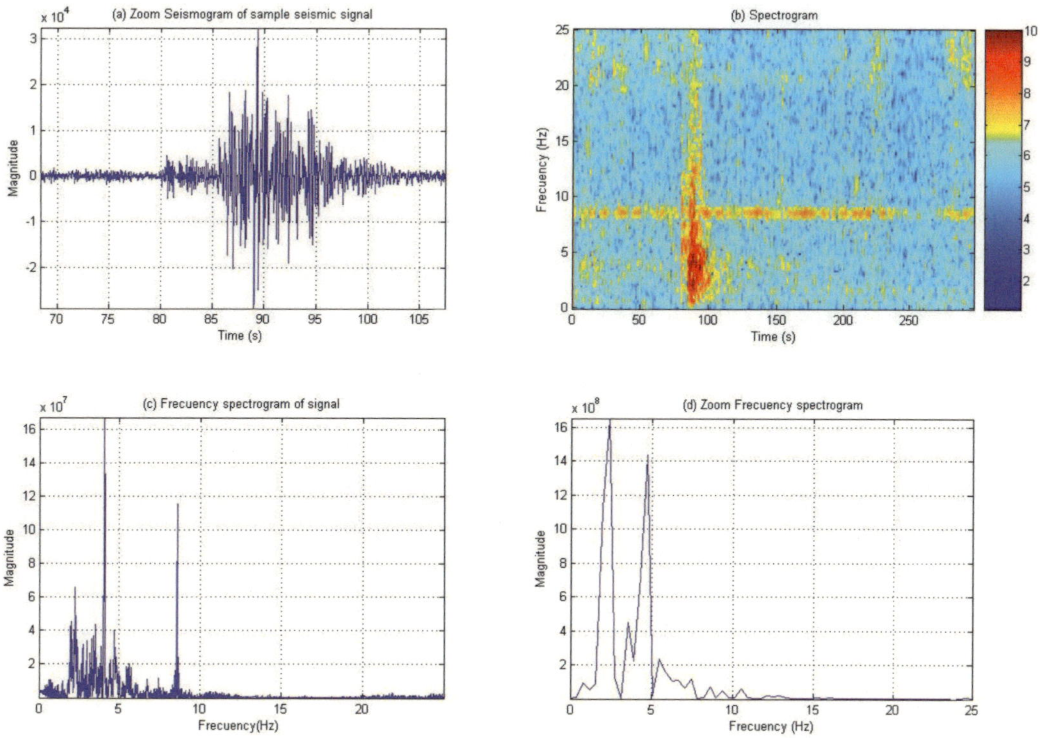

Fig. 3.6 **T4** seismic signal analysis at Telica volcano

follows. The signal is arranged into 4 seconds overlapping frames with a 0.5 seconds frame shit using a Hamming window. A 512-point FFT is used to compute the magnitude spectrum which serves as the input of an emulated filter-bank consisting of 16 triangular weighting functions uniformly spaced between 0 Hz and 20 Hz. The overlap between adjacent filters is 50%. The purpose of the filter bank analyzer is to give a measurement of the energy of the signal in a given frequency band. Then, the natural logarithm of the output filter-bank energies is calculated resulting a 16-parameter feature vector. Since the log-filter bank energies are highly correlated and the recognition system uses continuous observation HMMs with diagonal covariance matrices, it is necessary to apply a decorrelation transformation. Thus, the Discrete Cosine Transform (DCT) is used to decorrelate the features and reduce the number of components of the feature vector from 16 to 13 coefficients. Finally, the feature vector is augmented with linear regressions of the features (derivatives and accelerations) obtaining a total of 39 parameters.

4.6 Training

The recognition system [13,16,16a,16b] is based on continuous hidden Markov models (CHMM). CHMM are trained for each seismic event to be recognized and a noise model is used to represent sequences with no events. Both, training and recognition processes are performed using HMM Tool Kit (HTK) software (Young et al., 1997 [26]). In a CHMM the emission probabilities for a feature vector $\mathbf{o}_t$ in state $x(t)$, $b_{x(t)}(\mathbf{o}_t)$ are given by:

$$b_{x(t)}(\mathbf{o}_t) = \prod_{s=1}^{S} \sum_{k=1}^{K} c_{ik} N(\mu_k, \sigma_k, \mathbf{o}_t) \tag{3}$$

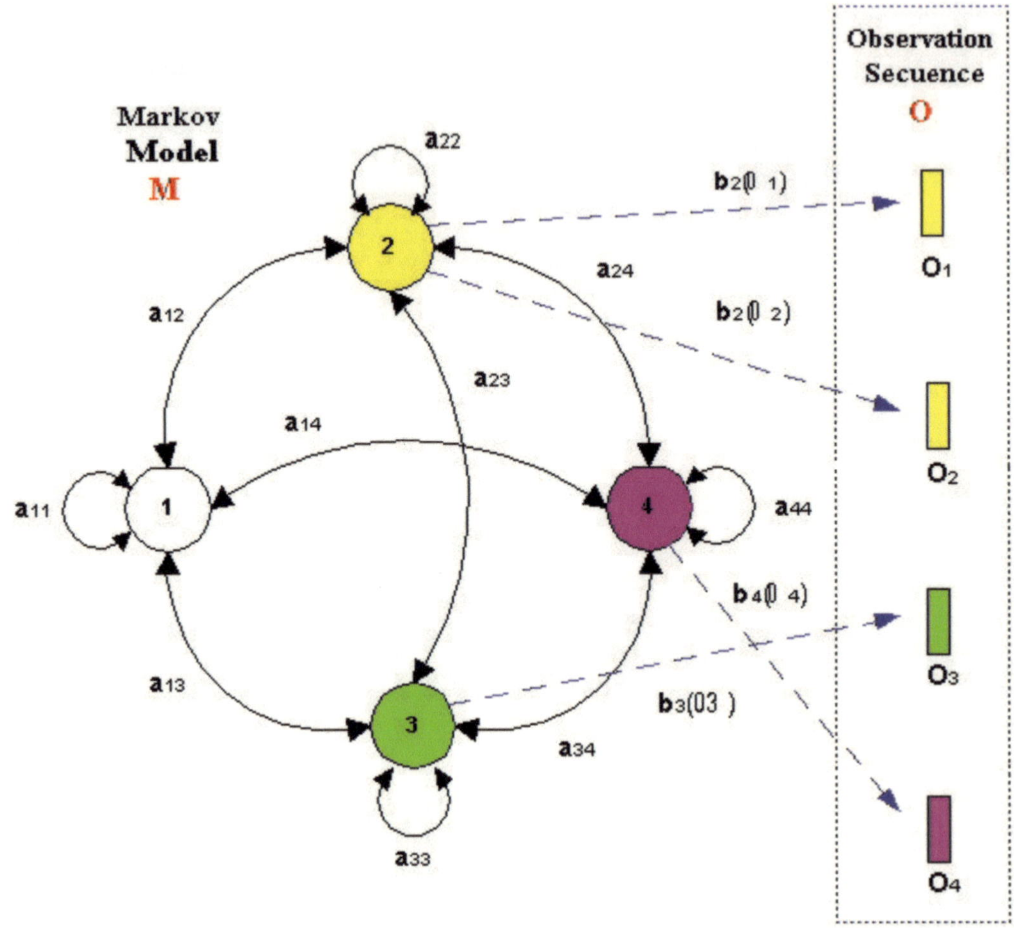

Fig. 4.1 Four state left-right HMM with non-emitting entry and exit states.

where S is the number of parameters in the feature vector, and K is the number of probability density functions (PDFs) considered.

The training algorithm for the HMM consists on finding the parameters of the model (i.e.: the weights for each state of the HMM, c_{ik}, and the transition probabilities between states a_{ij} of the model) from a previously labelled training database. Usually, the maximum likelihood criterion is chosen as the estimation function to adjust the model parameters that is, the maximization of the $P(\mathbf{O} \mid M)$ over M, where M defines an HMM. However, there is no known way to obtain a solution in a closed form. The Baum-Welch algorithm (Bahl et al., 1983 [27] and Dempster and Rubin, 1977 [28]) is an iterative procedure which provides a locally optimum solution to solve this problem (Fig. 4.4).

4.7 Recognition

The operation of the recognition system is described in equation 3. Note that $P(\mathbf{O} \mid \mathbf{w})$ is the conditional probability of the feature vector sequence $\mathbf{O}$ given the sequence of events $\mathbf{w}$ which can be computed by the HMMs while $P(\mathbf{w})$ is the probability of the sequence of events $\mathbf{w}$. As there is no statistical knowledge of possible event sequences, we assume that

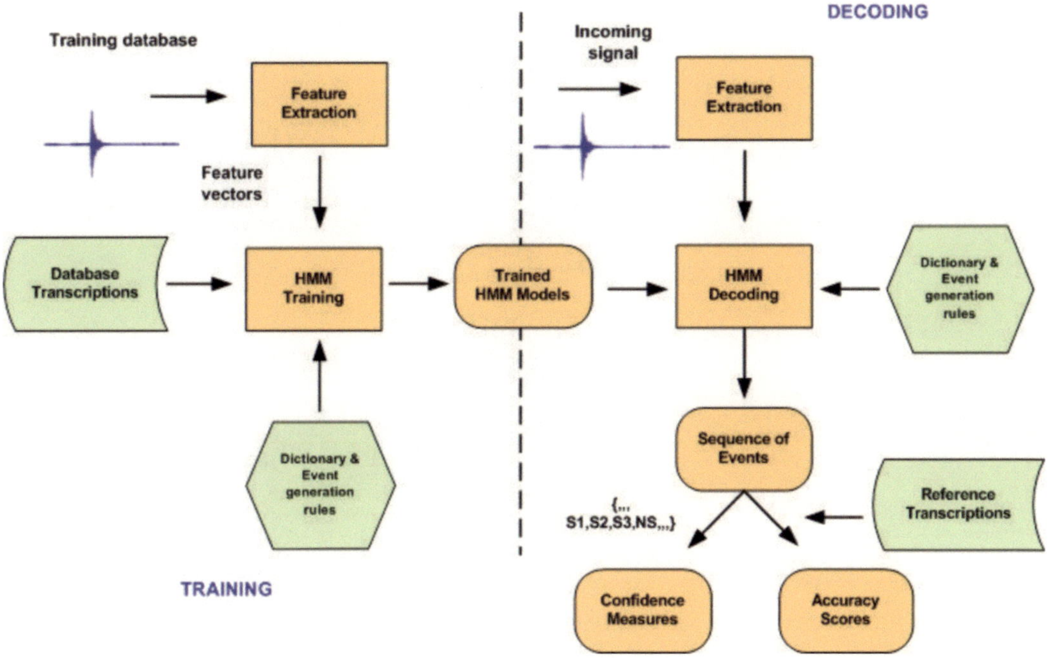

Fig. 4.2 Architecture of an HMM-based seismic event classification system.

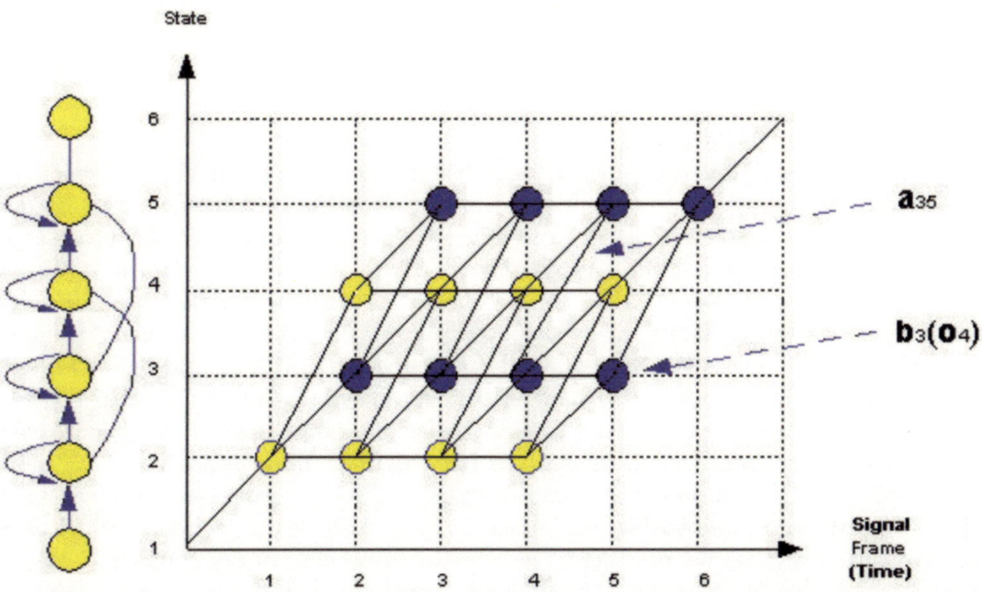

Fig. 4.3 Viterbi algorithm

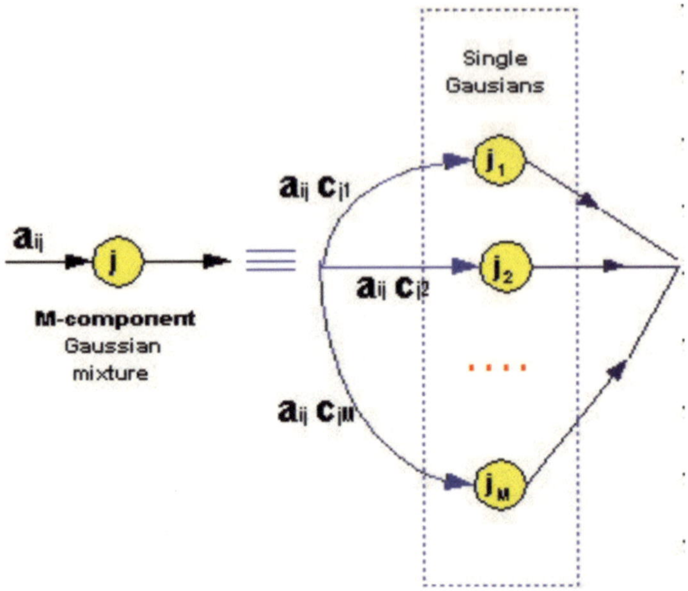

Fig. 4.4 Baum-Welch algorithm

after a particular event, any other one or noise could appear with the same probability. The recognition system combines the probabilities generated by the models and the probabilities obtained by the allowed transition for the seismic events. Equation 3 indicates that it is necessary to generate all the sequences of events and to evaluate all of them, thus selecting the one with maximum probability. Our recognition system solves this problem by means of the Viterbi decoding algorithm (Rabiner et al. 1993 [25], Furui and Soundhi 1992 [29], Young et al. 1997 [26]).

5. Results

5.1 Preparation of the database

The first step in the data analysis, after the revision of the files, is the visual inspection and segmentation of the signals. As commented before, each file is 300-s-long and could have different types of volcanic signals. For our study we proceeded to distinguish four types of events for Telica volcano and three types of event for San Cristóbal volcano, according with the volcanic activity of each one. For Telica volcano we define four types of seismic signals; Strombolian explosions, Telica explosions, Telica Long Period signal, volcanic tremor and background seismic noise. We have defined these types as T1, T2, T3 and T4. Additionally, we have defined the tremor background seismic noise as NT. In San Cristóbal volcano we identified three types of signals; Strombolian explosions, San Cristóbal explosions, volcanic tremor and background seismic noise. We have defined these types as S1, S2 and S3. Additionally, we have defined the tremor background seismic noise as NS. The rest of the volcanic signals were not considered. In fact, in order to have an adequate model of every class of volcanic signals we need as large as possible number of data, and only the above cited four class could provided a number of events to built a well defined model. The segmentation process consists in to mark over the seismogram the segment that corresponds to every class of events.(Fig. 5.1) This procedure was done by eye and by an unique expert who has decided the start and end of every signal. In this way we are confident of the use of the same criteria in the selection process. For San Cristóbal volcano we segmented 224 samples of S1, 330 samples of S2, 544 samples of S3 and 1,746 samples of background noise (NS) events. For Telica volcano we segmented 360 samples of T1, 502 samples of T2, 429 samples of T3, 298 samples of T4 and 2,855 samples of background noise (NT) events.

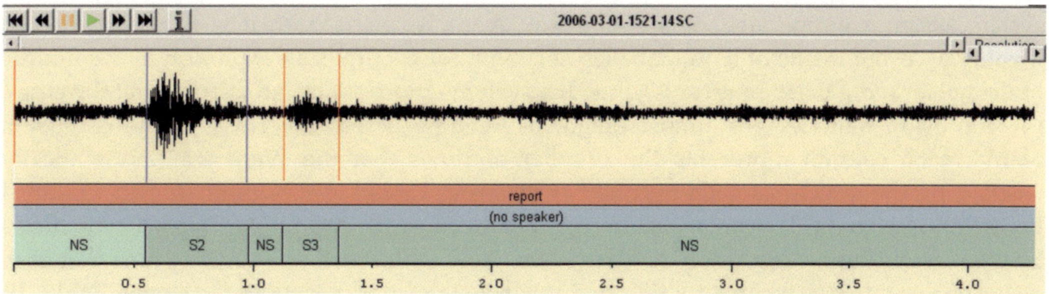

Fig. 5.1 Example of segmentation S2 and S3 signals in San Cristóbal volcano

5.2 Recognition system setup

Once the recordings were manually labelled during the data preparation stage, the recognition system was carefully trained using the available Baum-Welch reestimation algorithms [23] present in the Hidden Markov Model Toolkit (HTK) software [27]. The first step in the training process is the feature extraction process on a frame by frame basis as described above. The 39 parameter feature vector including static coefficients as well as dynamic features is used for training and testing. The training process consists of the initialization of an HMM for each of the events based on a training labelled data set. In this way, different HMMs were built for each of the events analyzed at the different volcanoes: that is, Telica and San Cristóbal event. Moreover, the different background noises observed at both volcanoes were also modelled using different HMMs. The models were defined as left-to-right HMMs where only transitions from state i to state $i+1$ are allowed. The optimal length of the HMMs is mainly determined by the mean duration of the types of events being modelled. Different experiments were carried out in order to determine the best choice. On the other, the HMM emission probabilities at each state were previously defined as Gaussian mixture densities and, during the training process, HMM models with increasing number of Gaussians were built in order to determine the best trade-off between recognition accuracy and performance.

To check the confidence of the method, two types of exercises have been done: closed and blind test. Closed test are done when the same data are used for train and test. For blind test the volcano database is divides in three subset and, rotary two subset are used to train the models and the other one for test; the final result is the average of the three different experiments carried out. Closed test could help to obtain an initial configuration of the recognition system, an initial valuation of the difficulty of the task and, even an idea of the quality of the supervised segmentation of the database. The blind test show objective results of the automatic classification system.

The direct application of the system, specifically trained for the San Cristóbal and Telica volcanoes, provided the following results: We obtained an 88.92% and 74.78% of accuracy in blind test (see table III and VI). Tables I, II, IV and V shows the confusion matrices for the

experiments conducted on the San Cristóbal and Telica volcanoes with 13-state HMMs defined with 16 Gaussians. Tables I and IV shows a set of closed test experiments for the different events for San Cristóbal and Telica database and Tables II and V shows a set of blind test experiments for the different events for San Cristóbal and Telica database.
These matrices indicate the different errors that appear in a automatic recognition system; substitution errors, insertion errors and deletion errors. A substitution error is when the system assign a wrong label to a well know event; a insertion error is when the system identify an event inside of a non labelled segment, for example, an explosion in the middle of the noise, and a deletion error is when the system ignore a labelled event. In all the cases, the confusion matrices are almost diagonal. Reading across the rows of the confusion matrix, each column represents the number of times that the event was automatically labelled by the system as such event. For example Table I shows that 102 San Cristóbal Long Period signal (S1) events were recognized as S1 event and 6 times was not identified by the recognition system ("del" row); the "ins" row indicates the number of time that each one of the events was incorrectly detected when just noise is present in the signal. Tables III and VI shows the percentage correct (%Corr) and the accuracy (%Acc) in closed and blind test.

	NS	**S1**	**S2**	**S3**
NS	**617**	**0**	**0**	**13**
S1	**0**	**102**	**0**	**0**
S2	**0**	**0**	**130**	**0**
S3	**0**	**0**	**1**	**193**
Ins	**0**	**1**	**0**	**1**
Del	**72**	**6**	**21**	**27**

Table I. San Cristóbal training result (closed test)

	NS	**S1**	**S2**	**S3**
NS	**422**	**0**	**0**	**0**
S1	**1**	**10**	**0**	**2**
S2	**2**	**1**	**46**	**3**
S3	**2**	**2**	**5**	**157**
Ins	**3**	**0**	**11**	**11**
Del	**13**	**3**	**5**	**12**

Table II. San Cristóbal test result (blind test)

	%Corr	%Acc
Closed test	88.16	87.99
Blind test	92.57	88.92

Table III. San Cristóbal % result (closed and blind test)

	NT	T1	T2	T3	T4
NT	2193	21	23	6	5
T1	1	210	6	3	6
T2	1	8	360	3	1
T3	1	2	3	330	3
T4	1	0	2	0	264
Ins	65	39	64	32	6
Del	164	28	59	38	30

Table IV. Telica training result (closed test)

	NT	T1	T2	T3	T4
NT	145	0	2	0	0
T1	0	9	2	1	9
T2	0	0	12	0	0
T3	0	1	3	13	3
T4	0	4	3	5	8
Ins	0	1	5	2	1
Del	8	3	2	3	4

Table V. Telica test result (blind test)

With these preliminary set of experiments we have set up the HMM-based recognition system and, in order to validate it, we have carried out experiments with a database containing recordings from both San Cristóbal and Telica volcanoes. With these tests we want to determine if the seismic signals as well as the background noises observed at San Cristóbal and Telica are clearly separable on a mixed data set. Table VII shows the confusion matrix for this test with 16-Gaussian HMMs. It is shown that it is almost diagonal and that San Cristóbal events, Telica events and the different background noises observed at San Cristóbal and Telica are effectively recognized with an accuracy of about 91.41%. In this way, no confusion occurred between the events at San Cristóbal and Telica so that no San Cristóbal event was classified as an Telica event and viceversa.

6. Discussion and conclusions

In the present work we have developed a volcanic seismic event discrimination system by using an automatic classification system based on Hidden Markov Models (HMM). The present system uses the statistical information compiled from a training set of data, when the event classification was supervised by an expert. From these data sets we have established a model of every event type. The present work used data from two active

	%Corr	%Acc
Closed test	**89.00**	**83.54**
Blind test	**78.24**	**74.78**

Table VI. Telica % result (closed and blind test)

======================== HTK Results Analysis ========================
-- Overall Results --

SENT: %Correct = 75.66 [H=917, S=295, N=**1212**]

WORD: %Corr = **93.52**, Acc=**91.41** [H=4531, D=274, S=40, I=102, N=4845]

	SAN CRISTÓBAL				TELICA				
	NS	S1	S2	S3	NT	T1	T2	T3	T4
NS	837	2	8	0	7	0	0	1	1
S1	0	248	1	0	0	0	0	0	0
S2	0	0	298	0	1	0	0	0	0
S3	0	0	0	84	0	0	0	0	0
NT	10	0	0	0	1964	4	3	0	0
T1	0	0	0	0	0	232	0	1	0
T2	0	0	0	0	0	0	351	0	0
T3	0	0	0	0	0	0	0	308	0
T4	0	0	0	0	0	0	0	0	209
Ins	19	0	3	0	67	1	6	5	1
Del	57	11	16	0	118	22	24	13	13

Table VII. Confusion matrix for mixed San Cristóbal/Telica recognition experiments.

MODELS	RECORDS		
	TELICA	SAN CRISTOBAL	MIXED RECORDS
TRAINING	83.29%	87.99%	--
TEST	74.48%	88.92%	--
TELICA DB TRAINING	SUCCESS	NO SUCCESS	--
SAN CRISTÓBAL DB TRAINING	NO SUCCESS	SUCCESS	--
TELICA AND SAN CRISTÓBAL MIXED DB TRAINING	--	--	SUCCESS TRA 91.41% But only with individual training

Table VIII. Telica and San Cristóbal mixed data bases training.?
DB = DATA BASE, TRA = TRAINING

volcanoes of Nicaragua, San Cristóbal and Telica, with different eruptive processes. We use data from two field surveys carried out in February to March 2006. At every volcano we have identified different types of events, three types and noise for San Cristóbal (S1,S2 and S3), and four types for Telica (T1, T2, T3 and T4) and background noise. The direct application of the system, specifically trained for every volcano, provided the following results:

6.1 San Cristóbal

We obtained, see table III, a 88.92% of accuracy in blind test, with a 11.1% of error. In the error estimate we include two types of results, the insertion of new events (20% of the errors), not labelled previously by the expert, and the deletion of signals. In this situation, the insertion of new events in the data base only could be considered as an error if these new events are not true events. In our case, more than the 90% of the insertions produced by the system correspond to true event that were no previously labelled in the training process. In figures 3.3 and 3.4 we show the seismogram, spectrogram and power spectra of samples of explosions (S2) and background tremor (NS) for San Cristóbal volcano. It is clear the difference between both types of signals.

6.2 Telica

Observing table VI, the application of the system for the data set of Telica has an accuracy of 74.78%, with an error of 25.22%. In this case, the insertions reach up to 69.2% of the total errors, and more than 90% of these insertions were a posteriori identified visually as a valid event. Thus the real accuracy of the system is higher than 80%. Comparing Figures 3.5 and 3.6, we find that the spectral and time-domain characteristics of T1 and T4 event are similar. In spite of these similarities, the system is able to discriminate between both of them.
We have to underscore that in the training process we selected those signals with good signal to noise ratio. We did not consider signals with low quality or with uncertainties in the classification process. However, the system seems to be able to recognize these dubious signals. Therefore, the system helps us to correct omissions performed in the initial training process of the data base. In this sense, the insertions could be considered as successes rather than errors. This ability of the system to detect events that were not previously recognized

by the expert is a consequence of the modelling of the temporal evolution of the power spectra of the seismic events, while the training process is made exclusively attending to the time-domain waveforms. The fact that our overall success rate exceeds 80% reflects the robustness and effectiveness of the proposed methodology.

We wondered if the recognition data base designed using data from a particular volcano and eruptive period could be applied to other volcanoes or different eruptive episodes. In the present work, we have used separately two data base from San Cristóbal and Telica volcanoes. To answer this question, we performed an experiment consisting in the mixing of both data bases, and its application to the discrimination of seismic signals from both volcanoes. There are nine event types in this new data base: S1, S2, S3 and San Cristóbal noise (NS), T1, T2, T3, T4 and Telica Noise (NT). The results are show in Tables VII and VIII. From these results, we conclude that: (a) We do not observe confusion or mixing in the event classification, that is, no event of San Cristóbal was identified as Telica event and viceversa; (b) The events of San Cristóbal was identified separately from the events of Telica; (c) We maintained the same high accuracy rate than in the previous experiments. It is remarkable that when we have mixed both data base we do not have confusion between all the signals. Also we point out that it is not possible to use the data base trained for San Cristóbal to recognize events of Telica, and viceversa. Thus each volcano and signal require an specific training process.

Finally, we conclude that the recognition and classification system based on HMM is a powerful, effective and successful tool. From the application performed over data belonging to two active volcanoes (San Cristóbal and Telica), we have demonstrated that in order to have a reliable result, it is necessary a careful and adequate segmentation process. Also, we proved that each type of signals requires its own characterization. That is, each signal type must be represented by its own specific model, which would include the effects of source, path and sites. Once we have built this model, the success level of the system is high.

7. References

[1] Chouet, B., 1996 *Monitoring and mitigation of volcano hazards*, chap. New methods and future trends in seismological volcano monitoring, pp. 23–97, R Scarpa and Tilling R ed.,Springer-Verlag.

[2] Chouet, B., 1996. Long-period volcano seismicity; its source and use in eruption forecasting, *Nature, 380* (6572), 309–316.

[3] Chouet, B., 2003. Volcano seismology, *Pure Appl. Geophys., 160* (3-4), 739–788.

[4] Baum, L. and Petrie, T. 1966 Statistical inference for probabilistic functions of finite state Markov chains. *Annals of Mathematical Statistics*, 37:1554-1563.

[5] Baum, L., Petrie, T., Soules, G., and Weiss, N., 1970 A maximization technique occurring in the statistical analysis of probabilistic functions of Markov chains, Ann. *Math. Statist.*, vol. 41, no. 1, pp. 164–171.

[6] J. A. Sánchez, C. M. Travieso, I. G. Alonso, M. A. Ferrer, Handwritten recognizer by its envelope and strokes layout using HMM's, 35rd Annual 2001 IEEE Internacional Carnahan Conference on Security Technology, (IEEE ICCST'01), London, UK, 2001, 267-271.

[7] M. A. Ferrer, J. L. Camino, C. M. Travieso, C. Morales, Signatura Classification by Hidden Markov Model, 33rd Anual 1999 IEEE Internacional Carnahan Conference on Security Technology, (IEEE ICCST'99), Comisaría General de Policía Científica,

Ministerio del Interior, IEEE Spain Section, COIT, SSR-UPM, Seguritas Seguridad España S.A, Madrid, Spain, Oct. 1999, 481-484.

[8] J. B. Alonso, C.Carmona, J. de León y M. A. Ferrer, Combining Neural Networks and Hidden Markov Models for Automatic Detection of Pathologies, 16_th Biennial International Eurasip Conference Biosignal 2002, Brno, Check Republic, June 2002.

[9] Renals, S., Morgan, N., Bourlard, H., Cohen, M. & Franco, H. (1994), Connectionist probability estimators in HMM speech recognition, IEEE Transactions on Speech and Audio Processing 2(1), 1994, 161-174.

[10] L.R. Bahl, P.F. Brown, P.V. de Souza, and R.L. Mercer, Maximum mutual information estimation of HMM parameters for speech recognition,. In Proc. IEEE Intl. Conf. on Acoustics, Speech, and Signal Processing, , Tokyo, Japan, December 1986, 49-52

[11] Yin, M.M., Wang, J.T.L., Application of hidden Markov models to gene prediction in DNA, Information Intelligence and Systems, 1999] Proceedings. International Conference on, 1999, 40 - 47.

[12] Cohen, A., Hidden Markov models in biomedical signal processing, Engineering in Medicine and Biology Society, 1998. Proceedings of the 20th Annual International Conf. of the IEEE, Vol. 3, 1998, 1145 - 1150.

[13] C. Benítez, J. Ramírez, J.C. Segura, J.M. Ibáñez, J. Almedros, A. García-Yeguas, and G. Cortés, "Continuous hmm-based seismic event classification at Deception island," *IEEE Trans. Geoscience and Remote Sensing*, vol. 45, pp. 138–147, January 2007.

[14] J.M. Ibáñez, C. Benítez, L.A. Gutiérrez, G. Cortés, A. García-Yeguas, and G. Alguacil, "Classification of seismo-volcanic signals using hidden Markov models: an application to Stromboli and Etna volcanoes," *Submitted for publication to Volcanology and Geothermal Research*, 2009.

[15] M. Beyreuther, R. Carniel, and J.Wassermann, "Continuous hidden Markov models: Applications to automatic earthquake detection and classification at Las Cañadas caldera, Tenerife," *Volcanology and Geothermal Research*, vol. 176, pp. 513–518, 2008

[16] Gutiérrez L., Ibañez J., Benítez C., Ramírez J., Almendros J, García-Yeguas A. "HMM-based classification of seismic events recorded at Stromboli and Etna Volcanoes" 2006 IEEE International Geoscience and Remote Sensing Symposium & 27th Canadian Symposium on remote sensing.

[16a] Ibáñez Jesús M., Benítez Carmen, Gutiérrez Ligdamis A., Cortés Guillermo, Yeguas-García Araceli and Alguacil Gerardo "The classification of seismo-volcanic signals using Hidden Markov Models as applied to the Stromboli and Etna volcanoes" Journal of Volcanology and Geothermal Research Volume 187, Issues 3-4, 10 November 2009, Pages 218-226

[16b] Cortes, G.; Arambula, R.; Gutierrez, L.A.; Benitez, C.; Ibaez, J.; Lesage, P.; Alvarez, I.; Garcia, L.; Evaluating robustness of a HMM-based classification system of volcano-seismic events at colima and popocatepetl volcanoes. Geoscience and Remote Sensing Symposium,2009 IEEE International, IGARSS 2009

[17] E. Del Pezzo, A. Esposito, F. Giudicepietro, M. Marinaro, M. Martini, and S. Scarpetta, "Discrimination of earthquakes and underwater explosions using neural networks", *Bull. Seism. Soc. Am..*, vol. 93, no. 1, pp. 215–223, 2003.

[18] S. Scarpetta, F. Giudicepietro, E. Ezin, S. Petrosino, E. Del Pezzo, M. Martini and M. Marinaro, "Automatic classification of seismic signals at Mt. Vesuvius volcano, Italy, using neural networks", *Bull. Seism. Soc. Am.*, vol. 95, no. 1, pp. 185–196, 2005

[19] M. Ohrnberger. *Continuous automatic classification of seismic signals of volcanic origin at Mt. Merapi, Java, Indonesia,* Ph.D. dissertation, Mathematisch-Naturwissenschaftlichen Facultat der Universitat Potsdam, 2001.

[20] Van Wyk de Vries B., 1993. Tectonic and magma evolution of Nicaraguan volcanic systems. Ph.D. Thesis. - Open University, Milton Keynes, 328 p.

[21] M. J. Carr and R. E. Stoiber Geologic setting of some destructive earthquakes in Central America *Geological Society of America Bulletin* (January 1977), 88(1):151-156

[22] L.R. Rabiner, "A tutorial on hidden Markov models and selected applications in speech recognition," *Proc. of the IEEE,* vol. 77, no. 2, February 1989.

[23] S. Young, G. Everman, M. Gales, T. Hain, D. Kershaw, X. Liu, G. Moore, J. Odell, D. Ollason, D. Povey, V. Valtchev, and P. Woodland, ," *The HTK Book (Version 3.4).* Cambridge University Engineering Department, 2006.

[24] M. Karnjanadecha, S. Zahorian. "Signal modeling for High-Performance Robus Isolated. Word Recognitions". IEEE Transactions On speech and Audio Processing. Vol 9 N° 6. September 2001.

[25] L. Rabiner and B. Juang, *Fundamentals of Speech Recognition*. Prentice Hall, 1993.

[26] S. Young, J. Odell, D. Ollason, V. Valtchev, and P. Woodland, *The HTK Book.* Cambridge University, 1997.

[27] L. Bahl, F. Jelinek, and R. Mercer, "A maximum likelihood approach to continuous speech recognition," *IEEE Trans. Pattern Anal. Machine Intell.,* vol. PAMI-5, pp. 179–190, 1983.

[28] A. Dempster and N. L. and D.B. Rubin, "Maximum likelihood from incomplete data via the EM algorithm," *J. Roy. Stat. Soc.,* vol. 39, no. 1, pp. 1–38, 1977.

[29] S. Furui and M. M. Sondhi, *Advances in Speech Signal Processing*. Marcel Dekker, Inc., 1992.

10

A Non-Homogeneous Hidden Markov Model for the Analysis of Multi-Pollutant Exceedances Data

Francesco Lagona[1], Antonello Maruotti[2] and Marco Picone[3]
[1,2]*Dipartimento di Istituzioni Pubbliche, Economia e Società - Università di Roma Tre and GRASPA Research Unit of Roma Tre*
[3]*Dipartimento di Economia - Università di Roma Tre and GRASPA Research Unit of Roma Tre*
Italy

1. Introduction

Air quality standards are referred to thresholds above which pollutants concentrations are considered to have serious effects on human health and the environment (World Health Organization, 2006). In urban areas, exceedances are usually recorded through a monitoring network, where concentrations of a number of pollutants are measured at different sites. Daily occurrences of exceedances of standards are routinely exploited by environmental agencies such as the US EPA and the EEA, to compute air quality indexes, to determine compliance with air quality regulations, to study short/long-term effects of air pollution exposure, to communicate air conditions to the general public and to address issues of environmental justice.

The statistical analysis of urban exceedances data is however complicated by a number of methodological issues. First, data can be heterogeneous because stations are often located in areas that are exposed to different sources of pollution. Second, data can be unbalanced because the pollutants of interest are often not measured by all the stations of the network and some stations are not in operation (e.g. for malfunctioning or maintenance) during part of the observation period. Third, exceedances data are typically dependent at different levels: multi-pollutants exceedances are not only often associated at the station level, but also at a temporal level, because exceedances may be persistent or transient according to the general state of the air and time-varying weather conditions may influence the temporal pattern of pollution episodes in different ways.

Non-homogeneous hidden Markov (NHHM) models provide a flexible strategy to estimate multi-pollutant exceedances probabilities, conditionally on time-varying factors that may influence the occurrence and the persistence of pollution episodes, and simultaneously accomodating for heterogeneous, unbalanced and temporally dependent data.

In this paper, we propose to model daily multi-pollutant exceedances data by a mixture of logistic regressions, whose mixing weights indicate probabilities of a number of air quality regimes (latent classes). Transition from one regime to another is governed by a non-homogeneous Markov chain, whose transition probabilities depend on time-varying meteorological covariates, through a multinomial logistic regression model. When these covariates are suitably chosen for measuring the amount of atmospheric turbolence, parameters of the multinomial logistic model indicate the influence of atmospheric stability on both the occurrence of typical pollution episodes and the persistence of these episodes. Conditionally on the latent class, exceedances are assumed independent and pollutant-specific exceedances probabilities depend on covariates that are proxies of the production of pollution. Because the information provided by these proxies is typically poor, latent classes accomodate for the influence of unobserved sources of pollution and, simultaneously, account for the dependence between multi-pollutant exceedances that were observed during the same day.

NHHM models generalize the class of homogeneous hidden Markov (HHM) models that are extensively discussed by MacDonald and Zucchini (1997). HHM models assume that the data are conditionally independent given the states of a (latent) homogeneous Markov chain and provide a flexible approach to model stationary categorical time series. An NHHM model is obtained as a generalization of a HHM model, by allowing the transition probabilities to be time-varying. On the other side, NHHM models generalize the class of mixtures of regression models with concomitant variables (Wang and Putermann, 1998), to allow for temporal dependence.

NHHM models have been already considered in the literature by several authors. Diebolt et al. (1994) have considered maximum likelihood estimation of the simple two-state Gaussian hidden Markov model with time-varying transition matrix. Applications of hidden Markov models with time-varying transitions include Durland and McCurdy (1994), Gray (1996), Peria (2002), Masson and Ruge-Murcia (2005), Kim et al. (2008), and Banachewicz et al. (2007). Wong and Li (2001) have considered a two-state non-homogeneous Markov switching mixture autoregressive model. All the above papers adopt classical inferential procedures. A Bayesian approach to inference for non-homogeneous hidden Markov model has been proposed by Filardo and Gordon (1998) and Meligkotsidou and Dellaportas (2010).

In environmental studies, NHHM models have found widespread application in meteorology and hydrology, in studies of climate variability or climate change, and in statistical downscaling of daily precipitation from observed and numerical climate model simulations (see, e.g., Zucchini and Guttorp 1991; Hughes and Guttorp 1994; Hughes et al. 1999; Charles et al. 1999; Bellone et al. 2000; Charles et al. 2004; Robertson et al. 2004; Betrò et al. 2008).

Fewer are the applications of homogeneous and non-homogeneous hidden Markov models in air quality studies, where this methodology has been mainly applied to study univariate pollutants concentrations under the assumption of normally-distributed data (Spezia, 2006; Dong et al., 2009) or to estimate exceedances probabilities (Lagona, 2005).

After describing the environmental data used in this study (Section 2), the specification of a NHHM for pollutants exceedances and the discussion of relevant computational details for estimation are outlined in Section 3. Section 4 illustrates an application to exceedances data of ozone, particulate and nitrogen dioxide, obtained from the monitoring network of Rome. Section 5 finally provides some concluding remarks.

2. Data

Our analysis is based on binary time series of occurrences and non occurrences of exceedances of air quality standards, as computed from hourly pollutants concentrations that are typically available from the monitoring network in an urban area.

station	type	PM_{10}	NO_2	O_3
Preneste	residential	34	2	
Francia	traffic		3	73
Magna Grecia	traffic		4	45
Cinecittà	residential	27	3	51
Villa Ada	residential	21	0	14
Castel Guido	rural	5	0	
Cavaliere	rural	3	0	
Fermi	traffic		22	64
Bufalotta	residential	16	0	18
Cipro	residential	7	2	31
Tiburtina	traffic		9	70
Arenula	residential		0	35

Table 1. Number of violations in 2009

In the application discussed in the present paper, we considered the concentrations data of particulate matter (PM_{10}), nitrogen dioxide (NO_2) and ozone (O_3), reported by the monitoring network of Rome (Italy) in 2009. These data are disseminated by the Environmental Protection Agency of the Lazio region (`www.arpalazio.net/main/aria/`). While six stations of the network are located in residential areas with moderate traffic, four stations are close to heavy traffic roads and two stations are located in rural areas.

Violations of air quality standards are defined differently for each pollutant, because most of the current legislation considers air quality standards separately for each pollutant. According to the most recent legislation, we recorded the day and the station where (i) the 24-hour average concentration of particulate matter was above the threshold of $50\mu g/m^3$, (ii) the maximum hourly concentration of nitrogen dioxide was above the level of 200 $\mu g/m^3$ and (iii) the maximum 8-hour moving average of ozone concentrations exceeded the level of 120 $\mu g/m^3$.

Table 1 displays the number of violations of the above standards, observed at the monitoring network in 2009. Empty cells indicate structural zeros, which are observed when a particular pollutant is not measured by the station. As expected, particulate and nitrogen dioxide exceed the standard in the neighborhood of traffic roads at a rate that is larger than that observed in residential areas, while most of the violations of ozone are observed in residential areas.

Although tables such as Table 1 are routinely reported to communicate the state of the air to the general public and to determine compliance with environmental regulations, these counts should be interpreted with caution, for a number of different reasons. First, some of the stations were not in operation during parts of the study period and hence the data are based on a time-varying number of stations. Second, the occurrence of exceedances is not only influenced by the location of the monitoring station but also by weather conditions. For example, global radiation and wind speed regulate the amount of atmospheric stability and can be responsible for stagnation or dispersion of pollutant concentrations. Atmospheric stability, i.e. the tendency of the atmosphere to resist or enhance turbulence, is related to both , global radiation and wind speed, leading to several stability classes. Stability classes are defined for different meteorological situations, characterized by wind speed and solar radiation (during the day) and can be classified according to the so-called Pasquill-Turner classification (Turner, 1994) As a result, these counts should be adjusted not only by the type of the station but also by weather conditions. This adjustment can be important when comparing exceedances data of several urban areas to address issues of environmental justice. We accordingly included daily means of wind speed and radiation into our analysis of exceedances data, as obtained by one of the most authoritative meteorological station in Rome (Collegio Romano, www.cra-cma.it/cromano.html).

3. A non-homogeneous hidden Markov model for binary data

Time series of exceedances data can be represented as a vector of $n \times H$ binary matrices, say $\boldsymbol{Y} = (\mathbf{Y}_t, t = 0, 1, \ldots T)$, where the (i, h)th element y_{iht} of matrix $\mathbf{Y}_t$ is equal to 1 if the hth event occurred in unit i at time t and 0 otherwise, $i = 1 \ldots n, h = 1 \ldots H$.
We introduce a latent vector $\boldsymbol{s} = (s_t, t = 0, 1, \ldots T)$, drawn from a vector $\boldsymbol{S} = (S_t, t = 0, 1, \ldots T)$ of discrete random variables S_t that take K categorical values. The product sample space of $\boldsymbol{S}$, say $\mathbb{S}$, includes K^T vectors. Without loss of generality, we write the distribution of the observed data, say $P(\boldsymbol{Y})$, as a mixture of conditional multivariate distributions, say

$$p(\mathbf{Y}) = \sum_{\boldsymbol{s} \in \mathbb{S}} p(\mathbf{Y}, \boldsymbol{s}) = \sum_{\boldsymbol{s} \in \mathbb{S}} p(\mathbf{Y}|\boldsymbol{s}) p(\boldsymbol{s}).$$

As a result, the marginal covariance between two occurrences, say Y_{iht} and $Y_{jk\tau}$, is given by

$$\begin{aligned} \gamma(i,j,h,k,t,\tau) &= \mathbb{E}Y_{iht}Y_{jk\tau} - \mathbb{E}Y_{iht}\mathbb{E}Y_{jk\tau} \\ &= \sum_{\boldsymbol{Y}_{(i,h,t),(j,k,\tau)}} p(\boldsymbol{Y}) - \sum_{\boldsymbol{Y}_{(i,h,t)}} p(\boldsymbol{Y}) \sum_{\boldsymbol{Y}_{(j,k,\tau)}} p(\boldsymbol{Y}), \end{aligned}$$

where $\boldsymbol{Y}_{(i,h,t),(j,k,\tau)}$ indicates any matrix $\boldsymbol{Y}$ with $y_{iht} = y_{jk\tau} = 1$ and, analogously, $\boldsymbol{Y}_{(i,h,t)}$ ($\boldsymbol{Y}_{(j,k,\tau)}$) indicates any matrix $\boldsymbol{Y}$ with $y_{iht} = 1$ ($y_{jk\tau} = 1$). These covariances can be arranged in a $\boldsymbol{\Gamma}$ blocks-matrix $\boldsymbol{\Gamma} = (\boldsymbol{\Gamma}_{t,\tau}; t, \tau = 0, 1 \ldots T)$, whose diagonal blocks, $\boldsymbol{\Gamma}_{tt}$, describe the covariance structure between contemporary occurrences, while the off-diagonal blocks, $\boldsymbol{\Gamma}_{t\tau}$, describe the autocovariances and the cross-autocovariances of the multivariate time series.
The above mixture is called HHM model when

1. exceedances patterns are conditionally independent given the latent states (conditional independence assumption), namely

$$p(\mathbf{Y}|\boldsymbol{s}) = \prod_{t=0}^{T} p(\mathbf{Y}_t|\boldsymbol{s}) = \prod_{t=0}^{T} p(\mathbf{Y}_t|s_t) \tag{1}$$

2. and the latent vector $\boldsymbol{s}$ is sampled from a Markov chain, namely

$$p(\boldsymbol{s}) = \delta_s \prod_{t=1}^{T} p(s_{t-1}, s_t),$$

where $\delta_s = p(S_0 = s)$ and the transition probabilities $p(s_{t-1}, s_t) = P(S_t = s_t | S_{t-1} = s_{t-1})$ do not vary with time (homogeneity assumption).

In a HHM model, multivariate time series data are therefore modeled by a mixture of multivariate distributions, whose parameters depend on the stochastic evolution of a

unobserved Markov chain. As a result, the hidden states of the chain can be interpreted as different regimes at which multivariate exceedances occur.
From a technical viewpoint, an HHM model greatly reduces the number of unknown parameters that drive the distribution of a multinomial time series. However, the K conditional distributions $p(\mathbf{Y}_t|S_t = s)$ still depend on $(2^{I\times J} - 1) \times K$ probabilities. Although a saturated log-linear re-parametrization of these probabilities is in principle possible, it would involve a model with high-order interactions that may be difficult to interpret. Moreover, estimation of saturated models can be unstable if data are unbalanced, as often happens with urban exceedances data. We therefore need to employ strategies to reduce the number of parameters. A parsimonious model that accounts for the multi-pollutant nature of the data and simultaneously allows for heterogeneous monitoring networks is a binary regression model, where pollutant-specific exceedances probabilities vary with the monitoring station. More precisely, we assume that

$$p(\mathbf{Y}_t|S_t = s) = \prod_{i=1}^{I}\prod_{j=1}^{J}\theta_{ijs}^{y_{ijt}}\left(1-\theta_{ijs}\right)^{1-y_{ijt}}, \tag{2}$$

where θ_{ijs} is the conditional probability that pollutant j exceeds the standard at station i, under regime s. Probabilities θ_{ijs} can be re-parametrized in a number of different ways, depending on the purpose of the analysis and the availability of specific covariates on single stations. In our application, the following two-way logit model was exploited

$$\text{logit}\,\theta_{ijs} = \beta_{0s} + \beta_{is} + \beta'_{js}, \tag{3}$$

where β_{0s} is a baseline parameter, while β_{is} and β'_{js} are respectively the station and the pollutant effects under regime s, with the identifiability constraints $\beta_{1s} = \beta'_{1s} = 0$, for each $s = 1 \ldots K$.
Parameters in equation (3) model exceedances data within multinomial regimes. In a HHM model, the temporal persistence of each regime during the period of interest is governed by the homogeneous (i.e., time-constant) transition probabilities of a latent Markov chain. Although at present the formation and evolution of air pollution episodes in urban areas is only understood in general terms, it is well known that meteorological covariates may have a significant influence on the persistence of exceedances, leading to a non-stationary behavior of exceedances data. Motivated by this, we extend the HHM model framework to allow for non-homogeneous transition probabilities that depend on a profile $\boldsymbol{x}_t$ of meteorological covariates. Specifically, we assume that latent vector $\boldsymbol{s}$ is drawn from a non-homogeneous Markov chain with distribution

$$p(\boldsymbol{s}) = \delta_s \prod_{t=1}^{T} p(s_{t-1}, s_t), \tag{4}$$

and exploit a multinomial logit model to re-parametrize the time-varying transition probabilities, as follows

$$p_t(s,k) = \frac{\exp\left(\gamma_{0ks} + \boldsymbol{x}_t^T \gamma_{ks}\right)}{\sum_{h=1}^{K} \exp\left(\gamma_{0hs} + \boldsymbol{x}_t^T \gamma_{hs}\right)}, \tag{5}$$

where γ_{0ks} is a baseline regime-specific effect ($\gamma_{0ss} = 0$, for identifiability) and the vector γ_{ks} are regression coefficients that measure the effect of weather conditions on transition probabilities.
Combining (2) and (4), we propose to model a time series of multivariate exceedances data by the following marginal distribution:

$$p(\mathbf{Y}|\gamma,\boldsymbol{\beta},\boldsymbol{\delta}) = \sum_{s_0} \delta(s) \sum_{s_1 \ldots s_T} \prod_{t=0}^{T} p_t(s_{t-1},s_t) \prod_{i=1}^{I} \prod_{j=1}^{J} \theta_{ijs}^{y_{ijt}} \left(1-\theta_{ijs}\right)^{1-y_{ijt}}, \tag{6}$$

known up to the parameters $\boldsymbol{\alpha},\boldsymbol{\beta},\boldsymbol{\delta}$. The above distribution modularizes the dependency structure of exceedance data, by separating temporal dependence, multivariate dependence, and non-stationary behavior. More precisely, the marginal covariance matrix of the multinomial time series $\boldsymbol{Y}$ can be viewed as a blocks-matrix $\boldsymbol{\Sigma} = (\boldsymbol{\Sigma}_{t,\tau}; t,\tau = 0,1\ldots T)$, whose diagonal blocks, $\boldsymbol{\Sigma}_{tt}$, describe the association between contemporary exceedances, while the off-diagonal blocks, $\boldsymbol{\Sigma}_{t\tau}$, describe the autocovariances and the cross-autocovariances of the multivariate time series. In particular, the generic element of $\boldsymbol{\Sigma}_{tt}$ is the (marginal) covariance between the exceedances of two pollutants j and l, recorded at two stations i and m at the same time t, namely

$$\begin{aligned}\sigma_{ijlm}(t) =& p(y_{ijt}=1,y_{lmt}=1)\\ =& \sum_{k=1}^{K} \pi_k(t)\theta_{ijk}\theta_{lmk} - \left(\sum_{k=1}^{K} \pi_k(t)\theta_{ijk}\right)\left(\sum_{k=1}^{K} \pi_k(t)\theta_{lmk}\right),\end{aligned} \tag{7}$$

where

$$\pi_k(t) = p(S_t = k) = \sum_{\boldsymbol{s}_{0:t-1}} \delta_{s_0} \prod_{\tau=1}^{t-1} p_\tau(s_{\tau-1},s_\tau) p_t(s_{t-1,k})$$

is the (time-varying) marginal probability for the latent chain of being in state k at time t. In general, for two different times t and τ, the generic element of matrix $\boldsymbol{\Sigma}_{t\tau}$ is given by

$$\begin{aligned}\sigma_{ijlm}(t,\tau) =& p(y_{ijt}=1,y_{lm\tau}=1)\\ =& \sum_{k,h}^{1\ldots K} \pi_{kh}(t,\tau)\theta_{ijk}\theta_{lmh} - \left(\sum_{k=1}^{K} \pi_k(t)\theta_{ijk}\right)\left(\sum_{h=1}^{K} \pi_h(\tau)\theta_{lmh}\right),\end{aligned} \tag{8}$$

where

$$\pi_{k,h}(t,\tau) = p(S_t = k, S_\tau = h) = \sum_{\boldsymbol{s}_{t:\tau-1}} \pi_k(t) \prod_{\tau'=1}^{\tau-1} p_{\tau'}(s_{\tau'-1},s'_\tau) p_\tau(s_{\tau-1},h)$$

is the joint probability for regimes k and h to act at times t and τ, respectively.
Examination of the above covariances clearly illustrates that model (6) includes, as particular cases, a number of simpler models that could be used for examining multivariate pollutants exceedances. For example, when the transition probability matrix takes a diagonal form, model (6) reduces to a simple mixture of K generalized linear models with concomitant variables (Wang and Putermann, 1998), which could be used when the data do not show a significant temporal dependency structure. When, additionally, $K = 1$, model (6) degenerates

to a logistic regression model for multivariate pollutants exceedances (Kutchenhoff and Thamerus, 1996), which can be exploited under a strong homogeneity of the data.
We take a maximum likelihood approach to estimate the parameters of the proposed NHHM model. To account for the presence of missing values, our analysis is based on the maximization of the log-likelihood function that is obtained by marginalizing (6) with respect to the missing values, namely

$$l(\gamma, \boldsymbol{\beta}, \boldsymbol{\delta} | \boldsymbol{Y}_{\text{obs}}) = \sum_{\boldsymbol{Y}_{\text{mis}}} \log p(\boldsymbol{Y} | \gamma, \boldsymbol{\beta}, \boldsymbol{\delta}), \tag{9}$$

where $\boldsymbol{Y}_{\text{mis}}$ and $\boldsymbol{Y}_{\text{obs}}$ denote the arrays of the missing and observed values, respectively. We recall the conditional independence that in our NHHM model holds between exceedances within the same latent state. As a result, the contribution of each missing value to $l(\gamma, \boldsymbol{\beta}, \boldsymbol{\delta} | \boldsymbol{Y}_{\text{obs}})$ is equal to 1. By introducing a missing indicator variable ($r_{ijt} = 1$ if y_{ijt} is missing and 0 otherwise), the log-likelihood function that we maximize is thus finally given by

$$l(\gamma, \boldsymbol{\beta}, \boldsymbol{\delta} | \boldsymbol{Y}_{\text{obs}}) = \log \sum_{s_0} \delta(s) \sum_{s_1 \ldots s_T} \prod_{t=0}^{T} p_t(s_{t-1}, s_t) \prod_{i=1}^{I} \prod_{j=1}^{J} \left(\theta_{ijs}^{y_{ijt}} \left(1 - \theta_{ijs}\right)^{1-y_{ijt}} \right)^{r_{ijt}}. \tag{10}$$

In the hidden-Markov-models literature, maximization of (10) is essentially based on the EM algorithm (see e.g. MacDonald and Zucchini, 1997; Cappé et al., 2005; and reference therein for details about the algorithm). As it stands, expression (10) is of little or no computational use, because it has K^{T+1} terms and cannot be evaluated except for very small T. Clearly, a more efficient procedure is needed to perform the calculation of the likelihood. The problem of computing these factors may be addressed through the Forward-Backward procedure (Baum et al., 1970; for a brief review see Welch, 2003).
We point out that the estimation algorithm involves the iterative evaluation of the solutions of the weighted score equations:

$$\sum_{t=1}^{T} \sum_{k=1}^{K} \sum_{s=1}^{K} Pr(S_{t+1} = k, S_t = j \mid \mathbf{Y}_{\text{obs}}, \hat{\boldsymbol{\theta}}) \frac{\partial \log p_t(s,k)}{\partial \gamma} = 0; \tag{11}$$

and

$$\sum_{t=1}^{T} \sum_{k=1}^{K} Pr(S_t = s \mid \mathbf{Y}_{\text{obs}}, \hat{\boldsymbol{\theta}}) \frac{\partial \log f(\mathbf{Y}_t \mid S_t = s)}{\partial \boldsymbol{\beta}}, \tag{12}$$

where $\hat{\boldsymbol{\theta}} = (\hat{\boldsymbol{\beta}}, \hat{\gamma})$ are the estimates found at a previous iteration. The above equations are the score equations of generalized linear models (GLM) with weights $Pr(S_{t+1} = k, S_t = j \mid \mathbf{y})$ and $Pr(S_t = s \mid \mathbf{y})$ respectively. Parameter estimates can therefore immediately be estimated by exploiting any GLM software, by simply including a component factor in a generalized linear model as suggested by Hinde and Wood (1987), which is conveniently (even if inefficiently) handled by augmenting the data matrix.
The E- and M-steps are repeatedly alternated until the log-likelihood (relative) difference changes by an arbitrarily small amount.
However, while the EM algorithm is useful for obtaining maximum likelihood estimates in such situations, it does not readily provide standard errors for parameters estimates.

We computed standard errors of parameter estimates using parametric bootstrap (Efron and Tibshirani, 1993), as standard errors based on the observed information matrix are often unstable (see e.g. McLachlan and Peel 2000). Specifically, we re-fitted the model to the bootstrap data that were simulated from the estimated model. This process was repeated R times, and the approximate standard error of each model parameter κ was computed by

$$\hat{se}_R = \left\{ \frac{1}{R-1} \sum_{r=1}^{R} [\hat{\kappa}(r) - \overline{\kappa}(R)]^2 \right\}^{1/2}, \tag{13}$$

where $\hat{\kappa}(r)$ is the estimate from the r-th bootstrap sample and $\overline{\kappa}(R)$ is the sample mean of all $\hat{\kappa}(r)$.

In a general framework, there are at least three different methods for computing standard errors (and confidence intervals) of hidden Markov model parameters, namely likelihood profiling, bootstrapping and a method based on a finite difference approximation to the Hessian (Visser et al., 2000). In this paper we adopt the parametric bootstrap approach generating bootstrap samples according to the parametric model using the maximum likelihood estimates of the parameters. Our choice is due to both the simplicity of implementing the parametric bootstrap and the results produced by this procedure. As shown by Visser et al. (2000), in the context of long time series (i.e. $T > 100$) computing the exact Hessian is not feasible and, via a simulation study, it can be proved that likelihood profiling and bootstrapping produce similar results, whereas the standard errors from the finite-differences approximation of the Hessian are mostly too small.

However, in the general hidden Markov model framework assessing the uncertainty about parameters can be difficult, as bootstrapping typically relabels states in different ways: the role of states can be exchanged at each simulation. Problems due to label switching will be most acute when data are not informative about the transition matrices.

There are several possible solutions to this label switching problem, motivated by the literature on mixture distributions (see e.g. Richardson and Green, 1997; Celeux, 1998; Boys et al., 2000; Spezia, 2009). The label switching problem can be tackled by placing an identifiability constraint on some parameter. This operation can be risky if no information on the ordering constraint is available to the investigator; so, the parameter space can be truncated wrongly and, consequently, estimators are biased. Hence, the identifiability constraint can be placed when the regimes are well separated, only.

Bayesian information criterion (BIC) is used to compare the models. Selecting an NHHM model that minimizes the BIC provides a relatively parsimonious model that fits the data well. The final decision on how many and which of the resulting summary variables are to be included in the model is evaluated in terms of physical realism, distinctness of the weather state patterns and model interpretation.

4. Results

We have estimated a number of different NHHM models from the exceedances data described in Section 2, by varying the number K of states of the latent chain. This section presents the results obtained by a three-states model, which was chosen on the basis of the BIC statistic, the degree of separation of latent classes and the physical meaning of the parameters.

The posterior probabilities of the three states (Figure 1) show that the three latent classes are well separated and that days can be clustered according to their maximum posterior probabilities of class membership. The resulting classification is intuitively appealing (Figure 2): under state 1, pollution episodes are mainly characterized by ozone exceedances, while state 3 is dominated by exceedances of particulate matter and a few violations of the nitrogen dioxide standard; finally, state 2 clusters days with acceptable air conditions. We however remark that days are clustered by jointly modeling the exceedances probabilities of the three pollutants and simultaneously accounting for the type of monitoring station where violations of standards are observed. Table 2 shows the estimated effects on the conditional exceedances probabilities, for each state. Effects are displayed by taking the log-odds of a particulate exceedance in a moderate traffic station as baseline. Under state 1 the log-odds of an exceedance of ozone are greater than the log-odds of an exceedance of the other two pollutants. The situation is reversed under state 3, where particulate and nitrogen dioxide dominate the probability of a pollution episode. As expected, the exposure to pollution sources is strongly significant only when a pollution episode occur (i.e., under state 1 or 3). When, conversely, the quality of the air is acceptable, most of the stations are likely to report concentrations that are below the standard, regardless of the locations where measurements are made. However, when a pollution episode occurs, the expected number of violations depends on the distribution of the type of monitoring sites that are functioning. As a result, when a few violations occur, the model predicts a serious pollution episode only when exceedances are observed in locations that are exposed to low pollution sources. This explains why days with a similar number of exceedances are given a different class membership by the model (Figure 2).

The estimated transition probabilities of the latent chain, varying with weather conditions, are depicted in Figure 3, according to the origin state (columns) and the destination state (rows). Examining the pictures in the second row of the figure, we observe that a regime of acceptable air quality (state 2) is persistent during the whole year, as indicated by the large probabilities of remaining in state 2 (middle picture). As a result, the probabilities of moving from state 2 to a different state are generally low. As expected, while the probability of moving from state 2 to state 1 (ozone episodes) increases during the warm seasons, moderate probabilities of moving to state 3 (particulate and nitrogen dioxide episodes) increase during the cold seasons. The high variability of the probabilities of remaining in state 1 (first row, left) and in state 3 (third row, right) confirm that pollution episodes, as measured by the number of exceedances, were not persistent during the period of interest.

Figure 3 has been computed by exploiting the estimates of Table 3, which display the log-odds of conditional transition probabilities of the latent chain, by taking the probability of remaining in the same state as a reference. Examination of the second column of this table shows that the probability of moving from a state of good air quality to a pollution episode decreases at high wind speed, in keeping with the known role that the wind plays in the dispersion of pollutants. On the contrary, solar radiation has a positive effect on the probability to move to ozone episodes, occurring in summer, and a negative effect on the probability to move to episodes of particular matter and nitrogen dioxide, which occur during the cold seasons. The estimates of the first column of the table confirm that, when wind speed increases, the probability to move from state 1 to a state of acceptable air quality is much greater than that of moving to a ozone episode. Interestingly, global radiation has a negative effect on a transition from state 1. Particularly in winter, when state 1 is often reached, high

estimate	state 1	state 2	state 3
intercept	-3.4993	-4.0985	0.4709
	(0.3381)	(0.1592)	(0.0900)
low emission	-2.7563	-0.2737	-14.0231
	(0.4545)	(0.7789)	(3.4449)
ozone	3.9124	-2.2011	-18.2600
	(0.3724)	(0.6044)	(3.4433)
nitrogen dioxide	-1.6443	-1.7206	-3.3205
	(0.7845)	(0.3790)	(0.2037)

Table 2. Log-odds of exceedances probabilities (standard errors in brackets)

	destination		origin	
		state 1	state 2	state 3
	state 1	0	-11.3842	-19.1536
			(1.0768)	(2.3051)
intercepts	state 2	5.8137	0	-1.8993
		(1.6782)		(0.3318)
	state 3	9.5675	0.8748	0
		(2.3389)	(0.3204)	
	state 1	0	-0.5000	-0.7198
			(0.0384)	(0.0502)
wind speed	state 2	-1.1085	0	2.2761
		(0.6023)		(0.0925)
	state 3	-4.3735	-1.2730	0
		(1.1265)	0.0916	
	state 1	0	0.3808	0.6482
			(0.0348)	(0.0092)
global radiation	state 2	-0.1891	0	-0.1539
		(0.0195)		(0.0976)
	state 3	-0.4796	-0.1132	0
		(0.1211)	(0.0201)	

Table 3. Log-odds of transition probabilities (standard errors in brackets)

levels of solar radiation create in the atmosphere the phenomenon of thermal inversion (a layer of warm air settles over a layer of cold air) preventing the mixing up among the different layers of the air, due to the convective currents, and, as a result, preventing pollutants from rising and scattering. Finally, the estimates in column three of the table indicate the influence of weather conditions on the probability to move from state 3, which occurs in summer. As expected, while wind speed is associated with an increasing probability to return to a regime of clean air, an increase in the levels of global radiation negatively influences the chances for the system to return to a state of acceptable air conditions.

5. Discussion

Although most of the current legislation considers air quality standards separately for each pollutant, recent studies stress the importance of a joint examination of exceedances with respect to several air pollutants. When we face multivariate variables, and the primary focus

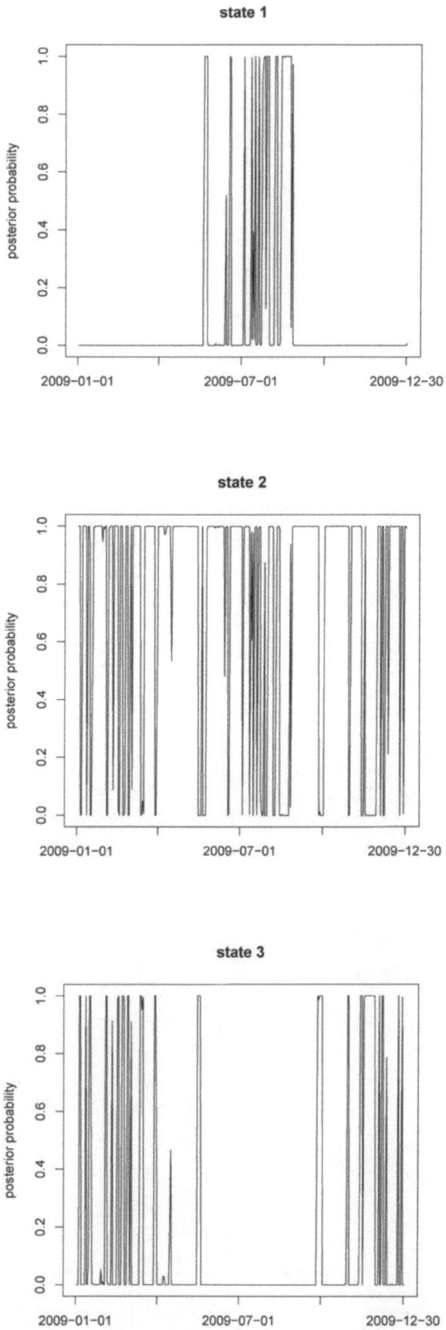

Fig. 1. posterior state probabilities, as estimated by a three-state non-homogeneous hidden Markov model.

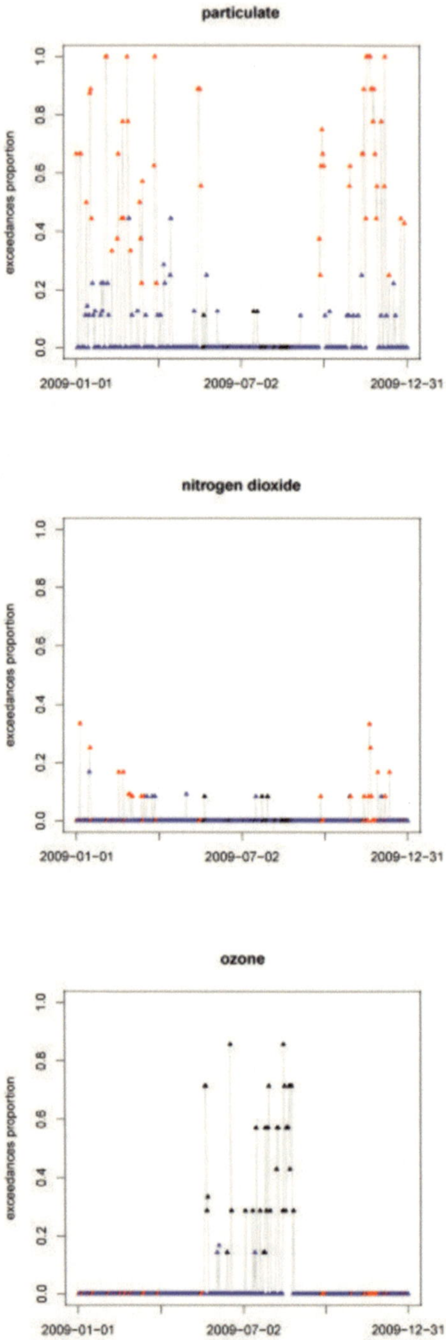

Fig. 2. observed exceedances proportions of three pollutants, clustered according to their posterior state probabilities, as estimated by a three-state non-homogeneous hidden Markov model; state 1 (black), state 2 (blue), state 3 (red).

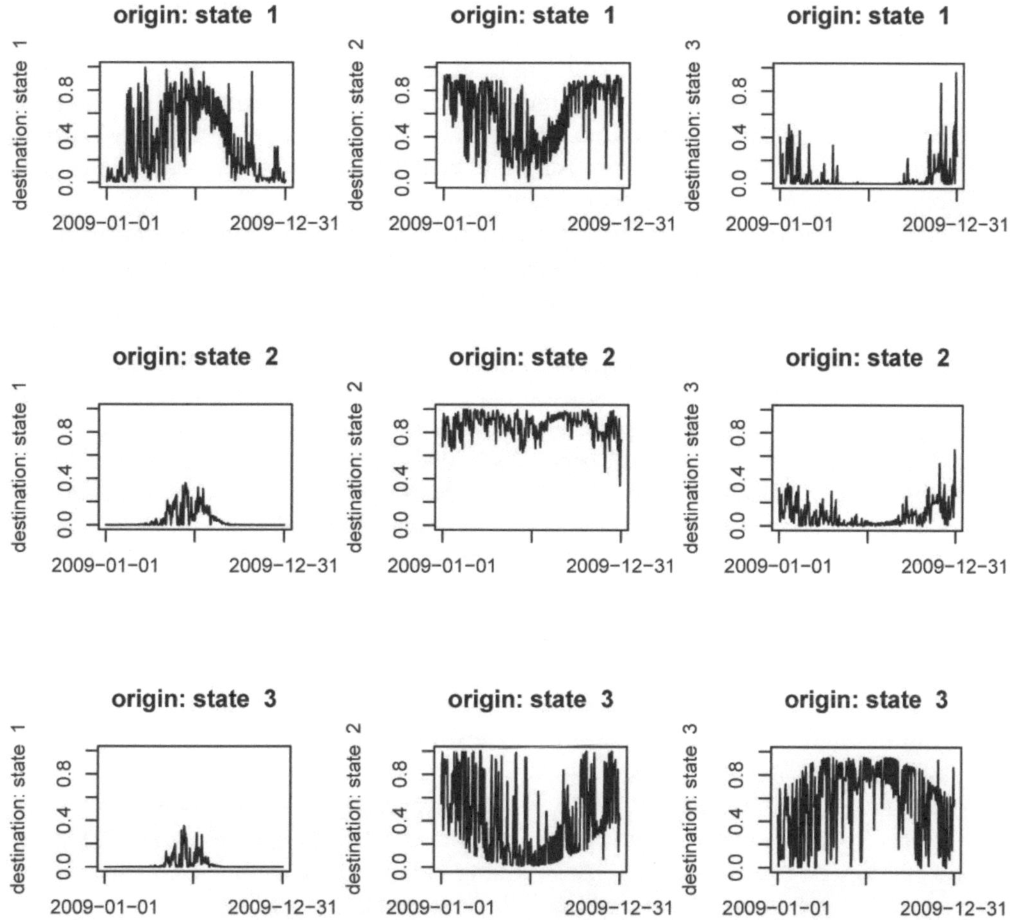

Fig. 3. Probabilities of transition from one state to another state, as estimated by a three-state non homogeneous hidden Markov model.

of the analysis is not only to build a regression model, but even to describe association among variables, the univariate approach is no longer sufficient and needs to be extended. In this context, we are likely to face complex phenomena which can be characterized by having a non-trivial correlation structure (e.g. omitted covariates may affect more than one variable), which can be captured by introducing a latent structure. Furthermore, it is well known that, when responses are correlated, the univariate approach is less efficient than the multivariate one.

To estimate multivariate exceedances probabilities, we have fitted a NHHM model to a time series of multivariate exceedances data. Non-homogeneous hidden Markov models are parsimonious specification of non-stationary time series and can be generalized along a number of dimensions, to accommodate continuous or discrete multivariate data and modularize the data dependence structure of the data according to the purpose of an analysis. In our case study, a NHHM model provides a parsimonious representation of a time series of multivariate exceedances by means of three latent regimes that are temporally persistent or

transient, according to time-varying weather conditions. Estimates of the effects of factors that may influence both the occurrence and the persistence of specific exceedances are in terms of log-odds, which helps to communicate results to nonspecialists. The clear-cut separation of the three latent classes supports a model-based clustering of days into periods of severe pollution episodes and periods of reasonable quality of the air. Estimated transition probabilities allow to interpret the persistence of pollution episodes in terms of the general conditions of the weather in the area of interest.
The NHHM model presented in this paper provides a model-based clustering of days, according to different patterns of multi-pollutants exceedances probabilities. Estimated posterior probabilities of the two latent regimes can be then interpreted as an air quality index, which exploits maximum likelihood estimates to provide a daily summary of multivariate exceedances data. Model-based air quality indexes are certainly more difficult to explain to the general public than data-driven indexes that are based on a deterministic aggregation of the hourly measurements on each pollutant at every site in a monitoring network. However a data-driven approach (Bruno and Cocchi, 2002) does not use probabilistic assumptions on the data generating process, and, as a result, there are no obvious methods either to construct these indexes in the presence of missing data or to predict their values.

6. References

Banachewicz, K., Lucas, A. and Vaart, A. (2007). Modeling Portfolio Defaults Using Hidden Markov Models with Covariates. Econometrics Journal, 10, 1-18.

Baum, L.E., Petrie, T., Soules, G. and Weiss, N. (1970). A maximization technique occurring in the statistical analysis of probabilistic functions in Markov chains. The Annals of Mathematical Statistics, 41:164-171.

Bellone, E., Hughes, J.P., Guttorp, P. (2000). A hidden Markov model for downscaling synoptic atmospheric patterns to precipitation amounts. Climatology Research, 15, 1-12.

Betrò, B., Bodini, A. and Cossu, Q.A. (2008). Using hidden Markov model to analyse extreme rainfall events in Central-East Sardinia. Envirionmetrics 19: 702-713.

Boys, R.J., Henderson, D.A. and Wilkinson, D.J.(2000). Detecting homogeneous segments in DNA sequence by using hidden Markov models. Journal of the Royal Statistical Society - Series C 49:269-285.

Bruno, F. and Cocchi, D. (2002). A unified strategy for building simple air quality indeces. Envirometrics, 13:243-261

Cappé, O., Moulines, E. and Rydén, T. (2005). Inference in hidden Markov models. Springer Series in Statistics.

Celeux, G. (1998) Bayesian inference for mixture: the label switching problem. In COMPSTAT '98. Proc. Comiplutationial Statistics Conf. (eds R. W. Payne and P. J. Green), pp. 227–232. Heidelberg: Physica.

Charles, S.P., Bates, B.C., Hughes, J.P. (1999) A spatiotemporal model for downscaling precipitation occurrence and amounts. Journal of Geophysical Research - Atmospheres, 104, 31657-31669.

Charles, S.P., Bates, B.C., Smith, I.N., Hughes, J.P. (2004) Statistical downscaling of daily precipitation from observed and modelled atmospheric fields. Hydrological Processes, 18, 1373-1394.

Diebolt, F.X., Lee, J.H. and Weinbach, G.C.(1994). Regime switching with time varying transition probabilities. In C.P. Hargreaves, editor, Nonstationary Time Series Analysis and Cointegration, pp. 283–302.

Dong, M., Dong, Y., Kuang, Y., He, D., Erdal, S. and Kenski, D. (2009) PM2.5 concentration prediction using hidden semi-Markov model-based times series data mining. Expert Systems with Applications, 36: 9046-9055.

Durland, J. M. and McCurdy (1994). Duration-dependent transitions in a Markov model of U.S. GNP growth. Journal of Business and Economic Statistics, 12, 279-288.

Efron, B. and Tibshirani, R.J. (1993). An introduction to bootstrap. Chapman & Hall: New York.

Filardo, A. J. and Gordon, S. F. (1998). Business cycle durations. Journal of Econometrics, 85, 99-123.

Gray, S. F. (1996). Modeling the conditional distribution of interest rates as a regime-switching process. Journal of Financial Economics, 42, 27-62

Hinde, J.P. and Wood, A.T.A. (1987). Binomial variance component models with a non-parametric assumption concerning random effects. In Longitudinal Data Analysis, R. Crouchley (ed.). Averbury, Aldershot, Hants.

Hughes, J.P. and Guttorp, P. (1994). A class of stochastic models for relating synoptic atmospheric patterns to regional hydrologic phenomena. Water Resources Research, 30:1535-1546.

Hughes, J.P., Guttorp, P. and Charles, S.P. (1999). A Non-Homogeneous Hidden Markov Model for Precipitation Occurrence. Applied Statistics, 48:15–30.

Kim, C., Piger, J. and Startz, R. (2008). Estimation of Markov regime-switching regression models with endogenous switching. Journal of Econometrics, 143, 263-273.

Lagona, F. (2005). Air Quality Indices via Non Homogeneous Hidden Markov Models. Proceeding of the Italian Statistical Society Conference on Statistics and Environment, Contributed Papers, CLEUP, Padova, 91-94

MacDonald, I.L. and Zucchini, W. (1997). Hidden Markov and other models for discrete valued time series, Chapman & Hall, London.

McLachlan, G.J and Peel, D. (2000). Finite Mixture Models. Wiley. New York.

Masson, P. and Ruge-Murcia, F. J. (2005). Explaining the transition between exchange rate regimes. Scandinavian Journal of Economics, 107, 261-278.

Meligkotsidou, L. and Dellaportas, P. (2010). Forecasting with non-homogeneous hidden Markov models. Statistics and Computing, in press

Peria, M. S. M. (2002). A regime-switching approach to the study of speculative attacks: A focus on the EMS cricis. Empirical Economics, 27, 299-334.

Richardson, S. and Green, P. J. (1997) On Bayesian analysis of mixtures with an unknown number of components (with discussion). Journal of the Royal Statistical Society - Series B 59: 731–792.

Robertson A.W., Kirshner S. and Smyth P. (2004) Downscaling of daily rainfall occurrence over Northeast Brazil using a hidden Markov model. Journal of Climate, 17(22):4407-4424.

Spezia L. (2006). Bayesian analysis of non-homogeneous hidden Markov models. Journal of Statistical Computation and Simulation, 76: 713-725.

Spezia, L. (2009). Reversible jump and the label switching problem in hidden Markov models. Journal of Statistical Planning and Inference, 139: 2305-2315

Turner, D.B. (1994). Workbook of Atmospheric Dispersion Estimates. Lewis Publishers.

Visser, I., Raijmakers, M.E.J. and Molenaar, P.C.M. (2000). Confidence intervals for hidden MArkov model parameters. British Journal of Mathematical and Statistical Psychology 53: 317-327.

Wang, P. and Puterman, M.L. (1998). Mixed Logistic Regression Models. Journal of Agricultural, Biological, and Environmental Statistics, 3:175-200.

Welch, L.R. (2003). Hidden Markov models and the Baum-Welch algorithm. IEEE Information Theory Society Newsletter, 53(4):10–15

Wong, C.S. and Li, W.K. (2001). On a logistic mixture autoregressive model. Biometrika 88(3): 833-846.

World Health Organization (2006). Air quality guidelines for particulate matter, ozone, nitrogen dioxide and sulfur dioxide. Global update 2005. WHO Press: Geneva.

Zucchini, W. and Guttorp, P. (1991). A hidden Markov model for space-time precipitaion. Water Resources Research, 27, 1917–1923.

Part 3

Hidden Markov Models in Image and Spatial Structures Analysis

11

Continuous Hidden Markov Models for Depth Map-Based Human Activity Recognition

Md. Zia Uddin and Tae-Seong Kim
Department of Biomedical Engineering
Kyung Hee University
Republic of Korea

1. Introduction

There is an enormous volume of literature on the applications of Hidden Markov Models (HMMs) to a broad range of pattern recognition tasks. The first practical application of HMMs is much based on the work of Rabiner et al (Lawrence & Rabiner, 1989) for speech recognition. Since then, HMMs have been extensively used in various scientific fields such as computational biology, biomedical signal interpretation, image classification and segmentation, etc.

An HMM can be described as a stochastic finite-state automation that can be used to model time sequential data. In general, there are four basic parts involved in the HMM: namely states, initial state distribution, state transition matrix, and state observation matrix. A state represents a property or condition that an HMM might have at a particular time. Initial state distribution indicates each state probability of an HMM at the time of starting the modeling procedure of an event. The state transition matrix represents the probabilities among the states. The observation matrix contains the observation probabilities from each state. Once the architecture of an HMM is defined with the four essential components, training of the HMM is required. To train, the first step is to classify features into a specific number of clusters, generating a codebook. Then from the codebook, symbol sequences are generated through vector quantization. These symbol sequences later are used to model spatiotemporal patterns in an HMM. The number of states and initial state distribution of HMM are empirically determined in general. The state transition and observation probabilities from each state are usually initialized with uniform distributions and later adapted according to the training symbol sequences. In practice, there are some well-established training algorithms available to automatically optimize the parameters of the HMM. The Baum-Welch (Baum et al., 1970) training procedure is a standard algorithm which uses the Maximum Likelihood Estimation (MLE) criterion. In this training algorithm, the training symbol sequences are used to estimate the HMM parameters. Finally, a testing sequence gets analyzed by the trained HMMs to be recognized.

In an HMM, the underlying processes are usually not observable, but they can be observed through another set of stochastic processes that produces continuous or discrete observations (Lawrence & Rabiner, 1989), which lead to discrete or continuous HMMs respectively. In the discrete HMMs, the observation sequences are vector-quantized using a codebook to select discrete symbols. Though the discrete symbols for the observations simplify the modeling, they have limited representation power. As the discrete symbols are obtained from the codebook, which is generated using some unsupervised classification algorithm such as the K-means (Kanungu et al., 2000) or the Linde, Buzo, and Gray (LBG)'s clustering algorithm (Linde et al., 1980), the quantized vectors may not be accurate: the quantized vectors represent incorrect symbols sometimes. In fact, modeling of an event is very much dependent on the codebook generation process in the discrete HMM that may result in unsatisfactory results. To mitigate this problem, continuous probability distribution functions for the observations can be used to model the time-sequential information that enables to get a model as accurate as possible. In the continuous HMMs, the observation probability distribution functions are a mixture multivariate of Gaussians. The architecture of a continuous HMM, the number of Gaussian components per state, and the number of training iterations are usually empirically determined. Once the event is modeled by the continuous HMM, one can calculate the probabilities of the observation sequence and the probable underlying state sequences. The principal advantage of using the continuous HMM is the ability to model the event directly without involving vector quantization. However, the continuous HMM requires much longer training and recognition time, especially when a mixture of several Gaussian probability density components is used.

Among a wide range of application areas in which HMMs have been applied to recognize complex time-sequential events, human activity recognition (HAR) is one active area that utilizes spatio-temporal information from video to recognize various human activities. In this video-based HAR methodology, it is essential to model and recognize key features from time sequential activity images in which various activities are represented in time-sequential spatial silhouettes. Once the silhouettes from the activity video images are obtained, each activity is recognized by comparing with the trained activity features. Thus, feature extraction, learning, and recognition play vital roles in this regard. In the video-based HAR, binary silhouettes are most commonly employed where useful features are derived from activity videos to represent different human activities (Yamato et al., 1992; Cohen & Lim, 2003; Niu & Abdel-mottaleb, 2004; Niu & Abdel-mottaleb, 2005; Agarwal & Triggs, 2006; Uddin et al., 2008a). To extract the human activity silhouette features, the most popular feature extraction technique applied in the video-based HAR is Principal Component Analysis (PCA) (Niu & Abdel-Mottaleb, 2004; Niu & Abdel-Mottaleb, 2005). PCA is an unsupervised second order statistical approach to find useful basis for data representation. It finds PCs at the optimally reduced dimension of the input. For human activity recognition, it focuses on the global information of the binary silhouettes, which has been actively applied. However, PCA is only limited to second order statistical analysis, allowing up to decorrelation of data. Lately, a higher order statistical method called Independent Component Analysis (ICA) is being actively exploited in the face recognition area (Bartlett et al., 2002; Kwak & Pedrycz, 2007; Yang et al., 2005) and has shown superior performance over PCA. It has also been utilized successfully in other fields such as speech recognition (Kwon & Lee, 2004). In (Uddin et al., 2008a), we introduced local binary silhouette features through ICA to represent human body in different activities usefully. To extend the IC features, we applied Linear Discriminant Analysis (LDA) on them to build more robust features and applied for improved HAR. To model the time-sequential human activity features, HMMs have been used effectively in many works (Yamato et al., 1992; Sun et al., 2002; Nakata, 2006; Niu & Abdel-Mottaleb, 2004; Niu & Abdel-Mottaleb, 2005; Uddin et al., 2008a; Uddin et al., 2008b). In (Yamato et al., 1992), the binary silhouettes were employed to develop some distinct discrete HMMs for different activities. In (Uddin et al., 2008a) and

(Uddin et al., 2008b), we applied the discrete HMM to train and recognize different human activities from binary and depth silhouettes features respectively. Continuous HMMs have also been applied in numerous HAR works (Sun et al., 2002; Niu & Abdel-mottaleb, 2004; Niu & Abdel-mottaleb, 2005; Nakata, 2006). In (Sun et al., 2002) and (Nakata, 2006), the authors utilized optical flows to build continuous HMMs for recognition. In (Niu & Abdel-Mottaleb, 2004) and (Niu & Abdel-Mottaleb, 2005), the authors applied binary silhouette and optical flow motion features in combination with continuous HMM to recognize different human activities.

Although the binary silhouettes are very commonly employed to represent a wide variety of body configurations, it sometimes produces ambiguities by representing the same silhouette for different postures from different activities. For instance, if a person performs some hand movement activities in the direction toward the camera, different postures can correspond to the same silhouette due to its binary-level (i.e., white or black) pixel intensity distribution. One example is shown in Fig. 1, which shows the RGB, binary, and depth images of right hand-up-down, left hand-up-down, both hands-up-down, clapping, and boxing activity respectively. It is obvious that the binary silhouettes are a poor choice to separate these different postures. Besides, from the binary silhouettes, it is not possible to obtain the difference between the far and near parts of human body in the activity video. For better silhouette representation than binary, in (Uddin et al., 2008b), we proposed IC features from the time-sequential depth silhouettes to be used with the discrete HMMs for robust HAR. The depth silhouettes better represent the human body postures than the binary by differentiating the body parts by means of different depth values. Thus, depth silhouettes can be utilized to overcome the aforementioned limitations available in binary silhouettes.

In this chapter, with a brief introduction of HMMs, especially the continuous HMM, we present its application to model various human activities based on the spatio-temporal depth silhouette features. Then, we show how to recognize various human activities from time-series depth maps (i.e., depth videos) of human activities. We demonstrate that superior recognition can be achieved by means of the continuous HMM and depth silhouette features in recognizing various human activities, which are not easily discernible with binary silhouettes. One of the aims of our HAR system is to be used in smart homes to monitor and recognize important daily human activities. This should allow continuous daily, monthly, and yearly analysis of human activity patterns, habits, and needs. In addition, when any abnormal activity is recognized, the system can automatically generate an alarm to draw attention of the smart home inhabitants to draw their attention to avoid unexpected injury and to provide assistance if needed.

The remaining sections of this chapter are structured as follows. Section 2 describes the basics of continuous HMMs. Section 3 explains the methodology of the HAR system from video image acquisition and depth silhouette feature extraction to modeling and training activity continuous HMMs for recognition. Section 4 shows the experimental results utilizing different feature extraction approaches with HMMs. Finally, Section 5 draws the concluding remarks.

2. Continuous Hidden Markov Model

HMM is considered to be one of the most suitable techniques for modeling and recognizing time sequential features (Lawrence & Rabiner, 1989; Kwon & Lee, 2004). Basically, a continuous HMM consists of two interrelated processes. The first process is related to an underlying, unobservable Markov chain with a finite number of states, a state transition

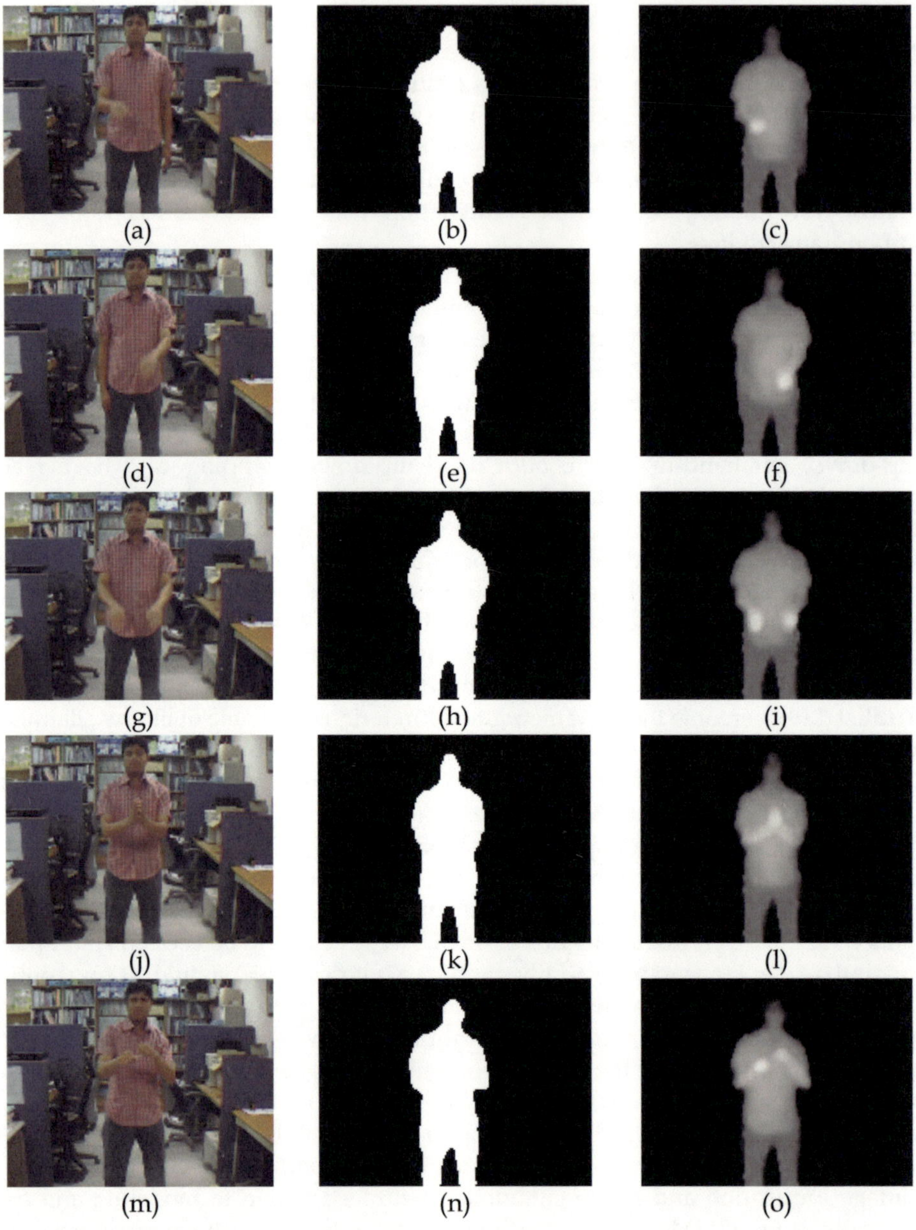

Fig. 1. RGB and their corresponding binary and depth images of (a)-(c) right hand-up-down, (d)-(f) left hand-up-down, (g)-(i) both hands-up-down, (j)-(l) clapping, and (m)-(o) boxing activity respectively.

probability, and an initial state probability distribution. The second consists of a set of density functions representing the observations associated with each state. As a continuous HMM can decode the time-sequential continuous information, it has been applied in many important applications such as speech recognition (Lawrence & Rabiner, 1989), human activity recognition (Sun et al., 2002), gesture recognition (Frolov et al., 2008) etc. A continuous HMM denoted as $H=\{\Xi,\pi,A,B\}$ can be expressed as follows. $\Xi=\{\Xi_1,\Xi_2,...,\Xi_q\}$ indicates the states where q is the number of states. The state of the model at time t can be expressed as $\Omega_t \in \Xi,\ 1\le t\le T$ where T is the length of the observation sequence. The initial probability of the states π can be represented as

$$\pi = \{\pi_j\},\ \sum_{j=1}^{q} \pi_j = 1. \tag{1}$$

The state transition probability matrix is denoted as A where a_{ij} denotes the probability of a changing state from i to j i.e.,

$$a_{i,j} = \mathrm{P}(\Omega_{t+1} = \Xi_j \mid q_t = \Xi_i),\ \ 1 \le i,\ j \le q, \tag{2}$$

$$\sum_{j=1}^{q} a_{i,j} = 1,\ \ 1 \le i \le q. \tag{3}$$

The observation probability matrix is denoted as B where the probability $b_j(d)$ represents the probability of observing d from a state j that can be expressed as

$$\mathrm{b}_j(d) = \mathrm{P}(O_t = d \mid \Omega_t = \Xi_j),\ \ 1 \le j \le q. \tag{4}$$

Though there are various types of HMMs (Lawrence & Rabiner, 1989), one of the popular HMMs is the left-to-right model as shown in Fig. 2. In this model, the initial probability of the states π be initialized as {1,0,0,0} if there are four states and the modeling procedure is to be started from the first state. The transition matrix A can be initialized according to the transition between the states. The initial transitions can be uniformly distributed based on the connections between the states. Thus, the transition matrix can be represented as

$$A = \begin{bmatrix} 0.333 & 0.333 & 0.333 & 0 \\ 0 & 0.333 & 0.333 & 0.333 \\ 0 & 0 & 0.5 & 0.5 \\ 0 & 0 & 0 & 1 \end{bmatrix} \tag{5}$$

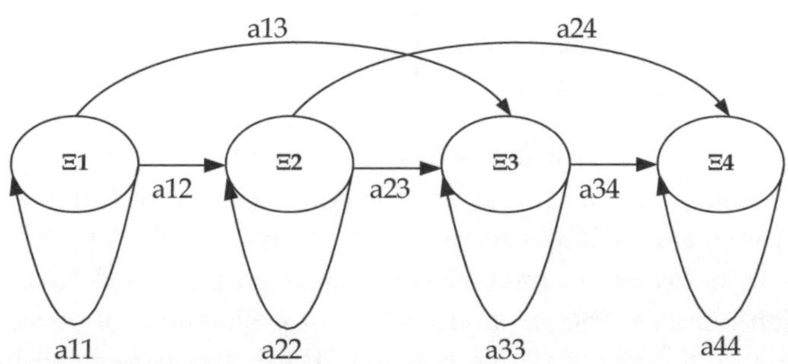

Fig. 2. A four state left-to-right HMM.

In the continuous observation probability density function matrix B, the commonly used distribution to describe the observation densities is the Gaussian one. To represent the continuous observation probability matrix, the mean and covariance are utilized. Weight coefficients are necessary to use during the mixture of the probability density function (pdf). Thus, the observation probability of O_t at time t from state j can be represented as

$$b_j(O_t) = \sum_{k=1}^{M} c_{j,k} b_{j,k}(O_t), \quad 1 \le j \le q, \tag{6}$$

$$\sum_{k=1}^{M} c_{j,k} = 1, \quad 1 \le j \le q \tag{7}$$

where c represents the weighting coefficients, M the number of mixtures, and O_t the observation feature vector at time t. The Baum-Welch algorithm (Baum et al., 1970) can be applied to estimate the HMM parameters as

$$\gamma_t(i) = \frac{\alpha_t(i)\beta_t(i)}{\sum_{i=1}^{q} \alpha_t(i)\beta_t(i)}, \tag{8}$$

$$\gamma_t(i,j) = \frac{\alpha_t(i)a_{i,j}b_j(O_{t+1})\beta_{t+1}(j)}{\sum_{i=1}^{q}\sum_{j=1}^{q} \alpha_t(i)a_{i,j}b_j(O_{t+1})\beta_{t+1}(j)}, \tag{9}$$

$$\xi_t(j,k) = \frac{\sum_{i=1}^{q} \alpha_t(i)a_{i,j}c_{j,k}g_{j,k}(O_t)\beta_t(j)}{\sum_{i=1}^{q}\sum_{j=1}^{q} \alpha_t(i)a_{i,j}c_{j,k}g_{j,k}(O_t)\beta_t(j)}, \tag{10}$$

$$g_{j,k}(O_t) = \mathrm{N}(x \mid \mu_{j,k}, \Sigma_{j,k}), \tag{11}$$

$$g_{j,k}(O_t) = \sum_{k=1}^{M} c_{j,k} \frac{1}{(2\pi)^{P/2} \, |\Sigma_{j,k}|} \exp\left\{-\frac{1}{2}(O_t - \mu_{j,k})^T \Sigma_{j,k}^{-1} (O_t - \mu_{j,k})^T\right\} \tag{12}$$

where $\gamma_t(i)$ represents the probability of staying in the state i at time t. $\gamma_t(i,j)$ is the probability of staying in a state i at time t and a state j at time $t+1$. α and β are the forward and backward variables respectively. T contains the length of the observation sequence. $g_{j,k}(O_t)$ indicates k^{th} mixture component probability at time t, P dimension of the observation feature vector, and $\xi_t(j,k)$ probability of selecting k^{th} mixture component in state j at time t. The estimated HMM parameters can be represented as follows.

$$\hat{a}_{i,j} = \frac{\sum_{t=1}^{T-1} \gamma_t(i,j)}{\sum_{t=1}^{T} \gamma_t(i)}, \tag{13}$$

$$\hat{c}_{j,k} = \frac{\sum_{t=1}^{T} \xi_t(i,j)}{\sum_{t=1}^{T} \gamma_t(j)}, \tag{14}$$

$$\hat{\mu}_{j,k} = \frac{\sum_{t=1}^{T} \xi_t(j,k)x_t}{\sum_{t=1}^{T} \xi_t(j,k)}, \tag{15}$$

$$\hat{\Sigma}_{j,k} = \frac{\sum_{t=1}^{T} \xi_t(j,k)O_tO_t^T}{\sum_{t=1}^{T} \xi_t(j,k)} - \hat{\mu}_{j,k}\hat{\mu}_{j,k}^T \tag{16}$$

where $\hat{a}_{i,j}$ represents the estimated transition probability from the state i to the state j and $\hat{c}_{j,k}$ the estimated k^{th} mixture weights in state j, $\hat{\mu}_{j,k}$ the estimated mean of kth mixture in state j, and $\hat{\Sigma}_{j,k}$ the estimated covariance of kth mixture in state j.

3. Continuous HMM-based HAR system

In our HAR system, we apply the continuous HMM to model and recognize various human activities from time-sequential depth silhouette features. Our HAR system consists of depth silhouette extraction, feature extraction, modeling, and recognition via the continuous HMM. Fig. 3 shows the key processes of our depth silhouette feature-based activity recognition system.

3.1 Depth silhouette extraction

A Gaussian probability distribution function is used to remove background from the RGB frames and to extract the binary Region of Interest (ROI) based on which depth ROIs are extracted from the corresponding depth images acquired by a depth camera. ZCAM™, a commercial camera developed by the 3DV system, is used to acquire the RGB and depth images of different activities (Iddan & Yahav, 2001). The image sensor in the ZCAM produces the RGB and distance information for the object captured by the camera.
To capture the depth information, the image sensor first senses the surface boundaries of the object and arranges each object according to the distance information. The depth value indicates the range of each pixel in the scene to the camera as a grayscale value such that the shorter ranged pixels have brighter and longer ones contains darker values. The system provides both RGB and depth images simultaneously. Figs. 4(a) to (e) show a background

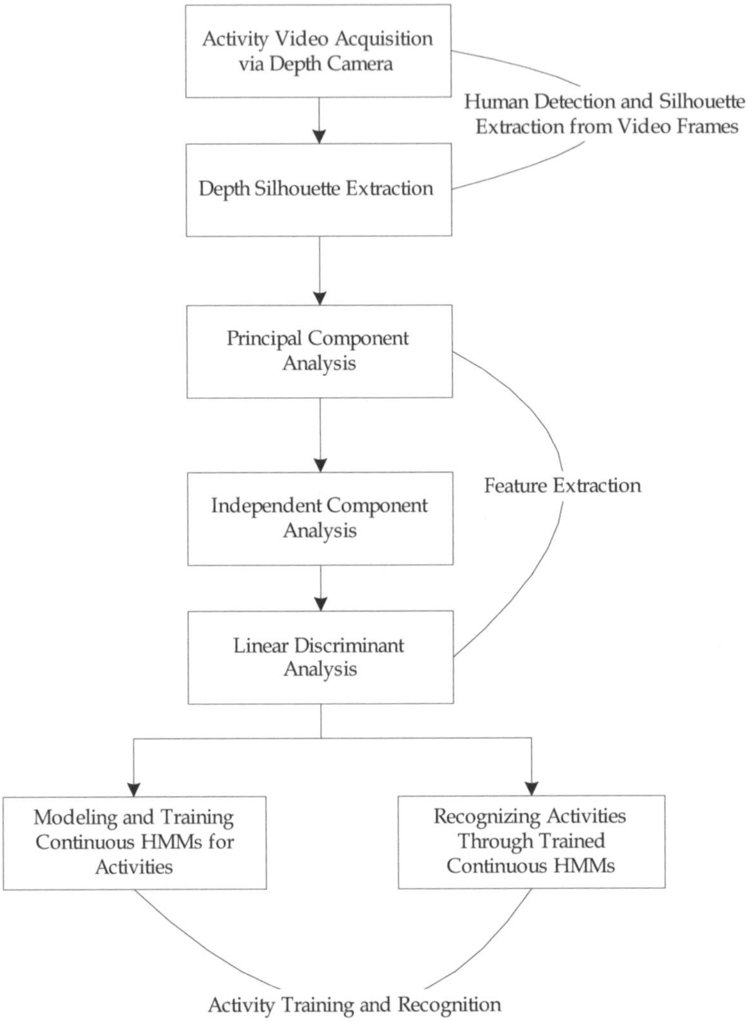

Fig. 3. Depth Silhouette-based human activity recognition system using continuous HMMs.

image, a RGB frame from a both hands up-down sequence, its corresponding binary, depth, and pseudo color image respectively. In the depth image, the higher pixel intensity indicates the near and the lower the far distance. For instance, in Fig. 4(d), the forearm regions are brighter than the body. Thus, different body components used in different activities can be represented effectively in the depth map or the depth information and hence can contribute effectively in the feature generation. On the contrary, the binary silhouettes contain a flat pixel value in the human body and hence cannot distinguish the body postures effectively. Consequently, by means of the infrared sensor-based camera, we obtained both the RGB and depth images of distinguished activities at 30fps to apply on our HAR system.

Since the raw depth images acquired by the camera consist of random noises, median filtering was applied on the depth images to make them smooth. Then, the depth silhouette was extracted from every depth image and resized to the size of 50x50. Fig. 5 shows sequences of depth silhouettes from right hand up-down, left hand up-down, both hands

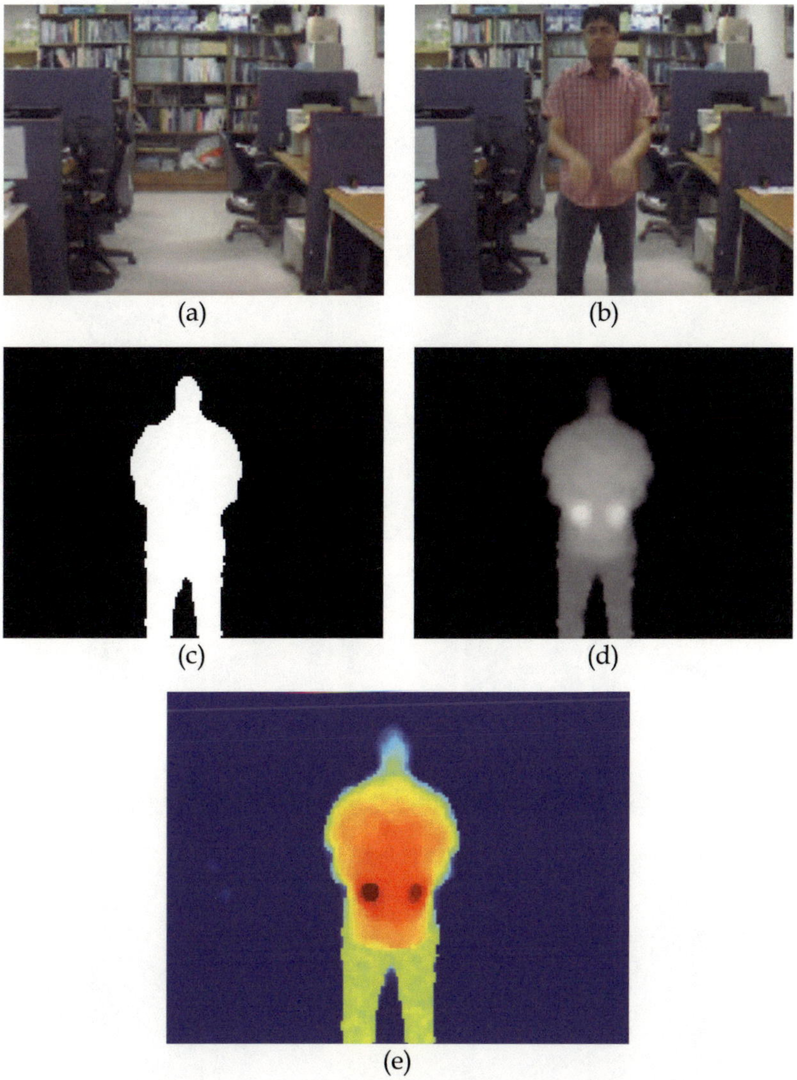

Fig. 4. Sample video images of (a) a background image, (b) a RGB frame from a both hands up-down sequence, (c) its corresponding binary, (d) depth, and (e) pseudo color image.

up-down, clapping, and boxing activities. To apply the feature extraction, each silhouette was converted to a vector with the size of the total pixels (i.e., 2500) in it. The first step before feature extraction is to make all the silhouette vectors zero mean.

3.2 Principal component analysis on depth silhouettes

After preprocessing of the silhouette vectors, we proceed to the dimension reduction process as the training database contains the silhouette vectors with a high dimension (i.e., 2500). In this regard, we applied PCA, one of the most popular methods to approximate original data in the lower dimensional feature space (Niu & Abdel-mottaleb, 2004; Niu & Abdel-mottaleb, 2005; Uddin et al., 2008a; Uddin et al., 2008b; Uddin et al., 2009). The main

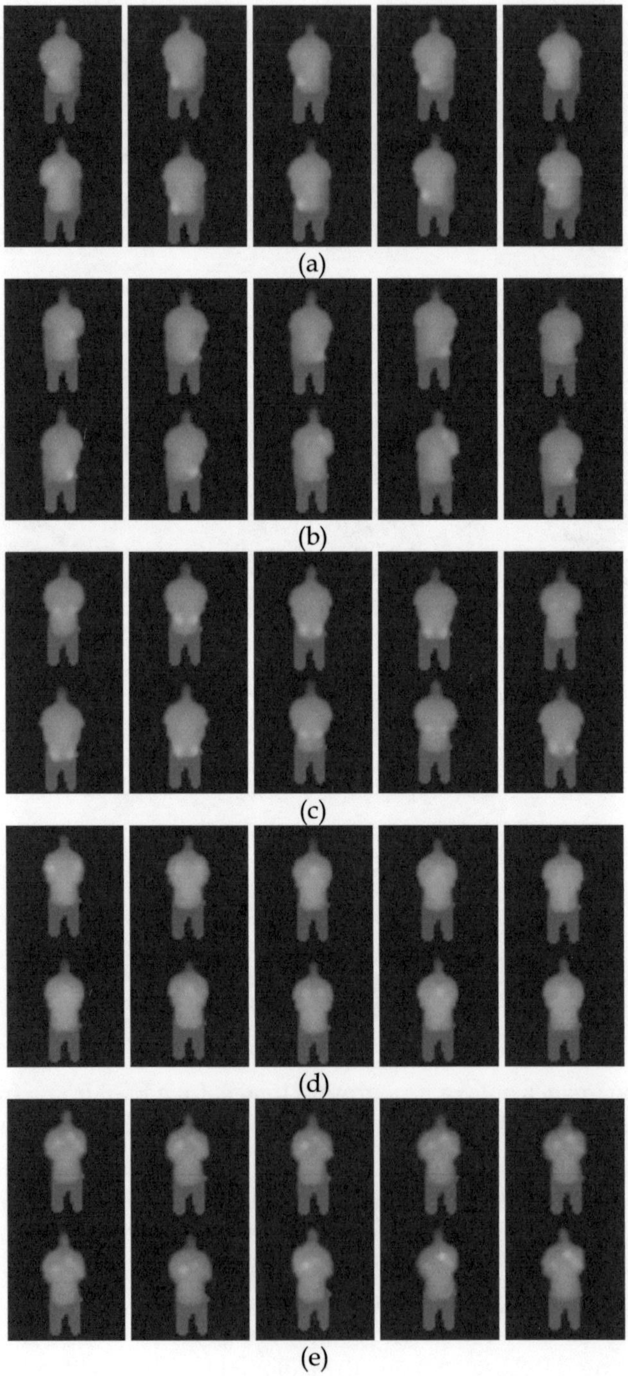

Fig. 5. Ten depth silhouettes from image sequences of (a) right hand up-down, (b) left hand up-down, (c) both hands up-down, (d) clapping, and (e) boxing activity.

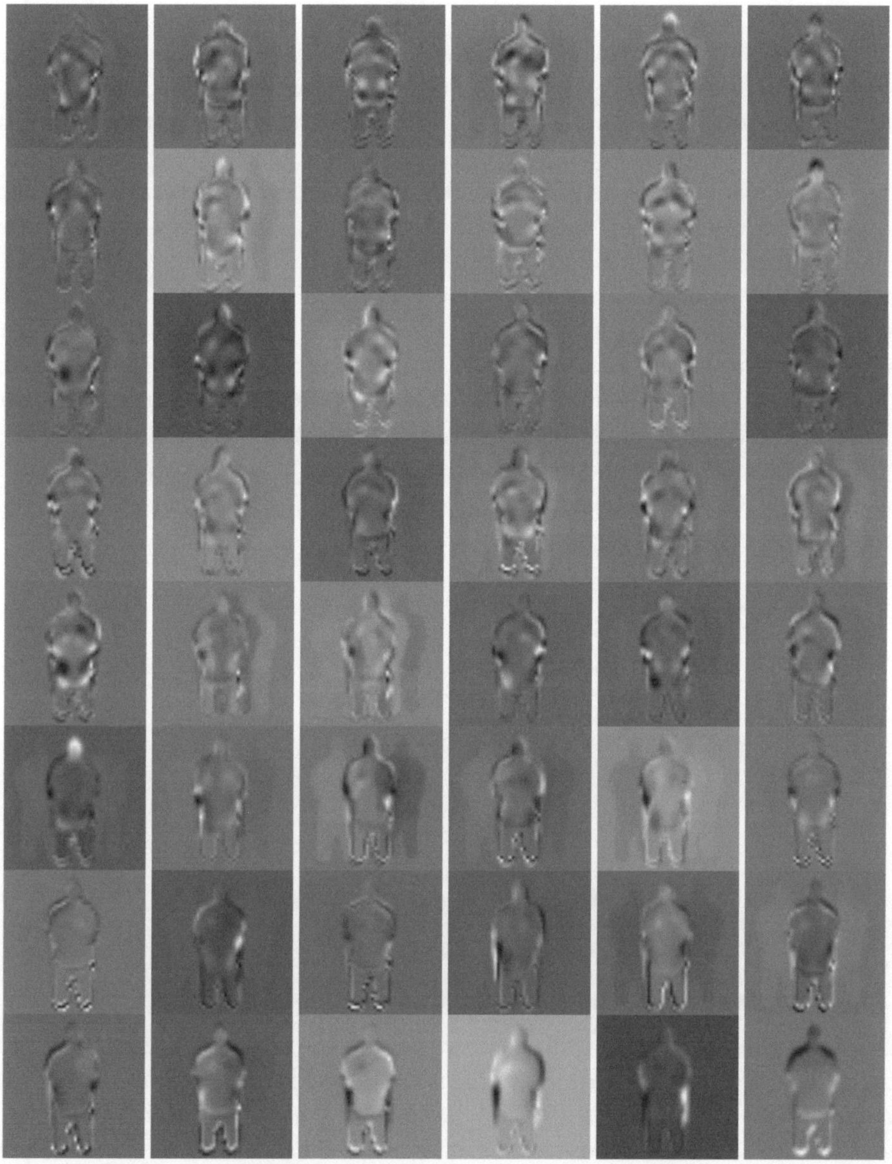

Fig. 6. Forty eight PCs of all the depth silhouettes of the five activities.

approach is to compute the eigenvectors of the covariance data matrix Q and then approximate using the linear combination of top eigenvectors. The covariance matrix of the sample training depth silhouette vectors and the PCs of the covariance matrix can be calculated as

$$Q = \frac{1}{T}\sum_{i=1}^{T}(\tilde{X}_i \tilde{X}_i^T), \tag{17}$$

$$\Lambda = E^T Q E \tag{18}$$

where E represents the matrix of eigenvectors and Λ diagonal matrix of the eigenvalues. The eigenvector corresponding to the largest eigenvalue indicates the axis of largest variance and the next largest one is the orthogonal axis of the largest one indicating the second largest variance and so on.

Basically, the eigenvalues close to zero carry negligible variance and hence can be neglected. So, the several m eigenvectors corresponding to the largest eigenvalues can be used to define the subspace. Thus, the full dimensional depth silhouette vectors can be easily represented in the reduced dimension. After applying PCA on the depth silhouettes of various activities, it generates global features representing most frequently moving parts of human body in all activities. However, PCA being a second order statistics-based analysis can only extract global information (Niu & Abdel-mottaleb, 2004; Niu & Abdel-mottaleb, 2005; Uddin et al., 2008a; Uddin et al., 2008b; Uddin et al., 2009). Fig.6 shows 48 basis images after PCA is applied on 2250 images of the five activities. The basis images are the resized eigenvectors (i.e., 50x50) normalized in a grayscale. Fig. 7 shows the top 150 eigenvalues corresponding to the first 150 eigenvectors.

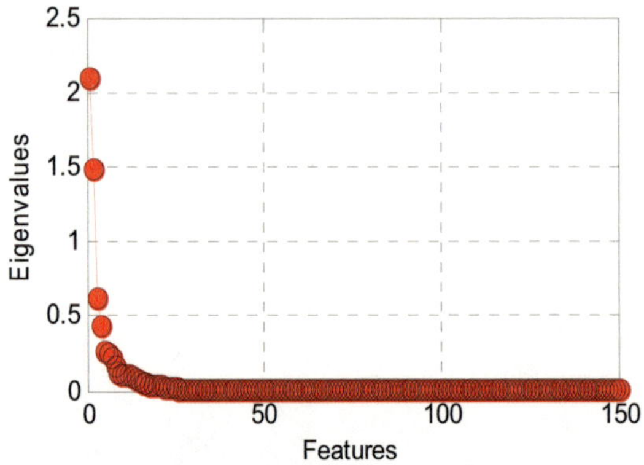

Fig. 7. Top 150 eigenvalues of the training depth silhouettes of the five activities.

If there are k number of depth silhouette vectors in the database where each vector is t dimensional and top m eigenvectors are chosen after applying PCA, the size of the PCA representations of all silhouette vectors becomes kxm where each silhouette vector represents the size of $1xm$. For our experiments, we considered 150 PCs after applying PCA over the training database of 2250 silhouettes of the five activities and as a result, m becomes 150 and the size of the E_m is 2500x150 where each column vector represents a PC. Thus, projecting each silhouette image vector with the size of 1x2500 onto the PCA feature space, it can be reduced to 1x150.

3.3 Independent component analysis on depth silhouettes

Independent Component Analysis (ICA) is a higher order statistical approach than PCA for separating a mixture of signals into its components. The most well-known applications of ICA are in the field of signal and image processing such as biomedical signals (Jung et. Al,

2001), speech (Lawrence & Rabiner, 1989; Kwon & Lee, 2004), face (Yang et al., 2005), etc. ICA has been recently applied in the field of facial expression analysis areas to focus on the local face features (Kwak & Pedrycz, 2007; Uddin et al., 2009).

Basically, ICA finds the statistically independent basis images. The basic idea of ICA is to represent a set of random observed variables using basis functions where the components are statistically independent. If S is a collection of basis images and X a collection of input images then the relation between X and S is modeled as

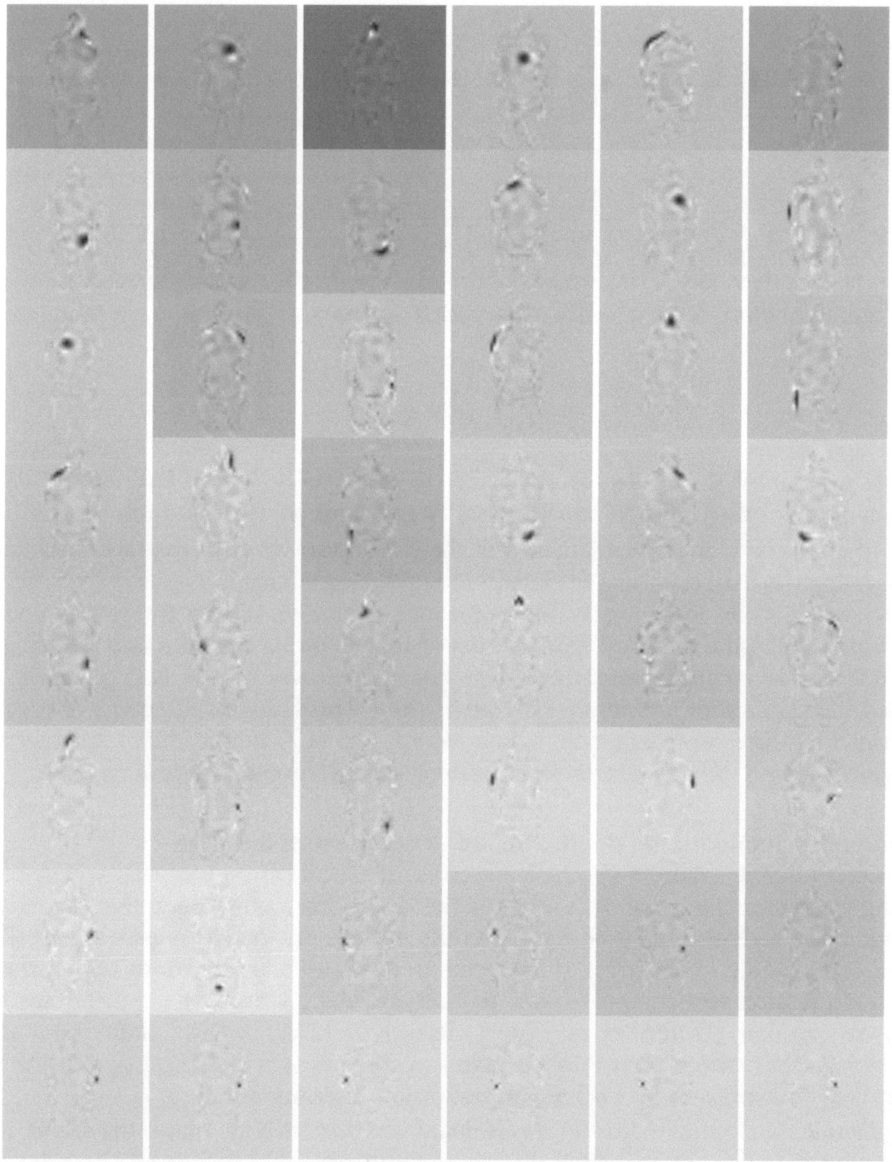

Fig. 8. Forty eight ICs of all the depth silhouettes of the five activities.

$$X = AS \tag{19}$$

where A represents an unknown linear mixing matrix of full rank.
An ICA algorithm learns the weight matrix W, which is inverse of mixing matrix A. W is used to recover a set of independent basis images S. The ICA basis images reflect local feature information rather than global information as in PCA. ICA basis images show the local features of the body parts in activity. Fig. 8 shows 48 ICA basis images for all activities. Before applying ICA, PCA is used to reduce the dimension of the image data. ICA is performed on E_m as follows.

$$S = WE_m^T, \tag{20}$$

$$E_m^T = W^{-1}S, \tag{21}$$

$$X_r = VW^{-1}S \tag{22}$$

where V is the projection of the images X on E_m and X_r the reconstructed original images. The IC representation I_i of ith silhouette vector $\tilde{X}_i$ from an activity image sequence can be expressed as

$$I_i = \tilde{X}_i E_m W^{-1}. \tag{23}$$

Since ICA is applied on the PC features in our HAR work, the size of the ICA representations of the depth silhouette vectors are same as PCA. As the top 150 PCs are chosen to apply ICA, therefore, the size of the IC features of each depth silhouette vector and the weighting matrix W are 1x150 and 150x150 respectively.
However, as PCA considers the second order moments only, it lacks information on higher order statistics. On the contrary, ICA considers higher order statistics and it identifies the independent source components from their linear mixtures. Hence, ICA provides a more powerful data representation than PCA as it tries to provide an independent rather than uncorrelated feature representation. Thus, we applied ICA in our depth silhouette-based HAR system to find out statistically independent local features for improved HAR.

3.4 LDA on the independent depth silhouette component features

Linear Discriminant Analysis (LDA) is an efficient classification tool that works based on grouping of similar classes of data. It finds the directions along which the classes are best separated by considering the within-class scatter but also the between-class scatter (Kwak & Pedrycz, 2007; Uddin et al., 2009). It has been used extensively in various applications such as facial expression recognition (Kwak & Pedrycz, 2007; Uddin et al., 2009) and human activity recognition (Uddin et al., 2008). Basically, LDA projects data onto a lower-dimensional vector space such that the ratios of the between-class scatter and the within-class scatter is maximized, thus achieving maximum discrimination.

LDA generates an optimal linear discriminant function which maps the input into the classification space based on which the class identification of the samples can be decided (Kwak & Pedrycz, 2007). The within-class scatter matrix, S_W and the between-class scatter matrix, S_B are computed by the following equations:

$$S_B = \sum_{i=1}^{c} J_i(\overline{m_i} - \overline{\overline{m}})(\overline{m_i} - \overline{\overline{m}})^T, \quad (24)$$

$$S_W = \sum_{i=1}^{c} \sum_{m_k \in C_i} (m_k - \overline{m_i})(m_k - \overline{m_i})^T \quad (25)$$

where J_i is the number of vectors in i^{th} class C_i. c is the number of classes and in our case, it represents the number of activities. m represents the mean of all vectors, m_i the mean of the class C_i and m_k the vector of a specific class. The optimal discrimination matrix D_{opt} is chosen from the maximization of ratio of the determinant of the between and within-class scatter matrix as

$$D_{opt} = \arg\ \max_{D} \frac{|D^T S_B D|}{|D^T S_W D|} \quad (26)$$

where D_{opt} is the set of discriminant vectors corresponding to the $(c-1)$ largest generalized eigenvalues λ problem as

$$S_B d_i = \lambda_i S_W d_i. \quad (27)$$

The LDA algorithm seeks the vectors in the underlying space to create the best discrimination among different classes. Thus, the extracted local feature-based ICA representations of the binary silhouettes of different activities can be extended by LDA. LDA on the IC features for the depth silhouette vectors can be represented as

$$F_i = I_i D_{opt}^T. \quad (28)$$

Fig. 9 depicts the 3-D representation of the depth silhouette features after applying on three ICs that are chosen on the basis of top kurtosis values. Fig. 10 shows a 3-D plot of LDA on

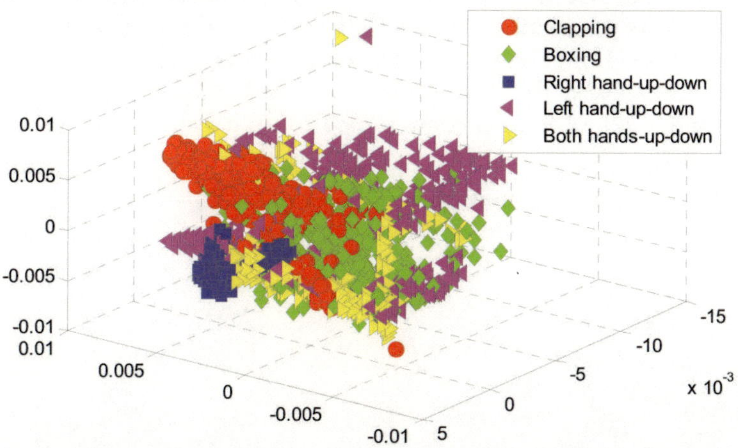

Fig. 9. A plot of the three IC features of 2250 depth silhouettes of all activities.

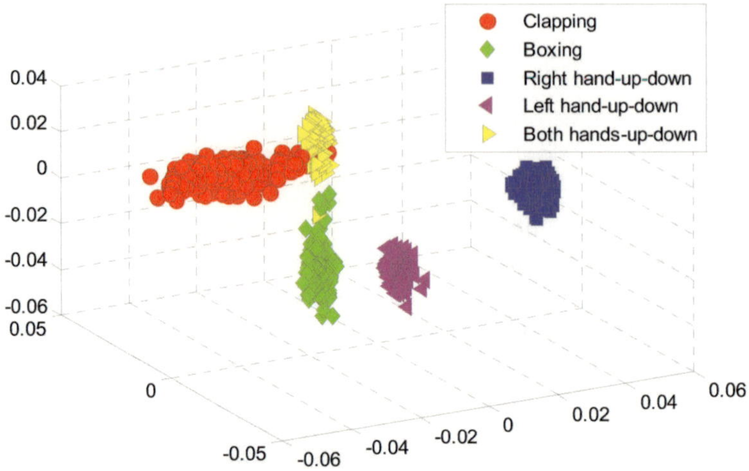

Fig. 10. A plot of the three LDA features of 2250 depth silhouettes of the activities.

the IC features of the silhouettes of the five activities where 150 ICs are taken into consideration. Fig. 10 demonstrates a good separation among the representations of the depth silhouettes of the five activities. Once the LDA algorithm is applied on a database of the depth silhouette vectors where each vector is 150 dimensional, the size of the LDA subspace becomes 4x150 as $(c-1)=4$. Hence, the LDA projection of the IC feature vector of each depth silhouette becomes 1x4.

3.5 Continuous HMM for depth silhouette-based activity training and recognition

Once human activities are represented in the time-sequential depth silhouette features, the continuous HMM can be applied effectively for HAR. In our system, we considered a four-state left-to-right HMM to model the human activities. The initial probability of the states π was initialized as {1,0,0,0}. The transition matrix A was uniformly initialized according to the transition between the states. Two mixtures per depth silhouette features were considered to model the activities by the continuous HMMs. Finally, the continuous HMMs were trained using the Baum-Welch parameter estimation algorithm. Each activity was represented by a distinct continuous HMM. Figs. 11 and 12 show the transition probabilities of a left hand up-down HMM before and after training respectively.

To recognize an activity, a feature vector sequence obtained from the activity image sequence was applied on all trained continuous HMMs to calculate the likelihood and the

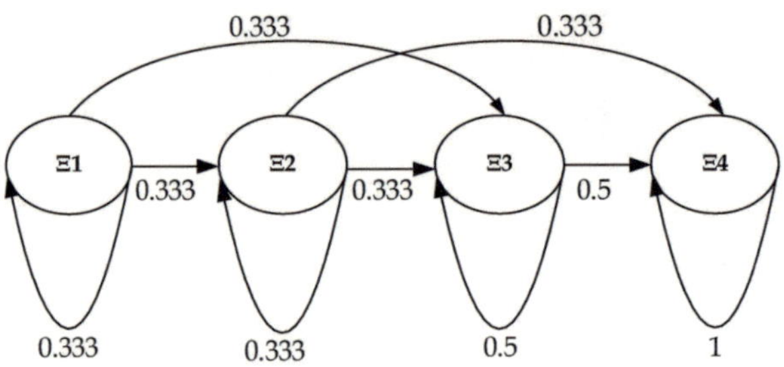

Fig. 11. A left hand up-down HMM before training.

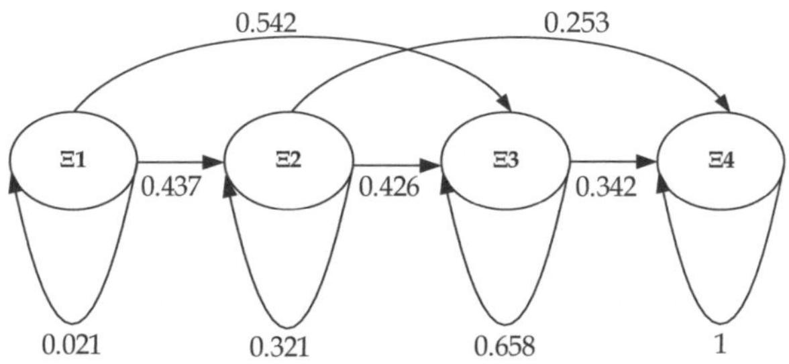

Fig. 12. A left hand up-down HMM after training.

one was chosen with the highest probability. Thus, to test a feature vector sequence O (i.e., $O_1, O_2, ..., O_T$), we found the appropriate HMM as

$$decision = \underset{i=1,2,...,N}{argmax}\{L_i\}, \tag{29}$$

$$L_i = \Pr(O \mid H_i) \tag{30}$$

where L represents the likelihood of O on corresponding trained activity HMM H.

4. Experimental setups and results

For the experiments, the binary (Uddin et al., 2008a) and depth silhouettes (Uddin et al., 2008b) were used as input to our HAR system. Five activities were recognized using different types of features with the continuous HMMs: namely right hand up-down, left hand up-down, both hands up-down, clapping, and boxing. Each activity sequence consisted of a time-series set of 30 silhouettes. A total of 15 sequences from each activity were used to build the feature space in training. Thus, the whole database consisted of a total of 2250 images. A total of 200 sequences (i.e., 40 sequences for each activity) were used in testing.

We started our experiments with the traditional binary silhouette-based HAR. After the background subtraction, the ROIs containing the binary silhouettes were extracted from the sequences. Since the binary silhouettes from the activities used in the experiments were similar to each other, the recognizer produced much low recognition rates for all the approaches (i.e., PCA, LDA on the PC features, ICA, and LDA on the IC features) as shown in Table 1.

In the following experiments, the binary silhouettes were replaced with the depth ones. The combination of PCA on the depth silhouettes with the continuous HMM were experimented first. PCA found the global depth silhouette features to be applied on the continuous HMMs, obtaining the mean recognition rate of 85.50%. By extending the PCA features by LDA, we obtained the mean recognition rate of 86.50%, improving the recognition marginally. We continued to apply ICA on the depth silhouettes to obtain improved local depth silhouette features, achieving the mean recognition rate of 93.50%. Finally, LDA on the IC features with the continuous HMMs produced the highest recognition rate of 99%. The recognition results using the various types of features from the depth silhouettes are shown in Table 2.

Approach	Activity	Recognition Rate	Mean	Standard Deviation
PCA	Right hand up-down	32.50%	36.50	6.02
	Left hand up-down	35		
	Both hands up-down	30		
	Clapping	40		
	Boxing	45		
LDA on the PC features	Right hand up-down	35	36	4.18
	Left hand up-down	32.50		
	Both hands up-down	37.50		
	Clapping	32.50		
	Boxing	42.50		
ICA	Right hand up-down	42.50	43	4.80
	Left hand up-down	37.50		
	Both hands up-down	50		
	Clapping	40		
	Boxing	45		
LDA on the IC features	Right hand up-down	45	45.50	4.11
	Left hand up-down	42.50		
	Both hands up-down	52.50		
	Clapping	42.50		
	Boxing	45		

Table 1. Recognition results using the binary silhouette-based approaches.

Approach	Activity	Recognition Rate	Mean	Standard Deviation
PCA	Right hand up-down	90%	85.50	4.47
	Left hand up-down	90		
	Both hands up-down	80		
	Clapping	85		
	Boxing	82.50		
LDA on the PC features	Right hand up-down	90	86.50	4.54
	Left hand up-down	92.50		
	Both hands up-down	82.50		
	Clapping	85		
	Boxing	82.50		
ICA	Right hand up-down	92.50	93.50	1.37
	Left hand up-down	95		
	Both hands up-down	92.50		
	Clapping	95		
	Boxing	92.50		
LDA on the IC features	Right hand up-down	100	99	1.36
	Left hand up-down	100		
	Both hands up-down	100		
	Clapping	97.50		
	Boxing	97.50		

Table 2. Recognition results using the depth silhouette-based approaches.

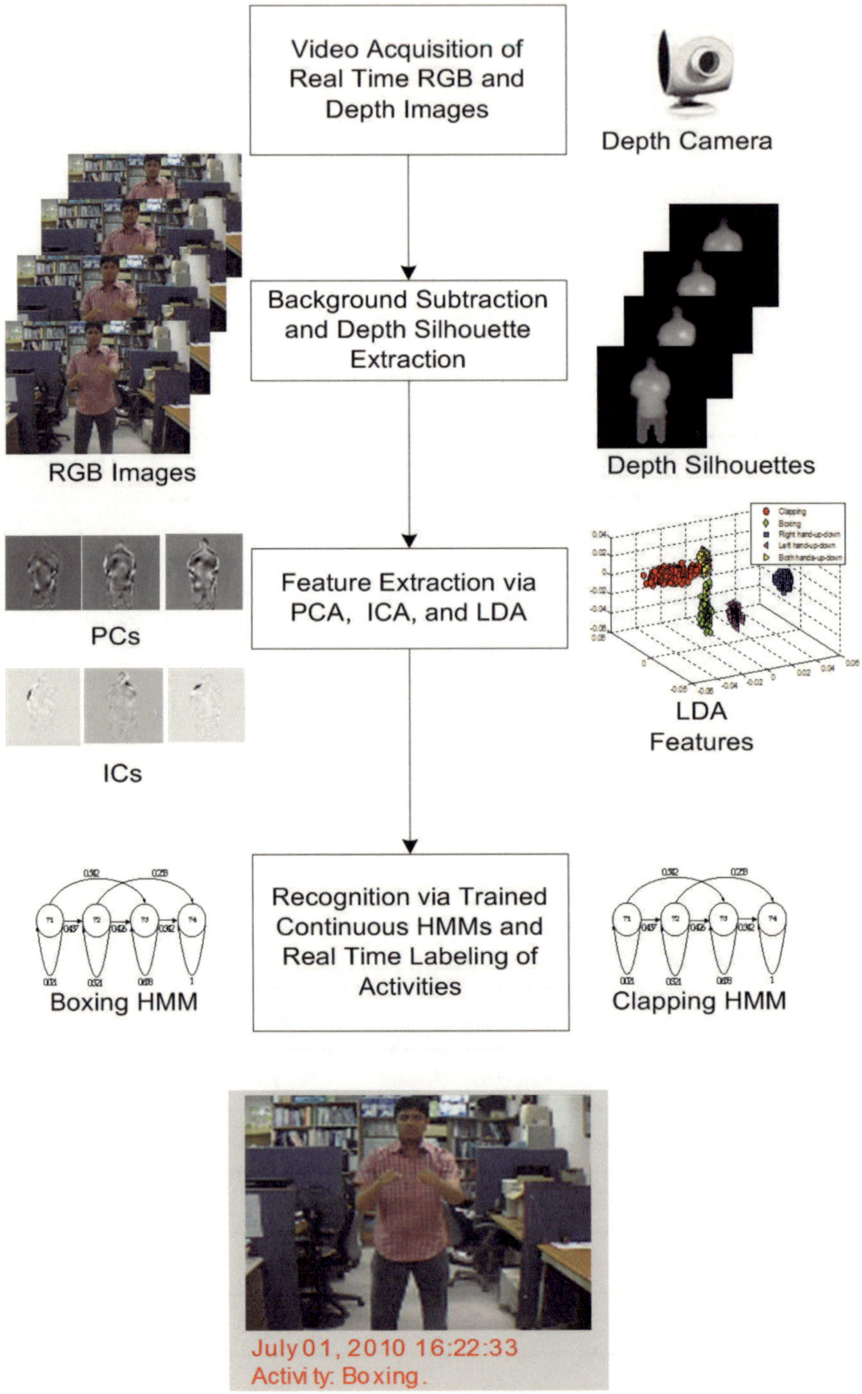

Fig. 13. Basic steps of our depth silhouette-based real-time HAR system.

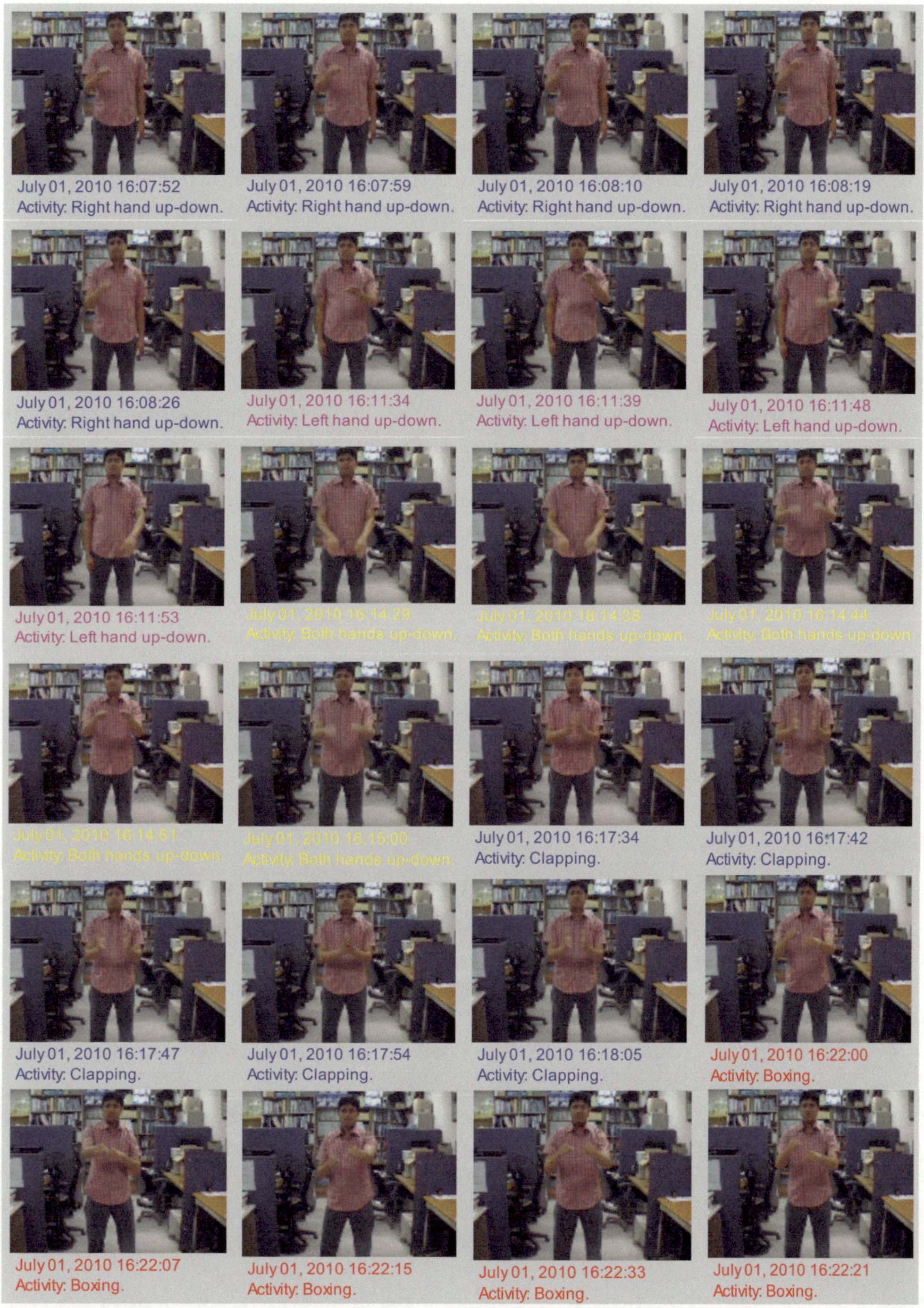

Fig. 14. Real-time human activity recognition results.

4.1 Real-time depth silhouette-based human activity recognition

After testing our system offline, we continued our study to recognize the five activities in real-time. We implemented a HAR system in a programming language, Matlab 7.4.0 to acquire the RGB as well as depth images of various activities in real-time and applied LDA on the IC features on the depth silhouettes with the continuous HMMs. We used a non overlapping window of 30 sequential depth frames from the real time video data and extracted the IC-based features to apply on the trained HMMs for recognition. Fig. 13 shows the architecture of our real-time HAR system. Fig. 14 shows some of our sample real-time recognition results with date and time where the result is shown at the bellow of the RGB images automatically. Here, the labeled RGB image is shown for the clarity of the activity though we used the depth silhouettes for activity recognition.

5. Conclusion

In this chapter, we have presented the basics of the continuous HMM and its application to human activity recognition. Our depth silhouette-based HAR methodology successfully incorporates the continuous HMM to recognize various human activities: we have shown that the depth silhouettes outperform the traditional binary silhouettes significantly, although the same HMM has been incorporated for recognition. We have also demonstrated real-time working of our presented HAR system. As presented, the HMMs can be effective in the field of HAR where pattern recognition of spatiotemporally changing information is critical.

6. Acknowledgement

This research was supported by Basic Science Research Program through the National Research Foundation of Korea (NRF) funded by the Ministry of Education, Science, and Technology (No. 2010-0001860).

7. References

Agarwal, A.; & Triggs B. (2006). Recovering 3D human pose from monocular images, *IEEE Transactions on Pattern Analysis and Machine Intelligence,* Vol. 28, pp. 44-58.

Bartlett, M.; Movellan, J. & Sejnowski, T. (2002). Face Recognition by Independent Component Analysis, *IEEE Transactions on Neural Networks,* Vol., 13, pp. 1450-1464.

Baum, E.; Petrie, T.; Soules, G.; & Weiss, N. (1970). A Maximization Technique Occurring in The Statistical Analysis of Probabilistic Functions of Markov chains. *Annals of Mathematical Statistics,* Vol., 41, pp. 164-171

Ben-Arie, J.; Wang, Z.; Pandit, P. & Rajaram, S. (2002). Human Activity Recognition Using Multidimensional Indexing, *IEEE Transactions on Pattern Analysis and Machine Intelligence Archive,* Vol., 24(8), pp. 1091-1104.

Carlsson, S. & Sullivan, J. (2002). Action Recognition by Shape Matching to Key Frames, *IEEE Computer Society Workshop on Models versus Exemplars in Computer Vision,* pp. 263-270.

Cohen, I. & Lim, H. (2003). Inference of Human Postures by Classification of 3D Human Body Shape, *IEEE International Workshop on Analysis and Modeling of Faces and Gestures,* pp. 74-81.

Frolov V.; Deml B.; & Hannig G. (2008) Gesture Recognition with Hidden Markov Models to Enable Multi-modal Haptic Feedback, Lecture Notes in Computer Science, Vol. 5024/2008, pp. 786-795.

Iddan , G. J. & Yahav, G. (2001). 3D imaging in the studio (and elsewhere…). *Proceedings of SPIE*, Vol., 4298, pp 48-55.

Iwai, Y.; Hata, T. & Yachida, M. (1997) Gesture Recognition Based on Subspace Method and Hidden Markov Model, *Proceedings of the IEEE/RSJ International Conference on Intelligent Robots and Systems*, pp. 960-966.

Jung, T.; Makeig, S.; Westerfield, M.; Townsend, J.; Courchesne, E.; & Sejnowski, T. J. (2001). Analysis and Visualization of Single-Trial Event-Related Potentials, *Human Brain Mapping*, Vol., 14, pp. 166-185.

Kanungu, T.; Mount, D. M.; Netanyahu, N.; Piatko, C.; Silverman, R. & Wu, A. Y. (2000). The analysis of a simple k-means clustering algorithm, Proceedings of 16th ACM Symposium On Computational Geometry, pp. 101-109.

Kwak, K.-C. & Pedrycz, W. (2007). Face Recognition Using an Enhanced Independent Component Analysis Approach, *IEEE Transactions on Neural Networks*, Vol., 18(2), pp. 530-541.

Kwon, O. W. & Lee, T. W. (2004). Phoneme recognition using ICA-based feature extraction and transformation, *Signal Processing*, Vol., 84(6), pp. 1005–1019.

Lawrence, R. & Rabiner, A. (1989). Tutorial on Hidden Markov Models and Selected Applications in Speech Recognition, *Proceedings of the IEEE*, 77(2), pp. 257-286.

Linde, Y.; Buzo, A. & Gray, R. (1980). An Algorithm for Vector Quantizer Design, *IEEE Transaction on Communications*, Vol., 28(1), pp. 84–94.

Mckeown, M. J.; Makeig, S.; Brown, G. G.; Jung, T. P.; Kindermann, S. S.; Bell, A. J. & Sejnowski, T. J. (1998) Analysis of fMRI by decomposition into independent spatial components, *Human Brain Mapping*, Vol., 6(3), pp. 160–188.

Nakata, T. (2006). Recognizing Human Activities in Video by Multi-resolutional Optical Flow, *Proceedings of International Conference on Intelligent Robots and Systems*, pp. 1793-1798.

Niu, F. & Abdel-Mottaleb M. (2004).View-Invariant Human Activity Recognition Based on Shape and Motion Features, *Proceedings of the IEEE Sixth International Symposium on Multimedia Software Engineering*, pp. 546-556.

Niu, F. & Abdel-Mottaleb, M. (2005). HMM-Based Segmentation and Recognition of Human Activities from Video Sequences, *Proceedings of IEEE International Conference on Multimedia & Expo*, pp. 804-807.

Robertson, N. & Reid, I. (2006). A General Method for Human Activity Recognition in Video, *Computer Vision and Image Understanding*, Vol., 104(2), pp. 232 - 248.

Sun, X.; Chen, C. & Manjunath, B. S. (2002). Probabilistic Motion Parameter Models for Human Activity Recognition, *Proceedings of 16th International Conference on Pattern recognition*, pp. 443-450.

Yamato, J.; Ohya, J. & Ishii, K. (1992). Recognizing Human Action in Time-Sequential Images using Hidden Markov Model, *Proceedings of IEEE International Conference on Computer Vision and Pattern Recognition*, pp. 379-385.p

Yang, J.; Zhang, D. & Yang, J. Y. (2005). Is ICA Significantly Better than PCA for Face Recognition?. *Proceedings of IEEE International Conference on Computer Vision*, pp. 198-203.

Uddin, M. Z.; Lee, J. J. & Kim T.-S. (2008a) Shape-Based Human Activity Recognition Using Independent Component Analysis and Hidden Markov Model, *Proceedings of The s21st International Conference on Industrial, Engineering and Other Applications of Applied Intelligent Systems*, pp. 245-254.

Uddin, M. Z.; Lee, J. J. & Kim, T.-S. (2008b). Human Activity Recognition Using Independent Component Features from Depth Images, *Proceedings of the 5th International Conference on Ubiquitous Healthcare*, pp. 181-183.

Uddin, M. Z.; Lee, J. J. & Kim, T.-S. (2009). An Enhanced Independent Component-Based Human Facial Expression Recognition from Video, *IEEE Transactions on Consumer Electronics*, Vol., 55(4), pp. 2216-2224.

12

Applications of Hidden Markov Models in Microarray Gene Expression Data

Huimin Geng, Xutao Deng and Hesham H Ali
[1]*Department of Computer Science, University of Nebraska at Omaha, Omaha, NE 68182 USA*

1. Introduction

Hidden Markov models (HMMs) are well developed statistical models to capture hidden information from observable sequential symbols. They were first used in speech recognition in 1970s and have been successfully applied to the analysis of biological sequences since late 1980s as in finding protein secondary structure, CpG islands and families of related DNA or protein sequences [1]. In a HMM, the system being modeled is assumed to be a Markov process with unknown parameters, and the challenge is to determine the hidden parameters from the observable parameters. In this chapter, we described two applications using HMMs to predict gene functions in yeast and DNA copy number alternations in human tumor cells, based on gene expression microarray data.
The first application employed HMMs as a gene function prediction tool to infer budding yeast *Saccharomyces cerevisiae* gene function from time-series microarray gene expression data. The sequential observations in HMM were the discretized expression measurements at each time point for the genes from the time-series microarray experiments. Yeast is an excellent model organism which has reasonably simple genome structure, well characterized gene functions, and huge expression data sets. A wide variety of data mining methods have been applied for inferring yeast gene functions from gene expression data sets, such as Decision Tree, Artificial Neural Networks, Support Vector Machines (SVMs) and K-Nearest Neighbors (KNNs) [2-4]. However those methods achieved only about 40% prediction precision in function prediction of un-annotated genes [2-4]. Based on our observations, there are three main reasons for the low prediction performance. First, the computational models are too simple to address the systematic variations of biological systems. One assumption is that genes from the same function class will show a similar expression pattern. However, clustering results have shown that functions and clusters have many-to-many relationship and it is often difficult to assign a function to an expression pattern (Eisen et al., supplementary data) [5]. Second, the measurements of expression value are generally not very accurate and show experimental errors (or noise). The observed expression values may not reflect the real expression levels of genes. For example, a correlation as low as 60% was reported between measurements of the same sample hybridized to two slides [6]. Third, none of the above methods explicitly address the less obvious but significant correlation of gene expressions. Our results indicate that the expression value of a gene depends significantly on its previous expression value. Therefore, Markov property can be assumed to simplify the non-independence of gene

expressions. In this application, we developed a gene function classification tool based on HMMs from time-series gene expression profiles (GEP) in yeast and the goal was to provide a better tool for more accurate gene function prediction as compared to other existing tools. We studied 40 yeast gene function classes which have a sufficient number of open reading frames (ORFs) in Munich Information Centre for Protein Sequences (MIPS), for example greater than 100, for the training purpose of HMMs. Each function class was modeled as a distinct HMM and the set of 40 HMMs compose a discriminant model for unknown gene function prediction. Cross-validation showed our HMM-based method outperforms other existing methods by an overall prediction precision of 67%.

In the second application, we developed a DNA copy number alteration (CNA) prediction tool based on HMMs to infer genetic abnormalities in human tumor cells from microarray gene expression data. The sequential observations in this HMM application were the discretized expression measurements for the genes along the chromosomal locations for each chromosome. Instead of the temporal order of gene expression in the time-series experiments in the first application, in the second application we used the spatial order of the genes according to chromosomal locations as the sequential data in HMM. It is well known that chromosomal gains and losses play an important role in regulating gene expression and constitute a key mechanism in cancer development and progression [7, 8]. Comparative Genomic Hybridization (CGH) was developed as a molecular cytogenetic method for detecting and mapping such CNAs in tumor cells [9, 10]. However, in the post-genomic era, the majority of the genome-wide studies in cancer research have been focusing on gene expression but not CGH, and as a result, an enormous amount of GEP data have been accumulated in public databases for various tumor types [11-15], but few CGH studies have been performed in large series of tumor samples [16]. The vast amount of GEP data represents an important resource for cancer research, yet it has not been fully exploited. We hypothesized that with a well-designed computational model, GEP data can be readily used to derive functionally relevant genetic abnormalities in tumors. From the literature review, most studies including GEP and CGH have been focusing on the impact of one on the other or combining the two for identifying candidate tumor suppressor genes or oncogenes [8, 17-25]. In this application, we proposed a novel computational approach based on HMMs to predict CNAs from the GEP data. It would significantly reduce the cost of CNAs detection in tumor cells, and more importantly, it will reveal functionally more relevant CNAs as compared to those identified by CGH, since CGH in principle defines only the structural changes which may or may not reflect functional effects, but GEP-defined CNAs must have the functional effects reflected by changes of gene expression. HMMs have recently been applied in array CGH for segmentation, a procedure to divide the signal ratios of each clone on the array into states, where all of the clones in a state have the same underlying copy number [26, 27]. In this application, HMM was used for an integrative analysis of GEP-to-CGH prediction which intended to capture two primary sources of uncertainty embedded in genomic data: First, the significant but subtle correlations between GEP and CGH; Second, the sequential transitions of DNA copy number changes along a chromosome. The purpose was to enhance the limited CGH data with the wealth of GEP data and provide an integrative genomic-transcriptomic approach for identifying functionally relevant genetic abnormalities in cancer research. In this application, we studied 64 cases of Mantle Cell Lymphoma (MCL) which had both GEP and CGH data associated. Since chromosomal gains and losses occur on individual chromosomes, we developed and trained a separate HMM for each chromosome and the set of 24 HMMs compose a discriminant model for the human tumor CNA prediction. Using cross validation, the training of the HMMs was done on the paired GEP and CGH data, and the prediction was made for a new tumor sample for its CNAs based on the trained HMMs from its GEP data. Our HMM method achieved 75% sensitivity, 90% specificity and 90% accuracy in predicting CNAs in 64 MCL samples when compared to the CNAs identified by experimental CGH on the same tumor samples.

2. Preliminary of HMM

Transition and emission probabilities

A HMM describes a doubly embedded stochastic process with one observable process {*Oi*} and one hidden process {*Hi*}. The hidden process {*Hi*} is an ordinary Markov model with state transition distribution defined as *aij*:

$$a_{ij} = P(H_n = j \mid H_0, H_1, \ldots, H_{n-1} = i) = P(H_n = j \mid H_{n-1} = i) \quad (1)$$

where ; a_{ij} is the transition probability from hidden state i to j.

The observable process $\{O_i\}$ is embedded upon the hidden process with a distinct probability distribution e_{ik} defined at each hidden state:

$$e_{ik} = P(O_n = k \mid H_1, H_2, \ldots, H_n = i) = P(O_n = k \mid H_n = i) \quad (2)$$

where e_{ik} is the emission probability of emitting symbol k at hidden state i.
Together with the initial hidden state distribution π, the HMM with discrete emission symbols can be readily represented as a 5-tuple (K, N, a_{ij}, e_{ik}, π), where K is the number of states of the hidden process and N is the number of observations at each hidden state. Given the observation sequence $O_1\, O_2 \ldots O_T$, and a HMM, M = (K, N, a_{ij}, e_{ik}, π), we can efficiently compute $P(O_1\, O_2 \ldots O_T \mid M)$, the probability of observing the sequence, by using the Viterbi or forward algorithms. In a HMM, the challenge is often to determine the hidden parameters from the observable parameters. To estimate the model parameters, when the state paths are known for the training datasets, Maximum Likelihood Estimation (MLE) or Bayesian Maximum A Posteriori (MAP) can be used; if the state paths are unknown, the Baum-Welch algorithm or Viterbi training can be used instead to learn the model parameters using a set of observation sequences. To estimate the hidden state path for a new case, two standard algorithms Viterbi and Forward-Backward can be used. Refer to Koski (2002), Durbin (1989) and Rabiner (1989) for details [1, 28, 29].

Viterbi, Forward and Backward Algorithms

Viterbi decoding is a dynamic programming algorithm. Suppose the probability $v_k(i\text{-}1)$ of the most probable path ending in state k with observation x_{i-1} is known for all the states k, then the probability $v_l(i)$ corresponding to the observation x_i with the state l can be calculated as in Eq. (3). The entire path π can be found recursively as in Algorithm (1).

$$v_l(i) = e_l(x_i) \max_k (v_k(i-1) a_{kl}) \quad (3)$$

where a_{kl} is the transition probability, $e_l(x_l)$ is the emission probability, k and l are states and x_i is an emission symbol.

Algorithm (1) Viterbi:

Initialization (i=0): $v_0(0)=1, v_k(0)=0$ for $k>0$.
Recursion (i=1…L): $v_l(i)=e_l(x_i)\max_k(v_k(i-1)a_{kl}); ptr(l)=\arg\max_k(v_k(i-1)a_{kl})$.
Termination: $P(x,\pi^*)=\max_k(v_k(L)a_{k0}); \pi_L^*=\arg\max_k(v_k(L)a_{k0})$.
Traceback (i=1…L): $\pi_{i-1}^*=ptr_i(\pi_i^*)$.

Posterior decoding is derived from Forward and Backward algorithms, which are similar dynamic programming procedures to Viterbi, but by replacing the maximization steps with sums to obtain the full probability for all possible paths. In Forward algorithm, $f_k(i)=P(x_1\ldots x_i,\pi_i=k)$ is the forward variable, representing the full probability for all the probable paths ending in state k with observation up to and including x_i. Then $f_l(i+1)$, which corresponds to the observation up to and including x_{i+1} and ending in state l, can be calculated by the recursion in Eq. (4). In Backward algorithm, the backward variable $b_k(i)=P(x_{i+1}\ldots x_L \mid \pi_i=k)$ is analogous to $f_k(i)$, but instead obtained by a backward recursion starting at the end of the sequence as in Eq. (5). The detailed Forward and Backward algorithms are shown in Algorithms (2) and (3).

$$f_l(i+1)=e_l(x_{i+1})\sum_k f_k(i)a_{kl} \tag{4}$$

$$b_k(i)=\sum_l e_l(x_{i+1})a_{kl}b_l(i+1) \tag{5}$$

where a_{kl} is the transition probability, $e_l(x_l)$ is the emission probability, k and l $\in\{H_+,H_-,H_o,L_+,L_-,L_o,M_+,M_-,M_o\}$ and $x_i\in\{H,L,M\}$.

Algorithm (2) Forward:

Initialization (i=0): $f_0(0)=1, f_k(0)=0$ for $k>0$.
Recursion (i=1…L): $f_l(i)=e_l(x_i)\sum_k f_k(i-1)a_{kl}$.
Termination: $P(x)=\sum_k f_k(L)a_{k0}$.

Algorithm (3) Backward:

Initialization (i=L): $b_k(L)=a_{k0}$ for $k>0$.
Recursion (i=L-1…1): : $b_k(i)=\sum_l e_l(x_{i+1})a_{kl}b_l(i+1)$.
Termination: $P(x)=\sum_l e_l(x_1)a_{0l}b_l(1)$.

Having $f_k(i)$ and $b_k(i)$, given the emitted sequence x, the posterior probability that observation x_i comes from a state k is shown in Eq. (6). The posterior probability that observation x_i comes from all possible states in the specific set is shown in Eq. (7), where $g(k)$ is a function defined on the states. Then we concatenate the most probable state at each position to form an entire state path.

$$P(\pi_i = k \mid x) = f_k(i) b_k(i) / P(x) \tag{6}$$

$$G(i \mid x) = \sum_k P(\pi_i = k \mid x) g(k) \tag{7}$$

3. Method

Application 1 – Yeast Gene Function Prediction

For a set of time-series expression data, we model the discretized expression measurements at each time point as observed emission symbols. Our goal is to train separate HMMs for each gene function class and use the set of HMMs as a whole discriminant model for unknown gene function prediction.

Data

The expression data set is obtained from http://rana.lbl.gov/EisenData.htm (Eisen, et al., 1998) [5]. The complete data set contains 2,467 genes with each gene having 79 experimental measurements recorded. Among the 2,467 genes, 2,432 have at least one function annotation at MIPS (http://mips.gsf.de/) [30]. For training purpose, we only include 40 function classes which have at least 100 open reading frames (ORFs) in MIPS.

The original data set is organized as a set of pairs $S = \{(\mathbf{X_i}, C_i) \mid 1 \le i \le n\}$ where $\mathbf{X_i}$= [X_{i1}, X_{i2},..., X_{iT}] is the expression vector and C_i is the class label for the ith training sample, T is the number of genes and n is the number of training samples. Expression vectors with the same class label are then grouped into the subset $S_j = \{(\mathbf{X_i}, C_i) \mid C_i = j,\ 1 \le j \le L,\ 1 \le i \le n\}$, where L is the number of classes. The entire prediction process can be performed in three steps: *discretization, training* and *inference. Discretization* is a data preprocessing step in which the continuous expression measurements are divided up into a fixed set of intervals (symbols). In the *training* step, the parameters of each distinct unit of HMM, M_i, are specified by using each training subset S_i. The whole model $M = \{M_i \mid 1 \le i \le L\}$ is a collection of unit models and used for *inference* of gene functions.

Model Structures

One advantage of HMMs is that designers can choose arbitrary transition and emission structures appropriate for modeling data from specific domains. In this application, two model structures were considered for modeling the sequential time-series microarray gene expression data (Figure 1). Model A defines states based on time sequence of experiments. This model is the backbone of the HMM for protein profiling [1, 31]. The advantage of model A is that the position-specific information is preserved. However, if we take a closer look, all transitions are of probability 1 and the HMM is actually degenerated into a weight matrix which doesn't consider the non-independence of data. To reflect the dependence of the expression data at different time points, we designed model B by combining the expression values and the experiment sequence as states. The state is defined as a pair, (*value, experiment*). If an expression value is below a predefined threshold at time point i, the state is "low-i"; otherwise it is "high-i". Model B is a more complex model which is able to capture the Markov property of expression data. However, model B has more parameters than model A and hence requires a larger number of training samples. The model A is referred to "chain HMM" and model B as the "split HMM".

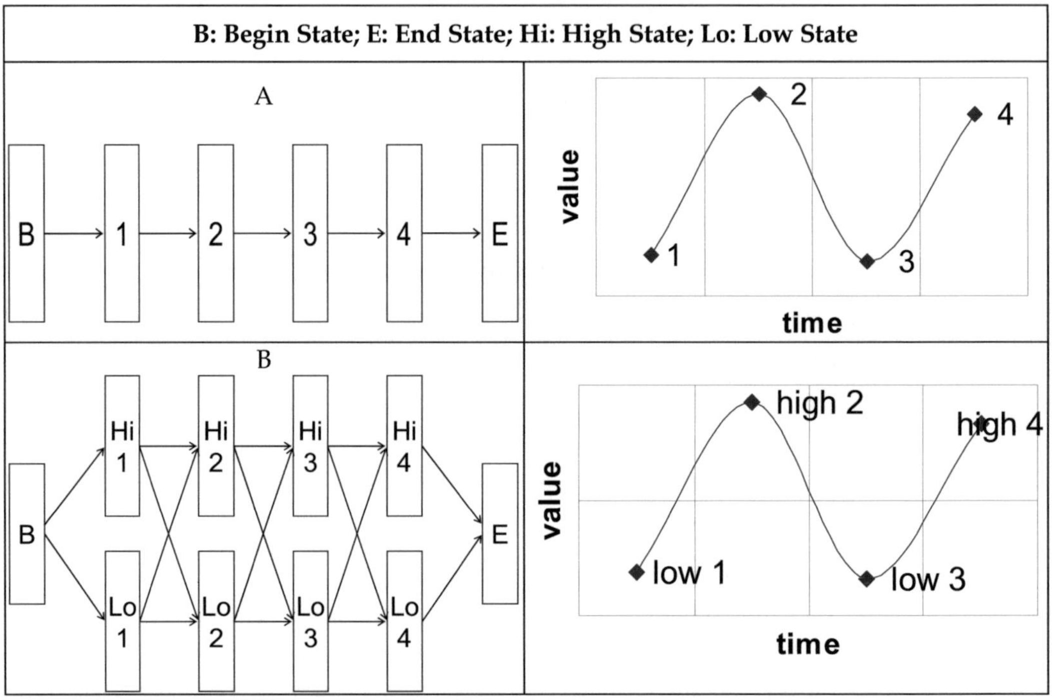

Fig. 1. Two HMM model structures for modeling yeast time-series microarray gene expression data. Left panels are state transition diagrams and right panels are expression patterns. A. States defined based on experiment order (i.e. time points). B. States definition according to both expression value and experiment order. Note that "B" and "E" are special dummy states without emission.

Training

In this section, we describe the training of prior distribution $P(M_i)$, transition distribution (a_{ij}) and emission distribution (e_{ik}) for each gene function class. All the distributions are considered as a multinomial distribution with certain unknown parameters. We will use Bayes' learning to determine the point estimator of all unknown parameters from the data.

The prior probability density function $P(M_i)$ is estimated by the Maximum Likelihood Estimator (MLE) of a multinomial distribution as in Eq. (8):

$$\hat{P}(M_i) = \frac{|S_i|}{\sum_{i'=1}^{L} |S_{i'}|} \tag{8}$$

where $|S_i|$ is the number of training samples in the ith class and L is the number of classes.

The transition probability distribution can be modeled as a multinomial distribution $Mul(a_{i1}, a_{i2}, ..., a_{iKi})$. We use a Dirichlet distribution $Dir(1, 1, ..., 1)$ as the conjugate prior to avoid the problem of zero probability. Therefore, the Mean Posterior Estimator for the transition probability a_{ij} is defined as in Eq. (9):

$$\hat{a}_{ij} = \frac{A_{ij} + 1}{\sum_{j'=1}^{K_i} A_{ij'} + K_i}, 1 \le i \le K, \ 1 \le j \le K_i \tag{9}$$

where A_{ij} is the count of transitions from state i to j in the training samples, K is the number of states defined in the HMM, and K_i is the out-degree of state i (i.e., K_i=1 in the chain HMM, , and K_i =2 in the split HMM). Similar to the transition probabilities, emission probabilities can be estimated by counting the frequencies as well in Eq. (10),

$$\hat{e}_{ij} = \frac{E_{ij} + 1}{\sum_{j'=1}^{N} E_{ij'} + N}, 1 \le i \le K, \ 1 \le j \le N \tag{10}$$

where E_{ij} is the count of emissions of symbol j at state i in the training samples, K is the number of states defined in the HMM, and N is the total number of symbols at each state. The training was performed for each function class.

Inference

Given an expression vector **X** and the model M (a collection of each unit model M_i), inferring the function of **X** is performed based on Bayes' theorem:

$$P(M_i \mid \mathbf{X}) \propto P(\mathbf{X} \mid M_i) P(M_i) \tag{11}$$

In order to calculate the posterior probability $P(M_i \mid X)$, we need the prior probability of each $P(M_i)$ and the likelihood $P(\mathbf{X} \mid M_i)$. $P(M_i)$ is specified in Eq. (8). The likelihood $P(\mathbf{X} \mid M_i)$ can be considered as the marginal probability of **X** across all hidden state paths π.

$$P(\mathbf{X} \mid M_i) = \sum_{\pi} P(\mathbf{X}, \pi \mid M_i) = \sum_{\pi} a_{0\pi 1} \prod_{l=1}^{T} a_{\pi(l)\pi(l+1)} e_{\pi(l)X(l)} \tag{12}$$

where $\pi(l)$ is the lth hidden state in the path π and $X(l)$ is the symbol at the lth state. Once the parameters of the HMM M_i have been determined from training data, the likelihood term can be efficiently computed by the forward algorithm, as described previous section *Preliminary of HMM*. The inference of function class is then made by choosing the most likely class given the data, as in Eq. (13).

$$M^* = \arg\max_{M_i} P(M_i \mid \mathbf{X}) = \arg\max_{M_i} P(\mathbf{X} \mid M_i) P(M_i) \tag{13}$$

Application 2—Human Tumor CNA Prediction

In the second application, HMMs are used to address the following question: "Given a sequence of gene expression data along chromosomal locations as observations, predict the hidden CGH status of the chromosomal gains or losses."

Model Structure

In the HMM-CNA prediction, the observable process $\{O_i\}$ describes discretized gene expression values of genes along a chromosome, where O_i ="H", "L" or "M" for *high, low* or *medium* expression, respectively; the hidden process $\{H_i\}$ describes the underlying CNAs, where H_i ="+", "-" or "o" for *gain, loss* or *normal* copy number status of a gene, respectively. In Figure 2A, the HMM model was illustrated as a Bayesian network, where the shaded nodes $S_1, S_2, \ldots, S_n$ represent hidden state variables, and the visible nodes $E_1, E_2, \ldots, E_n$ represent the observations for the variables, for the genes along a chromosome. The emission space consists of three symbols $\{H, L, M\}$ and the hidden state space consists of nine states that the gene expression values superimposed on the CNAs $\{H_+, L_+, M_+, H_-, L_-, M_-, H_o, L_o, M_o\}$, where E_α emits E, $E \in \{H,L,M\}$ and $\alpha \in \{+,-,o\}$. Figure 2B showed the state transition diagram. The model is a single chain incorporating three Markov sub-chains. In each sub-chain, there is a complete set of state transitions, describing the elongation of a DNA segments with a gain, loss or normal copy number. The state transitions between sub-chains are also allowed to describe the state change of a gain, loss or normal CNA. This design of intra- and inter- sub-chain transitions in HMM makes it possible to identify alterative gain, loss and normal regions of variable length automatically.

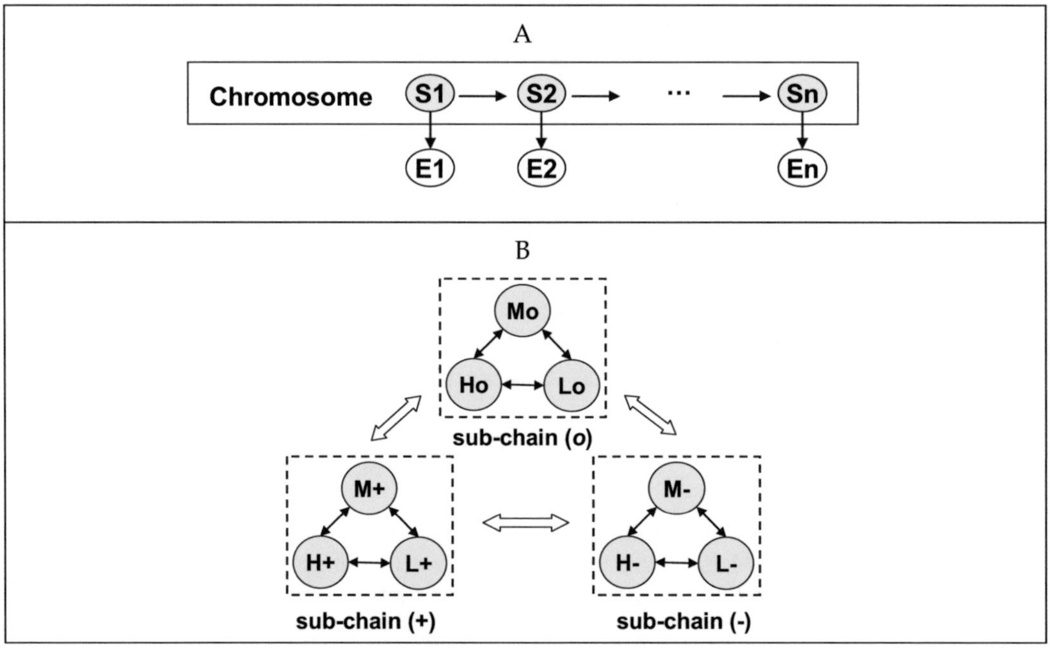

Fig. 2. HMM model structure for human CNA prediction. (A) HMM model presented as a Bayesian network. The shaded nodes $S_1, S_2, \ldots, S_n$ represent hidden state variables and the white nodes $E_1, E_2, \ldots, E_n$ represent the observations for the variables. (B) State transition diagram of HMM-CNA model. The model is a single HMM chain integrating three Markov sub-chains: (+), (-) and (o). In each sub-chain, a Markov chain is graphically shown as a collection of states, with arrows between them describing the state transitions within a gain, loss or normal CNA. There are also arrows between sub-chains, describing the state transitions from a gain, loss or normal CNA to another.

Training

Since chromosomal gains and losses are based on individual chromosomes, we developed and trained a separate HMM for each chromosome accordingly. The whole HMM-CNA prediction model was made of individual HMMs. In our training dataset, given the paired GEP and CGH data, the hidden state path for each observation sequence is known. Therefore, the transition and emission probabilities can be estimated using MLE as in Eq. (9) and (10).

Inference

Having the model parameters trained by training data, we used Viterbi or Posterior (also called Forward and Backward) decoding algorithms [1] to infer hidden CNA states for a new tumor sample based on its GEP observations. Viterbi algorithm works by finding the highest probability path as a whole as a hidden state path, while alternatively, Posterior algorithm finds the most likely state for each position and then concatenate those states as a hidden state path. The detailed algorithms of Viterbi and Posterior decoding were shown in *Preliminary of HMM* section.

An alternative inference method for HMM when given only emissions (i.e. GEP observations) as training data is the Baum-Welch algorithm [1], which estimates the model parameters (transition and emission probabilities) together with unknown CGH states by an iterative procedure. We chose not to use this algorithm as there are many parameters in the model, but relatively few data points at each gene position to estimate these parameters. Instead, we use the true CGH states to guild the HMM prediction using the Viterbi or Posterior algorithms.

Smoothing Algorithm

Since gains and losses identified by our experimental CGH had the resolution on cytobands, we determined the gains and losses on cytoband resolution as well by applying the following smoothing method. Basically, a multinomial probability was used to measure the likelihood of a cytoband harboring a gain/loss or not. In Eq. (14), L is the likelihood under a hypothesis H, where H_1 for the alternative hypothesis that "a cytoband is harbouring a gain or loss", and H_0 for the null hypothesis that "a cytoband is not harbouring a gain or loss"; n_+, n_-, and n_o are the numbers of genes in the gain, loss and normal status within this cytoband, and n is the total number of genes on this cytoband, $n=n_+ + n_- + n_o$; θ_+, θ_- and θ_o are the corresponding multinomial parameters which can be estimated using MLE in Eq.(15). Under H_1, $\theta_{1,+}$, $\theta_{1,-}$ and $\theta_{1,o}$ are estimated by the number of genes n_+, n_- and n_o on a cytoband ($n=n_+ + n_- + n_o$), while under H_0, $\theta_{0,+}$, $\theta_{0,-}$ and $\theta_{0,o}$ are estimated by the number of genes N_+, N_- and N_o on the whole genome as background ($N=N_+ + N_- + N_o$). Log-of-odds (LOD), which is *Log*10 of the ratio of the two likelihoods, was used to measure how likely that the cytoband harbors a gain or loss in Eq. (16). The higher the LOD score, the more likely this cytoband harbors a genomic gain or loss.

$$L(n_+, n_-, n_o \mid H) = \frac{n!}{n_+! n_-! n_o!} \theta_+^{n_+} \theta_-^{n_-} \theta_o^{n_o} , \tag{14}$$

$$\theta_{1,+} = \frac{n_+}{n},\ \theta_{1,-} = \frac{n_-}{n},\ \theta_{1,o} = \frac{n_o}{n} \text{ and } \theta_{0,+} = \frac{N_+}{N},\ \theta_{0,-} = \frac{N_-}{N},\ \theta_{0,o} = \frac{N_o}{N} \tag{15}$$

$$LOD = \log_{10}\frac{L(n_+, n_-, n_o \mid H_1)}{L(n_+, n_-, n_o \mid H_0)} = \log_{10}\frac{\theta_{1,+}^{n_+}\theta_{1,-}^{n_-}\theta_{1,o}^{n_o}}{\theta_{0,+}^{n_+}\theta_{0,-}^{n_-}\theta_{0,o}^{n_o}} \tag{16}$$

Other Simple Methods

To compare with HMM, we also made two other simple methods, rGEP (raw GEP) and sGEP (smoothing GEP), to map the GEP status to CGH status without a sophisticated learning and inference process. By rGEP, we mean that a high expression status of a gene is mapped to a gain (i.e. "H" → "+"), low expression to a loss (i.e. "L" → "-"), and medium expression to a normal (i.e. "M" → "o") status. In sGEP, a smoothing method (a multinomial model, as described above) was applied after rGEP to get a gain or loss status for a cytoband across a number of consecutive genes.

Data

The data we used in this application include 64 MCL samples performed with both GEP and CGH experiments [22]. The GEP data were obtained using Affymetrix HG-U133 plus2 arrays and normalized (global median normalization) using BRB-Array Tool [32]. 1.5-fold change was adopted to determine high (>1.5 fold increase), low (>1.5 fold decrease) or medium (<1.5 fold change) expression of each gene in a tumor case as compared to the median expression of this gene across all tumor cases. The CGH experiments were performed by Vysis CGH kits (Downers Grove, IL). aCGH-Smooth [33] was used to determine breakpoints and relative levels of DNA copy number. The company recommended 1.25 and o.75 signal ratio of tumor to normal cells was used to segregate gain (>1.25), loss (<0.75) and normal (between 0.75 and 1.25) regions. Small-sized chromosomes and sex chromosomes were excluded from the study due to technical limitation and lack of gender data, including chromosomes 19-22, X and Y. The chromosomal locations of genes and cytobands were obtained by Affymetrix probesets alignments and NCBI Human Genome database Build 36.1. The LOD score of 2 was used as the cutoff to call a gain or loss for a cytoband after the smoothing algorithm.

4. Results

Evaluation criteria

The prediction performs were evaluated using cross validation, in which the set of samples was divided up into the training set and the test set. The total n samples were randomly split into k subsets of equal size. We use each subset as the test set and the other k-1 subsets as the training set (which is called k-fold cross validation). In the extreme case where one case was used in the test set and all the other n-1 cases were used in training, it is called leave-one-out cross validation (LOOCV). K-fold cross validation or LOOCV were used to validate the HMMs in the two studies.
The performance of predictions was evaluated using the criteria of *precision, recall, sensitivity, specificity* and *accuracy*, defined as below:

$$precision \equiv \frac{|TP|}{|TP| + |FP|} \tag{17}$$

$$recall \equiv sensitivity \equiv \frac{|TP|}{|TP| + |FN|} \tag{18}$$

$$specificity \equiv \frac{|TN|}{|TN|+|FP|} \tag{19}$$

$$accuracy \equiv \frac{|TP|+|TN|}{|TP|+|TN|+|FP|+|FN|} \tag{20}$$

where $|TP|$ means the number of true positive, $|FP|$ for false positive, $|TN|$ for true negative, and $|FN|$ for false negative.

Application 1 – Yeast Gene Function Prediction

Many factors affect prediction performance, such as the model structure, the size of training data and the number of predictions made. We performed experiments for different settings and search for the setting at which the best performance was achieved. A graphical output of a trained split HMM model is shown in Figure 3 for function class 32 (cell rescue, defense and virulence in Table 1). Only the first eight expression measurements are shown. Six emission symbols plus a missing symbol are color-coded corresponding to the relative expression level in the microarray image. The thickness of each edge represents the transition probability. The width of each vertical bar represents the probability of each symbol at a specific state. It is obvious that in the high expression value state (at top of the chain), the observed expression measurements are also relatively high (the bar widths are wider at 3 to 6); while in the low expression value state (at bottom of the chain), the observed expression measurements are also relatively low (the bar widths are wider at 0 to 2).

Since a single gene may have multiple functions, we can make multiple predictions for a testing gene. Besides choosing the function class with the highest posterior probability, we

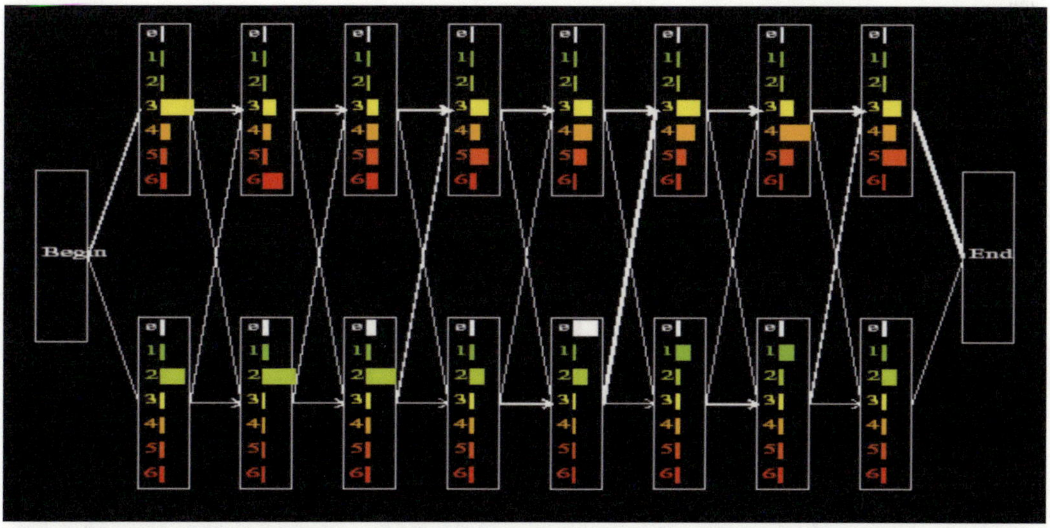

Fig. 3. HMM training results for class 32 (cell rescue, defense and virulence). Only the first eight expression measurements are showed here. Six emission symbols plus a missing symbol are color-coded corresponding to the relative expression level in the microarray image (red high expression and green low expression). The thickness of each edge represents the transition probability. The width of each vertical bar represents the probability of each symbol at a specific state.

can choose the second highest, the third highest, and so on. This procedure is termed single-dip, double-dip, and trip-dip, etc. The prediction performance at different dips was shown in Figure 4c. The *precisions* achieved for single- and double- dip settings are about 60% or higher and for triple-dip is about 50%. The *recalls* are around 30% for single-dip, but can reach 51% when multiple predictions are made (triple-dip). The overall prediction accuracy is significantly higher than that of SVMs and KNNs (40% precisions, 30% recalls). From Figure 4c, we can also see that *precision* and *recall* are inherently conflicting measures such that improving one will often be at a cost of the decrease of the other if other conditions are same.

From Figure 4a and Figure 4b, the number of *TPs*, the number of predictions (*TPs*+*FPs*), *precision* and *recall* generally increase as the size of training set increases. At the *n*-fold cross validation (i.e. LOOCV), HMM-based method achieved an overall prediction *precision* of 67%, which outperforms other existing methods (40% *precisions* in SVMs and KNNs). From Figure 4a and 4b, we also observed that the split HMMs seem to be a more conservative method than the chain HMMs. At the same level of fold, the chain HMMs tend to have higher *TPs* and *recalls* than the split HMMs, but lower *precisions* than the split HMM.

Precision is the most important evaluation measurement for prediction, because it tells directly how likely the prediction is correct. *Recall*, on the other hand, tells how sensitive the prediction is. Figure 4d shows that the split HMMs generate higher *precisions* than the chain HMMs at the same level of *recall*. However, in general the chain HMMs show higher *recalls* than the split HMMs. Table 1 shows the detailed prediction results for each function class of genes. Only five classes have a precision less than 60%.

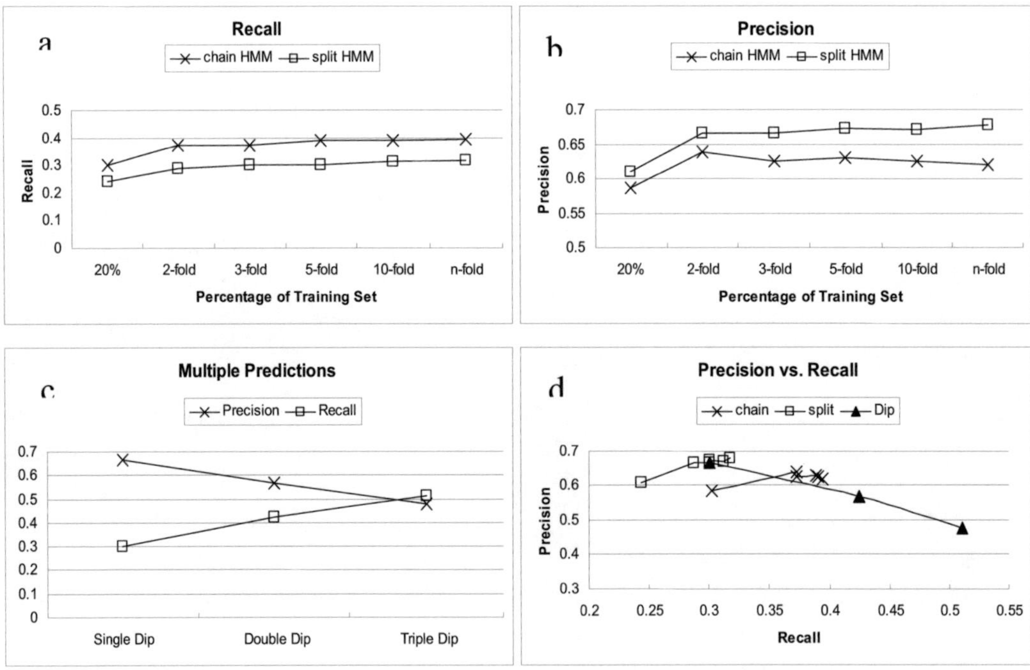

Fig. 4. Testing results of various experiment settings. ***a***. comparison of *recalls* between chain HMM and split HMM. ***b***. comparison of *precisions* between chain HMM and split HMM. ***c***. pattern of *precisions* and *recalls* for multiple predictions. ***d***. relationship between *precisions* and *recalls*.

Function Entry	Annotation	|TP|	|TP|+|FP|	|TP|+|FN|	Precision	Recall
01	metabolism	199	295	631	67.5%	31.5%
01.01	amino acid metabolism	24	29	137	82.8%	17.5%
01.03	nucleotide metabolism	15	24	94	62.5%	16.0%
02	energy	72	105	159	68.6%	45.3%
10	cell cycle and DNA processing	203	342	388	59.4%	52.3%
10.01	DNA processing	42	47	186	89.4%	22.6%
10.01.03	DNA synthesis and replication	3	3	77	100%	3.9%
10.03	cell cycle	44	64	265	68.8%	16.6%
10.03.01	mitotic cell cycle, cell cycle control	16	17	217	94.1%	7.4%
10.03.02	meiosis	1	1	44	100%	2.3%
11	transcription	346	623	553	55.5%	62.6%
11.02	RNA synthesis	92	157	354	58.6%	26.0%
11.04	RNA processing	56	76	170	73.7%	32.9%
11.04.01	RNA processing	21	34	54	61.8%	38.9%
11.04.03	mRNA processing (splicing, 5'-, 3'-end proc)	16	16	100	100%	16.0%
12	protein synthesis	162	204	300	79.4%	54.0%
12.01	ribosome biogenesis	105	108	176	97.2%	59.7%
14	protein fate (folding, modification, destination)	176	285	448	61.8%	39.3%
14.07	protein modification	16	16	139	100%	11.5%
14.13	protein degradation	40	43	116	93.0%	34.5%
14.13.01	cytoplasmic and nuclear protein degradation	29	29	83	100%	34.9%
20	cellular transport, transport facilitation and routes	207	392	431	52.8%	48.0%
20.01	transported compounds (substrates)	36	42	151	85.7%	23.8%
20.03	transport facilitation	7	7	79	100%	8.9%
20.09	transport routes	64	112	367	57.1%	17.4%
20.09.18	cellular import	5	5	95	100%	5.3%
32	cell rescue, defense and virulence	43	56	143	76.8%	30.1%
32.01	stress response	21	27	92	77.8%	22.8%

Function Entry	Annotation	|TP|	|TP|+|FP|	|TP|+|FN|	Precision	Recall
32.07	detoxification	5	6	49	83.3%	10.2%
34	interaction with the cellular environment	42	45	212	93.3%	19.8%
34.01	ionic homeostasis	9	9	89	100%	10.1%
34.01.01	homeostasis of cations	3	3	83	100%	3.6%
34.11	cellular sensing and response	21	22	125	95.5%	16.8%
34.11.03	chemoperception and response	21	22	125	95.5%	16.8%
42	biogenesis of cellular components	72	108	263	66.7%	27.4%
42.01	cell wall	7	7	84	100%	8.3%
42.04	cytoskeleton	6	7	71	85.7%	8.5%
42.16	mitochondrion	36	46	71	78.3%	50.7%
43	cell type differentiation	12	12	193	100%	6.2%
43.01	fungal/microorganismi c cell type differentiation	12	12	193	100%	6.2%
Total		2307	3458	7607	66.7%	30.3%

Table 1. Detailed prediction results on 40 gene classes in yeast time-series gene expression dataset [5]. For training purposes in HMM, only 40 gene classes were included which have at least 100 ORFs in MIPS. The results were based on the split-HMMs using 3-fold cross validation.

Application 2 – Human Tumor CNA Prediction

Using cross validation, HMM-CNA was applied to 64 MCLs, on which both GEP and CGH experiments were performed [22]. The entire dataset was split into training and testing datasets. In the training dataset, the HMM model was trained by the paired GEP and CGH data on the same tumor samples, and in the testing dataset, the specified HMM model was applied to the GEP data for a new tumor sample to predict its CNAs. The predicted gains and losses were compared with those identified by experimental CGH on the gene level for the sensitivities and specificities, and on the cytoband level for the recurrent genetic abnormalities.

Gene-Level Validation

We first evaluated HMM Viterbi decoding method by *sensitivity*, *specificity* and *accuracy* against experimental CGH in predicting gain and loss of each gene for all the samples using LOOCV. For comparison purpose, the performance of rGEP and sGEP methods were also included. Table 2 summarized the average *sensitivity*, *specificity* and *accuracy* for all chromosomes on 64 MCL samples. Figures 5 showed the performance on individual chromosomes for *sensitivity* (A) and *specificity* (B). In general, *sensitivity* was improved from 40% in GEP to 45% in sGEP and to 75% in HMM, and *specificity* from 70% in GEP to 85% in sGEP and to 90% in HMM, in predicting gain; in predicting loss, *sensitivity* from 30% in GEP to 50% in sGEP and to 60% in HMM, and *specificity* from 80% in GEP to 90% in sGEP and

HMM. These results suggested that the HMM were able to capture the hidden genomic CNA information buried in the GEP data; while directly mapping GEP status to CGH status without any learning process, such as rGEP and sGEP methods, could not predict well.

		Sensitivity (%)	Specificity (%)	Accuracy (%)
Gain	rGEP	38.45± 2.93	71.43± 0.58	69.46± 1.50
	sGEP	42.77± 10.42	86.33± 2.97	83.59± 3.48
	HMM	**74.49± 17.77**	**88.56± 4.78**	**87.50± 5.59**
Loss	rGEP	28.26± 3.70	80.94± 0.70	77.71± 3.47
	sGEP	50.66± 24.13	**92.71± 2.00***	89.19± 3.63
	HMM	**59.63± 17.22**	90.63± 4.91	**89.30± 5.69**

Table 2. Sensitivity, specificity and accuracy of HMM, rGEP and sGEP as compared to experimental CGH.

The HMM prediction were good for the majority of chromosomes, but we noticed that on some chromosomes HMM prediction was not good, such as chromosomes 1, 6, 9, 10 and 13 for gain and chromosomes 4, 5, 15 and 18 for loss. This is due to infrequent aberrations and hence insufficient training data for the gains or losses on those chromosomes. For example, in the CGH data of the 64 MCL cases, only one, three, one, two and one cases were observed with gain on chromosomes 1, 6, 9, 10 and 13, respectively, and two, one, one and two cases with loss on chromosomes 4, 5, 15 and 18, respectively.

Cytoband-Level Validation

Cytobands are defined as the chromosomal areas distinguishable from other segments by appearing darker or lighter by one or more banding techniques for karyotype description. To compare HMM prediction with the "gold standard" experimental CGH on the same resolution (our experimental CGH detected gains and losses on cytobands), we also determined cytoband-level gains and losses from HMM by applying a smoothing algorithm as described in *Method* section.

Figures 6 showed the results of cytoband level gains and losses on MCL dataset. The two HMM decoding methods, Viterbi and Posterior, were shown in panels A and B, respectively, where loss frequencies for cytobands (i.e. the number of cases harboring a loss on a cytoband) were shown on left-sided bars and gain frequencies on right-sided bars. In Posterior decoding (Figure 6B), as expected, the frequencies of gains and losses decrease as posterior probability increases (p=0.5, 0.6, 0.7, 0.8 and 0.9), and those frequencies are highly correlated (Pearson's correlation coefficients around 0.99, Table 3). Comparing the results from Viterbi (panel A) and Posterior (panel B), a high concordance was also observed (Pearson's correlation coefficients around 0.98, Table 3). Therefore, the Viterbi method was used to represent HMM in comparison of the experimental CGH side by side in panel C.

Table 3 showed that Pearson's correlation coefficients between HMM and CGH are around 0.8 for gains and losses. In Figure 6C, gains and losses were shown separately with CGH results colored yellow above X axis and HMM results colored red below X axis. Apparently, the majority of the frequent gains and losses predicted by HMM are in good concordance with those identified by experimental CGH, such as gains of 3q, 7, 8q, 15q and 18 and losses

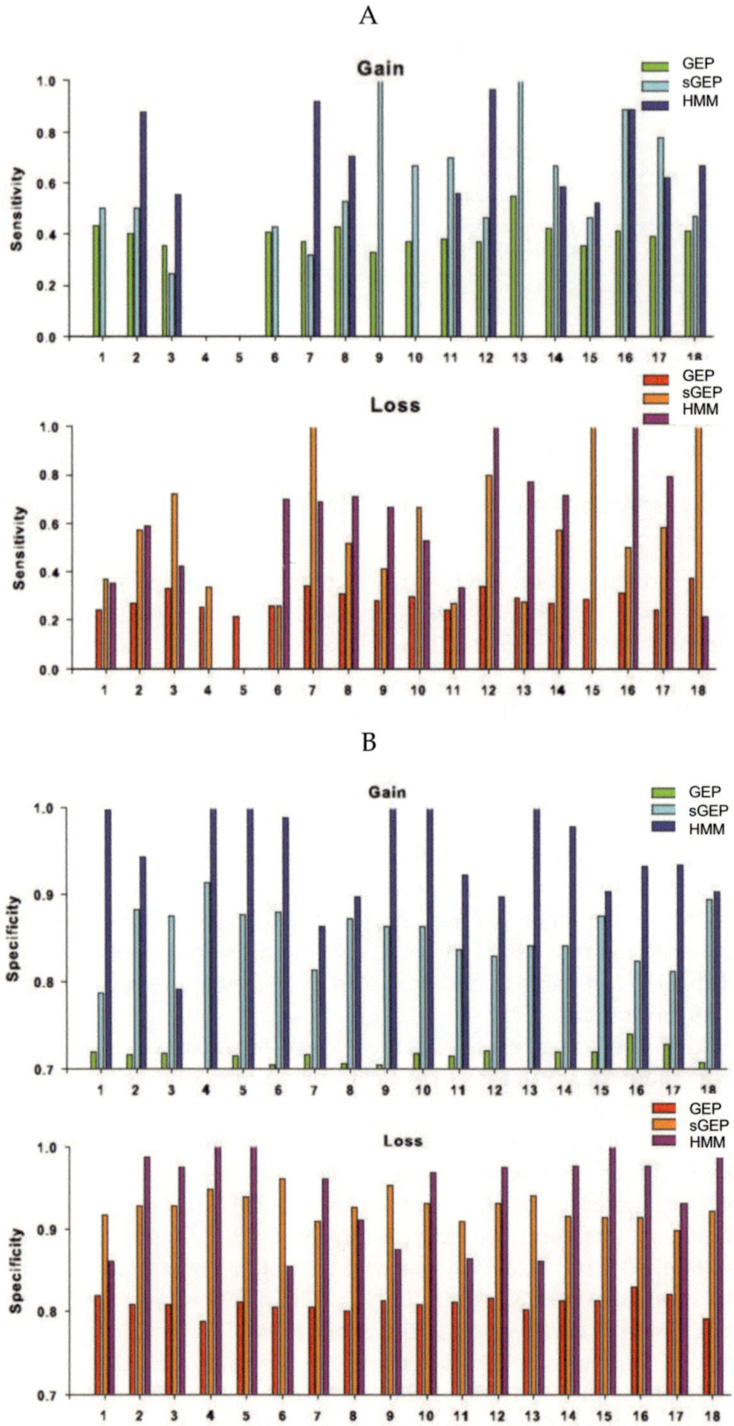

Fig. 5. Sensitivity (A) and specificity (B) in predicting gain and loss regions by GEP, sGEP and HMM in 64 MCL.

of 1p21-p31, 6q, 8p, 9p, 9q, 11q21-q23, 13 and 17p13-pter. Those regions have also been revealed as high-frequency chromosomal alteration regions in various studies using conventional cytogenetics, CGH and array CGH {Bea, 2005 #38}.

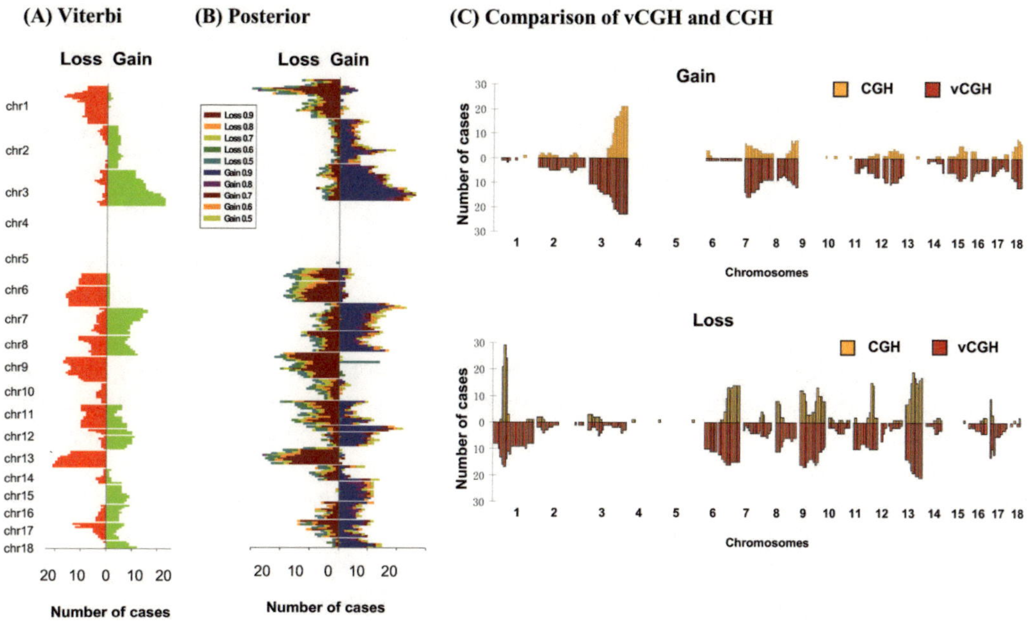

Fig. 6. Cytoband-level gains and losses by HMM and CGH on 64 MCLs. (A) HMM Viterbi method. (B) HMM Posterior method with a series of probability cutoffs (p=0.5, 0.6, 0.7, 0.8 and 0.9). In (A) and (B), left-sided bars correspond to losses whereas right-sided bars to gains. On Y axis are the cytobands ordered from pter to qter (from top to bottom) for each chromosome and on X axis, the length of each bar indicates the gain and loss frequencies, i.e. the number of cases harboring a gain or loss on a cytoband. (C) Comparison of HMM and CGH where Viterbi method was used to represent HMM. Gain and loss were shown separately. CGH results were shown in yellow (above X axis) and HMM prediction were shown in red (below X axis). On X axis, each bar represents a cytoband ordered from pter to qter for chr1 to chr18. On Y axis, the height of each bar indicates frequency, i.e. the number of cases horboring a gain or loss on a cytoband.

There are also some limitations of the approach due to utilization of transcripts-based GEP data. For example, it may not predict well for regions with few genes (also called "gene desert"), or if the genes in a region are not expressed at a sufficiently high level for GEP. The HMM approach is also limited by the design of the GEP arrays. For example, on Affymetrix HG-U133 plus 2 platform, there are no probes distributed on the p arms of chromosomes 13, 14, 15, 21 and 22, and hence those regions are unpredictable for gains or losses by HMM.

5. Conclusions

In this chapter, we demonstrated two applications using HMMs to predict gene functions and DNA copy number alternations from microarray gene expression data. In the first application of HMM on yeast time-series expression data, the overall prediction accuracy of

		CGH	HMM Viterbi	HMM Posterior				
				p_0.5	p_0.6	p_0.7	p_0.8	p_0.9
CGH		1	0.766	0.734	0.745	0.744	0.752	0.756
HMM Viterbi		0.828	1	0.970	0.978	0.978	0.978	0.973
HMM Posterior	p_0.5	0.831	0.978	1	0.990	0.986	0.982	0.969
	p_0.6	0.828	0.980	0.996	1	0.996	0.991	0.978
	p_0.7	0.828	0.983	0.992	0.995	1	0.993	0.981
	p_0.8	0.827	0.985	0.988	0.992	0.996	1	0.990
	p_0.9	0.820	0.981	0.983	0.986	0.991	0.993	1

Table 3. Pearson correlation of cytoband-level gain and loss frequencies between CGH, HMM Viterbi, and HMM Posterior. Gain were shown in the bottom, and loss in the top triangles.

our model is significantly higher than that of SVMs and KNNs. A properly designed HMM is capable of modeling the three features of expression data: pattern variation within a class, experimental noise, and Markov property. The extraordinary flexibility of HMMs allows us to extend the current model in several directions. One of the current developments is to extend the HMM model to Bayes nets for functional prediction from heterogeneous data sets. With appropriately constructed conditional distribution, all kinds of available data can be applied for training and inference using Bayesian network model. Besides the functional prediction of unknown ORFs, one potential application of this method is to search for ORFs of functional homology in databases. To do this, a proper cut-off likelihood value (or equivalently a LOD score) must be specified. Whenever a homolog is found (i.e., beyond the cut-off value), it may be included as a training set to reinforce the training process.

In the second application of HMM on the human tumor microarray gene expression data, we proposed a novel computational approach based on HMMs to predict genetic abnormalities in tumor cells. Taking advantage of the rich GEP data already publicly available, HMM may significantly enhance the identification of genetic abnormalities in cancer research. Our model is among the first which employed HMM for the purpose of GEP-to-CGH prediction. We expected the HMM to capture two primary sources of uncertainty embedded in genomic data: the significant but subtle correlations between GEP and CGH, and the sequential transitions of CNAs along chromosomes. We applied the HMM model to 64 MCL samples and using cross validation, HMM achieved 80% sensitivity, 90% specificity and 90% accuracy in predicting gains and losses as compared to the experimental CGH on the same tumor cases. The recurrent gains and losses predicted by HMM on cytobands were concordant with those identified by CGH. In addition, our model does not only highlight DNA CNA regions but also served as an integrative tool cross-linking genomic and transcriptiomic data for functionally relavent genomic abnormal regions. As this HMM-based method is a general computational tool which can be applied to any types of tumors, it may significantly enhance the identification of genetic abnormalities in cancer research. To improve the model, we plan to add relevant biological parameters to preprocess or filter the data in prediction. We will consider gene densities, transcriptional units, regional epigenomic silencing, genes that not expressed in normal samples, common "genomic aberrations", and human genomic copy number polymorphism in the model.

6. References

[1] Durbin R, Eddy S, Krogh A, Mitchison G: Biological sequence analysis: probabilistic models of proteins and necleic acids. New York: Cambridge Unisersity Press; 1998.

[2] Brown MP, Grundy WN, Lin D, Cristianini N, Sugnet CW, Furey TS, Ares M, Jr., Haussler D: Knowledge-based analysis of microarray gene expression data by using support vector machines. *Proceedings of the National Academy of Sciences of the United States of America* 2000, 97(1):262-267.

[3] Kuramochi M, Karypis G: Gene Classification Using Expression Profiles: A Feasibility Study. In: *Proceedings of the 2nd IEEE International Symposium on Bioinformatics & Bioengineering (BIBE 2001)*. 2001: 191.

[4] Pavlidis P, Weston J, Cai J, Grundy WN: Gene function classification from heterogeneous data. In: *Proceedings of the 5th International Conference on Computational Molecular Biology (RECOMB 2001)*. 2001: 242-248

[5] Eisen MB, Spellman PT, Brown PO, Botstein D: Cluster analysis and display of genome-wide expression patterns. *Proceedings of the National Academy of Sciences of the United States of America* 1998, 95(25):14863-14868.

[6] Churchill GA: Fundamentals of experimental design for cDNA microarrays. *Nature genetics* 2002, 32 Suppl:490-495.

[7] Cahill DP, Kinzler KW, Vogelstein B, Lengauer C: Genetic instability and darwinian selection in tumours. *Trends Cell Biol* 1999, 9(12):M57-60.

[8] Phillips JL, Hayward SW, Wang Y, Vasselli J, Pavlovich C, Padilla-Nash H, Pezullo JR, Ghadimi BM, Grossfeld GD, Rivera A *et al*: The consequences of chromosomal aneuploidy on gene expression profiles in a cell line model for prostate carcinogenesis. *Cancer Res* 2001, 61(22):8143-8149.

[9] du Manoir S, Speicher MR, Joos S, Schrock E, Popp S, Dohner H, Kovacs G, Robert-Nicoud M, Lichter P, Cremer T: Detection of complete and partial chromosome gains and losses by comparative genomic in situ hybridization. *Human genetics* 1993, 90(6):590-610.

[10] Kallioniemi A, Kallioniemi OP, Sudar D, Rutovitz D, Gray JW, Waldman F, Pinkel D: Comparative genomic hybridization for molecular cytogenetic analysis of solid tumors. *Science (New York, NY* 1992, 258(5083):818-821.

[11] Stanford Microarray Database [http://smd.stanford.edu/]

[12] Gene Expression Omnibus, NCBI [http://www.ncbi.nlm.nih.gov/geo/]

[13] UPenn RAD database [http://www.cbil.upenn.edu/RAD/php/index.php]

[14] caArray, NCI [https://cabig.nci.nih.gov/tools/caArray]

[15] ArrayExpress at EBI [http://www.ebi.ac.uk/microarray-as/ae/]

[16] SKY/M-FISH & CGH Database at NCBI [http://www.ncbi.nlm.nih.gov/sky/]

[17] Bea S, Zettl A, Wright G, Salaverria I, Jehn P, Moreno V, Burek C, Ott G, Puig X, Yang L *et al*: Diffuse large B-cell lymphoma subgroups have distinct genetic profiles that influence tumor biology and improve gene-expression-based survival prediction. *Blood* 2005, 106(9):3183-3190.

[18] Hyman E, Kauraniemi P, Hautaniemi S, Wolf M, Mousses S, Rozenblum E, Ringner M, Sauter G, Monni O, Elkahloun A *et al*: Impact of DNA amplification on gene expression patterns in breast cancer. *Cancer Res* 2002, 62(21):6240-6245.

[19] Iqbal J, Kucuk C, Deleeuw RJ, Srivastava G, Tam W, Geng H, Klinkebiel D, Christman JK, Patel K, Cao K *et al*: Genomic analyses reveal global functional alterations that

promote tumor growth and novel tumor suppressor genes in natural killer-cell malignancies. *Leukemia* 2009, 23(6):1139-1151.

[20] Lenz G, Wright GW, Emre NC, Kohlhammer H, Dave SS, Davis RE, Carty S, Lam LT, Shaffer AL, Xiao W *et al*: Molecular subtypes of diffuse large B-cell lymphoma arise by distinct genetic pathways. *Proceedings of the National Academy of Sciences of the United States of America* 2008, 105(36):13520-13525.

[21] Pollack JR, Sorlie T, Perou CM, Rees CA, Jeffrey SS, Lonning PE, Tibshirani R, Botstein D, Borresen-Dale AL, Brown PO: Microarray analysis reveals a major direct role of DNA copy number alteration in the transcriptional program of human breast tumors. *Proceedings of the National Academy of Sciences of the United States of America* 2002, 99(20):12963-12968.

[22] Salaverria I, Zettl A, Bea S, Moreno V, Valls J, Hartmann E, Ott G, Wright G, Lopez-Guillermo A, Chan WC *et al*: Specific secondary genetic alterations in mantle cell lymphoma provide prognostic information independent of the gene expression-based proliferation signature. *J Clin Oncol* 2007, 25(10):1216-1222.

[23] Virtaneva K, Wright FA, Tanner SM, Yuan B, Lemon WJ, Caligiuri MA, Bloomfield CD, de La Chapelle A, Krahe R: Expression profiling reveals fundamental biological differences in acute myeloid leukemia with isolated trisomy 8 and normal cytogenetics. *Proceedings of the National Academy of Sciences of the United States of America* 2001, 98(3):1124-1129.

[24] Linn SC, West RB, Pollack JR, Zhu S, Hernandez-Boussard T, Nielsen TO, Rubin BP, Patel R, Goldblum JR, Siegmund D *et al*: Gene expression patterns and gene copy number changes in dermatofibrosarcoma protuberans. *The American journal of pathology* 2003, 163(6):2383-2395.

[25] Varis A, Wolf M, Monni O, Vakkari ML, Kokkola A, Moskaluk C, Frierson H, Jr., Powell SM, Knuutila S, Kallioniemi A *et al*: Targets of gene amplification and overexpression at 17q in gastric cancer. *Cancer Res* 2002, 62(9):2625-2629.

[26] Fridlyand J, Snijders AM, Pinkel D, Albertson DG, Jain AN: Hidden Markov Models Approach to the Analysis of Array CGH Data. *J Multivariate Anal* 2004, 90:132-153.

[27] Marioni JC, Thorne NP, Tavare S: BioHMM: a heterogeneous hidden Markov model for segmenting array CGH data. *Bioinformatics (Oxford, England)* 2006, 22(9):1144-1146.

[28] Koski T: Hidden Markov Models of Bioinformatics: Kluwer Academic Pub.; 2002.

[29] Rabiner L: A tutorial on hidden Markov models and selected applications in speech recognition. In: *Proc IEEE*. vol. 77; 1989: 257-286.

[30] Mewes HW, Frishman D, Guldener U, Mannhaupt G, Mayer K, Mokrejs M, Morgenstern B, Munsterkotter M, Rudd S, Weil B: MIPS: a database for genomes and protein sequences. *Nucleic Acids Res* 2002, 30(1):31-34.

[31] Eddy SR: Profile hidden Markov models. *Bioinformatics (Oxford, England)* 1998, 14(9):755-763.

[32] BRB-Array Tool [http://linus.nci.nih.gov/BRB-ArrayTools.html]

[33] Jong K, Marchiori E, Meijer G, Vaart AV, Ylstra B: Breakpoint identification and smoothing of array comparative genomic hybridization data. *Bioinformatics (Oxford, England)* 2004, 20(18):3636-3637.

13

Application of HMM to the Study of Three-Dimensional Protein Structure

Christelle Reynès[1], Leslie Regad[2], Stéphanie Pérot[3], Grégory Nuel[5] and Anne-Claude Camproux[4]
[1,2,3,4]*Molécules Thérapeutiques in silico (MTi), UMR-S973 Inserm, Université Paris Diderot, Paris*
[5]*MAP5, UMR CNRS8145, Université Paris-Descartes, Paris*
France

1. Introduction

Hidden Markov models (HMM) have been successfully applied in molecular biology, especially in several areas of computational biology. For example, it is used to model protein families, to construct multiple sequence alignments, to determine protein domains in a query sequence or to predict the topology of transmembrane beta-barrels proteins (Bateman *et al.*, 2004; Durbin *et al.*, 1998; Krogh *et al.*, 1994; Pang *et al.*, 2010).

Proteins are macromolecules responsible for performing many important tasks in living organisms. The function of proteins strongly depends on their shapes. For example, carrier proteins should recognize the molecules they carry such as hemoglobins should recognize oxygen atoms, anti-bodies their antigens,... Protein misfolding may cause malfunctions such as Parkinson and Alzheimer diseases. Therefore, it is necessary to know the structure of a protein to understand its functions and the disturbances caused by the inappropriate behavior derived from misfolding. Precisely this knowledge makes it possible to develop drugs and vaccines and synthetize proteins which, for example, disable the regions of virus activity, preventing them from acting on the cells.

The exploration of protein structures, in its initial phase, consisted in simplifying three-dimensional (3D) structures into secondary structures, including the well-known repetitive and regular zone - the α-helix (30% of protein residues) and the β-sheet (20%). The remaining elements (50% of residues) constitute a category called loops, often considered as structurally variable, and decomposed into some subcategories such as turns (see Frishman & Argos, 1995, for example). Although the prediction of secondary structure types can be achieved with a success rate of 80%, the description of the secondary structures of a protein does not provide *per se* an accurate enough description to allow the characterization of the complete structure of proteins.

Moreover, protein structures are determined experimentally mostly by X-ray crystallography and nuclear magnetic resonance (NMR) techniques. Both require sophisticated laboratories, are time and cost expensive and cannot be applied to all proteins. On the other hand, the methods consisting in protein sequencing are easier and less expensive than methods implying structure determination. The recent genome sequencing projects (Siva, 2008; Waterston *et al.*, 2002) have provided sequence information for a large number of proteins. Consequentely, Swiss-Prot database release 57.6 (Boeckmann *et al.*, 2003), a curated protein sequence database provided by the Universal Protein Knowledgebase (UniProt) consortium, contains sequences of more than 13,069,501 distinct proteins (Consortium, 2010), whereas the Protein Data Bank (PDB) (Henrick *et al.*, 2998) contains 70,000 distinct protein structures. Thus, there is an increasing gap between the number of available protein sequences and experimentally derived protein structures, which makes it even more important to improve the methods for 3D structure protein prediction.

Thus, an important challenge in structural bioinformatics is to obtain an accurate 3D structural knowledge about proteins in order to obtain a detailed functional characterization and a better understanding. With the increase of available 3D structures of proteins, many studies (Baeten *et al.*, 2010; Brevern *et al.*, 2000; Bystroff *et al.*, 2000; Kolodny *et al.*, 2002; Micheletti *et al.*, 2000; Pandini *et al.*, 2010; Unger *et al.*, 1989), have focused on the identification of a detailed and systematic decomposition of structures into a finite set of generic protein fragments. Despite the fact that some libraries provide an accurate approximation of protein conformation, their identification teaches us little about the way protein structures are organized. They do not consider the rules that govern the assembly process of the local fragments to produce a protein structure. An obvious mean of overcoming such limitations is to consider that the series of representative fragments describing protein structures are in fact not independent but governed by a Markovian process. In this chapter, the first part presents the development of a HMM approach to analyze 3D protein architecture. We present the use of a HMM to identify a library of representative fragments, called Structural Letters (SLs) and their transition process, resulting in a structural alphabet, called HMM-SA, decomposing protein 3D conformations. The aim of this part is to assess how much HMM is able to yield insights into the modular framework of proteins, i.e. to encode protein backbones into uni-dimensional (1D) sequentially dependent SLs. The HMM-SA is a very performant tool to simplify 3D conformation of proteins and such a simplification can constitute a very relevant way to analyze protein architecture. Different applications of HMM-SA for structure analysis are listed, such as loop modelling, protein structure comparison, analysis of protein deformation during protein interactions, analysis of protein contacts, detection and prediction of exceptional structural patterns.

The second part of the chapter presents a contribution to the important challenge of protein structure prediction by predicting through another HMM the presence/absence of functional patterns identified thanks to HMM-SA. The method can be decomposed into two steps: in a first time, a simple link between amino-acids (AAs) and SLs is learned through boolean functions, then, a HMM is used to take into account the results of the first step as long as the dependencies between successive SLs. The first step is independent on the studied pattern whereas a new HMM is automatically built for each new pattern. The method will be illustrated on three examples.

2. HMM-SA obtention

2.1 Datasets and description of three dimensional conformations

The data extraction of HMM-SA is performed from a collection of 1,429 non-redundant protein structures (Berstein *et al.*, 1977) extracted from the PDB. The selected proteins have a crystallographic resolution lower than 2.5 Å and less than 30% sequence identity with one another (Hobohm *et al.*, 1992). Because the structure of the model is based on local dependence between successive residues in each protein, all non-contiguous protein chains (i.e. those containing fragments that spanned gaps) were eliminated from the dataset. The polypeptide chains were scanned in overlapping windows that encompassed four successive α-carbons (C_α), thereby producing a succession of short-backbone chain fragments. As in some previous studies (Pavone *et al.*, 1996; Rackovsky, 1993; Rooman *et al.*, 1990; Smith *et al.*, 1997), we used four-residue lengths, which contain enough information to find basic structural elements: four-residue turns for α-helices, bridges for β-sheets and undefined loop structures. Moreover, a four-residue segment is small enough to keep the number of SL categories reasonable. Increasing the number of residues per segment would introduce larger variability and would lead to a larger number of categories.

The collection of 1,429 proteins represents a total of 332,493 four-residue fragments. Protein structures are described using the distances between C_α, see Figure 1a, as series of overlapping fragments of four-residue length (Camproux *et al.*, 1999a). Let $C_{\alpha_1}, C_{\alpha_2}, \ldots, C_{\alpha_n}$ be the n carbon atoms of the backbone structure of the protein. From these data, we build a sequence $X_0, X_1, \ldots, X_{n-4}$ such as $X_i = (X_i^1, X_i^2, X_i^3, X_i^4) \in \mathbb{R}^4$ with:

$$X_i^1 = ||\overrightarrow{C_{\alpha_{i+1}} C_{\alpha_{i+3}}}||; \quad X_i^2 = ||\overrightarrow{C_{\alpha_{i+1}} C_{\alpha_{i+4}}}||; \quad X_i^3 = ||\overrightarrow{C_{\alpha_{i+2}} C_{\alpha_{i+4}}}||;$$

$$X_i^4 = \frac{\overrightarrow{C_{\alpha_{i+1}} C_{\alpha_{i+2}}} \wedge \overrightarrow{C_{\alpha_{i+2}} C_{\alpha_{i+3}}}}{||\overrightarrow{C_{\alpha_{i+1}} C_{\alpha_{i+2}}} \wedge \overrightarrow{C_{\alpha_{i+2}} C_{\alpha_{i+3}}}||} \times \overrightarrow{C_{\alpha_{i+3}} C_{\alpha_{i+4}}}.$$

The three values X_i^1, X_i^2, X_i^3 correspond to distances between the non consecutive $(C_{\alpha_1}, C_{\alpha_2}, C_{\alpha_3}, C_{\alpha_4})$ and X_i^4 the oriented projection of the last α-carbon C_{α_4} onto the plane formed by the three first ones, as shown in Figure 1a. The three distances between consecutive C_α are not considered in this approach because fewly variable.

The first and third distances (X_i^1, X_i^3) describe the opening of the beginning and end of a four-residue fragment and X_i^2 describes the global length of this fragment. X_i^4 is proportionnal to the determinant of the three vectors defined by the successive C_α pairs normalized by the norm or modulus of the first two vectors. This descriptor is proportional to the distance of the four C_α to the plane P built by the first three C_α. The sign of X_i^4 indicates the topological orientation of the fragment relative to P : trigonometric, i.e. the fourth α-carbon C_{α_4} is located above P (for a positive value of X_i^4) and inverse trigonometric, i.e. the fourth α-carbon C_{α_4} is located below P (for a negative value of X_i^4). X_i^4 not only gives the direction of the fragment fold but also provides direct interpretable information about the volume of the fragment. A *flat* fragment, i.e. with no volume, corresponds to a value of X_i^4 close to 0.

2.2 HMM modelling

In the first work, the idea was to consider the model of Figure 2 where all X_i are generated independently from each other conditionally to one out of the K hidden states $S_i \in \mathcal{S} = \{1, 2, \ldots, K\}$ such as:

$$\mathcal{L}(X_i | S_i = r) \sim \mathcal{N}(\mu_r, \Sigma_r) \quad \forall r \in \mathcal{S} \tag{1}$$

with $\mathcal{N}(\mu_r, \Sigma_r)$ four-dimensional multi-normal density with parameters (μ_r, Σ_r) describing the average descriptors, the variability of each descriptor and the covariance between descriptors as estimated on the associated fragments. We additionally consider two types of model to identify a structural alphabet corresponding to K SLs: (i) a simple process without memory or (ii) a HMM process with memory of order 1.

Model without Memory, denoted MM(order 0), assuming independence of the K SLs, is

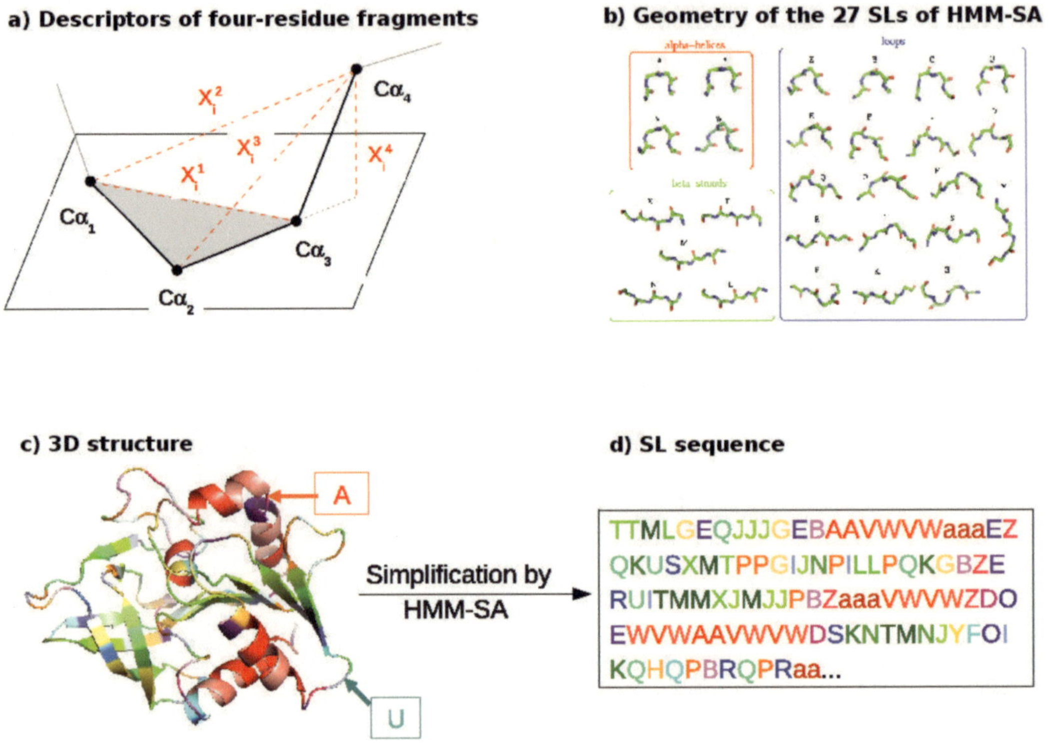

Fig. 1. Encoding of 3D conformation of proteins using HMM-SA with 27 SLs. (a) Representation of the four descriptors $(X_i^1, \ldots, X_i^4)$, used to describe the 3D conformation of four successive C_α fragments. (b) Geometry of the final 27 SLs, ranked by corresponding secondary structures. (c) 3D representation of the B chain of protein 1gpw colored according to its SL encoding. (d) Final 1D SL encoding of the B chain of protein 1gpw.

identified by training simple finite mixture of four-dimensional multi-normal densities. Model assuming that the sequence (S_i) is distributed according to a homogeneous Markov chain with starting distribution ν and transition matrix τ is defined by:

$$\mathbb{P}(S_1 = r) = \nu(r) \quad \text{and} \quad \mathbb{P}(S_{i+1} = s | S_i = r) = \tau(r, s) \quad \forall r, s \in \mathcal{S}. \tag{2}$$

It hence results in a model with $(14K + K^2 - 1)$ parameters.

2.3 Model selection: Statistical criteria to determine the optimal number of SLs

The classical model selection approach is based on the parsimony principle: we want to select the model that better fits the data with the smallest possible complexity. This typically leads to penalized likelihood criteria like the Bayesian Information Criterion (BIC, Schwartz, 1978) which balances the log-likelihood of the model and a penalization term related to the number of parameters of the model and the sample size. In the first work, structural alphabets of

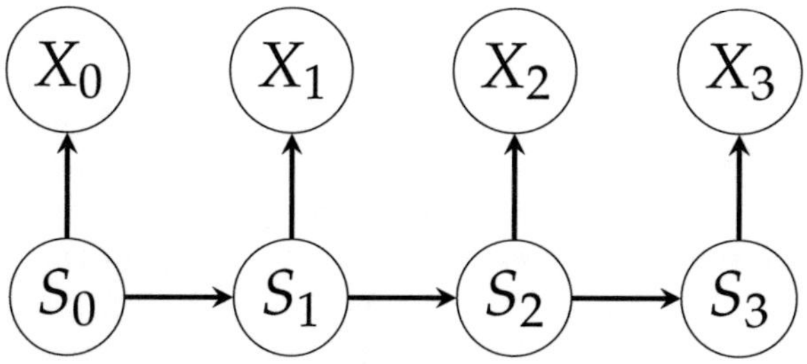

Fig. 2. Graph of dependencies in the simplest model with $n = 7$ C_α hence resulting in a total of $n - 3 = 4$ SLs.

different sizes K, denoted SA$-K$ were learned on two independent learning sets of proteins by progressively increasing K, and using the two types of model detailed in section 2.2 (with or without memory) and compared using BIC.

2.4 Encoding proteins

One ultimate goal is to reconstruct the unobserved (hidden) SL sequence of the polypeptidic chains, given the corresponding four-dimensional vectors of descriptors, and to provide a classification of successive fragments in K SLs. For a given 3D conformation and a selected model (fixed number K of SLs), the corresponding best SL sequence among all the possible paths in $\mathcal{S}^n = \{1, 2, \ldots, K\}^n$ can be reconstructed by a dynamic programming algorithm based on Markovian process.
Once a model has been selected and its parameters estimated, we classically use the Viterbi's algorithm (Rabiner, 1989) in order to obtain the Maximum A Posteriori (MAP) encoding:

$$\hat{s}^{\text{MAP}} = \arg\max_{s} \ell(\hat{\theta}|X = x, S = s). \qquad (3)$$

We used this approach to optimally describe each structure as a serie of SLs. This process of compression of 3D protein conformation into 1D SL sequence is illustrated in Figure 1c,d, on the structure of chain B of the amidotransferase (pdb ID: 1gpw_B). This protein is coloured after HMM-SA encoding, according to its corresponding series of SLs.
Assessing the discretization of protein structures
For a given SL, the average Root-Mean-Square deviation (RMSd) between C_α coordinates, that is an Euclidean distance of the fragments to their centroid best superimposed, is used to measure the structural variability of each SL. For two given fragments, the RMSd between C_α coordinates of superimposed fragments is used to measure their structural proximity.
To reconstruct the protein 3D structures from their description as a series of SLs, and to keep some possible comparisons, we use the building procedure employed by Kolodny *et al.* (2002). Briefly, the fragments are assembled using an iterative concatenation procedure to adjust 3D conformation.

3. HMM-SA as a general concept to simplify 3D protein structure analysis ?

3.1 Results of HMM-SA identification

HMM-SA is weakly dependent on the learning set

Structural alphabet of increasing sizes using either HMM or MM are learned and compared on the basis of their goodness of fit. The influence of the Markovian process is large. For MM, no BIC optimum is reached until alphabet sizes of 70 whereas, for HMM, a larger optimum is reached for 27 hidden states, which means a better fit of the data using HMM. Interestingly, the Markov classification takes advantage of information implicitly contained in the succession of observations to greatly reduce the number of SLs, while keeping a more homogeneous repartition of fragments into the different SLs (the least frequent SL represents 1.5% of fragments).

Similar results are obtained using two independent learning sets of 250 proteins with similar BIC curves evolution. It follows that, at the optimum, structural alphabet is very weakly dependent on the learning set, which in turn suggests that the learned model can be considered as representative of all protein structures. The optimal structural alphabet, HMM-SA, obtained by using statistical criterion BIC, corresponds to 27 SLs and their transition matrix. Main characteristics of HMM-SA (Camproux *et al.*, 2004) are briefly summarized below.

Geometrical and logical description of HMM-SA

The 27 identified SLs are denoted as (case sensitive) structural letters: namely $a, A, B, ..., Y, Z$. The set of SLs, sorted by increasing stretches is presented in Figure 1b and their transitions constitute the structural alphabet, HMM-SA. The *local fit approximation* is low, as quantified by the average C_α RMSd to the centroid associated with each SL (0.23 ± 0.14 Å). Concerning description of logic of protein architecture, 66% of the 729 possible transitions between SLs have frequencies of less than 1%. The existence of pathways between SLs is observed, obeying some precise and unidirectional rules. These results are detailed in Camproux *et al.* (1999b; 2004).

Actually, SLs associated with close shapes have been distinguished by different logical rules. SLs A, a, V, W appear almost exclusively in α-helices (more than 92% of associated fragments assigned to α-helices) while five SLs L, N, M, T, X are mostly located in extended structures (from 47% to 78% of associated fragments assigned to strands). Interestingly, the other 18 SLs are involved in loops description, which is particularly interesting given the variability of loop structures and their implication in numerous important processes.

The stochastic HMM approach allows (i) the characterization of different short structural 3D SLs (ii) the description of the heterogeneity of their corresponding short fragments and (iii) the study of their global organization by quantifying their connections. The transition matrix only shows a limited number of transitions between SLs, indicating that the connections by which the SLs form the protein structures are well organized.

Moreover, the learning process attempts to optimize the likelihood associated with the entire trajectories of the proteins, resulting in propagation of such long range conditioning to the short range constraints that are learned. Our model fits well the previous knowledge related to protein architecture organisation and seems able to grab some subtle details of protein organisation, such as helix sub-level organisation schemes. For instance, the two closest SLs A, a in terms of geometry, close to canonical α-helix, are distinguished by different prefered transitions. Taking into account the dependence between the states results in a description of local protein structures of low complexity. Although we use short fragments, the learning process on entire protein conformations captures the logic of the assembly on a larger scale. HMM-SA shows very reasonable performance in terms of reconstruction of the whole protein structure accuracy, (RMSd value less than 1 Å), compared to other recent fragment libraries optimized in a purpose of reconstruction (Kolodny *et al.*, 2002; Micheletti *et al.*, 2000).

Subsequently, HMM-SA provides some kind of compression from the 3D protein coordinate space into the 1D structural alphabet space (see Figure 1 c,d). From such 1D encoding and the associated logical rules, it is possible to tackle the exploration of 3D protein conformations using 1D techniques, as performed in classical sequence analysis. This widens the perspective of being able to work with a 1D representation of 3D structures much beyond the simple search of exact words, through the use of the classical 1D AA alignment methods. We have explored different directions in which this facility could be of interest.

3.2 Different sucessful applications of HMM-SA

Different applications of HMM-SA have been explored, such as:

- study of conformations of side chains in protein structures (Gautier *et al.*, 2004). It establishes a set of tools for analyzing lateral chain conformations of proteins in the server Ressource Parisienne en Bioinformatique Structurale (RPBS, http://bioserv.rpbs.jussieu.fr/cgi-bin/SCit);
- improvement of protein fold recognition from AA content compared to classical methods by adding Markovian information (Deschavanne *et al.*, 2009);
- performing fast 3D similarity search (RPBS, http://bioserv.rpbs.jussieu.fr/cgi-bin/SA-Search). The detection and analysis of structural similarities of proteins can provide important insights into their functional mechanisms or relationship and offer the basis of classifications of the protein folds. The global 3D alignment of two proteins is NP-hard (Lathrop, 1994). Therefore, approximate methods have been proposed to achieve fast similarity searching, based on the direct consideration of protein α-carbon coordinates (Gibrat *et al.*, 1996; Holm & Sander, 1993; Shindyalov & Bourne, 1998). Using HMM, the lod-score matrix of similarity between SLs allows the quantification of the similarity of protein fragments encoded as different series of SLs. It is possible to use it with classical methods developed for the AA sequence similarity search and thus to reduce 3D searches as a 1*D* sequence alignment problem (Guyon *et al.*, 2004);
- analyzing protein contacts (Martin *et al.*, 2008b). This study showed that the description of protein contacts (intra and inter-molecular) by the local structure residues (described by HMM-SA) involved in these contacts is more sensitive than that provided by type of AAs involved in contacts;
- analyzing the deformation of proteins during interaction (Martin *et al.*, 2008a): HMM-SA has also been used to analyze the regions of protein/protein interactions before and after contact (Martin et al., 2008b). This study identified regions undergoing deformation, and the identification of common structural motifs from the strain involved in the interaction of two proteins;
- deciphering the shape and deformation of secondary structures (Baussand *et al.*, in press). The conformation of secondary structures can be further analyzed and detailed thanks to HMM-SA which allows a better local description of protein surface, core and interface in terms of secondary structure shape and deformation. Induced-fit modification tendencies should be valuable information to identify and characterize regions under strong structural constraints for functional reasons;
- in addition, HMM-SA was shown to be a powerful tool for the analysis of protein loops, the most variable and flexible regions in proteins (Camproux *et al.*, 2001; Regad *et al.*, 2006). They are, however, often known to play an important role in protein function and stability

(Fetrow, 1995; Fernandez-Fuentes *et al.*, 2004). The HMM-SA was optimised in terms of 3D local description of proteins and resulted in precise and detailed description of 3D conformations into 27 SLs: 18 SLs being focused on loop description. Indeed, the encoding of loop structures allowed the establishment of a systematic methodology to extract all the structural motifs of seven residues in all the loops, especially long loops. Analysis of these patterns and their environment has enabled a quantification of structural redundancy in loops. An analysis of their distribution in the short and long loops has shown that the short and long loops share a number of structural motifs (Regad *et al.*, 2008);

- concerning the information of AA sequence, all the SLs of HMM-SA have some significant AA sequence specificity compared to the profiles of a collection of protein fragments (Camproux & Tuffery, 2005). This dependence can be used to generate direct candidate folds from AA sequence in a two-steps scheme of prediction. First, the goal is to predict local SL series from AA sequence. For short fragments, available 3D conformation can be found in the PDB (using Guyon *et al.*, 2004); for longer ones (SL-fragments not available in the PDB), local SLs or SL-words could be assembled to generate 3D structures, following the same principles as Maupetit *et al.* (2009);
- concerning the 3D reconstruction, a recent paper (Maupetit *et al.*, 2009) has shown the performance of HMM-SA for peptides (short SL-fragments). Rational peptide design and large-scale prediction of peptide structures from AA sequences remain a challenge for chemical biologists. This paper proposed a *de novo* modelling of 3D conformations for peptides between 9 and 25 amino acids in aqueous solution. Using HMM-SA, PEP-FOLD assembles the predicted SL fragment profiles by a greedy procedure driven by a modified version of the OPEP coarse-grained force field;
- in addition, the HMM methodology of building structural alphabet has been proven to identify a specific structural alphabet for porin proteins (i.e. transmembrane proteins). This alphabet has helped to describe how fine these proteins are, specifically in terms of beta strands composition (Martin *et al.*, 2008c).

Actually, HMM-SA is a very interesting tool to study protein structures and hence function. In particular, it is interesting to identify conserved SL-patterns having particularities such as being associated to a specific function or to turns, for example. Then, the natural continuation of such identifications is to provide a method being able to detect those patterns directly from AA sequence. Thus, it makes it possible to annotate AA sequences with annotations identified from 3D structure without knowing the conformation of the considered sequence.
The last section focuses on the prediction of patterns identified as specific to a function for example.

4. Using HMM to detect interesting HMM-SA patterns

As previously introduced, sequencing technologies are constantly providing new AA sequences with often few functional knowledge. Hence, being able to retrieve information about new protein sequences is a critical problem.
In this context, automatic tools allowing to provide such information are of big interest. The most common way to perform such a search is to identify patterns specific from a given function for example and to design a prediction method. Information taken into account can consist in different levels: only sequence (Ansari & Raghave, 2010; Sigrist *et al.*, 2010), sequence and structure (Halperin *et al.*, 2008; Pugalenthi *et al.*, 2008), only structure (Manikandan *et al.*, 2008; Polacco & Babbitt, 2006) or use of more general classifications: GO (Espadaler *et al.*,

2006), SCOP (Tendulkar *et al.*, 2010) ... In this section, the objective is to design a prediction method only based on AA sequence in order to provide information for only sequenced proteins.
However, sequence-based methods are likely to be limited with regards to structure-based ones as structure is known to be better conserved than sequence (Chothia *et al.*, 2003). Hence, the proposed method will use HMM-SA as a structure-based middle step to identify interesting structural patterns. As loops are very often implied in interactions (Ansari & Helms, 2005; Saraste *et al.*, 1990), stress is laid on patterns of interest found in loops. Those patterns will be defined here as four SL words encoding seven AA residues. This length has been chosen to obtain satisfying representativities (Regad *et al.*, 2006). However, the prediction method is independent on the pattern length and could be applied to any identified pattern.

4.1 Looking for interesting patterns

In bioinformatics, it is common to look for a pattern of interest in a potentially large set of rather short sequences (upstream gene regions, proteins, exons, etc.). In DNA sequences, it has been observed that functional sites have unusual frequencies: very frequent or rare. Some methods used this observation to extract functional sites by defining them as over- or under-represented sites. Their identification is usually achieved by considering a homogeneous m-order Markov model of the sequence, allowing the computation of p-values (probability that the expected occurrence of a word is larger than its observed occurrence). Stationarity of the model is often assumed for practical reasons but this approximation can result in some artifacts especially when a large set of small sequences are considered. No specific development has taken into account the counting of occurrences in a large set of short independent sequences as loop trajectories in HMM-SA space. A study aiming at addressing this problem by deriving efficient approaches and algorithms to perform these computations for both low and high complexity patterns in the framework of homogeneous or heterogeneous Markov models has been developped in Nuel *et al.* (2010). More precisely, this article proposed an exact method, enabling to take into account both non stationarity and fragmentary structure of sequences, applied it on simulated and real sets of sequences and actually illustrated that pattern statistics can be very sensitive to the stationary assumption.
Subsequently, a detailed analysis of statistically exceptional motifs, identified by HMM-SA, with regards to SCOP superfamilies, groups of proteins with similar structure and function, shed a new light on candidate patterns. Indeed, this study confirmed the link of those potentially interesting patterns with functional motifs in loops and provide a systematic way of identifying such patterns (Regad *et al.*, in revision).
Then, once a pattern has been confirmed as interesting, it is of big interest to be able to predict its presence and thus, the presence of the identified function, directly from a protein AA sequence, even if the 3D structure is unknown. It is important to notice that among identified patterns only the ones showing AA sequence specificities will be likely to be predicted directly from AA sequences. The proposed prediction method is divided into two steps: the first one aims at assigning to each four-AA sequence a SL profile, this will not be deeply describe as outside the scope of this chapter. The second step makes use of a HMM model to combine the profiles provided by step 1 and compute a final probability of finding the considered motif at each position in the sequence.

4.2 The initial data

We use the AA sequences and corresponding SL encoding of 16,995 loops extracted from the PDB with at most 25% of sequence identity. This limited sequence identity rate aims at avoiding any bias in the learning step. The length of loops ranges from 1 to 1,261 SL (hence from 4 to 1,264 AA) with an average of 116 and a standard deviation of 129. They are extracted from 7,778 different proteins.

4.3 First step outline: from four amino-acids to one structural letter profile

The first step input is a 4-AA sequence fragment. In a practical point of view, each overlapping 4-AA words of the considered AA sequence will successively become input. The goal is to find what should be the SL encoding for this fragment. However, as there is no exact bijection between AA and SL sequences, it would be unappropriate to give only one possible SL for each 4-AA fragment. Hence, a SL profile will be the first step output. It consists in a score quantifying the probability of finding each SL at the considered location. This score is based on votes provided by 351 rules: there is one rule for each SL couple ($27 \times 26/2$).

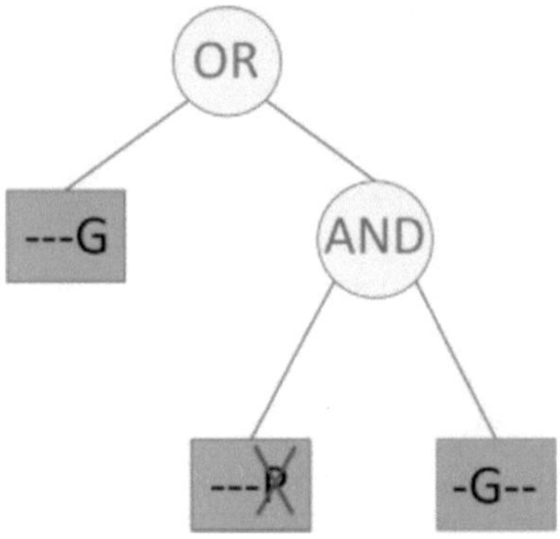

Fig. 3. Example of classifier used to discriminate between two letters A and B: if there is *(G in second position)* AND *(no P in fourth position)* OR *(a G in fourth position)* then the sequence is affected to A else to B.

It is really appropriate to illustrate those rules through a tree-like representation. Indeed, each rule is a combination of binary questions about the presence or absence of a given AA for a given position (between 1 and 4) in the considered 4-AA fragment. For instance, Figure 3 gives an example. Contrary to classical decision trees, this tree has to be read from leaves to root: by sequentially answering to each leaf question (there is or there is not such and such an AA at such and such a position) and combining the answers through the AND/OR operators contained in nodes, a global yes/no answer is obtained allowing to affect the AA sequence to one of the two SLs compared through this classifier. Hence, the 351 rules will provide votes concerning the 4-AA fragment which constitute a kind of profile for the *true* encoding of this sequence into one structural letter. The optimization of the rules is performed through genetic programming (Koza, 1992; Langdon & Poli, 2002) by scoring the rules through their parsimony and the entropy gain they achieve.

4.4 Second step: specific pattern modelling and application to prediction

Due to the complexity of the prediction problem (impossibility to build an easy bijection between AAs and SLs), the first step cannot be sufficient to answer the problem. Indeed, some SLs are easy to discriminate through their AA sequence. For example, SLs B and M are

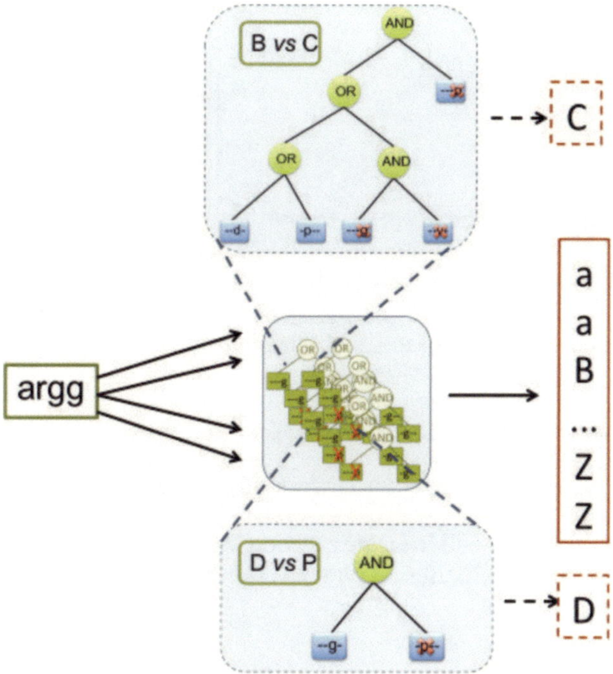

Fig. 4. Global unfolding of Step 1 and two examples of classifiers. A 4-AA long fragment (argg) is given as input of the 351 classifiers, each one voting for one out of the two SLs it compares (ex.: B vs C and D vs P). Finally, a vector of 351 votes is obtained.

very well discriminated through their classifier: one out of the two subgroups obtained after applying the classifier contains 3.2% of the B SL and 98.0% of the M. On the other hand, SLs a and M are particularly difficult to distinguish through their AA sequence: one out of the two subgroups obtained after applying the corresponding classifier contains all the SLs a and 80.6% of SLs M, which is a very poor classification. Hence, further information has to be taken into account to be able to make decisions about a four-SL word. In this context, a particularly interesting knowledge is about dependencies between SLs. It is the goal of the second step.

The aim of this step is to decide, given the results of the first step for four consecutive SLs and through a scoring function, if the conformation adopted by the considered seven residue fragment is likely to be encoded into a given four SL word identified to be linked to a functional pattern.

As emphasized earlier, a real dependency exists between successive SLs, especially because of overlaps. Hence, this dependency can be favourably used to build a model. A HMM has been chosen to model the link between first step outputs and a given four SL word. This HMM is described in Figure 5. In this model, hidden states are the *true* SLs while observed states are outputs of step 1 for the corresponding AA sequence. Arrows between S_i and S_{i+1} symbolizes the dependency between successive letters called *transition probabilities* in HMM context and arrows between S_i and O_i represent the link between true SLs and step 1 outputs, namely the *output probabilities*.

Thanks to this model, the objective of the second step is to compute the probability of the four true SLs being the target functional pattern given the step 1 outputs for four successive (and

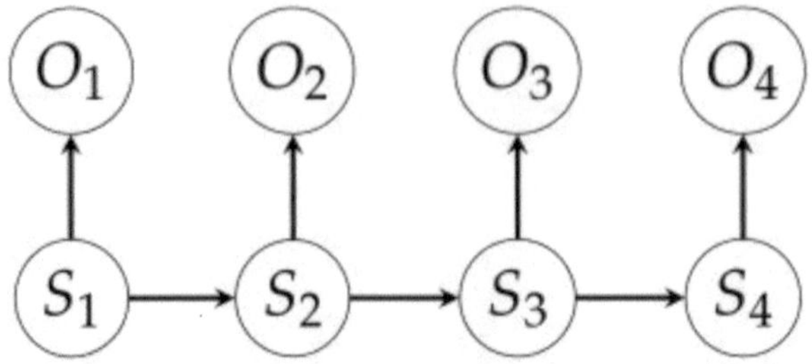

Fig. 5. Structure of the HMM used to model the relationship between first step outputs and *true* SLs for a seven residue fragment: (S_1, S_2, S_3, S_4) are the *true* SLs and $O_i = (o_i^1, o_i^2, \ldots, o_i^{351})$ is the vector of votes obtained from step 1 for the four AA fragment encoded by S_i.

overlapping) four-AA fragments. Hence, we have to compute

$$\mathbb{P}(S_{1:4}|O_{1:4}) = \mathbb{P}(S_1, S_2, S_3, S_4|O_1, O_2, O_3, O_4). \quad (4)$$

High values of this probability will indicate a strong assumption that the considered fragment is likely to be encoded into the identified pattern and then to have the target function. According to the chosen model,

$$\mathbb{P}(S_{1:4}|O_{1:4}) = \mathbb{P}(S_1|O_1) \prod_{i=2}^{4} \mathbb{P}(S_i|S_{i-1})\mathbb{P}(S_i|O_i).$$

Now, $\mathbb{P}(S_i|O_i)$ has to be computed. Assuming that the results of the 351 different trees are independent,

$$\mathbb{P}(S_i|O_i) = \mathbb{P}(S_i|o_i^1, o_i^2, \ldots, o_i^{351}) = \prod_{j=1}^{351} \mathbb{P}(S_i|o_i^j).$$

This assumption is wrong for some comparisons (especially comparisons implying a common SL which is well predicted) but most of pairs of comparisons can be considered as independent (results not shown).
Then, by Bayes theorem, and by denoting by $\bar{S}_i$ the absence of S_i, that is to say there is any of the 26 other SLs,

$$\mathbb{P}(S_i|o_i^j) = \frac{\mathbb{P}(o_i^j|S_i)\mathbb{P}(S_i)}{\mathbb{P}(o_i^j|S_i)\mathbb{P}(S_i) + \mathbb{P}(o_i^j|\overline{S_i})\mathbb{P}(\overline{S_i})}.$$

Finally, $\mathbb{P}(S_i)$, $\mathbb{P}(o_i^j|S_i)$ and $\mathbb{P}(S_i|S_{i-1})$ are estimated on the dataset.

4.5 Applications

4.5.1 Prediction of an ATP-binding site specific motif

Previous studies (as described at the beginning of this section) have shown that fragments encoded into the four SLs *YUOD* (see Figure 6(a)) are very often associated to ATP/GTP binding sites. Indeed, in our database, 95% of fragments encoded into *YUOD* are associated to this functional annotation in SwissProt database. Hence, being able to predict the encoding into *YUOD* is really useful to predict this function for a new AA sequence.
The superimposition of several fragments encoded into *YUOD* is shown in Figure 6. Moreover, this structural word has a high sequence specificity as shown in Figure 4, especially

positions 1, 6 and 7. Thus, this structural word, involved in protein function (binding to ATP/GTP), is a very good candidate for our approach.

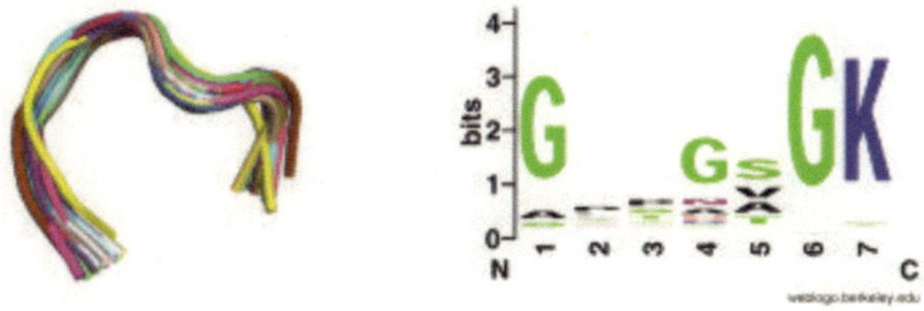

(a) (b)

Fig. 6. (a) Representation of several fragments encoded into *YUOD*. (b) Logo of the AA sequences encoded into *YUOD*.

In our dataset, *YUOD* can be found 183 times in 181 proteins (two proteins contain two occurrences). The model is applied on the whole proteins to study the ability of the computed probability (Eq. 4) to discriminate between *YUOD* and $\overline{YUOD}$ (*not YUOD*). The ROC curve associated to the logarithm of this probability is shown in Figure 7. It displays the sensitivity (ability to retrieve *YUOD*) and specificity (ability to recognize $\overline{YUOD}$) according to the probability threshold chosen to split the words into *YUOD* and $\overline{YUOD}$. The AUC (area under curve) associated to this ROC curve is 0.9866. Hence, the computed probability is really efficient to identify *YUOD* among all other words. Indeed, such a discrimination quality is particularly valuable because of the ratio between the two classes: *YUOD* only represents 0.52% of studied words. Then, according to the application requirements, several thresholds can be defined providing different balances between sensitivity and specificity. Some interesting threshold values and their corresponding parameters are enclosed in Table 1. Very high values of specificity have been chosen, indeed the $\overline{YUOD}$ class is really large and then only 1% of false positive ($\overline{YUOD}$ predicted as *YUOD*) can be a large number when applied to big proteins or to several proteins.

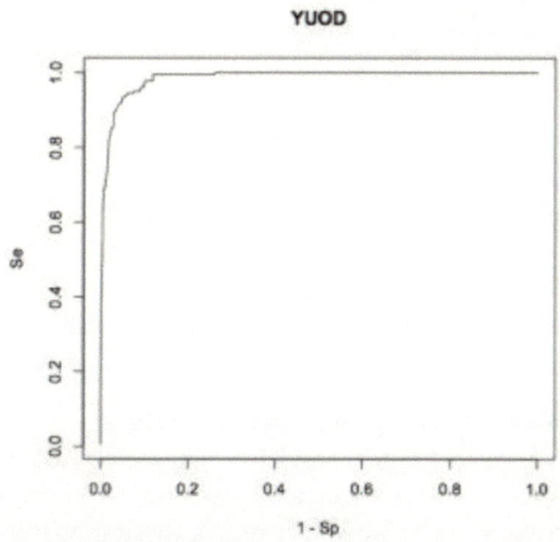

Fig. 7. ROC curve (AUC = 0.9866) associated with the probability of having *YUOD* for a given seven AA fragment (Se=sensitivity, Sp=specificity).

Threshold	-4829	-4805	-4732
Specificity	90.02	95.07	99.00
Sensitivity	97.81	93.44	69.95

Table 1. Sensitivity and specificity obtained for the identification of *YUOD* according to the chosen log(probability) threshold.

An example of *YUOD* detection is given in Figure 8. It concerns the chain A of the Circadian clock protein kinase kaiC (pdb ID: 2gbl_A). It originally contains two true *YUOD* occurrences and four have been predicted through our model. Two out of the four positives (numbers 1 and 2) are exactly located at co-crystallized ATP binding sites (A and B). Moreover, among the two false positives, number 3 adopts a 3D conformation which is really close to the one observed at ATP binding sites. This example demonstrates the difficulty of evaluating a prediction method for annotations. The evaluation of true positive and false negative can be really precise when dealing with manually annotated and reviewed databases such as Swiss-Prot but false positives may be true positive that have not yet been experimentally verified. It is impossible to make a decision in this case.

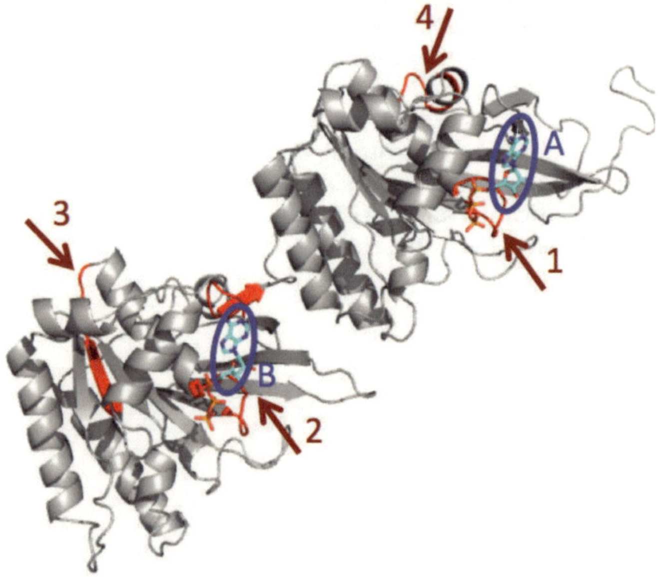

Fig. 8. 3D representation of 2gbl_A co-crystallized with two ATP molecules (indicated by lettered circles). The fragments identified as *YUOD* are indicated with numbered arrows.

4.5.2 Prediction of a SAH/SAM-binding site specific motif

S-adenosyl-methionine (SAM) and S-adenosyl-homocysteine (SAH) are molecules associated to some methylation processes and are particularly studied in the context of antiviral drugs research. It is then interesting to be able to predict their binding to proteins. The four-SL word *RUDO* has been identified to be most of time associated to SAH/SAM in Swiss-Prot. Moreover, it has a certain sequence specificity (results not shown).

In our dataset, *RUDO* is found 39 times in 39 different proteins. The AUC associated to the ROC curve corresponding to the log(probability) computed by our method is 0.9606. The specificity and sensitivity obtained with different thresholds for the log(probability) are given in Table 2. Thus, results are satisfying and allow us to recover more than two thirds of the *RUDO* motifs without wrongly assigning more than 1% of the other words.

Threshold	-4903	-4806	-4712
Specificity	90.00	95.00	99.00
Sensitivity	87.18	84.62	69.23

Table 2. Sensitivity and specificity obtained for the identification of *RUDO* according to the chosen log(probability) threshold.

An illustration can be found in Figure 9. It concerns isoloquiritigenin 2′-O-methyltransferase (pdb ID: 1fp1) which was here co-crystallized with a SAH molecules. Four words were predicted as *RUDO* with a threshold of -4712 whereas only one has been encoded as *RUDO*. However, looking of the 3D conformation, it appears that all four identified fragments are really closed to the ligand. Thus, the method using the HMM-SA as a tool to discover patterns, is not limited to the fragments being strictly encoded into the identified fragments but is also able to discover fragments with close encodings and thus structures, as only sequence is finally taken into account. Hence, fragments which are likely to adopt a *RUDO*-like conformation can be as well identified by the method.

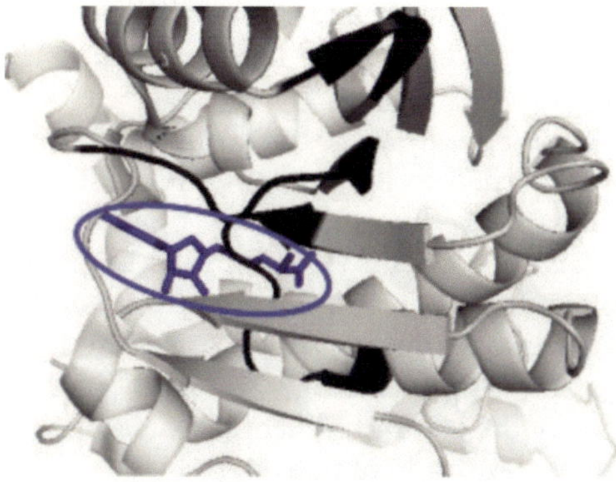

Fig. 9. 3D representation of 1fp1 (light grey cartoons) co-crystallized with a SAH molecule (indicated by a circle). The fragments identified as *RUDO* are black-coloured.

4.5.3 Prediction of a specific β-turn

The prediction of turns is also of special interest in protein study (Fuchs & Alix, 2005). The four-SL word *HBDS* can be linked to β-turns: the corresponding fragment conformations are shown in Figure 10. This is a frequent word, in our database, it was found 1,633 times in 1,363 different proteins (there are one to six occurrences in those proteins). The AUC associated to the prediction of *HBDS* is 0.9359. Table 3 indicates the specificities and sensitivities associated to different log(probability) values. The results are a bit less efficient than previous ones (due to a lower sequence specificity) but enable to locate 85% of those turns with a specificity of 90% (knowing this specificity is likely to be underestimated because of close fragments which have not been strictly encoded into HBDS).

Fig. 10. 3D representation of several fragments encoded into *HBDS*.

Threshold	-4013	-3844	-3777
Specificity	90.17	95.11	98.88
Sensitivity	84.71	71.07	28.93

Table 3. Sensitivity and specificity obtained for the identification of *HBDS* according to the chosen log(probability) threshold.

4.6 Prediction method outcome

The automatic annotation of simply sequenced proteins is a very important task in the present context of high-throughput sequencing programs. The method proposed in this section is based on the identification of motifs of interest directly on structures using HMM-SA. The *input data* of the described method are *only AA sequences* and as a consequence, only patterns having sequence specificities will be likely to be handled with this method. But for this kind of motifs, the method is really powerful. One method (Maupetit *et al.*, 2009) has already been proposed to predict the 3D structure of small peptides through HMM-SA but the motif-oriented aspect of the method proposed here makes it much more precise and time efficient.

As much information as possible is extracted from data. The dependence between AA sequences and 3D structures is learned in the first step through the use of HMM-SA. Then, the second step takes advantage of two different sources of information by building a HMM. Firstly, the strength of dependence between AAs and SLs is quantified and used through observation probabilities: some observations will be really trusted (when a strong link has been found in the first step) whereas others will be considered with care as less reliable. Secondly, the dependence between successive SLs (some SLs favourably follow other ones) is also taken into consideration by the computation of transition probabilities. Finally, a really complete model is obtained by the addition of both steps.

Moreover, as HMM-SA is only an intermediate between sequence and function (or any other interesting pattern), the method, as shown in some illustrations, is able to identify fragments as close to the target word even if this fragment would not be encoded into the exact SL target word. Hence, relying on sequences is a good way to overcome some cases of flexibility: in the crystallization conditions, the fragment has not been found in the strict conformation associated to the target word, but its AA sequence specifities can be recognized by the prediction method. Eventually, HMM-SA encoding and the proposed prediction method are interestingly complementing each other in the prediction of patterns of interest.

Furthermore, the important adaptability of the prediction method is of large interest. Indeed, in this paper we focused on pattern which had been identified directly through HMM-SA but it is completely possible to identify 3D motifs as interesting for any other reason, to encode it into HMM-SA and to build the model on the obtained word. Let us recall here that the size of considered fragments is not limited. Earlier, only seven-residue fragments have been considered but any length would be possible. Furthermore, as illustrated through the three examples, the size of the learning dataset can be really variable (from 35 to 1633 occurrences of the pattern) as the model is always the same. The only variable parameter is the log(probability) threshold. However, preliminary studies seem to indicate that this threshold depends on the strength of the sequence specificity of the structure. Hence, further work could be able to set this threshold directly from the quantification of this dependence.

5. Conclusion

Interest and limits of the HMM to study 3D protein organisation
In contrast to supervised learning strategies (Levitt and Chothia, 1976; Kabsch and Sander, 1983; Richards and Kundrot, 1988; Prestrelski et al., 1992; Hutchinson and Thornton, 1993; Zhu, 1995), the SLs emerged from the HMM without any prior knowledge of secondary structural classification. In that sense, the HMM is able to classify conformations that template studies must describe as undefined or random structures and also to subdivide conformation classes previously defined as a single class, resulting in a finer description of the 3D conformations. For instance, the HMM approach allows different levels of variability within each SL. Classical methods have recently been used to extract and classify local protein backbone elements but these methods did not take into account any local dependence between SLs: all these studies used only the structural characteristics to identify structural 3D letters and reconstructed a posteriori the organization of these 3D conformations. One major contribution of HMM is that this model implicitly takes into account the sequential connections between the SLs. It is striking that structurally close SLs can have different roles in the construction of 3D structures.
HMM-SA learning has shown to be stable over different protein sets. Our model fits well the previous knowledge related to protein architecture organisation. Using such a model, the structure of proteins can be reconstructed with an average accuracy close to 1.1 Å root-mean-square deviation and for a low complexity of 3D reconstruction (see Camproux *et al.*, 2004, for details). This stochastic HMM approach allows the characterization of different SLs with different fragment heterogeneity by taking into account their global organization and quantifying their connections. It results in a fine and pertinent description of the 3D structures and a very performant tool to simplify 3D conformation of proteins. Different successful applications of HMM-SA for 3D analysis have been performed.
This ability has allowed to design several methods of protein studies, such as the prediction of interesting patterns detailed in this chapter. This method has shown to be really efficient for patterns having a certain AA sequence specificity. Further work should allow to predict the efficiency and the threshold to be used directly from a quantification of this dependency. Moreover, this prediction method has the main advantage to be really adaptive, to different pattern lengths or to different alphabets for example. In this study, HMM-SA has been used because of its very interesting abilities of precise description especially for loops, but the same methodology could be applied on other types of alphabets. Finally, the method is bounded by the function specificity of the pattern. Indeed, a function might be associated to different patterns. Thus, our method is able to predict one type of realization of a given function at a time. Of course, it is completely possible to learn several patterns linked to a function and to give a global prediction for all of them. But for the moment, this limit prevents us to compare with prediction methods for specific function (such as Ansari & Raghave, 2010) encoded through different patterns. This should be quickly possible by the identification of new patterns which is in progress.

6. Further HMM improvements

Concerning the HMM-SA identification, a number of improvements can be brought into the HMM modeling by taking into account deterministic dependency and local descriptors, the criterion of model selection and posterior probabilities of different structural letters in the encoding.

In the previous work, the idea was to consider the model of Figure 2 where all X_i are generated independently from each other conditionally to a hidden state $S_i \in \mathcal{S} = \{1, 2, \ldots, K\}$ as detailed in Section 2.2. One problem of this approach is that it does not take into account the correlation between X_i and X_{i+1}. We alternatively suggest to consider the model where the distribution of X_{i+1} depends on S_{i+1} (like in the previous model) and from X_i. For example, if we assume that $X^1_{i+1} = X^3_i$ and that $(X^2_{i+1}, X^3_{i+1}, X^4_{i+1})$ has a Gaussian distribution whose parameters only depend on S_{i+1}, the resulting model both improves the existing one and reduces its number of parameters.

A critical point of the HMM-SA approach is also related to the model selection: how many structural letters should we use in order to get the best structural alphabet ? For this problem however, our objective is not only to select the most parsimonious model providing the best fitting but also to provide a reliable classification of the fragments in order to allocate a given fragment to a specific structural letter with the least possible uncertainty. For that purpose, it might be interesting to replace the used BIC criterion by classification orientated criteria like the ICL (Biernacki *et al.*, 2000; McLachlan & Peel, 2008) or the Discriminative Information Criterion from Biem (2003). The idea of these approaches is to introduce in the penalization a term related to the entropy of the classification which purpose is to avoid to select a model where two structural letters are too close to each other.

Another important issue is related to the encoding of 3D structures into sequences of structural letters. For that purpose, it is both natural and classical to use the Viterbi's algorithm in order to obtain the MAP encoding. However, it often exists many alternative suboptimal configurations that might be of interest. In order to check this, it might be interesting to compute the posterior distribution $P(S = s | X = x, \widehat{\theta})$ using the Forward/Backward quantities and hence to point out regions where the structural alphabet encoding has a low confidence. One may then either exclude this low reliability regions or take into account the uncertainty of the encoding by sampling several encoding for these regions.

It also might be of great interest to introduce in the HMM-SA model a descriptor of the structure flexibility in its learning process. Initially, a unique 3D structure was supposed to correspond to one protein sequence (Mirsky, 1936). The constant and rapid increase in the number of experimentally solved protein structures has shown the flexibility of 3D structure proteins to adapt to different conditions and partners. Thus, this property is at the heart of the fundamental functions of proteins. This flexibility is being quantified by parameters such as the B-factor. The inclusion of this information in the construction of a new alphabet could be used to define classes of structures particularly flexible and to better model the complexity of proteins. For instance, knowledge and prediction of these flexible regions could significantly improve docking protocols, including the choice of starting structures.

Actually, if the HMM-SA original model only considered the 3D structure of the protein, the additional work presented in this chapter has shown that the original AA sequences also bear useful physicochemical information that can improve the prediction. It is hence very tempting to combine these two approaches together by introducing the AA sequence into the HMM-SA model from the beginning like suggested in Figure 11.

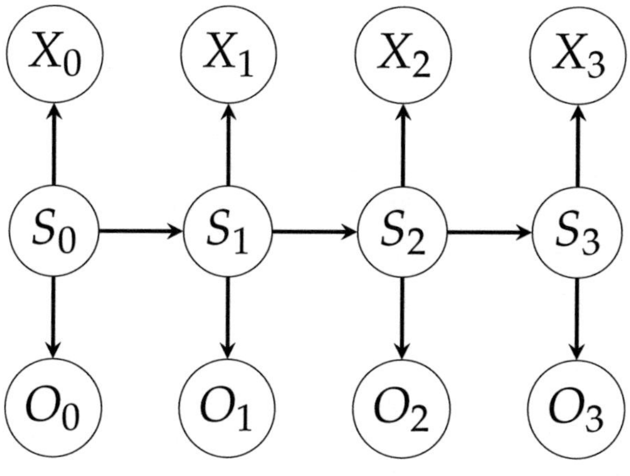

Fig. 11. Graph of dependencies in the model combining both the 3D structure and the primary sequences. The model is drawn for $n = 7$ C_α hence resulting in a total of $n - 3 = 4$ SLs.

7. References

S. Ansari and V. Helms, Statistical analysis of predominantly transient protein-protein interfaces. *Proteins*, 61(2): 344-355, 2005.

H.R. Ansari and G.P.S. Raghava, Identification of NAD interaction residues in proteins. *BMC Bioinformatics*, 11(160), 2010.

L. Baeten, J. Reumers, V. Tur, F. Stricher, T. Lenaerts, L. Serrano, F. Rousseau and J. Schymkowitz, Reconstruction of protein backbones from the BriX collection of canonical protein fragments. *PLoS Comput Biol.*, 4(5), 2010.

A. Bateman, L. Coin, R. Durbin, R.V. Finn, V. Hollich, Griffiths-Jones S., Khanna A., Marshall M., Moxon S., E. L. L. Sonnhammer, D. J. Studholme, C. Yeats and S.R. Eddy, The Pfam Protein Families Database. *Nucleic Acids Research*, 32: 138-41, 2004.

J. Baussand and A.-C. Camproux, Deciphering the shape and deformation of secondary structures using a structural alphabet approach, in press in *BMC structural biology*.

F.C. Berstein, T.G. Koetzle, G.J.B. Williams, E.F. Meyer, M.D. Brice, J.R. Rogers, O. Kennard, T. Shimanouchi and M. Tasumi, The Protein Data Bank: a computer-based archival file for macromolecular structures. *J. Mol. Biol.*, 112, 535-542, 1977.

A. Biem, A model selection criterion for classification: Application to hmm topology optimization, *Proc. 17th ICDAR*, Edinburgh, U.K, 104-108, 2003.

C. Biernacki, G. Celeux and G. Govaert, Assessing a mixture model for clustering with the integrated completed likelihood. *IEEE Transactions on Pattern Analysis and Machine Intelligence*, 22(7):719-725, 2000.

B. Boeckmann, A. Bairoch, R. Apweiler, M. Blatter, A. Estreicher, E. Gasteiger, M.J. Martin, K. Michoud, I. Phan, R. Pilbout and M. Schneider, The swiss-prot protein knowledgebase and its supplement tremble. *Nucleic Acids Res.*, 31: 365-370, 2003.

A.G. De Brevern, C. Etchebest and S. Hazout, Bayesian probabilistic approach for predicting backbone structures in terms of protein blocks. *Proteins*, 41: 271-87, 2000.

C. Bystroff, V. Thorsson and D. Baker, HMMSTR: a hidden Markov model for local sequence-structure. *J. Mol. Biol.*, 301(1): 173-90, 2000.

A.C. Camproux, P. Tuffery, J.P. Chevrolat, J.F. Boisvieux and S. Hazout, Hidden Markov model approach for identifying the modular framework of the protein backbone. *Protein Eng*, 12(12): 1063-73, 1999.

A.C. Camproux, P. Tuffery, L. Buffat, C. Andr, J.F. Boisvieux and S. Hazout, Using short structural building blocks defined by a Hidden Markov Model for analysing patterns between regular secondary structures. *Theoretical Chemistry Accounts*, 101: 33-40, 1999.

A.C. Camproux, A.G. De Brevern and S. Hazout, Exploring the use of a structural alphabet for structural prediction of protein loops, *Theoretical Chemistry Accounts*, 106: 28-35, 2001.

A.C. Camproux, R. Gautier, and P. Tuffery, A Hidden Markov model derived structural alphabet for proteins. *J. Mol. Biol.*, 339: 591-05, 2004.

A.C. Camproux and P. Tuffery, Hidden Markov Model derived Structural Alphabet for proteins: the learning of protein local shapes capture sequence specificity. *BBA*, 1724(3): 394-403, 2005.

C. Chothia, J. Gough, C. Vogel and S.A. Teichmann, Evolution of protein repertoire. *Science*, 300(5626):1701-1703, 2003.

T.U. Consortium, The Universal Protein Resource (UniProt). *Nucleic Acids Res*, 38, D142-148, 2010.

P. Deschavanne and P. Tuffery, Enhanced protein fold recognition using a structural alphabet. *Proteins*. 76(1):129-37, 2009.

R. Durbin, S. Eddy, A. Krogh and G. Mitchison, Biological sequence analysis. (1998) Probabilistic models of proteins and nucleic acids.

J. Espadaler, E. Querol, F.X. Aviles and B. Oliva, Identification of function-associated loop motifs and application to protein function prediction. *Bioinformatics*, 22(18): 2237-2243, 2006.

J.S., Fetrow, Omega loops: nonregular secondary structures significant in protein function and stability. *FASEB J*, 9: 708-17, 1995.

N. Fernandez-Fuentes, A. Hermoso, J. Espadaler, E. Querol, F.X. Aviles and B. Oliva, Classification of common functional loops of kinase super-families. *Proteins*, 56(3): 539-55, 2004.

D. Frishman and P. Argos, Knowledge-based protein secondary structure assignment. *Proteins*, 23(4): 566-79, 1995.

P.F.J. Fuchs and A.J.P. Alix, High accuracy prediction of β-turns and their types using propensities and multiple alignments. *Proteins*, 59(4): 828-839, 2005.

R. Gautier, A.C. Camproux and P. Tuffery, SCit: web tools for protein side chains conformation analysis. *Nucleic Acids Research*, Web Server issue : W508-11, 2004.

J.F. Gibrat , T. Madej and S.H. Bryant, Surprising similarities in structure comparison. *Curr Opin Struct Biol*, 6(3): 377-85, 1996.

F. Guyon, A.C. Camproux, J. Hochez and P. Tuffery, SA-Search: a web tool for protein structure mining based on a Structural Alphabet. *Nucleic Acids Res*, 32: W545-48, 2004.

I. Halperin, D.S. Glazer, S. Wu and R.B. Altman, The FEATURE framework for protein function annotation: modeling new functions, improving performance and extending to novel applications. *BMC genomics*, 9(Sup 2): S2, 2008.

K. Henrick, Z. Feng, WF. Bluhm, D. Dimitropoulos, JF. Doreleijers, S. Dutta, JL. Flippen-Anderson, J. Lonides, C. Kamada, E. Krissinel, CL. Lawson, JL. Markley, H. Nakamura, R. Newman, Y. Shimizu, J. Swaminathan, S. Velankar, J. Ory, EL. Ulrich,

W. Vranken, J. Westbrook, R. Yamashita, H. Yang, J. Young, M. Yousufuddin and H.M., Berman, Remediation of the protein data bank archive. *Nucleic Acids Res*, 36, D426-D433, 2008.

U. Hobohm, M. Scharf, M. Schneider and C. Sandres, Selection of representative protein data sets. *Protein Sci.*, 1: 409-417, 1992.

L. Holm and C. Sander, Protein structure comparison by alignment of distance matrices. *J. Mol. Biol.*, 233(1): 123-38, 1993.

R. Kolodny, P. Koehl, L. Guibas and M. Levitt, Small libraries of protein fragments model native protein structures accurately. *J. Mol. Biol.*, 323(2): 297-07, 2002.

J.R. Koza, Genetic Programming: On the Programming of Computers by Means of Natural Selection, MIT Press, 1992.

A. Krogh, M. Brown, I.S. Mian, K. Sjolander, D. Haussler, Hidden Markov Models in Computational Biology: Applications to Protein Modeling. *J. Mol. Biol.*, 235(5): 1501-31, 1994.

R.H. Lathrop, The protein threading problem with sequence amino acid interaction preferences is NP-complete. *Protein Eng*, 7(9): 1059-68, 1994.

G.J. McLachlan, and D. Peel, *Finite mixture models*. New York: Wiley, 2000.

K. Manikandan, D. Pal, S. Ramakumar, N.E. Brener, S.S. Iyengar and G. Seetharaman, Functionally important segments in proteins dissected using Gene Ontology and geometric clustering of peptide fragments. *Genome Biol.*, 9(3): R52, 2008.

J. Martin, L. Regad, C. Etchebest and A.C. Camproux, Inter-residue contact analysing using local structure descriptors. *Proteins*, 9; 73(3): 672-689, 2008.

J. Martin, L. Regad, H. Lecornet and A.C. Camproux, Structural deformation upon protein-protein interaction: a structural alphabet approach. *BMC Structural Biology*, 8:12, 2008.

J. Martin, A. de Brevern and A.C. Camproux, In silico local structure approach: a case study on Outer Membrane Proteins. *Proteins*, 11; 71(1): 92-109, 2008.

W.B. Langdon and R. Poli, Foundations of Genetic Programming, Springer-Verlag, 2002.

J. Maupetit, P. Derreumaux and P. Tuffery, PEP-FOLD: an online resource for de novo peptide structure prediction. *Nucleic Acids Research*, 37, 2009.

C. Micheletti, F. Seno and A. Maritan, Recurrent oligomers in proteins: an optimal scheme reconciling accurate and concise backbone representations in automated folding and design studies. *Proteins*, 40: 662-74, 2000.

A.E. Mirsky and L. Pauling, On the structure of native, denatured and coagulated proteins. *Proc. Natl. Acad. Sci.* USA, 22: 439-447, 1936.

G. Nuel, J. Martin, L. Regad and A.C. Camproux, Exact distribution of a pattern in a set of random sequences generated by a Markov source: applications to biological data. *Alg. Mol. Biol.*, 5:15, 2010.

A. Pandini, A. Fornili and J. Kleinjung, Structural alphabets derived from attractors in conformational space. *BMC Bioinformatics*, 11:97, 2010.

X. Pang, L. Zhou, M. Zhang, F. Xie, L. Yu, L. Zhang, L. Xu & X. Zhang. A mathematical model for peptide inhibitor design. *J. Comput Biol.* , 17(8): 1081-93, 2010.

V. Pavone, G. Gaeta, A. Lombardi, F. Nastri, O. Maglio, C. Isernia, and M. Saviano, Discovering protein secondary structures: Classification and description of isolated alpha-turns. *Biopolymers*, 38: 705-721, 1996.

B.J. Polacco and P.C. Babbitt, Automated discovery of 3D motifs for protein function annotation. *Bioinformatics*, 22(6):723-730, 2006.

G. Pugalenthi, K.K. Kumar, P.N. Suganthan and R. Gangal, Identification of catalytic residues from protein structure using support vector machine with sequence and structural features. *Biochemical and Biophysical Research Communications*, 367(3): 630-634; 2008.

L.R. Rabiner, A tutorial on hidden Markov models and selected applications in speech recognition, *Proc. of the IEEE*, 77(2): 257-85, 1989.

S. Rackovsky, On the nature of the protein folding code. *Proc. Natl Acad. Sci. USA*, 90: 644-648, 1993.

L. Regad, J. Martin and A.C. Camproux, Identification of non random motifs in loops using a structural alphabet. *Proceedings of IEEE Symposium on computational intelligence in bioinformatics and computational*, 92-100, 2006.

L. Regad, F. Guyon, J. Maupetit, P. Tuffery, A.C. Camproux, A Hidden Markov Model applied to proteins 3D structures analysis. *Computational statistics and data analysis*, 52: 3198-3207, 2008.

L. Regad, J. Martin and A.C. Camproux, Dissecting protein loops with a statistical scalpel: functional implication of structural motifs. *BMC Bioinformatics*, in revision.

M.J. Rooman, J. Rodriguez, and S.J. Wodak, Automatic definition of recurrent local-structure motifs in proteins. *J. Mol. Biol.*, 213: 327-336, 1990.

M. Saraste, P.R. Sibbald and A. Wittinghofer, The P-loop: a common motif in ATP- and GTP-binding proteins. *Trends in Biochemical Science*, 15: 430-434, 1990.

I.N. Shindyalov and P. E. Bourne, Protein structure alignment by incremental combinatorial extension (CE) of the optimal path. *Protein Eng*, 11 (9): 739-47, 1998.

G. Schwartz, Estimating the dimension of a model. *Annals of statistics*, 6: 461-64, 1978.

C.J.A. Sigrist, L. Cerutti, E. de Castro, P.S. Kangendijk-Genevaux, V. Bulliard, A. Bairoch and N. Hulo, PROSITE, a protein domain database for functional characterization and annotation. *Nucleic Acids Research*, 38: D161-D166, 2010.

N., Siva, 1000 Genomes project. *Nature biotechnology*, 26(3): 256, 2008.

P.E. Smith, H.D. Blatt, and B.M Pettitt, A simple two-dimensional representation for the common secondary structural elements of polypeptides and proteins. *Proteins*, 27: 227-234, 1997.

A.V. Tendulkar, M. Krallinger, V. de la Torre, G. Lopez, P.P.Wangikar and A. Valencia, FragKB: structural and literature annotation resource of conserved peptide fragments and residues. *PLoS one*, 5(3), 2010.

R. Unger, D. Harel, S. Wherland and J.L. Sussman, A 3D building blocks approach to analyzing and predicting structure of proteins. *Proteins*, 5: 355-73, 1989.

R.H. Waterston, E.S. Lander and J.E. Sulston, On the sequencing of the human genome. *Proc. Natl. Acad. Sci.USA*, 99: 3712-16, 2002.

C.H. Wu, R. Apweiler, A. Bairoch, D.A. Natale, W.C. Barker, B. Boeckmann, S. Ferro, E. Gasteiger, H. Huang, R. Lopez, M. Magrane, M.J. Martin, R. Mazumder, C. O'Donovan, N. Redaschi and B. Suzek, The Universal Protein Resource (UniProt): an expanding universe of protein information. *Nucleic Acids Res.*, 34: D187-D191, 2006.

L. Zou, Z. Wang, Y. Wang and F. Hu, Combined prediction of transmembrane topology and signal peptide of beta-barrel proteins: using a hidden Markov model and genetic algorithms. *Comput Biol Med.*, 40(7): 621-8, 2010.

14

Control Theoretic Approach to Platform Optimization using HMM

Rahul Khanna[1], Huaping Liu[2] and Mariette Awad[3]
[1]*Intel Corporation, 2111 NE 25th Ave., Hillsboro, OR 97124*
[2]*School of EECS, Oregon State University, Corvallis, OR 97331*
[3]*American University of Beirut, (ECE) Riad El-Solh, Beirut 1107 2020*
[1,2]*USA*
[3]*Lebanon*

1. Introduction

Power optimization and power control are challenging issues for server computer systems. A system can be represented as a set of components whose cooperative interaction produces useful work. These components may be heterogeneous in nature and may vary in the power consumption and power control mechanisms. Server system components may coordinate power control actions using embedded controllers or special hardware. System development tends to be a complex process that competes for performance in the presence of design constraints. These constraints may be on manufacturing cost, validation cost, area, form-factor, or operational costs. Operational cost is related to the cost of operating a system for a unit of work. Operational cost reduction requires observability, controllability, and adaptability. These features come at a price that may increase the manufacturing, design, and validation costs.

Energy efficient design helps in realizing a system that minimizes power and thermal dissipation for a given performance constraints. These systems can perform one or many functions related to power/thermal management for a given performance policy: 1. Parameter tuning to reduce energy consumption for a given performance policy. This may require collective (or coordinated) tuning of system components for minimum power usage at given performance levels. 2. Limiting the power of an individual component (or set of components) in a power constrained system. Power is allocated (or de-allocated) in a manner such that performance degradation is minimized to the extent possible. 3. Power prediction and forecasting to avoid sudden state changes. This prediction can be at the component level or at the system level. For example, we may predict the inactivity periods between bursts of memory traffic, which allows us to proactively prepare the system for an appropriate sleep state. This avoids reactive latencies and hence increases performance. 4. Distributing the available power to system components in a manner that maximizes the overall performance. One strategy may involve individual allocation (or de-allocation) due to each component's share in performance gain. 5. Using activity vectors to perform thermally balanced computing, thus avoiding hot spots. Activity data can also be used to co-schedule tasks in a contention-free and energy-efficient manner.

Furthermore, energy-efficient systems design involves complex choices due to a variety of degrees of freedom for power parameter tuning. The process involves modeling methodology, implementation choices, and dynamic tuning. Modeling methodology includes the choice of algorithms or heuristics that tunes the state transition. Implementation choices involve the hosting of executable code in a manner such that it can access the appropriate telemetry data in an efficient manner at runtime. Additionally, it should have enough computation power to perform policy-related functions while being non-intrusive during sleep states.
In recent years energy-efficient design in servers has received much primarily due

- The need to reduce heat dissipation, thereby reducing the cooling costs
- The need to reduce energy consumption, thereby reducing the energy-related operating costs
- Strict current limits in a power-limited server rack. It may therefore be desired to maximize the rack consumption while keeping the energy limits within regulations
- Capacity planning that requires efficient use of existing real-estate, which necessitates the optimal use of available racks.

In general, energy efficient design helps in realizing a system that minimizes power and thermal dissipation for a given performance constraints. These systems can perform one or many functions related to power/thermal management for a given performance policy:

- Parameter tuning to reduce energy consumption for a given performance policy. This may require collective (or coordinated) tuning of system components for minimum power usage at given performance levels.
- Limiting the power of an individual component (or set of components) in a power constrained system. Power is allocated (or de-allocated) in a manner such that performance degradation is minimized to the extent possible.
- Power prediction and forecasting to avoid sudden state changes. This prediction can be at the component level or at the system level. For example, we may predict the inactivity periods between bursts of memory traffic, which allows us to proactively prepare the system for an appropriate sleep state. This avoids reactive latencies and hence increases performance.
- Distributing the available power to system components in a manner that maximizes the overall performance. One strategy may involve individual allocation (or de-allocation) due to each component's share in performance gain.
- Using activity vectors to perform thermally balanced computing, thus avoiding hot spots. Activity data can also be used to co-schedule tasks in a contention-free and energy-efficient manner.
- Profiling task characteristics related to (a) Task priority (b) Energy and Thermal profile (c) Optimization methodology regarding latency targets proportional to task priority.

2. HMM approach

We face several challenges in the establishment of power/thermal monitoring infrastructure that can uncover complex deviance from an established norm. The correlation of sensors is typically separated by a significant amount of time that makes it difficult to model. In such cases, the Hidden Markov Model (HMM) is particularly useful because it can exploit the pattern in the sequence of events to predict the state. Since HMM uses and correlates observations with hidden states, it may very well be a consideration in system design. Observation points can be optimized using a reasonable set of system-wide QoS checkpoints (QC) or sensors. Hidden states can be created using explicit knowledge of probabilistic relationships with these observations. These probabilistic relationships, which are also called profiles, are hardened and evolved with the constant usage of the multiple and autonomous systems. These profiles, HMM parameters and observation probability density function (pdf) are stored in a central storage where they are re-estimated based on the HIT/MISS data collected. If observation checkpoints can be standardized, then the problem of predictability can be reduced to profiling the existing and new hidden states to standard observations. In terms of modeling a large number of temporal sequences, HMM can serve as an excellent alternative, because it has been widely used for speech recognition, image identification, microbiology, Internet attacks, and misuse based on operating system calls. In all these applications, the aim is to map a pattern to one of the many states. If we consider an abnormal behavior to be a pattern of an observed sequence, HMM should be appropriate to map those patterns to one of several states. Furthermore, it is essential to build an adaptive strategy based on embedding numerous policies that are informed by contextual and environmental inputs. The policies govern various attributes of behavior, enhancing flexibility in order to maximize the efficiency and performance in the presence of high levels of environmental variability.

Power autonomic environment comprises of cooperating elements that play an optimization game among themselves in order to optimize its resource usage while adhering to the global policies related to power and thermal constraints. A real-time mechanism can to be devised independent of the behavior of the cooperating components. This mechanism enhances the ability to detect abnormalities or policy drifts by monitoring unusual activities (or drifts) in the system by comparing it to a user's profile. It analyzes the trending in a system's behavior as it evolves with usage. We may utilize relevant observations (such as changes in system performance parameters or fault frequency) to predict hidden states (operational degradation, performance loss). These methods detect and report system abnormality as a result of drift for an acceptable profile. According to Denning (Denning, 1987), a profile characterizes the behavior of a given subject with respect to a given object, thereby serving as a signature or description of normal activity for its respective subject(s) and object(s). Observed behavior can be characterized using statistical metric represented by a random variable x monitored over a period of time. Metric can typically be defined using a counter, interval and evaluation data. Observations records along with statistical models can be used to determine the conformity of the normal process (or activity). Two of the profiles that aid in QoS analysis are the following:

- System Usage Profile. This profile is the summary of system usage trends for a given subject (or user DNA). It contains information related to users' best-known practices (or trends) such as most used application, average system activity, or user preferences.
- System Activity Profile. This profile is the summary of system resource usage trends over a period of time (or system DNA). It contains information related to resource usage (CPU usage, memory usage, input/output (IO) usage, number of tasks, execution-time, and system calls).

Any deviation from a standard profile identifies a potential anomalous state and triggers a policy based method supported by autonomics. A false positive trigger acts as a feedback for retraining the model. A functional approach would correlate the system observations (using usage and activity profile) and state transitions to predict the most probable state.

The state in this case describes the component's ability to operate constructively in an optimization game for a given objective. These objectives could be related to improving system's performance/watt for a given power limits, reducing performance de-gradation as a result of component fault, or identifying the components that have been compromised as a result of intrusions or other events.

2.1 Power optimization in server platforms

This chapter presents a framework of modeling and optimization for stochastic power management using HMM. It describes the essential ingredients that is responsible for building the profile and detecting any deviations from that profile. The objective is to anticipate the power/thermal policy deviations while reducing the number of false positives. The model has to fulfill several objectives related to accurate profile deviation detection using different ingredients such as:

- QoS checkpoints (QC) that analyzes the sensor activity which predicts the transition from a normal state to an abnormal state.
- Creation of an activity profile that identifies the abnormal activity of the observable states by measuring the sensor deviation from the normal behavior. In short, it characterizes the behavioral signature corresponding to the normal activity of a given subject with respect to a given object.
- Concept drift that measures the change in the user behavior over a period of time.
- Control loop that adapts the checkpoint trigger according to the weighted sum of proportional, average, and derivative sensor measurements over derivative and integral time window.
- Model that predicts the most probable state based on previous state (normal/abnormal) as well as observed states.

HMM based model utilizes the distributed checkpoints in a platform. These checkpoints are in a form of sensors, activity counters, error counters, performance counters and energy counters. A series of observations from these checkpoints are utilized to identify the HMM model applicable for an evaluation period that describe the workload behavior. Workload behavior is a characteristics of the resource utilization patterns. For example, workload may be I/O bound, CPU bound, Network bound or idle. Workload behavior patterns are then used to tune the system for optimal performance/watt. The methodology essentially use the HMM based stochastic power management techniques to tune the system effectively in order to:

- Avoid reactive response to power state change demand.
- Optimal distribution of power states between silicon components according to the performance gains.
- Optimal tuning of the entry/exit timings of the power states according to the workload profiles.
- Optimal operation of the fans by evaluating the effectiveness of the changes in Fan speeds wrt. component heating, power consumption and performance variations.

Depending upon the complexity of workload relationship to the utilization of several active components in a system, the solution space could involve large number of variables with high dimensionality. These variables tend to be noisy and discontinuous with little or no information about the corresponding interactions between there respective components. The problem is further aggravated by the fact that hardware/software based power/thermal optimization functions kicks in autonomously, thus making the complete solution highly non-linear. The effectiveness of a potentially significant variable for one workload may cease to be effective for other depending upon the underlying relationship to the output (estimated power). Conversely, formerly insignificant variable may play a significant role in determination of estimated power in the newer workloads. Hence, before calibrating a non-linear equation with a set of selected variables, we also need to select an optimal set of variables within a large search space that will eventually lead to an accurate solution. Higher accuracy targets present a larger search space with a potential to uncover currently unknown non-linear behaviors.

2.2 Variable reduction & consolidation

Complex variables are essential ingredients of building the HMM model. They extract the observed states functions that are modelled to predict one of the HMM states (QoS, QDP or QV) (Figure 3). Variable Reduction (Fig. 1) helps to selects the weight for the input variables of a component (CPU, Memory, HDD etc.) after identifying those which: (1) Are most correlated with the output values, (2) Cause discontinuities and contribute to the threshold effects in the output values and (3) Are eliminated as they possess a high degree of linear correlation with another variable such that both influence the analyzed output variable in a very similar (if not an identical) way.

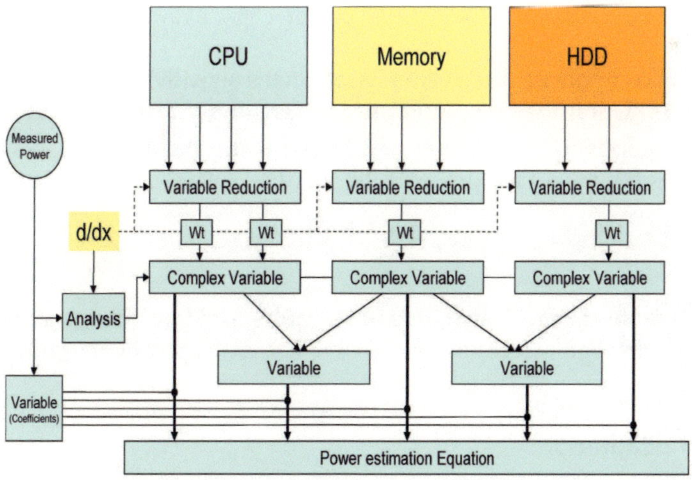

Fig. 1. Synthesis of optimal power estimation equation using variable reduction. Reduced variables construct complex variables that can then be used as emissions in the *Hidden Markov Model*

The main objective of variable reduction is to help analyze and compare the slope coefficients of a system's model where component's input variable is regarded as the most significant which is related to the slope coefficient of the largest absolute value. A large slope coefficient indicates high sensitivity to very small changes in the input variable that results in very large changes in the output variable. In our approach we extract consequetive models that are created by shifting sampling window of the data points. Each model shares the sampled data with consequetive models. This helps in converting a multidimension non-linear model into a series of linear models:

$$\chi_i = \frac{dP_i}{dt} = \sum_{j=0}^{N}(\lambda_i^j * \frac{dV^j}{dt}), \quad \sum_{j=0}^{N}\lambda_i^j = 1 \tag{1}$$
$$t_i \in (i * d, i * d + M)$$

where, χ_i represents the estimated rate of change of power, P_i represents the estimated power of the ith model, λ_i^j represents the coefficient of the jth variable of ith model, V^j represents the jth input variable, and t_i represents the modeling window of the dataset of size M shifted by d samples. Coefficients λ_i^j of each model i is determined by curve-fitting using Genetic Algorithm (GA) with the fitness represented by:

$$F_i = \frac{1}{M}\sum_{t_i}|max(0, \frac{\hat{\chi}_i - \chi_i}{\hat{\chi}_i})| \tag{2}$$

where $\hat{\chi}_i$ represents the measured rate of change of power. λ_i^j represents the significance of the corresponding variable X^j for model i. Finally average of λ_i^j determines the overall significance of each variable as given by equation 3:

$$\lambda^j = \frac{\sum_{i=0}^{M}\lambda_i^j}{M} \tag{3}$$

Variable X^j of each component are selected based on the sensitivity of the variable represented by λ^j (Equation 3). Upon the completion of the sensitivity analysis, a reduced equation is formed for each component (CPU, memory, HDD) using the adjusted weighted sum $\hat{\lambda}^k$ of dominant variables V_x^k, where k represents the set of all selected dominant variables:

$$V_x = \sum_k \hat{\lambda}^k * V_x^k \tag{4}$$

Reduced set of variables form a distributed observables for identifying a change in a workload conditions that would require a control action to balance the power, thermal and performance parameters.

3. Attributes of adaptation

Adaptation is primarily achieved by steering each platform component to its optimal state. Normally, users are subjected to arbitrary performance and environmental variations. Adaptive systems exist to solve such problems that result due to a great deal of variability, flexibility, and dynamism. Adaptation may also serve functions that may be mutually hostile and pull in different directions. This results in making compromises between solutions in an effort to maximize the fitness of the overall solution. For example, increase in performance is generally associated with an increase in power that results in a further increase in power due to cooling pressures. An adaptation function will optimize the power in a manner that delivers the desired performance as perceived by the application. It is noteworthy that desired performance may not necessarily be the highest performance. In real systems, it is impossible to improve all aspects of the target policy to the same degree simultaneously. Traditional adaptation techniques use single point optimizations and do not employ multiple adaptations synergistically. For complex platforms, adaptation approach migrates to multi-point space exploration that chooses the optimal configuration that can continue to achieve homeostasis. This requires a prediction-based classifier that determines the survivability of a particular configuration. An important step in adaptation is to generate on-line (or off-line) behavioral profiles of different configurations under varying resource conditions. Necessary requirements for the adaptation process are:

- The ability to monitor resource conditions in a continuous mode using sampling rates according to observed data redundancy and the control periods.
- The ability to determine when adaptation should be performed.
- The ability to determine how the adaptation should be performed by modeling control behavior.
- The QoS profile that describes the real-time constraints and its resource requirements for a given autonomic element.
- Choice of available execution paths for a given autonomic element.

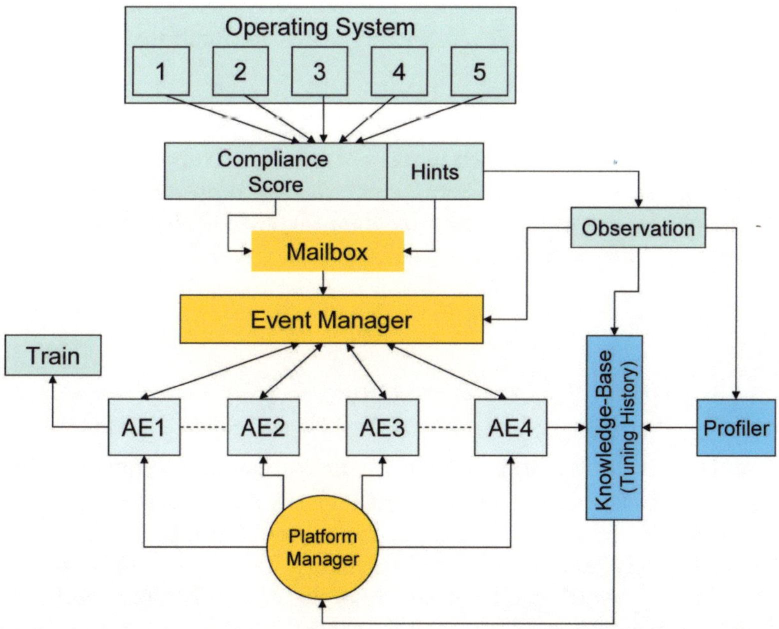

Fig. 2. Adaptation as a function of compliance scores/hints and the history of Adaptation. An autonomics manager acts as a conduit to the knowledge base. AEs make a process control decision using the previously tuned parameters based on applicability of the historical trends due to workload changes.

The QoS profile governs an appropriate level of resource reservation by indicating the output quality levels in a dynamic fashion. In general, the QoS maximization process starts with an initial resource allocation which it revises according to changing application demands and satisfaction levels. For example, applications can specify the satisfaction level at a scale of

0-9, with 9 being extremely satisfied. Additionally, applications can offer potential hints into the basis of performance loss. This information is consumed by the competing objectives functions that engage in an optimization game and generate an alternate configuration to maximize the application satisfaction score. Fig. 2 shows the adaptation infrastructure where an application produces a satisfaction score and associated hints.

Models may utilize these hints based on their applicability using an event manager filter. Once compliance score and hints are evaluated, each model identifies a set of tuning parameters that can maximize the compliance score. Resulting decisions steer each model to dynamically train itself based on the historical trends and scores. The dynamic training process transparently includes the competing strategy in order to play the optimization game that leads to a stable equilibrium. Traditional adaptation techniques (especially power optimization) have remained seemingly incognizant of the strategies employed by other components and the interplay between them. The adaptation techniques are built with an assumption that other components are not operational at the time of adaptation. Global optimization is only possible if tradeoffs between competing components are identified. In the absence of tradeoff study, only the most aggressive strategy, although suboptimal, may survive. We can characterize the operations of the various components as a non-cooperative dynamic game (Γ) played at interval T when game strategies are evaluated. Each player represents its strategy space by aggregating its goal management strategies. For example, the CPU can represent its power management strategy space using a set of N+1 "P" states, as illustrated in Equation 5:

$$S^{T}_{cpu} = [S^{0}_{cpu}, S^{1}_{cpu}, S^{2}_{cpu}, S^{3}_{cpu}, \cdots S^{N}_{cpu}] \tag{5}$$

Where S^{T}_{cpu} represents the strategy space that is not attached to any CPU power management scheme. The strategy space for other components is also represented in the same manner. Cumulative strategy space is used to optimize the usage of the shared resource as described by the global policy specification, as shown in Equations 6 and 7:

$$f(R(t)) \geq \sum_{i}(S^{R}_{i}(t)) \tag{6}$$

$$f(R(T+1)) = f(R(T)) - \sum_{i}(\delta^{R}_{i}) \tag{7}$$

Where, $S^{j}_{i}(t)$ represents the strategy at time "t" for component "i" and shared resource "j". $f(R(t))$ represents the policy specification of shared resource "R" at time "t". δ^{R}_{i} represents the reduction in resource "R" by component "i" in the subsequent interval (T+1). Consequently, higher δ^{R}_{i} may not directly translate to a higher quality. The objective is to determine a value for δ_i such that both the overall quality of service of the device is maximized.

Once automated, adaptation maximizes the performance of the target system without manual intervention. It tunes a system that trades off resource requirements over time for a desired level of quality of service. Furthermore, it provides flexibility in allocating resources to competing elements in a manner such that all objectives' goals meet their real-time requirements. Tuning History acts to correct the model throughout the life of the platform optimization objectives. Complex variables, compliance scores, hints and component performance counters act as standard emissions that construct the basis of HMM model. Furthermore, adaptation step is performed by changing the operating functions of cooperating component (power state, frequency, off-lining, changing idle timings etc.)

3.1 Control modeling ingredients

This section describes the essential ingredients for a profile detection system (PDS) that is responsible for building the profile and detecting any deviations from that profile. The objective of the PDS is to anticipate the power, thermal or performance policy deviations while reducing the number of false positives. An instantaneous deviation from a normal profile can be expected due to a momentary change in the system environment. Therefore in PDS we have to fulfill objectives related to accurate profile deviation detection using different ingredients such as:

- *Checkpoints* to analyze the sensor activity to predict the transition from a normal state to an abnormal state.
- *Activity profile* to identify the abnormal activity of the observable states by measuring the sensor deviation from the normal behavior. In short, it characterizes the behavioral signature corresponding to the normal activity of a given subject with respect to a given object.
- *Concept Drift* to measure the change in the user behavior over a period of time.
- *Control Loop* that adapts the checkpoint trigger according to the weighted sum of proportional, average, and derivative sensor measurements over derivative and integral time window.
- *Model* to predict the most probable state based on previous state (normal/abnormal) as well as observed states. This can be accomplished using hidden Markov model (HMM) as described later in this section.

4. Hidden Markov Model

HMM-based approaches correlate the system observations (usage and activity profile) and state transitions to predict the most probable state sequence. It represents a stochastic model of discrete events and a variation of the Markov chain. Like a conventional Markov chain, an HMM consists of a set of discrete states and a matrix $A = a_{ij}$ of state transition probabilities. The states of the HMM can only be inferred from the observed symbols, hence the use of the term hidden. HMM modeling schemes consist of observed (checkpoints) states, hidden (quality of service) states, and HMM (activity) profiles. HMM training using initial data and continuous re-estimation creates a profile that consists of transition probabilities and observation symbol probabilities. Steps involved in HMM modeling include:

- Measuring observed states that are analytically or logically derived from the QoS indicators. These indicators are test-points spread all over the system representing competing risks derived analytically or logically using QoS checkpoint (QC) indicators. Profile deviation can be considered to be a result of several components competing for occurrences of the deviation. In this model QoS checkpoint (QC) engine derives continuous multivariate observation, which is identical to the mean and standard deviation model except that it is based on correlations among several metrics.
- Resource activity trend that corresponds to resource activity monitored over a larger sampling period and represent characteristics that repeat over that sampling period. For example, CPU activity changing depending upon the time of the day. Each period of activity can be thought of as an extra dimension of activity measure.
- Event interval that represents a time period between two successive activities. For example, logging attempts between two consecutive intervals fall in this category.

- Estimating an instantaneous observation probability matrix that indicates the probability of an observation, given a hidden state $p(S_i|O_i)$. This density function can be estimated using explicit parametric model (usually multivariate Gaussian) or implicitly from data via non-parametric methods (multivariate kernel density emission).
- Estimating hidden states by clustering the homogeneous behavior of single or multiple components together. These states are indicative of various QoS states that need to be identified to the administrator. Hidden states $S = \{S_1, S_2, , S_{N?1}, S_N\}$ are the set of states that are not visible but each state randomly generates a mixture of the M observations (or visible states O). The probability of the subsequent state depends only upon the previous state.
- Estimating hidden state transition probability matrix using prior knowledge or random data. This prior knowledge and long-term temporal characteristics are an approximate probability of state components transitioning from one QoS state to another.

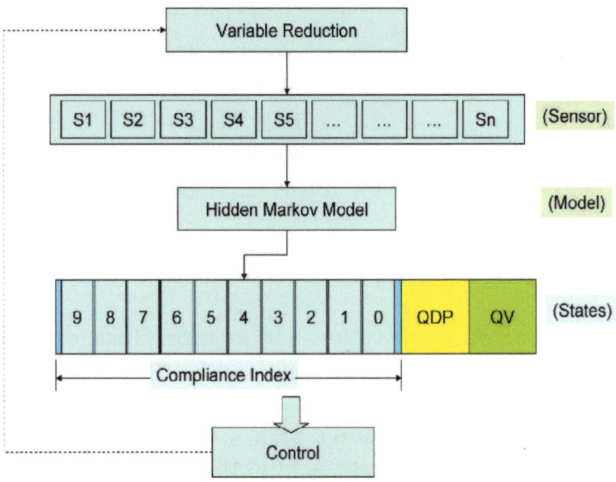

Fig. 3. Hidden States representing the platform policy compliance. These states are estimated from the checkpoints spread over the system in the form of sensors. Checkpoint sensors can be configured for accuracy.

The complete HMM model is defined by the following probabilities: transition probability matrix $A = \{a_{ij}\}$, where $a_{ij} = p(S_i|S_j)$, observation probability matrix $B = (b_i(v_m))$, where $b_i(v_m) = p(v_m|S_i)$, and an initial probability vector $\pi = p(S_i)$. The observation probability represents an attribute that is observed with some probability if a particular failure state is anticipated. The model is represented by $M = (A, B, \pi)$. The transition probability matrix is a square matrix of size equal to the number of states and represents the state transition probabilities. The observation probability distribution is a non-square matrix whose dimension equals the number of states by the number of observable, and represents the probability of an observation for a given state. The PDS has the following states:

- HMM state indicates the anticipated degree of compliance by the platform. This compliance follows the policy that governs the power, thermal and performance (Service Level Agreement) requirements. Therefore HMM state exists as Compliance Index (CI) that ranges from 0-9. While a factor of 9 indicates a stable system that is fully compliant, a value of 0 indicates a compliant but un-stable system with over(or under) resource allocations, frequent variations and reactive control.

- QoS Deviation in progress (QDP) indicates an activity that is setting itself up and expected to cause the overall quality of service to deteriorate.
- QoS Violation (QV) indicates a successful QoS violation. A successful violation will be accompanied with unusual resource usage (CPU, memory, IO activity, and so on) and a low compliance indicator.

Power, Thermal and performance variations in a system can result in sub-optimal states that may need correction for platform policy compliance. The sub-optimal states need to be predicted well in advance such that corrective actions can be employed within an opportunistic window of time. Such conditions can be predicted using a set of sensors that share probabilistic relationship with the available states. In a platform these sensors are available as activity counters, temperature monitors, power monitors, performance monitors etc.

4.1 CPU power variables

Contribution of CPU power consumption can be measured by calculating fetched micro-operations ((μops)). This metric is directly related to power consumption and also represents the amount of internal paralleism in the processor. On the other hand, instructions retired matric only reflects the useful work and neglects the work done in execution of incorrect branchs and pipeline flushes. The processor decomposes x86 instructions into multiple micro-operations which are then sent to the execution units. Complex instruction mix can result in a false calculation of the amount of computations performed. μops acts independent of complex instructional mix and normalizes this metric to give useful counts. Apart from using the CPU HW counters, we also use O.S performance meters. One such matrix is CPU utilization that can be used in lieu of μops with a reduced degree of accuracy.

4.2 Memory power variables

It is possible to estimate power consumption in DRAM modules by using the number of read/write cycles and percent of time within the precharge, active and idle states (Janzen, 2001). Since none of these events are visible to the microprocessor, we indirectly estimate them by measuring memory bus accesses by the processor and other events that can be monitored at the CPU. Whenever a memory transaction cannot be satisfied by an L2 cache, it triggers a cache-miss action and performs a cache-line sized access to the main memory. Since the number of main memory accesses is directly proportional to the number of L2 misses, it is possible to approximate memory access count using L2 cache-miss count. In reality the relation is not that simple, but there is still a strong causal relationship between L2 misses and main memory accesses. TLB Misses is another variable that can be significant to power estimation. Unlike cache misses, which mainly cause a cache line transfer from/to memory, TLB misses results in the transfer of a page of data. Due to the large page sizes, they are stored on the disk and hence power is consumed on the entire path from the CPU to the hard disk.

4.3 I/O power variables

Three major indicators of the I/O power are (1) DMA Accesses, (2) Un-Cacheable accesses and (3) Interrupt Activity. Out of these three indicators, Interrupt/cycle is the dominant indicator of the I/O power. DMA indicators perform suboptimal due to presence of various performance enhancements (like write-combining) in the I/O chip. I/O interrupts are typically triggered by I/O devices to indicate the completion of large data transfers. Therefore, it is possible to correlate I/O power to the appropriate device. Since this information is not available through any CPU counters, they are made available by the operating system (using perfmon).

4.4 Thermal data

Apart from various performance counters defined in previous sections, we also consider using thermal data which available in all the modern components (CPU, Memory) and accessible via PECI BUS.
The heat produced by a component essentially corresponds to the energy it consumes, so we define it as:

$$Q_{component} = P(Util) \cdot Time \tag{8}$$

where, P(Util) represents the average power consumed by the component as a function of its utilization. For most components, a simple linear formulation correctly approximates the real power consumption:

$$P(Util) = P_{base} + Util \cdot (P_{max} - P_{base}) \tag{9}$$

where, P_{base} is the power consumption when the component is idle and P_{max} is the consumption when the component is fully utilized.

5. QoS Checkpoint control

QoS represents a fitness component that maximizes the work-load compliance index by using a minimal amount of resources. The QoS contribution of each element is dependent upon optimal resource allocation that would maximize the CI index and not violate the platform policy (Power Budgeting etc.). A high CI may still demonstrate low QoS due to non-compliant resource distribution. While HMM model predicts the new HMM state, contributing elements predict the desired resource allocation to maximize the CI. CI acts as a feedback path for training purposes that demonstrates the sensitivity of the resource allocation (or de-allocation) throughout the life of the platform. Individual components can build proprietary cost functions (as described below) to predict the desired resource allocation. Once a steady state condition is reached, where the compliance index is sustained by a given set of resources, any deviation from that profile can be construed as a QoS (or profile) violation. QoS indirectly measures the workload compliance efficiency and tries to maximize the compliance factor, as shown in Equations 10 and 11:

$$QoS = CI \cdot \left(1 - \frac{1}{N} \cdot \sum_{i}^{N} R_i\right) \tag{10}$$

$$R_i = \frac{max[0, (R_i^d - R_i^a + \epsilon)]}{R_i^d} \tag{11}$$

where CI represents the compliance index of the workload, R_i^d represents the desired (profiled) resource requirement for component i, R_i^a represents the current resource allocation and N is the number of components that shares that resource. It should be remembered that variations in workload demands may require changing the resource allocation (R_i^d) to maintain the maximum compliance index.

In this section we discuss the applicability of the control theoretic architecture that drives the defensive response based on hysteresis to reduce the incidence of false positives, thereby avoiding inappropriate ad hoc responses. Excessive responses can slow down the system and negatively impact the effectiveness of the PDS. PDS control responses are related to adjusting component functionality (such as throttling), alert generation (to predict QoS violation state) and analyzing concept drift. We introduce checkpoint control loop that acts as the first state of a multistage QoS detection system of sequential PDS. The process output of the control loop provides the observability of an individual QoS checkpoint that aids in the state estimation. Collective observations from several checkpoints are fed into the statistical model (in this case HMM) responsible for predicting the state transition. It is imperative that any such output should be stable and free of oscillations. Response measures are delayed to account for delay involved in the estimation of QoS state based on observations from other checkpoints.

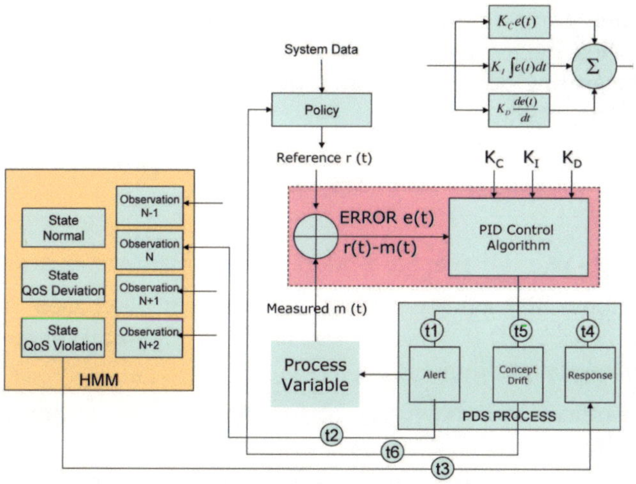

Fig. 4. PID control loop for QoS checkpoint. The Process output (alert) constitutes the observation (emission) in an HMM. A true-positive response is fed back to the process response unit of the PID control to aid runtime retraining. Concept drift analysis aids in re-setting the reference point.

An appropriate response can be built into the QoS checkpoint approach that predicts the QoS divergence pattern and triggers the selective response to a control loop. The PID controller (Fig. 4) may execute one such control loop that takes a measured value from a QoS checkpoint and compares it with a reference value. The difference is then used to trigger alert (abnormal activity) to the process in order to establish the process' measured value back to its desired set-point. It is built with a weighted integral and differential response to the trigger mechanism along with the reactive response to an instantaneous measurement. PID controller can adjust the process outputs based on the history and rate of change of the error signal, which gives more accurate and stable control. This avoids the situation where alerts may not be the true representation of QoS activity due to false positives. Such miscalculations can result in either disproportionate and costly corrective (or defensive) measures or complete failure. The reference (set-points) values are dynamic in nature and set as a part of coarse grain settings that are estimated over long periods of time. These re-estimates are required to account for the changing user behavior, also referred as concept drift. While the set-point (reference) may remain constant over a long period of time, it can change due to user behavior or system policy driven by a temporary change in the operating environment. System data and the process feedback provide hints that are then used to change the set-point (or set-point weights) in steps based on system policy. System policy is driven by long-term hysteresis based on the system's behavior and the well-known relationship with various checkpoints.

5.1 QoS attributes

Local policy operates within the server node construct and is managed by a management container (manageability Engine, Base Board Management Controller etc.). The goal of local policy is to maximize performance per watt while it operates within total allocated power ($P^t_{alloc}(t)$). In order to implement local policy, the following conditions are desired:

- Ability to accurately monitor power at sub-component granularity.
- Ability to accurately control power at sub-component granularity. Sub-Component power limits are controlled by managing its energy within a given interval. Since energy is equivalent to integrating power over time, power limits are controlled by managing its running averages over time.

$$E^i_T = \int_0^T N_i(t)dt; \;\; N_{i,avg} = \frac{E^i_T}{T} \tag{12}$$

- Ability to accurately monitor average workload performance at runtime.
- Ability to distribute the power among sub-components based on a performance maximization function. This function can be realized using simple random walk or complex evolutionary algorithms.
- Ability to communicate any power or performance credits accumulated in successive evaluation periods.

Felter et al propose a power shifting policy (Felter, 2005) that is analogous to optimal power distribution discussed in this section. This policy reduce peak power consumption by using workload-guided dynamic allocation of power among components incorporating real-time performance feedback, activity-related power estimation techniques, and performance-sensitive activity-regulation mechanisms to enforce power budgets. In addition to the necessary elements required to implement local and global policies, following autonomics infrastructure items are required to build the power distribution model that can be summarized as follows:

5.1.1 Adaptive sampling Infrastructure (LSI)

LSI is responsible for setting the optimal size of the monitoring/control interval. While shorter intervals are better for accuracy, they can overwhelm the natural behavior of the workload. Furthermore, short control intervals impose stronger than necessary constraint of power budgets. Therefore it is desirable to construct the sampling scheme that is statistically proportional to the proximity of the process to the critical threshold according to following equation:

$$T = T_{base}\left(1 + \alpha \cdot \frac{N_{alloc} - N_{avg}}{N_{alloc}} + \beta \cdot \frac{Pr_0 - Pr_{avg}}{Pr_0}\right); \;\; \alpha + \beta = 1 \tag{13}$$

5.1.2 Local Cost Minimization Function (LCMF)

LCMF performs the power distribution amongst node sub-components (DIMM(s), CPU(s), I/O, LAN(s), Storage etc.) in a manner that maximizes the performance while operating under a constant power budget. This function trains itself by utilizing historical trends, identifying repeating patterns. These patterns can be represented in the form of discrete HMM CI states (Sec. 4) that can predict the degree of policy compliance in the future. For example, system sub-components power allocation function is given by:

$$N_{alloc} \geq \sum_{k=1}^{n} (N_k = [f(x_k) + N_{k,min}]) \qquad Pr_o \leq Pr_{avg} \tag{14}$$

$$Pr_{avg} = \sum_{k=1}^{n} C_k \cdot (N_k)^{c_k} \tag{15}$$

Where:
$f(x_k)$ = Power consumed by component k as a function of performance state x_k
$N_{k,min}$= Minimum power of component k
C_k and c_k= Trained coefficients of performance equation. For linear model, $c_k = 1$.
N_{avg} = Average power consumption
N_{alloc} = Node Power Budget allocated by global policy
Pr_o = Desired performance
Once performance model is trained, N_k can be adjusted for maximum performance gain. Discrete states prediction triggers the control action that pro actively mitigates the effects of the performance loss (required to enforce a given policy).

5.1.3 Global Cost Minimization function (GCMF)

GCMF works similar to local cost maximization function on server nodes. It performs the power distribution amongst server nodes in a manner that maximizes the performance while operating under a constant global power budget.

5.1.4 Running Average Power Synthesizer (RAPS)

RAPS is a running average power calculator for a monitored quantity over an enforcement window. RAPS measurement allows for all the sub-components and server nodes to control average power over a given interval.

5.1.5 Running Average Performance Synthesizer (RAPrS)

RAPrS is a running average performance calculator of the node workload. This is monitored for each individual workload running in a server node.
Running average power and performance calculator can be utilized to dynamically monitor the power and performance trends over an adjustable evaluation window of time and maintain the average power at or below a given threshold.

6. Profile deviation detection (PDS) architecture

This section characterizes components of the PDS that cooperate with each other to predict a QoS noncompliance (violation) state. PDS is deployed as a part of an autonomic element (AE) that detects the signs of QoS violation locally and independent of other AEs.

The PDS architecture comprises multiple stages with an information feedback mechanism between stages. These stages can be roughly defined as follows:

- QoS Checkpoint Control Stage (QCCS) is the observability stage with an objective to produce stable emissions using continuous estimations. This stage is also responsible for detecting temporary changes due to legal activity and concept drift signifying changing long-term application behaviors. This decision is crucial because a drift in the normal behavior may also be falsely predicted a QoS violation. Observation can be rejected as a noise, or classified to a valid state based on the trending, similarity between unclassified states tending toward certain classification, and feedback from state machine based on other independent observations.
- QoS State Detection Stage (QSDS) receives the observability data from multiple checkpoints and predicts the transition to one of the hidden states (normal, QoS violation) based on trained statistical model. An estimated QoS decision is fed back to QCCS, which helps re-estimating the usage trends while avoiding any false positive preemptive responses.
- QoS Response Stage (QRS) is responsible for initiating the corrective (healing) actions due to state transition. These actions may scale back any abnormal activity as seen in the observability data. A mis-predicted state transition may initiate an inappropriate response and will have negative effect on checkpoint activity.

After various components of the model are trained, it enters a runtime state where it examines and classifies each valid observation. Various components of a QoS detection system are explained in the following sub-sections.

7. QoS checkpoint control stage (QCCS)

QCCS represents the feedback control component (Figure 5) for an individual QoS checkpoint. It comprises a measurement port, PID controller, observation profiler, concept drift detector (CDD), and feedback path to the process input.

Measurement Port is composed of fast-acting software and silicon hooks that are capable of identifying, counting, thresholding, time-stamping, eventing, and clearing an activity. Examples of such hooks are performance counters, flip counters (or transaction counters), header sniffers, fault alerts (such as page faults), bandwidth usage monitors, session activity, system call handling between various processes and applications, file-system usage, and swap-in/swap-out usage. Measured data is analyzed as it is collected or subsequently to provide real-time alert notification for suspected deviant behaviors. These fast-acting hooks are clustered to enact an observation. Measurements can be sampled at regular intervals or cause an alert based on a user-settable threshold.

Observation Profiler monitors various inputs for maintaining/re-estimating activity profile that ascertains a rough (partially perfect) boundary between normal and abnormal activity and characterized in terms of a statistical metric and model. A metric is a random variable representing a quantitative measure accumulated over a period. Measurements obtained from the audit records when used together with a statistical model analyze any deviation from a standard profile. An observation profiler receives multiple feedbacks from PID control output, event trigger and QSDS, and performs recursive estimations that generate successive probabilistic profile data estimates with a closed-form solution. A trigger event is generally followed by a change in the PID control output that initiates a recovery response. A true

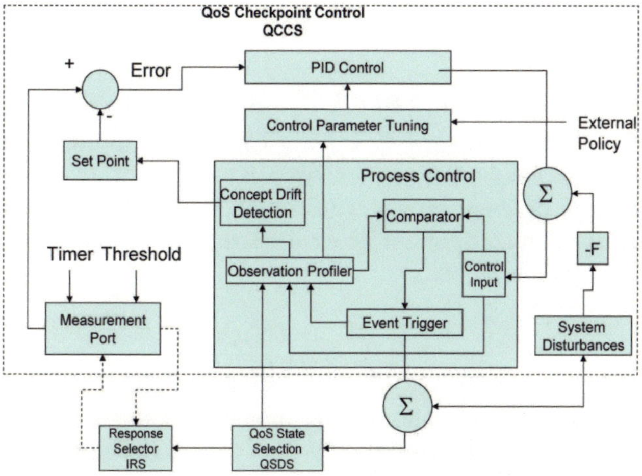

Fig. 5. QCCS is responsible for providing the stable observability data to the QoS state detection stage. This data is profiled for variances due to changing user behavior and temporary changes in system environment (also referred to as disturbances).

positive recovery response will scale back the checkpoint activity to normal. A false positive action will instead cause oscillations, degraded system performance, or little change in the measured error. Activity profile data consists of probability distribution function (pdf) and the related parameters (e.g. variance, mean, activity drift factor etc). Successive observations are evaluated against this profile which results in its new profiles and drift detection. An observation (emission) can also be a set of correlated measurements but represented by a single probability distribution function. Each of these measurements carries different weights as in multivariate probability distribution. Such relationship is incorporated into the profile for the completeness of the observation and reduces the dimensionality for effective runtime handling. Observability in this case is derived out of the profile that represents a consolidated and single representation of activity. A sample profile data structure is defined as follows.
NFS Profile {
  Observation Name = NFS Activity
  Input Events = {Disk I/O, Network I/O, $\cdots$ }
  Output Emissions = Function (Input Events)
  PDF Parameter = $\{D[N], D[HI], D[FI], D[IP], D[IS]\}$
  Unclassified Observation = $\{U[t_1], U[t_2], \cdots, U[t_n]\}$
  Concept Drift Data = $\{\eta_{t1}, \eta_{t2}, \cdots\}$
  }

Concept Drift Detector detects and analyzes the concept drifting (Widmer, 1996) in the profile where training data set alone is not sufficient, and the model (profile) needs to be updated continually. When there is a time-evolving concept drift, using old data unselectively helps if the new concept and old concept still have consistencies and the amount of old data chosen arbitrarily just happen to be right (FAN, 2004). This requires an efficient approach to data mining that helps select a combination of new and old (historical) data to make an accurate re-profiling and further classification. The mechanism used is the measurement of Kullback-Leibler (KL) divergence (Kullback, 1951), or relative entropy measures the kernel distance between two probability distributions b(.|.) of generative models as expressed in Equation 16:

$$\alpha_t = KL(b(v|\theta'_t), b(v|\theta_t)) \tag{16}$$

Where: α_t = KL divergence measure θ'_t = New Gaussian component θ_t = Old Gaussian component at time . v = Observation vector We can evaluate divergence by a Monte Carlo simulation using the law of large numbers (Grimmett, 1992) that draws an observation θ'_t from the estimated Gaussian component , computes the log ratio, and averages this over M samples as shown in Equation 7.7 as:

$$\alpha_t \approx \frac{1}{M} \sum_{i=1}^{M} \log \left(\frac{b(v_i|\theta'_t)}{b(v_i|\theta_t)} \right) \tag{17}$$

KL divergence data calculated in the temporal domain are used to evaluate the speed of the drift, also called drift factor ( ). These data are then used to assign weights to the historical parameters that are then used for re-profiling.
Feedback Path is responsible for feeding back the current state information to the profile estimator. The current state information is calculated by running the ISDS module using the current model parameters. This information is then used by the profiler to filter out any noise and re-estimate the activity profile data. If a trigger event is not followed by a state transition, then a corrective action is performed to minimize the false positives in the future.
PID Controller (Fig. 4) generates an output that initiates a corrective response applied to a process in order to drive a measurable process variable toward a reference value (set point). It is assumed that any QoS activity will cause variations in the checkpoint activity, thereby causing a large error. Errors occur when a disturbance (QoS violation) or a load on the process (changes in environment) changes the process variable. The controller's mission is to eliminate the error automatically. A discrete form of PID controller is represented by Equation 18:

$$u(nT) = P + I + D + u_0 \tag{18}$$

where,

$$\begin{aligned} P &= K_p \cdot e(nT) \\ I &= K_i \cdot T \cdot \sum_{i=(nT-w)}^{nT} e(i) \\ D &= K_d \cdot \frac{e(nT) - e(nT-1)}{T} \end{aligned}$$

where e(t) is the error represented by difference between measured value and set-point, w is the integral sampling window, nT is the n-th sampling period, and K_p, K_i and K_d are the proportional, integral, and derivative gains respectively. Stability is ensured using the proportional term, the integral term permits the rejection of a step disturbance, and the derivative term is used to provide damping or shaping of the response. While integral response measures the amount of time the error has continued uncorrected, differential response anticipates the future errors from the rate of change of error over a period of time. The desired closed-loop dynamics are obtained by adjusting these parameters iteratively by tuning and without specific knowledge of a QoS detection model. Control parameters are continuously tuned to ensure the stability of the control loop in a control-theoretic sense, over a wide range of variations in the checkpoint measurements. While control parameters are evaluated frequently, they are updated only when improvement in stability is anticipated. These updates can be periodic over a large period of time.

7.1 Relevant profiles

This section look into events that forms input to the profile structure. Exploiting temporal sequence information of event leads to better performance (Ghosh, 1999) of profiles that are defined for individual workloads, programs, or classes. An abnormal activity in any of the following forms is an indicator of a QoS variation:

- CPU activity is monitored by sampling faults, inter-processor interrupt (IPI) calls, context switches; thread migrations, spins on locks, and usage statistics.
- Network activity is monitored by sampling input error rate, collision rate, RPC rejection rate, duplicate acknowledgments (DUPACK), retransmission rate, timeout rate, refreshed authentications, bandwidth usage, active connections, connection establishment failure, header errors and checksum failures and so on.
- Interrupt activity is monitored by sampling device interrupts (non-timer interrupts).
- IO utilization is monitored by sampling the I/O requests average queue lengths and busy percentage.
- Memory activity is monitored by sampling memory transfer rate, page statistics (reclaim rate, swap-in rate, swap-out rate), address translation faults, pages scanned and paging averages over a short interval.
- File access activity is monitored by sampling file access frequency, file usage overflow, and file access faults.
- System process activity is monitored by sampling processes with inappropriate process priorities, CPU and memory resources used by processes, processes length, processes that are blocking I/Os, zombie processes, and command and terminal that generated the process.
- System faults activity represents an illegal activity (or a hardware error) and is sampled to detect abnormality in the system usage. While rare faults represent a bad programming, but spurts of activity indicate an attack. n System calls activity measures the system-call execution pattern of a workload. It is used to compare runtime system-call execution behavior with the expected pattern and detect any non-expected execution of system calls. Pattern-matching algorithms match the real-time sequence of system-calls and predict a normal or abnormal behavior (Wespi, 1999).
- Session activity is monitored by sampling the logging frequency, unsuccessful logging attempts, session durations, session time, session resource usages, and so on.
- Platform Resource Activity is monitored by sampling CPU, DIMM, I/O power consumption, and thermal data. Additionally CPU, memory, and I/O bandwidth performance can also be measured using performance counters available within the CPU core or un-core logic.

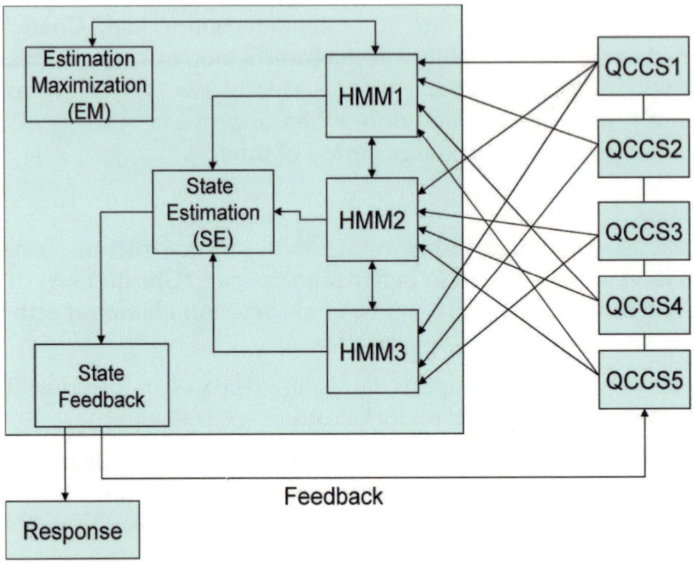

Fig. 6. QoS state detection stage (QSDS)

7.2 QoS State Detection Stage (QSDS)

QSDS defines the statistical model that is responsible for predicting the current QoS state based on observable data inputs received from QCCS modules. In this context we may choose HMM where states are hidden and indirectly evaluated based on model parameters. QCCS trigger output acts as an emission to a specific HMM model and weighted according to its significance relative to that model. HMM emissions are defined as processed observation, derived from one or more temporal input events using a processor function. They represent competing risks derived analytically or logically using checkpoint indicators. Platform states can be considered to be a result of several components competing for the occurrences of the anomaly. Observed inputs may be expressed as a weighted fraction of individual observations from multiple checkpoints in an attempt to enhance the performance of QoS state detection. Similar observed inputs (emissions) may be distributed among mixture of models, usually Gaussian, with weights given to each model based on trivial knowledge and continuous training. This approach is advantageous as it allows one to model the QoS states at varying degree of granularity while retaining the advantages of each model. Depending upon the data characteristics (amount of data, frequency); models can be adapted by modifying weights such that complex models are favored for complex inputs and vice versa. Such mixture model can be represented as Equation 19:

$$p(v) = \sum_{k=1}^{K} a_k b(v|\theta_k) \tag{19}$$

$$a_k > 0 \ and \ \sum a_k = 1$$

Where: v = Observation vector $p(v)$ = Modeled probability distribution function a_k = Mixture proportion of component K = Number of components in the mixture model θ_k = Distribution Parameters of component $b(v|\theta_k)$ = Distribution function for component

Figure 6 illustrates the HMM-x sub-block which is responsible for receiving the abnormal activity alert and processes the interrupt to service the hidden-state (QoS) estimation. It maintains the HMM data and interacts with the expectation-maximization (EM) block and the state-estimation (SE) block for retraining and state-prediction flows. This block also implements reduced dimensionality by combining multiple inputs into a single observation with its own probability distribution function. This observation is then fed into the EM and SE block for state estimation. The EM algorithm Grimmett (1992) provides a general approach to the problem of maximum likelihood (ML) parameter estimation in statistical models with variables that are not observed. The evaluation process yields a parameter set which it uses to assign observations points to new states. The EM sub-block is responsible for finding the ML estimates of parameters in the HMM model as well as mixture densities (or model weights) and relies on the intermediate variables (also called latent data) represented by state sequence. EM alternates between performing an E-step, which computes an expectation of the likelihood, and an M-step, which computes the ML estimates of the parameters by maximizing the expected likelihood found on the E-step. The parameters found on the M-step are then used to begin another E-step, and the process is repeated. In the HMM mixture modeling, QoS checkpoint events under consideration have membership in one of the distributions we are using to model the data. The job of estimation is to devise appropriate parameters for the model functions we choose, with the connection to the data points being represented as their membership in the individual model distributions. SE is responsible for modeling the underlying state and observation sequence of HMM mixture to predict state sequences for new QoS states using the Viterbi algorithm (to find the most likely path through the HMM). Trained mixture appears to be a single HMM for all purposes and can be applied as a standard HMM algorithm to extract the most probable state sequence given a set of observations. Estimates for the transition and emission probabilities are based on multiple HMM models and are transparent to the standard HMM models. The Viterbi algorithm is a dynamic algorithm requiring time $O(TS^2)$ is the number of time steps and S is the number of states) where at each time step it computes the most probable path for each state given that the most probable path for all previous time steps has been computed. The state feedback sub-block feeds back the estimated state to the observation profiler in ICCS, which then uses this data for recalibrating the profile.

8. System considerations

Profile detection in local platform components (CPU, DIMM etc.) is limited to profiling local activity using floating QCCS modules. The intent is to reduce the system complexity and enhance the likelihood of software reuse. These hooks exist to accelerate the combined measurements of the clustered components with an ability to send alerts based on a systems-wide policy. It contains the hardware and software that act as a glue between transducers and a control program that is capable of measuring the event interval and event trend with an ability to generate alerts upon departure from normal behaviors (represented by system policy). In this specific case, the feedback control loop is implemented partially in the silicon (QCCS block) with configurable control parameters. To further enhance the auto-discoverability, modularity, and re-usability, configuration and status registers may be mapped into the capability pointer of the PCI Express configuration space. Similar mechanisms exist today in the very basic form as performance counters (PerfMon), leaky-bucket counters, and so on. These counters need to be coupled with QCCS modules that contain a PID controller, profilers, threshold detectors, drift detectors, and coarse-grain tuners. QCCS modules should be implemented in isolation from the measured components such that a single QCCS component can multiplex between multiple measurement modules.

While some of the checkpoints are used for local consumption, others are shared with the monitor nodes to aid in cooperative state estimation. These checkpoints share the trigger data with the monitor nodes and contribute as the node's contribution to the mixture of HMM. The enormous amount of measurement data and computational complexity are a paramount consideration in the design of an effective PDS system.

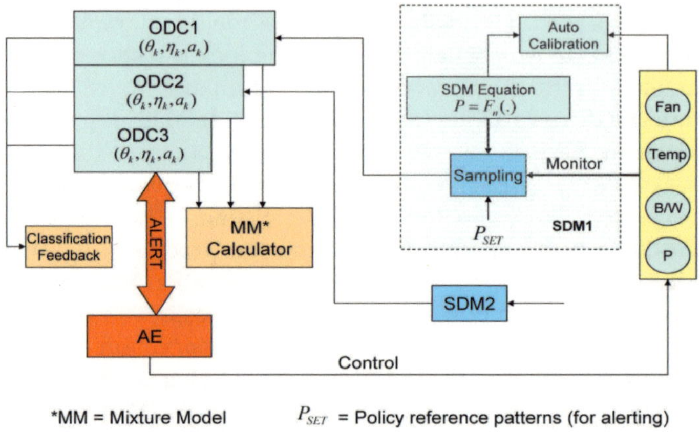

Fig. 7. Illustration of the relationship between events (circles), sensors (SDM) and classifiers (ODC). Clusters of events (marked by similar colors) are registered to an SDM. SDM upon evaluating the event properties, generate an event to ODC. ODC is responsible for classification, trend analysis and drift calculation.

8.1 Sensor data measurement (SDM)

SDM hooks reduce the system complexity and increase the likelihood of software reuse. SDM accelerates the combined measurements of the clustered components with an ability to send alerts using a systems policy. Hardware and software acts as glue between transducers and control program that is capable of measuring the event interval, event trend with an ability to generate alerts on deviation from normal behavior (represented by system policy). The SDM hardware exists as a multiple-instance entity that receives alert vectors from various events spread all over the system. A set of correlated events form a cluster and are registered against a common SDM instance. This instance represents the Bayes optimal decision boundaries between set of pattern classes with each class represented by an SDM instance and associated with a reference vector. Each SDM instance is capable of trending and alerting and integrates the measurements from the event sensors into a unified view. Cluster trending analysis is unusually sensitive to small signal variations and capable of detecting the abnormal signals embedded in the normal signals by supervised learning (Kohonen, 1995).

As illustrated in fig. 7, policy based reference patterns are manually (or automatically) identified that would result in alerts to ODC. Simple patterns may be represented in a form of RAW thresholds. More complex patterns would require statistical processing of the RAW data into meaningful information which is then matched against reference patterns.

8.2 Observation Data Classifier (ODC)

ODC hooks accelerate the classification of an observation alert generated by SDM. This is multiple-instance hardware (Figure 7) capable of handling multiple observations in parallel.

Each registered observation instance of the ODC hook consists of probability distribution parameters of each state. Upon receiving an SDM alert, the observation corresponding to this alert is then classified to a specific state. Reclassification of observed data may cause changes in the probability distribution parameters corresponding to the state. ODC is capable of maintaining the historical parameters, which are then used to calculate concept drift properties (drift factor, drift speed, and so on) using drift detector.

8.3 Mixture Model (MM) Calculator

The MM calculator determines the probability of the mixture (usually Gaussian) for each state, using the current observation. During the system setup, event vectors are registered against SDM instance. These events are clustered and processed in its individual SDM. The processing includes trigger properties that initiates an observation. These observations then act as single-dimensional events that are registered to its ODC. Upon receiving the trigger, ODC performs reclassification of the observation (derived from the trigger) and calculates the concept drift. It should be noted that this hardware is activated upon a trigger by its parent.

9. Summary

Since the QoS state resulting from service-level-agreements (SLA) compliance cannot be inferred directly by monitoring any specific parameters, we need to predict QoS violations based on a mixture of observable data points, events, and current states. This leads to a statistical mechanism for QoS prediction using HMM where observed data are represented as a weighted mixture component. Using this mechanism, an observed deviation from a normal behavior carries a higher probability of being in a sub-optimal state. We define HMM based statistical model that predicts the QoS state based on observable data inputs received from checkpoint control modules. This chapter also introduces the concept of a feedback control mechanism that regulates the defensive response to every perceived sub-optimality (or abnormality). As explained earlier, this helps reduce the false positive rate, which is one of the major problems in Profile Detection System (PDS). Modern silicon (CPU, I/O hubs, PCI Express devices) contains performance counters that can be measured at moderate granularity. To avoid software overhead, these counters can be mapped to the feedback control modules. Various functional units of the silicon should be able to profile the activity trends supported by the eventing mechanism in a power efficient manner. Physical layer design should support protocols related to optimal monitor-node selection based on user-defined policies and authentication. PDS needs to understand relationships, relevance, and correlation between multiple triggers (or emissions) in a computationally efficient manner.

10. References

Denning, Dorothy E. (1987). An Intrusion-Detection Model, *IEEE TRANSACTIONS ON SOFTWARE ENGINEERING*, VOL. SE-13, NO. 2, FEBRUARY 1987, 222-232.

Fan, W. (2004). Systematic data selection to mine concept-drifting data streams. *ACM SIGKDD*, 2004.

Felter, W.; Rajamani, K.; Keller, T.; and Rusu, C. (2005). A performance-conserving approach for reducing peak power consumption in server systems. In Proceedings of the *19th Annual international Conference on Supercomputing*, Cambridge, Massachusetts, June 20 - 22, 2005.

Ghosh, A. K.; Schwartzbard, A. and Schatz, M. (1999). Learning program behavior profiles for intrusion detection. In Proc. *Workshop on Intrusion Detection and Network Monitoring*, pp. 51-62, Santa Clara, USA, Apr. 1999.

Grimmett, G. R. and Stirzaker, D. R. (1992). Probability and random processes. *Oxford, U.K.: Clarendon Press*, 2nd edition, 1992.

Janzen, J. (2001). Calculating Memory System Power for DDR SDRAM. *Micro Designline*, Volume 10, Issue 2, 2001.

Kohonen, T. (1995). Self-organizing maps. *Springer Press*, 1995.

Kullback, S. and Leibler, R. A. (1951). On information and sufficiency. *Annals of Mathematical Statistics*, vol. 22, pp. 79-86, Mar. 1951.

Wespi, A.; Debar, H. and M. Dacier (1999). An intrusion-detection system based on the Teiresias pattern-discovery algorithm *Eicar'99, Aalborg*, Denmark, Feb. 27-Mar. 2, 1999.

Widmer, G. and Kubat, M. (1996). Learning in the presence of concept drifting and hidden contexts. *Machine Learning*, vol. 23, pp. 69-101, 1996.